Of Time and Knoxville

Of Time and Knoxville

FRAGMENT OF AN AUTOBIOGRAPHY

Anne W. Armstrong

Edited by Linda Behrend

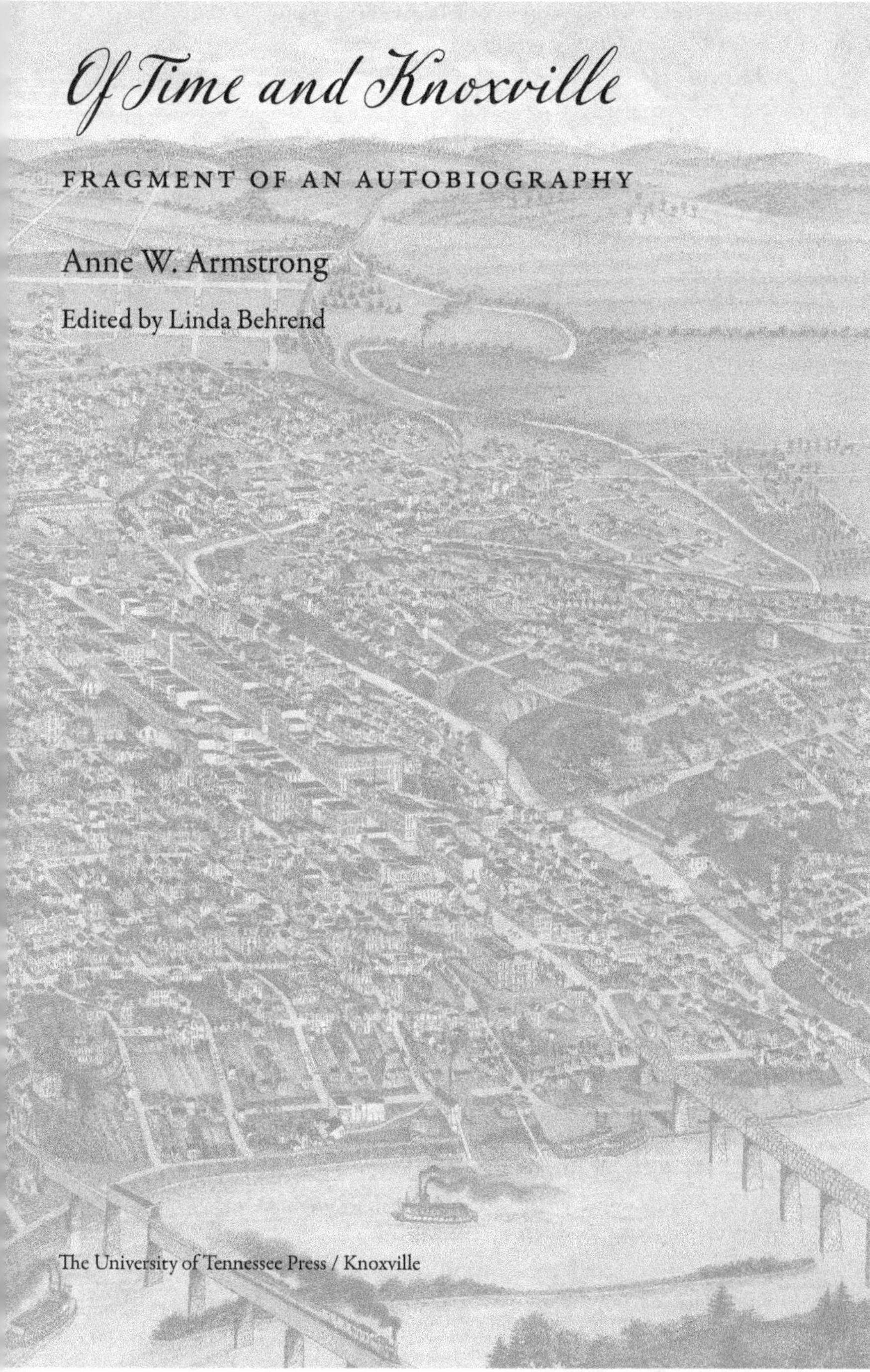

The University of Tennessee Press / Knoxville

First Edition.

Images are courtesy of the Calvin M. McClung Historical Collection, Knox County Public Library, unless otherwise noted.

Frontis: Anne Wetzell Armstrong's passport photo, 1924. Wikimedia Commons.
Background: "Knoxville, Tenn. County Seat of Knox County 1886." Henry Wellge, Beck & Pauli, and Norris, Wellge & Co., 1886. Map. Library of Congress.

Cover illustrations: Armstrong's passport photo, Wikimedia Commons; Armstrong's handwriting sample courtesy of the editor; "The Hill" courtesy of the University of Tennessee Libraries; remaining images courtesy of the Calvin M. McClung Historical Collection, Knox County Public Library.

Library of Congress Cataloging-in-Publication Data

Names: Armstrong, Anne W. (Anne Wetzell), 1872–1958, author.
Title: Of time and Knoxville : fragment of an autobiography / Anne W. Armstrong.
Other titles: Fragment of an autobiography
Description: First edition. | Knoxville : The University of Tennessee Press, [2022] | Includes bibliographical references. | *Summary:* "This scholarly edition of Anne Armstrong's autobiography, *Of Time and Knoxville*, published here for the first time, provides a snapshot of Knoxville in the late nineteenth and early twentieth centuries as the city was becoming a modern, industrialized urban center. Armstrong moved to Knoxville as a teenager in 1885 and spent her early formative years there. Her memoir discusses the University of Tennessee, a growing west Knoxville (Cumberland Avenue and Kingston Pike, in particular), and other notable areas in what we now know as the university and downtown districts. Armstrong is also author of *This Day and Time*, an Appalachian novel credited as the first fictional account to depict the region realistically. Linda Behrend has written a critical introduction and meticulously annotated Armstrong's work"— Provided by publisher.
Identifiers: LCCN 2022036531 (print) | LCCN 2022036532 (ebook) | ISBN 9781621907060 (paperback) | ISBN 9781621907077 (pdf)
Subjects: LCSH: Armstrong, Anne W. (Anne Wetzell), 1872–1958. | Knoxville (Tenn.)—Social life and customs—19th century. | Knoxville (Tenn.)—History—19th century. | Knoxville (Tenn.)—Biography.
Classification: LCC F444.K7 A76 2022 (print) | LCC F444.K7 (ebook) | DDC 976.8/85092 [B]—dc23/eng/20220805
LC record available at https://lccn.loc.gov/2022036531
LC ebook record available at https://lccn.loc.gov/2022036532

To Ed and Roger Naylor
great-grandsons of Anne Wetzell Armstrong,

and

In memory of
Robert J. (Jack) Higgs (1932–2015)
professor emeritus, East Tennessee State University,
who kept her memory alive.

Contents

Illustrations

Preface

> The greatest part of a writer's time is spent in reading, in order to write; a man will turn over half a library to make one book.
>
> —Samuel Johnson: in James Boswell's *Life of Samuel Johnson* (1791)

The first time I heard the name "Anne Wetzell Armstrong" I was working in the library at East Tennessee State University (ETSU) in Johnson City, Tennessee. The technical services archivist had come to my department to verify her name in an online database. I immediately associated her with Annie Armstrong, the Southern Baptist missionary for whom an annual offering is named. I soon learned that this was a different "Annie Armstrong" and that the Archives had acquired a photocopy of her typewritten manuscript "Of Time and Knoxville."

Through unforeseen circumstances, within a year I was working in the ETSU Archives myself—and learning more about Anne Wetzell Armstrong and the manuscript. The more I learned, the more interested I became. The manuscript had been donated to ETSU by Marshall D. Hogan, M.D., of Kingsport, Tennessee, probably through the efforts of Dr. Robert J. "Jack" Higgs, an English professor who had arranged for the Research Advisory Council at ETSU to reprint Armstrong's Appalachian novel *This Day and Time* in 1970. I contacted Dr. Hogan (who has since died) and asked to interview him. He had known Mrs. Armstrong from his childhood and also knew her grandson, Roger "Bob" Naylor, who was around his age. He had kept in touch with Mrs. Armstrong over the years and told me of visiting with her in Abingdon, Virginia, up until the time of her death. He said that a mutual friend had given the manuscript to him after her death. When I visited him on September 6, 1999, he gave the original typescript to me, saying: "You're young; you can do something with it."

For a long time, "doing something" with the manuscript was on hold. The copy at ETSU had restrictions stating that it could not be reproduced for publication. The whereabouts of Roger "Bob" Naylor were unknown. Dr. Hogan and Dr. Jack Higgs had told me that Mrs. Armstrong had two great-grandsons in Texas, but I had not been successful in locating them. They had been born in Houston, but were now living in Austin. However, I continued to learn about Armstrong and to accumulate documentation on her life. Beginning in 2003, I gave several presentations about her at annual conferences of the Appalachian Studies Association. I also wrote entries on her for both the *Encyclopedia of Appalachia* (2006) and *The New Encyclopedia of Southern Culture* (Volume 9: Literature, 2008). Meanwhile, I changed jobs and moved to Knoxville.

In 2005 I was working in Hodges Library at the University of Tennessee when I received a telephone call from Roger Naylor, great-grandson of Anne Armstrong. To quote his brother Ed: "We found you as we were going over the copyright records for Anne's book *This Day and Time* and Roger googled her name and you popped up." They had run across a grant application I submitted in 2004 seeking funds to travel to Houghton Library at Harvard to examine a collection containing some of her correspondence with Thomas Wolfe.

I talked with both Ed and Roger Naylor on the telephone, and we kept in touch via e-mail until January 2006 when I was able to visit them in person while in Texas for a library conference. We shared information about Armstrong, and they allowed me to examine boxes of her papers and memorabilia that were in their possession. I presented them with the original typescript of their great-grandmother's memoir—making it clear that I would like to edit it for publication. Not long afterward, Ed Naylor let me know that he had found a handwritten manuscript which appeared to be Part 2 and a continuation of the memoir I already had. Ed performed the monumental task of transcribing the handwritten chapters of Part 2 and putting it into digital form.

The brothers had known very little about their great-grandmother. Their father, born October 7, 1921, had been barely a year old when his father, Roger Franklin Armstrong, died on October 26, 1922. When their father's mother (the former Anne Marie Baker) remarried, she and her new husband, Charles Edward Naylor, moved to Houston, Texas; and her child, who had been named Roger Armstrong (after his father), assumed the surname of his step-father, becoming Roger Armstrong Naylor, later nicknamed "Bob." He died in November 1984, leaving Mrs. Armstrong's great-grandsons to carry on her legacy.

Editing the manuscript and researching the history involved has been quite a journey. I wish to thank both Ed and Roger Naylor for allowing me to edit this work for publication; my thanks especially to Ed for his diligence in transcribing the handwritten portion. Thanks also to Roger and his wife, Ann, for graciously receiving me in their home and making me feel welcome. Our mutual goal has been to tell Anne's story; I hope that my part in this effort has succeeded in doing it justice.

At this point, I feel that I need to make a couple of disclaimers. First, I am not a historian. However, if not the credentials, I *do* have a background that, I feel, helped prepare me for this endeavor. My first work experience and training were in journalism, where the facts—and documenting the facts—are of utmost importance. After that, I became an information specialist (AKA librarian), which involved learning and using the skills needed for research. Secondly, like Anne Armstrong, I am not a native Knoxvillian, although my mother grew up in Knox County and most of her extended family still lives in the area. During my growing up years I came to Knoxville frequently to visit relatives and friends of hers.

I spent four years in Knoxville earning a B.A. in English from the University of Tennessee. Twenty years later, I again studied at UT, receiving a Master's degree in Library Science. I had wanted to live in Knoxville for a long time before I was able, in 2001, to make it my permanent home.

Although I felt that I knew Knoxville fairly well, preparing Mrs. Armstrong's memoir for publication has been an education for me, not only in the history of Knoxville and the late 1800s, but also in the books she read and the authors to whom she referred. I have consulted a lot of books about Knoxville and the time period in order to create annotations that I felt would best provide background material and, in some cases, bring the information about people and places in her story up to date.

Acknowledgments

First of all, I need to again acknowledge Ed and Roger Naylor, who trusted me with their great-grandmother's manuscript. I cannot thank them enough for allowing me to edit her memoir and for their support during this endeavor.

I wish to thank Norma Myers Riddle, director, and Marie Tedesco, Ed Speer, Ned Irwin, and Georgia Greer, staff members in the Archives of Appalachia at East Tennessee State University during the time I was working there, for introducing me to Anne Wetzell Armstrong and for their many kindnesses to me during that time. I acknowledge the University of Tennessee Libraries, Knoxville, for awarding me two Faculty Research Incentive Program grants which supported my research on Armstrong and enabled me to visit her great-grandsons in Austin, Texas.

My thanks to Jack Neely and another individual who read first drafts of my edited and annotated version of the manuscript, enthusiastically recommended its publication, and offered helpful suggestions for improving the work.

Knoxville is indeed fortunate to be home to the Calvin M. McClung Historical Collection, which came after but actually figured into Anne Armstrong's story during a time when Calvin McClung was still living and she visited in his home. We owe a great debt to Ed and Roger Naylor for generously donating their great-grandmother's manuscripts, photographs, books, and other papers to the McClung Collection. I have spent many hours there using its wonderful resources, and I thank manager Steve Cotham, archivist Joanna Bouldin, and all the staff for their assistance. Many of the pictures in this book, as noted, are part of the McClung Collection. In addition, classes in genealogical research, provided by the East Tennessee History Center, were of immense help in preparing me for work on this publication.

Thomas Wells, my editor at the University of Tennessee Press, has patiently guided me through the publication process, and I thank him.

I thank my children for their support—my son Kevin Akard for technical assistance with computer issues, his wife Kathy for help with maps and family trees, my daughter Alison Akard for help with genealogical research and the initial construction of genograms for the Wetzell, Armstrong, and Naylor families, and my son Keith Akard and daughter Lucy Reynolds for their support and encouragement.

Finally, I want to thank my friend Martha Whaley, who is a constant source of encouragement.

Critical Introduction

In *Of Time and Knoxville*, Anne Wetzell Armstrong claims Knoxville, Tennessee, as her home town—even though she was not born there—saying that it was "where I had spent the most impressionable years of my life." Her memoir provides important primary source material on the history of Knoxville and its people during the last several years of the nineteenth century at a time when major railroads were connecting Knoxville to the rest of the country and the town grew into a city.

In the 1850s the East Tennessee & Virginia (ET&V) and the East Tennessee & Georgia (ET&G) railroad companies built lines that connected Knoxville with other already existing railroads; from 1869–1894, Knoxville was the headquarters for the ETV&G Railroad. Knoxville was especially important during the Civil War, because both sides needed the railroads for transporting troops and supplies. After the war, Knoxville became a boom town and great southern jobbing center, with the railroads providing transportation for goods into and out of the city. According to Bruce Wheeler, "By 1885 Knoxville was the fourth leading wholesaling center in the entire South . . ." and by 1896, "the South's third largest wholesaler."[1] Other sources (MacArthur, Rothrock, Deaderick) agree.

People were coming to Knoxville from the northeast and midwest and even from other countries, most notably England and Canada. They came to teach school or to invest in Knoxville's businesses or as speculators in Knoxville's growing economy. Knoxville was full of immigrants who came to work in the mills, marble quarries, and factories that were springing up. Some immigrants, such as Peter Kern and Peter Staub, who both appear in *Of Time and Knoxville*, would make important contributions to Knoxville's cultural life. This was Knoxville's "Golden Age," into which our heroine arrived in 1885.

Born Anne Audubon Wetzell on September 20, 1872, in Grand Rapids, Michigan, Mrs. Armstrong was close to thirteen when she came to Knoxville. Her father, Henry B. Wetzell, moved his family to establish a timber and lumber business in the town's post-Civil War economy. Wetzell and his brothers had a successful lumber business in Michigan, but he had been to East Tennessee as a Union soldier and knew the area's abundant resources. Other members of the family were her mother, Lorinda, sometimes called Linnie; her older brother, Harry, who was enrolled as a cadet at the University of Tennessee; and her younger sister, Mary, usually referred to as "May" in this narrative. The family found housing in a part of Knoxville known at that time as "West End" (the present-day Fort Sanders neighborhood).

Looking back on her teenage years, Mrs. Armstrong takes us on a tour of Knoxville as it was in the late 1880s through the end of the century. She paints a vivid picture of the town at that time: the people, schools, churches, food, clothing, social customs, and the lingering effects of the recent Civil War, including a poignant story about her father's involvement in the Battle of Fort Sanders. She describes African-American cooks and her family's interactions with their household help. She gives detailed accounts of shopping with her mother at the Market House and of attending Second Presbyterian Church, where she first saw her future husband, Robert F. Armstrong, son of the couple for whom Knoxville's Bleak House was built.

She tells about influential businessman and landowner Perez Dickinson, whose "Island Home" was a social center of the time. Others who stand out in her narrative are Miss Molly Hayes (her favorite teacher), her neighbor and chum Mary Gaines, and her school friend Laura McAdoo, whose brother, William Gibbs McAdoo Jr., later became U.S. Secretary of the Treasury. Of all the local townspeople whom Mrs. Armstrong mentions, it is clear that she came close to idolizing Lizzie Crozier French, who led Tennesseans in the fight for women's suffrage, and that she had an equally strong dislike for Mary Boyce Temple, a local socialite who, nevertheless, is credited with saving Knoxville's Blount Mansion from demolition.

Mrs. Armstrong's "fragment of an autobiography" is really more a reminiscence, rambling and episodic, lapsing into flashbacks and stream of consciousness at times, as she remembers her experiences as a young girl in Knoxville and relates them to happenings later in her life. She often goes off on tangents, but her style is sophisticated and witty, with an occasional barb; her tongue can be acerbic. Some readers may find her speech quaint, but it is a reflection of the time in which she lived, and I have preserved it in order to contribute to her depiction of Knoxville at that time.

Similarly, her depiction of African Americans is a reflection of her time. Despite some deprecating remarks about black people, she does not seem to have had any ill will toward those with whom she came into contact; most of them she knew as servants or household help. In fact, one of the reasons she gave for breaking her engagement to Jim Ramsey was his attitude toward African Americans. But Knoxville also had a number of influential middle-class professional African-American citizens at the time, such as businessman Cal Johnson, lawyer William Yardley, and Charles W. Cansler, who became a teacher about the same time Armstrong was teaching in Knoxville. Others served as elected officials, such as aldermen.

Mrs. Armstrong's narrative is full of literary allusions; everything makes her think of a book or author she has read. She was obviously enamored with authors

Henry James, Charles Dickens, and, later on, others such as Walt Whitman and Robert Browning. She writes of "[her] own insatiate curiosity about books," and, in her own inimitable way, relates many of her stories to literary works of her time and to literature in general. She was highly educated and extremely well-read. By the time she wrote her memoir, she had lived in many different places and had traveled widely. Her literary allusions could almost be said to constitute a reading list for the latter half of the nineteenth century through the first half of the twentieth, and her way of expressing herself a window into that time. Authors with local ties whom she mentions include Mary Noailles Murfree, James Agee, Frances Hodgson Burnett, and Joseph Wood Krutch.

Anne W. Armstrong, as she most often identified herself, became a well-known author in her own time. Her first pieces were published while she was still a student at Mount Holyoke Seminary and College in South Hadley, Massachusetts. She went on to publish in *Atlantic Monthly, Harper's Monthly, Saturday Review of Literature, Yale Review,* and other prestigious periodicals of that time. Her first novel, *The Seas of God*, was published anonymously by Hearst in 1915 and by Mills and Boon in Great Britain in 1916, at which time she revealed her identity as the author. This story, based somewhat on her own life, is partially set in Knoxville (although she calls the town "Kingsville") and contains the first known description of Market Square in a novel.[2]

Other authors with a Knoxville connection who have included scenes on Market Square in their novels are James Agee, David Madden, Cormac McCarthy, and Richard Marius. Agee, whose autobiographical novel *A Death in the Family* was set in a thinly-disguised Knoxville, had even more in common with Anne Armstrong. Both of them had a devout church-going mother and a father who, although known as a good man, was "not a member of any church." Armstrong, after her father's death, expresses fear that the minister performing his funeral will say that he was not a Christian because he was not a member of the church. In the case of Agee's father, the priest refuses to read the complete burial service over him because he had never been baptized. Armstrong grew up attending Second Presbyterian Church, but she also went to St. John's Episcopal Church (where Agee was a member several years later) with her first husband, and she had her son christened by its minister. She was acquainted with Agee's grandparents and even visited in their home, in which Agee was later born. She and he, although over a generation apart in age, both lived on Highland Avenue during their time in Knoxville. And each of them, in telling a story about growing up in Knoxville, included a walk up to the ruins of Fort Sanders—Armstrong with "Theodore" and Agee (as Rufus) with his uncle following his father's funeral. Perhaps most striking, both of their fathers died as the result of an accident involving a motor vehicle—a train wreck in the case of Armstrong's father, an automobile wreck in Agee's.

Some of David Madden's books have other things in common with Armstrong's story. His novel *Sharpshooter* (1996) imagines a young Confederate soldier's war experiences and gives a fictionalized account of him shooting General William P. Sanders from the tower of Bleak House (the Armstrong home which Longstreet commandeered as his headquarters during the siege of Knoxville). Madden's earlier novel *Bijou* (1974) concerns the movie theatre that was made out of Lamar House by expanding the building and adding a stage—the same Lamar House where General Sanders was taken after being shot and later died. Madden's youthful fascination with the movies echoes Armstrong's interest in the performing arts, to which she was exposed in Knoxville at Staub's Opera House, just across the street (until it was torn down) from the Lamar House/Bijou.

Cormac McCarthy described Market Square in his first book, *The Orchard Keeper*, but his best remembered scene is from *Suttree*, when his title character wanders down Market Street through the square with a sack of fish to sell. Armstrong knew something about people like Cornelius Suttree from teaching their children. In Part 2, Chapter Nineteen of her memoir, she writes: "With the river only a block or so below the Bell House, some of them [the boys] came from tough families who lived in dilapidated houses along the river-front, piecing out a precarious existence. . . ."

Another creative figure with Knoxville (and Armstrong) ties is film director, producer, and scriptwriter Clarence Brown, who, like Armstrong, was not born in the south but spent his formative years there. Most sources report that he came to Knoxville at the age of ten or eleven (he was born May 10, 1890), when his father was appointed to a position at Brookside Mills. He graduated from Girls' High School (GHS) in 1905 at a time when high school ended with the tenth grade. Not only did GHS include boy students, it also had classrooms for grades three through seven. Based on his year of graduation, Brown would have been in seventh grade at GHS during the 1901/02 school year, Armstrong's final year of teaching in Knoxville, and could even possibly have attended sixth grade at GHS in 1900/01. In her memoir Armstrong mentions that, although officially the ninth-grade teacher, she would at times go to other classrooms to teach rhetoric and literature "to less or more advanced classes." I cannot help thinking that Clarence Brown was Armstrong's student, or at least fell under her influence since she, as Supervisor of Literature, developed a new course of study in literature for the high school grades (which was adopted beginning with the 1898/99 school year), and she also prepared a supplementary reading list for the lower grades.

In midlife, Mrs. Armstrong held positions in personnel and industrial relations with National City Company of New York City (1918–1919) and Eastman Kodak Company (1919–1923), and she later wrote numerous articles dealing with business and labor relations that were published in nationally-circulated journals and magazines. On the other hand, she had an abiding interest in the mountains of the southern highlands and a facility for describing the land and its people. (Readers of her memoir will be amused to hear her tell about a family trip to "the wilds" of Jonesboro and Erwin.) Her novel *This Day and Time* (1930) is considered by many to be the first book of realistic writing about Appalachia. It portrays the life, speech, and customs of the mountain people in upper East Tennessee during the early twentieth century. Mrs. Armstrong and her husband had built a home in the Big Creek section of rural Sullivan County, Tennessee, in 1916, and the mountain people of that area provided the setting and many of the characters for *This Day and Time*. Readers who are familiar with the heroine of *This Day and Time* will notice a marked similarity between her and the mountain woman hired as a cook for the Wetzell household in *Of Time and Knoxville*.

One of the features in *This Day and Time* for which Armstrong has been consistently recognized is her use of dialect to create authentic speech for her mountain characters. In 1971 Earl J. Schrock Jr. published an article entitled "An Examination of the Dialect in *This Day and Time*" in the *Tennessee Folklore Society Bulletin*. It was anthologized in *Voices from the Hills: Selected Readings of Southern Appalachia* and has been frequently cited.[3]

In her memoir, Armstrong includes quite a few examples of her penchant for dialect—beginning in the first chapter when Bithe, the maid, comes in to "do up" the room and in the conversations of washerwomen in the street below her window. In addition to other instances of African-American speech throughout the book and her use of the Appalachian speech of their cook, she puts dialect in the mouth of Mr. Barnes, whom she dislikes, and Mr. Joy (the janitor), whom she does like. She counts visiting Marblehead, scene of "Skipper Ireson's Ride," as one of the most rewarding experiences during her summer in New England and quotes the refrain from Whittier's poem, which is made even more terrible by his use of dialect.

After the rush of business articles that Mrs. Armstrong published in the 1920s and *This Day and Time* in 1930, she wrote on a wide variety of topics. Two still-cited articles are "The Southern Mountaineers" (*Yale Review*, March 1935)[4] and "As I Saw Thomas Wolfe" (*Arizona Quarterly*, Spring 1946). Mrs. Armstrong met Thomas Wolfe in April 1937 when he stopped in Bristol, Tennessee/Virginia, on his way to Asheville, North Carolina, to spend the summer. In September that year, on Wolfe's return trip to New York, he spent several days (or just a few, accounts vary) in a cabin on Mrs. Armstrong's property in northeast Sullivan County, Tennessee, before she took him to meet Sherwood Anderson in nearby Marion, Virginia.[5] Mrs. Armstrong described Wolfe's visit in "As I Saw Thomas Wolfe." She and Wolfe also corresponded, and some of their letters are archived in the "William B. Wisdom Collection of Thomas Wolfe" (MS Am 1883-1883.3) in Houghton Library at Harvard University. Like Wolfe, Mrs. Armstrong found that the thinly veiled semi-autobiographical novel she set in Knoxville (calling it "Kingsville" as Wolfe called Asheville "Altamont" in his first novel *Look Homeward, Angel*) stirred up hard feelings among local residents.

It seems obvious that Mrs. Armstrong patterned the title of her memoir after *Of Time and the River*, the title of Thomas Wolfe's semi-autobiographical novel published in 1935 by Charles Scribner's Sons. Perhaps Wolfe's subtitle, "A Legend of Man's Hunger in His Youth," gives a clue to her choice. Or perhaps her intention was just to reflect on what Knoxville was like at a particular time in her past, a theme she muses on in her introduction to her book.

But her memoir is also a "coming of age" story. She seems to be infatuated with boys—what we used to call "boy crazy"—although her stories are probably just a reflection of her age and the customs of her time. However, we can be sure that when she says her beaux "made love to her" she did not mean what it would mean today. She shows an open-minded attitude toward sex and did not hesitate to talk about it in her book, including prostitutes (e.g., the madams of Crozier Street), sadism, and sexual as well as physical abuse. She seems to have had more than a passing interest in fallen women—Mrs. Hamilton (supposedly), Em Parham, and Lydia, the character she created in her novel *The Seas of God.* Given the history of her disastrous first marriage, it is no wonder that in both her novels the main character is a strong "single" woman raising a son by herself under adverse conditions. On the other hand, she feels confused about "marrying a man I did not love and had never wanted to marry" and shamed by being a divorced woman. She is convinced that Knoxvillians look down on her because she is unconventional and does not belong to any church.

Mrs. Armstrong acknowledges that the stimulus which prompted her desire to write about Knoxville was John Gunther's insult to what she considered her home town. His remark was: "Knoxville is the ugliest city I ever saw in America, with the possible exception of some mill towns in New England. Its main street is called Gay Street; this seemed to me to be a misnomer."[6] (It must be remembered that Knoxville was, at one time, something of a mill town.) Armstrong had lived in Knoxville, except for brief periods, from 1885 until 1902 and remembered it quite differently. Nevertheless, she thanked him because, she said, writing the memoir "has furnished me a rewarding experience as I have groped my way back through the mists of time to a town . . . even whose blemishes are still dear to me."

She also objected to the book she calls the "*History of Knox County Tennessee*," published in 1946,[7] just a year before Gunther's *Inside U.S.A.* appeared. This book's actual title is *The French Broad-Holston Country*, indicating the important role these rivers played in the history of Knox County. The point at which they come together, a few miles above Knoxville, is still called the "Forks of the River." The Tennessee River, along which Knoxville was founded, was still called the Holston all the way to the mouth of the Little Tennessee (several miles below Knoxville) until 1890, when a federal statute recognized the confluence of the Holston and French Broad as its beginning.[8] In Armstrong's time the river was used not only for transportation, but also for recreation, like swimming and boating, as she recounts. Knobside, the home that Armstrong and her husband built in Sullivan County, was on the South Fork of the Holston River in upper East Tennessee.

Her memoir is the story of Knoxville as she knew it near the end of the nineteenth century, but she wrote it some fifty years later, during the middle of the twentieth century, when she was in her late seventies and early eighties. Based on her date of birth and the date that *Inside U.S.A.* was published, Mrs. Armstrong would have been at least seventy-five when she began her memoir. A 1952 newspaper article about the production of a play by Mrs. Armstrong mentions that she, in her eighties by that time, had completed a two-volume autobiography (the work at hand).[9]

Anne Wetzell Armstrong was indeed "one of the most remarkable women ever to live in Knoxville" as stated in *Heart of the Valley: A History of Knoxville, Tennessee.*[10] Perhaps the very eclectic nature of her writings, plus the fact that her first book was published anonymously, are reasons why she is not better known as an author today even though *This Day and Time* is still considered an important example of realistic writing about the Appalachian region. We can be glad that her "tell-all" memoir survived to give us such a vivid picture of Knoxville as it was just before the beginning of the twentieth century.

NOTES

1. William Bruce Wheeler, *Knoxville, Tennessee: A Mountain City in the New South*. 3rd ed. (Knoxville: University of Tennessee Press, 2020), 18.
2. Jack Neely, *Market Square: A History of the Most Democratic Place on Earth* (Knoxville: Market Square District Association, 2009), 114.
3. Earl J. Schrock Jr., "An Examination of the Dialect in *This Day and Time*," *Tennessee Folklore Society Bulletin* 37 (June 1971): 31–39; Robert J. Higgs and Ambrose N. Manning, eds., *Voices from the Hills: Selected Readings of Southern Appalachia* (New York: Ungar, 1975), 460–473.
4. "The Southern Mountaineers" was later anthologized and also reprinted in *Reader's Digest.*
5. Ted Mitchell, *Thomas Wolfe: A Writer's Life*. Rev. ed. (Raleigh: North Carolina Division of Archives and History, 1999. Published in cooperation with the Appalachian Consortium), 73, 78–79; Andrew Turnbull, *Thomas Wolfe* (New York: Charles Scribner's Sons, 1967), 272–273.
6. John Gunther, *Inside U.S.A.* (New York: Harper & Bros., 1947), 761.

7. Mary Utopia Rothrock, ed., *The French Broad-Holston Country: A History of Knox County, Tennessee* (Knoxville: East Tennessee Historical Society, 1946).
8. Anne Toplovich, "Tennessee River System," *Tennessee Encyclopedia of History & Culture*, ed. Carroll Van West (Nashville: Tennessee Historical Society / Rutledge Hill Press, 1998), 943-44.
9. Ralston Matheny, "Granny's Millions," *Knoxville News-Sentinel*, September 22, 1954: 15, knoxnews.com, accessed July 11, 2017.
10. Lucile Deaderick, ed., *Heart of the Valley: A History of Knoxville, Tennessee* (Knoxville: East Tennessee Historical Society, 1976), 449.

Editorial Note

Anne Armstrong was such a good writer that I have made very few changes to her text. I have endeavored, as much as possible, to let her speak for herself in her "fragment of an autobiography." Just as her story is about Knoxville in the last decades of the nineteenth century, I felt that the style and wording should reflect the language and spelling of that time. Therefore, I have preserved certain spellings and conventions of the day, such as "Michael Angelo," "Hayti," "Tolstoi," "can not," "to-day."

Also, given the time period of the story, certain racial terms appear that would not be appropriate today. These have been retained as part of the historical record. Armstrong does not seem to have felt any ill will toward blacks with whom she came in contact. Although she uses words such as "slatternly" when talking about some African-Americans, she also uses them in reference to poor whites.

Armstrong tended to use the British spelling for certain words (e.g., fibre, centre, furore, neighbour), and I have retained her spelling. I have also kept her capitalization of the seasons and certain other words (e.g., Spring, Southern, Century) that we do not now capitalize. Inconsistencies and minor errors in spelling have been silently corrected or explained in a note. In several instances, Armstrong misspells the names of people or misstates their relationships. In these cases, I have inserted bracketed information to correct her error or have added a note of explanation.

At this point, I feel that I need to say something about names: especially, Annie Wetzell, the name by which our author was known growing up. After her first marriage and divorce, she retained her married surname and went by Annie Wetzell Waldron. When she married again, she was often referred to (especially in newspaper articles) as Mrs. Robert F. Armstrong, but she almost always used "Anne W. Armstrong" (occasionally, "Anne Wetzell Armstrong") as her by-line, although she admits that, early on, she sometimes put "A. W. Armstrong" on submissions because of the reluctance of publishers to accept articles by a woman. I have used AWA instead of her name in most footnotes, partly out of convenience and partly for reasons of space.

In her memoir, she chose to use the name "Theodore De Groot" for the man who became her first husband. If she had a reason for choosing this name, I do not know it and will not speculate about it. His real name was Leonard T. Waldron.

She calls one of her boyfriends "Hu White," but I have not been able to find any information that might identify him. Possibly she changed or made up his name.

When I first read Mrs. Armstrong's memoir, I doubted some of her stories. However, as I began checking sources and verifying information about the people and places she was telling about, I came to find that, for the most part, she is accurate in her reporting. She may have fabricated or embellished some of her stories, of course, but in only a few places does she get things mixed up. I have added notes to correct the details where Mrs. Armstrong has either misremembered, or confused relationships or the timing of events. Errors in some proper names (e.g., Schmitt instead of Schmidt, Midland—not Midlands—Bank) have also been explained in notes. Other annotations have been added to flesh out and provide background information on people and places that Mrs. Armstrong mentions but which may not be familiar to present-day readers or to those not familiar with Knoxville (or Knoxville as it was before the turn of the century).

Changes that I have made include substituting italics for underlined words in Mrs. Armstrong's text, standardizing the style for decades (e.g., the '80s instead of 80's), and using a single *em* dash for multiple dashes and spaces within and at the end of sentences. Where ellipses appear, they were hers.

In the interest of space (Part One of the manuscript consists of 368 double-spaced typed pages and Part Two of 1,017 handwritten pages), some sections have been omitted, but in such a way that the story proceeds seamlessly. Therefore, I have not used ellipses to indicate omissions. Only in the case of Mrs. Armstrong's story "The Branner House" (Chapter Six: Mama and the Gaines Family) and Robert Houston Armstrong's "Trip to Texas" journal (Chapter Thirteen: Bleak House) did I insert an editorial note explaining that part of Armstrong's original text has been deleted.

Chronology

1867	Henry Bower Wetzell marries Lorinda "Linnie" Snyder on December 5
1870	Henry "Harry" Wetzell born April 24 in Brooklyn, New York
1872	Annie Audubon Wetzell born September 20 in Grand Rapids, Michigan
1877	Mary E. "May" Wetzell born May 7 in Grand Rapids, Michigan
1885	Wetzell family moves to Knoxville, Tennessee, in September
1888	Harry Wetzell drowns on June 5
1889	Flat Creek train disaster, August 22
1889/90 & 1890/91	Annie Wetzell attends Mount Holyoke College
1892	Spring – teaches at Miss Ogden's School in Knoxville
1892	marries Leonard T. Waldron on July 1 in Chicago
1892	Fall – lives on Whiskey Row in Snohomish, Washington
1893	January – moves to Fargo, North Dakota
1893	Summer – visits Waldron's sister on South Side of Chicago and spends a few days at the Chicago World's Fair
1893	August – returns to parents' home at 306 Highland Ave., Knoxville
1893	son Roger Waldron born on September 8
1893	late November(?) – moves w/Waldron to little house "out near Bell Ave."
1894	early June – moves back to her parents' home on Highland Ave.
1894	divorced from Leonard T. Waldron on August 22 (final decree)
1894	Henry B. Wetzell dies on September 11
1894	takes job as traveling "general agent" in October(?)
1895	accepts position teaching third grade at Bell House School in late January; moves with her mother to North Knoxville; moves back to West End (500 White Ave.) at end of summer

1895	Fall – begins teaching at Girls' High School (will teach there seven years: 1895/96, 1896/97, 1897/98, 1898/99, 1899/1900, 1900/01, 1901/02)
1897	July – visits Tennessee Centennial Exposition in Nashville
1897 or '98?	visits Tullahoma during summer and runs into Jim Ramsey
1898	enrolled in summer quarter at the University of Chicago
1898/99	named "Supervisor of Literature" at Girls' High School; introduces new course in English and American classics
1899	May Wetzell marries Leon L. Roach on February 27 in Franklin, Ohio
1900	spends summer visiting literary shrines in New England
1900 or '01	moves to Miss Hilton's boarding house at 708 Walnut
1902	leaves Knoxville at end of school year (presumably to marry Jim Ramsey)
1902-04	[unknown]
1905	Annie Wetzell Waldron marries Robert Franklin Armstrong on June 14
1915	publishes *The Seas of God* anonymously
1922	son Roger Franklin Armstrong (born Waldron) killed on October 26
1930	publishes *This Day and Time*
1930	visits Knoxville in September, "Thirty Years After"
1931	Robert Franklin Armstrong dies on March 24
1958	Anne Wetzell Armstrong dies March 17 in Abingdon, Virginia

Of Time and Knoxville

"... mingled yarn, good and ill together"

Author's Preface

During the palmiest days of the *American Mercury,* Henry Mencken, then its Editor, commented in its pages, in his inimitably insulting fashion, on some place or other that it had sunk to the cultural level of Port-au-Prince, Hayti, and Knoxville, Tennessee.[1]

At the time, I still considered Knoxville my home town, although I had long lived far from it. But I relished Mr. Mencken's reference to a spot on the earth's surface where I had spent the most impressionable years of my life. I could not forget certain smug aspects of the town and its all too frequent evidences of religious bigotry. Since the Scopes' Trial[2] the very name of the state had become a synonym for abysmal ignorance. More than this, I had recently heard a report, whether true or false, that Joseph Wood Krutch, the distinguished critic and essayist, member of a highly respected and admired Knoxville family, had been pilloried in the local press in an article headed, "A Son of Knoxville but Knoxville not Proud of Him."[3] About the same time a report reached me that an able professor at the University of Tennessee (located at Knoxville) had just been asked to resign when he confessed having read Robinson's *Mind in the Making*, considered by the University authorities to be subversive.[4]

I wrote Mencken: "I know nothing about Port-au-Prince, Hayti, but a good deal about Knoxville, Tennessee. Would you like it?"

The answer came: "We would."

Circumstances, however, prevented my supplying the article I had in mind. But in the quarter of a century that has intervened between that time and this every once in a while I have speculated on just what *was* the cultural level of Knoxville. Was it really lower than the cultural level of other Southern towns, or for the matter of that of other towns of like size in the United States in the same period? Today, my response to Mr. Mencken would be somewhat different from the one that in the 1920s I solicited space for on the pages of the *American Mercury.*

Nevertheless, I should never have attempted any rebuttal to Mr. Mencken's now ancient though still provocative charge except for the publication in 1947 of John Gunther's *Inside USA.* What fired me here was Mr. Gunther's tagging Knoxville as the ugliest city he had ever seen in the USA—a statement which, coming from a man who had seen Gary, Indiana, and Los Angeles, California, aroused me to such an unreasonable pitch of resentment as to make me wonder anew what it was in this dirty old town of Knoxville that could still command from me an allegiance I had never felt for any other place.

I got to thinking about Knoxville. I have no acquaintance whatever with the sprawling, overcrowded city which TVA,[5] for all the compensating blessings it has showered upon the surrounding region, together with Oak Ridge, in close proximity to Knoxville (with the more dubious benefits it has conferred upon the human race), have made of this town. But the desire grew in me to recapture, if I could, something of the old Knoxville which still lives in my mind, a Knoxville of the '80s and '90s and of the turn of the century.

I am aware, of course, that there are as many Knoxvilles as people who have called it home, or known it even fleetingly. This is simply a *Knoxville To Me*: full of the trivia which after all make up the lives of most of us. Though there are facts in it, it is not primarily a book of facts. It is a tissue, if I may call it so, woven of memory, legend, of myth, of gossip, even of scandalous tittle-tattle—and of dreams, for often in dreams I still walk the streets (streets whose very names have changed), climb up and down the hills of old Knoxville.

But while I do not claim this to be in essence a factual work, I have thought it desirable to base it on a certain irreducible minimum of fact, and to this end have read, conscientiously I hope, the rather recent *History of Knox County, Tennessee*; a bulky volume, most of its pages devoted to the founding and development of the town of Knoxville, and sponsored by the East Tennessee Historical Society,[6] to which I hereby acknowledge my indebtedness for such services as it has rendered me. Chief among them is the realization that for a completely denatured history of Knoxville, none will ever surpass it. It is, in fact, incredible that what I had always known as a highly colorful community could be so completely drained of all its color. Far from being a story of the flesh and blood men and women who in the course of long years acted out their infinitely varied parts on the Knoxville scene, it refrains from all references which might be considered in even the slightest degree damaging. It may be looked upon as a Calendar of Saints. The only sinners listed in its long roll of pioneers, civic leaders, and their descendants from 1786, when the town was founded, until 1945, when this volume appeared, was one Sam Rutherford who, in 1813, in the course of a brawl bit off part of the ear of a fellow citizen of Knoxville, one John Garod; and a Peggy McMahon who got herself preserved in print through having been, also in 1813, indicted by the "Grand Inquest" on the score of being a common scold.[7]

Now all this is very curious to one who was in a position to know and early recognized that despite its prodigious display of piety and its strong streak of Puritanism of our deadly Southern variety, there was probably as much pure worldliness, as large a proportion of rascality and lubricity in Knoxville, as many young rake-hells among its first families, as in any equal area in the United States.

What I have attempted then, is the Profane History of Knoxville; or rather, to state the much more modest aim I have had in view, a small segment of that history. Many individuals whose names appear in the pages of the *History of Knox County*, I knew, knew well, and as a child in their midst long ago, unconsciously taking notes, I have had things to say about a considerable number of them, in my effort to show something of what it felt like to be growing up in Knoxville in the 1880s and 1890s.

NOTES

1. This statement did appear in *The American Mercury*. However, it was not H. L. Mencken but Charles Angoff, assistant to the editor, who wrote: "Once the Athens of America, Boston now plunges downward toward the cultural level of Port au Prince and Knoxville, Tenn." Charles Angoff, "Boston Twilight," *American Mercury* (December 1925), 439.
2. In July 1925, John T. Scopes was tried for teaching evolution in the public schools of Dayton, Tennessee. See George E. Webb, "The Scopes Trial," in *The Tennessee Encyclopedia of History & Culture*, ed. Carroll Van West (Nashville: Tennessee Historical Society, Rutledge Hill Press, 1998), 830–31.
3. Krutch was not named in the *Knoxville Sentinel* editorial that said, in part, "We wish this native son to know that we are not proud of him" in response to an article that Krutch wrote for *The Nation*, which had assigned him to cover the Scopes trial. In his biography of Krutch, John Margolis discussed at length the article and Krutch's reporting on the trial. *Knoxville Sentinel*, July 10, 1925; John D. Margolis, *Joseph Wood Krutch: A Writer's Life* (Knoxville: University of Tennessee Press, 1980), 56–61.
4. According to the Finding Aid for a 1923 diary held in the University of Tennessee Special Collections Library, University President Harcourt A. Morgan allegedly dismissed Professor J. W. Sprowls because Sprowls had assigned a text, *The Mind in the Making*, which discussed evolution. The diary was kept from April 9 to August 20, 1923, by Philip M. Hamer, professor of history at UT during that time. *The Mind in the Making: The Relation of Intelligence to Social Reform* was written by James Harvey Robinson and published by Harper in 1921. Hamer, Philip M., (Philip May), 1891–1971. Finding Aid for the Philip M. Hamer Diary, MS.0526. 1923. http://dlc.lib.utk.edu/spc/view?docId=ead/0012_002914_000000_0000/0012_002914_000000_0000.xml (viewed March 5, 2018).
5. Tennessee Valley Authority.
6. Mary U. Rothrock, ed. *The French Broad-Holston Country: A History of Knox County, Tennessee* (Knoxville: East Tennessee Historical Society, 1946).
7. Rothrock, *French Broad-Holston Country*, 63, 64.

PART ONE

Annie Wetzell, about age 9. Taken in Grand Rapids, Michigan, before moving to Knoxville.

Chapter One
Gay Street

Like James McNeil Whistler, who did not "choose" to have been born in Lowell, Massachusetts, but in Baltimore, Maryland, St. Petersburg, Russia, or where he would,[1] at the moment, I choose—whatever my birth certificate may state—to have been born in Knoxville, Tennessee. It is certainly true that, while presumably by train, I have not the faintest recollection of arriving in Knoxville. My first memory of the place is of sitting at an open window, facing on Gay Street, in old Schubert's Hotel, old even then, in 1885.[2] Once a log tavern, and in the intervening years a fashionable gathering place which advertised in the *Knoxville Journal* its "elegant bar-room, spacious ballroom, and large open fire-place in the commodious lobby," Schubert's at the time of my own first acquaintance with it, had become pretty dingy. Only the "elegant bar-room," whose slightly sour and powerful fumes pervaded the whole hotel, survived to suggest its earlier grandeur. Soot-stained, however, and generally grimy though it was, it still retained a certain air of old-fashioned comfort and dignity and my parents had probably been given to understand that Schubert's was better, whatever its failings, than its only two rivals in the town, the pillared, dilapidated yet statelier looking Lamar House on the corner below, or the somewhat more modern, if unimpressive, Hattie House, farther up the street.[3]

It was September, late in the afternoon, and from various connecting circumstances of which I retain vague memories, I think the day must have been Saturday. My parents had placed my younger sister in my charge when they started out in a livery carriage on what promised to be a prolonged excursion. They were house hunting and with prospects thus far, it seemed, far from encouraging.

I think, if my dream-like memory of it all can serve as guide, that I must have been sitting for most of the day, gazing, sometimes leaning, out of the open windows, guiltless of screens (one of those "Northern ideas" to which Knoxville was not yet ready to yield). Meantime my little sister May played with her dolls, or dozed in the sweltering heat on the big black-walnut bed, above which was suspended a voluminous canopy of white mosquito-netting, now in the day-time draped back over the bed's towering head-board. But the room, with its drab walls, lofty ceiling, massive and ornate Early Victorian furniture, its huge wardrobe, marble-topped washstand bearing on it a china bowl and pitcher decorated with water-lilies, its worn and rather badly spotted crimson carpet and its musty smell, though different from any I had known before was not sufficient in itself to hold my interest—not with so much happening down below on Gay Street, the origin of whose name, incidentally, I have never been able to discover, and one to which Mr. John Gunther objected, in his *Inside USA*, as a misnomer,[4] but which presented, on that long past September day, if not a gay scene, at least a far from very grim one, to my own young unjaundiced eye.

But it was not, to be truthful, a wholly innocent eye with which I contemplated Gay Street for the first time. Considering my years—I had not yet reached my teens[5]—I was already, measured by the standards of the day, what might almost have been regarded as a traveled person. Child of traveling parents, whether traveling merely for pleasure or where my father's far-flung business interests called him—of parents, moreover, who were wont, at a moment's notice and in the face of vigorous protests from teachers, to take any or all of their children out of school in the middle of a term and traveling with them, I had had more than a passing glance at a host of cities, large and small, from New York and Boston and Philadelphia to the raw young town of Duluth, perched above the steely waters of Lake Superior. I knew Long Branch, New Jersey, Greenwich, Connecticut, Mackinaw Island, and the Falls of Minnehaha. But here, in this Knoxville, were new sights, sounds, smells—an utterly new feel.

Down below, on the street, bulky or lean Negro women were slopping by, pieces of shoes tied on their feet with rags, and balancing on their heads great willow baskets heaped up with what it was plain were freshly laundered clothes they were carrying home to their white folks somewhere. I could catch the sally a Negro woman threw out to another, with jovial insolence in passing: "Lord 'a mercy, nigger, where *you* gwine?" and again the mincing exchange as two black acquaintances met: "How's you-all?" "Why, we's tol'able, thankee." All of the time shackly wagons were clattering by, wagons hitched to mules, loaded with women and children, or with men in the wagon-box, eating water-melons as they rode, spitting out seeds into the street. There were a good many men, too, black and white, on mules or horse-back, all going, as the afternoon waned, in the direction of the bridge over the river, down at the end of Gay Street, only a few blocks away; shouting to each other, guffawing, going home to the country, you could tell, after a day's trading or idling in town. Often, in striking contrast, genteel surreys, with or without fringe on top, would pass, and occasionally a Victoria, the black coachman on the box in livery, and in the back the prettiest ladies and young girls I had ever seen, I thought, and all in the daintiest of summer toilettes, their voile or organdy dresses trimmed with ruffles and narrow lace frills; on their heads broad-brimmed Leghorn hats with ribbons streaming from the low crowns.

What puzzled me, though, and gave me the feeling of slight anxiety were groups of men on the corners below and gathered here and there along the curb opposite—

young men, well-dressed, often handsome, and others older, seedier. The groups kept forming and re-forming, but the men in them always talked in hushed voices, though with gestures and evident heat, about something that seemed, secretly, to concern them in common. What were they so excited about? In a few more hours I would know. Meantime, directly across the street, in front of an empty store building, stood a blind man with a ragged, dirty-faced little girl beside him who held out a cup for coppers. The blind man sang over and over, in a loud, high-pitched, nasal voice, with each syllable long drawn out, a ballad which began:

> His name was Hicks Car Michael,
> His char-ac'-ter was bad.

But what attracted me most in the view from the hotel windows was Staub's Opera House,[6] on a corner obliquely across from Schubert's, a squarish brick building, then of a soft yellowish tone, as I recall it, and with out in front what obviously were bill-boards announcing future attractions, a lure I finally was unable to resist, so that some time during the day I had deserted my post, and slipped across the street, stopping to drop a few pennies into the cup of the ballad singer and receiving in return a printed copy of the ballad from which I learned that the man whose

Staub's Opera House, corner Gay Street and Cumberland Avenue.

name was Hicks Carmichael had killed someone, unhappily run afoul of the Law and met his own "sad fate" when not long before he had been hanged in Knoxville. It was a ballad, I may add, whose mournful strains were to sound now and then from corners of Gay Street for years to come.[7]

At the theatre, I read on the bill-boards that Emma Abbott was to be heard the coming week in Donizetti's popular *Daughter of the Regiment*, in *Martha* and *The Bohemian Girl*. I had heard of these operas, though never gone to an opera, notwithstanding the fact that my parents, along with constantly interrupting the schooling of their children to take them traveling, had also taken us, at a very tender age, to see Edwin Booth in *Hamlet*, the great Salvini, the Elder, in *Othello*, Joseph Jefferson in *Rip Van Winkle*, Madame Modjeska, the Polish star, in *Adrienne Lecouvreur*, Ristori, the Italian tragic actress who had been a rival of the immortal Rachel, in *Francesca da Rimini*, and many other famous players of the day. As for Staub's Opera House itself, though I had seen much more imposing opera-houses, as theatres in general were called then in the United States, yet immediately it took on for me a romantic aspect such as no other theatre had ever worn, or ever was to, not even the *Comédie Française*.

It was, I believe now, looking back, more than anything else, the *old* look of things in Knoxville—even things like Staub's Opera House that were not, in reality, very old, but that Knoxville's damp sooty winters, its long, moist, hot summers, had combined to make look so—it was this, I think that began at once working its magic on me. Main streets with which heretofore I had been familiar were broad well-kept thoroughfares, plate-glass windows flashing along their lengths. Here, the very shabbiness on every hand: across the way the scarred mouldy store-fronts of stores that looked dim and cool inside, their windows half-shrouded in indigo-blue shades; the uneven brick pavements, moss pushing up in places between the bricks; the steep, shadowy narrow street which I could see opposite, plunging down the hill at the side of the Opera House—why, this was like some place I had read about and seen pictures of in *St. Nicholas*, that children's monthly on which I had been brought up and only recently discarded in favor of the more sophisticated delights of Thackeray's *Vanity Fair*. It was like some worn and ancient town in the Old World with narrow steep streets, dark and malodorous but tinged with history. And Knoxville itself was tinged with history. The Battle of Fort Sanders, in "the late War," had been fought here.[8] My father had helped throw up its earth-works. The heart knows its own climate when it finds it, and where I had always wanted to be—from the beginning—was in Knoxville!

Then the smells—fumes from the bar-room downstairs and from nearby saloons up and down the street; the ammoniac reek from Pryor Brown's Livery Stable, biggest and best in town and directly back of Schubert's Hotel;[9] the stench—as it can only, in candor, be called—arising from the open ditches, instead of closed sewers, through which the city's waste was still disposed—these smells, old and evil though they were, old as sin, yet in some mysterious and exciting way blended, in time, with impressions of the bewitching ladies in the Victorias, of the blind ballad-singer, the wicked man, Hicks Carmichael, who had been hanged, of black faces constantly in sight, served only to enhance the spell which Knoxville was beginning to exert.

The heat became more oppressive as the sun went down. My thin summer dress clung to my skin and I kept mopping my forehead and fanning with a big palm-leaf fan I had found in the room. But suddenly my attention was turned from the heat to a magnificent equipage lumbering into view from further up Gay Street, an open landau, two stalwart mulattoes in high hats on the box and on the back seat, alone, the corpulent figure of an old man in a white linen suit, with an abundance of snowy hair escaping from under the wide-brimmed hat he wore and framing his broad, clean-shaven, florid face. His hands were resting on a gold-headed cane. This, as I was soon to know, was the Hon. Perez Dickinson, born in Amherst, Massachusetts, and a close kinsman of the poetess, Emily Dickinson, "Uncle Perez," as the irreverent in Knoxville called him.

Merchant, planter, banker, one of Knoxville's wealthiest and most influential men, at seventeen he had come South—as had so many other New England men

Perez Dickinson (ca. 1893).

and women—to teach school. But after three years of school-teaching had abandoned it for a more lucrative enterprise, shortly becoming silent partner in the emerging firm of Cowan, McClung & Company, wholesale drygoods, groceries, and shoes, with Knoxville, developing then—in the 1830s and '40s—as a wholesale distributing center for all the surrounding Southern States.

Childless, over seventy, a widower for forty years past when I first caught sight of Col. Dickinson, as he was generally called (a title inescapable in a time when all men of any importance in Knoxville were Colonels, Majors, or at very least, Captains), he maintained not only what was referred to as his "princely mansion" in town, but a sumptuous country house, "Island Home," on his great plantation near Knoxville, entertaining lavishly in both.[10]

Of all this I knew nothing, of course, when, from a window in Schubert's Hotel, his resplendent figure arrested my attention, though neither then, nor later, could I have imagined Col. Perez Dickinson against a measured New England background. Ironically enough, this son of Massachusetts, with his spacious ways, was, and ever remained, Knoxville's outstanding example of that romantic and legendary figure, the Southern planter, at his flamboyant best. None I had seen on the stage was pictorially his equal, though everything now in Knoxville was beginning to take on the character of a play or story, and after Col. Dickinson had passed in his landau I should hardly have been surprised to see golden chariots rolling down Gay Street.

But I had been prepared—conditioned, I might say, in previous months, to expect marvels in Knoxville. My father had first seen the old town—old for an American town—as a soldier, during the War; been impressed by its climate and its splendid situation— "built, like Rome, on seven hills." I had heard, or overheard, much, in fact, about the whole great valley of East Tennessee, rimmed by mountains—one of the most beautiful and potentially rich valleys in the United States, and with Knoxville, "The Marble City,"[11] at its very heart, the strategic center of a region abounding not only in marble, but in iron and coal, with endless tracts of timber, an all but inexhaustible supply, to which the axe had not yet been laid. Fabulous fortunes would be made here!

It is true my father had already made a fortune, or so I had inferred from words let drop by our eccentric but able and prosperous Cousin Simon: "By George, Henry a millionaire, and not yet forty!"

It was almost dark now and in a strange place (as any birth-place is bound to be), I was getting a little anxious for my parents' return. When they opened the door, Mama—I can see her plainly—, beautiful all her life, and in a modish dress of cream-colored batiste, a touch of scarlet about it somewhere, its overskirt bordered, as were the sleeves, with a deep flounce of English eyelet embroidery in the same delicate creamy shade; with a bustle—which no lady of the period would have been seen without—, and her hat, gloves, parasol, all in harmony with the rest of her costume. I can see the refinement, and the dignity, without stiffness, which she never lacked, but a look of being a trifle wilted now, her face unusually flushed, perhaps from the heat, and in her dark eyes a faintly fretted expression. She went into the adjoining bedroom to freshen up and my father lit the gas and sat down, taking my sister in his lap.

"Your Mama," he said, "is a little disappointed in the house. It was all we could find to rent, or to buy, for that matter—any we would consider. It's not in very good repair and it's not *very* clean!" He burst into a laugh at this, a boyish, yet not boisterous laugh. "Well, I think your Mama will like it better," he said, "when it's been scrubbed and scoured and maybe some fresh paper and paint applied. Anyway, we won't have to live in it very long, only till we know Knoxville better and where we want to build. But children," he said, lowering his voice and a mischievous look in his eyes, "I'll tell you something, a secret—I sort of like that old house we found out there near Fort Sanders. We'll move in as soon as the owners move out. Of course it's an old-fashioned house and hasn't many conveniences, but it has little wooden balconies—regular Romeo and Juliet balconies—hanging around it from the upstairs rooms. It has a big yard, plenty of room for Trix [the dog] to run around in. It has some wonderful magnolia trees in front and apple trees and pear trees and cherry trees in the back, and a grape trellis hanging just full of grapes—."

By this time, I could hardly wait to see the place.

But it was always thus when Papa appeared. Tall, broad-shouldered, with no superfluous flesh, yet not exactly lean, all his movements were easy. But it was not alone that he was the very image of physical vigor united with flexibility, of abounding health. It was more than this. He was one of those people, those vital and decisive people, in whose presence we felt a power to cope with whatever arose, felt instantly secure. And so it was now.

We went down to supper. The old Negro waiters in their not too clean white coats hovered around Papa obsequiously. It was a little cooler here in the dusky ground-floor dining room which opened, on its Gay Street side, directly on to the sidewalk. There were no printed menus but appetizing odors from dishes on all the tables mingled with the pungent, all-enveloping winey fumes from the adjacent bar-room. There were grapes and peaches and melons, platters of golden-brown fried chicken, of ham and of steak, platters of steaming corn on the cob, which the waiters called "roastin' ears." There were heaped-up dishes of string beans that had been boiled with bacon; dishes of lima beans and of the smaller, more tender variety of limas—butter beans; there were sweet potatoes, just dug from the ground, cucumbers and tomatoes only a few hours off the vines—all the fresh, rich, home-grown products of Knoxville's market, of which there was none better then, it is safe to say, in the whole South, or certainly not in the Mid-South. There were new-made jams and jellies, too, of every description and on every table a high glass compote of deep amber honey, made, Papa explained, from the blossoms of sourwood trees, and the best honey, he said, in the world. And there were the old waiters scurrying back and forth on their flat feet, constantly bringing fresh supplies of small flaky biscuits, piping hot, of strong hot coffee, and big glass pitchers from which they refilled your glass with sweet milk, or with buttermilk still with little blobs of butter floating on it as it had come from the churn, and while Mama might find the string beans too greasy, the thin fried steak that had been dipped in flour and was crisp and brown, a poor substitute for rare, juicy Porterhouse, so far as I was concerned never before, nor after, was a supper quite so delicious as that first supper at old Schubert's Hotel.

Just the same, all of the time we were eating, I was not quite easy. The dining-room was getting crowded. Young men kept coming into it from the Gay Street entrance, or through the swinging-doors from the bar-room, joining other young men at the tables in the back of the room. With the few and poor lights in the room and its thick smoky atmosphere, I could only see the young men dimly, but I could tell, from their heads close together, they were conferring about something or other. I noticed that the old Negro waiters, as they hurried back and forth, with their huge trays, held aloft, exchanged keen furtive glances with each other and occasionally that one of them gave a quick backward, almost imperceptible but knowing nod in the direction of the young men, several of whom I recognized now as the same I had seen from the bedroom windows, gathered in knots on the street below. I became conscious of a feeling of suppressed excitement diffused through the whole dim, crowded, sultry room, merged with its heavy smell of good food and drink. Something was afoot in this highly charged atmosphere and instinct told me it was nothing good.

But when I questioned Papa he put me off lightly. It was only when Mama questioned him that in turn he questioned the waiter. I strained my ears.

"Dey's young men," the old waiter said in low tones, his grizzled head bent down, "who's come up from Loudon, Sweetwater, Athens—all de little towns round about. You see, suh, der was a young man kilt heah in Knoxville a couple o' days back, a travelin' man, mighty well liked. Oh, yas, suh, de Law got de man dat kilt him. He's in de jail-house heah, but dere might be a little trouble. Of co'se I don't know nothin' about it 'cep'n what I heahs, but some says . . ."

That was all I could catch, but I saw across our cluttered and now disordered table a look of slight alarm rise in Mama's somber eyes. What sort of a place *was* this to which her husband had brought her?—this man whose adventurous lead she had followed many years and heretofore without a moment's misgiving.

Papa spoke reassuringly. The city authorities, he was confident, were well advised. They would take all precautions.

Next morning Mama and Papa went to church. Mama was to present to the Second Presbyterian Church in Knoxville her "Letter" from the church of which she had previously been a member. Papa was not a member of any church. When he and Mama lived in New York during the early years of their married life they had attended the Plymouth Church in Brooklyn and for its pastor, Henry Ward Beecher, he always expressed high respect, as later for Spurgeon, the famous English preacher, whom he went to hear whenever he was in London.[12] But in general—I was already aware—neither religious denominations nor religious dogmas made any strong appeal to my father, although he dutifully put on his frock coat and every Sunday morning accompanied Mama.

A fat, slatternly, good-humored black chambermaid, with a white rag around her head, came in to do up the room. She said her name was Tabitha, but just call her Bithe. She kept talking more or less to herself as she went around, draping the voluminous folds of the mosquito canopy over the back of the bed, changing the dingy bluish linen for some fresh but smelly linen of the same hue; as she slapped with her dust-cloth here and there and emptied the slops. "Law, honey, you-all best not be roamin' aroun' ter-night. Dey's gwine ter be trouble in dis ole town shore as Jedgment Day."

But she gave some attention now to my little sister, bent over a book of fairy tales, her shy face almost hidden by the long fair ringlets which fell below her shoulders. "Ain't she sweet as a angel?" Bithe said, but then, turning quickly to where I was standing in front of the windows, looking out, and at the same time trying to braid my hair in the two braids I wore down my back, "But you're sweet, too, honey. Lawd 'a mercy, sech fine hair—fine as silk! Want Bithe to he'p you plat it?"

It was the first compliment I had ever received on my hair, which was perfectly straight and ash brown. Bithe's honeyed words, in her deep, soft, rich voice, seemed to establish an immediate bond between us. She remained at the windows, pointing a black finger and half whispering now: "Right down dere, down de hill, on Crozier Street—second street below dis heah one, Gay—dat's where de man—white man—was kilt, in one o' dem whorehouses down yonder."

A shiver ran through me. I had seen the word "whore" in the Bible, but never before heard it spoken. I understood its meaning, however, if vaguely, and recognized at once that in this good-natured black chambermaid I had a source of knowledge about the mysterious subject of sex. I must have asked some questions. At any rate, Bithe explained that Crozier Street (long since, I believe, Central Avenue) was Knoxville's "bad street," with whorehouses, she said, from one end to the other. She pointed now in another direction, toward the "jail-house," down by the river, close to the bridge. They kept bloodhounds there. Sometimes of a night you could hear the hounds. It made your blood curdle. And that's where the young man was they were going to "string up." Bithe was full of excitement, her eyes, with their

Annie and May Wetzell (ca. 1880).

yellowish, blood-shot whites, bulging as she poured all this into my eager if horrified young ears. "De young mens shore is a-gatherin'," she went on, mutteringly, "but yet an' still I don't reckon dey'd lynch him of a Sunday, de Lawd's day. But dey might. Ain't no tellin'—"

A strong, unfamiliar, musky and animal smell still lingered in the room after Bithe had left with her slop-bucket and broom. But she had left behind her, as well, something warm and human and comforting, despite the fact that some of the new knowledge she had imparted had made me feel faintly sick.

But at noon my brother Harry came to have dinner with us and Crozier Street lost, for the time, the powerful and disturbing impression its name had made on my mind.

Three years older than I, a tall slim youth with dark, waving hair and dark eyes, not sharp eyes, but smouldering, like Mama's, Harry was strikingly handsome. Of course I should have liked to be as handsome as Harry, as pretty as my little sister May with her long bright curls. But I can not remember that the matter gave me any particular concern. Certainly it did not prevent my being impressed by Harry's appearance in his natty new uniform and jaunty cap. He had entered the University of Tennessee—which at the time was a military establishment as well—and was living there until we had established a home.

It was after Harry had returned to the Hill (as Knoxville referred to the university in its midst) that I went for a walk with Papa.

Gay Street, so lively the day before, proved now as dull, deserted, as lifeless, as utterly depressing as the main streets in most American towns of the period (and many since) on Sunday afternoon. Not even a horse and buggy went by.

We stopped on the corner of a narrow cross-street called Clinch and my father pointed out where his offices would be, opposite us, on the ground floor next the Hattie House (later the Imperial, and still later in belated honor of Admiral Farragut, born in a log cabin close by,[13] the Farragut). Beyond the Hattie House the wholesale houses that lined the street for a block or two—wholesale drygoods, clothing, hardware, shoes, drugs—had their indigo-blue window shades pulled all the way down, giving the street all the more a funereal air.

But Gay Street, with Knoxville's "bad street" scarcely more than a stone's throw below—Gay Street, for all its Sabbath solemnity had staged its own riotous scenes. Only a year or so before, on a busy market day, the street thronged, Thomas O'Conner, who had amassed a fortune through building railroads and other early ventures in East Tennessee, president of Knoxville's oldest and most important bank, owner of its finest home, "Melrose," had shot and killed the two hot-headed young Mabry brothers, who looked upon Tom O'Conner as an upstart, while the Mabry brothers had shot and killed O'Conner in the same fray; all three dead, a matter of minutes, in front of the stores from which they had just emerged.[14]

But as Papa and I turned from Gay Street into Clinch, I had not yet heard of the O'Conner-Mabry feud and its tragic termination, for all that the town was still

Harry Wetzell.

Post Office and Custom House. Art Work of Knoxville, 1895.

ringing with it, and as we crossed the street to the Custom House (as the Postoffice was called then) to mail some letters,[15] my attention was arrested by the sight of some of the same young men standing around outside in knots that I had seen the evening before at supper and earlier from the hotel windows. They were in their black Sunday suits now, though still talking together in ominously hushed tones. The words of the Negro chambermaid ran through me, "Dey *might*. Ain't no tellin'—"

Papa did not seem to notice the young men. We came out of the Custom House, and there, obliquely across from us, was the lovely old Second Presbyterian Church, which Papa and Mama had attended in the morning, and which, I reflected, not too joyfully, Harry and May and I later would be expected to attend with them, whether we wanted to or not. Nevertheless, this church made its instant and lasting impression on me. Built close to the ground, it stood far back from the street, and with its graceful spire, tall pointed windows, its mellowed red-brick walls partly overgrown by ivy, and a broad brick walk leading from the gate to its few shallow steps, it looked, I thought, just as a church ought to look, at once stately, simple, and somehow humanized by time. All around—for the church yard occupied almost a block—were tall ancient trees with ivy clambering over them, and at the side and back of the churchyard were old graves, their rounded, weather-stained head-stones embroidered with lichens, their inscriptions almost obliterated, and still older graves, above ground, burial vaults, a marble slab, with worn carving, resting on the low brick walls of each of these tombs.[16]

Papa and I walked slowly along Prince Street (now Market) at the side of the churchyard, which, like almost everything else in the Knoxville of that day, was not very well kept, but softened, like the church itself, by the English ivy which covered much of the ground, by the deep green carpet of periwinkle spread here and there, by the neglected but blooming roses and the tangles of honeysuckle blooming too, now in September for the second time, and whose heavy sweet perfume, with its sensuous, faintly sour under-scent, we could catch as we leaned over the low stone wall, trying to make out inscriptions on the tombs nearest us, a scent, a mere whiff of which, to this day, wherever I am, can recreate for me instantly, disturbingly, as nothing else, the old Knoxville I knew in my youth.

For me, as for Papa, there was nothing melancholy, nothing morbid, in the attraction which the old churchyard held for us. I found in it the same strong appeal I had found in the narrow shadowy streets, fouled by weather and dirt, which I had gazed down into from the windows of Schubert's Hotel. As for Papa, while he was not in the least afraid of new things, especially of new ideas—which he went out to meet—, yet he liked old churches, old streets, old towns, filled with a sense of the past; and what he liked, I liked, so my mind was at ease as we crossed over into Market Square behind the churchyard, my father pointing out, in passing, Peter Kern's Ice Cream Parlor, a red-brick building (for Knoxville was a red-brick town in those days) on the corner of the Square nearest the churchyard, and a favorite social resort and gathering place of the period.[17] Long afterwards, in old towns in Spain and Italy and Southern France, where markets and marketing were cheek-by-jowl with scarred old churches in open squares—often conducted on the very steps of the churches—, I would be carried back nostalgically to Knoxville, with the bustling swarms of people coming and going to its Farmer's Market on Market Days, to the peaceful tree-shaded old churchyard of its Second Presbyterian Church and Peter Kern's Ice Cream Parlor—all pleasantly jumbled together in the heart of the town. It was after my time in Knoxville that, mindless of the fact that New York had preserved its Trinity Church and Churchyard in the very heart of its own downtown district and notwithstanding grown to be one of the great cities of the world; that Boston had saved not only her Common with its ancient graves but many of the narrow, crooked, historic streets leading into the Common and still grown mightily in power and wealth and population—it was after my time that the city fathers of Knoxville, to widen Prince Street in the interest of "civic progress," and obliterating the name the street had borne from frontier days, re-naming it Market,[18] tore down the Second Presbyterian Church, reducing to rubble what

Peter Kern's Confectionery.

in architectural proportions and setting was not only the town's most beautiful church, but one of the most beautiful in the Mid-South; that they laid waste the old churchyard, disgorging graves that for a hundred years had remained undisturbed in their midst; deprived the town for all time, of an open space at its centre, a daily vision of beauty and tranquility to refresh the spirits of its people—destroyed, in a word, in a single operation, sturdy vestiges of the town's bygone history worth more than all the thousands of pages of emasculate [*sic*] print that would ever be issued on the subject.[19]

It is, however, perhaps too much to ask of city fathers that they be possessed of aesthetic appreciation, or be sensitive to imponderables that would enrich beyond measure a community life over which, for their little day, they preside. In any case, happily for me, none of these civic crimes of time to come cast their shadows athwart our path on that Sunday afternoon when I walked with my father across from the cool shadowy churchyard of the Second Presbyterian Church to the narrow thoroughfare leading along the east side of Market Square.

The old wooden Market House, built in the '50s, capacious but shed-like, and that still stood then in the center of the Square, was tightly shuttered on Sundays, and the farmers' wagons that on week-days would be backed up to the curb, with the farmers noisily crying their wares—all this was absent now. Only some wisps of straw, and bits of refuse which a miserable, mangy stray dog or two were picking up from the gutter, attested to the furious activities of Market Square on week days.[20]

We looked through the dusty windows of closed-up shops where dry groceries were sold—dark, disorderly, overcrowded shops, but which carried, we would know in time, the widest variety and choicest quality of supplies; rare cheeses, Bombay chutney, kegs of pickled oysters, *pâté de fois gras*—all manner of exotic specialties to meet the demands of the town's gourmets and *bon vivants*, of which there were many, and shops from which even now a smell of spices reached us mingled with the aroma of freshly roasted coffee. We glanced into cheap-Jack shops where shoddy clothing was displayed in the windows, and then, emerging from the Square at its far end, crossed another narrow street and started up a hill bordered on either side by substantial, dignified, rather aristocratic-looking old houses, set amidst trees and shrubbery.

But it was an old square red-brick house, a rather handsome home, which stood on a corner at the foot of the hill, on Wall Street, facing the rear of the Market House, which was to make a more lasting impression on me than anything else on this first brief journey in discovering Knoxville—and not exactly the house either, but a large wire enclosure we came upon as we climbed the hill, and in it some deer, among them a doe and a little fawn. We stopped to look at the deer, delighting in their color, dainty movements and pretty black muzzles; and saw now, at a slightly higher elevation, but belonging to the same house, a rose garden, in riotous bloom, for in a day when no one sprayed or had so much as heard of black spot Knoxville was full of blooming roses in September, and there were few Knoxville homes, rich or poor, of whites or blacks, without their larger or smaller garden of roses—Jacqueminot, LaFrance, Malmaison—all the old-fashioned, full-scented roses people grew then.

I had seen deer before—many of them in parks and a few in the wild. I had seen rose gardens, roses blooming with equal and perhaps greater profusion, but for some reason these deer, these roses, so near to the grimy Gay Street, to Market Square, remain with me as something in an all but forgotten dream, and a little different from any I would know again.[21]

NOTES

1. American artist James Abbott McNeill Whistler (1834–1903) was born in Lowell, Massachusetts, but during the trial resulting from his libel suit against critic John Ruskin "claimed St. Petersburg, Russia, as his birthplace, declaring, 'I shall be born when and where I want, and I do not choose to be born in Lowell.'" Whistler had lived in St. Petersburg as a boy; he later lived in Baltimore as a young man. Lisa N. Peters, *James McNeill Whistler* (New York: Smithmark, 1996), 11; Ronald Anderson and Anne Koval, *James McNeill Whistler: Beyond the Myth*, (New York: Carroll & Graf, 1994), 38.

2. Schubert's Hotel was on the northwest corner of Gay Street at its intersection with Cumberland Avenue.
3. The Lamar House, onto which the present-day Bijou Theatre was built as an addition in the early 1900s, still stands on the southwest corner of the same intersection. Hattie House, on the northeast corner of Gay Street at Clinch Avenue, was on the site where the Farragut Hotel opened in 1919.
4. After calling Knoxville "the ugliest city I ever saw in America . . ." John Gunther goes on to say: "Its main street is called Gay Street; this seemed to me to be a misnomer." John Gunther, *Inside U.S.A.*, 1st ed. (New York: Harper & Bros., 1947), 761.
5. Annie Wetzell and her family arrived in Knoxville on Wednesday, September 3, 1885, according to an article in the *Knoxville Daily Journal* on the next day (p. 4). Her thirteenth birthday would be September 20.
6. A performing arts venue on the southeast corner of Gay Street and Cumberland Avenue. Built in 1872 by Peter Staub, a Swiss immigrant. Lucile Deaderick, ed. *Heart of the Valley: A History of Knoxville, Tennessee* (Knoxville: East Tennessee Historical Society, 1976), 463–4.
7. Although there *was* a local ballad telling the story of Hicks Carmichael, the murder for which he was hanged did not occur until May 1888, nearly three years after the day that Armstrong describes. *Knoxville Journal*, May 22, 1888, July 21, 1888. William D. Mercer, of the University of Tennessee, Knoxville, published a research article, "The Ballad of Hicks Carmichael: Law, Music, and Popular Justice in Urban Appalachia," in the online peer-reviewed journal *Law, Culture, and the Humanities* (June 1, 2018). The "Ballad of Hicks Carmichael" was first recorded by folk song collectors Edward Capers Kirkland and Mary Neal Kirkland in 1937. *The Kirkland Recordings: Newly Discovered Field Recordings from Tennessee and North Carolina, 1937–39*, notes by Kip Lornell (LP Record, Tennessee Folklore Society, 1984).
8. This Civil War battle took place Sunday, November 29, 1863. For a description of the siege of Knoxville, the battle and its aftermath, see Mary U. Rothrock, ed., *The French Broad-Holston Country: A History of Knox County, Tennessee.* (Knoxville: East Tennessee Historical Society, 1946), 138–141.
9. In 1925, Pryor Brown built a mixed-use parking garage on the corner of Market and Church, where his livery stable had been, and added to it in 1929. Known for a time as the "House of Brown," this four-story building was a transit center with a fleet of taxis and a freight transfer service in addition to providing parking for automobiles. Jack Neely, *The Legend of the Gold Bricks, and Other Knoxville Stories*, ed. Paul James (Knoxville, Tenn.: Knoxville History Project, 2018), 27–31. In 2016, developers, along with Knoxville city leaders, announced plans to turn the historic Pryor Brown parking garage into a mixed-use facility with upper level residential units and storefronts on the street level. *Knoxville News-Sentinel*, June 2, 2016.
10. Perez Dickinson, born in Amherst, Massachusetts, and a cousin of poet Emily

Dickinson, came to Knoxville in 1829 and became Knoxville's foremost citizen, a merchant and banker—one of Knoxville's "merchant princes"—and first president of the Knoxville Board of Trade. He married Susan Penniman, also of Massachusetts, in 1845, and brought her to Knoxville, but she died the next year following the birth of their child, which also died. Although Dickinson's principal residence was on Main Street, he owned some six hundred acres outside the city, where he developed a model farm and had his "Island Home," a show place for entertaining visitors and giving parties. The house is now the residence of the superintendent of the Tennessee School for the Deaf, which is located on Dickinson's former property. See: Rothrock. *The French Broad-Holston Country,* 411–412; Betsey Beeler Creekmore, *Knoxville!* (Knoxville: East Tennessee Historical Society, 1991), 103–122.

11. Because of its many marble companies and their importance in the marble industry, Knoxville came to be known, at that time, as the "Marble City." Michael J. McDonald and William Bruce Wheeler, *Knoxville, Tennessee: Continuity and Change in an Appalachian City* (Knoxville: University of Tennessee Press, 1983), 21–22.
12. Charles Haddon Spurgeon (1834–1892).
13. Admiral David Glasgow Farragut (1801–1870), born at Lowe's Ferry on the Holston River in west Knox County, was the first Admiral in the United States Navy. Rothrock, *The French Broad-Holston Country,* 416.
14. Killed in the October 19, 1882, gunfight were O'Conner, Joseph A. Mabry, Jr., and his son (not brother) Joseph A. Mabry III. Deaderick, *Heart of the Valley,* 565. Mark Twain includes a detailed description of the shootout in a lengthy footnote in Chapter 40 of *Life on the Mississippi.*
15. Built of Tennessee marble between 1871 and 1874 at the corner of Clinch Avenue and Prince (now Market) Street, Knoxville's Custom House served as U.S. Post Office and federal building until 1933. It later housed the main offices of the Tennessee Valley Authority (TVA). Today, after a major renovation and expansion in 2004, it is home to the East Tennessee History Center, comprising the Calvin M. McClung Historical Collection, the Knox County Archives, and the East Tennessee Historical Society and Museum. Knox County Public Library, http://www.knoxlib.org/local-family-history/custom-house-history-center (viewed October 10, 2016); Knox Heritage, http://knoxheritage.org/our-work/neighborhood-tours/historic-downtown-knoxville-walking-tour/us-custom-house-post-office/ (viewed October 10, 2016)
16. Second Presbyterian Church was founded in 1818. The church building to which Armstrong refers, on the west side of Market Street between Clinch and Union Avenues, was erected in 1860. Rothrock, *The French Broad-Holston Country,* 281–282.
17. Peter Kern (1835–1907), a German immigrant, began his business life in Knoxville as a baker. The three-story building constructed in 1876 to house his bakery/confectionary, ice cream parlor, and the Oddfellows Hall, is still standing at the corner of Market Street and Union Avenue. Today, its space is occupied by two restaurants and the

Oliver Hotel, which is at the back of the building and faces Union Avenue. Peter Kern was elected mayor of Knoxville in 1890. Jack Neely, *Market Square: A History of the Most Democratic Place on Earth*. 2nd ed. (Knoxville: Market Square District Association, 2011), 33–35, 48–50, 52–53.

18. Prince did not become Market Street until around 1914. There had been an earlier Market Street, at the north end of Market Square. It was later called Asylum and, eventually, Wall Avenue. Neely, *Market Square,* 29; Ronald R. Allen, comp., *The Street Has Changed* (Knoxville: R. Allen, 2003), unpaged, (under: "Wall Avenue").
19. The building that Anne Wetzell Armstrong (hereafter referred to in footnotes as AWA) knew as Second Presbyterian Church was dedicated on Nov. 10, 1860. The church had occupied an earlier building on the same site since 1820. In 1905, they sold their property near Market Square to help finance a new, larger building at Church Street and Walnut. The graves in the original graveyard were probably only eighty-five years old. Max Arnstein bought the property and opened a department store on it. The Arnstein building, at the corner of Prince and Union, is still standing. Lowell L. Giffen, *A History of Second Presbyterian Church* (Knoxville, Tenn.: *s.n.*, 1994), 6, 14, 20, 40; Neely, *Market Square*, 108.
20. The old Market House to which AWA refers opened in 1854 on land donated to the city by William G. Swan and Joseph A. Mabry for a market place. It was replaced in 1897 by a "new" two-story market house with a public hall on the second floor where various meetings, ceremonies, and political rallies were held. Knoxville's downtown Market Square shopping area has been designated a historic commercial district on the National Register of Historic Places, but the Market House, which was once its centerpiece, no longer stands. AWA used wording very similar to what appears here in describing Market Square and the Market House in her novel *The Seas of God.* For more information about Knoxville's Market Square, see: Neely, *Market Square.*
21. The TVA Towers, built in the 1970s for the Tennessee Valley Authority, now occupy the hill above Wall Avenue facing the rear of Market Square, which AWA describes. The narrow street going up the hill, its houses, deer enclosure, and rose gardens are all gone.

Chapter Two

Mrs. Clotworthy's and Young Gentlemen in a Hurry

It proved a sweltering night. Tossing and tossing, I slept fitfully under the mosquito canopy, turning my big pillow over and over for a cool side. There was the sound of distant thunder and my earlier fears that something brutal, fiendishly savage, and terrifyingly near was going to happen, fears stilled during the happy afternoon walk with Papa, once more took possession of me. Again and again I was on the point of arousing Mama and Papa in the next room. My heart kept pounding. I thought I heard hoarse shouts from the direction of the river and once I heard, or believed I did, the deep-toned baying of the blood-hounds which I knew now were kept at the jail and which were associated in my mind with such ferocity and horror that at the sound, whether real or imagined, suddenly I became so cold that in spite of the heat, I shook all over. But then all would be quiet again except for the rumble, farther and farther off, of occasional thunder, and in the morning there was no report of any violence out of the ordinary having occurred during the night. It was that same morning we moved from Schubert's Hotel to Mrs. Clotworthy's on Church Street.

I try to see Church Street as I saw it then. It was a nice, leafy, restful street with no tawdry or raw-looking houses on it; a few frame, more of them brick, but none of them ornate, and whether of one or two stories, houses that looked comfortable, as if they had been lived in a good while, unpretentious and yet with a kind of dignity about them, while on the corner of Church and Walnut was a really charming, if slightly shabby old brick house, of a dark rich red, standing some distance back from the street and close to the ground, built in the simple, rather severe lines of an earlier period, but its walls softened by that English ivy which in the moist, highly favoring climate of Knoxville grew everywhere with such luxuriance; the house, for all its simplicity, with an air of bygone elegance about it; and the yard, a bit neglected, but with holly trees, and full of somewhat overgrown shrubs—syringa and lilac and snowball and crepe myrtle. The house vanished many years ago, but an old Dr. Humes lived there then, a man of such independence of mind and outstanding courage that after being educated for the Presbyterian ministry, when he found he could no longer subscribe to the Westminster Confession of Faith, left the church, subsequently becoming rector of St. John's; afterwards, for many years, president of the University of Tennessee,[1] and now in his last tottering years, reduced to renting out rooms to tubercular guests from the North, when it was still thought that merely to get to a less severe climate might cure the disease. His home was presided over by two gentle, refined and aging spinster daughters, scarcely less frail than himself, and who, in spite of having been born and lived all their lives in the South, through a certain primness of carriage and manner, a certain precision of speech, seemed to have come straight out of New England, as indeed they had, on their mother's side, a native of Connecticut, and former teacher in Knoxville's "Female Seminary."[2] But this was true of all New England residents in Knoxville during the nineteenth century, many of whom left their mark on the place. With the sole exception of the Hon. Perez Dickinson (transformed, bone and marrow, into a Southern gentleman of the old regime), they retained, even to the third and fourth generation, characteristics which instantly revealed their New England ancestry.

Near the Humes house was the old Southern Methodist Church, and further along, on the opposite side of the street, Mrs. Clotworthy's boarding-house.[3]

I do not know why my father and mother decided to move to Mrs. Clotworthy's. The rates were no doubt less than at the hotel, but my father was still a man of very considerable means, and my parents, if not exactly reckless with money, were both of them extravagant by nature and never indulged in small economies for economy's sake, so I can only surmise that they thought here, at Mrs. Clotworthy's, they might find it cooler, less grimy perhaps, and more homelike than at Schubert's Hotel. Already, however, I was conscious that the spell which Knoxville, from the first, had cast over me, it had not cast over Mama, and my father was probably overlooking nothing which he thought might win her over to a more favorable impression of the place where she was destined to live henceforth for many years, and in whose future, whatever its present imperfections, he himself had boundless faith.

Mrs. Clotworthy's was one of half a dozen excellent boarding-houses on Church Street then, or nearby in the same part of town. It was on the corner of what I believe was Henley,[4] a square, roomy frame house, painted a light grey, as I recall it, with a commodious porch across the front, partly shaded by matted honeysuckle vines, and with a two-story ell at the back. Inside, a wide airy hall ran the length of the house, so that with the outside blinds partly closed during the day, the house seemed cool, in spite of the wilting midsummer heat which still persisted in September.

Although this boarding-house was invariably spoken of as "Mrs. Clotworthy's," and boarding-houses in Knoxville were almost always run by widows; often, at the time, by widows of Confederate soldiers, left with a family to bring up, and with few other ways open in which a Southern gentlewoman could make a living; yet, in this case, there was a *Mr.* Clotworthy, a short, sturdy, unobtrusive man, who had an outside occupation of some sort, I suppose,[5] but whose sole function in the boarding-house seemed to be to conduct family prayers which were held every morning in the parlor and which the boarders were expected—nay, pressed, to attend.

I had frequently stayed in hotels in traveling here and there with my parents, but this was the first time I had ever stayed in a boarding-house, and as part of the whole new world I was exploring I found it of as fresh and exciting interest as Schubert's Hotel and Gay Street.

Mrs. Clotworthy welcomed us with great effusion. She was a plump, middle-aged highly emotional woman, dressed in as deep mourning as summer clothing permitted in a climate where the summers were not only extremely hot but extremely sticky. A perpetual smile played tremulously over her round, rosy, rather pretty face, although at the same time she was perpetually on the verge of tears. Almost at once—while my parents were unpacking, I presume—she led me into her mother's downstairs room, back of the parlor, a large, dusky, untidy chamber, smelling strongly of St. Jacob's Oil, or some other liniment then in favor. The mother, a heavy-set woman, crippled with rheumatism, and whose name, if not herself, I have long ago forgotten, was also in deep mourning. She welcomed me as effusively as had her daughter, although she wept unrestrainedly when she began talking, as she did immediately, of another daughter who had died a year or two earlier and was apparently the person for whom mourning was being worn. (Knoxville was full of women in mourning then. You were seldom out of sight of a long crepe veil hanging down some woman's back.) The daughter who was dead had been married to a Presbyterian minister, one of some prominence, it seemed, and I gained the impression, not without a slight shock, that this made her loss more devastating to the mother and sister than had she been married to a man—to their minds—of less importance.

The intermittent weeping and smiling through their tears of the two women, on such short acquaintance with them, was something completely new to me in adult behavior. It embarrassed me a little, I remember, without arousing in me the least sympathy. All the same, I was drawn to the women. Between their showers of tears they felt of the material in the simple summer dress I was wearing, pronounced it "exquisite," —noted that the narrow lace with which the neck and sleeves were edged was "real Val," and insisted that the dress was "mighty becoming." They even had admiring words for my plain high-buttoned black kid Burt's shoes. I had never been at all content with the clothes Mama selected for me. Although I was (and am) one of those mortals born happy, as they say, every morning, yet I had envied, at times with an all but aching heart, girls I had known or seen, of about my own age, who wore what to me were far prettier dresses and fancier, immeasurably more attractive shoes than I was permitted to wear. Here, at Mrs. Clotworthy's, I was to hear, for the first time, flattering words about my clothes, and even more surprising, about my looks. They spoke to each other, mother and daughter, in soft cooing voices, almost as if I were not present, of my "beautiful fair complexion, my very blue eyes, my very white teeth." I was sadly conscious of childhood freckles that had not entirely disappeared, and that my teeth, if very white, were also very crooked. This was heady stuff. I was twelve years old and it was the first time in my life, to my remembrance, that anyone, except the black chambermaid at Schubert's Hotel the day before, had ever praised anything about my looks. It began to dawn on me, if hazily, that I had come to dwell in the delectable land where people, white and black, had honey on their lips, honey at their hearts, and a warmth that was something more than Knoxville's sweltering September heat irradiated the closely-shuttered, gloomy, liniment-smelling old bedroom and surged through me.

Mrs. Clotworthy's mother leaned across the high fat-looking bed, puffed up by featherbeds, and beside which her chair was placed, and drew from it the morning paper, pointing to my father's name in large type on the front page with after his name the word "Capitalist," a word that had not yet gathered to itself any odious significations, or certainly none in circles to which I had been exposed myself.

So that's what Papa was—a Capitalist!

I had only the vaguest idea what the word meant, but from the article it appeared that the town was to be congratulated on gaining Papa as a resident.[6]

"We're certainly proud, honey," the old lady said, with her tearful smile, as I handed her back the paper, "to have you-all with us," and then in the next breath, "and we're so glad you're Presbyterians. We love mighty well to have good Presbyterians in our home."

What did she mean by that? The glow in the room grew dimmer. I had never heard my parents speak of Presbyterians as better than anyone else, and I even doubted that Papa would consider himself a Presbyterian at all, to say nothing of a "good Presbyterian." He certainly always got up and left church on Communion Sundays as soon as Communion service started.

But the lovely new kind of warmth in which I had just been immersed soon returned. There were such pleasant people in the house; so friendly and gay-mannered, so ready, like Mrs. Clotworthy and her mother, to say things which made you feel good. There were a few married couples; two or three school-teachers of disarmingly amiable aspect; some bachelors—traveling men of good family and courtly manners who lived at Mrs. Clotworthy's when they were off the road; there was the inevitable tubercular guest from somewhere in the North, a shaky young man with a wistful smile who, somebody whispered, was "dying with consumption"; there were a couple of girls from out of town studying music in Knoxville; and then, standing out as the star, an alluring young matron from South Carolina who had been spending the summer at Tate Spring,[7] not far from Knoxville and at the time (and for long afterwards) a fashionable resort, and who was lingering in the higher altitude of Knoxville with her little boy and his turbaned black nurse before plunging back into the fiercer heat of the Deep South. Slender, dark-eyed, high-spirited, completely self-assured, with a vibrant voice and great chic, with her air of conscious superiority, along with a dash of deviltry, a touch of latent insolence, yet at the same time exhibiting the utmost graciousness toward the other boarders—those lesser beings who surrounded her at Mrs. Clotworthy's—this glamorous young woman with whom I had only a brief casual contact long fulfilled my idea of what a princess should look and be like, although none of the actual princesses from various royal families whom I had opportunity to observe in later life (often conspicuously dowdy) ever equaled or even approached her in their power to charm. She became for me, in truth, a sort of embodiment of all that I was to find at once most irresistible and most disquieting in a South which, from the beginning, I had adopted for my own.

All this assorted company sat down together at the two or three long tables in Mrs. Clotworthy's dining-room; tables covered with long white table-cloths; supplied with good-sized starchy linen napkins; and with the same superabundant food there had been at Schubert's Hotel, only here it was more delicious, and incredibly, of even greater variety.

At midday dinner, besides the freshest of the many fresh vegetables then in season, there was corn-bread in one of its innumerable Southern forms, and invariably heaped up platters of chicken (chicken that had never known the rigors of cold storage, but taken from the coop only a few hours before)—smothered chicken, accompanied by rice that was dry and flaky, according to Southern culinary tradition; or fried chicken that was served with cream gravy and corn fritters in the identical fashion later known to menus all over this country as *Chicken à la Maryland*, but that would never be anything for me but *Chicken à la Knoxville*. For dessert, there were apple and peach cobblers; steamed blackberry rolls with hard sauce into which sherry or brandy had entered liberally; all manner of cooling sherbets—lemon and orange and pineapple and grape and peach, as well as home-made peach ice-cream; sometimes frozen custard, rich with eggs and cream, or Charlotte Russe.

When supper came, at the nicest hour of the day, the sun going down now, and a light breeze, bearing whiffs of honeysuckle, beginning to blow into the dining-room through Mrs. Clotworthy's screenless western windows, we would find, whatever else, platters of cold ham, wafer thin—ham, not pink in color, half raw in taste, cured by chemicals, but honestly hickory-smoked, properly aged before it was eaten, of a dark winey red, and never tough or coarse textured, for a poor ham was practically unknown in the Knoxville of that day, when connoisseurs of food could be found among all classes of its citizens, an expert knowledge of food and drink ranking among the fine arts and part of the education of every Knoxville gentleman.

But in addition to the ham, there would be veal loaf or cold smoked tongue for supper, cold jellied chicken perhaps, or chicken salad of the old-fashioned sort, finely minced; while, as often as not, hot fried chicken would appear again, as at noon, and now, to go with it, small, thin, piping-hot buttermilk biscuits, or "gems" that had been baked in deep iron gem-rings and that in all but name were popovers. Then occasionally for supper we would be treated to that special delicacy, spoon bread; or to baked grits in the shape of a soufflé; while always scattered the lengths of the tables and making splashes of color were dishes of sliced scarlet tomatoes, lightly bedded in ice, and a bewildering choice of freshly-made damson preserves, red raspberry or blackberry jam, apple and dewberry jelly; supper ending with ambrosia, apple snow, or with peaches and cream and cup cakes still warm from the oven.

It was breakfast, though, at Mrs. Clotworthy's, which I recall even more vividly than her other meals: the fried apples, half jellied, that were served with the broiled or fried breakfast ham; the delicate golden-brown fingers of fried grits or fried mush, and all the tempting breakfast breads, among them Sally Lunn, made with yeast, set to raise the night before, and better than any Sally Lunn I was ever to taste in England, its native home.[8] Almost every morning there were waffles, too, with honey—the same dark-colored, tangy, incomparable sourwood honey we had had at Schubert's Hotel; or, if not waffles, pancakes of wheat flour (known as "batter cakes" in Knoxville), or lacey little corn griddle cakes so tender and fragile they would break at the touch of the fork. Toast, I might add, never appeared. It was supposed, in the time and place, to be only for people too sick to be out of bed. I soon learned, however, that the most highly esteemed, the true aristocrats, among all the breakfast breads at Mrs. Clotworthy's, were the small cracker-like "beaten biscuits," whose dough, placed on the square marble slab with which every proper kitchen in Knoxville was provided, had been beaten with a rolling-pin till the dough blistered, a full half hour, and the sound of which, rising from a nearby kitchen, the steady rhythmic pounding, accompanied by some old Negro cook's low moaning voice, as she sang those heart-breaking, haunting songs, which we now call "spirituals," would be the first sound to reach me during all the years of my life in Knoxville.

What now strikes me as little short of miraculous is that this extraordinarily good, this superlative Knoxville food, albeit most of the cooks had been trained in slave times, could come out of the Knoxville kitchens of the day. I never entered Mrs. Clotworthy's kitchen then or later, but beyond the shadow of a doubt it was much like the others; almost without exception unbelievably dark at all hours, devoid of what now are the commonest conveniences, poorly equipped to the last degree when it came to utensils, with grease-splattered walls and splintery floors over which roaches scampered by day and marched in armies at night, and everything covered with soot where the only stove was a battered iron range burning soft-coal, its top, much of the time, winter or summer, red-hot, and over which every day, the year around, from dawn till long after dark, bent the sweating old Negro cook, concocting with consummate skill all those delightful, infinitely varied dishes which we would devour later—the kitchen's one concession to kitchen hygiene, a white cloth (often far from white) bound around the cook's head. But the last room in her house that any sensible Knoxville matron of the day would have thought of examining too closely—far less of putting forth what she would have considered useless efforts to make cheerful and attractive, even sanitary—was the kitchen.

"Niggers won't take care of things," was a common saying. And the kitchen at Mrs. Clotworthy's, in that long past time, assuredly claimed none of my own attention. What interested me were the boarders.

The era of "light-housekeeping," when innumerable couples or single persons would live in a room or two and manage on one solid meal a day eaten at the nearest boarding-house, was not to arrive in Knoxville for another decade or so. But in this earlier time families in all parts of town when their cooks fell ill, or in some other domestic crisis, would take their meals at Mrs. Branner's on Church Street,[9] or at Mrs. Clotworthy's in the next block, so that there were a good many people outside the house whom we saw at dinner and supper, and talk at table was always animated and often exciting. Remarks were tossed back and forth about the rip-roaring, if generally good-natured, campaign for governor of Tennessee then going on, with the candidates brothers; Bob Taylor, one of the most popular of the flowery orators of the day, the Democratic candidate, and his brother Alf, fiddling his way through the State, the Republican candidate. Nothing could have better attested the split political character of East Tennessee than this contest between two brothers, but it is also evident to me, looking back, that there must have been more culture then in the region than it is sometimes credited with, and a livelier sense of history, or the brothers would hardly have chosen emblems reminiscent of the War of the Roses between the rival houses of York and Lancaster in England in the fifteenth century, with every man you saw in Knoxville that fall wearing either a white or red rose in his button-hole.[10]

Another subject of engrossing interest in the table-talk was the approaching marriage of the president, Grover Cleveland, to his handsome young ward, Frances Folsom. After several colorless presidents and president's families in the preceding administrations, the fact that the wedding was to take place in the White House was looked upon as the most romantic scene to be enacted there since the days of Dolly Madison.[11]

There was a couple, however, among those who came in for meals, who never took part in this lively talk. Their name was Mickey, I believe.[12] In any case, they lived in an old-fashioned one-story red-brick house at the rear of the Clotworthy property and facing Henley (if the street *was* Henley). A solidly built man with sparse grey hair standing up like bristles on his large squarish head, Mr. Mickey always wore black clothes, while Mrs. Mickey, her face fiery red and with an oily glisten, also wore black, including a small black bonnet tied under her chin with broad black ribbons. They both ate gluttonously, with strict attention to their plates. An occasional grunting "Ach! Ach!"—denoting disapproval—would escape Mr. Mickey, involuntarily, it seemed, but aside from that the only words either one of them uttered were when Mrs. Mickey, baring her teeth, in the semblance of a smile, but with a distinctly menacing effect, would arrest the attention of the Negro waiter and speaking in a guttural voice, with a strong German accent, demand peremptorily that some dish or other be passed them again.

The Mickeys had not been long in Knoxville then and few people there ever knew much, if anything, about their past. But it is a long road which leads back to the September days when, hardly more than a child, I watched the greedy, evil-looking old Mickey couple wolfing their food at Mrs. Clotworthy's, and there is another, quite different, but ineradicable memory connected in my mind with this boarding-house.

On that first morning we stayed there, while things were still strange, I found my way into the parlor, which was cool, with its partially closed blinds, and sat down on a sofa covered with hair-cloth which stood in one corner, in front of a walnut whatnot. I could catch whiffs of honeysuckle from the vines on the porch outside. A flighty young woman, past early girlhood, one of the boarders studying music in Knoxville, and who was from Athens, a little town below Knoxville, was seated at the big square piano, singing over and over, in a tremulous, passionate voice, with dramatic fervor:

In the gloaming, oh, my darling,
When the lights are dim and low.[13]

I was enraptured with the song, which I had never heard before, and it was to be forever connected in my mind with what followed. Facing the doorway into the hall, I became aware of a tall young man standing there, good-looking for all that his face was flushed, his eyes a little blood-shot, and he appeared somewhat unsteady on his feet. Though I was not yet familiar with the looks of young men who had been drinking, I decided that that was the case, but I was not alarmed until he spoke.

"Sis!" he brought out in a thick voice and the young woman at the piano, with a quick lift of her head that had been bowed over the keys, whirled around on the piano stool and, rushing to the door, threw her arms around him.

"Oh, brother, brother!" She clung to him hysterically. "Don't tell me," she said breathlessly, though in an undertone, "you've come up to get into that thing to-night? Oh, my Lord, I'm so scared you'll—" But she broke off as, weaving a little, he drew her into the hall for some further whispered talk and I knew now, for a certainty, what was going to happen.

The whole town knew. The young man who was murdered had traveled for one of the big wholesale houses in Knoxville.[14] Popular not only in Knoxville but in all the little towns in East Tennessee which made up his territory, there never seemed to have been the slightest doubt that his murderer would be promptly tried, convicted, and sentenced. But the friends of the murdered man were in a hurry. The fact that he was a hard drinker and killed in one of the houses of ill fame he frequented did not lessen their burning resentment. They were bent on vengeance, a vengeance not the Lord's, nor yet the Court's, but to be taken into their own hands, as in frontier days.

From the hour when this tipsy young man appeared at Mrs. Clotworthy's and almost as quickly disappeared, I was conscious of mounting tension. In the hall, at meals, lingering on the porch, hanging over the gate, on the street—people were talking in undertones.

We were too far away, six or seven blocks, to hear more than a dull roar, some time after midnight, from the mob that stormed the jail and dragged the prisoner they were after down to the bridge across the river, at the foot of Gay Street. But I knew in the morning, from the absence of chatter, the strange, overhanging silence, that the lynching had taken place.

After breakfast, however, as if nothing had happened, Mrs. Clotworthy herded as usual all the boarders who were unable to escape gracefully into the parlor. Accompanying herself on the piano, she led in singing "Jesus, Lover of My Soul." Then Mr. Clotworthy read a chapter from the Bible, following it with what seemed an interminable prayer while the rest of us remained on our knees, our heads bowed on the chairs or sofas where we had been sitting. It seemed an even more dreary proceeding than I had remembered it from similar occasions during my childhood at the home of one of my grandfathers. But for the time being, so far as I was concerned, everything joyous in life had been blotted out. And there were other stirrings within me. "Why didn't someone *do* something? Why didn't people get together and prevent this thing they *knew* was going to happen?"

As we came from prayers I noticed that the girl from Athens had red eyes, as if she had been crying. No one said anything about the lynching but there was a scramble to get hold of the morning paper. Finally I had my chance.

"Oh, honey, I *wouldn't* read it!" Mrs. Clotworthy implored, coming upon me with the paper in my hands.

I shrank from being so impolite, but I resisted her pleading, and there it was, with big headlines, spread all over the front page of the *Knoxville Journal*, where only the morning before had been the piece about Papa.[15]

The lynching, it seemed, had been badly bungled. The young men directing it, befuddled with drink, in the darkness, and amidst the general delirium, had failed to tie the noose properly, so that somehow or other their victim pulled himself up onto the girder above him and began crawling across it. It was then that the mob, yelling and cursing, began shooting up at him and he began crying down to them, "Oh, my God, boys, don't shoot! I wasn't the one killed him. Oh, God, boys—!" But they went on shooting. He was able to crawl all the way across the girder, still pleading, till riddled with bullets, he fell into the river below, landing on the base of a stone pier, his voice at last silent, body a bundle of blood and broken bones.

It made me very sick as I read about the lynching in the *Knoxville Journal*, but I kept on reading. It seemed that except for the darkness it was almost a carnival scene. There was even an air of fashion about it. Circulating among the mob, so the paper said, were young men who had left the dance that was going on at Sans Souci Club in its club-rooms on lower Gay Street, its members specimen young Southern aristocrats of impeccable descent who had come in their tail-coats, their dancing pumps, to witness, perchance participate in this *mise à mort*. It might, indeed, viewed from to-day, without too gross exaggeration, have been called a Gentlemen's Lynching, for what David Cohn has said of the Delta country where, in his own phrase, he was born and raised, might with equal truth have been said of Knoxville: "This is a church-going and whiskey-drinking society."[16] And in a society composed of such elements, incongruous things can and do happen.

But however that may be, the old wooden bridge over the Tennessee, mute witness to this bit of Knoxville history, has long since vanished, as have so many other things, both beautiful and ugly, in the old Knoxville, and in the afternoon of that day of the lynching Colonel Dickinson came to take us to Island Home, his plantation across the river, and then Knoxville's great show-place.[17]

Mama sat beside him on the back seat of the landau, while my little sister and I sat with our father on the seat opposite. It is all pretty much like a dream now, but I can still see how Colonel Dickinson looked; his corpulent figure in a slightly rumpled white linen suit, his puffy hands resting on his gold-headed cane, his courtly, deferential manner toward Mama, the type of woman, the *only* type, as was well known—a beautiful woman, dressed with taste and elegance—, he ever arranged to have sit beside him as he drove through town, a sort of royal progress, on his way to show Island Home to distinguished visitors or newcomers to Knoxville. I can see the glow which the crimson lining of the lace-bordered parasol Mama carried in the open landau threw over her face with its finely carved yet not austere features and its faint olive tinge underneath a fine-textured, flawless skin.

As we drove down the short but steep hill that led to the bridge, on either side of us appeared a stream of people coming and going, and when we were actually on the bridge, the mulatto coachman had to drive cautiously to avoid driving over some of the men, women and children who were milling around there, but as they scattered a little to allow the landau to pass, in a shuddering glance I caught sight of the big brownish-red splotches on the floor of the bridge which they had been gazing at, and saw people leaning over a railing at one side, pointing down to the stones at the foot of the pier where the body of the man who was lynched, though it was no longer there, had landed.

The coachman could only drive slowly. It was not allowed then to drive fast over

Old River Bridge from South Knoxville (1890s?).

a bridge. But Colonel Dickinson's smooth florid face under his broad-brimmed planter's hat betrayed no awareness of the crowd of morbid sight-seers with which we were hemmed in. He made no comment. As Knoxville's foremost citizen and president of its first Board of Trade, it was awkward, to say the least, to have a lynching follow on the very heels of my father's arrival in town with his family. And my parents, with no wish, I suppose, to embarrass him further, said nothing either; though I felt sick now myself as when I had read the newspaper account of the lynching in the morning.

But as we turned into a woodland drive that led to Island Home and followed the windings of the river, which constantly came into view through breaks in the trees, shining and sparkling, excitingly alive, its overhanging trees canopied with Virginia creeper, already showing a few scarlet tendrils, or draped with wild clematis, now, in September, a witchery of snowy fluff—with before my eyes all this lavish, lovely wild growth which softens the borders of the ever-curving Tennessee, and with goldenrod and purple asters everywhere along the roadside, the scene behind us on the bridge faded a little and my mind became calmer.

We stopped in front of a quaint white cottage, half hidden in shrubbery, which served as porter's lodge, while some little darkies ran out to open the gates for us, and then we drove a mile or two through broad acres, a thousand or so, with white fences, cattle grazing in the pastures, and immense flocks of turkeys here and there in the fields. An old plantation which Colonel Dickinson had bought at the close of the War, no doubt at a bargain, he had developed into a model stock farm. But it was when, still some distance away, we came in sight of the mansion that the place began to work its magic. Though no massive columns appeared, no classic façade usual in the ante-bellum architecture of a wealthy Southern planter's home, yet with a double flight of curving stairs mounting to the broad front gallery, a long alley of box leading from either side, and in its setting of old oaks, overgrown with ivy and hung with mistletoe, of towering cedars, magnificent magnolias, their lower limbs extending far out over the ground, of holly trees, and huge crêpe myrtles now a glory of deep pink bloom, I had never seen a place that seemed to me so charming, so romantic. Built by slaves, and like its setting softened and enriched by age, this story-book manor made the same appeal, greatly magnified, that I had found in the old red-brick houses in Knoxville, in its narrow steep old streets, its old uneven pavements with moss pushing up between the bricks. Only here was no look of decay, no dilapidation.

The drawing-room, library, all the lofty oversized bed-rooms were on the first floor of the mansion, on either side of a hall of noble proportions, running from the brick-paved gallery in front to one of identical design in the rear which overlooked landscaped gardens, a carriage-house and barns further away, and a row of old brick cottages, once slave-quarters, but that now housed the servants on the place, ex-slaves or their descendants.

On the ground floor was the dining-room. Whether the kitchen was on this floor or in a separate building, according to the custom on plantations in the Old South, I can not recall, in spite of many subsequent visits to Island Home after I

Island Home Plantation.

had reached the age to go to its "princely entertainments," as the *Knoxville Journal* invariably called any party given by the Hon. Perez Dickinson.

What I *do* recall is the furnishing of the mansion: massive mahogany pieces and in every bed-chamber a stately four-poster; Aubusson carpets on the floor; damask hangings, but no pictures on the walls, no ornaments on the mantels—no frippery anywhere. A man's house and yet its owner, this Yankee who, *mirabile dictu*, had become indistinguishable from a native-born Southerner, asserted with what seemed pride that while he drove out to Island Home every day and had entertained countless guests there, he had never himself spent a night in the house.

We sat on the front gallery. A middle-aged Negro house-keeper brought us out a tall pitcher of lemonade with big goblets to drink it from, and then we visited the green-houses, on a terrace a little below and at one side of the mansion and famed for their Maréchal Niel roses, which hung now, thousands of them, from trellises overhead, clambered over the glass walls—those golden roses one seldom sees nowadays, with their great heavy heads, their incomparable fragrance, and a cluster of which was presented to Mama by Colonel Dickinson with one of his sweeping bows.

But the golden haze through which I saw Island Home for the first time on that September afternoon faded out as we reached the bridge again on the drive back to town. The sun had gone down, but people, though fewer, and some in wagons, were still streaming on to the bridge, eager to gaze before it was too dark at the blood-stained planks on the bridge floor. And so powerful was the impression this made on my mind that for years afterwards in nightmarish dreams I would see, in an unrecognizable locality, but against a glowering sky, a group of uncouth and sometimes subhuman figures peering down at the floor or ground, and the thing they were staring at, though I could never see it, and there was no bridge, would always be blood that had dripped down from a man overhead who had been lynched.

Remembering these dreams brings back, too, a story that in later years went the rounds in Knoxville and was generally believed at the time. The madam of a house on Crozier Street,[18] so the story ran, sent on her death-bed for Knoxville's best beloved physician, Dr. John Boyd, whom the woman had known previously only through his reputation for kindness and understanding.[19] There was something, she said, she must tell him before she died. She then confessed that the man who had been lynched in 1885 was not the one who had committed the crime. It had been committed in the establishment she still presided over. She had turned State's evidence, but it was her own lover, in a fit of jealousy, who had killed the young traveling man, and as her lover had been killed himself later, somewhere in the West, there was no longer any reason for shielding him. The thing, she said, had been bothering her for a long time.

"I've kept studyin' about it," she was quoted as saying, "and I want to get it off my mind before I go to meet my Maker."

NOTES

1. A Knoxville native, Thomas William Humes (1815–1892) was elected president of East Tennessee University (of which he himself was a graduate) in 1865 and served in that capacity until 1883. East Tennessee University became the University of Tennessee in 1879 during his administration. Before becoming university president, Humes had been rector of St. John's Episcopal Church in Knoxville. He was also an author and served as librarian of the Lawson McGhee Library (Knoxville) for the last few years of his life. See biographical entry in Rothrock, *French Broad-Holston Country*, 431–32.
2. After the death of his first wife in 1847, Humes married Anne Betsy Williams, of New Hartford, Connecticut, in 1849. She was teaching in the Knoxville Female Seminary at the time. They had two children before her death in 1879. Rothrock, *French Broad-Holston Country,* 432. Knoxville's "Female Seminary" is not the same institution as Knoxville Female Academy. Laura E. Luttrell, "One Hundred Years of a Female Academy: The Knoxville Female Academy, 1811–1846; the East Tennessee Female Institute, 1846–1911" in *The East Tennessee Historical Society's Publications,* no. 17 (1945), p. 78, note. Knoxville Female Seminary was established by the Rev. Robert Burns McMullen in 1846 and was in operation for eight to ten years (Rothrock, 451).
3. The 1885 *Knoxville City Directory* lists a "Mrs. Laura Clotworthy, boarding," at 148 Church Street.
4. At that time, Henley Street "ran from Union to the river and was primarily residential." Knoxville Woman's Building Association, *Knoxville Cook Book: a Collection of Practical Tested Recipes by Many of the Best Housekeepers Throughout the Entire United States* (S.l.: B. Warters, 1901). Reedited by Frank Tipton Rogers (Knoxville, TN: V. B. Rogers, c1985), 315.
5. Mrs. Laura Clotworthy's husband is listed as John B., soap manufacturer, in the 1885 *Knoxville City Directory.*
6. Although a search of September 1885 Knoxville newspapers did not reveal an article naming Henry Wetzell a capitalist, in 1889 a *Knoxville Journal* article with the headline "Local Capitalists Interested in Tennessee Lumber" mentions H. B. Wetzell as one of the directors of a timber company, "organized about four years ago," with headquarters in Knoxville. *Knoxville Journal* (April 5, 1889), 7.
7. Tate Spring (or Springs), a resort known for its natural mineral water, was about 40 miles northeast of Knoxville near Morristown.
8. Sally Lunn bread originated in Bath, England, toward the end of the eighteenth century and is named for the woman who sold it there.
9. An Eliza C. Branner (widow of William A.) is listed in the 1887 *Knoxville City Directory* as having a boarding house at 113 Church Street.
10. Robert L. Taylor (Democrat) and his brother Alfred A. Taylor (Republican) ran against each other in Tennessee's 1886 gubernatorial campaign, a contest called the

"War of the Roses." Although Bob won the 1886 election and served three terms, Alf later became governor of Tennessee in 1920. For more information on Bob and Alf Taylor and their "War of the Roses" see *The Tennessee Encyclopedia of History & Culture,* Carroll Van West, editor-in-chief (Nashville: Tennessee Historical Society, Rutledge Hill Press, 1998).

11. [Frances Folsom] "was married to President Cleveland on June 2, 1886, in the Blue Room of the White House." *The National Cyclopaedia of American Biography*. Reprint. (Ann Arbor: University Microfilms, 1967, original c1891, 1899, 1921), vol. 2, p. 403.
12. Probably "Michie." City directories of that time include M. J. Michie and L. P. Michie, student, both boarding at 148 Church St. in 1885; additionally, John W. Michie at 93 Henley in 1888, 1890, and 1891. *Knoxville City Directory*, 1885, 1888–1891.
13. Popular 1877 song with words from a poem by Meta Orred and music by Annie F. Harrison.
14. During the last quarter of the nineteenth century, "Knoxville . . . was the wholesale distribution center for the upper South." Betsey Beeler Creekmore, *Knoxville!* (Knoxville: East Tennessee Historical Society, 1991), 103; Deaderick, *Heart of the Valley*, 411–12. The Travelers' Protective Association of America was formed in 1890 for the benefit of the men who were, at that time, called "commercial travelers." Post "C" of the Travelers' Protective Association was organized in Knoxville in 1894. William Rule, ed., *Standard History of Knoxville, Tennessee,* (Chicago: Lewis Publishing Co., 1900), 571.
15. The *Knoxville Daily Journal* and the *Knoxville Daily Chronicle* both reported the murder, and the lynching it led to, in great detail on their front pages during the first week of September 1885. The story of the lynching, which had occurred the night before, appeared Saturday, September 5. Jack Neely, Knoxville journalist and local historian, includes an account of the week's events under the title "The Stranger: A Late-Summer Murder Story" in his book *From the Shadow Side, and Other Stories of Knoxville, Tennessee* (Oak Ridge, Tenn.: Tellico Books, 2003), 151–159.
16. Quotation from *Where I Was Born and Raised* (Boston: Houghton Mifflin, 1948), p. 15, by David L. Cohn (1894–1960), nonfiction writer born in Greenville, Mississippi.
17. Although a wooden bridge from Gay Street across the river had been built in 1874, it was blown off its piers in 1875. The south side of the river (and Dickinson's Island Home) could be reached only by ferry before construction, in 1880, of the bridge to which Armstrong refers. Rule, *Standard History of Knoxville, Tennessee*, 302–303; Creekmore, *Knoxville*, 114–116.
18. "Knoxville's 'bad' street with whorehouses from one end to the other" (see Chapter 1 of this narrative). Present day Central Street.
19. Dr. Boyd, a Knoxville native, practiced medicine in Knoxville and the surrounding counties for over fifty years. A marble gateway, placed at the entrance to the Court House grounds in his memory, bears the inscription "Our Beloved Physician, Dr. John Mason Boyd." Rothrock, *French Broad-Holston Country*, 383–385.

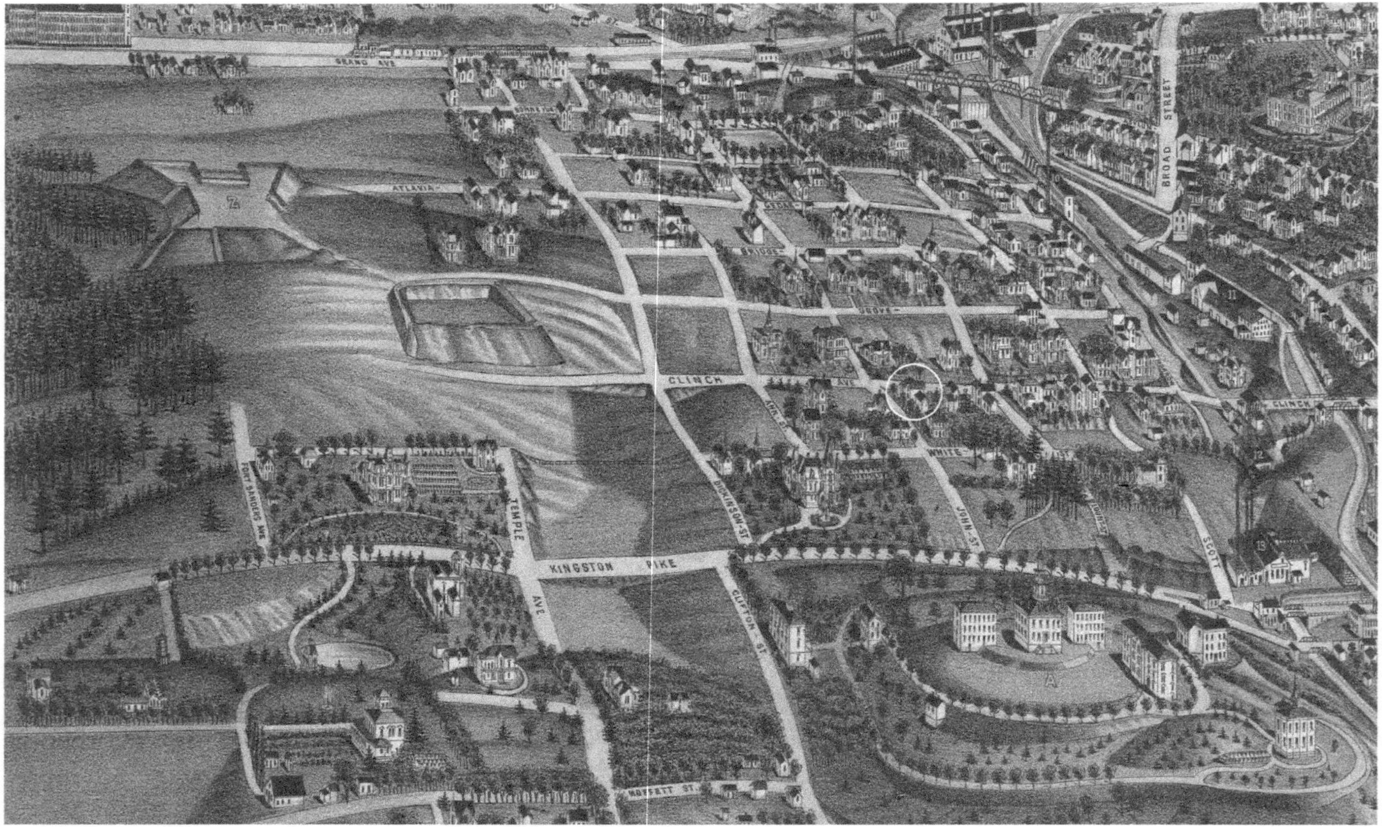

West End (showing Barnes House at corner of Clinch and John; Fort Sanders at left). Library of Congress.

Chapter Three

The Barnes House

Later in our lives we always referred to our first home in Knoxville as the Barnes house, from the name of the people from whom we rented it and who apparently somewhat grudgingly gave us possession when they moved out of it and on to a farm they owned, some six or seven miles from Knoxville, on the river, near Lyon's View.

Long ago torn down, the house was on Clinch Street,[1] in the part of town then known as West End,[2] with its impressive suggestion of the fashionable West End of London, and with a few "princely residences," in the jargon of the day, already built there. On the heights, only a short distance beyond, the battle of Fort Sanders had been fought,[3] while the entrance to the University, at the foot of the hill which its buildings crowned, was hardly more than a block from our side gate.

The strange thing to me now, in recalling the Barnes house, is that just as I have no recollection whatever of arriving in Knoxville, so I have none of seeing for the first time the house in which we were to spend five fateful years. I have no memory either, not the faintest, of moving in; of the hub-bub, inseparable, one would suppose, from settling in a new home in an unfamiliar region. At the farthest point to which my memory of the Barnes house carries me back, we are already living in it, with an orderly pattern of family life well established. Papa is going back and forth to his offices on Gay Street; Harry is rooming and having his meals at home now; Trix, his Llewelyn setter, with her forepaws resting on top of the side gate, is waiting quiveringly every afternoon for his whistle as he nears the house, coming home from classes or drill at the Hill; my little sister and I are both in school; we are all going to the Second Presbyterian Church on Sunday; I am having regular music lessons twice a week from Professor Ellenberger, organist of the Second Church, and have resumed my detested daily hour of practicing on the piano.

I know, however, that when I saw the Barnes house for the first time I was not let down. I would have remembered a shock of that sort. It would have left its slight but ineffaceable scar. An old house and not very large (though not so small either, when I count up the rooms, ten in all), it stood on a corner, not far back from the street, with two immense spreading magnolias, one on either side of the brick walk leading up from the front gate, and a picket fence around the pleasant roomy yard. The house, in spite of being painted a dark grey, presented a by no means gloomy appearance. There was nothing forbidding about it. In fact, as I see it now and saw it then (though I doubt if anyone else who ever lived in Knoxville and knew the Barnes house saw it that way), what with its two pairs of French windows that opened on to the front porch, its many gables, and the little balustraded balconies which depended from each of the upstairs bedrooms, it was not only rather cozy-looking but picturesque. In its unpretentious way, it had something of the same story-book charm to which I was so susceptible and which I was finding now on every side.

The old-fashioned yard, too, although plainly long neglected, had its appeal. There were the many fruit trees at the side and back; golden pears and purplish-red plums both ripe, oozing with juice, in the September when we first knew the place. There was a big crêpe-myrtle that had only begun to shed its brilliant crinkly little flowers of water-melon pink; a wealth of shaggy white chrysanthemums that grew in clumps along the base of the house and honeysuckle that almost hid a sagging side porch with its weight of matted vines; while at the back a long grape-arbor led to what was then called, euphemistically, by people of more than ordinarily delicate sensibilities, the "garden house"—an appendage, incidentally, still far from uncommon in the Knoxville of that day, when city water-works had only very recently been established and city sewers not yet among Knoxville's amenities.

But to Mama, the Barnes house, outside and in, was something quite different from what I found it. For her, there was no touch of romance in a garden-house, under whatever name. A kitchen separated from the dining-room, not by a butler's pantry, but by a considerable stretch of uncovered porch, was not an arrangement she considered "quaint," nor was a bath-room, located at the back of the downstairs hall, with its rusty tin tub entirely unconnected with any supply of hot water. The truth is, in every particular the grimy old Barnes house was utterly different from the cheerful immaculate home she had presided over heretofore, with its well equipped bath-rooms, central heating, gilt wall papers, its billiard-room, gay red and white awnings in summer, close-clipped lawns, well-tended formal flower-beds, its urns and fountain—all the appurtenances of an elegant home of the era.

No word, however, although she was far from the most patient of women, ever escaped my mother indicating her disappointment in our new surroundings, or none I ever heard, unless in a humorous vein. It was only from an expression I now and then surprised in her unfathomable eyes, a sort of brooding look, that I derived this impression, one that troubled me faintly. But wherever my father led, there she would go, and she set about with characteristic energy and efficiency to make what she could out of an extremely inconvenient old house with primitive plumbing and heating—a house that had never possessed, from Mama's late-Victorian standpoint, the slightest claim to distinction.

On one side of the hall, with its soot-darkened wall-paper, depicting in repeated squares a scene from the Swiss Alps (one of my own delights), was the room we

Mama (Lorinda "Linnie" Snyder Wetzell).

would use as a parlor. With a bay-window overlooking the tree-shaded side-yard, French windows in front, and a black marble fire-place, in this room presently were assembled many, if not all, of the parlor furnishings with which we had long been familiar: the delicately patterned lace curtains, touching the floor and with their crimson plush lambrequins; the tall carved ebony easel bearing on it a portrait of my brother as a lad of thirteen; the ebony cabinet of many brackets, surmounted by a white marble replica of Canova's graceful and elegant Hebe; on the wall the same landscape paintings in their heavy gilt frames we had always known; the same ebony chairs with their gold inlay, upholstered in delicate grey satin brocade; and here and there the same bisque figurines, cloisonné vases, pieces of Rookwood pottery, Wedgewood and Royal Worcester, the same white Staffordshire hound—all the bric-à-brac people collected then, and in front of the fire-place the self-same velvety Persian rug with its pale golds and soft greens, black and orange markings—the rug on which more than one Christmas morning I had curled up to open my gifts before the fire. Yes, very cluttered, this parlor, viewed from the middle of the twentieth century, but in 1885 it was marked, one would have said, I believe, by fastidious taste, that it was beautiful, and to me, whatever it was to Mama, it was home.

Even more was it home in a room across the hall which now housed those tall walnut bookcases with their glass doors which we had known since we knew anything at all. There were the same sets of Thackeray and Dickens and George Eliot and Hawthorne in fine leather bindings, the rows and rows, in some of the cases, of sober black or brown bound volumes of *Harper's Magazine, Scribner's,* the *Century,* and *St. Nicholas*; on the lowest shelf of one of them the long line of the *Encyclopaedia Britannica* in calf; above another book-case a Rogers group, "Bringing Home the Cows," on the walls of the room the same Whistler etchings, the same French engravings, a series of four, with their French titles and glossy ebony frames, that seemed always to have gone with the books, and here in this room was the marble bust of Charles Dickens which my parents had purchased after the memorable occasion when, as bride and groom, they had heard him in New York, in 1867, read from *Oliver Twist* and other of his works, and dearest to them, I believe, of all their household goods. Here, too, was the piano and the old deep easy-chairs in dark red velvet or leather. In this room now we would live, despite the fact that no one yet talked of a "living-room." Here, in the evening, we would gather around the gas drop-light on the commodious library table: Mama in her old-rose cashmere tea-gown with cascades of lace down the front, her long slender fingers busy with her crocheting, or pricking back and forth through the embroidery hoops she held; my father engrossed in Thoreau's *Walden*, or perhaps in *Fresh Fields* by John Burroughs, just off the press; my little sister, her long fair curls hanging down over her book of fairy-tales, lost in the story of Cinderella; Harry poring over one of *The Little Classics*, trying to memorize "The Charge of the Light Brigade" for the next meeting of Chi Delta, the literary society he had joined on the Hill, and I absorbed in *Pendennis*. I see it all, the quiet group (how safe they all look!), see it plainly after more than sixty-five years, far more plainly than I saw it then—an American family, *déraciné*, as Henry James would put it, the more closely knit that they had not sent down roots—if they ever would—into alien soil.

But it was, I believe, old Mr. Barnes, who owned the place, more than any of the inconveniences and discomforts of the Barnes house, which disturbed, and at times infuriated, Mama.[4]

The Barnes family, like the Clotworthys, were "good Presbyterians," members of the Second Presbyterian Church we now attended ourselves; Mr. Barnes, as I recall it, an elder; his unmarried daughter, "Miss Mamie," active in its sociables, Sunday School picnics, and other church affairs; a second daughter, "Miss Lula," married to one of its former and popular pastors, the Rev. Sturgis, a widower—a marriage regarded as a great feather in Miss Lula's cap and which seemed to have thrown a certain aura over the whole Barnes family, at least in the formidable little Presbyterian world that was part of the Knoxville of that day.

A great raw-boned slovenly old hulk of a man, Mr. Barnes had come South in his youth from Vermont, probably, and like most New Englanders who settled in the South prior to the Civil War, to teach school, but unlike other New Englanders in Knoxville, notably the Hon. Perez Dickinson, he had acquired none of those special social graces prevalent in the region of his adoption, he had only taken on the worst it had to give. Never, before nor since, have I heard any native Southerner, any ex-slave-holder, of whom I knew many in my youth, rant with such bitter violence as old Mr. Barnes about the "niggers," as he called them. "Ain't no more fit to be educated than a possel o' hogs. Ought to be back in slavery, where they belong, every mother's son of 'em!" With his uncouth speech and ruffianly manners, his long untidy gray locks and the stubbly fringe of Horace Greeley whiskers encircling his chin and cheeks, he reminded me of the horrendous figure of Simon Legree I had seen once in my early childhood in a stage version of *Uncle Tom's Cabin.* Without bothering to clean the red clay off his boots when he came in from the farm, or to ring the door-bell, he would stalk through the halls upstairs and down as if he were still living in the house himself, opening doors that he found closed, staring a moment into this room or that, dismissing what he saw with a snorting "Humph!" and going on to another. If my mother were home and he encountered her in his rounds, he would explain that he just wanted to see how we were gettin' on or would make a pretext that he was looking for something or other he thought he had left behind. He seemed to take prodigious pleasure in the fact that the mosquitoes, always at their worst in Knoxville in the fall, were still so pestiferous that Mama had had to have mosquito-canopies installed over all our beds and showed unmistakable satisfaction when he observed she had had to purchase a wardrobe for every bed-room in a house without closets.

I can never forget, either, how the old man liked to goad my mother, and how fiercely I resented it when he seemed bent on taking her down a peg. He gloated especially, it was plain, over the troubles she was having in her first experience with Negro servants.

"Oh, you'll get used to niggers," he would tell her with a great guffaw. "You'll get used to 'em stealin' you out o' house and home. You'll get used to mosquitoes and cockroaches and flies and bed-bugs—everyone has 'em."

A woman of much dignity, old Mr. Barnes was Mama's greatest trial during our early months in the Barnes house. But she never lost control of herself, however strong the provocation he offered. Proud, high-spirited, ambitious, she was yet far from heartless and I believe she sensed that old Mr. Barnes' boorish behavior, his sneers, were but outward manifestations of some grievous inner hurt. She sensed, in all probability, that he was humiliated by the transformation the house and even the yard had undergone in her own and my father's hands. Old now, lean days had come upon him. The move back to his little farm had been dictated by necessity; and a coarse-grained man to start with, it was this seeing others occupying a home he had been forced to relinquish which had aroused such animosity in him.

But however all that may be, I think there was never any other individual for whom our family entertained unitedly a more cordial dislike than for old Mr.

Barnes. In my own case, no doubt his loutishness has remained more strongly imbedded in my memory for the reason that of the many men, of all classes, I came to know, first and last, during my crowded youthful years in Knoxville, I can recall only two who were ill-mannered, and of the two, one was old Mr. Barnes. I doubt, indeed, if any Southern city ever lived up to the South's traditional reputation for courtesy more fully than Knoxville. Whatever its limitations, whatever it has become since, the old Knoxville at least, with the all but universal kind and friendly manners of its men, their marked gallantry, lives glowingly in my mind as the most courteous city I have known.

But it would have taken, in any event, more than a Mr. Barnes to dampen permanently the spirits of a family as adventurous by nature as I have reason to believe ours was, as curious about life in its multitudinous forms, and with all the new interests opening up.

West End, at the time, still preserved to a large extent a rural—an all but Arcadian—atmosphere. There were no street-cars; only a stuffy old horse-drawn bus, "The Rosebud," to take people to and from Gay Street, if they had no horses themselves, or preferred, as many did, not to take them out at night, or on Sunday. Almost everyone, however, had horses, and stables to keep them in. To own a horse then or even a span of horses was no more an indication of comfortable means or social importance than to have servants. They were both regarded, as cars in the 20th Century, not as luxuries, but necessities. Cows were still generally kept, too, in West End, families tethering a Jersey or two in their own ample yards or having one of the young Negro boys always available drive them back and forth to Fort Sanders, where no streets had yet been run through the fortifications, only a few houses erected on its uppermost rim, and there was free and unlimited pasturage.

There was no crowding anywhere but an exhilarating feeling of space all around us. Behind the Barnes house, between us and the Hill, was the old White place, with a big old-fashioned weather-beaten frame house, in its grove of locust trees, where some of the White descendants lived, and many acres of untilled field, neglected orchard and rough pasture, part of the former estate of James White, founder of Knoxville and owner once of all the land now known as West End.[5] To the west, separated from the White property only by a rutted lane that led down the hill to the gates of the University, was the home of one of Knoxville's early "merchant princes," Captain Woodruff, who had made his fortune in wholesale hardware and during the '70s built one of the cupaloed castles that Hudson River gentry were erecting in the same period, and that with its landscaped if somewhat informal grounds, facing the University, covered a whole block.[6]

At the time there was no residential district in Knoxville where the houses were uniformly of more or less imposing appearance—no "restricted" area, and in West End, as elsewhere, homes like the Woodruffs and other less impressive but still stately mansions would be found next to the simplest of cottages—often cheek-by-jowl with the most disreputable of shacks. But this, after all, was a period when the Old South, with its lingering aristocratic traditions, was just beginning to merge with the new commercial South, and while *émigrés* or native apostles of progress might deplore the spotty look of the town, to me, this grandeur and destitution side by side—the castle on the hill, the hut below, with its faintly feudal flavor—fitted perfectly into the story-book Knoxville growing up in my mind.[7]

It was in no such illusions, however, that Harry found any attraction. Rushing home from the Hill in the late afternoon, he would start with Trix at his heels for the long grassy slopes to the west and north of Fort Sanders, up which the Confederates had made their gallant charge, only to be repulsed with the loss of thousands[8]—slopes grown up sparsely now with small scrub pines and cedars, and beyond which was open country, and here he would search for the big lead bullets used in the Civil War, or for Indian arrow-heads, seldom coming home without some of both in his pockets. Often, though, he would take his gun. Quail were so plentiful that frequently we would hear the call of a cock, "Bob White! Bob White!" right under our windows in the Barnes house, and if Trix flushed a covey or so of birds on Fort Sanders, Harry was sure to bring some back.

Harry would come through the side gate, and trying to dissemble his youthful pride, lay them out in a row on the zinc-covered kitchen table for the rest of us to exclaim over—one of the few times, at least during our first year or two in the Barnes house, when I ever had the courage to enter the kitchen. It was a horrible room. Even I, with my adolescent passion for Knoxville and all its works, could find no fascination here. Long and narrow, with a preposterously high ceiling and walls kalsomined a hideous blue, it was dreary in the extreme, and off it was a servant's room of similarly abnormal proportions, with the same hideous blue walls and an even more bleak and prison-like air.

But we would never linger long in the kitchen. If Harry laid the birds on the kitchen table, it was with no expectation that big old fat Aunt Caroline would clean them. My father held that a sportsman should clean his own game and accordingly Harry would carry the pretty little creatures, still warm, but with their limp and lifeless heads—which I could hardly bear to look upon—, out to a bench underneath the grape arbor where he would pluck and draw them if we were to have quail on toast for supper or for breakfast next morning.

On Sunday afternoons we would take long drives in the surrey on the country roads around Knoxville, with Trix trotting along behind. We would follow Kingston Pike for miles along the island-dotted river, winding below us in slow, willow-fringed curves; on the other side of the river here and there fields that had been newly plowed for fall sowing, the soil rich red and sentinel cedars marking the fence-rows between them. Constantly the Smokies[9] were coming into view;

often, now in the autumn, veiled in mist, but sometimes, when there was no haze in the air, on the nearest mountains a bloom of wonderful blue, as of blue flowers, and beyond the blue mountains, other ranges fading to paler and paler gray in the distance, vague outlines at last, merging into the pearly clouds that wreathed their summits.

Frequently, however, Papa would turn off the main highway to explore less traveled roads and here he and Mama seemed to miss nothing, whether a picturesque old water mill, still in operation, with its mill-race and great wooden wheel, the old rail fences patched with gray lichens, a clear little stream in which water-cress grew, or the plushy maroon plumes of sumac bushes along the road. They would remark on the beauty of the cedar trees covered at this season with their little berries of robin's-egg blue and speak of the scarlet berries that everywhere brightened the dogwoods and hollies; and they shared so completely each other's tastes, not only in books, the theatre, in worldly gayeties (of a dignified order), but equally in trees and birds and flowers—in the whole world of nature, that their keen interest in this world to a certain extent was communicated on these Sunday drives—at least in latent form—to all their children.

It was still that period, as I contemplate it now, so fleeting in our own, as in most families, so piercing in remembrance, when it was Life with Father and Mother. I recognize now that I myself had not yet retreated more than a step or two into the dreamy world of adolescence where parents are not admitted. I had not yet formed those connections which would have their own absorbing, if furtive interests, their own importunate demands, that would soon make a long drive with the family on Sunday afternoon the last diversion I would seek. But even now, it is true, I was finding that going to market with Mama on Saturday was of livelier interest than Sunday drives in the surrey.

Sometimes Uncle Pompey, the old Negro who drove for us in addition to various domestic duties, would draw up on Union Street, at the back of the Second Presbyterian churchyard and other times Mama, for some reason, would decide he should wait further away, but wherever it was we left the carriage there would always be clean if ragged little Negro boys running to meet us, eager to pick up a nickel or dime, clamoring for the privilege of carrying the good-sized willow market basket we had brought with us. A little darky behind us, we would proceed then toward the Market House. If we chose the side of Prince Street that borders the churchyard we would find backed up to the curb a solid line of farmers' wagons from which watermelons were sold and which had given this section of the street its name of Watermelon Row. It was perilous walking on a pavement slippery with multitudinous watermelon seeds that had been spat out upon it, and to a person of Mama's orderly habits it was very distasteful to observe the number of melon-rinds that loafers buying melons from one of the wagons, ripping them open and eating

Old wooden Market House, east side looking north (ca. 1890).

them on the spot, had tossed over into the churchyard, to land there on its lovely carpet of periwinkle and English ivy, often directly on top of a slab covering one of the burial vaults.

Farmers' wagons were backed up, too, all around the three sides of the narrow cluttered thoroughfare surrounding the Market House and as we approached it nearer and nearer we would have to make our way through the throng always gathered there on Saturday, not only people who had come to do their marketing but innumerable loafers, spitting tobacco juice recklessly in any direction, swarms of beggars—ragged, dirty-faced, miserable-looking "poor white" boys and girls pursuing you with their whining, "Miss, gimme a nickel!"—and little bare-footed pine-sellers, who always met you when you drew near to the Square and ran along beside you until you disappeared into the Market House, begging you to buy one of the small bundles of rich pine they carried, the sappy pine used for kindling-wood in Knoxville. There were country lads trying to sell you for a few pennies one of their chains of chinquapins, strung on a thread, like beads, or chestnuts from a sack they carried or out of their pockets, in a day when "chestnut blight" had not yet destroyed all the magnificent chestnut trees in the Southern mountain country. Under your feet, whichever way you turned, were little mangy mongrels nosing around for scraps. But an even more shocking sight than these waif dogs covered with sores were some of the beggars; a face among them pitifully askew, twisted till it was hardly human, as a result of salivation, when calomel was still the sovereign remedy for innumerable ills; faces with a patch that barely concealed a nose or ear being eaten away by cancer; faces disfigured, bodies maimed, in some other sickening fashion. Long, long after my life in Knoxville, when I would see beggars in Southern Spain, with their pock-marked, deeply-pitted faces, holding up to you fearful-looking naked stumps of arms or legs as the train made its brief stop at Bobadilla, some other station, or seeing them at market in Rondo or Triana, my thoughts would fly back to Market Square in Knoxville, and especially to a monstrosity that was wheeled around there regularly in a cart, a middle-aged woman with a huge head, a broad, clay-colored, vacant face, and who had been born without legs, though she had given birth to numerous progeny, some of whom, wretched semi-idiotic creatures, pushed her around as they begged for pennies or nickels.

But once inside the Market House all was order and decency. Mama would visit the meat market first; next the middle section of the Market House, where, besides the stalls with their arrays of home-grown fruit and vegetables, dressed and live poultry, were more than a hundred tables allotted free in the central aisle to farm women for the display of their produce—butter and eggs, honey from their own hives or from a bee-tree, persimmons, after frost had touched them and made them sweet, home-made cottage cheese and apple butter, often big hominy which, soaking their corn in lye to remove the husks, they had prepared laboriously themselves, and always for sale stiff, crowded bunches of fiery cockscomb, pink and purple China asters, blazing African marigolds and other vivid, inharmonious flowers from their country gardens. Finally we would reach the Fish Market, at the rear of the building, opening on to Wall Street.

Mama seldom bought anything from the noisy vendors in the wagons backed up to the curb alongside the Market House, though thrifty marketers who didn't mind being jostled usually found their best bargains there. Mama preferred the relative decorum of the less crowded indoor market. Her first trip through it was one of inspection. Occasionally she stopped to ask the price of something, for here, in brisk, bustling, competition, prices might differ greatly in stalls only a few feet apart. But Mama was no bargainer. She delighted in giving things away, but had been endowed with no trading instinct, a weakness—one that greatly complicated their lives—which she handed down to her children. In marketing, she was concerned almost solely with the quality of the food she was after, whether dressed guinea-fowls, late peaches, green tomatoes for pickling, a beef heart for stuffing and baking, an ox-tail for soup; and when she found what she wanted she filled our big market-basket rapidly, for in these early days in Knoxville, when our acquaintance there was still very limited, she was seldom delayed by visiting with other women at market.

I myself was always loath to leave the market. Here, here alone, not in the churches, not in the schools—nowhere else, met the town and the country, blacks and whites, young and old, the rich and the poor, the pious and the impious, the saints and the rogues, the fashionables and the disreputables of Knoxville, and with the wonderful profusion of alluring food on every side—a thing to put on canvas—, with the cheerful, laughing, joshing crowds, the exuberant pagan joy that surged through the whole Square on market days and furnished its shifting color, I found some of the same sort of excitement I felt at the theatre to which my parents exposed all their children at so early an age. Even the beggars, in their rags and misery, seemed to fit appropriately, as dark shadows in the background, into the *mise en scène*. And there was ever present in my own mind, too, from the first time when I went to market with my mother, a sense (not yet clearly defined, perhaps, but hovering on the edge of my thoughts) of the spectacular contrast between this scene, humming with human activity and happiness, throbbing with life, and the blue-nose Puritan Knoxville Sunday which would follow on the morrow, when Market Square would seem to belong to a city of the dead, and over the whole town would settle a pall from under which you could never quite escape, however hard you tried, any more than you could escape the all-enveloping pall of soft-coal smoke which settled over the town in its short but sooty winters.

There was another thing I observed when my vision of Market Square had not yet been dulled by too great familiarity. It served, I saw, for Knoxville women of more or less leisure as a meeting place from which they could expect to bring home not only food, but savory bits of town talk. Throughout the Square, and especially inside the half-open Market House, we would come upon groups of matrons, simply yet attractively dressed in their summer lawns and ginghams, laughing, talking, whispering together, while waiting around a short distance away were the little darkies who carried their baskets for them, and holding by the feet, heads dangling, the live hens or fryers the ladies had been buying. Sometimes the ladies were so absorbed in the confidences they were exchanging they seemed hardly aware they were blocking the way. But I soon noticed that in one of these groups it was always the same tall, angular, red-faced woman, in mourning and with a long crepe veil hanging down her back, who, towering above the others in the circle, darting her small black-bonneted head back and forth excitedly, held them in rapt attention. If we passed near I could catch the curious sound of her prolonged intake of breath, followed by an explosive exclamation which sent the other women into fits of laughter. Once seen, it was impossible ever to forget this woman, and as long as I knew her, many years—for she lived to a great age—, my first horrified impression of her as a harpy, that fabulous monster of Greek mythology, ravenous, rapacious, and filthy, with the face of a woman and body of a vulture, was never, I am sorry to say, entirely obliterated. Nor could I ever quite erase from my mind an early impression of the women who habitually flocked around her that they were scavengers, as eager to pick up any morsel of scandal she let drop, as the little waif dogs to pick up their bits of offal around the Market House.

The woman was Mary Aiken, and the Market House at the time a veritable clearing house for Knoxville gossip. Later, her comfortable home on Cumberland Street, where she presided daily over what I suppose might be termed a *salon de scandale*, shared with the Market House the dubious distinction of providing a focal point for its exercise of Mrs. Aiken's talents. And make no mistake, she had them. Collecting gossip as a connoisseur might collect early paintings by Cézanne, or choice specimens of carved jade, she seized upon the most sensational hints that were brought her, fused and heightened them through the employment of a far from torpid imagination, and with matchless gusto distributed the end product. She raised gossip in Knoxville, if not to a fine art, to a science, and was the terror of the indiscreet among its socially prominent, for she was seldom wrong in her facts, no situation being too delicate, or too disgraceful, for her to explore. Donning her mourning bonnet with its long crepe veil, she would go directly to the house where a sudden death was suspected of being a suicide and inquire in her intrepid manner whether the member of the family, not yet buried, had or had not cut his own throat; or to get the straight of an unusually crooked and sorrowful matter, call on an old and eminent family and ask outright whether it was true, as rumored, that their idolized but dissolute only son had married the madam of a "sporting house" on Crozier Street and settled down to live there with her. Equally dreaded and courted, a flock of youngish and older sycophants always gathered around her, Mrs. Aiken was as firmly established in her self-appointed bureaucratic position as any mayor or chief of police in Knoxville's history, and much more secure in her tenure of office, for it lasted as long as she did. She made gossip her career, as other women might make music, teaching, civic affairs, or simon-pure domesticity, and all in all, it is safe to say that no woman in Knoxville ever wielded, whether for good or ill, a more powerful influence, not even that unbelievably fantastic spinster, Miss Temple (a legend in her own life-time), who reigned over Knoxville society—over its more submissive elements—for more than four decades.

Seeing her, however, as I now do, retrospectively, Mary Aiken was by no means basically evil. Nobody ever accused her of being a liar or particularly malicious. If she could destroy a reputation, she could also, and on occasion did, with great spirit, save one. Daughter of the celebrated "Parson" Brownlow,[10] originally an itinerant Methodist preacher, a violent Union man who had upheld as violently the institution of slavery, she had inherited from her father, Tennessee's Governor through the bitter and tragic Reconstruction Era, and later, United States Senator, not only the "Parson's" dynamic spirit and whip-tongue, but his superior mind and robust sense of humor. Her case, then, seems to be one pointed out by Voltaire: "All people are good except those who are idle."[11] Secure in her social position, her husband a successful business man and "good provider,"[12] there was nothing that she *had* to do, and though one of the gun-powder women always a danger to society, it is possible that under different circumstances she might have made valuable social contributions. As it was, when she failed to find sufficient outlet for her excess mental energy, either through the social diversion of the time and place, or in the direction to which most ladies of leisure turned then in Knoxville—the Missionary Society of the church they belonged to, or teaching in its Sunday School—, Mary Aiken, with no spiritual props, it would seem, no hunger and thirst for "culture," but with a remarkable sense of drama, found her release, to the extent she found release, in the *Comédie Humaine* as it presented itself in her native town.

And it was this redoubtable lady, as it happened, who is linked in my own mind with one of the most memorable occasions of my girlhood.

It was in 1889 that Lily Langtry, the "Jersey Lily," famed as the most beautiful woman in the world,[13] came to Knoxville on her first American tour. At her feet had knelt England's illustrious Prime Minister, "the Great Commoner," William Ewart Gladstone, no less than his prospective sovereign, the Prince of Wales, later Edward VII. She was to appear at Staub's Opera House in *As in a Looking Glass*.[14] By this time I was sixteen and for a year or more past had been allowed, reluctantly, to "date," as the expression is in the present, more rowdy century. There was a frenzy of excitement among girls of my age in their eagerness to see this toast of two continents, about whom many stories—most of them not in print—were being circulated. Very few, however, of our young beaux had enough pocket money to afford seats—at least in the parquet or in the dress circle, where we would wish to be seen—, with the sharply advanced prices for the one night's performance, so that I was all but delirious with joy when Alex Carter, a senior at the University, asked to take me.

At sixteen, to go to a performance of any sort at Staub's Opera House was an ecstatic experience. Built by Swiss-born Peter Staub, one of Knoxville's finest and most cultivated citizens, it had been opened, fittingly, in 1872, with Sheridan Knowles' *William Tell*. But on this evening in late May from the moment we reached our seats in its crimson and gilt interior, with its glittering crystal chandeliers, its mysterious shadows, with the hum of subdued talk from the audience already assembled, the violins in the orchestra-pit tuning up, I was lost, as never before, in a realm of enchantment.

The play itself is pretty dim to me now. I have an idea that it was rather rubbishy, and concocted principally as a vehicle for exhibiting the Jersey Lily's peerless beauty. As a matter of fact, I haven't the faintest notion today what it was all about, and whether Mrs. Langtry was playing the part, thinly veiled, of a *demi-mondaine*, or of a great lady in the London world of fashion. One thing, however, I *do* remember, that the play ended with her taking poison and writhing around on the floor in her dying agonies—the wages of sin, I suppose. But, at the time, I viewed this final scene, as the previous ones, with no levity, and no one, I believe, in the Jersey Lily's audience was more thrilled than I when she appeared in one magnificent gown after another, with their long trains, wasp waists, mountainous bustles surmounted by satin bows and streamers, their extreme *décolletage*, revealing without stint the swan-like shoulders and bosom which, like the classic profile, had been painted by Millais and all the great artists of the time—elaborate *fin du siècle* costumes, banded with sable, embroidered with crystals, glittering with brilliants—taffeta and velvet and brocade, in mauve and sea-green, pale amber, shell pink, and one an ivory satin with sprays of water-lilies trailing over a shoulder and down the lengths of the skirt.

But the high point of the play came when in the last act but one this international beauty who had basked in the smiles of royalty, the best known woman of the day, for whom saloons and even towns on our wild Western plains were being named, with the aplomb of a woman of the great world, with nonchalant grace, lighted and smoked a cigarette—an act so daring, off or on the stage, in 1889, that the audience fairly gasped, and one that sent, I am sure, as they sinned by proxy, a shiver of vicarious delight from end to end of the house.

For myself, all this, I confess, would have been still more exciting had I attended the play with someone else than Alex Carter, whose deplorable nickname, incidentally, was "Piggy." He was a stalwart, well-built youth of dignified mien and a beautiful dancer, I thought, so that at hops on the Hill he was the one with whom I loved to dance the Military Schottische. But he was rather solemn, even a bit pompous, sitting beside me through the entire performance with hardly a word of comment, so that I wondered, I remember, whether he was sharing my own thrills and tremors.

What I remember even more distinctly, however, was that the dauntless Mrs. Aiken sat that evening almost directly behind us, two rows further back, and in one of the *entr'-acts* when a crony of hers, in the row between, remarked on how crowded the opera-house was, every seat filled and the aisles jammed, Mrs. Aiken leaned forward and in a loud whisper hissed: "Ye gods, she can't act! They've only come to see a woman who's slept with the Prince of Wales."

There was a ripple of suppressed laughter all around us. I felt my cheeks suddenly hot. I was painfully embarrassed. This was the boldest remark I had ever heard in public. *What would Piggy think?* Piggy made no sign. The town's deadliest wit had made certain, however, that everyone in Knoxville would hear her *mot* by noon on the morrow.

But in those earlier days when, my braids down my back, I walked submissively beside Mama in the Market House, offering no suggestions, but my eyes and ears busy, neither Mama nor I knew even the name of the tall red-faced woman in the mourning bonnet, the movements of whose small head, thrusting it out only to draw it back as suddenly, suggested startlingly an angry turkey-cock.

But soon Mama would have innumerable callers and her mother-of-pearl card-case be constantly in use, for what seems to me now the most insensate of social customs still prevailed then, obliging her to return first calls within three weeks. There was a custom, brand-new to her, too, to which she must conform. Formal calls in Knoxville, as elsewhere then in the South, were made in the morning, which heretofore Mama had devoted to household affairs, needle-work, or writing letters.

We were getting acquainted also with our neighbors. During summery weather, which continued in Knoxville through October, neighbors did most of their visiting with each other on their porches in the evening. Directly opposite on Clinch Street lived Charles Waring, an Irish gentleman with a family of children and an easy-going, merry Irish wife who, despite the frowzy reddish wig she wore, in the absence of hair of her own, was a woman of considerable charm. The gentleman himself, a graduate of Trinity College, Dublin, an engineer by profession,[15] and an able one, was a man of some eccentricities. With his aloof air, British gait, his monocle worn, not in the usual manner, but affixed to the brim of his hat, he was looked upon, we soon found, as the rarest sight in West End, with the possible exception of an amiable brown-bearded professor who lived in the block below us and used to pass daily on his way to the Hill, completely unconcerned, apparently, with the figure he cut, his arms both filled with books and his big black cotton umbrella hooked into his coat-collar and dangling down his back.

There must have been more individualists then than now. At any rate, our Irish neighbor was one. Regularly, after supper, he crossed the street, and asking only for my father, taking a chair close beside him on the porch, he would talk, unremittingly, for hours on end. Long after the rest of us had gone to bed, I could hear him from my room upstairs, his loud, toneless voice droning on, and as he was stone deaf, Papa unable to make any reply, unless an occasional nod of his head. It must have been no small trial to Papa, a capital talker himself, one I had witnessed again and again holding a roomful of people spell-bound as he recounted some of his own adventures in this or other countries. But he bore patiently with this Irishman, the sole member of his race I have ever known who was completely devoid of a sense of humor. After all, he was a near neighbor, and it was one of the cardinal virtues of my parents that they maintained friendly relations with all their neighbors, at whatever cost.

In a neat story-and-a-half white cottage, facing the side street which ran between their corner and ours, lived a Mr. and Mrs. Ault, an elderly childless couple who likewise were unique, at least in the West End of that day. Already white-headed and stooped when we first knew him, always in black clothes and a long coat, Sam Ault was an accountant in one of the more important wholesale houses in Knoxville.[16] At once genial and cautious, the pair were "well fixed," so people said, and lived well, in their thrifty fashion, with a broken-down but reliable old colored man to help Mrs. Ault with her roses and a staid middle-aged Negro woman to tend the house and cook their meals, suspected to be excellent, though few had ever been asked to sample them.

In the cool of the morning any day you could see Mrs. Ault, a woman of ample proportions, in a loosely-girded light percale dress of a grayish tone, a battered black straw hat on her head, pottering among her roses. She took great pride, as she had reason to, in her rose garden, and was always more than ready to show it to any visitor. Calling attention as she led you around to all its beauties, naming each of its many varieties, and with hundreds upon hundreds of glowing roses and buds in top condition loading the bushes, at the end of the tour she would take the garden shears always in her hand, carefully cut a single fading overblown blossom ready to shatter at the lightest touch, and with a pretty speech, quite a little ceremony, present it to the departing caller.

But it was not her way with her roses, or not that alone, which would embalm this lady, and a lady she was, in the memory of her neighbors. It was more her way with her magnolias. There was a row of immense magnolia trees, inside the fence, all along the Clinch Street side of her property, and the showy magnolia blossoms with their heavy scent, in a day when as yet there were few, if any florist shops in Knoxville, were always in great demand, not only for weddings and funerals, but for Commencement exercises both of the public schools and the University, customarily held in Staub's Opera House. Everyone gave freely of their magnolias for such uses, as of any other flowers they had in bloom; so it was with dismay that people learned one June, at Commencement time that Mrs. Ault was no longer *giving* away her magnolias. She was *selling* them henceforth.

"Who ever *heard* of such a thing—charging for magnolias!" the indignant cry went up. And little boys and girls passing on the way to school, spying Mrs. Ault bent over a rose bush, her back toward them, would stick up their noses at her. "She *sells* her magnolias!"

But it was not the time for the blooming of magnolias in our early days in the Barnes house. October was at hand, October steeped in its warm pensive haze, the little dry click of insects everywhere filling the air, the snail's slimy iridescent trail along the old brick walks, honeysuckle clambering over the crumbling stone walls and the picket fences, and roses still blooming, if less lavishly, in all the gardens. And it was in October that Dr. Scott, pastor of the Second Presbyterian Church,[17] and his wife invited us to the Manse for supper. My brother, sister, and I had never before been asked out in the evening with our parents. But for all of us it was a special occasion, the first home in Knoxville to which we had been bidden as guests.

The Scotts were to leave shortly for a new pastorate in some distant part of the country. We had seen little of them and would not see them again, yet that evening gleams like a jewel, to this day, among the keepsakes of my mind.

I had heard Dr. Scott preach on several successive Sundays, and from the pulpit he had made no impression on me one way or the other, except that he did not wear a beard, as most ministers did then, along with doctors, lawyers, and Presidents of the United States, but a feature to which I had a strong intuitive aversion, and the absence of which may have predisposed me in Dr. Scott's favor. But however that may be, seeing him now in his home, with his open, frank, clean-shaven face, with the direct gaze from his kind and comprehending eyes, with his dignity and grace, and no suggestion at all about him of Church or Sunday School, he became the first, and for many years thereafter was the only clergyman who appealed to me as a human being and to whom I was drawn personally in even the slightest degree. It was, however, probably the house where we found the Scotts which wrought most of the magic of that October evening.

Demolished so many years ago that most of the people who would have remembered it are now in their graves, the house, used temporarily as a Manse by the Second Church, stood on West Main Street, which then, and for long afterwards, though so close to down-town, was a fine tree-shaded residential street. Midway of the block, it was between, as I recall it, Walnut (so delightfully once called Crooked Street) and Locust, and with its entrance flush with the street, it must have been one of the earliest houses of any pretentiousness built in the town, and was the only brick house I remember in the Knoxville of the '80s whose bricks had been painted white, so that, together with its simple yet dignified Colonial design, it had a distinctive charm and seemed suitable as the former home of a diplomat, Horace Maynard, who had recently died, but who had been our Minister to Turkey during President Grant's administration. Born in Massachusetts and a graduate of Amherst, Horace Maynard, like Perez Dickinson, was one of the New Englanders who, coming South early in life, had left a stamp on Knoxville.[18]

Inside the house (which retained many furnishings which Mr. Maynard had brought from Constantinople), a short curving flight of steps led from the small entrance hall up to the landing from which, at the right, the dining-room opened, and then another short curving flight brought you to a foyer onto which opened the drawing room, extending from the front of the house to the rear, where French windows led directly into the garden, some distance above the level of the street, completely hidden from it, and sloping gently upward.

Although supper in the Maynard house differed, no doubt, in actuality, not very greatly from many other "company meals" with which I was familiar, yet from the moment I had stepped into this home, so sharply and excitingly different from any other I knew, so redolent of the past, I was riding a cloud and can never forget the gleam of the table, its damask and silver, the lean old jet-black maid, in her snowy turban, who waited on us—the look of the room with its white panelled walls, its gigantic (as it seemed to me) antique fire-place, its corner cupboards of a bygone day. I can never forget the moment when the minister's wife, a wholesome youngish woman with a delightful laugh and like the minister himself with nothing stuffy or oppressive about her, lifted the lid of the big white and gold tureen at her place and a cloud of steam arose from the oyster soup which she started to ladle. I can see the silver ladle itself, the very pattern of its handle, in the shape of a shell at the tip. Never was silver so bright, damask so satiny—never, never again would oyster soup be so delicious. But the whole room, in my memory, wears a festal air. The little lights from its tapers have never ceased to twinkle.

For all that, however, it was the drawing-room, where we went from supper and where we could look through the open French windows into the garden, that was the marvel and the miracle. With its glassy parquet floor, its great cushiony divans and immense ottomans still in their summer covers of pale grey linen, its absence of bric-a-brac, but a pier-glass heavily framed in gilt between the front windows and another gilt-framed mirror, reaching clear to the ceiling, above the white marble mantel with its ormolu clock and girandoles, it had such a feeling of space, of elegance and distinction, it seemed such a noble room, that while it may have resembled no drawing-room that ever existed in Constantinople, it certainly bore little resemblance to parlors in my native country at the turn of the century. It opened casements for me to far-off, exotic lands of which I was dreaming more and more; and when twilight began to steal over the trees outside, giving them a gauzy look, to veil softly a tangle of old shrubs, the few lingering roses, and a little silvery fountain, at one side, that broke the deepening green of a wall of ivy—the garden itself became now a part of the marvelous room, although to be perfectly candid about the fountain, while I see it as plainly as any fountain I have ever seen in my life, after sixty-five years and more, I'm not quite sure it was really there. But if it was not there, it ought to have been, and for years to come when I was not living in my secret thoughts in the ante-bellum mansion at Island Home, approached by its long avenue and in its splendid setting, it was in the old Horace Maynard house on Main Street.

But these were halcyon days. Even for Mama there was an enormous amount of fresh interest in the new environment. For one thing, there were the Southern mountaineers close to us now—our contemporary ancestors,[19] as they came to be called much later by psychologists and sociologists, but a recent discovery then for the country at large. Papa and Mama had read with enthusiasm a collection of stories, *In the Tennessee Mountains*, which had appeared only a year before in the *Atlantic Monthly*. At present they were reading *A Prophet in the Great Smoky Mountains*,[20] a novel, just published, by the same author, Charles Egbert Craddock, the first writer to make widely known this left-behind people who for two centuries had been pocketed, by reason of natural boundaries, in between the East and West of American civilization. People were talking of the great literary sensation of the day, harking back to the time of George Sand, George Eliot, and Currer Bell.[21] Invited by the editor of the *Atlantic* to Boston, when "Mr. Craddock" was ushered into the editorial sanctum, the editor was astounded to see before him, not the double-fisted man he had pictured to himself as the writer of these virile stories and to whom he had been addressing his letters, but an extremely refined, slightly lame little lady, one Mary Murfree, of Murfreesboro, Tennessee.[22]

The Southern mountaineer, however, had not been made known to our own household solely through Miss Murfree. For several years my father had been making trips, mostly on horseback, into the mountain country of East Tennessee and Western North Carolina, seeking options on mining and timber properties for both English and American investors. He had spent many nights in remote mountain regions, as much at home in the cabins of the elemental lusty folk who inhabit the Southern mountains as in Indian tepees in the wild country above Lake Superior, to which other of his business interests took him, as he was in his club in New York or London. He had shared the shelter of one mountain man, never jailed, far less tried, yet reputed to have killed, first and last, no less than six of his fellow mountaineers, through disputes over a boundary line, over a "bench-legged fice, best squirrel dog in these-here mountains," or some such matter. Lodged for the night in a one-room cabin by a friendly young couple with eleven children, he had been equally dismayed and touched when to do him honor, following what they had heard was the custom of "town folks," they had taken a sheet off the bed they were using and laid it next morning for breakfast over the rough planks of their table for a table-cloth.

Papa had, in fact, brought back his own tall tales of the most hospitable people in the world, a people possessed at once of a barbarism that would make them sink their teeth into the lip of a refractory horse, precisely as a wild Indian would do, and of a tact so deep and innate, a kindness so spontaneous, a politeness so marvelous, as to shame any but the most insensitive of visitors from the outside world. He had enthralled listeners by his tales of the Southern mountain folk as he had with stories of his experiences, wherever they had been.

But now Papa had something more in mind. Even before we moved into the Barnes house, while we were still at Mrs. Clotworthy's, he had insisted on taking my mother, my sister and myself with him, so that we should have a taste ourselves of this primitive life, a first-hand impression of the beautiful mountain country he had come to love as no other he knew.

We had gone by train as far as Jonesboro, oldest town in the State, where we stopped at a sagging old inn with a neglected rose-garden and feasted memorably at supper on chicken salad and peaches and cream—an inn where three Presidents of the United States—Jackson, Polk, Johnson—had stopped before us, and even (a name, to me, far more quickening) the immortal Charles Dickens.[23]

From Jonesboro we had traveled by wagon, jolting over roads strewn with such enormous boulders that time after time we got out and walked, uncertain whether the horses could make it even with the wagon empty. At Erwin, to-day a thriving industrial town, then a black-smith's shop, a store to which the mail was "fotched" and a house or two, we stopped for a couple of days; then on through endless virgin forests, over the mountains into North Carolina, where we stayed, a day or two at a time, among the places I remember, with a family named Byrd in their log cabin on the Cane River, and later, a few miles distant, in a two-story log house, with another Byrd, "Uncle Neely," the big man of the region, with his thousands of acres of mountain land. Everywhere we slept on feather beds, ate coarse mountain fare, beans boiled with fat-back, corn pone, boiled sweet potatoes, thick pale sad-looking soda biscuits—food always unappetizing, often none too clean, and for a toilet not even a "garden-house," only the bushes to hide behind.

For Mama, though she was moved as deeply, I do not doubt, as my father, by the breath-taking beauty of the wild mountain scenery, yet anything in the nature of roughing it was entirely outside the range of her own desires and Victorian tastes; so that she endured, I suspect, rather than enjoyed, this one effort on Papa's part to broaden the understanding of his family by exposing it to ways of living other than their own.

To me, that whole expedition into the mountains is exceedingly dim now, though it left certain lovely impressions: the sweet spicy smell of the pines when the sun was on them; the green Cane River dancing and dimpling down below the Byrds' cabin, at sunset glowing like a burnished rose; and more vivid than any other, an impression of early morning, the river still lightly veiled with mist, and the garden beside the Byrds' or some other cabin, overgrown with weeds at this season, but with wild morning-glories trailing over the weeds, everywhere lifting up their silky cups, still sparkling with the heavy September dew, an enchantment of color, deep rose and milk-white and sapphire-blue.

But if much of the experience is hopelessly hazy now, where not a complete blank in my mind, there was an incident connected with it that I doubt I shall ever forget.

To start with, while Papa with apparently effortless ease hit it off, as we say, with any and all of these sturdy people, I myself, on first acquaintance with them, felt a little afraid of the mountaineers, especially of the men, many of whom looked like stage brigands and some of them known to be "killers." I was repelled, too, by the women in their long bedrabbled skirts and with snuff-sticks in their mouths. Even the tow-headed mountain children, though I was not constitutionally timid, I could find nothing to say to when they gazed at me without saying anything themselves, so it was with consternation I heard Papa's announcement one day late that fall that Uncle Neely Byrd had come down to Knoxville—on my father's invitation, I gathered—and brought with him four nieces, mountain girls about my age. Papa had found accommodation for the party at the Haynes House, a small hotel, patronized by country people, on Prince Street, just off Market Square.[24] But he would drive the girls out to our house during the afternoon and asked me to entertain them while he was showing Uncle Neely some of the sights of the town.

I think no afternoon in my life every dragged so interminably. The four girls, in new woolen dresses, plaid or in dark shades, and not looking so outlandish as in my youthful snobbery I had feared, sat on the couch or in the big leather or velvet easy-chairs in the sitting-room, perched on the edge of their seats, as if for instant flight in case of need, and looking straight in front of them, as if seeing nothing, their faces expressionless, eyes guarded, but seeing, in reality, everything, as I would know in course of time.

Mama was not at home, or at any rate did not appear, so I was left to my own devices. I brought out first various curios we had; shells picked up at the seashore, little birch-bark canoes made by the Indians on Mackinaw Island, and so on. When these elicited no response, I tried books of views with pictures in them of Niagara Falls, the Pyramids of Egypt, the Taj Mahal, and other wonders of the world. Then I brought over from the parlor the large plush-bound album containing family photographs and explained who they all were: the gentleman with sideburns, my Uncle Daniel; the pretty black-eyed child wearing a chain and locket, my little cousin Bessie who died of diphtheria; the lady whose hair was arranged in a "waterfall," my Aunt Sarah; the old man with a flowing white beard and who looked like God, my grandfather.

When all this failed, seemingly, to arouse any interest, I had Hester, our Negro house-girl, bring in some cookies which Aunt Caroline, the cook, had just baked and a pitcher of lemonade. One of the girls refused the lemonade with a decisive shake of her head. The others drank it gingerly and ate the cookies, but still said nothing. At last, in desperation, I offered to play the piano, and while there was no assent to the proposal, there was no dissent, so I sat down and played in rapid succession some of Mendelssohn's "Songs Without Words"; "Listen to the Mocking Bird"[25]—one of my father's favorites, to which he had a sentimental attachment, having heard it first when a soldier in Knoxville during the War—; after that, "Nearer My God to Thee,[26] with Variations," and finally my own favorite, "The Polish Dance,"[27] a fiery piece which I played with such dash and abandon, such reckless pedaling and thunderous crashing down on the keys, that I thought surely it must provoke response of some sort. But the girls still sat motionless, without uttering a word.

I felt I had failed miserably. I was a trifle resentful, too, at having had this put upon me. I was acutely uncomfortable and I was baffled—these mountaineers were even harder to understand than I had thought. What did not cross my mind was that for the mountain girls, never before out of the remote mountain region where they were born—shy, fiercely proud—however humble they might appear—, everything around them strange, the afternoon had probably been a more fearsome experience than for me.

Perez Dickinson's Town Home, southeast corner of Main and Locust (1890s?).

It *did* occur to me, however, that had Papa been there, he would have had the girls talking, laughing, singing "Barbara Ellen."[28] But even Papa, versed though he was in the art of getting along with all sorts and conditions of men, had something of a surprise in store for him that afternoon. Mountain folk in their native habitat, it turned out, and in Knoxville, were not quite the same. I do not know whether Uncle Neely himself had been in Knoxville before. In any event, as a special attention my father took him to visit the palatial town-house of Perez Dickinson on Main Street. Under Colonel Dickinson's personal and hospitable guidance the old mountain man was shown through all its luxurious rooms, with his attention called particularly to the white marble bath-tub, imported from Italy, and the first (perhaps the last) of its sort in Knoxville. Like his nieces whom I was making, at the same hour, such earnest if ineffectual efforts to entertain, the hardy lynx-eyed old man took in every room, every sight, then passed on to the next, without a word of comment. But at last, departing with my father, as they walked together down to the gate, Uncle Neely made a single grim observation: "A man who lives in a house as fine as that-there won't never go to heaven."

How little I thought then that in years to come the endless windings, twistings, of my life would bring me eventually into long and intimate and happy association with this elemental folk. I would even write a book about them, *This Day and Time* (Alfred Knopf's, 1930), a protest against the saccharine Southern mountaineers appearing in contemporary American fiction. But it was the same year that Uncle Neely Byrd came down to Knoxville—when I was just turning thirteen—that I had contact with another of the mountain people, and again at home.

It came about through Mama's difficulties in the beginning in dealing with Negro servants. It could not be learned in a day. She was not, I believe, unreasonable in her demands; on the contrary, measured by the mores of the day, inclined to be considerate of servants.

I remember a mulatto maid dropping an immense overloaded tray of dishes as she was passing through the back porch in the Barnes house on her way from the kitchen to the dining-room.

Hearing the crash, Mama went to investigate. She found the girl shaking with terror, her face a greenish-white as she stared down at the porch floor, every dish broken.

Mama placed her hand on the girl's arm. "Don't worry about it, Bonnie," she said quietly. "Just don't try to carry so many at once another time."

That was Mama. She could be extremely impatient over some trifle, but in a crisis the bigger side of her nature rarely failed to assert itself.

It was Mama, when she could not bring herself to take the advice of a West End neighbor that she measure out the flour, meal, grits, sugar, coffee and other supplies needed daily, then lock up the rest and carry the key herself. It was Mama, when she refused to follow another bit of advice—that she lift the cloth covering the basket every cook carried home with her at the end of her long day's work to make sure there was nothing in the basket except such remnants of broken food as went, through immemorial custom, to Negro cooks.

It may be that Mama realized, vaguely, if not clearly, that with the starvation wages then paid even by families of ample means, the only choice for a Negro cook, if she was to keep the bodies and souls of her always big brood of children together—to keep (somewhere in the shambles of "nigger town") even a roof that leaked like a sieve over their heads—the only choice was to steal.

Stealing was expected, Mama saw. It was generally condoned. And who was she, she may have asked herself, to balk a system that was not even a system, simply an inevitable state of affairs which had arisen with the old slave economy dissolved now, and another economy barely beginning to shape itself? At all events, however lenient and understanding Mama may have been, our Negro cooks in the Barnes house came and went. The good cooks were in the old families, or in the many boarding-houses that throve then in Knoxville. Cooks who came to us could not cook; they were incurably slovenly; they arrived late in the morning or failed to turn up at all when occasionally it snowed, though this last flaw, when I look back, seems easy enough to explain. In the cast-off threadbare nondescript garments, the only ones most of them possessed in those days, they were seldom clad warmly enough to buffet winter storms. Better huddle over their own wretched spark of fire than wade through snow or icy slush with their naked feet half out of their pieces of shoes tied on with rags.

It is true that Hester, our Negro "house-girl," a middle-aged woman in reality, with a houseful of children, always in trouble, and a whining woman whom I never liked for that reason (and for a more irrational and finicky one that did me no credit—because she had six fingers on each hand), was nevertheless honest, dependable, and a beautiful laundress, so that Mama valued her highly. But Hester was no cook. A cook was the problem and after Mama dismissed Aunt Caroline for habitual drunkenness, some time late in the winter she heard of a white woman from somewhere in the Smokies who was said to be clean and an excellent plain cook, and decided to try her.

I have no idea how long the mountain woman remained with us and have forgotten her name, but evidently she was proving fairly satisfactory and my mother intending to keep her, for it was when Mama became aware the woman herself was dissatisfied that she called upon me.

"She may be homesick," Mama said. "I told her she could sit in the dining-room. You go in and talk to her. You won't have to stay long and maybe you can cheer her up."

I sensed that the situation was serious. It would be hard to imagine two more dolorous places in which to spend one's solitary evenings than the hideous blue-walled kitchen in the Barnes house and the bleak prison-like servant's room adjoining it, but while there were "servant's halls" in English novels, no servants of ours—none before this tall, lanky mountain woman—had ever been allowed to spend their scant leisure any place else than in their own rooms or the kitchen.

Reluctantly I put down the story I was reading. It was Ouida's *Dog of Flanders*,[29] I remember, oddly enough, amidst so much else long forgotten.

I opened the door into the dining-room, a long queer room with dreary slate-gray wall-paper, our handsome and ornate walnut dining-room furniture looking entirely out of place in its present setting, and crowding the room, the only one in the house without an open fire-place, so that an ugly smallish iron stove with a flat top and an apron had been installed against one wall.

The mountain woman sat near the wall, her feet in their worn and clumsy men's shoes resting on the apron, her big-knuckled work-coarsened hands in her lap, her shoulders hunched, head drooped, her eyes downcast, in an attitude of utter despair.

The woman lifted her eyes as I came into the room, the eyes, with something wild in them, of a trapped animal. Then she dropped them again. I think, as I look back on it now, with my later knowledge of the mountain people, of their fanatical clinging to their independence and feeling of losing caste with their fellow mountaineers if they worked as a servant, that no black woman for sale on the block in the old slave-markets ever felt more debased than this forlorn creature whom I had been sent to cheer up.

I stayed with her a while. I don't think I sat down and I don't know what I talked about, but nothing that brightened her it is certain, for a few days later she left, telling my mother she couldn't stand it longer, it was too lonesome.

"Town folks," she said in leaving, not exactly resentfully, but as if to explain the irresistible urge that was upon her, "is the curiousest folks ever I knowed. Seems like folks in town don't never make a body feel much welcome, so I reckon I'd best get back to the hills an' hollows where I were raised up an' my fathers afore me." She made quite a lengthy speech. "You-all's been nice to me," she said, "accordin' to your lights, but I don't reckon I could ever be satisfied in no town. I'd sooner be dead an' the grave-vine a-growin' on my grave, as to live in ary town on earth."[30]

The words stuck in my mind, in the minds of all of us, but they amused us, at the time, I fear, more than moved us. When I read Ouida's *Dog of Flanders* I had such a big lump in my throat I could hardly swallow; Papa and Mama had been deeply affected, even wept, over the sufferings of the neglected Florence in Dickens' *Dombey and Son*;[31] yet we were alike insensible to the heartache within the walls of our own home. My father was, in truth, one of the most humane of men and with what in his day was considered an advanced social view-point, but it never occurred, I am confident, either to him or my mother that we could have found a place for this desolate mountain woman in our family circle, in the glow of the open fire, where even Trix, stretched on the hearth-rug, had her place and where there was human companionship, or at least there were humans.

This nameless mountain woman has kept coming back to me, however, ever since, and the way she looked when I opened the door to the dining-room that winter evening so long ago. She stands a shadowy ghost at my elbow even now as I write these lines in the middle of another century, on the eve of what promises—or threatens, to be a servant-less age, one which in such large measure we have brought upon ourselves, or beyond denial have hastened.

As it happened, that first winter in Knoxville was an unusually severe one. Snow would stay on the ground for two or three days at a time and with only small grates and most of the heat going up the chimney it was impossible to keep the rather large rooms in the Barnes house comfortable. Accustomed to central heating, none of us had ever been so cold before, though I can not remember minding this myself. If no one's cook came and everyone's pipes burst, also whenever it snowed the schools closed, which seemed a special dispensation of Providence. Then when Uncle Pompey came in the winter dawns to make the fire in the bedroom I shared with my sister, and snug under the covers I caught the acrid scent of the resinous pine kindling as it burst into flame, heard the crackle and roar, while the tin blower was on, of the coal breaking up, and still abed, watched the ceiling above us flicker with golden light and the dusky walls begin to bloom rosily, nothing could have exceeded my sheer sensuous joy in this early morning experience, while to take a bath piece-meal, with a china bowl and pitcher or tin foot-tub in front of the fire at bed-time seemed vastly more delightful, if somewhat more laborious, than immersion in any conventional bath-tub I had known.

On Christmas Eve, around the fire in the parlor, Papa read us, as always, Dickens' *A Christmas Carol*, a family custom not quite extinct to-day but then widespread throughout the United States. We had wound ropes of ground-pine around the picture frames, hung mistletoe from the chandeliers, massed the mantels with holly until the whole house was pervaded with the aromatic, exciting smell, like no other, of Christmas greens. There would be guests at the two o'clock Christmas dinner next day. Already the table had been set and even the dining-room had lost its usual dismal look and taken on a holiday air.

I can see now the massive carved and marble-topped side-board and buffet, the bowls of sultanas and English walnuts, tangerines and hot-house grapes, set amidst the sparkling cut-glass and freshly-polished silver pieces they held; see the table, stretched to its full length, the long lustrous "banquet-cloth" which covered it, the huge dinner napkins *de rigueur* in the Eighteen Eighties; see the glowing ruby spheres of jellied cranberries, one at either end of the table, the pearl-handled knife and tiny gold spoon for the after dinner coffee among the array of silver at each place. Everything was in readiness; Uncle Pompey and Hester instructed in their respective duties; the oyster-plates, with their little hollows, to be chilled for the raw oysters; the plum-pudding to be brought in blazing for Mama to serve. There was no one of us, however, who did not realize that the success of the dinner rested mainly on old Aunt Caroline, a superlative cook, even now in her dotage, when she was in condition to cook at all, though Mama had been assured by one of Aunt Caroline's former employers that she could cook even better when she was drunk than when she was sober. In any case, whatever misgivings Mama still harbored had been quieted to some extent by Aunt Caroline's fervent promises: "Yas, Missy, don' yo' hab no fears. Lawd, yas, Lawd, yas, ef I'm a-livin' I'll be heah soon in de mornin'—dat big turkey, big as a mountain, still ter be stuffed, an' a heap o' things us got ter do."

Christmas morning, long before daylight, we were awakened by the explosion of fire-crackers from every direction, the small white boys in the neighborhood, no less than the little darkies, following the custom that had originated in slave times of bringing in Christmas in this noisy fashion. As soon as it was light, and earlier than usual, Uncle Pompey and Hester appeared, and all Hester's children, besides various other Negroes who had worked for us at some time, or some way, during the past months, and whom we had not seen since, but on hand now with their grinning salutation the instant they caught sight of any of us, "Christmas gif'!"—an open bid, almost never disappointed, for a Christmas remembrance in the shape of a little "jingling money."

There was the welter, too, of opening Christmas gifts and still Aunt Caroline had not come. Finally Hester prepared a slim breakfast for us—no waffles, no treats of any kind, but which, to keep from disarranging the dining-room, we ate on a card-table in front of the sitting-room fire, an irregularity which seemed fun to all of us except Mama, whose brow was beginning to cloud more and more.

The morning wore on. No sight or sound of Aunt Caroline and all the saloons in Knoxville on Gay Street or back streets, sending forth potent fumes from their steaming bowls of Christmas cheer.

The worst of it was that although Mama liked to market and plan meals, she did not like to cook. She would make her own fruit-cakes in the fall, her own brandied mincemeat to be packed down in crocks for the winter—a sort of yearly ritual with many Victorian ladies in a day when such things could not be bought—but aside from that she seldom even entered a kitchen, so seldom that I do not remember ever seeing her there during the whole of my childhood, except when my father had brought game into the kitchen on his return from some hunting or fishing trip.

Mama rose, however, to the occasion. Somehow or other the turkey was roasted, other dishes prepared. She had changed into her green velvet princesse with the moss-agate buttons, and though several hours later than the appointed hour, Uncle Pompey was just about to announce at the parlor door that dinner was served when a tremendous uproar reached us, and staggering in from the side gate, shouting at the top of her voice, Aunt Caroline crashed down on the back porch.

In spite of her bulk, with Papa's and Uncle Pompey's aid, she managed to regain her feet and to mutter thickly, "Christmas gif'!" Then straightening herself, weaving back and forth, her eyes glazed and bloodshot, she grumbled defiantly, "I'm a-goin' ter hab my Tom and Jerry on Christmas day, an' I ain't a-carin' what *no* pu'son says!"

But there was another party this Christmas time, one attended by no disaster. It was given by Mrs. Rhea, my Sunday School teacher, for her Sunday School class, and she had invited Harry also. The Rheas lived at the time in Maplehurst, an imposing home, with grounds around it, on Hill Street; the house with a tower and overlooking the river.

On the evening of the party as Harry and I followed the winding driveway up to the door of Maplehurst, Harry in his dress uniform, tall and slender, with his fine bearing, dark hair and eyes—with Mama's good looks—, and I, less pictorial, in the high-necked, long-sleeved white cashmere party dress then the mode—far from a glamorous one—for girls of my age, we might well have felt slightly intimidated. But if so, the feeling was dissipated the instant we stepped inside.

I do not, it's true, recall how the house looked inside, save for a general impression of elegance combined with comfort. I can not recall the games we played, nor the supper except that we all put on the fanciful little paper caps we had pulled out of our snapping mottoes; that there was chicken salad, ice cream in the form of Santa Claus or a reindeer; that there was light and color, endless laughter; that we each had a present at our place, the one at mine a little garnet velvet casket with a gilt clasp and in it three cut-glass flasks of perfume popular in that innocent day—*Jockey Club, New Mown Hay* and *Ylang-ylang.* But what I am conscious of now above everything else, is that there was not an instant of feeling strange. At once we belonged, Harry and I, or if I can not speak with complete confidence in regard to Harry, who already was growing grave, for a lad of sixteen, I can speak for myself. More than ever I felt I had come to my own country. I would remember always, too, the grace and geniality of Dr. Rhea, our host, a personable and charming man, although most unforgettable of all was Mrs. Rhea herself, small, blonde, delicate, and with a gentle spirit that hovered over, though never intruded unduly upon all these lively young people she had gathered together.

A niece of Colonel Perez Dickinson, to whom she frequently referred with pride and affection as "Uncle Perez," Mrs. Rhea was a daughter of Colonel Dickinson's sister,[32] and though the most lavish, the most gracious, of hostesses, with a flattering manner and soft Southern speech, there was yet something about her that came straight down from her Massachusetts mother—that more than a touch of primness which characterized all the women of New England ancestry in Knoxville.

I was to have a reminder of this prudery—if we would call it so—years after I had said farewell to Knoxville, never to return. When my first novel, *The Seas of God*, came out in 1914,[33] although anonymously (at the instigation of the publishers), it leaked out shortly in Knoxville that I was the author and that while its later scenes were laid in New York and Italy, the locale of the earlier was, under a thin disguise, Knoxville. Naturally, a good many copies were sold there, but what astounded me, as I believed I had written a highly moralistic work and been sustained in the belief by more than one critic, was when many Knoxville readers found the book shocking, and among them Mrs. Bella Rhea, who, it was reported to me, said sadly: "And to think that Annie was once in my Sunday School class!"

This amused me at the time. To-day, however, when I look back with some tenderness on happy hours Mrs. Rhea furnished me when I was very young, I am inclined to regret that I should ever have given this most lovable of proper Knoxvillians even a moment of sorrowful concern.

But whatever my regrets, I like to look back on that first winter in Knoxville. Soon my father, American manager of an English syndicate with investments in the Southern mountain region, and with an office now at 39 Hanging Ditch, Manchester, would be leaving us often, constantly crossing back and forth to England. Soon his children—I, specifically—would be chafing under parental restraint, finding stronger attractions outside the Barnes house than within it. But now there was real delight in the Sunday evenings when, the servants gone, we would eat supper before the fire in the sitting-room, remains of the roast of beef, roast ducks or chicken, left from dinner, toasting bread over the coals in the grate, and Trix close beside us, waiting quiveringly for the bites we would slip her, with my father affecting to be unconscious of what was going on, and Mama's attention diverted for the moment by the spirit-lamp and tea she was brewing, or busy cutting the iced layer-cake, always a feature of these Sunday suppers. Mama, it must be owned, was no true lover of dogs. She would do her duty by them but, to start with, never approved of dogs being in the house at all, and never, never would have sanctioned their being fed from the table.

It was after the supper things were cleared away, however, that the evening really began. Sometimes, before the gas was lighted, with only the warm glow from the fire suffusing the room, Papa and Mama would want me to play the piano. Without musical instinct to speak of, and despite all their opera and concert going, with very limited musical development, they were able to enjoy my simple performances and even, I believe, entertained hopes—baseless ones—that one day I would become a brilliant pianist. But usually it was directly after supper that my father started the reading.

He read us that winter Dickens' *A Child's Dream of a Star*, which seemed to have profoundly impressed him, for like many of his generation, like Dickens himself, while he had long since rebelled against the God of orthodoxy and discarded the orthodox Hell, he still clung to the orthodox Heaven, where, as in *A Child's Dream of a Star*, we would find waiting to welcome us after death, in familiar guise, those we had loved and lost. I did not myself, at the bottom of my heart, very much like this story. I did not like anything in the nature of an allegory and shied away also from mystical suggestions. But Dickens all the same was a household word with us; Micawber, Sairey Gamp, Pecksniff, Little Nell,[34] more familiar than the people who lived next door now or across the street; and when my father read us that same winter another of Dickens' short stories, *Dr. Marigold*, I found it irresistible. With his cart, his horse and dog, peddling everything from frying pans to chronometer watches, living with his wife and child inside the cart, Dr. Marigold pitched it now in the market-place of some ancient English town, again drew off upon a bit of turf in a green lane where he would hobble his horse, turn him grazing, swing the kettle and cook the stew outside, gypsy fashion—then over the hills and far away, and all of the time inside the cart a bed with curtains, a fire-place for cold weather, even a little shelf for books. What more could a mortal want? And sometimes now, in my mind, I was dwelling, not in the dignified Horace Maynard house in Knoxville, nor yet in Island Home, Perez Dickinson's ante-bellum mansion, but going cozily up and down the length of England, living in Dr. Marigold's cart, or one very like it.

It was a golden time, as I think of it now.

One evening Papa read *The Man Without a Country*[35] which stirred us as no story he had read us before, although it may be that it was his way of reading which had much to do with the effect it produced. I have often wondered, in fact, if my father had not been a business success early in life, whether he might not have had equal success as an actor, or an artist, urged as he had been by George Inness, greatest of American landscape painters, who had examined some of his youthful drawings, that he follow art as a career.

But there was one of these Sundays which stands apart. That evening my father elected to read us from a diary he had kept through the War, even the existence of which we had not known heretofore. He had run away from home at sixteen, enlisted in the 51st Pennsylvania Volunteers, served till the end of the War, and still a lad of only seventeen taken part in the Battle of Knoxville, at Fort Sanders.[36]

This time we had not yet had supper. It was in the late afternoon when he began reading. The diary was a small cheap-looking account-book, soiled, weather-stained, and its lined pages, written in pencil, blurred now, sometimes almost obliterated, were often hard for him to make out. Although he had preserved the diary, he had never re-read it till this winter evening in the Barnes house, as he sat by the west window in the sitting-room, to catch the last rays of the setting sun.

Henry B. Wetzell, 51st Pennsylvania Volunteers. From a tintype taken during the Civil War.

We listened, tense with excitement. This was nearer to War than we had ever expected to get. We were learning now something of how it feels to be in one. But as my father read on, and came to his bare, fragmentary recordings of the last days of the Siege of Knoxville in November, 1863, when the Confederates had blocked the Union supply lines and my father and his comrades were faced with starvation, reduced to a cracker a day for each man, when hunger gnawed him, when it was bitterly cold and his feet in their worn-out shoes left bloody tracks in the snow, when all around him were the wounded and dying—all at once as he read to us of the sufferings of that boy he had once been, a great sob tore through him, he was overcome, he closed the diary and hid his face in his hands.

We could never have conceived of such a thing—that our father, that stalwart, self-confident, resourceful man, inspiring others with his own sense of self-reliance—that Papa, so full of fun and high spirits, and with his marked air of authority along with his great good humor—that *he* could break down and sob.

Mama crossed the room. She stooped down and laid her hand on his shoulder. "Why, Henry!" she said.

The very props that held up the universe seemed to have given way.

NOTES

1. On the south side at the corner of John Street. Knoxville City Directories, 1880s.
2. After the Civil War and into the 1890s, the name of a community immediately west of the original city of Knoxville, stretching from Henley Street westward, and including the University of Tennessee "hill" and the area from the river northward to Grand Avenue. Most of this area became West Knoxville, incorporated in 1888, and part of the city of Knoxville in 1897. Allen, *Knox-Stalgia* 154.
3. The battle took place in the early morning hours of November 29, 1863. The fort, originally called Fort Loudon, was renamed by Union forces in honor of their General William P. Sanders after he was wounded by a sharpshooter on November 18 and died the next day. Rule, 170.
4. Azro A. Barnes, *Knoxville City Directory, 1884–1885*. Ellen Renshaw House mentions "Mr. Barnes house" in her diary, recording that the Yankees had taken out a window and made it into a fort during the siege of Knoxville. Mr. Barnes is identified as Azro A. Barnes (1821–1901), a Vermont native with a wife and two children. Ellen Renshaw House, *A Very Violent Rebel: The Civil War Diary of Ellen Renshaw House*, ed. Daniel E. Sutherland, Voices of the Civil War Series (Knoxville: University of Tennessee Press, 1996), 46, 50–51, 61, 224n35.
5. "All of what is now the Fort Sanders Neighborhood was owned by Hugh Andrew May White. The property, which included the Civil War fort, was subdivided by his heirs in the 1870s, and was known as 'White's Addition.'" Betsey Beeler Creekmore, *Knox*

County, Tennessee: A History in Pictures (Norfolk, Va.: Donning Company, 1988), 137; Ron Allen, *Knox-Stalgia* (Knoxville, Tenn.: R. R. Allen, 1999), 156. Hugh A. M. White (1802–1860), son of Moses White, was a grandson of Knoxville founder James White. After H.A.M. White's death, his daughter, Lucy Graham White Rodgers (Mrs. Thomas Rodgers), and her family continued to live in the home, called Sunnyside, until the 1920s, when the University of Tennessee built their College of Home Economics on the site. *U.S. Census*, 1900, 1910, 1920. Hugh Lawson White (1773–1840), oldest son of James White and well-known statesman, judge, senator, and, in 1836, candidate for President of the United States, was H.A.M. White's uncle. Rothrock, 501–02; Creekmore, *Knoxville!*, 52–62.

6. The Woodruff mansion faced the entrance to the University of Tennessee until 1930, when the University purchased and cleared the property. Hoskins Library was built on the site, but the original carriage house remains at 1410 White Avenue. Creekmore, *Knox County, Tennessee: A History in Pictures*, 142.
7. Today, the Fort Sanders neighborhood—including the site of the battle near the corner of present-day Laurel Avenue and Seventeenth (17th) Street (which was originally Fort Sanders Avenue)—is a congested area, with Fort Sanders Regional Medical Center, East Tennessee Children's Hospital, doctors' buildings, Fort Sanders Educational Development Center (formerly Fort Sanders Elementary School), parking garages, apartment buildings, and old houses divided into rooms for students of the nearby University of Tennessee, all in close proximity.
8. Although the Confederates suffered many more casualties than their opponents, their losses were not thousands. When General James Longstreet's Confederate troops made their assault, they found that the Union defenders had cleared the hillside of trees, strung telegraph wire between the stumps, and dug a deep trench, which filled with icy water, outside the walls of the fort. The battle lasted only twenty minutes. The Confederates had 813 casualties (129 killed, 458 wounded, 226 missing); Union losses were only thirteen (five dead and eight wounded). Rule, 172–174; Digby Gordon Seymour, *Divided Loyalties: Fort Sanders and the Civil War in East Tennessee,* 2nd ed., rev. (Knoxville: East Tennessee Historical Society, 1982), 191–204, 205.
9. Great Smoky Mountains.
10. William Gannaway Brownlow (1805–1877). See Rothrock, *French Broad-Holston Country*, 386–387.
11. Voltaire, *Romances* (New York: Peter Eckler, 1889) 12; quoted in Will Durant, *The Story of Philosophy* (New York: Washington Square Press, 1961) 200.
12. Mary B. Aiken's husband was Henry Martyn Aiken (1844–1923), manager or president of the Tennessee & Ohio Railroad and a founder and president of Holston National Bank. *Knoxville City Directory*, 1886; *U.S. Census*, 1890; Rule, 257.
13. English actress (1852–1929) born Emily Charlotte Le Breton. Famous for her great

beauty and known as the "Jersey Lily." William Rose Benét, *The Reader's Encyclopedia.* 2nd ed. (New York: Thomas Y. Crowell, 1965). 565.

14. Stage adaptation of the novel by Francis Charles Philips (1849–1921).
15. Charles Waring, C. E., University of Dublin. Rule, *Standard History of Knoxville, Tennessee,* 364.
16. Samuel B. Ault, corner John and Clinch, West End, bookkeeper. *Knoxville City Directory,* 1886.
17. Rev. T. S. Scott, pastor of Second Presbyterian between 1885 and 1887. Rule, *History of Knoxville,* 429.
18. Horace Maynard (1814–1882) came to Knoxville in 1838 to teach at East Tennessee College (now the University of Tennessee). He studied law and was admitted to the bar in 1844. He was first elected to the U.S. Congress in 1857. A staunch Unionist, he fled to Kentucky in August 1862 to escape arrest and, when re-elected even though Tennessee had seceded, made his way to Washington, DC where he continued to represent Tennessee in the federal Congress. He was attorney general of Tennessee under Military Governor Andrew Johnson and, after Tennessee was re-admitted to the Union, was again elected Tennessee's representative in the U.S. Congress. After sixteen years in congress, he served five years as minister to Turkey before being appointed U.S. Postmaster General by President Rutherford B. Hayes. The people of Maynardville, county seat of Union County (just north of Knoxville), named their town in his honor. Rule, 485–86; Rothrock, *French Broad-Holston Country,* 453–54; Thomas William Humes, *The Loyal Mountaineers of Tennessee* (Knoxville: Ogden Brothers, 1888), 126–28.
19. From the title of an essay, "Our Contemporary Ancestors in the Southern Mountains," by William Goodell Frost, president of Berea College (Berea, Kentucky). Published in the *Atlantic Monthly,* vol. 83 (March 1899), and, although only nine pages long, issued later in book form.
20. The actual title of this work is *The Prophet of the Great Smoky Mountains* (1885).
21. Masculine pen names of the female authors Amantine Lucile Aurore Dupin (Baronne) Dudevant, Mary Ann (or Marian) Evans, and Charlotte Brontë, respectively.
22. For more information on Mary Noailles Murfree (1850–1922), see Allison Ensor, "Mary Noailles Murfree," in *Tennessee Encyclopedia of History & Culture,* ed. Carroll Van West, (Nashville: Tennessee Historical Society, Rutledge Hill Press, 1998) 651–52; Thomas Daniel Young, *Tennessee Writers* (Knoxville: University of Tennessee Press, 1981) 11–16.
23. The town of Jonesborough (formerly spelled "Jonesboro") was chartered by the State of North Carolina in 1779 and became part of Tennessee when it was granted statehood in 1796. Dr. William P. Chester opened Chester Inn on the Great Stage Road in 1797. Now fully restored and a historic site owned by the State of Tennessee, it is on Jonesborough's Main Street. Carroll Van West, "Chester Inn," in *Tennessee Encyclopedia*

of History & Culture, ed. Carroll Van West (Nashville: Tennessee Historical Society / Rutledge Hill Press, 1998), 148–49; Town of Jonesborough, "Chester Inn Museum," https://jonesborough.com/locations/chester-inn-museum/ (viewed Oct. 16, 2020). The U.S. Presidents mentioned did stay at Chester Inn; according to Chester Inn Museum staff, there is no evidence—only anecdotes—reporting that Dickens stayed there. Telephone conversation with editor, Oct. 16, 2020.

24. Haynes House was at 146 ½ Prince Street (now Market), an area which today is occupied by the western side of Krutch Park. *Knox-Stalgia,* comp. by Ronald R. Allen (Knoxville: 1999), 70.
25. American folk song popular during the nineteenth century, first published in 1855. Words by Septimus Winner (under the pseudonym "Alice Hawthorne"), with music arranged by him from a melody he heard whistled by a street musician named Richard Milburn.
26. Hymn with words by Sarah F. Adams, tune (called BETHANY) by Lowell Mason.
27. Chopin's Prelude No. 7.
28. Popular ballad also known as "Bonny Barbara Allan" (sometimes Allen).
29. Children's book (1872) by English novelist Marie Louise de la Ramée (1838–1908) under the pen name Ouida.
30. Armstrong's heroine Ivy Ingoldsby speaks very similar lines in her Appalachian novel *This Day and Time* (Alfred A. Knopf, 1930; repr., Johnson City: Research Advisory Council, East Tennessee State University, 1970), 70–71.
31. Novel (1848) by Charles Dickens.
32. Bella Cowan Rhea's mother, Lucinda Dickinson, married Knoxville merchant and businessman James Hervey Cowan. His partnership with Perez Dickinson grew into the prominent wholesale firm Cowan, Dickinson, and McClung. Rothrock, *French Broad – Holston Country,* 401-02; Wheeler, *Knoxville, Tennessee*, 10.
33. *The Seas of God: A Novel* (New York: Hearst's International Library Co., 1915). AWA's identity was revealed when her book was published the next year by Mills and Boon in Great Britain.
34. Characters from Dickens' novels *David Copperfield, Martin Chuzzlewit*, and *The Old Curiosity Shop*.
35. By Edward Everett Hale (1863).
36. Whether the diary survived is not known. However, H. B. Wetzell later wrote an article entitled "Two Days at Campbell's Station" in which he vividly describes leaving Lenoir's before daylight the morning of November 16, 1863; being attacked and fighting Longstreet's Confederate forces at Campbell's Station; and then helping draw Benjamin's battery along the road to Knoxville that night, arriving at Fort Sanders early the morning of November 17. He contrasts that day with June 18, 1887, when he and his family took a carriage ride to the site of the battlefield at Campbell's Station. His account appeared in a special souvenir edition of the *Knoxville Journal* published for the October 1890 Blue

& Gray Reunion of Civil War veterans in Knoxville. *Knoxville Journal,* October 7, 1890, 7; available online through Calvin M. McClung Historical Collection, Knox County Public Library at: http://cmdc.knoxlib.org/digital/collection/p15136coll4/id/4379 (viewed September 19, 2020). A copy of the article is in the Charles Ducloux Scrap Book, held by the McClung Collection, and is cited by Earl J. Hess in *The Knoxville Campaign: Burnside and Longstreet in East Tennessee* (Knoxville: Univ. of Tenn. Press, 2012), 288–89, 371.

Chapter Four

The Barton Building and the Lost Cause

The Barton Building vanished so long ago that there must be few Knoxvillians living to-day who remember that there ever was such a building. It stood on the east side of Gay Street, at the corner of Church, a two-story building painted a light gray, as unimaginative and unimpressive a building as ever stood on a town's main street. I only remember it myself because it had been taken over by the city and converted from a retail store into use as a school while the new Girl's High School was being built.[1]

There had been some question in my parents' minds, it seemed, as to whether they should enter me in Knoxville's public schools or in the East Tennessee Female Institute, founded before the Civil War and the direction of which had recently been assumed by Mrs. Lizzie Crozier French and her sister, Miss Lucy Crozier.[2] Mrs. French had called on Mama to solicit her patronage. Recognizing her as a woman of exceptional mind and vigorous character, Mama had been inclined to send me to the Institute. Had my father, as well, met Mrs. French, a militant liberal, at the time the matter was under discussion, I am quite sure I should have been placed under her direction. As it was, my father, a profound believer in the Public School system of the United States, felt that this was the kind of school all children—or certainly his own, in their earlier years—should attend, so that in the end his judgment prevailed and I became a seventh grade pupil in the Barton Building.

As usual, I was late. School had opened a month earlier. The trip to the mountains had delayed me this time, but there had always been a trip somewhere to prevent my starting school when other children did, and looking back on it now, I am less and less inclined to believe that this was either careless or merely accidental on the part of our anything but easy-going parents. If opportunity for travel offered, we would gain as much from it, they evidently believed, as from the days we would otherwise have spent in school. This seems to fit in with the pains they took, wherever we were, to have us, at so early an age, visit historic sites, art galleries, and to see the great plays and actors of the day. And they were strengthened in their purpose no doubt by the fact that while none of their children ever aspired to high marks in their classes, far less attained them, yet none of us, for all the irregularity of our early schooling, ever failed to pass, somehow or other, into the next grade.

What astonishes me now is that I have no recollection of entering school in the

Barton Building—and entering late at that. This should have been a crucial experience, and the more so that there could scarcely have been a more striking contrast than between the imposing school buildings I had known heretofore and the all but ridiculous school quarters afforded by the Barton Building. But there was a witchery in those first years in Knoxville which transformed in my eyes even the ugliest of indigenous objects and conditions. School in the Barton Building became just one more delightful adventure in the most delightful of all possible worlds, and so in my first memory of it I am already coming and going by a side door at the rear of the building, climbing a steep narrow flight of stairs to the barrack-like second floor, passing through one school room after another, separated by the flimsiest of temporary partitions, till I reach my own, where the teacher, Miss Molly Hayes, is sitting on a small platform, facing me, and I am sharing a double-desk and seat with Birdie Thomas.

It must have been very soon after I entered the grade that some girl during study period slipped a tightly wadded sheet of paper to me on which she had drawn a picture of Miss Hayes, caricaturing outrageously, mercilessly, Miss Hayes' long drooping nose, with scribbled underneath, *She's a Catholic!*

It was against the rules to pass notes. I must have fumbled the pass. Anyway, Miss Hayes stepped down from the platform. Tall and graceful in her dark blue dotted Swiss with its little touches of white lace, her long full skirts swinging slightly from side to side, she advanced majestically down the aisle. The room was deadly still and I was petrified. Without seizing it forcibly she extracted the paper from me, unfolded it, and standing in the aisle surveyed it.

"A very good portrait," she said at length, without raising her voice and her blue Irish eyes brimming with laughter, "—only it's too flattering." She handed it back, and resuming her seat on the platform, went on marking the arithmetic papers piled on her desk.

Miss Hayes' face was always red, as if her skin was so thin that the blood was trying to burst through; her hair was crinkly and even then turning grey; she had the long pendulous nose of Dante, Savonarola, George Eliot, and Cardinal Newman. But she was always dainty; when she moved to the black-board or up the aisle, she moved like a queen; and with no fuss about it, she maintained such order as few teachers ever achieve.

There were no boys in the room. Boys and girls still went to separate schools in Knoxville except for a handful in the three High School grades who passed through our room in order to reach their own in the front of the building. But with the girls, those who would soon become my intimates, I felt immediately at home. We shared the same unconscientious attitude toward our studies as evils which could only be endured where they could not be evaded; the same boundless zest for youthful gayety, effervescent good times—and I thought there could never have been girls more attractive. The fact that I had traveled widely while they had never been anywhere to speak of except Knoxville, that I had seen famous theatrical stars that were only names to them, gave me, I am confident, not the slightest feeling of superiority. On the contrary, I envied them far more than they could possibly have envied me, when they talked of the wild fun they had at Montvale, Lea Springs, or Tate's, nearby resorts where they went with their families in summer. Mama might think much more highly of Long Branch or Narragansett Pier as watering places, but all through my girlhood I longed to go to one of the half-dozen gay and popular "springs" where the other girls went; resorts which no longer flourish, I imagine, or even exist.[3]

Two of them lived beyond the railroad tracks and the "depot" (as we called the railroad station then), in North Knoxville, where there were a few widely scattered old homes of some dignity, and where many new homes of a more or less fussy type were going up on the wide level new streets that were being laid out, but to me the whole region a remote Hinterland that seemed to bear no relation to the older Knoxville; to have none of the charm of the narrow hilly old streets in the heart of the town, or even of West End—not a vestige, except for Old Gray Cemetery, named for the author of the "Elegy [Written] in a Country Churchyard,"[4] the cemetery where generations of representative Knoxville families had buried their dead, where English ivy clambered over ancient oaks and elms, where there were borders of box, paths that wound and dipped, a great central fountain and hollies that stood guard beside old brick burial vaults. Here alone was a beauty, if tinged with melancholy, that almost reconciled me to my classmates living in a part of the town that ever impressed me as dull and depressing.

As a matter of fact, they lived very near old Gray. Ida (later Idalia, from Ouida's novel *Idalia*,[5] when girls were beginning to change their names to more romantic ones, or back to the statelier ones of their grandmothers)—Ida lived less than a block below the cemetery in one of the old square red-brick houses with pairs of tall narrow upstairs windows rounded at the top, green blinds, broad comfortable porches, flower and vegetable gardens at the side and back—houses that still preserved some of the aroma of their antebellum past.

Ella (later Helen) lived even closer, directly across the street from the gates of Old Gray, in a frame house painted an unpleasant shade of brown and the clapboards running vertically instead of in the usual fashion—a house with a look of never having been intended for human habitation and of such forbidding ugliness that you could never forget it.

Both Ella and Ida were blondes; Ida petite and vivacious; Ella with classic features, a colorless skin, eyes as near violet as eyes get to be, and a rather indifferent air. Both, in a few years, would be beauties, belles, and inevitably rivals.

But there was Maggie, too, in the little group I knew best in Miss Hayes' room.

After she came back from a year or so at "Miss Cary's Select School for Young Ladies" in Baltimore, she would be Margaret, but now she was just Maggie, who lived on Asylum Street in a neat old-fashioned one-story cottage with a pretty yard full of flowers in front of it, and opposite the Deaf and Dumb Asylum[6] which had given its name to the street.[7]

Ella, Ida, Maggie—these were the little girls beside whom I stood at the blackboard in Miss Molly Hayes' room, diagramming sentences; with whom I shared the tortures of Mental Arithmetic, standing up before the class to do an example in your head that was hard enough for me, at least, to do on paper; the girls with whom in a few years I would be going to boating parties on the river, cotillions at the Sans Souci Club, the girls with whom I grew up.

There *was* a girl, however, one I first saw in the Barton Building, who was to leave her impress on me. I remember as if it were yesterday when this Junoesque young creature came swinging through Miss Hayes' room on the way to her own in the 10th grade. Tall, moulded generously, with dark wavy hair, and somewhat irregular features, our whole room was galvanized, suddenly began to crackle, sparks shooting in every direction, when the handsome girl, about sixteen then, I imagine, though mature for her age, merely passed through our room. With a practically impassible gulf between the 7th and 10th grades, we gazed at her in awe. We could hardly hope to know her well. But we were constantly hearing about her and about her unbelievable brilliance. Her name was Laura McAdoo. She was the youngest sister of a McAdoo that would one day be Secretary of the Treasury of the United States and marry a daughter of President Woodrow Wilson,[8] and the family lived then in a big square old-fashioned white frame house, in no way remarkable, but on one of the streets down near the river (East Hill, it may have been) and very near the dilapidated riverside tavern where King Philippe of France had stopped[9] when, in exile, as the Duke of Orleans, he passed through Knoxville on a wilderness journey planned for him by President George Washington, and a monarch whom I would never cease to associate in my mind with the McAdoos (a kind of royalty in exile themselves) from the time I knew where they lived and knew the name of the high-voltage girl with the dark, luminous rather heavy-lidded eyes, the swinging gait, the rich, spontaneous laughter—this young goddess, as she seemed to me.

It would be a year or so till I knew her, and a good many more years till Laura, married to a French scientist and become herself more French than the French, would be Madame Gagey, living in Paris, etched by the famous Paul Helleu, who with his bold yet delicate art had captured in dry-point that atmosphere, at once indefinable and intoxicating, in which Laura was always enveloped; painted by the fashionable portrait painter, Boldini, at the zenith of her beauty, in a portrait which showed her remarkable resemblance to the great Eleonora Duse[10]—many years before Laura and I would be hastening together to the Chamber of Deputies, not to miss a word of witty and fiery sessions more exciting than performances at the *Grande Guignol*; or chatting over the tea-cups in the salon of her apartment on the Parc Monceau with Anatole France,[11] her distinguished and devoted friend, with his Old World gallantry, his aware and avid old eyes.

But at the time and in the place of which I am writing, it was the custom on Friday afternoons, in the 10th grade room, which faced on Gay Street, for pupils to recite verses they had selected themselves and memorized and the authorship of which other pupils in the room must guess; and there came a Friday when the authorship of an unusually grandiose selection proved difficult to detect. It was not Longfellow, not Poe, not Byron—all the guesses were wrong.

Suddenly a youth in one of the back seats sprang into the aisle, waving his hand frantically. He *had* it.

"Laura McAdoo or Shakespeare!" he shouted in a triumphant tone.

It was a story told, in more or less good-natured raillery ("Laura McAdoo or Shakespeare" became a byword), for years afterwards in Knoxville; one that no one enjoyed more than the McAdoos themselves, never blind to their own superior endowment, but blessed with a sense of humor. It was one of the many legends starting to form around a family marked, from the beginning, one and all, for eventful lives.

There were, however, two girls in Miss Hayes' room who, in some respects, made a far deeper impression on me than any of the others. They were Birdie Thomas, with whom I sat, and her sister Marguerite. These girls brought to me, personally and permanently, a sense of what the South had suffered from the War Between the States, as it was then referred to in Knoxville, when not merely as "the War."

The Thomas girls were in mourning for their mother who had recently died. They lived on Asylum Street, opposite the Deaf and Dumb Asylum, in a few rooms upstairs in a cheap rooming-house, with their grandmother, two younger brothers, and their father who, it was whispered, was always drunk. The family was very poor, as everyone in our room knew. The girls' black dresses, of the cheapest material, were often soiled, their hair appeared sometimes to have not been combed, their slender shapely fingers were inclined to be grimy, and they hobbled around in shabby black buttoned shoes they had long outgrown. Both girls, moreover, though not actually emaciated, were very thin, and I believe, still growing, as they were, they must have been always hungry. When we gathered in little groups to eat our lunches together at noon we tried not to see (or not to have them see us see) the miserable little lunches they had brought; a couple of biscuits that looked as if they had nothing between them, not even butter. But if one of us offered them a piece of fried chicken or slice of cake from our own boxes, they invariably refused it. It was mighty sweet of us, mighty sweet, but they just never seemed to be hungry at noon time, accustomed as they were, to eating their hearty meal in the evening. I believe their pride would have sustained them to the very brink of starvation before they would have betrayed the true state of their family affairs.

But if the Thomas girls were very poor, very proud, they were also very popular. Of the two, Marguerite was later the one to be called a beauty but with her finely carved features, thin lips, dead-white skin, even in her heyday to me there was something about her face a trifle chilling. It was like a white camellia, beautiful but without fragrance. To me, too, so white, so sad, it was a tragic face, though partly no doubt this was a reflection from my awareness of the plight of her family. In any case, I much preferred the looks of my desk-mate, her sister Adele, called Birdie, the younger though taller of the two, her head drooping a little, like a flower on a too slender stem, her face one that would grow rosy when she was pleased or excited, and that instead of remaining fixed in its original mould, somehow seemed to ripple on the slightest provocation.

The Thomas girls, at this time, had not lived long in Knoxville. Why the family had come there no one ever seemed to know, but they were from South Carolina, I believe it was, and—so it was generally understood—descended from a long line of rich and cultivated planters who had been ruined by the War, while the girls' father had never recovered from wounds received in the Confederate Army, which, coupled with grief over the recent death of his wife from "consumption," was assumed to have led to his present state.

I think I first became acutely conscious of Birdie Thomas as different from anyone I had known previously when during study hour she pointed in her own book to a picture of Jefferson Davis in the Barnes *History of the United States* which we were studying. Encircling his head she had sketched something resembling a nimbus and above it written, "The Uncrowned King." It was from her, too, I heard in low tender tones, tones of religious fervor, of "The Lost Cause," the most sacred thing, it seemed, in her life.

This prepared me then, in a way, for what would happen when our grade started studying a subject on which feeling could still be so easily aroused. Although Tennessee, as a State, had gone overwhelmingly Confederate, Knoxville had gone two to one against Secession and in Miss Hayes' room the girls' fathers were almost equally divided between those who had fought on the Union and the Confederate sides. The fathers themselves were fraternizing freely now, but not so their daughters, at least not those from Confederate families, from whom the slightest reference to the War could draw fire. For one thing, increased tension had recently been created through the Confederate General John B. Gordon's having referred on some public occasion to "Winnie" Davis, daughter of Jefferson Davis, as "The Daughter of the Confederacy," and although the United Daughters of the Confederacy was not to be founded for another decade, yet in Knoxville, as elsewhere, the local Ladies' Confederate Memorial Association now adopted this appealing name. Little girls, no less than women, were joining the burgeoning movement and some of its repercussions were felt in the 7th Grade History Class in the Barton Building in the form of daily battles, only restrained through Miss Hayes' invariable fairness, deft handling of the belligerents, unfailing vein of Irish humor, and her almost superhuman patience.

We were obliged at the time, in accordance with the iniquitous methods of teaching history then employed, to memorize every word in the account of battles in our text-book. When one day some girl recited verbatim "The Battle of Bull Run," emphasizing dramatically that the Confederates under General Joseph E. Johnston had routed the Union Army, "which had fled from the field in wild disorder," suddenly the air was rent by a terrific cry, one of the new little Daughters of the Confederacy giving the Rebel Yell at the top of her lungs, with the room thrown into a near panic and startled teachers rushing in from the adjoining school-rooms.

When someone a week later recited that the Union Army in Chattanooga, following the Confederate success at Chickamauga, was shut up so closely that it nearly starved, another girl shouted, "Goody! Goody!" then clapped her hand to her mouth and muttered, though with a saucy spark in her eye, "Excuse me, please, Miss Hayes. I didn't mean to."

These were of course unseemly incidents and dealt with accordingly, though Miss Hayes ever made allowance for youthful spirits, and never forgot that the girls under her were at their most hysterical age. It was harder, however, to know what to do with a girl when she was reciting "The Battle of Gettysburg" and coming to the lines: "When the sun set, the battle of Gettysburg was over, and Lee was defeated," and the girl burst into tears; hardest of all perhaps for Miss Hayes to restrain her own feelings when, as the term drew toward a close, it fell to the lot of one of the pupils to repeat a section headed "Lee's Surrender," and when she came to the lines, "Lee's troops were only to promise to bear arms no longer against the United States. They were to give up public property except that they were to keep their horses for use in the Spring ploughing," the girl choked, and in her mind doubtless all she had heard at home of what her parents and *their* parents had suffered in blasted homes, in privation, in pride, she sank to her seat, bowed her head on her arms and sobbed. These were not mere words in a text-book the girl had recited—not to most of the girls in the room, not to Miss Hayes, whose father had been killed fighting for the Confederate cause, passionately believed in. These, twenty years after, were wounds, still bleeding.

And sorrow was, after all, a thing that could be allowed for. But when bitterness, small-mindedness, had been shown in the history class, Miss Hayes, stealing time, if need be, from Etymology, the study which came next, would say: "Now, girls, let me read you a few lines that will do none of us any harm," and she would open a book on her desk that contained "The Blue and the Gray" and read quietly, like saying a prayer:

Under the sod and the dew,
Waiting the judgment day;
Love and tears for the Blue
Tears and love for the Gray.[12]

Molly Hayes! There must be citizens of Knoxville living now, in the middle of the 20th Century, who went to school to her. In the later years of her teaching she taught boys too, and was no less successful than with girls.[13] Thousands upon thousands of Knoxville children during the fifty years, starting as a young girl, she taught in the Knoxville Public Schools were under the sway of this noble teacher, this great Irish Catholic lady. Hers was ever the happy school-room, as there are "happy ships" in the Navy—and those that aren't. I was to have news of her death long after I had left Knoxville—to learn she had died in the Charity Ward of a Knoxville hospital. Underpaid through all her earning years, she had supported her widowed mother as well as herself through most of her life, and there was nothing for her but this—at the end.

So far as I know there is no town in the United States that has ever erected a memorial to a surpassingly skillful and greatly loved teacher in its public schools. But if one should ever decide to do so, I think it might fittingly be Knoxville, in honour of Molly Hayes.[14] Personally, I would go further. If I had any influence in canonical circles I would have her canonized—enrolled among all the saints of Christendom as St. Molly of Knoxville. There have been Hermit Saints, Warrior Saints—why not Teaching Saints? I know of no profession that calls for more saintliness. For miracles, I could point to her miraculous handling of school-children. I would, in fact, as St. Martha is especially the patroness of female discretion and good housekeeping, make St. Molly the patroness of good teaching: have her represented, as in life, tall and slender and graceful, her robe not rich and heavily adorned, yet with a suggestion of quiet elegance about it, and of a deep blue; her face, not mawkishly sweet, as in the images of some saints, but alive with intelligence, distinguished (mark enough of martyrdom) by its long pendulous nose, but its blue eyes lighted with laughter; a starry diadem set upon her crinkly iron-gray hair; for her personal and pictorial attributes a black-board, a map, an open text-book, and where Saint Ursula has eleven thousand virgins sheltered under her mantle and St. Martha a dragon bound at her feet, I would have St. Molly with an adolescent boy and girl standing beside her, one on either side, each clasping one of her magical hands.

But these reflections on a teacher who occupies in my memory a niche all her own, and before whom I would fain burn a candle, are made long, long after the Barton Building was reduced to rubble, and in the days when I was her pupil, my thoughts, I have reason to believe, were turned, more often than in any other direction, toward my class-mates, Birdie and Marguerite.

It would be after school, or perhaps on Saturday, I would go to see them, and always with other girls. Though I do not remember that the Thomas girls ever came to the comfortable homes of any of the rest of us, the favorite meeting place for us all was the fairly large sitting-room, upstairs, in front, in the commonplace house on Asylum Street where the Thomas family was lodged at the time. I was to know them later in still poorer quarters and in more remote and less respectable neighborhoods (they were always moving, a circumstance for which the girls were able to furnish ingenious explanations), but this barely furnished room where I first knew them at home, with tattered matting, discolored walls with the plaster off in spots, never enough chairs, a small, badly-worn collection of books in a walnut what-not in one corner, an age-stained Confederate flag hanging over the mantel—this is the room in which I see them most plainly. But the Thomas girls had only to wave their wands, their shabby, ugly surroundings disappeared and you entered the romantic, if shadowed, realm where persons lived who had been nurtured on grand traditions, but whose only riches now were supplied by their minds and imaginations.

Sometimes their grubby, neglected-looking little brothers, stockings down, would streak past the door toward mysterious rooms in the rear which were never open to visitors. The family had no servant, not even a piece of one (at least we never caught sight of any), which meant abject poverty indeed in the Knoxville of the '80s. Their grandmother was far too frail to have done whatever cooking and cleaning was done, so presumably it was done by Marguerite and Birdie, which accounted no doubt for some of the spots on their dresses. It was plain, at any rate, that they did not intend to have even the friendliest of eyes observe them at their menial offices, or peer into the places where they performed them, and never, at any time, did they let so much as a word slip to indicate that they lived any differently than the young friends from well-to-do or wealthy families whom they drew to them in such numbers, or that their own family situation in general was less than ideal.

Quite often their father would come back—back from heaven knows where—before we had left. This always made me a trifle nervous, not knowing what might occur. Occasionally he would fumblingly open the door from the hall into the sitting-room and sweeping off his broad-brimmed black hat, without saying a word, though signifying that he was a gentleman even in his cups, make us a deep Chesterfieldian bow. Darting to the door at such a time, Birdie would take his arm and with "Papa, dear!" and her hand on his arm, guide his uncertain steps till they disappeared together. Once or twice we heard the ominous sound of his stumbling up the stairs from the front door and when he appeared, from the condition of his long black coat and bashed-in hat, it was evident he had fallen into the gutter or somewhere else on the way home. But Birdie was equal to this, too. She would spirit him out of sight and when she returned to the sitting room, her face only a little rosier than before, murmur in a tender tone, "Poor Papa, he just isn't well!" and then, as if nothing out of the way had happened, resume her part in the gay, silly talk which normal girls of that age habitually indulge in when their elders are absent.

There was, however, an elder whom we genuinely welcomed when once in a while she joined us for a few moments—the Thomas girls' grandmother. Tall, fragile to the last degree, tremulous, though very erect, when she entered the room in deep mourning, in her rusty black Henrietta banded in crepe, in the fashion of a long past day, and a small net cap on her head, Marguerite and Birdie could not have shown her greater deference had it been an empress they were conducting to the rickety rocking-chair (the only chair in the room with even a semblance of comfort), nor shown greater pride when we had all sprung from the floor or from wherever we were perched, and they presented us to her.

She was their living patent of nobility, the stamp on her for us to see—their heritage, their only tangible one, from a fabulous world they had been born too late to know at first hand. But there she sat, this *grande dame* of the old regime, a ghostly pillared mansion rising behind her; enthroned, incongruously, in a broken-down rocking-chair, amidst the dingiest, meanest of surroundings, yet completely at her ease, exhaling as authentically as Cape Jasmine the fragrance of the Old South, of a social order that had vanished forever. I do not pretend I see her face now. It is as blank as are the faces of those who appear to us in dreams. I recall clearly, however, my impression at the time that Birdie's tall, slender figure, the soft roundness of her face, must have come down to her from her grandmother; recall, too, my realization, however vague, that generations of gently-bred women before her had gone into the gracious, cultured tones of the grandmother's voice when she took my hand in hers: "So this is Annie Audubon, of whom Marguerite and Birdie have told me! My dear, what a beautiful and distinguished name your parents gave you." I remember that although before this I had never thought much about my baptismal name, and if anything disliked it, that now it took on a certain luster.

The Thomas girls had read precociously, under the inspiration of their grandmother, nearly all of Shakespeare and both of them, with what still seems to me phenomenal verbal memories, could always find a passage from Shakespeare to apply, in a humorous sense, to whatever thing or person—usually person—was the center of our girlish discussions. Most of the few books in their what-not were, in fact, classics, and almost all of them poetry, and while it was the surface gayety of Birdie and Marguerite which charmed all their young acquaintances, deeper currents in them, running underneath, were revealed from time to time. It was Poe,[15] and not merely his melodrama and tunefulness, but his melancholy, mournfulness, even morbidity—his "Nevermores," dark tarns, ghouls, haunted woodlands, his biers and dirges, tombstones and tolling bells, gaping graves, funeral palls, sepulchres by the sea—which fed the secret sorrow of a conquered people that was in the Thomas girls and made Poe appeal to them more powerfully, it was plain, than any other poet—or any save Father Ryan, the priest and poet who had served as Chaplain in the Confederate Army.

Even before the Thomas girls had introduced me to the poems of Father Ryan,[16] their gallant behavior in a heart-breaking situation, along with their other engaging traits, had influenced me so strongly that the pedestrian jingling of "Yankee Doodle" moved me no more now than: "To market, to market, to buy a fat pig," while I responded with all the fervor of the Thomas girls to:

> In Dixie land, I'll take my stand,
> And lib and die in Dixie,
> Away, away,
> Away down south in Dixie,

and when, in a tense passionate voice, one of them would read or recite Father Ryan's "The Conquered Banner":

> Furl that Banner, for 'tis weary;
> Furl it, fold it, it is best;
> Furl it, hide it, let it rest!
> Furl that Banner, softly slowly!
> Treat it gently—it is holy—
> For it droops above the dead.
> Touch it not—unfold it never,
> Let it droop there, furled forever,
> For its people's hopes are dead!

—at times like this, overcome with sorrow, I would get the feeling that it was the Conquered Banner "wreathed around with glory, though its folds are in the dust,"—and not the Stars and Stripes to which I owed allegiance.

It was the memory of all this—of the Barton Building, the Thomas girls, "The Conquered Banner," that made me understand, long afterwards, the feelings of a little grandson of mine[17] whom I had taken to Lexington, Virginia, that he might see the town where Robert E. Lee seems to have lived only yesterday. Having had two great-grandfathers on the Confederate side in the Civil War, two on the Union side, Bobby was somewhat perplexed as to where his own sympathies should lie. Visiting the chapel of the Virginia Military Institute, he gazed in silence at the realistic painting of the Battle of New Market which hangs there; listened intently to the affecting story of how the whole battalion of cadets had marched out into that nearby battle, many to be killed; he seemed impressed with various spots in the town connected with its great hero; when at last we descended into the crypt of the chapel where Lee rests, a recumbent statue of him above the tomb, he gazed at that also in silence. It was only when his eyes turned from the tomb and rested upon the skeleton of "Old Traveler" opposite—perpetuating a man's devotion to his horse—that his doubts were resolved and he confided to me in a whisper, "I believe, Grandmother, that I'm a Confederate!"

NOTES

1. The Barton Building (or Block) housed the Girls' High School from 1885 to 1886, when it moved into its new permanent home at 431 Walnut Street. Rule, *Standard History of Knoxville,* 407.
2. East Tennessee Female Institute had been founded as Knoxville Female Academy. Following the Civil War, during which it was used as a hospital, it reopened as East Tennessee Female Institute. Luttrell, "One Hundred Years of a Female Academy"; Rothrock, *French Broad-Holston Country* 258.
3. Montvale Springs was a popular resort in Blount County, Tennessee, during the 1800s and into the twentieth century. Lea and Tate Springs were resorts developed in the late 1800s in Grainger County, Tennessee, to attract tourists to visit mineral springs in that area. *Tennessee Encyclopedia of History & Culture,* 73, 379; National Park Service Data Sheet <focus.nps.gov/pdfhost/docs/NRHP/Text/75001754.pdf> viewed December 9, 2016. See also: Mary Fanslow, "What Do They Do at the Springs?: An Overview of Five East Tennessee Resorts," *Journal of East Tennessee History* 80 (2008): 1–27.
4. English poet Thomas Gray (1716–1771).
5. *Idalia: A Romance* (London: Chapman & Hall, 1876) by English novelist Marie Louise de la Ramée, who used the pen name Ouida.
6. Established by the Tennessee legislature in 1844, the Deaf and Dumb Asylum was renamed Tennessee School for the Deaf and moved to a new campus in the Island Home section of Knoxville in the early 1920s. Rothrock, *French Broad-Holston Country,* 267. The original school site was used as a hospital during the Civil War, and later as Knoxville City Hall from 1924 until 1980. The buildings have been placed on the National Register of Historic Places and today house Lincoln Memorial University's Duncan School of Law. "LMU to Renovate Historic Building for Legal Aid of East Tennessee" <https://www.lmunet.edu/law-site-news/view/359/lmu-to-renovate-historic-building-for-legal-aid-of-east-tennessee > (viewed January 6, 2017).
7. Asylum Street is now part of Summit Hill Drive where it borders the original campus of the Deaf and Dumb Asylum; west of Henley Street, it is called Western Avenue.
8. William Gibbs McAdoo, Jr. (1863–1941).
9. Probably Chisholm's tavern. Rule, *Standard History of Knoxville,* 56, 89. According to Rothrock, "Louis Philippe, Duke of Orleans (afterward King of France)" was a guest at Blount Mansion in 1797. Rothrock, *French Broad-Holston Country,* 380.

10. Eleonora Duse (1859–1924). Italian actress.
11. Anatole France (1844–1924). French novelist, poet, and critic.
12. Lines from "The Blue and the Gray," 1867 poem by Francis Miles Finch.
13. During a 1939 visit to Knoxville, the famous film director Clarence Brown, when asked for his outstanding memory of school days in his hometown, replied: "That one's easy—Miss Molly Hayes. Miss Molly was our teacher in the old Girls' High School." Bob Cunningham, "Big 'If' for Tennessee Is How Season Goes This Year," *Knoxville News-Sentinel*, October 21, 1939.
14. Mary Agnes "Miss Molly" Hayes (1856–1913) was buried in Calvary Catholic Cemetery, Knoxville. In 1936 friends and former pupils raised money to place a tombstone on her grave with the inscription: "The influence of a great teacher abides / She served 40 years with untiring zeal." *Ibid.*; "Find A Grave Index," database, *FamilySearch* (https://familysearch.org/ark:/61903/1:1:QVK5-X7BL : 13 December 2015), Mary Agnes Hayes, 1913; Burial, Knoxville, Knox, Tennessee, United States of America, Calvary Catholic Cemetery; citing record ID 50482382, *Find a Grave*, http://www.findagrave.com (viewed January 3, 2017).
15. Edgar Allan Poe (1809–1849), American poet and short-story writer.
16. After serving the Confederacy, Father Abram Joseph Ryan came to Knoxville as pastor of the Catholic Church of the Immaculate Conception. A historical marker, placed by the Knoxville—Knox County Civil War Centennial Committee at the corner of W. Vine Ave. and Walnut St., near the front entrance to the present-day church building, reads:

    "Father Abram J. Ryan (1838–1886)–Confederate chaplain, poet of the Confederacy, author of the requiem of the Lost Cause, "The Conquered Banner," written at Knoxville soon after Lee's surrender at Appomattox Courthouse April 9, 1865, and pastor of the Immaculate Conception Parish, 1865–1867."

17. Roger "Bob" Armstrong Naylor, (1921–1984).

Chapter Five

Clinch Street and the Court of the Grand Duke of Hesse

On Sunday morning there would always be a procession of families either who owned no horses, or [were] opposed to taking them out on Sunday, walking past our house on Clinch Street on their way to church. Almost all the churches in Knoxville then were in or near the center of town and from its West End, where we lived, it was rather a long walk. But long or short, nobody seemed to mind walking in those days. Even people with horses and carriages did a great deal of it.

For some reason, we never started to church as early as most of West End, and this furnished an opportunity for me to observe some of our neighbors taking part in the passing procession, notably the Pitman family, on their way to the Plymouth [*sic*] Congregational Church;[1] natives of Rhode Island and like all other New Englanders in Knoxville, through their walk, speech, and other less definable characteristics, instantly discerned as New Englanders, and as such, to the average Knoxvillian of the period, white or black, only a little funnier than Northerners in general.

On the Sunday mornings when I watched the Pitmans going to Church, with the narrow board-sidewalks of the West End of the day, they followed the usual pattern of church-goers on Clinch Street; Papa and Mama in front, and in their case a very tall young daughter in her late teens following them, two gangling half-grown boys behind her, and all of them with the same sort of stride. It was not their walk, however, which arrested my attention. It was the fact that at a time when bustles were universally worn, a time when practically every woman, of every class, in the United States was wearing a bustle of more or less fantastic proportions, Mrs. Pitman and her daughter presented to the public eye the startling phenomenon of perfectly flat posteriors. Even the cooks in West End would watch from their quarters in hope of catching a glimpse of this recurring Sunday sight, shaking with laughter when they caught it. The truth is, Mr. Charles Pitman, with a hundred estimable qualities, was nevertheless something of a domestic tyrant. Having decided that bustles were immodest, he had refused to allow his wife and daughter to wear them, only a little later to issue another edict when, following the vogue of the bustle, there was one of those not unusual, sharp reversals in fashions for women, when almost overnight bustles became hopelessly *passé* and the "habit back," another extreme, came in with the female posterior now clearly defined. But if the feminine silhouette had suffered a change, the Puritan urges of Mr. Pitman had not. Finding the new fashion, with its bold outlines and carnal suggestions, even more offensive than the former one, he decreed now that his wife and daughter should assume the previously condemned bustle, so that once again these two excellent women furnished a mirth-provoking Sunday spectacle for all the light-minded of Clinch Street.

There was no comic flavor, however, to the long sultry Sunday evenings in summer when, partly screened by two great magnolia trees, I could sit on our front porch and observe those who strolled by in the twilight on their way back and forth to Fort Sanders, where the Battle of Fort Sanders had been fought, and whose grassy slopes, open widely to the sky and to any air that might be stirring, served as a sort of park for that part of town.[2] Lovers would meet there after dark, but in earlier hours there was something special that held me on our porch steps—something which, secretly, I found exciting. Some time before dark a most beauteous lady, a Mrs. Hamilton, was almost sure to pass, with her tall, handsome son, a lad in his teens, her arm lightly tucked in his. She lived on the opposite side of the street, on a corner a block below us, in a good-looking house of generous proportions that was set above a terraced yard attractively planted and always well tended. There appeared to be no *Mr.* Hamilton,[3] at least none was ever in evidence, and she was never seen with anyone save her slim handsome young son, and with him only on those oppressive Sunday evenings when they strolled, arm in arm, back and forth to Fort Sanders in the gathering dusk, and on Sunday mornings when, prayer-book in hand, on their way to St. John's, they made part of the "Sabbath" procession—the only noticeable break in it, in point of fact, as the other church-goers, with instinctive caution, kept well ahead of the pair, or well behind them. Though the lady was not young—or young as at thirteen we measure age, her extraordinary beauty and extreme elegance made me exceedingly curious about her, and the more so that she was the only woman near us on Clinch Street who had never exchanged calls with my mother, so that I had questioned Mama about her, only to receive an evasive and rather chilling answer, one which made me realize that Mrs. Hamilton was a person not to be talked about, even referred to.

The truth is, Mrs. Hamilton was Knoxville's Lost Lady. Even the most censorious—the most indignant, that she should be living in the very heart of one of the most respectable, indeed select, neighborhoods, could not quite dismiss her as merely a brazen strumpet. She was so palpably well-born, well-bred. With her perfect aplomb, she had that air, possessed that elusive attribute, which, for want of a better word, we call "class." Although she bore no resemblance to the bewitching Mrs. Hamilton[4] whom Romney[5] immortalized on canvas, on whom Lord Nelson's thoughts dwelt in his dying hours at Trafalgar, yet a little above medium height, with ample breasts, tidy waist, her dusky hair piled high, with her luminous yet unfathomable eyes, her fashionable dress with its long overskirt and bustle of the period, in her India silks, Swiss mulls—in whatever she wore, never overdressed but *soignée* to the last detail, this scandalous lady was the most alluring mortal, I thought, that I had ever beheld. In later years when I saw the lovely ladies of Renoir, those subtle beauties with their vibrant yet delicate color, their expression at once imperious and ever so faintly demure—enchanting portraits that made French bourgeois existence of the 19th Century look like the golden age, I saw again Mrs. Hamilton, the mysterious "lady" who lived a block below us on Clinch Street.

There was a flaw in her face. Strangely, I can not recall what the flaw was, only that far from marring, it furnished a piquant touch which seemed to enhance her beauty. What remains with me most clearly is, however, her carriage, her light, spirited step, with its slight suggestion of hauteur—that, and the way her dark beautiful eyes were habitually focused far ahead, like a sleep-walker's. While she looked without a shadow of hesitation straight at whomever she met, she looked at the same time straight through them, so that if no one spoke to her—and no one did—at least no one cut her, for to all appearances she was utterly unaware of the bodily existence of other Knoxvillians she might encounter here or there on the street, or in the course of her devotions at St. John's where she was a regular attendant.

There was, I remember, a great row at St. John's, the whole church torn asunder over the question of whether Mrs. Hamilton should be confirmed there, as she had expressed a desire to be, and though I do not recall whether or not she was ever permitted to kneel at the chancel and partake of the sacrament, what I do recall is that no one ever seemed to know where Mrs. Hamilton came from, or where she went when she disappeared from the Knoxville scene after lending it color, however dubious the tone, for a decade or so, and leaving no trace behind her, or only an imponderable one.

Many years afterward when I was entertained in the former home of the glamorous "Lost Lady,"[6] who had once dwelt among us, now the home of a Mr. and Mrs. Tyler (grandparents of the yet unborn James Agee),[7] to my surprise (and I fear disappointment!) there was not the faintest sign anywhere of its previous occupant—already become half-mythical. It was just like any other home of refined and cultivated people.

This house, with its shrouded windows and what seemed to me its sinister air, never ceased in the year after year I passed it to evoke a certain disquieting interest. But it was a house in the same block, obliquely across and further down the street, as different a *ménage* as could well be imagined, in which I was to spend some of the most rapt hours of my girlhood.

The house itself was one you would pass a hundred times without noticing—not the ugliest house you ever saw, but utterly commonplace, a tallish two-story white frame structure, one of two exactly alike, with a small square porch at one side in front, a mere patch of lawn between it and the street—a house, if you *should* notice it, you would recognize at once for what it was—built to rent.

The Bauers lived there, an elderly couple who had moved South a year or two earlier from some town in Illinois where they had been living, and as Mr. Bauer had come to Knoxville to assume the responsible position of auditor, I believe it was, with the East Tennessee, Virginia, and Georgia Railroad,[8] they could presumably have afforded a better house. It is possible, however, that at least Mrs. Bauer, who was excessively thrifty, may have welcomed the moderate rental of their present abode. It may, in fact, have been this propensity on Mrs. Bauer's part, the chance to turn an honest penny, which led to my parents' initial acquaintance with the pair, which has remained something of a mystery to me, as the Bauers lived two blocks below us and—like Mrs. Hamilton!—never exchanged calls with anyone, though for the quite different reason that they were completely sufficient unto themselves.

At any rate, one Spring Mama went to New York for several weeks, but before leaving, as we had a poor cook at the time, she decided she would feel more at ease if my little sister and I and our father, when in town, took our meals out, while she was gone. Then, through some channel, a hint reached her that Mrs. Bauer might give us our meals, "as an accommodation," during her absence, and it was thus I came to enter a house which looked so ordinary on the outside, but which, once I had passed through its unpromising portal, opened up to me some of the atmosphere, the absorbing interest, the endless romance of the Old World, where both Mr. and Mrs. Bauer had been born and lived until, approaching middle life, they came to the United States to make it their permanent home.

Mrs. Bauer was English and probably from the professional class. No Cockney, she spoke our common language as only the cultivated English speak it. But the astounding thing about her was that she looked so like Queen Victoria (still on the throne at the time) that she could easily have sat for a portrait of her Britannic Majesty. Of about the same age, squat, outrageously homely, with the same projecting eyes, beak nose, drooping mouth, slightly receding chin, her hair worn in precisely the same fashion, when she went shopping or marketing in Knoxville, in her full long skirts, black dolman, with her small black bonnet perched high on her head, tied with broad ribbons under her sloping chin, and above all, with the imposing presence, the majestic gait, which, like Her Majesty, she had managed to achieve despite what would have seemed insurmountable handicaps nature had imposed—with all this, she was so like the pictures of Queen Victoria appearing then in *Harper's Weekly* and other publications of the day, that people encountering her for the first time on the street would gape at her, hardly believing their eyes; in stunned silence turn and stare after her when she had sailed by.

I was always itching to ask Mrs. Bauer, after I knew her, whether she realized her remarkable resemblance to the Queen, but could never quite screw my courage to the sticking point. Early in my acquaintance with this formidable lady I had become aware that she was not one to suffer fools gladly.

As for Mr. Bauer, you could be sure of a patient answer whatever you asked him. Young for his age, smooth-shaven, his light brown hair worn a little longer than American men of the time wore theirs; modest, a trifle shy, with his candid blue eyes, gentle, gracious, courtly manner, August Bauer was the type of German that many of us (after two wars with Germany) have almost forgotten ever existed. Born in Hesse-Darmstadt, August had grown up in the very shadow of the Grand Duke's palace in Darmstadt, and as his father was Court Botanist (with whatever privileges that quaint office may have enjoyed), August had had for playmates, from his earliest recollection, little German princes and princesses—nephews and nieces of the reigning childless Grand Duke. Moreover, in his youth, August had taken part in the festivities accorded Princess Alice, daughter of Queen Victoria, when Prince Louis,[9] heir presumptive to the throne of Hesse, and August's former playmate, brought her home as a bride to Darmstadt; that Prince Louis whom Lord Melbourne[10] had called "one of those German beggars," not wanting his sovereign's daughters to marry princes of small German houses; and Alice, the princess one of whose daughters, Alix, would, in this century, meet a tragic fate as the last Czarina of Imperial Russia.[11]

August Bauer was the first man I had known of European education and culture. I listened, wide-eyed, to all he had to tell me of his native Rhineland, and of Darmstadt itself, with its ancient market place and chiming bells. It all fitted into the old fairy-tale Germany on which my generation was nurtured in childhood, with German governesses preferred then to French in American homes where a governess was part of the household staff.

But I was no less enthralled when he talked of England. An elder sister of Mr. Bauer had gone to that storied land, a young woman, to become German governess to all Queen Victoria's children except the Prince of Wales, and now that the Queen's children were grown up, the last of them, Princess Beatrice, wed in 1885 (only a few months before my acquaintance with the Bauers began) to Prince Henry of Battenberg (Mountbatten, as we know that family since World War I), another of those "German beggars" to whom Lord Melbourne had objected, the Queen still retained Fräulein Bauer as a member of her household, one her brother August had often visited in his youth, at Windsor, at Osborne, in the Highlands—wherever Her Majesty might be in residence, and who had been treated "very kindly" by the great Queen herself.

It was on a holiday visit to his sister in England that August met the English girl who would become his wife and though it was hard to imagine that the dictatorial Sophie Bauer I knew had ever been the blooming, yielding lass she must have been then, yet all my previous experience paled now in interest beside the world into which, between them, this elderly Clinch Street couple inducted me. At the Bauers, these were bona-fide flesh and blood princes and princesses, queens and kings, about whom I was hearing in the most intimate fashion. I could never hear enough. And I became so familiar with the Houses of Hesse and Hanover, the Hapsburgs and Hohenzollerns and Bourbons—with all the royal families of Europe and their intricate inter-marryings, that while much useful information I once possessed has slipped from me, never to be recovered, yet absurdly enough, if all existing copies of that royal stud-book, the *Almanach de Gotha*,[12] were destroyed, I believe that even to-day I could reproduce not a few of its pages.

But neither Mr. nor Mrs. Bauer, it must be added, were blind worshipers of royalty. Mr. Bauer expressed frankly his concern over Prince William (later the Kaiser). Already, with his father still alive, this conceited, bumptious, hot-headed young man, hooking up with Bismarck, was usurping imperial prerogatives, giving himself imperial airs.

"It does not bode well," Mr. Bauer, shaking his head, would say thoughtfully, "for the future of the German people."

Mrs. Bauer, for her part, had no patience with the heir to the British throne (afterwards Edward VII), who, she insisted, did nothing but amuse himself, and I recall vividly a Sunday when we appeared at the Bauers for breakfast and my father remarked on the earthquake at Nice which the morning paper reported along with the news that the Prince of Wales, then in Nice, had behaved with exemplary calmness, refusing to get up when his bed was shaken violently.

"Humph!" Mrs. Bauer sniffed. "Too drunk to get out of bed, I dare say."

But from the moment I opened the front door at the Bauers I became immediately aware of a *milieu* distinctly different from any I had known before. The very smell that met my nostrils was different—a mingled scent of curry and celery seed, basil and thyme and marjoram and bay leaves and chives and parsley (most of which Mrs. Bauer grew in her own tidy little herb garden), so that even now, long familiar with them, when I catch a medley of these savory scents I am carried back to the Bauers on Clinch Street.

The door to the Bauers' parlor, at the right of their narrow front hall, was always closed. They used the room behind it, where we had our meals, also as sitting-room. In that day when rooms in general were loaded with gimcracks, it seemed rather bare, but like every inch of the Bauers' house it was miraculously clean. Everything in the house that could be scrubbed had been scrubbed, and in this room where we ate, the andirons, fender, the brass scuttle on the hearth, were always polished till they gleamed, so that notwithstanding its bareness, the room had a sort of cozy charm. By the side windows were Mrs. Bauer's rocker and basket-work sewing-stand and Mr. Bauer's Morris-chair; against one wall was a sofa with folded across its end a Scotch plaid blanket—a gift from Victoria, the Queen, which at her behest, the famed John Brown, her bibulous body-guard, had picked out for August during one of his early visits to his sister at Balmoral; and hanging above the sofa, the only picture in the room, a large, heavily-framed engraving depicting a dramatic scene from the life of the German hero, Wallenstein.[13] This engraving, with its somber historic subject, seemed to my youthful mind to lend a special and great dignity to the otherwise simple sitting-room of the Bauers. There were no books visible, but on a drop-leaf side-table always neatly folded newspapers of recent date: the *Chicago Tribune* as well as the *New York Tribune,* the *London Times,* and a German daily, the *Frankfurter Rundschau,* I believe it was.

We seldom arrived for meals that we did not find one or both of the Bauers enveloped in a newspaper. They would rise immediately, Mrs. Bauer in an immaculate percale dress, made, with complete disregard for current fashions, with a full skirt and tight basque buttoned up to a narrow turn-over collar fastened by an oval mosaic gold-encircled broach depicting the Roman Coliseum. She would hasten out to the kitchen. Although a wizened old Negro woman did much of the scullery work and labored for her daily from daylight till dark in the unceasing, inexorable warfare which Mrs. Bauer waged against Knoxville's sooty grime, yet Mrs. Bauer did most of the cooking herself and memorable cooking it was that came out of that shining kitchen of hers, probably one of the few in Knoxville that in 1886 could have stood up under any very exacting sanitary inspection.

It is the custom, of course, even among the English, to indulge in a blanket indictment of English cookery, but no one could, justifiably, who had tasted the hot scones, the crumpets, which Mrs. Bauer served us at supper, her Yorkshire Pudding that, baked in the pan with the rare rib-roast of beef, soaked in its drippings, and cut in blistery golden-brown squares, bordered the roast when it came on at dinner—no one who had ever tasted her deep-dish apple-pies, her green-gooseberry tarts, her English Beefsteak and Kidney Pie—above all, her Melton Mobray[14] Pie, that time-honored masterpiece, with its flaky puff-paste encasing the tender jellied contents, the pork pie which had made a fox-hunting center in Leicestershire famous for its pork pies. The fact is, however rare it may be among the English, Mrs. Bauer had a gift for cooking. For all her gruff voice and autocratic ways, she took no end of pains, too, to please us, and whatever her penny-pinching propensities, it must be said that they did not extend to her table.

There was always, though, among the varied delights I found at the Bauers, a thing which distressed me. The lot on which their house was built, like many others in West End, sloped sharply down at the rear, so that coal from the coal-shed in the back yard must be carried up a long steep flight of outside back steps when it was brought to the house. Apparently for the sake of economy, a Negro boy or man was not employed by the Bauers for this work. It was Mr. Bauer himself who, after his return from his office, each evening was observed to carry coal and kindling up his back steps.[15] White men in Knoxville—certainly white *gentlemen*, did not split kindling, carry successive buckets of coal for their grate fires into the house themselves—not in the '80s, and it became a grave scandal in West End when it was known that Mr. Bauer carried in his own coal. It was almost more offensive to the neighborhood's sensibilities than the presence of Mrs. Hamilton in its midst.

I had heard the talk and when I came sometimes to the Bauers in the late afternoon, if Mr. Bauer was inclined to linger for a moment's chat before he started on his chores, or exhibited an inclination to keep on the genteel black coat in which he had returned from the office, Mrs. Bauer would remind him, peremptorily, "August, change your coat!"

This would make my blood boil. And it hurt me even more when August would answer, softly, "Yes, Sophie, yes, yes!" and with a look of faint amusement in his blue eyes go out meekly to the back hall where an old coat hung on a peg ready for him to put on.

The pair had, however, so much in common, were so congenial in their tastes and interests, I doubt, thinking of it now, if August Bauer suffered unduly from his wife's merciless bossing, or felt it so humiliating as the neighborhood supposed to be seen carrying his own coal and kindling up his back steps. He had been brought up in frugal fashion. Money had been very scarce even in the royal household in Darmstadt, and at this stage of his life he may have been no more averse than she to living simply and saving any penny they could.

In any case, there was one direction in which Mrs. Bauer's magisterial manner met with little success. Putting on her bonnet and gloves, she would regularly march across the street and, mounting one flight of steps and then another to the roomy, ramshackle, high-perched house of the Gaines family, demand that she see its mistress, her landlady, the Widow Gaines, whose principal object in life, as she had no hesitation of acknowledging, was to marry off four daughters of marriageable age, and with her income derived almost solely from rent she received from the Bauers and one or two other houses she owned nearby.[16]

The name (as I happened to know) by which Mrs. Bauer went in the gay and harum-scarum Gaines family was John Bull in Petticoats, and when someone at the Gaines' spied their *bête-noire* approaching, a hushed warning would ring through the house: "For heaven's sake, Mama, there comes John Bull!"

Lou, the Gaines' good-natured slatternly mulatto house-girl, her head wound in a white rag, would meet Mrs. Bauer at the door and show her into the dim, dusty Gaines' parlor with its rose-wreathed Aubusson carpet worn to the thread.

"Set down, ma'am," in her oiliest tones, Lou would urge Mrs. Bauer. "Won't you have a fan? Miss Pink, she'll be down in jes' a minute."

Like most families in Knoxville then, the women in the Gaines family lived all day long in their bed-rooms upstairs, except for meals and if callers came. There was always sewing going on there, and dresses to be tried on, in a day when dresses could not be bought ready-made, and when "Miss Pink" appeared below there would be sure to be a threaded needle stuck in the front of her cambric wrapper, though she would be wearing her diamond ear-rings and her soft pretty face would be liberally coated with rice powder.

In her suave flattering manner, Mrs. Gaines would express much pleasure at seeing her tenant from across the street; inquire solicitously after Mr. Bauer's health and her own.

But Mrs. Bauer would have none of these blandishments. The chimney in their parlor still smoked; their roof was still leaking; the cellar, still a puddle whenever it rained.

Quite unruffled, the Widow Gaines would be so *surprised* that these matters had not already been attended to. She had spoken about them several times to the man who looked after her property. Well, she would just have to get after him again. . . .

This was the way things usually went. But huff and puff as Mrs. Bauer might, in the end, if any repairs were made, the Bauers made them.

Mrs. Gaines was a favorite topic of conversation with Mrs. Bauer whenever I was alone with her. She warned me against the whole family. "Feather-brained," she called them. As for Mrs. Gaines, "I wouldn't trust her around the corner. The most outrageous liar I have ever known. Not an honest bone in her body! But all Southerners," she would wind up, "are liars." So far as I was concerned, if it made them like the Gaines, I would have had the whole human race possess this trait.

Once I had the temerity to put in a feeble word of defense for Mrs. Gaines, whom, like all her family, I was beginning to find dazzlingly attractive, but Mrs. Bauer, flashing a look, squelched me with even more than her customary vigor: "Nonsense! Nonsense! The woman's a perfect humbug!"

In the main, however, Mrs. Bauer was surprisingly tolerant of such silliness as I expressed in her fearsome presence, and in spite of everything I found her almost as fascinating as the Gaines. It was her foreignness, her Englishness, that captivated me. She was a composite of the many domineering female figures, half or wholly comic, which enlivened all those English novels I was devouring at the time. She seemed to have stepped right out of their pages. But my respect for her grew, too, especially when I saw the part she took in discussions between my father and Mr. Bauer at table, or after breakfast on Sunday mornings. As August Bauer was the first man I knew with a cultured European background, Sophie Bauer was the first woman I knew (and it would be a long time till I knew another) who, equally well-informed, could enter with men into serious discussion of national and world affairs.

After breakfast on Sunday there was more time. Dinner would not be till two and though Mr. Bauer had been reared a German Lutheran and Mrs. Bauer in the

Church of England, after listening to a few sermons in Knoxville soon after their arrival there—sermons which Mrs. Bauer in her forthright fashion characterized as "extraordinarily stupid," they had compromised now by going to no church at all, while my father was in no haste, either, to be off, so that they would settle down for talk whose flavor, once tasted, I would make any excuse not to miss, pleading a headache—anything, to get out of going to Sunday School, and could settle down under the big engraving of Wallenstein, only disturbed by the clanging of the early Sunday School bells which filled me with a sense of joyous relief mixed with a slight sense of guilt.

Germany was always what they talked about first. Notwithstanding Mrs. Bauer's dictatorial attitude in personal matters, she shared with her husband his democratic ideals. It was those ideals which had led them to hope that all Germans of liberal views would rally around Crown Prince Fritz and the Crown Princess, Queen Victoria's daughter, in their efforts to advance the more liberal ideas already prevailing in England. It was, in point of fact, the Bauers' belief in democracy, as against the Divine Right of Kings, that had ultimately brought them to this country. But they were anxious at present, as was also my father. Bismarck,[17] they agreed, was the evil genius of Germany. There had been the grab of Schleswig-Holstein a few years before; and now there was Germany's growing chauvinism, its increasing slavery to militarism. They talked very earnestly about all this and what small grounding I ever got in modern European history I got more from Sunday mornings at the Bauers than from any class-room or text-book.

From time to time Mrs. Bauer would rise and, with her air of command, sweep into the kitchen, where from my seat on the sofa I could see through an open door what was going on there; old black Jerusha, preparing, it might be, a leg of lamb for the oven under Mrs. Bauer's expert direction, chopping mint in a wooden bowl for the mint sauce, scraping new potatoes, shelling the little early peas, but, whatever it was, never dreaming—as no one else did—that she could sit down to the job.

When Mrs. Bauer came back, the talk had often turned in a different direction, and sooner or later on public affairs in this country. I find people now, in the middle of the 20th Century, who look upon strikes not only as diabolic by nature, but as a rather recent plague sent upon the American people. There is nothing, however, which I remember better than those Sunday morning talks at the Bauers in 1886. There were railroad strikes; women laundry workers (the "Joan of Arc Assembly" of the Knights of Labor) striking; strikes in the stock-yards—strikes everywhere, all over the country, and overshadowing everything else the recent Haymarket Riot in Chicago.

While my father, no less than the Bauers, had an inordinate horror of socialism, yet he was in complete sympathy with the current strikers, almost without exception fighting for an eight-hour day. And it was here that the Bauers could not quite go along with him; here that he put up his strongest arguments in favor of labor's rights and aspirations, moreover as a stabilizing force in our rapidly expanding economy; here that he showed himself, I realize, looking at it retrospectively, more than ordinarily broad-gauged for a man of his day, and a large employer himself.[18]

After we had taken our meals at the Bauers, Mrs. Bauer quite often would call me in as I was passing on my way from school. She would have some chicken livers, which she had noticed I liked, made into a little *pâté* for me; a tempting piece of Scotch short-bread, thick with caraway seeds, or some other *bonne bouche*. Though she was as brusque as ever, she always seemed pleased to see me, and when the Bauers' daughter, Marie, came home that summer on vacation from the girls' boarding-school where she taught, somewhere in the Middle West, it was made very pleasant for me at the Bauers and I was there a good deal.

In her late twenties then, her dark hair, brushed back plainly and already streaked with grey, Marie Bauer had the stocky build of her mother, her mother's beak nose, but the kind, amiable nature of her father. I took to her at once, and she had little choice but to take to me, for it was her first visit to Knoxville, and her parents, except for tradesmen and Mr. Bauer's office associates, had no acquaintance there with whom they were on terms [of] even the slightest intimacy, save for my own family.

Marie and I proved companionable despite the discrepancy in our ages. I had read much of Thackeray, Dickens and George Eliot, and at the time was reading William Dean Howell's latest novel, *The Rise of Silas Lapham*, so that we had a meeting ground in books; then Marie had much to tell me of her own school days in Switzerland, part of that magic "Europe," the very mention of which never failed to quicken my pulses.

Sometimes she would take me up to her bed-room, over the parlor, and the room was enchanting to me, with its cuckoo clock, Swiss music-box that played little silvery selections from *The Beggar Student* and *Bohemian Girl*,[19] its collection of books in German, French, English. But what really bewitched me was the row of five or six dolls arrayed on top of a painted Swiss chest under one of the windows. I had long ceased playing with dolls and the dolls on the chest were nothing as pretty as some I had owned myself. But these dolls had once belonged to Princess Beatrice (that daughter of Queen Victoria recently married to Prince Henry of Battenberg). She had sent them from Windsor Castle, one by one, as birthday gifts to another little girl of the same age in whom her German governess, Fräulein Bauer, had interested her—to little Marie Bauer in the United States of America. And here they were, upstairs in one of the most commonplace of frame houses on Clinch Street; quite ordinary in themselves, but each one, when I knew their history, with a halo encircling its bisque or cloth or china head.

NOTES

1. Presumably Pilgrim Congregational Church, listed in Rule, 459; and Rothrock, 298. Knoxville City Directories during this period also list a Pilgrim (but no "Plymouth") Congregational Church in Knoxville.
2. In the latter part of the nineteenth century there was some interest in turning the remains of Fort Sanders into a public park or national battlefield. However, by 1898 streets had been laid out through the fortifications and homes built along those streets, and the opportunity for a permanent structure preserving or commemorating the fort slipped away. Today, the site of the battle, near the corner of present-day 17th Street (originally Fort Sanders Avenue) and Laurel Avenue, has only a Tennessee State Historical marker and a vandalized UDC monument nearby to remind passersby of what took place there. Rule, 177; Allen, *Knox-stalgia,* 57.
3. Contrary to what AWA says, apparently there *had* been a Mr. Hamilton at one time. The 1884 and 1885 Knoxville City Directories list a "Fritz W. Hamilton" on Clinch Avenue at the northeast corner of Clinch and Blount (there were no house numbers in West End at that time), a location which agrees with Armstrong's description in relation to where the Wetzells were living on Clinch. His name also appears in the 1880 census record, along with wife "Cassie," or possibly "Carrie." In later Knoxville City Directories Mrs. Hamilton, alone, is listed variously as Mrs. Carrie Hamilton, Mrs. Cary M. Hamilton, and Mrs. Carolina M. Hamilton. Only in the 1891–92 directory is she listed as "wid[ow] Fitz [*sic*]."
4. Lady Emma Hamilton (1761?-1815), wife of Sir William Hamilton, and mistress of Lord Nelson. Benét, *Reader's Encyclopedia,* 437.
5. George Romney (1734–1802), English painter.
6. Possibly a reference to Willa Cather's 1923 novel, *A Lost Lady*.
7. James Agee (1909–1955), writer, journalist, film critic, and scriptwriter, was born in Knoxville and spent his early childhood in the same West End neighborhood where Armstrong and her family lived only a few years earlier. Much of Agee's posthumously published novel, *A Death in the Family* (1957), is set in that neighborhood. The novel, which won a Pulitzer Prize in 1958, was made into a movie (re-titled *All the Way Home*) which was filmed in Knoxville and had its premier there in 1963. Neither Agee's family home, which was on Highland Avenue, nor the house where his maternal grandparents, Mr. and Mrs. Joel C. Tyler, lived on Clinch is still standing.
8. The 1886 *Knoxville City Directory* lists Augustus Bauer as a civil engineer; the 1887 directory, as a draughtsman with ETV&G Railroad.
9. Later Ludwig IV, Grand Duke of Hesse from 1877 to 1892.
10. Prime Minister of the United Kingdom and advisor to Queen Victoria.
11. Empress Alexandra of Russia, who, along with her husband, Czar Nicholas II, and their children were executed in 1918 by Bolsheviks following the Russian Revolution.

12. European diplomatic and social register, beginning in 1763. Benét, *Reader's Encyclopedia,* 26. Official Website: www.gotha1763.com/
13. Albrecht von Wallenstein (1583–1634).
14. Also, Melton Mowbray.
15. This scene will remind readers of Mr. Poole in AWA's novel *The Seas of God.* The Bauers appear the obvious models for Mr. and Mrs. Poole.
16. She was the widow of Matthew Ambrose Gaines, a grocer and merchant, and son of Matthew M. Gaines, mayor of Knoxville in 1843. Ambrose Gaines died August 12, 1885, just before the Wetzells came to Knoxville. The four Gaines daughters were Margaret, Etta, Blanch, and Mary; there were also two sons, George Towns Gaines and Ambrose Gaines. Mrs. Gaines, born Mary Winston Towns in Macon, Georgia, was the daughter of George Washington Bonaparte Towns (governor of Georgia from 1847–1851) and his wife Mary Winston Jones Towns. U.S. Census, 1850, 1880; Find-A-Grave database, < findagrave.com/memorial/7116407/george-washington_napoleon_bonaparte-towns> (viewed September 8, 2020).
17. Otto von Bismarck (1815–1898).
18. A dealer in timber and mineral lands, Henry B. Wetzell had his own business, H. B. Wetzell & Company, in partnership with George A. Rumsey. Andrew Morrison, *Knoxville, Tennessee 1891,* Engelhardt Series: American Cities 25. (St. Louis, Mo.: Geo. W. Engelhardt & Co., 1891; repr., Knoxville: Charles A. Reeves, 2002), 38.
19. Operas of the time.

Chapter Six

Mama and the Gaines Family

It was the fall after we came to know the Bauers, the fall I entered the new Girls' High School on Walnut Street,[1] that my intimacy began with Mary Gaines. Just how the intimacy started I can not recall, but in Mary's spirit I found something that chimed with my own, and in my efforts to throw off restraints from which Mary was so largely free, a new era opened in my life. I began to feel more at home in other girls' homes, especially in the Gaines' house, with its mad disorder, its warmth and glow and color, than in the orderly, well-regulated, seemly home of my parents.

My mother, though, did not like the Gaines at all. She had come south too late in her life ever to amalgamate with people so radically different, and the Gaines stood to her, I think, for everything in the South which she mistrusted, and more or less disapproved. Coming as a child, with me, it was different.

Dwelling in later years on my youth in Knoxville and the unbounded delight I had found in the Gaines family, they became in my mind the archetype of families I had known there, not beggared by "the late War," not utterly ruined, as the family of the proud Thomas girls who lived on Asylum Street had been, but greatly reduced, yet who still presented a high-spirited and sparkling front.

It was, in fact, in memory of the Gaines family that I wrote a story, "The Branner House," published in the *Yale Review* in 1938. [Armstrong's story, omitted from this chapter, is available in *Yale Review* 27, no. 3 (March 1938): 587–600. An excerpt is included in the anthology *Writing Appalachia*, ed. Katherine Ledford and Theresa Lloyd (Lexington: University Press of Kentucky, 2020), 248-51.]

NOTES

1. The new Girls' High School at 431 Walnut Street (on the corner of Union Avenue) opened in 1886. Rule, 404.

Chapter Seven

The Year I Was Fourteen

Like that inspired and wayward Irishman, George Moore, to use an illustrious example, I would only know what I wanted to know, and not until I entered the new Girls' High School had I taken a book home from school,[1] but now I was so enamored with the idea of learning a foreign language, albeit a dead one, that I lugged home my Latin grammar and reader every afternoon and next morning after breakfast would shut myself up in the parlor, and as I had started Ancient History the same year and was much impressed with the Peripatetic School of Philosophy,[2] imitating the pupils of Aristotle in ancient Athens, I would walk up and down from the black marble fire-place in the back of the room to the French windows in front, round and round past the tall easel bearing Harry's portrait, the ebony cabinet surmounted by the marble Hebe, in and out among the ebony chairs, repeating over and over:

> *qui, quae, quod,*
> *cuius, cuius, cuius*

—or whatever the conjugation assigned for the day; then, as I danced down the hill a little later, and not to be late, hurried up another hill that was still Clinch Street, I would be all the time chanting a string of prepositions:

> *a or ab, absque, corum, cum, de,*
> *e or ex, prae, pro, sine, tenus,*

which in my dream-like memory of that long past day had something to do with the Ablative Case.

Going to school in the handsome new building on Walnut Street—in which grammar and elementary grades were still housed along with the High School—was altogether different from going to school on Gay Street. It was something like returning to a well regulated home from the zestful informalities of a camping trip. We had left behind all sorts of inconveniences and makeshifts, but a good deal of fun too that had arisen out of our crude, crowded temporary quarters in the Barton Building.[3] The self-same teachers seemed different here, a trifle more rigid—all except Miss Molly Hayes, who had a room now on the second floor, where we were; a big fine front corner room of many windows, in which she moved with all her old sweeping grace, and there was the old smile, the old mischief in her understanding Irish eyes, for us to warm ourselves by whenever we could contrive a minute's chat with her in the new setting.

To be sure, in the Eighth Grade we had a big fine corner room too, and on the platform sat (I can only see her sitting, never moving) Miss Nona McAdoo, a member of that exotic and extraordinary family of McAdoos, many of whom would become known in years to come far beyond the boundaries of Knoxville and Nona herself, in later days, a rich young American widow living in Europe, referred to in our native press as an international beauty. But it took more than beauty to move our young hearts, at once so flinty and so susceptible, in that first year in High School. Miss Nona taught us adequately, I suppose, such subjects as she taught, but there was something mincing and affected in her speech and she seemed so wrapped up in her own beauty that not one of us, I believe, ever got very near her. We even objected to the rather fanciful clothes she wore, finding her "overdressed," for a teacher, a charge that I venture to assert was never brought against any other teacher in Knoxville in those days, when teachers' salaries there as elsewhere were still niggardly in the extreme, and no Southern gentlewoman taught, or labored as yet in any gainful field, unless pressed by sad necessity.

Miss Nona made little impression on me, however, of any sort, though there were girls in the room who, when they discovered her patrician profile did not lend itself so readily to caricature as had Miss Hayes' drooping, inglorious nose, found satisfaction in sketching her sizable feet and hands (which they had decided were "plebian"), grossly exaggerating them on the fly leaves in their text-books or on notes they passed around.

But I can not quite forget that it was through Miss Nona I came to know, or know as early as I did, her younger sister Laura, that young goddess who used to pass through our room in the Barton Building, leaving in her wake a long stream of very upsetting incandescent light.

Laura had graduated now. Every once in a while during noon recess she would stop by the High School on her way somewhere else, to see her sister Nona about something or other, and tarry to chat with those of us who, irresistibly attracted, and sufficiently audacious to approach, clustered around her.

Laura was about sixteen at the time.[4] Like Mary Gaines, whose hair had been cut for the same reason, Laura's head had been shorn during the intervening summer, after typhoid, which almost everyone in Knoxville had then, sooner or later. But Laura, with her tall, full, graceful figure, which she carried with just the suggestion of a swagger, with her crop of short dark curls, was handsomer than ever. She was going on with her studies, reading Horace and other advanced Latin with Professor

Ruth, short, sturdy, irascible superintendent of the Knoxville Public Schools,[5] generally referred to, from his ruddy complexion and stubby projecting auburn beard, as Rufus, the Red; a hard-driving martinet of whom pupils and teachers alike were scared out of their wits, but of whom Laura alone was totally unafraid.

When one of us called him a holy terror, Laura burst into a merry laugh. "Why, he's perfectly adorable!" she insisted. "I'm going to start Greek with him soon."

Meantime, by herself, with the aid of an Italian dictionary, she was reading Dante's *La Vita Nuova.*

Despite her taste for the classics, however, Laura would talk with equal enthusiasm of the gay times she had had in visiting "kin" up in Abingdon, Virginia,[6] a spot thenceforth invested for me with such charm as no other on earth for a time; or of Neb Hazelhurst, with whom she danced and rode horseback when she visited other kin down in Georgia—an aristocratic daredevil, a sort of Rhett Butler,[7] with whom she had all the rest of us madly in love, though we had never laid eyes on this handsome rascal, and never would.

Gradually, as the year wore on, Laura and I would get off by ourselves when she stopped at the High School. I was flattered, of course, in this recognition by an older girl. She fired me, too, with a desire to enter that larger, richer life of the mind, an expanding world in which she was beginning to move herself with such ease, it seemed. But there was Mary Gaines, swaying me in an opposite direction, toward the butterfly existence which was the only one she aspired to, and the only one I aspired to myself, most of the time.

Mary had become my boon companion; Laura, an idol. But for all that[,] the Thomas girls had not lost their original attraction, one considerably strengthened by a party they engineered at this time. On the appointed evening a dozen or more of us were to meet with them where they lived now, and thence proceed to the place where the festivities were to be held. I was to go with Rob Simmonds, a slim, good looking, amiable lad who lived in West End, some little distance beyond us, on a street leading up to the summit of Fort Sanders, where it was planned our own new home would shortly rise. It was the first time I had gone to a party with any boy but Harry—an event in itself.

The Thomas girls no longer lived on Asylum Street. As one in an endless series of moves, they had landed this time on Bell Avenue, a continuation of Mabry, which led off Gay, and both known now, I believe, as East Vine; a street on which a horse-car ran then, through a hopelessly forlorn region of dilapidated one-story houses with weedy vacant lots between, here and there a tumble-down soot-blackened grog or grocery shop and among them an occasional raw yellowish frame store-building, still unpainted, which had just been run up.

It was in some rear upstairs rooms over one of these flimsy new store-buildings that Rob and I, after some little difficulty, finally located the Thomas girls on the night of the party. This latest move of theirs was recent. None of us had been there before. But I do not remember anyone seeming in the least shocked or depressed by the surroundings in which we found them, though the bare room whose door opened to our knock was filled with the resinous smell of newly-cut pine lumber mixed with a less agreeable one of plaster that was still wet—a clammy room beside which the dingy old sitting-room on Asylum Street seemed now, by comparison, almost elegant, and the only reminder of it that same stained old Confederate flag, "The Conquered Banner,"[8] hanging on one of these damp grayish evil-smelling walls.

But the Thomas girls themselves were here. What else mattered? They were not only here, they appeared utterly unaware that they had descended yet one notch lower in coming to live in this remote section of the town, and on Bell Avenue—of all streets! For the rest of us, I suspect that our youthful code, whatever other virtues it may have excluded, recognized valor, so that the valiant Thomas girls would have had their following wherever they lived. Then besides, they were chockfull of ideas, far more resourceful, far more ingenious, I realize now, than any of those they drew around them, and here on Bell Avenue they possessed the same magic they had possessed on Asylum Street. They waved their wands. On the instant all of us were alive in every fibre, tip-toe for adventure, brimful of excitement over what was ahead, for it was Friday night—and Hallowe'en!

Only the Thomas girls with their fertile imaginations and marked initiative would ever have thought of the long deserted mansion, a few blocks further out on the disreputable street where they had come to live, as affording perfect conditions for the age-old revels of Hallowe'en.

A little later than the autumn of which I write, the Bell Avenue Street-car line was extended several miles into the country, ending at Lake Ottosee, for some years a popular resort for picnics and summer concerts.[9] Going back and forth to Lake Ottosee we would pass this stately abandoned mansion, the overgrown shrubbery in its extensive grounds gray with dust which rose from the unpaved road it faced, its fountains dry, yet with its vestiges of bygone grandeur standing out unforgettable amidst the cheerless wastes which surrounded it. Then one day it was gone—the dust-laden trees, tangled shrubbery, fountains—everything. Not even mounds of rubble to show where it had once stood and machines at work, the ground being prepared for some new structure on the site.

I have an idea that in earlier days it had been the center of a plantation, embracing lands later to become part of the growing town. But I could never in the years after it disappeared learn who had built or ever lived in this mansion. Many who had passed it as often as I could not recall it, and in recent years when I have mentioned the place to surviving Knoxvillians of my own generation, I gain the impression they think the house I describe is purely a figment of my imagination.

But however flattering this may be to my imaginative powers the house existed. It stood there, right enough, exactly where I have placed it, all through the '80s, maybe later, and on this long past Hallowe'en, when observance of the Eve of All Saints' Day had not yet been given over largely to small boys ringing door-bells, carrying off gates and committing other depredations not ordinarily allowable; when old Scotch and Irish and Welsh customs were still followed to some extent, our little party, talking in subdued voices, entered it secretively by a back door on the ground floor. Whether the Thomas girls had secured a key, or how it was we were able to enter, I can not recall.

What I remember is our making our way, as we approached the house, through paths overgrown with brambles, the boys carrying pumpkins they had cut in the semblance of faces and stone jugs of sweet cider; the girls with baskets of fruit, sandwiches and cake, and with mirrors and other paraphernalia essential to rites that would reveal our future husbands or wives. I remember how black the sky was that night; the frosty gleam of the stars, how sharply cut and high overhead they seemed; the acrid smell of dry leaves; the tang in the air. But what I remember best is the silence that suddenly fell upon us when we had gropingly made our way inside and as the boys lit one by one the candles in the pumpkins that served as lanterns we made out by their dim light that the great musty room where we found ourselves had once been a kitchen. The floor was of brick and a huge brick fire-place confronted us at one end, its andirons still standing in ashes that had never been removed, a rusty iron kettle hanging from the crane.

We heard a few squeaks; the sound of scampering mice in the walls; the sudden snap, frighteningly loud, of timbers contracting in the cold.

The boys set a lighted pumpkin at each end of the long high chimney-shelf and others on the broad window-sills in the room. I could not take my eyes off the shadowy, cavernous, barely-discerned fire-place. People had lived here. Slaves had toiled in this ancient brick-paved kitchen, preparing rich and splendid meals. A warm-blooded spacious way of life had gone on in this ghostly old house with its tomb-like chill. But slaves had vanished. Masters had vanished. Everything vanishes. The thought was a trifle sobering, if you dwelt on it. . . .

We piled our baskets and other burdens on the floor in a corner, and whispering now, as Birdie and Marguerite warned that only by keeping quiet could we hope to see or hear anything uncanny, started our explorations with the aid of a couple of extra candles the boys had brought; tip-toeing through other rooms in the basement—apparently store-rooms—, big and bare, paved with brick, like the kitchen, and all of them clean, save for dust and cobwebs. No refuse anywhere.

But it was on the floor above, the main floor of the house, we found a surprise. Instead of the stately staircase leading to chambers overhead that we had expected, there was an unsupported spiral iron stairway, the first I had ever seen, and with a balustrade of fretted iron-work in a beautiful design of grapes and grape leaves. There was a surprise, too, in the bed-chambers when we reached them; square lofty rooms with their windows in pairs, though not placed at the usual height, but with a semi-circular set of shallow steps mounting to a little platform from which the casements opened, and with a seat running along underneath. What a wonderful place, I thought, as these secluded windows were revealed through the darkness by the flickering, uncertain light of our candles, for a girl (myself of course) to sit and read, or dream.

All the time, however, as we passed from one creepy chamber to another, incredulous yet my heart beating fast, I was listening for the hollow groans and moans we were supposed to hear, and when we were entering one pitch-black chamber, more terrifying to the girls at least than if a witch had appeared, a bat, traditional to Hallowe'en, the Devil's own spawn, and suggesting a vast, invisible, obscene realm on the edge of our own, swooped down so close to our heads that we could catch the gnashing sound this weird mammal emits in hunting.

There was no chaperone. But there was nothing that could have caused even Mama, had she known, a moment's concern. No kissing; nothing more, at most, than some lad's quick furtive pressure of a girl's hand. The age of premature and promiscuous "petting" had not yet arrived.

After we got back to the basement the boys found logs in an out-house, and with some dry branches they picked up, started a fire.

Seated on the brick floor, we ate our supper. Some of the chill began to die out of the room. We placed chestnuts on the hearth, near the fire, nuts in pairs, for a boy and girl, not quite sweethearts, but making eyes at each other, and if the two nuts burned together, the boy and girl were sure to marry. We ducked for apples set afloat in a tub filled with water from a cistern outside. Each of us in turn carried a lighted candle in one hand, a mirror in the other, downstairs in the dark, and saw the face of the one we were to marry come into the mirror. Marriage, viewed romantically, was a subject of growing interest. It was years, to be sure, before any of us would marry; but this did not lessen the zest with which we sought to peer into the future. And then, as the night wore on, and we sat around the fire, with the logs slowly burning down to embers, the great black empty house rising above us, impenetrable blackness outside, and the stillness broken only by a coal falling now and again into the ashes, or the tick of a death-watch in the wall—in this atmosphere, with our youthful appetite for the grisly, the ghoulish, not yet appeased, we started telling all the horror stories we had heard or read, among them "The Black Cat," "Premature Burial" and other[s] from Poe, until, thrilled to the marrow, some of us were shivering from genuine fright.

There would never be, for any of us, I suppose, another Hallowe'en party that in the true spirit of the night would come up to this one.

But who were they, I wonder, pondering it now, the boys and girls in that little band which sat around the fire frightening each other? No names come back, no faces, no forms; only those of the Thomas girls and Rob Simmonds—those and the house itself where the party was held, far out in a street in Knoxville that once was called Bell Avenue.

It was the same fall of the Hallowe'en party that Jim Fletcher started bringing me bouquets. He would hand them to the house-girl or whoever met him at our front door and state explicitly that they were for "Miss Annie."

Heliotrope, tuberoses, fuchsias, sprays of delicate shell-pink begonia blossoms, Cape jasmine, a rose here and there, and all set in a pattern and interlaced with smilax, they were magnificent bouquets, no mere garden flowers, but fine hot-house products in the day when Knoxville still had no florist's shop and only Colonel Perez Dickinson and a few others greenhouses of their own.

I was a bit more embarrassed, at first, than pleased by these tributes.

A well-born but brash, loud-voiced youth, not too prepossessing in appearance, Jim lived on the corner below us in a rather attractive house with a porch that was near to the ground running around two sides of it and only one other house between it and our own. A member of the family who had aroused more interest in me than Jim was his older sister, a beautiful young lady who was always smiling, though without much warmth, but had attracted my own attention mainly, I think, because of her name, Johnny, after a youth "Uncle Johnny" killed in the War. There were many girls in Knoxville then, when we were still so close to "that sad Brothers' War"—girls with boys' names, Johnny or Willy or George or Hugh, for uncles not old enough to have had sons to carry the name when they fell, sacrifices to the Lost Cause.

When Mary Gaines saw one of those bouquets in our parlor, and heard who had brought it, she was seized with convulsions of laughter.

"Old big-mouth Jim!" she hooted. "Well, what did I tell you? He's always sayin' how sweet you are."

"Sweet!" I sniffed.

Who wanted to be "sweet?" You were "sweet, mighty sweet," in Knoxville, when people didn't know what else, what else that was nice, to say about you.

"I can tell you," Mary said, "where old Jim gets 'em—right out of Mrs. O'Conner's green-houses."[10]

Mrs. O'Conner was Jim's aunt. She was the widow of that Tom O'Conner, president of the Mechanics National Bank in Knoxville at the time he had figured as both murderer and murdered in Knoxville's most sensational shooting affray, only a few years before; "died"—as the *History of Knox County*,[11] in the nature of such eviscerated works, puts it discreetly, without elaboration—"died in October, 1882."

Haunted by memories, the childless Widow O'Conner lived quite by herself,

Melrose Park, Knoxville, Tennessee (1885).

save for servants, at Melrose. Built by slave labor in the 1850s, in classical design with Tuscan detail and long French windows in the lower story, Melrose had been between battle lines in the '60s. Soldiers of both sides had been killed within the walls of the mansion. Then, after the War, a Knoxville lawyer of rising importance named Temple had acquired the property, renamed it, calling it Melrose after his mother-in-law's former home near Melrose Abbey in Scotland, and selling it later to O'Conner.[12]

Standing at a slight elevation in park-like grounds which extended all the way down to Kingston Pike and along the pike as far as the toll-gate,[13] this beautiful estate on the edge of town, with its iron stags, conservatories, artificial sheet of water and little ornamental boat-house[14]—with all the adornments of a gentleman's place in that era, Melrose was now Knoxville's outstanding show-place after Perez Dickinson's Island Home. But unlike Island Home, Melrose was not shown, or more than one could see for himself as he drove along the pike. Since her husband's sensational death, Mrs. O'Conner saw no one, people said, except members of her own family, so I was surprised when Jim stopped one day on his way to his aunt's and urged me to go along. I hesitated, knowing I would have to face Mary's gibes later, but in the end I consented, walking along self-consciously beside Jim as we started out from our side gate and hoping we would meet no one I knew, though by the time we reached a woodsy lane that ran along at the rear of Melrose I was laughing and joking with him freely. Jim might be slightly ridiculous, but he was full of good will and good humour [*sic*]. I couldn't dislike him. I didn't object, either, to his calling me "Miss" Annie. It made me feel reasonably sure that in another year I'd dare put my hair up on top of my head.

Coming in the back gate, near the green-houses, we found Mrs. O'Conner herself in the first one we entered, a slender, frail, elegant little lady in her deep widow's weeds, with an onyx and pearl broach among the ruches at her throat, matching earrings, and a face so deathly white it startled me. Jim, however, was not in the slightest degree abashed by his aunt's tragic appearance. He was as cheery, noisy, as bumptious, as ever—completely himself, and his aunt, though the essence of refinement, seemed to like him this way. (Maybe big Tom O'Conner, "that Irish upstart," as the Mabry brothers[15] called him, had been something like this.) With the utmost graciousness she talked to Jim and me as if we were her age, consulting us, asking our advice and aid, as she cut flowers for us lavishly and arranged them herself, instead of calling on her green-house man.

After this first visit I would often go out to Melrose with Jim. I got to looking forward to these little excursions, although they were always, for me, an odd blend of delight and sadness.

It wasn't only the resplendent, heavy-scented bouquets we would bring away which impressed me. Not only the Italianate house with its noble lines, walls partially clad in ivy—an old house, ripened by time and commanding grounds which swept down splendidly below it. No, there was something connected with Melrose that stamped itself even more enduringly on my mind. It was Mrs. O'Conner's look each time when Jim and I were leaving. I was too young then to analyze it, but now it seems to me that she was almost clinging to us at the moment of parting. Living in the shadowed world where she dwelt now, in proud exile; alone, weighed down by heavy mourning garments banded with crepe, nursing her grief—as she would, in approved Victorian fashion, to the end of her days—, tormented perhaps to some extent by shame, she seemed bent on catching a gleam or two of light and warmth, even if evanescent, from that world which Jim and I inhabited. We were touched, it is true, by her sorrow. But untouched ourselves as yet by the sterner realities of human existence, we could not hide, however hard we might try, the unbounded buoyancy, the gladsome vitality, that filled us. Our faces betrayed us, too, I suppose—their features not yet set, but "morning faces" she was loath to let slip from sight.

"Come again," she would say, with a wistful, almost pleading expression in her dark stricken eyes. One hand, with its diamond rings, too large now, on Jim's shoulder, the thin cold fingers of the other clasping mine, "Son," she would say, "you and Annie come again soon, won't you? I dearly love to have you."

Jim taking me out to Melrose, Rob to the Hallowe'en party—so now boys were beginning to notice me a little. It didn't mean much to me, though, I believe—not yet. What meant more was Mary's extending my education on a subject of great and ever deepening mystery. Mary's opportunities to find out things were better than mine.

True, Mary seldom came to our house. Notwithstanding the touch of gamin that was in her, notwithstanding that she was daunted by few things or persons, she stood in as great awe of Mama as I of Queen Victoria in the guise of Mrs. August Bauer. I think, too, that after the wild disorder of her own home, the regulated life in ours, its extreme orderliness, with a place for everything and everything in its place, oppressed her. But Mary's rich and powerful voice that would one day sound forth from a church choir in Knoxville was beginning to get some training now and after her vocal lesson she would often stop by the Girls' High School, we would walk home together and she would be bursting with what she had to tell me; stories—there was always a fresh one—she had picked up (overheard) from her popular older sisters and girl friends of theirs, several of them to be married soon, and who made the Gaines house their gathering place. Some of the stories were quite bawdy. The older girls, according to Mary, "liked to died laughin' over 'em."

To Mary and me, these stories, relating largely to the private lives of married couples, if of no less burning interest, were sometimes less funny. Frequently one of them puzzled us. We were not too sure we had caught its point. A more reliable, at least clearer, source of sex education was the Gaines' cook. I had never been allowed in our own kitchen long enough to reach intimate terms with the cook, whether black or white, as Mama held, with firmness, that you could not expect results from a cook you allowed children to hang around.

In the Gaines house it was different. "Miss Pink" never bothered herself about a matter of that sort. Mary, like all the Gaines "brats" before her, spent all the time she wanted to in the huge, ill-lighted, grimy, greasy, roach-infested but hospitable Gaines kitchen, where she could question at will Aunt Melissa, a black initiate who, without benefit of clergy, had had innumerable progeny of her own during the many years she had toiled for the Gaines family, and was still having them.

Mary's questions were mainly directed to how babies actually got born, of which we had only the vaguest notion, and of which Aunt Melissa was able to furnish realistic, if some of them rather sickening, details. If Mary ventured too far, however, in her inquiries, trying to get a little nearer to understanding that greatest mystery of all, how babies got started in the first place, Aunt Melissa would push out her thick rubbery lips with a show of indignation: "Oh, go 'long, Miss Mary! I'm gwine ter tell Miss Pink—you a-wantin' ter know so much." She would shoo her out of the kitchen.

Meanwhile, with such limited light as even Aunt Melissa could, or would, throw on the subject, it continued to occupy the thoughts and color a good deal of the conversation not only of Mary and myself but of the other girls of our age we knew well. Not all my reading of George Eliot, Dickens, and Thackeray, my surreptitious dips into the wicked Ouida,[16] had offered a clue to things we wanted to know most. I had seen Powers' Greek Slave[17] at an exhibition in New York and other nude female figures in marble, yet in that most prudish era in the world's history, so ignorant were we of female anatomy, including our own, that while we laughed about it together, there was not one of us who was not a trifle troubled. Could the miracle of procreation really take place within our own bodies? Each of us was afraid she was not made right.

But it was not Mary, however much she may have contributed to my knowledge of this agitating subject, who first made me aware of Em Parham's.

I can not recall exactly over so great a span of time, but I believe it was when I still knew Mary only slightly, while I was going to school in the Barton Building, that I became conscious of Em Parham's, and at least hazily of the nature of her establishment. It was virtually impossible, indeed, for children of school age in West End to remain ignorant of Em Parham's, and of what it was, passing it every day, as they did, on their way to and from school, to church, to Peter Kern's Ice Cream Parlor—to almost anywhere they were going.

I remember perfectly, at any rate, the feeling that started coming over me when on the way to school in the morning I had crossed the viaduct, left behind the grocery shop and saloon on opposite corners and begun to climb the hill ahead, one I would climb hundreds and hundreds of times in my life, as it turned out. Half way up the block there was a Negro family, very light-colored, who lived in a two-story house, dark red, a much better house than most Negroes lived in then, or do now, but down below the level of the street, and with some of them, decently dressed, though with something I fancied was secret and sly in their looks, always sitting on their front porch, where they had a red-bird hanging in a home-made wooden cage from one of their porch posts. They would nod politely and murmur "Howdy" if I glanced down in their direction. I always began to get nervous at this point. I was getting close now to Em Parham's. I wanted to run past the place but the bricks in the old brick pavement on this stretch of the hill were extremely uneven and sunken in spots. If I ran, I might fall. But I would walk fast, my heart knocking against my ribs. I was gripped by an icy fear that someone might come out of Em's while I was passing, or that I might see something else I was not intended to see. What I dreaded especially was that Em might appear. She was only a name to me, but one that stood for the dark and hidden, for bottomless evil, and I quailed before the very thought of ever laying eyes upon the depraved woman herself.

But no one ever came out of her door as I passed—or not for a long time. Em, as everyone knew, was only a Parham by marriage. Her maiden name was one of the most respected in Knoxville. She was a cousin, no distant one, of some of its prominent citizens, and how she came to take up her infamous trade I never learned, but there her establishment stood on West Clinch for as many years as I knew Knoxville; a tallish frame house painted a light gray, spic and span, its shutters all tightly closed, day and night; the steps that mounted to its small latticed front porch only a few feet back from the street; close beside it the First Colored Presbyterian Church in Knoxville, and diagonally across (with that juxtaposition of the sacred and the profane by no means uncommon in the old Knoxville) another church, a substantial red-brick structure of pseudo-classical design with garish stained-glass windows—a church for whites, though of what denomination I am no longer certain. With its location, outward appearance, the standing of the elderly lechers and young libertines allegedly among its patrons, Em Parham's was regarded as the town's most high-toned bordello. Even the *unco guid*,[18] the most naïve adults, in West End could not remain perpetually oblivious to its existence, while for West End children, passing constantly, closer acquaintance with it, sooner or later, was inevitable.[19]

Ordinarily I was one of a smaller or larger group of girls who walked home from school together in the afternoon and we would stop laughing, invariably drop our voices, as we neared Em Parham's, glance at each other meaningly [*sic*] and not resume our normal behaviour until we were well down the hill, beyond the place. There was a girl among us, however, a good deal of a hoyden, who one afternoon as we reached Em's, to our consternation ran up boldly on to the porch and rang the door-bell, which responded with a muffled jangling. As nothing more exciting happened, the girl repeated the prank every afternoon, but there came a day when the hour of our passing apparently had been taken note of. As we came abreast the house and the girl rang the bell as usual, we were aghast to see the door suddenly swing open and on the threshold a figure, who, in my fright, appeared to be Satan himself, albeit a woman—raw-boned, somewhat above medium height, with black hair that was plainly dressed, heavy mannish features, cold but smiting black eyes, and the hardest face I had ever looked upon. In spectacular contrast to Mrs. Hamilton three or four blocks further West on Clinch, sin could certainly never have materialized in a less glamorous form than in the person of Em Parham.

She shook her fist after the girl, calling her by her full family name. "You young devil, you, I'll tell your papa on you!" she threatened in a raucous though not overloud voice.

The girl never again rang Em's bell. The mention of her father, with its intimation of Em's personal acquaintance with him—this hint sobered her and we all walked down the rest of the hill that day in silence.

It was a good while after this that one morning as I came up the hill alone I was horror-stricken by the sight of two women fighting in front of Em's establishment, very near to the side-walk. I took in at a glance that they were young, one of them rather pretty, with frizzed tow-colored hair, and both of them in Mother Hubbards,[20] the brand, in those days, of their profession, as were the fancy high-heeled buttoned shoes they wore when they walked the streets. They were slugging each other soundlessly, biting and clawing, parts of their Mother Hubbards torn off them, shamelessly exposing their nakedness underneath, their hair streaming down over their dazed, drunken eyes.

I had never realized before that women—women I would ever see, could fight. My heart seemed to stop beating. But in the nightmarish vision which remains with me like some hideous half-forgotten dream, the feature of the scene that stands out most prominently is of Em, the arch-fiend, all at once appearing, jerking the women apart, seizing each, and with the brutish and prodigious force of a cave woman, starting to drag them out of view.

Years afterward there was another scene centering around Em Parham's that would fix itself in my mind. It was during the Spanish-American War, "that summer frolic of 1898," as it has been referred to since. I was no longer a child now. Many of the mysteries of sex had been resolved. I had been married and held the hand of a child of my own, a little boy of five, as we climbed the Clinch Street hill on a Sunday morning, inescapably passing Em's.

The Armistice had already been signed but troops not yet disbanded had been moved from Chickamauga, where many had died of typhoid, in the hope of a more healthful location at Camp Poland, which had been established in the immediate vicinity of Knoxville.[21] The town was full of soldiers and as Roger and I, part of the customary lengthy procession of Church and Sunday School goers, climbed the hill we encountered a line of men in uniform extending all the way down from Henley with another long line on the opposite side of the street, waiting their turn for admittance to Em Parham's.

A member of so august a body as the United Nations has recently (as I write) stated before one of its sections occupied with the problem of regulating prostitution, "There will be prostitutes as long as there are planets." This may well be so and I know nothing of the present-day mores of Knoxville, but in the course of a long and extraordinarily varied life, I have witnessed nothing that for sheer bestiality surpassed this scene, nothing that more blatantly outraged the decencies which civilized men commonly observe among themselves.

Whether it was before or after this unholy spectacle I can not recall, as events long past, to the inconvenience of the annalist, seldom, in recollection, arrange themselves in chronological order, but it must have been about this time that Em Parham achieved a new and amazing prominence in the community.

The small inconspicuous corner saloon at the bottom of the hill, below her establishment, was kept by a man whose name I retain only as "Joe."[22] We hardly ever walked on his side of the street, as there was no sidewalk behind the saloon, only a weedy path between it and the viaduct, but from our side, looking across the street, although we never saw any roughness around his corner, often we would see the saloon-keeper himself sitting on a bench out in front, with a Dalmatian bitch somewhere near him and sometimes with a whole litter of little pups she was suckling or that were playing around her. We noticed the Dalmatian because of her marking—Dalmatians were unusual in Knoxville—and we noticed Joe, a mild looking man with a drooping moustache, because of the talk that he was Em Parham's "lover," and lived with her, in her house, as a sort of husband. One day the *Knoxville Journal* announced Joe's sudden death.[23] The saloon was closed. There was crepe on the door. I do not recall whether or not his death was violent. What I recall were rumors afloat that Em Parham might have had some part in it, as Joe had carried a large insurance policy in her favor.

She must have cleared herself, however, at least with officers of the Law, for she was never tried in the courts and shortly after Joe's death the town was electrified by seeing her drive down Gay Street seated in a luxurious new barouche drawn by a span of strawberry roans with their flaming cream-colored tails and manes, and with a Negro coachman in a high hat on the box. Even Colonel Perez Dickinson's regal progress through town in his lumbering landau, with both liveried coachman and footman on the box, paled now beside a sight almost any fine afternoon of Em on the back seat of her open carriage; Em in her widow's bonnet and veil, an immaculate snowy ruche encircling her heavy-featured masculine face; seated beside her one of her "girls," elaborately, though perhaps in concession to the nature of the outing, not too gaudily, dressed; and another opposite, where the flowers were piled, as they proceeded in the direction of North Knoxville and Old Gray to lay flowers on Joe's grave. A calliope with its steam whistle, all pipes blowing, would not, in fact, have drawn more heads to doors and windows along Gay Street than word that Em, in all her sinful glory, was rolling by.

Joe's grave itself became shortly, too, an object of such popular interest that people made special trips to see it on Sunday afternoon. It was in the newer part of Old Gray, where beyond, separated from it only by a low stone wall, lay the National Cemetery with its thousands of small uniform headstones. It was close to a main driveway, facing it, and over the grave Em had erected a monument that would have attracted no particular attention in any Latin country, accustomed to such embellishments, but in Knoxville was a novelty. In the white shaft which rose above it, instead of the usual quotation from Scripture accompanying the name of the deceased and dates of his birth and death, she had had inserted under glass a cabinet photograph of the saloon-keeper, taken standing, in a slouch hat, and at his feet the Dalmatian with a row of her pups, ten in all, ranged beside her.[24]

Whatever became—as we have a way of asking about flamboyant individuals—of this most improper of improper Knoxvillians? I haven't the ghost of an idea. But for all I know, the handful of dust she is now may rest beside saloon-keeper Joe in Old Gray,[25] among ambassadors, senators, scholars—Knoxville's most distinguished dead; saints and sinners alike.

Each in his narrow cell for ever laid.[26]

NOTES

1. George Moore (1852–1933), Irish novelist, playwright, poet, and critic, said: "Never could I interest myself in a book if it were not the exact diet my mind required at the time, or in the very immediate future." *Confessions of a Young Man* (1886), Chapter 2.
2. The Peripatetic School of Philosophy took its name from the Peripatos, a covered walkway in the Lyceum, along which Aristotle walked as he was teaching his disciples. *Reader's Encyclopedia*, 775.
3. See Chapter 4.
4. Born September 18, 1870, Laura McAdoo was almost exactly two years older than AWA.
5. Albert Ruth, Superintendent of Knoxville City Schools, 1881–1897. Deaderick, *Heart of the Valley*, 243, 652.
6. A small town in southwest Virginia, not far from its border with Tennessee. Incidentally, Armstrong would later make her home nearby in the mountains of upper east Tennessee. By the time of her death, she herself was living in the town of Abingdon, where a stage adaptation of her novel *This Day and Time* was performed at the Barter Theatre.
7. Major romantic character in Margaret Mitchell's novel *Gone with the Wind* and the movie adaptation.
8. Title of the poem by Father Abram Ryan.
9. Now Knoxville's Chilhowee Park. Deaderick, *Heart of the Valley*, 218.
10. Jim Fletcher was the son of Ellen Renshaw House, whose Civil War diary was published as *A Very Violent Rebel*, ed. Daniel E. Sutherland (Knoxville: University of Tennessee Press, 1996). Ellen, who married James W. Fletcher, named the first of their four children "Johnnie" after her beloved brother John, who was shot and killed by robbers shortly after the war ended. The Widow O'Conner was Ellen's sister Frances "Fannie" Renshaw House, xviii, 192, 201–2, 203, 258n; U.S. Census, 1880.
11. A reference to *The French Broad-Holston Country: A History of Knox County,* ed., Mary U. Rothrock (Knoxville: East Tennessee Historical Society, 1946), 442.
12. Around 1858, John J. Craig, a Knoxville marble dealer, began building a house, named Lucknow, at the top of a hill just west of what was then East Tennessee University. After the War, the house and surrounding grounds became the country estate of Judge Oliver Perry Temple (1820–1907), his wife, the former Scotia Caldonia Hume, and

their daughter, Mary Boyce Temple. Melrose Mansion occupied the site where the University of Tennessee's Hess Hall now stands. It was purchased by the Nicholson Art League in 1925 and later served as the University of Tennessee Art Center before its demolition. Rothrock, 496–497; Deaderick, 417, 510; Betsey Beeler Creekmore, *Knoxville*, 3rd ed. (Knoxville: University of Tennessee Press, 1976), 305.

13. In 1866, the Tennessee legislature chartered several turnpike companies, among them the Kingston Turnpike Company, which was authorized to build a road from Knoxville to Kingston and beyond. The turnpike company could erect a toll gate, beginning five miles from Knoxville, and collect tolls to raise funds for extending and macadamizing its road. Rule, 272–275; Rothrock, 236–238.
14. According to Creekmore: "At the foot of Melrose hill, Lake Street begins where a little lake once ornamented the mansion's extensive grounds." Creekmore, *Knoxville*, p. 305.
15. As noted in Chapter 1, footnote 14, the two Mabrys whom O'Conner killed were father and son, not brothers.
16. Pen name of Louise de la Ramée (1838–1908), English novelist, "widely known for her flamboyant romances of fashionable life." Benet, *Reader's Encyclopedia*, 840.
17. "The first publicly exhibited, life-size, American sculpture depicting a fully nude female figure"; by Hiram Powers (1805–1873). First toured in America between 1847 and 1851. National Gallery of Art Website < https://www.nga.gov/content/ngaweb/Collection/art-object-page.166484.html > (viewed April 22, 2017)
18. Allusion to "Address to the Unco Guid, or the Rigidly Righteous," a poem by Robert Burns.
19. Knoxville City Directories during the 1880s and 1890s list a "Parham, Mad. Emma" at 152 W. Clinch (at its intersection with Henley). For a lengthy discussion and listing of Knoxville's "Madams," including Emma Parham, see Ronald R. Allen, *Knoxville Miscellany: People, Places and Events in Old Knoxville* (Knoxville, 2008), 220–246. An 1894 Tennessee Supreme Court Case, *Emma Parham v. Board of Mayor and Aldermen of the City of Knoxville,* states: "Plaintiff, also referred to as 'Em,' was accused of running a Bawdy House out of her home located at 152 Clinch Street in Knoxville, Tennessee." Tennessee Supreme Court Cases, Tennessee State Library and Archives Website, <http://supreme-court-cases.tennsos.org/> (viewed April 28, 2017). Sanborn maps for March 1890 show 152 Clinch and Shiloh Presbyterian Church (colored, acc. to Rule, 434) next door at 150 Clinch.
20. A loose usually shapeless dress.
21. For more information about Camp Poland, see Rule, *Standard History of Knoxville,* 189–191. According to Rule's count, on September 1, 1898, nearly 9,000 men were encamped there.
22. Joseph R. Cole was owner and operator of a saloon at 529 High Street, on the northwest corner of West Clinch. *Knoxville City Directory,* 1891–92, 1893, 1894.
23. Cole died March 20, 1894, "in the rear room" of his saloon ("at the corner of Clinch

and Henley streets") from a gunshot to the head, ruled to have been self-inflicted. "Not Appalled by Death," *Knoxville Daily Journal,* March 21, 1894.

24. The monument to Joe Cole (March 27, 1856 - March 20, 1894) still stands, but there is no picture in the rectangular indentation where one could have been placed. Editor's visit to Lot No. 806, Old Gray Cemetery, May 24, 2017.
25. "Emma (d. March 7, 1913)" is not directly beside Joe Cole, but only a few feet away from him in the Parham Plot (Lot No. 806) at Old Gray Cemetery. Robert A. McGinnis, transcriber, *Graves of Old Gray Cemetery* ([Knoxville: R.A. McGinnis], 2007), 207. Editor's visit to Old Gray Cemetery, May 24, 2017.
26. From Thomas Gray, *Elegy in a Country Churchyard* (1750).

Second Presbyterian Church. Art Work of Knoxville, 1895.

Chapter Eight

The Second Presbyterian Church and the Human Heart

Through all my years in Knoxville I never lost a sense of joy at the sight of the old Second Presbyterian Church; simple, stately, in the heart of the town and with its peaceful old churchyard shadowed by ancient oaks over which English ivy clambered—joy, that is, in its outward appearance, a joy which grew less when I entered the church, particularly if the congregation had already gathered, and one that disappeared entirely when I contemplated the detached Sunday School building at one side, some little distance away, in a front corner of the churchyard, and very inappropriately, so far as its appearance was concerned, called the "chapel"—a sturdy two-story red-brick structure of no distinction, built much later than the church itself and conforming to it in no degree in its design.

According to custom, Sunday School in the Second Presbyterian Church preceded Church and I do not remember that in the beginning I especially minded going to it. It was just one of those things you couldn't get out of, or not often. Then there were girls in my Sunday School class I saw daily at school. We could whisper and giggle together over our personal affairs and certainly there could not have been two more gracious and patient Sunday School teachers than frail, dainty little Mrs. Robert Rhea I had first and the sister-in-law who succeeded her, Miss Ellen Rhea, an elderly erect spinster, always in dignified black silk, a jet aigrette trembling atop the narrow but tall black bonnet which, in the mode of the '80s, she wore perched high on her head. Besides being "good Presbyterians," both Mrs. Rhea and Miss Ellen were—which might or might not be the same thing—good women. They did their best, beyond a doubt, to infuse interest into the Sunday School lesson for the day, but under their teaching, whatever passage or story taken from the Bible they touched upon became straightway, for me, dry as dust, utterly and absolutely dead.

To be sure, there was never, I suppose, a more unregenerate Sunday School pupil. I never knew my Sunday School lesson. A mere glance at the Westminster leaflet which contained it and every bone in my vigorous young body became as wax. I never knew the Golden Text, however brief, for any particular "Sabbath," and though not inclined to be impertinent, was never embarrassed, far less troubled by pangs of conscience, when I knew none of the answers, as the other girls did, to questions about Esau, Elijah, John the Baptist, the Pool of Siloam—whatever it might be. I was vaguely aware that the other girls had been prodded into learning their Sunday School lesson, so far as they knew it, by their parents, a thing my own never did. Brought up in strict Presbyterian families, subject from their infancy to a lengthy and solemn grace before each meal; to family prayers every morning and whenever the minister called; to Church, Sunday School, and the rigors of the Long Catechism on Sunday morning; to Church services again in the evening and Prayer Meeting in the mid-week—reared in this atmosphere, both Papa and Mama had apparently revolted inwardly at an early age, and when they came to establish a home of their own it was on a pattern more consistent with their ideas of the good life; so that they never urged upon their children at any time more than the most conventional religious observance; sending us to Sunday School as they sent us to dancing school, to our music lessons, as part of their general program for bringing up their children. They would expose us to this and that, among other things to Sunday School, and then later, I judge they thought, we could interpret the Bible in the light of our reason and make—if we made one—our own approach to God.

My own invariable failure to learn my Sunday School lesson, as I look back on it now, was as much a matter of indifference as of anything else. But there were other aspects of Sunday School which aroused in me emotions of a much more positive nature. Its superintendent at the time, a tall bulky man, one of the rather numerous New Englanders who had come to Knoxville and prospered there, lived now in a fine old red-brick house with grounds around it a few miles out of town on Kingston Pike. I still retained at this age a propensity to see in persons for whom I had conceived a distaste a resemblance to various fowls of the earth and air, and when I watched Mr. Washburn swinging his weight from side to side as he proceeded ponderously down the aisle of the assembly room, he reminded me of an old red rooster strutting around a barnyard; an impression reenforced [*sic*] when mounting the platform to conduct the opening or closing Sunday School exercises, without a single gleam of geniality on his large, stern face he would give out even the simplest announcement with a magisterial air which seemed to suggest that the Sunday School of the Second Presbyterian Church was his private demesne which some—at least of the younger members—had contrived to enter without permission. This superintendent became, in fact, inextricably associated in my mind with all the things I found uncongenial in Sunday School.

Then there were the Sunday School cards handed out weekly. They must have been distributed indiscriminately, and not as an award for any especial Sunday School diligence, or I never would have received one. As it was, I acquired, in time, quite a collection. Crudely colored, the Biblical characters depicted on them might be walking along the seashore with a couple of palm trees somewhere in view, but regardless of the scene, those cards made me feel that the last place I would ever wish to see would be the Holy Land. Nothing could have been less appealing, susceptible though I was to the charms of antiquity. Incredibly, they even exerted an influence when, years later, I neglected more than one opportunity to visit Palestine; only at length, more or less by accident, to find myself there; to find a beauty, even a physical beauty, that nothing had led me to expect; and most astonishing of all, as I looked upon scenes pictured on those Sunday School cards of anything but fond memory—Bethany and Jerusalem, Jericho and the River Jordan, the Sea of Galilee, and the Garden of Gethsemane—, to find a Bible, intolerably boring as it had been taught in Sunday School and prosily presented in Church, now so revitalized that for the first time I began to read it in earnest, discovering in it, not a book to be worshipped, yet nonetheless—as millions before me had and would after me—the most fascinating and glorious book in the world.

When Sunday School was over, I would watch from the doorway of the Sunday School building until Papa and Mama came into sight, starting up the long brick walk from the street. Joining them at the church steps, I would follow them into the bare-walled vestibule where a formidable array of black-coated elders stood ready to welcome all arrivals with a sort of subdued jocularity, a hearty shake of the hand for a newcomer, an encouraging pressure on the arm for any less regular member of the congregation who might appear unexpectedly.

Mama would enter our pew first, then I, and next my timid little sister May who would snuggle close to Papa in his seat next the aisle. Harry would be with other cadets from the Hill, who sat together somewhere in the rear, under the choir loft. Our pew was one of a double row which ran through the center of the church, with its two aisles, its row of pews on each side under the windows, and its opposite amen corners in front, flanking the pulpit, below which, on separate pedestals, stood the two sumptuous bouquets always furnished by Colonel Perez Dickinson from his gardens or green-houses at Island Home.

Before services began, on the rare occasions when we were early and there were only a few other people at wide distances apart as yet in their seats, my eyes would wander through the great empty spaces around us, and with the dark wood of the pews, their deep-red cushions, the hush that pervaded the whole church, and in the subdued light which sifted through the tall narrow windows whose stained glass was without strong color or pronounced design—in this brief and blessed interval the Second Presbyterian Church came near to fulfilling the idea of a "sanctuary" that had been gradually forming in my mind. Something far down inside me stirred then. But I responded, I confess, if less deeply, yet with keen interest, when a few moments later stately matrons in the sober elegance of their silks and satins, velvet and furs, in bonnets and hats bearing plumes and birds, or ribbons and flowers, according to season, poured now into the church in rapid succession, accompanied by charmingly dressed young girls and portly frock-coated gentlemen emitting a faint scent of bay rum or Florida Water.

With the Easter parade not yet established in our nation as an annual fashion display with religious undertones, here was a parade, every Sunday. When the congregation poured out of church at the close of services the church steps would be surrounded by young men who had hurried from every other church in town not to miss the spectacle, while to observe the parade at a more respectful distance many had gathered in knots along the brick walk leading down to the street, for the Second Presbyterian Church was, indubitably, in the '80s and '90s, whatever its worldly status since, Knoxville's most fashionable church.

True, this church was often referred to as the "Northern Presbyterian Church," as it was a member of the Northern Presbytery, and many of its congregation were of Northern descent or had been Union sympathizers. There were of course prominent families who attended St. John's. There were Whites and other descendants of early settlers, strong adherents to the Confederacy, unbending in their pride though many of them impoverished now, who went to the old *First* Presbyterian Church, almost as old as the town itself. At least one family of social prominence attended the showy new red-brick Baptist Church on Gay Street and some of the contemporary elite the Southern Methodist Church. But the preponderance of Knoxville's wealth and fashion in the Knoxville of the day would be found in the Second Presbyterian Church. Here were most of those "merchant princes" who had made their fortunes in coal and lumber and marble, in wholesale drugs and dry goods, groceries and hardware. Among the pillars of the church there were, I have not forgotten, the Lynns, a large family of modest means, no pretensions, and across whose plain kindly faces was written *God's Own*. But there were no seedy persons in the church, no shabby ones—no poor folks.

It was not, however, when the Lynns began to file into the pew they occupied under the west windows, across the aisle from our own, that I emerged from my earlier dreamy state and centered my gaze on the aisle farther away. I had a feeling that the Doxology itself, through some sort of maneuvering behind the scenes, would be held up, if need be, until Colonel Dickinson, the Temples, and the Armstrongs were in their pews.

In the days I remember best, usually Colonel Dickinson was the first of them to arrive. Pink-faced, corpulent, and benign, leaning on his gold-headed cane, limping a little, he would advance slowly toward his pew, somewhat forward of the center of the church, and with his valet, a tall, straight, broad-shouldered mulatto, following closely behind. Once in his pew, the Colonel would dispose his vast bulk in its inside corner, his valet would carefully place the Colonel's foot with a gouty toe on the plush cushion underneath, and then retreat, marching back up the aisle with great dignity. As I looked at the back of Colonel Dickinson's round snowy head rising above the velvet collar on his black broad-cloth coat, I wondered why, if he was as iniquitous as people said, the Second Presbyterian Church paid him such honor.

I seldom dwelt lengthily, however, on the matter for, as nearly always happened, the Temples, who had the next pew but one behind his, would arrive shortly after Colonel Dickinson and to see them advance majestically down the aisle—father, mother, and with an interval between, their middle-aged daughter, Miss Mary—was to begin to feel I was at a play.

These were the Temples who had lived for a few years in the beautiful suburban estate now the property of the widow O'Conner; the Temples who, by changing its previous name to Melrose, in honor of Mrs. Temple's Scotch mother, had contrived to convey even to their contemporaries in Knoxville the completely erroneous impression that it had been the ancestral home of the Temples. These were the Temples after whom an attractive residential street in West End had been named;[1] and who lived now in an old red-brick corner house on Cumberland Street, only a block from Gay and opposite Pryor Brown's Livery Stable—a fine house in its day, but for all that it opened directly on the street, yet with its tall chimneyed but windowless Colonial wall at either end, a disorderly garden at the rear enclosed by a tall board fence, and its generally unlived-in air, as uninviting a house from the outside as you could find then in town.

A busy-browed, glum man, smooth-shaven and stiff as a ramrod, Judge Temple would stand at the entrance to his pew till his tall dour-faced wife, plumes tossing on her poke bonnet, took her seat. Then their daughter, who had been to Vassar, with a leisurely swish of her heavy moiré skirts, and her head wagging slightly, patronizingly, from side to side, like an automaton, would make her own regal advance toward the family pew—regal despite the fact that, though somewhat above medium height and of matronly figure, she walked with a waddle.

Even to see Mary Temple was hardly to believe her, and although I saw her often through the years, saw her in the setting of her own imposing if dingy home, in countless other social settings, served with her on many a committee for this or that, yet always she was herself, pompous, drawling, inordinately affected, simpering at times—preposterous.

A sort of elephantine coyness characterized her manner when gentlemen—gentlemen desirable to impress—were present, and in her slit-like mouth, and the glassy stare from her protuberant, uncomprehending eyes, there was a certain cruel though inescapable batrachian suggestion.

When I first gazed spell-bound, at this grotesque and incredible woman, who, like Mrs. Aiken, was to wield no small influence, such as it was, over the Knoxville cosmos of her day, I was so fascinated that the mere sight of her there was almost sufficient inducement to make me endure the endless tedium of Sunday morning

Mary Boyce Temple.

services at the Second Presbyterian Church. She was like a drawing by Cruikshank,[2] one of those hilarious caricatures of Dickens' characters which enlivened his novels. Even more she was like "The Dame of Rank" which Thomas Rowlandson portrays in *The English Dance of Death*, a work among my parents' books whose illustrations in color I had pored over with delight before I could read. It was only long afterwards, when I first saw Goya's portraits of the Court of Charles IV of Spain in the Prado at Madrid, that it came to me (with Knoxville always somewhere in the back of my thoughts) that here was a painter, one who refused to gloss the truth, to flatter even royalty, and if a king was a fool, for all the ribbons and stars arrayed on his royal breast, made him a fool—here was an artist who could have conveyed to posterity, under her resplendent raiment, her furbelows, her monumental pretentiousness, her smirking aplomb, the real Mary Temple.

On the pages of the *History of Knox County*, where Mary Temple's wan effigy appears, in biographical form, along with other Knoxville worthies, purged of all human weaknesses, nothing could be more misleading than the classification of her as a "welfare worker." Entirely accurate, on the other hand, is its statement, "Many interesting legends cluster around Miss Temple and her social reign."[3] The work refrains, however, from mentioning the nature of the legends. It may be told now, I make bold to think, that if Miss Temple failed to add to the gayety of nations, at least throughout most of her long lifetime, her fatuities added to the gayety of Knoxville. No gathering there was ever so dead that it did not spring to life with the latest story, true or invented, about Mary Temple. She was, in a word, Knoxville's perennial laughing-stock.

But her full flowering came only after her grim parents both had been laid in Old Gray; when, with a substantial fortune, she became mistress now, and sole occupant of the dreary, grubby cold house on West Cumberland where, first and last, she entertained innumerable visiting big-wigs, entertained with an ostentation in sharp contrast to the miserly inner workings of her ménage, for which she had early become famous.[4] It was told—one of hundreds of tales—that to save on the number of chickens she must provide, she would have the chicken salad for her parties made in two batches; one entirely of white meat, the other of dark, and that in her serving pantry, for the guidance of William, her wizened faithful old Negro butler, she posted a list of guests to whom the salad made from the breast of the chicken was to be served, with the less choice variety allotted to guests of less social or financial prominence.

It was generally believed, from the languishing looks she lavished upon him when they were seen together at receptions or other affairs, that Miss Mary would have liked to marry Colonel Tom Williams (grandfather of present-day playwright Tennessee Williams). During the '90s there was much speculation on the subject. A widower with two attractive daughters, of distinguished appearance and manners, a member of the Knoxville bar, a wit, a raconteur, a *bon vivant*, a man of elegant and expensive tastes, Colonel Tom was possessed of almost everything except an adequate income, and encouraged in the idea by his cronies at the Cumberland Club (Knoxville's first "gentleman's club")[5] with whom he whiled away his afternoons playing poker and imbibing Scotch and soda, Miss Temple seemed the perfect solution for his situation. Accordingly, every afternoon he would have the definite intention of going around to Miss Mary's, only two or three blocks away, and proposing to her. Thoroughly mellowed now, he would pick up his hat and cane, muster his courage, make a start, yet before he reached his destination his heart would fail him.

This story was very likely purely a concoction of convivial spirits at the Cumberland Club, though no story touching Miss Temple was so improbable that it fell short of wide circulation.

In these expansive years (some forty of them) she traveled extensively, as the annals of the East Tennessee Historical Society correctly states, and years after I had seen the last of Knoxville, of Mary Temple and the more sycophantish elements in Knoxville society, the toadies and tuft-hunters, for whom, with all her absurdities, her home had become an unrivalled center—in these later years I would meet people here, there, everywhere, in Europe or in this country, who, if I happened to mention Knoxville, would say, ruminatingly, "Knoxville . . . Why, *we* met a woman from Knoxville—." Perhaps they had met her at our embassy in London, our embassy in Rome; perhaps at White Sulphur,[6] or in Washington, where she was wont, toward the end of her life to entertain Congressmen, Senators, and minor representatives of the diplomatic corps with luncheons at the Willard; but wherever it was they had met her, an identical smile arose in their eyes, lurked around a corner of their lips, as they pondered: "Miss . . . ? Let's see . . . what was her name?" and always I could supply the name.

But at church when I was still in my early teens, Mary Temple afforded me a measure of comic relief while I waited, a feeling of boredom already creeping over me, for the sermon that must shortly begin.

There were still the Armstrongs, however, with their pew between Colonel Dickinson's and the Temples', more often late than not, but whom I hailed with a burst of joy in my heart when they finally appeared, although sometimes this was not until the congregation with an all-enveloping rustle (a sound, bringing the inevitable nearer, which never failed to depress me), were on their feet and starting to sing with mingled complacency and resounding fervor:

Praise God, from whom all blessings flow.[7]

When the Armstrongs were late, supposedly it was because, as frequently occurred, their carriage had stuck in the mud and had to be pulled out on their way into town from their plantation, which was on Kingston Pike and extended for some miles, on both sides, along the river. The islands in the river were theirs too. It was on the islands they raised their finest melons and had buried their silver—pieces they valued most—during the War, to keep the Yankees from getting them. Their home, Bleak House,[8] a mansion with a tower, overlooking the river and all the plantation, had been General Longstreet's[9] headquarters during the siege of Knoxville. Minié balls were imbedded in its walls and in the big square rosewood piano in the drawing-room. In the ball-room above, with its prism chandeliers and fire-place at either end, great log fires roared on nights when the Armstrongs were giving balls—those balls where, as at all the Armstrong parties, such superlative food and drink were served as nowhere else even in a region famed then for its food and drink—balls where on cold winter nights not only ladies and gentlemen in ball-room attire but their Negro coachmen waiting outside were kept so bountifully supplied with hot rum punch that, according to report, often when guests, on leaving, were ready to enter their carriages, they would find their coachmen beyond the point of being able to handle the horses on the drive back to town, if even in shape to mount the box. Wild tales, during the '80s, as long before and long afterwards, were told of the Armstrongs and the royal scale on which they entertained, and whatever of fable may have entered into these stories, yet beyond the peradventure of a doubt, there was never, in its great days, any cheese-paring either in the ante-bellum brick-paved basement kitchen at Bleak House, or in the more modern one which, in later years, supplemented it on the floor above.

They were exciting people, these Armstrongs. They drew me as the moon the tides. They had about them, one and all, the seigniorial air of a family long accustomed to landed grandeur, yet at the same time were singularly free from any suggestion of smugness, far less of stuffiness. In a picture of her that dominates all others in my mind I see Mrs. Armstrong scuttling, I might call it, for her movements were habitually rapid and her carriage none too erect, into her accustomed inside seat in the Armstrong pew. Always, on Sunday, elegantly though quietly clad in black, there was nonetheless something saucy about her. That she was a bit of a madcap could be read into her looks as she flashed her black eyes, as sharp as her tongue was known to be, around her once or twice before settling herself in her corner and reaching for the hymn-book in the rack in front of her. Save for her nose which, though well-shaped, was a trifle too prominent, she would have ranked as one of the great beauties of her day. As it was, many considered her so when, as Louise Franklin, an outstanding belle, the motherless sixteen year old daughter of a rich planter in Cocke County,[10] she had come down to Knoxville on a visit and captured its most eligible bachelor, Robert Houston Armstrong, some twenty years her senior.[11] As the dashing young mistress of Bleak House during the War, afraid of no horse or man that ever lived, she had been the toast of both armies, and to the end of her life carried with her that *je ne sais quoi* of women who have had more than ordinary attraction for men.

Now she was still in her heyday, and although Colonel Armstrong had reached his sixties, with his ruddy complexion, his snow-white hair, side-burns and moustache, a tall courtly figure in an Inverness cape, he seemed the perfect foil as he

Louise Franklin Armstrong.

Robert Houston Armstrong (ca. 1890).

followed her into their pew. From his bearing you might have mistaken him for a retired military man. In reality, he had never been a soldier. His title, like Colonel Dickinson's, was purely complimentary. Yet he was by no means without distinction. The kindliest of men, he was also the most gallant. Moreover, he was a man of markedly cultivated tastes and scholarly inclinations. In his leisure (and the truth is, save for a few orders he issued from the back porch to the overseer of his plantation, his life was completely one of leisure), he would paint (many of his paintings once hung in Bleak House), play the flute, compose Latin poems, read the classics—Ovid, Marcus Aurelius, Plato.

To his wife, extremely active and efficient, and though not without appreciation herself of the fine things in literature and the arts in general, yet the nature of her elderly husband's pursuits amused, if it did not, as some surmised, actually irk her. She was determined, at all events, that he should not take himself too seriously, and with the rather raffish streak of humor that was in her, would announce to a group of guests, in his presence, "When Colonel Armstrong dies, I'm going to have engraved on his tomb-stone: 'Here lies a man who never did a lick of work in his life.'"[12]

She delighted to shock him even more, if possible, than she delighted to shock others, and abhorring prigs, was even a bit resentful, it appeared, that he indulged in none of the Southern gentleman's legendary vices. Notwithstanding that he had brought a wine-grower all the way from Switzerland to have charge of his vineyards, and that he entered as fully as his high-spirited wife into the gay parties they gave, yet he was very abstemious himself, preferring, quite frankly, lemonade or buttermilk, not only to wines made on his plantation from special grapes, but to the imported vintages with which the wine-cellar at Bleak House was stored and which he dispensed so liberally to his guests.

It was in this connection, and not entirely in jest one may guess, that Mrs. Armstrong had told some of her cronies (willing no doubt for them to repeat it, as they promptly did) that she wanted her son Bob,[13] whatever else he became, not to turn out a milk-sop. A mere lad and in Bingham's Military School in North Carolina at the time, she wanted him, she declared, when he grew up, to drink, swear, gamble—be a *man*! And according to all accounts, the son, an only one, and now a young man, was by way of fulfilling even the wildest dreams his mother had ever entertained in regard to his future.

He drank, swore, gambled—that was the least of it.

After returning from school in North Carolina and a few restless terms on the Hill, at his parents' behest he had accompanied an older sister to Washington where she was to study painting at the Corcoran Art Gallery and he was to act as her escort and protector.[14] But quickly bored by these polite responsibilities and having exhausted the sights of the Capitol, he took to hanging around the office of the Commissioner of Indian Affairs. Here reports were coming in daily from Dakota Territory, where the Sioux Indians, many of whom, or their fathers, had fought only a few years before in the battle of Little Big Horn, were threatening fresh trouble. This set the blood of young Armstrong on fire. He applied for a job, any job, that would take him into the heart of the present Indian disturbance. And no sooner had he delivered his sister Adelia back safely at Bleak House than, to the dismay of his parents, a document arrived from the Department of the Interior appointing him to a post on the Cheyenne River Indian Agency in Dakota Territory[15] and ordering him to proceed thence at once. There, for all their efforts to persuade him to return home, all the inducements they held out, he remained for five years. There was even, during this time, a rumor that he intended to marry a Sioux, a half-breed, as one of his Dakota friends had done, a young lieutenant lately out of West Point and stationed at Fort Bennett, on the border of the Indian Reservation.

But whatever the rumors, one thing became certain; their son and heir was even more of a problem to the Armstrongs after his return from the Indian country than before he had left.

After five years in the saddle, his hunting knife, his six-shooter, always thrust through his belt, rifle across his saddle-bow; after learning to speak the Sioux language fluently, coming and going freely in countless teepees, pursuing buffalo across the boundless prairie in company with his "Sioux brothers"—Spotted Eagle, Little Bull, Crazy Horse; after feasting on stewed dog with Turning Heart, Swift Bird, Hunts the Enemy; and, at the other extreme, at the imminent peril of his life,

Robert Franklin Armstrong.

helping break up those Indian ceremonial dances which the United States government had prohibited as too inflammatory—after years of this, Bleak House, the plantation, any social gayeties Knoxville could offer, seemed tame indeed. Even the fifty-thousand acres in the Great Smokies owned by his grandfather, Drury Paine Armstrong, banker and planter, whose plantation, Crescent Bend, adjoined their own—the mountains where he had hunted deer and bear in his earlier youth and shared the primitive life of the mountaineers were no lure for him now.

A few months at home and he was off on a bicycle tour of England and Scotland; then shortly abroad again for a tour of the Continent with his mother; and following that a year's stay in Paris, where presumably he was pursuing studies of some sort, but in reality only a final attempt, everyone believed, on his parents' part, to wean him from his love of what was literally then the Wild West, from the Sioux, for whom he had formed a strong attachment, and a semi-savage existence which he had reveled in.

This was the era in our national history when Europe was considered the cure for every ill which might afflict a wealthy well-placed American family. But the Armstrongs' efforts along this line were later than the memorable Sunday when I caught my own first glimpse of the most talked of member of a much talked of family. He had only recently returned from Dakota Territory. Two store windows on Gay Street were filled with Indian war-clubs, pipes, moccasins, spoons carved from buffalo horns, head-dresses of eagle feathers—all manner of trophies, which he had brought back, among them a ghost-cloth, that elaborately-beaded skin of a young deer which the Sioux spread on the ground beside their dead with food for the journey to the next world, and attracting even more attention, an Indian painting of such rare artistry as to be destined ultimately for the Smithsonian Institute.

On the particular Sunday which comes back to me now with extraordinary vividness, Mrs. Armstrong had reached her accustomed seat in church, with Colonel Armstrong, in his Inverness cape, following in his stately manner, and there in the aisle stood for an instant, quite at ease, waiting to enter, this dare-devil of dare-devils, their erratic and picturesque son, a tall, broad-shouldered, slim-hipped, virile yet graceful figure in a dark suit, not dandified, but wearing his clothes well (a man who would be as at home in his opera hat as in fringed buckskin racing his cow pony across the Dakota plains), and his hair, with a just perceptible wave, so light you could see why the Indians had named him Tow Head. He had, so people said, his mother's devastating wit, and his nose, like hers, was prominent, though better suited to his man's face than to hers, and a balance for the extremely sensitive, almost tender mouth he had inherited from the old Colonel, hidden, in his father's case, by a flowing moustache, but which, exposed in his own, and combined with his vivid blue eyes, his conspicuously Saxon coloring, might have given a faintly feminine cast to his open, smooth-shaven youthful face, save for the prow-like nose. I see him before me at this moment as I write. He was not exactly handsome, but he was above everything else very much a man.

My heart gave a leap. Suddenly the stiffly-patterned dim interior of the Second Presbyterian Church was filled with a glow not there before. How startled I would have been had some voice whispered that in future years the life of this man would be intricately interwoven with my own.

By now I was fifteen. I was going with cadets, going to hops on the Hill. Yet I was forced to reflect that this was no young boy. He would never throw a glance my way. This was a returned hero, a polished young man of the world; with his father's chivalrous air despite his years among the Sioux—a young man going around with girls who had been out a season or two, taking them to Staub's Opera House, the races, here and there.

All the same, my heart was beating fast. There was a great tumult within me. But outwardly meek, I sat up straight between Mama and Papa, trying to drown out with my thoughts the sound of the minister's voice, with its affected ministerial quaver, one of the sounds in church I disliked most. I thought about Bob Armstrong and Bleak House. . . .

The minister's voice went on and on but I had little notion of what he was saying. In the ten years, in truth, that I was to listen almost continuously to his sermons, nothing he said ever made more than a momentary impression, if it even reached me at all.

This was the minister who had followed Dr. Scott[16] (with whom I had had such brief contact, but the first minister I had ever thought of as primarily a human being). Short and plump, the present incumbent,[17] with a genial, if impersonal, expression on his round, rubicund face, and with twinkling, sometimes swimming, eyes, was a rather jolly looking little man. In the later years of his incumbency his drinking habits were freely discussed, even among his congregation. He was said to have been seen on several occasions, once coming out of a hotel on Gay Street, in a state of advanced intoxication. But his congregation in general preferred to disbelieve, or disregard, these stories. In any event, it may be said in his defense, if one be needed, that he probably indulged in drink to no greater extent than the average clergyman of British extraction, who took his port, his sherry, his whiskey toddy, in moderation, and as a matter of course. It is indubitably true, at any rate, that none of the *joie de vivre* ascribed to him ever got into his sermons, which followed the "good" Presbyterian pattern, not only free from sensationalism, but from dynamic appeal of any sort, sermons than which, at the time, I could not have imagined any more tiresome except for those when he went on vacation and the pulpit was filled by one of the Bachmans, a family that supplied a number of parsons to East Tennessee, and this one, if I remember correctly, Dr. Nathan Bachman,[18] with a long stringy brown beard, a saintly man, but with a dry and droning voice and his discourses so utterly devoid of light and warmth as to have destroyed any incipient interest I might ever have had in orthodox institutionalized religion.

It was not the sermons, however, to which, after all, I need pay little attention, but communion service which I dreaded most in the Second Presbyterian Church. On a Sunday when I entered church and noticed, inescapably, that the communion table beneath the pulpit was shrouded in a thick white cloth, instantly a feeling of revulsion swept through my whole body. I did not know then that the custom of eating bread sacramentally as the body of a god had its origin in savagery, long before Christ, but I knew that I was never so acutely miserable as when the whole church was permeated with the drowsy fermentative odor of wine arising from "the Lord's Supper," an odor heavy with the suggestion at once of sin, of death and the tomb. I knew that I was never so deeply disturbed as when I glanced sideways at Mama's bowed head, her face dark, withdrawn, and as if she were gazing into depths, invisible to me, but which the light of the sun would never reach. I watched her nibble at the small white square of communion bread in her gloved hand and crumbs of which, it seemed to me, from the movements of her throat, she swallowed with an effort. I saw why Papa left before all this began, and I longed to get away myself, out of this gloom, this morbid atmosphere, out again under the cheerful sky—anywhere else.

But however unimpressed I was by the devotional aspects of religion as I observed them in church and Sunday School, however unreceptive and insensitive to them, even so, strange as it may seem, I was intensely interested in religion, a subject that none of the romantic or purely frivolous interests natural to my age ever crowded entirely out of my mind, whether I was sitting silently in church, or wherever I was.

Brought up in the happiest, most wholesome of homes, neither of my parents ever talked to their children about religion. But just as when Papa discussed European, and especially German, affairs with our neighbor on Clinch Street from Hesse-Darmstadt, or talked with the Bauers about strikes and what he felt were, at the time, in this country, the legitimate grievances of labor, I would give rapt attention to every word they said, however engrossed I seemed to be in something else, so it was that at home, from almost as far back as I can remember, I would sit a little apart, a book in my hands, and if my father was discussing religion with an old friend from New York or London who was visiting us, I would cock my ears. It was thus I became gradually aware that while my father and his close and congenial friends accepted the teachings of the New Testament as a guide to human conduct, they rejected the doctrines of the Christian Church. I became clearly aware also that regarding, as they did, the primary purpose of religion as the achievement of the good life, they found it more persuasive when lived than preached; thought little of lip-faith and lip-service, believed that love of Christ and his teachings was by no means inconsistent with independence of formal religion.

I have said that my parents never talked to their children about religion, but that is not strictly accurate. There were two religious subjects Papa, at least, had no hesitation in broaching—God and Hell. At a very early age he gave us to understand that the "fires of Hell" were not "real flames"; that if you did wrong, you had to suffer for it, but that God would never condemn anyone to *everlasting* punishment because, if so, God would not be as good, as just and merciful, as even a good man. Papa, I suspect, while he might rationalize God as a spirit, never quite rid himself of the idea of an anthropomorphic God. In any case, he looked upon him as a wholly beneficent being and did not propose that his children should ever be saddled with the God of orthodoxy.

For a good many years, however, in spite of my father's attempts to condition his children against traditional impressions of God that were still widely prevalent, and though the Sunday School card might carry, imprinted on it brightly as the Golden Text, "God is Love," yet God remained to me as an extraordinarily tyrannic, disagreeable, bearded old man who must be eternally wheedled and cajoled. But, at all events, I merely disliked God. I suffered no terror at the thought of him, as none at the thought of Hell, while Heaven, pictured with golden-haired angels in beautiful flowing garments of rainbow hues, arrayed around the throne of God, playing harps and viols, and with nothing else apparently to do, offered no attraction whatever. Getting to Heaven or avoiding Hell, I may say in sum, and without the slightest equivocation, are the last things that have concerned me throughout my life.

But if never, at any time, was I to be tortured with doubts about the Hereafter, if Heaven and Hell, particularly Hell, long before I was fifteen were, to me, completely dead issues, they were extremely live ones, in the '80s and '90s, to a large part of the population of Knoxville. A Hell of literal fire and brimstone was still being preached then in many of its churches, while the town periodically was shaken to its foundations by revivals and revivalists. Even Barnum's circus—"white elephant" and all—did not call out the enormous crowds (riff-raff, illiterates, semi-literates, people of social position and some pretensions to refinement and culture—all classes) who flocked to hear Sam Jones, like Billy Sunday a first-rate showman, and the most popular of the evangelists who came to Knoxville.[19]

The meetings where Sam Jones poured forth his fiery diatribes on sin and sinners would go on for a whole week without even standing room in the great tent where they were held; with nothing talked about anywhere but who had gone up to the Mourners' Bench, "got religion," shouted, shrieked (the terrific tumult could be heard a block or two away), who had wept, had hysterics, or fainted and been carried out; and with only one voice, so far as I ever knew, raised openly against all these orgiastic proceedings, the voice of Mrs. Lizzie Crozier French, that stout-hearted little Knoxvillian who never failed to come out in her calm, outspoken fashion against religious bigotry and fanaticism in any form, and who had replied to some of her women acquaintances urging her with tears in their eyes, even sobs, to attend these "great meetings" of Sam Jones: "But why should we look for Christian leadership to a man who lacks the two prime requisites of Christianity—charity and humility?"

After a Sam Jones revival and the frenzied wave of Puritanism with which it was accompanied had spent itself, quite soon the card-players, dancers, theatre-goers, would go back to their card-playing, dancing, theatre-going, but while the town was still immersed in this delirium, *I* had problems, too.

Mary Gaines—almost all the girls I knew, went to revivals, went either through fear of what others would say if they failed to show up, lest their own "salvation" might perchance be at stake, or because of the rousing spectacle provided, with excitement running as high as ever at a bull-fight in a provincial town in Spain. Mary would beg me to go with her, but lacking the courage of Mrs. French, I did not speak out. I made specious excuses, often hard pressed to think one up, for not going. I would sooner, I think, at the age I was then, have died than to seem to the boys and girls I associated with in any way "different," so I kept my burgeoning ideas on the subject of religion to myself.

It would be some years yet until I knew Whitman, restorer, as William James put it, of the eternal natural religion—"the religion of healthy mindedness," and it would be even longer until the fateful moment when reading George Sand's *In-*

timate Journal,[20] I came upon the passage which thenceforth would give my own thoughts on religion their permanent direction:

God is not a force outside us. He is the sun and the stars and the gold in the chalice. He is the bread. He is all the elements of the earth. He is the heart of man; and all men, with all their yearnings and fortunes, are in Him. He is the universal Spirit. He reveals Himself in man. He is I and I am He.[21]

Neither had I come yet to look upon religion—all religions, as fundamentally symbolic myths. But I was no longer dependent largely, if not solely, on candid overheard conversations between my father and his friends for my religious convictions. I was dipping now into all sorts of books I found lying on our library table in the Barnes house, or on the shelves in our book-cases. No salacious ones were there, not even a classic like the *Decameron*, but there were the works of Huxley, Darwin, and Tyndal[e], of Voltaire, Gibbon's *Decline and Fall of the Roman Empire*, and Renan's *Life of Jesus*,[22] that beautiful but explosive work which, not only in France but in the entire Western world, had been the great literary and philosophical event of the '60s, and the name of whose author was still execrated, now in the '80s, among the orthodox; a work which insisted that every man was entitled to his own definition of God and which presented Jesus, with all his divine compassion, yet not as the gentle, joyless, often anaemic [*sic*] Jesus of portraits that hung on the walls of Sunday School rooms, pictured on the Sunday School cards, the Jesus of sermons beyond counting, but as a dynamic personality—a thorough revolutionary. On the same shelf with Renan there was, too, another of the hotly discussed books of the 19th Century, Charles Hennell's *Inquiry Concerning the Origin of Christianity*,[23] the book that made so profound an impression on George Eliot that she had rejected in her twenties and never returned to a Christianity that meant, not the wisdom of Jesus, not the inspiration of his example, but that system of belief invented by a succession of theological committees during the four centuries following his death.

None of these books in the family library had ever been urged upon any of us as we were growing up, though neither had they been forbidden. They were simply there. We could read them, if we chose to. Looking at the matter, retrospectively, I can only conclude that my father's ideas of education, education beyond the elementary stage, were closely in tune with those of the yet unborn Dr. Robert Maynard Hutchins as president of the University of Chicago—that it should be a process not of "settling" students' minds, but of *unsettling* them, if their horizons were to be widened, their intellects inflamed.

Certain it is that no mind ever took more kindly to this type of education than my own. The books I was reading now, on my own initiative, were furnishing me the most joyously exciting experience I had ever known. An instinctive rebel, it would seem, I was primed then, when it appeared, for Mrs. Humphry Ward's[24] *Robert Elsmere*, a closely reasoned attack on evangelical religion published in this country in 1888, selling nearly a million copies here after creating an unparalleled furore in England, where it had agitated bishops, set cabinet ministers at bitter variance, and called forth from Gladstone, then Prime Minister, his famous answer, "'Robert Elsmere' and the Battle of Belief."[25]

Granddaughter of the celebrated Dr. Arnold of Rugby, sister of the poet and critic, Matthew Arnold, aunt of Julian and Aldous Huxley;[26] from a family of scholars and eminent educators, Mrs. Ward had been brought up in Oxford, in an atmosphere of scholarship, skepticism, and inquiry, and in *Robert Elsmere* wrote a book which, dramatizing the intellectual tendencies of her generation, shook the literary world of the day—a time of new ferment in English thought—as had Renan's *Life of Jesus* twenty years before.

It was to Mrs. Humphry Ward's generation that Papa and Mama belonged. I noted the more than ordinary absorption they both showed in this novel, and when one or the other of them laid it down, picked it up. A novel of some six hundred pages of fine print, completely humorless, and with none of the robust and rollicking appeal I had found in Dickens or Thackeray, the penetrating power of George Eliot in delineating the characters that people her books, yet this story of the rector of an English country parish who resigned his orders because he could no longer accept the creed of the Church of England, gripped me as no book I had come upon heretofore.

I shall always be able to see and feel that Spring when I read *Robert Elsmere.* It was in late February, or March perhaps. Spring comes early in Knoxville. After school, if Mama had gone shopping or to the dressmaker's, I would pick out a more or less secluded spot in the side yard, seat myself on the ground, and read feverishly. The air was full of the smell of new-turned earth from the garden behind me which had just been spaded. The faint, sweetish, slightly suffocating scent of plum blossoms reached me from the plum trees, now a drift of powdery white, along our back fence. Crocuses twinkled in the grass along the narrow brick walk that led to the side gate where Trix, her fore-paws planted on top, always waited at this hour for Harry's whistle as he came from the Hill. Red birds were singing madly and if I lifted my eyes for an instant they were met by the sign of flaming bushes of flowering quince and long golden nodding rows of daffodils in the Aults' yard across the street.

There was one of these afternoons I remember particularly. Never had I been so filled with the rapturous joy just of living, breathing, and somehow all this fresh revelation of the beauty and wonder of the world seemed to connect itself quite naturally with the excitement, the unbounded joy, I was drinking in from *Robert Elsmere*. To this day, in fact, the special slightly rank scents, the sights, sounds, of early Spring in the Mid-South never fail to bring back to me some of the mingled emotions, the ecstasy, of those hours when I was reading a book which would mark a definite mile-stone in my life.

If I was not consciously in search of a faith, nonetheless I had found one. Like millions of others then, Americans, British, Continentals, who refused to accept religious or other opinions simply because they were held by most of the people around them, I resented, I resisted with all the small might I possessed, the vengeful, petty God of the Old Testament, that monster of Judaism, yet I wished to retain Jesus—a Jesus my reason would let me believe in. Renan had been reassuring in his insistence that Jesus can not be looked upon as belonging exclusively to those who call themselves his disciples, but that he is the common honor of all who share a common humanity. But here, in *Robert Elsmere*, it was all put in a form for me to grasp more readily, more surely, as tense in every fibre of my being, I followed its hero, grappling, in agony of spirit, with the problem of ridding himself of the deeply incrusted ideas of Jesus he had inherited; struggling, heart-brokenly, with his devoted yet rigid-minded wife, Catherine, who held with obsessive fundamentalist fervor that if the Gospels were not true in fact, in history, they were not true at all; a hero who triumphed at last, if at the cost of his life, in the clear image which finally emerged from his years of anguished doubt, the image of a purely human Christ, the true Jesus of Nazareth, whose life had been wreathed in legend through the love of his first ignorant followers; not the Jesus disfigured and misrepresented by the churches, not the risen and ascended Jesus, but a Jesus in which God was manifested preeminently, as in all great souls, but not otherwise *in kind* than in himself, Robert Elsmere, and in all men—all sharing equally with Jesus the divine sonship, and with nature and man the continuing and only revelation of an Eternal Goodness, an Eternal Mind.

It was *Robert Elsmere* that made me see, too, that stories in the Gospels, such as the raising of Lazarus, the exquisite fable of the Resurrection, if not true in the historical sense, were still full of poetical truth, of *true* truth; that if Jesus of Nazareth never existed, yet love of Jesus remains "resurrection and life," that you can not escape him, his life and death underlying, as they do, our institutions as the alphabet our literature; and that as every great religion is a concentration of great ideas, capable of infinite expansion and adaptation, the special task of our own age was to re-conceive a Christ whose story from the beginning had been obscured by error.

Many puzzling matters seemed to be clearing up as I sat on the grass, impatient of interruption, rushing through *Robert Elsmere*. Far away from West End and Clinch Street on one of these afternoons, my mind seething, I was suddenly aware of Mary Gaines coming around the corner of the house from our front gate. With her tall lithe figure, gypsy beauty, devil-may-care way of carrying herself, audacious way of speaking, she usually captured me on the instant. Mary was still a potent influence in my life.

"What you readin'?" she called out, as she came striding toward me.

I jumped up from the ground but before I could answer she had snatched the book from my hands and was glancing at a page in it here and there.

"What's it about?" she asked impatiently, her brow puckered.

"Oh, just about an English minister and his wife," I answered as off-handedly as I knew how.

"A *minister*—! Lordy!" Mary stared at me incredulously as she handed back the book.

The books we read in common, and with equal zest, were *Molly Bawn* and *Airy Fairy Lillian* [or *Lilian*] by "The Duchess,"[27] a popular Irish novelist of the day among writers of light, very light, fiction.

"Is it a love story?" Mary persisted, with just a shade of irritation in her voice. Why should I be reading anything so dull as a story about a minister and his wife?

"Well, sort of," I hedged. "There's a love story *in* it—"

I felt a little embarrassed, a bit disloyal. But I could never tell Mary Gaines what *Robert Elsmere* was about. There was no one then in Knoxville, or anywhere else, with whom I could, or wanted to, talk about "religion," religion as it was gradually taking shape in my own mind. This was my secret life.

When I contemplate those long past days when already my inner, hidden life was at wide variance with my light-hearted, irresponsible outer life, I understand of course better than at the time why I was unable to respond to the Second Presbyterian Church.

Santayana[28] has been quoted in regard to his own religion, Catholicism (which he has never ceased to follow after his own uniquely heretical fashion and in whose celebrations and sacraments he continues to find satisfaction), that it should not be judged as an institution based upon "the more or less hypothetical sayings of the alleged founder of Christianity, but as an expression the human spirit and an almost superhuman answer to the needs of the human heart."

Judging the Second Presbyterian Church, for the moment, by this standard, I am well aware that numberless men and women must have found in its services what their hearts sought. But be that as it may, it was not there—it was in a hundred different directions, I would find answers to the needs of my own. Only the mellowed exterior of this lovely old church in its setting of ancient oaks invariably gave a lift to my spirit. As for the sermons that poured from its pulpit, after seventeen years of almost continuous exposure to them, only two left a durable impression, and one of these, or a fragment of it, sticks in my mind, ironically, through the ludicrous note that was injected into it on a solemn occasion.

A memorial service was being held for President William McKinley, assassinated by the Polish anarchist, Czolgosz.[29] For some reason the service was not conducted by the pastor of the Second Church, but by Dr. James Park of the old First Presbyterian Church.

Dr. Park was in a class by himself among Knoxville parsons, a specimen of *homo Knoxvillianus* at its best. Though his father[30] had been born in Ireland, he himself was born, lived ninety years, and died in the same house (a rare occurrence in the United States), a plain red-brick L-shaped house on Cumberland, built in the 18th Century by John Sevier, first Governor of Tennessee,[31] still standing (1950) and open now to the public as typical of the large dwellings erected by wealthy builders in Knoxville in pioneer days.

At the time of which I write, with a long white beard, short and sturdy, and in his clerical black, Dr. Park was a familiar figure as he stumped around the neighborhood of his church or home, poking his cane playfully at this or that acquaintance, at children he met, sometimes at a complete stranger he thought he would like to know. Past eighty now, stories about him were legion. He had served as chaplain in the Confederate Army; nevertheless had discouraged his daughters when they wished to join the Daughters of the Confederacy. The War Between the States was over, he said. We were all one nation. Let us nourish no past bitterness. But his behavior in the pulpit was equally unpredictable. He would stop his sermon any Sunday, point his finger at girls on a back pew who were whispering to each other, or at any others he thought were not giving serious attention to his discourse, and admonish them by name. But he would always give a whimsical twist to this admonition, one that robbed it of its sting, sent a titter through his congregation, and knit the erring one to him more firmly than ever.

At the memorial service, as he drew to the close of his final and unconscionably lengthy prayer, he suddenly electrified his hearers by a plea in loud fervent tones for the President's assassin. "And, oh Lord, have mercy upon the soul of that miserable creature with the unpronounceable name!"

It was on a Sunday some years before this that the pulpit of the Second Church had been occupied by Julia Ward Howe, famous author of the "Battle Hymn of the Republic," and now approaching eighty. President of the New England Woman's Suffrage Association, Mrs. Howe had been brought to Knoxville, among a group of nationally known women interested in "Woman's Rights," through the efforts of Mrs. Lizzie Crozier French, an ardent suffragist herself, and as I have no hesitation in saying, then, and for long afterwards, Knoxville's most progressive citizen.

Although never ordained, Mrs. Howe had frequently preached in Unitarian churches, occasionally before other denominations. In opening her sermon, she explained with at once deep religious feeling and delicate sense of humor, that there was a time when women had had to leave church before benediction, because it was thought they had no souls, but now they were permitted to remain and *pronounce* benediction.[32]

Sitting in our family pew on this Sunday in the early nineties, dressed in deep mourning, when one tragedy after another had befallen our family and my personal world gone to pieces[33]—in one of the darkest hours of my life, when I had been for weeks past in seclusion, seeing almost no one, and only at the insistence of Mrs. French had come to hear Mrs. Howe, all at once the thick cloud in which I had been enveloped seemed to lift a little. I seemed to awaken from my stupor. This was to be none of those tedious sermons to which, bored and rebellious, I had listened so often. Never before had a voice so cultivated, so soft yet so clear and strong, so richly resonant, sounded through the Second Presbyterian Church.

This was the Julia Ward Howe who had written those smiting lines that had helped decide the fate of a nation:

Mine eyes have seen the glory of the coming of the Lord;
He is trampling out the vintage where the grapes of wrath are stored;
He hath loosed the fateful lightning of His terrible swift sword.

So old, so small, this was the woman, belonging to a wealthy and aristocratic family of New York and Newport, an attractive debutante at twenty, gayest of the gay, but who, with serious-mindedness and ambition underlying her gayety, had turned from her frivolous existence to an arduous life in the service of humanity, and now, a little old lady in black velvet, with a tiny ruched cap of white net on her snowy head, a bit of point lace and the gleam of diamonds at her throat—still a figure of worldly charm and distinction, but enchanting by the power of her character and spirit, her ineffable radiance—now was preaching that the aim of life is to learn, teach, serve, enjoy.

Never before had I received from this pulpit what might be called mental stimulus; what I considered a challenge.

But it was only toward the close of her sermon when her voice rose, still soft and musical, yet seeming to soar above and beyond the very church roof overhead, as she referred movingly to Raphael and Michelangelo, "who had died with their tools in their hands"—it was only then that I perceived for the first time in my life the nobility, the redeeming force, of work, of the task that, undertaken, must never be laid down.

I did not yet know it, but this little lady in black velvet with her marked and wrinkled but beautiful old face—it was she who set my feet on a path, a long hard path it proved, but a path. She who brought me to see that if all my roseate girlhood dreams had come to naught, if the world we had known as a family was gone, gone forever, nevertheless I could build a new one, of some sort. I did not have, it is true, the vaguest notion of how I was to build, how to start. But she had aroused my daimon, the will to work, to achieve, perhaps in a small way to serve, and as I went out of church, down the long brick walk to Clinch Street, I felt less confused than for a long time past. My heart was less like a stone.

NOTES

1. West End's Eighth Street (Knoxville's present-day Sixteenth Street) became Temple Avenue at its intersection with West Cumberland Avenue and extended to Circle Park. This formerly residential neighborhood has long since been taken over by the University of Tennessee campus in its westward expansion. What was once Temple Avenue has become part of Volunteer Boulevard, and the Torchbearer statue with its eternal flame stands at the entrance to Circle Park with McClung Museum on the right at the beginning of its circular drive and UT's combination Communications and Student Services Building along its back. The only residence which has survived is the home of General Lawrence D. Tyson, facing Volunteer Boulevard and separated from the massive John C. Hodges Library on Melrose Avenue. Tyson House, "encroached upon by dormitories, shorn of its balustrades, and minus one columned portico" (in the words of Betsey Beeler Creekmore in her book *Knoxville!,* 137), is now used by the University of Tennessee for the offices and meeting space of its Alumni Association.
2. George Cruikshank (1792–1878), English illustrator and caricaturist.
3. Rothrock, *French Broad-Holston Country,* 495.
4. In 1922 Mary Boyce Temple purchased a 1907 Queen Anne-style mansion at 623 W. Hill Avenue, where she lived and entertained until her death in 1929. The house, still standing on the northeast corner of Hill and Henley Street, is one of the last remaining structures in downtown Knoxville built to be a single-family home. Local architect Brian Pittman purchased the house, which had fallen into disrepair, in 2006 and has restored it to its original condition. Knox Heritage, "KH Invites Members to Tour Mary Boyce Temple House," http://www.knoxheritage.org/news/kh-invites-members-to-tour-mary-boyce-temple- house/; "Historic Downtown Knoxville Walking Tour: Temple-Pittman House (58)," http://www.knoxheritage.org/our-work/neighborhood-tours/historic-downtown-knoxville-walking-tour/temple-pittman-house/ (viewed September 26, 2020).
5. At the corner of Walnut Street and W. Clinch Avenue. Organized in 1892, the Cumberland Club originally met in the Doctor's Building at 601 Walnut Street. *Knoxville News,* Wednesday, April 12, 1922, p. 1.
6. Greenbrier resort at White Sulphur Springs, West Virginia.
7. Opening line of the Doxology.
8. Bleak House, named after Charles Dickens' novel, has been preserved as Confederate Memorial Hall (3148 Kingston Pike), home to Knoxville Chapter 89, United Daughters of the Confederacy. Deaderick, *Heart of the Valley,* 561–62. Creekmore, *Knoxville!,* 86.
9. Confederate General James Longstreet.
10. Louise (or Louisa) Franklin was the daughter of Lawson D. Franklin, considered to have been the first millionaire in the state of Tennessee. Her mother, Sarah Elizabeth B. (Rogers) Franklin, died in 1846, when Louise was only eight years old. The family

home, listed in the Register of Historic Places, was at Leadville (or Leadvale), near White Pine in Jefferson (not Cocke) County, Tennessee. National Register of Historic Places Digital Archive on NPGallery <npgallery.nps.gov/NRHP/>, Franklin, Lawson D., House, White Pine, Jefferson, Tennessee, National Register #73001796 (viewed July 25, 2017).

11. Robert Houston Armstrong (1825–1896) was twelve years older than Louise Franklin (1837–1910). They were married Dec. 9, 1856. "Tennessee, County Marriages, 1790–1950," database with images, *FamilySearch* (https://familysearch.org/ark:/61903/1:1:X8YJ-VNT : 21 December 2016), Robert H. Armstrong and Louise Franklin, 09 Dec 1856; citing , Jefferson, Tennessee, United States, Marriage, p. 224, Tennessee State Library and Archives, Nashville and county clerk offices from various counties; FHL microfilm 968,301 (accessed July 20, 2017).

12. Robert Houston Armstrong read law, in the same class with Oliver P. Temple, under the direction of the late Judge Robert J. McKinney and was admitted to the bar in 1846. In addition to managing his family's extensive property, he represented Knox County in the state legislature from 1855–1857 and 1859–1861. Oliver P. Temple, *Notable Men of Tennessee From 1833 to 1875: Their Times and Their Contemporaries*, comp. and arranged by Mary B. Temple (New York: Cosmopolitan Press, 1912), 13–14, 191; *Two Centuries of Knox County, Tennessee: A Celebration in Photographs* (Knoxville: McClung Historical Collection, 1992), 39.

13. Robert Franklin Armstrong (1864–1931).

14. His sister, Adelia Armstrong (1859–1931), became a well-known Knoxville artist. She married John Edwin Lutz in 1885, and they built their home, called Westwood, on the opposite side of Kingston Pike a little west of Bleak House on property given them by her father. Historic Westwood is now home to Knox Heritage, an organization that "works to preserve the structures and places with historic or cultural significance in Knox County, Tennessee." Knox Heritage Website, accessed July 26, 2017, http://knoxheritage.org/.

15. Dakota Territory, as created by Congress in 1861, included the present states of North and South Dakota and much of Wyoming and Montana. *Concise Dictionary of American History* (New York: Scribner's, 1962), 275.

16. Who lived in the former home of Horace Maynard.

17. The Rev. Dr. Robert R. Sutherland became pastor of Second Presbyterian Church in September 1887 and remained there until March 1896. He was later minister at Ramsey Memorial Church, also in Knoxville, beginning in 1898. Knoxville's Sutherland Avenue was named for him. Rule, *Standard History of Knoxville,* 429, 463; *Herald and Presbyter* 69, no. 28 (July 13, 1898): 16.

18. The Reverend Nathan Bachman was pastor at Second Presbyterian from 1865 until 1876, with the Reverend Robert L. Bachman becoming pastor on September 27, 1896, following Dr. Sutherland. Rule, *Standard History of Knoxville,* 429.

19. Samuel P. Jones (1847–1906), itinerant Methodist preacher from rural Georgia, conducted revival meetings in the South beginning in 1872. William A. "Billy" Sunday (1863–1935), former baseball player for the Chicago White-Stockings, turned to evangelism after his conversion in 1886. Sydney E. Ahlstrom, *A Religious History of the American People* (New Haven: Yale University Press, 1972), 746, 747.
20. George Sand was the pen name of Amandine Lucile Aurore Dudevant, née Dupin (1804–1876). Her *Journal Intime* (translated *Intimate Journal*) was published posthumously in 1926.
21. The exact wording is: "God is not a force outside of us. Nor is he a shining luminary lifted above the skies. Nor is he, in any special sense, the consecrated bread in the chalice of gold. God is the sun and the skies and the gold of the chalice. He is the bread. He is all the elements of earth. He is the heart of man. He is in us and outside of us. We are in him and never outside of him. He is universal spirit. He reveals himself in man, whom he animates with his breath and whom he sometimes enfolds in his love." *The Intimate Journal of George Sand*, trans. Marie Jenney Howe (New York: Haskell House, 1975), 87. The discrepancies in Armstrong's version of the passage may be the result of her attempt to recall it from memory (or from notes she had made).
22. Translation of: Ernest Renan, *Vie de Jésus* (1863).
23. First published in 1838.
24. English novelist Mary Augusta Arnold (1851–1920) wrote under her married name. She was the wife of T. Humphry Ward, himself a journalist and writer.
25. W. E. Gladstone's review under this title was published in *The Nineteenth Century*, Vol. 23 (May 1888), 766–788.
26. Mrs. Ward was indeed the granddaughter of Thomas Arnold (1795–1842), headmaster of Rugby. However, she was the niece, not sister, of the poet Matthew Arnold, who was the brother of her father (also named Thomas Arnold [1823–1900]). Julian and Aldous Huxley were the sons of her sister. John Sutherland, *Mrs Humphry Ward: Eminent Victorian, Pre-eminent Edwardian* (Oxford: Clarendon Press, 1990), 1, 408.
27. Irish novelist Margaret Wolfe Hamilton Hungerford (1855–1897) signed most of her books "The Duchess." *Molly Bawn* (1878) was the best-known of her more than thirty novels. Benét, *Reader's Encyclopedia*, 486.
28. George Santayana (1863–1952). Spanish-born American philosopher, critic, poet, and novelist.
29. President McKinley was shot September 6, 1901, and died eight days later; Leon Czolgosz was executed October 29.
30. Also named James Park. For more information about the Reverend James Park (1822–1912) and his family, see Rothrock, *French Broad – Holston Country*, 464–466.
31. Only the foundation was built by John Sevier; the house itself was completed in 1812 by the elder James Park. The Park House has had several owners and uses, and in 1974 was listed in the National Register of Historic Places. It was purchased in 2002 by Pete

Claussen and his wife, Linda, to be used as headquarters for the Gulf and Ohio Railways (of which Claussen is CEO). With the help of architect Lee Ingram of the firm Brewer Ingram Fuller, the Claussens restored the house to its 19th century appearance. G&O Headquarters web page, viewed August 12, 2017, http://www.gulfandohio.com/go-headquarters/.

32. William Rule corroborates the remarks that Armstrong attributes to Mrs. Howe, adding the date of the occasion, November 4, 1894. *Standard History of Knoxville,* 429.

33. Armstrong is no doubt referring to the 1888 drowning death of her brother, the 1889 Flat Creek train wreck which seriously injured her father, her failed marriage which ended in divorce on August 22, 1894, and the death of her father on September 12, 1894.

Chapter Nine

The Hill and the River

It was the same year I read *Robert Elsmere,* in the previous autumn, that I went to the Thanksgiving hop on the Hill.

I never quite understood why the University came to be known in Knoxville as "The Hill,"[1] inasmuch as it was Knoxville's proud boast that, like Rome, it was built on seven hills. But *the* Hill it remained as long as I knew it, and I see it now as I saw it then: its fine old trees, oaks and elms, which cast their shadows everywhere in the grounds and overspread the driveway that wound around and around up to the old red-brick buildings in simple Georgian Colonial style which still, at the time, crowned its summit, the chapel with its little bell-tower in their midst—buildings which had been closed when the War started because most of the faculty and student body had volunteered either in the Confederate or Union forces, though reopened during the War, both armies, in their alternate occupation of the town, using them as barracks and hospital.

If by remote chance any Knoxvillian of the present day should wish to know what these plain but substantial buildings really looked like, they have only to visit the Yard at Harvard, where dignified old red-brick rectilinear buildings of the same period and almost identical in appearance continue to serve Harvard University. With Knoxville's positive genius, however, for demolishing all the noblest evidences of its past, its own early University buildings, with all their historic associations, long since were demolished to make way for the flamboyance of Collegiate Gothic.[2]

Earlier presidents on the Hill had been graduates of Harvard or Dartmouth, but now, in the '80s, its new incumbent was the stalwart, impressively handsome Dr. Charles Dabney,[3] of a distinguished Virginia family, a graduate of its university and with a PhD acquired at Göttingen. Thirty-two when he became president of the University of Tennessee, he used to explain laughingly in later years that it was not through any remarkable precocity he gained the office at such an age, but because PhDs were still so uncommon in this country when he brought his back from Germany that he could have had almost anything he chose. In any case, the faculty on the Hill began now to acquire more and more graduates of the University of Virginia, often with their doctor's degree from Leipsic [i.e., Leipzig] or some other German university, some of them men of social charm, occasionally, if truth be

"The Hill." Courtesy of the University of Tennessee Libraries.

told, erudite boors, but as a whole making the influence of Virginia felt not alone on the Hill but in the town's more cultivated social circles.

But nothing, I need hardly say, was of less concern to me, at fifteen, than the character of the University buildings or its faculty. My sole interest was in the cadets (it had had a strong military department before the War and now again had one), those spruce lads who came mostly from somewhere in Tennessee, though a few of what seemed the more exotic types from the Deep South, Mississippi or Louisiana.

The cadets had begun now to include me in their round of Sunday afternoon calls. With no movies, no baseball or other sports—with the automobile, like movies and the radio, not yet invented—and buggy riding with a girl on Sunday unthinkable, all in all there was nothing else for them to do on this free afternoon save call on the girls.

They usually came in twos or threes and soon the walnut hat-rack in the hall at the Barnes house would have caps hanging on every hook. As a rule the same cadets did not stay long, but the parlor would be filled all afternoon, most of them full of lively talk and the parlor constantly filled with laughter, though the laughter, like the talk, never overly loud, for Mama, just across the hall, could hear every word unless, blessedly, the weather was so cold that even with the glowing coal fire in the parlor grate the door into our unheated draughty hall had to be kept closed. But there was plenty of merriment, notwithstanding a certain formality. Emily Post would have been charmed; the cadets sitting bolt upright, buttoned up to the chin, in our ebony parlor chairs upholstered in their silvery brocade; no lolling, no smoking (their fathers might smoke cigars, but only youths supposed to be straight on the road to perdition smoked cigarettes at the time, and never indoors). The cadets never thought, either, of addressing me other than as "Miss Annie." And they never forgot the gallant, flattering manners instilled in them from early childhood. "Miss Annie, you certainly are lookin' mighty pretty this evenin'," a statement I knew to be untrue, but none the less music on that account.

I reveled in it all, the truth is, especially, I confess, in being the lone girl among this throng of boys. There was invariably, however, a certain tension. My blood was ever one to boil at low temperature, and surrounded by cadets, I kept thinking excitedly that our talk would sound so *foolish* to Mama, if she overheard. Just the knowledge she *might* overhear kept me on edge. Mama always made me feel so *young* when she appeared or I thought she was listening. I knew instinctively that she made the cadets feel young too, if she encountered them in the hall as they were coming or going, when if not actually uncivil, which she was incapable of being, there was yet a touch of severity, even suspicion, in her manner—Mama, so gracious, so genial, so hospitable, with her own friends, but dismayed by a social pattern she had not foreseen, this swarm of young men coming to see a daughter not yet "out," far even from being through school.

The pattern, as a matter of fact, was probably much the same as in any smallish college town in the South in that day and for a girl to have a steady stream of student callers on Sunday afternoon did not indicate necessarily that she was a belle. All the girls I knew had as many as I, or more, if their parlor was larger. The only girls who had few, if any, were *thin* girls, this being one of those recurrent periods in the Western world when feminine curves were in vogue and a figure sufficiently curvaceous, as we say now in our frank and flippant way, would redeem the most hopeless face. I was not angular, I may add. Even so, I marvel to-day that I could have competed with any degree of success with girls most of whom, to start with, were much prettier than I, and in whose homes the cadets were made to feel welcome by all the members of the family they ever came in contact with. At Ida's, in North Knoxville, Miss Mallie always saw to it that freshly-baked cake along with hot chocolate, lemon sherbet, raspberry shrub, or blackberry vinegar, according to season, were served to Ida's callers. At the Bradley girls' on Summit Hill all manner of good things, chicken salad, smoked tongue, minced oysters, beaten biscuits—a regular collation, was set out. At our house, there was only myself and some elegantly upholstered, more or less comfortable chairs to offer and I can only explain the mystery of my receiving such attention as I did on two possible grounds.

Mama (so Mary had confided to me) had gained the reputation among the cadets of being something of an ogre. Perhaps they regarded it a sporting venture to face her, elegance itself, and her icy politeness, should they meet her in the hall with her obvious displeasure that they should be there at all. Too well-bred to hint of such a thing to me, nevertheless I was conscious of a sort of conspiratorial air in the always rather highly charged atmosphere in our parlor when cadets were there. From time to time a nightmarish fear assailed me. Mama might suddenly appear at the door and with a stern word disperse the whole gathering. I suspected that the cadets were visited by similar unvoiced fears, and this, I felt vaguely, seemed to draw us closer together through the danger of a common embarrassment we shared.

But there was the further circumstance that I had no difficulty in talking to the cadets, no matter how many; no difficulty, when it comes to that, in talking to any member or members of the human race. I am a born talker, I suppose. Although I have written a good deal, first and last, in the course of my life, I have never been under any illusion that I was a born writer. When I have written, it has been to release excess energy not otherwise employed at the time, or because there was something I burned to get over to more people than I might through other channels, as, for instance, in mid-life, my views on labor-management relations after intimate contact with the problems involved.[4] But I am, I insist, constitutionally a talker. There are few things I have enjoyed more in my life than talking, and thus a propensity which showed itself, apparently, while I was still in my teens, may have stood me in good stead on those Sunday afternoons which seemed to fly by so swiftly, though lasted in reality several hours.

But what, in heaven's name, I ask myself now, did we talk about on those afternoons?

One thing is certain, it was not about books. Though I had developed early a lust for reading and belonged to a rather bookish family, I would have sensed that the cadets would probably not be interested in the same sort of reading: in the *Atlantic Monthly* and the *North American Review,* the latest issues of which could always be found on our library table, together with *Harper's Weekly, Harper's Magazine, Harper's Bazaar, Harper's Young People* for my little sister, now that Harry and I had outgrown it (how the House of Harper did flourish then!). The *Manchester Guardian,* in its weekly edition, was always there too, my father's favorite among English weeklies, and with no American ones then, such as *Life* and *Time,* that *everybody* reads.

No, our talk was not of a literary nature, and I am equally sure it was not on politics. The War was over. People in Knoxville talked less and less now of the Lost Cause, unless they happened to meet on the street, a perpetual reminder of it, old Mr. Mitchell who had sworn, "By God!" he would never cut his beard if the Yankees won, and with it reaching now to his waist and part way round it, people said, though he kept it closely buttoned from view, inside his black coat. But even the Carpetbag Era was fast becoming only an ugly dream, and there was no issue before the country as a whole likely to interest normally frivolous young people such as we were.

There might have been an occasional play at Staub's Opera House we discussed, but assuredly it was not sports we talked of. There *were* none, no collegiate sports, none on the Hill at any rate. The day was far distant when the University of Tennessee would have to make the decision whether to be a great university or have a great football team, and made it. There was not even a baseball team on the Hill in the '80s, and only one professor, a Virginian, an able if ungainly and brusque professor of mathematics, Professor Schmidt [i.e., Schmitt],[5] who gave the students any encouragement (thereby winning their everlasting devotion) when some years later a team was formed. Most of the cadets could, of course, swim and a few, like my brother, had their own row-boats for use on the river. As for the girls then who could swim, they were as rare in Knoxville as everywhere else. A few cadets, Harry among them, played tennis, but on the one or two private courts in West End. There were none on the campus. Racing, again, was hardly a subject for conversation. True, Knoxville had its trotting races every fall, but it was not a racing center, and most of the cadets, from small towns, had probably never seen a horse race, unless at a county fair. It was several years yet until the first lad in Knoxville to be referred to as an athlete, a young Apollo named Cary Spence (later, in World War I, a Brigadier General), would come home from Sweetwater Military Academy, down in lower East Tennessee, with a medal pinned on his breast for his prowess as a sprinter.[6]

No, it was not sports that kept us talking animatedly for hours on end. The worship of sports had not yet begun in the United States. Our conversation centered generally, as I recall it, on little affairs, flirtations, going on between this or that boy and girl, though what amused us most (and I recall this clearly) were various lads taking off their professors.

Some of the cadets had been to Bell Buckle. They had great tales to tell of this unique institution, the Webb School in Middle Tennessee, the first boys' preparatory school in the Mid-South, designed originally, when the Public School system was still feeble in the South, to give sons of the Confederate soldiers a sound foundation for a classical education; famed for its rude buildings, rough life, for the floggings administered freely, vigorously, impartially, by "Old Sawney" and "Old Jack," those two already legendary Webb brothers who had founded the school and who were famed as well for their success in beating Greek, Latin, and Mathematics into even the most resistant skulls.[7]

Alone among the cadets was one from Mississippi who came and went by himself on Sunday afternoons. Short and dark-skinned, Jack could hardly be considered handsome, but with his aristocratic yet devilish air the girls without exception were more flattered by attention from Jack Kirby than from any "man" on the Hill. He stood out for one reason because he spent money freely. Where other cadets might bring a pound box of candy on Sunday, Jack would bring a five-pound box. He was prodigal also at Christmas time, giving quite costly gifts to such girls as were permitted by their mothers to accept them, mothers of whom Mama was not one. It was a bitter moment when I had to return to him a beautiful soft leather purse with sterling silver corners.

But what set Jack Kirby apart more than anything else was that we could not quite figure him out, though we could see behind him a pillared mansion set amidst great live-oaks dripping with moss, surrounded by boundless cotton fields, and his father a courtly Mississippi planter in the grand tradition, so that we were a bit let down when after Jack graduated and went back to Mississippi we learned that his father was, and had long been, something less romantic, a conductor on the Illinois Central.

The thing, however, that would keep him green in my own memory long after I had forgotten even the names of scores of other youths I knew then, was a thing altogether different. Coming from the Deep South, with his thinner blood, Jack would usually appropriate the chair nearest the fire. I haven't the remotest notion now what we were talking about at the time, but at some point or other Jack's low-pitched lazy voice came from beside the fire: "When you tell a lie, you've got to have ten to back it up."

Nothing I would hear or read later on the subject ever made so profound an impression on me, not even the historian Macaulay to the effect that honesty is the best policy even for a *temporal* policy.[8]

Open by nature, I never became an adept at fabrication, yet it may well be that this moralistic warning thrown off casually by Jack made the deeper imprint because now that boys had entered it my life was becoming daily more complicated and I was becoming ever closer acquainted with that "tangled web we weave when first we practice to deceive."[9]

In any case I do not think I had yet fallen from grace at the time I went to my first dance on the Hill. I remember no struggle beforehand. Very likely permission to go had been granted more readily because Harry would be there.

Harry had helped decorate the bare barn-like old Mess Hall where the dance was held with autumn leaves, pumpkins, and other emblems of Thanksgiving. But he would neither take a girl to the hop nor dance himself, though like all of us he had had instruction in dancing from the time he could walk, and tall, slender, graceful, he danced well. An odd change had come over Harry. I do not believe I gave it a thought at the time, only later. But while he was not bashful, and was so good-looking that the girls were always trying to attract him, he never responded with more than "Hello!" and a friendly wave of the hand. There had been a time, several years earlier, when he had shown a tendency to be "wild," as wildness was measured then; running around a bit in the evening, staying out later than expected, smelling suspiciously of cigarettes. Papa and Mama, I knew, had been worried. But now he had become serious beyond his years, and a model student, meticulously fulfilled all his duties on the Hill as at home.

In a few more months we would know one at least of the reasons for the change; know the vastly different effect of the Second Presbyterian Church and Sunday School on Harry than on a congenital non-conformist like myself.

But nothing was farther from my thoughts than Harry on the soft November night when in a state of high and blissful excitement, my new evening cape over my shoulders, a satin party-bag with my dancing slippers inside dangling from my arm, I walked with Archie Hicks the two or three dimly lighted blocks to the Hill and up the winding driveway to the Mess Hall, an unpretentious red-brick building on a slope at a lower level than the other buildings, with a porch running across the whole length of its front and lights streaming now into the darkness from every window.

Archie was the cadet of cadets to escort me to my first dance on the Hill. A personable blondish lad from over in West Tennessee near Memphis, he came from a family of many physicians and would become a physician himself. He stuttered a little but had a light humorous way with him and was very protective in his manner. He made me feel completely comfortable and the more so that although I liked him very much he did not have that thing about him, whatever it was, that made my heart flutter.

The hall was thronged. The floor may not have been too smooth and the orchestra was of only a few pieces, but to be whirled around by one cadet in dress uniform after another to the magic of violins, to circle rapturously from end to end of the long room, to be lost in the dashing movements of the Military Schottische, in the gay polka, the wilder gallop, and in between to be waltzing, waltzing, waltzing madly, till the last waltz reluctantly at midnight to the slower happy-sad strains of *Home, Sweet Home*—this was as near heaven as I could possibly conceive.

The *valse triste*, in various forms, with couples moving solemnly around a dance floor as if to the mournful measures of a funeral hymn only appeared (perhaps as a portent) in our present barbarous and unhappy century. Dances in the late 19th Century were magnificent frolics. Romps.

But there would never of course be another dance like this one, although long afterwards Mama told that when we were living in the Barnes house and I came home from a dance I would always come into her and my father's bed-room, stand at the foot of their big walnut bed, and say breathlessly that I had danced twenty miles, each time insist that this was the best dance I had ever gone to.

But I do not remember this. What I remember is that my eyes hardly closed until daylight after my first dance on the Hill. I was still waltzing, waltzing, waltzing, a cadet's arm clasped firmly around my waist, a little weary now, but every note of the dance tunes still sounding softly, over and over, in my enchanted ears. Even the mattress under me danced. I seemed to be floating on it, billowing through space, and half asleep, half awake, was only aroused from this delicious delirium as the wintry dawn crept through the windows and the familiar sound reached me of the Aults' old Negro cook beating the dough as she made beaten biscuits for their breakfast, the steady, rhythmic pounding with her rolling-pin accompanied by her low moaning voice in one of those heart-breaking songs which came out of slave times.

This was the year I was in Ninth Grade in the Girls' High School, the last year I would go there and I have only the faintest remembrance of what went on in the large corner room of the third floor which we occupied. I do, however, make out the blurred outlines of myself seated at one of its double desks in a row next the inside wall with the blackboards and, my mind full of cadets, finding it difficult to keep them out of Caesar's *Commentaries on the Gallic Wars.* They had a way of getting between me and the sentences I was struggling to translate, albeit neither then nor at any time was I burdened with anxiety about my grades. Few pupils were, I believe, in those days, and fewer parents, who assumed that if their children were in school they must be learning *something*, and seemed to let it go at that.

The only clear memory connected with school I have of that year is also connected with the Thomas girls. I recall hazily that through some sort of windfall their family fortunes had improved slightly by this time and that they were living, though still in rooms, in a more reputable part of town. At all events they continued to be more resourceful and enterprising than any other girls I knew.

One of our studies in the Ninth Grade was botany, a study I detested. Tearing petals off a lovely little flower, counting its sepals and stamens, pressing it between newspapers and then affixing it in its lifeless state to one of the loose sheets in a herbarium, was not my idea of fun. But the Thomas girls succeeded in transforming even this dry study into an adventure, a series of them. As soon as the first wild flowers appeared, arbutus and hepatica peeping up shyly through the winter's leaves, Birdie and Marguerite formed a small group, girls and boys, and after school or on Saturday we would troop across the bridge at the foot of Gay Street, always stopping to identify what we imagined were blood stains on its plank floor (grim reminders of the lynching there) and then scramble by zigzag trails up the bluffs on the far side of the river, heavily wooded then and with columbine and dwarf iris growing in every crevice in the rocky steeps; blood root among the ferns; spring beauties, anemones, trillium, colonies of May apples, and occasionally a lady's slipper in rich little hollows back of the bluffs.

Sometimes on Saturdays we took our lunch with us and after we had finished botanizing made a picnic of the occasion as we rested at the top of the bluffs, where we could look down at the broad, willow-fringed, curving river below us and across to the town, its old red-brick buildings, spires and chimneys, softened by distance.

There was no other spot near Knoxville at that time so entirely unspoiled, so idyllic, and the botanizing expeditions having proved a success, shortly were converted into reading circles. Each of us carried a volume of Shakespeare (heavy though they usually were) and settling ourselves on the ground or on some mossy boulder, through long mild spring afternoons we sat around under the trees, still in their first fresh golden green, reading the play selected, its *dramatis personae* divided so that everyone had a part or parts to read as the play unfolded.

I remember (and it surprises me that I do) precisely the plays we read in that woodsy setting: *As You Like It* (appropriately, for it was veritably a Forest of Arden around us), *Julius Caesar, Hamlet, King Lear, Romeo and Juliet,* and (very ambitiously, it strikes me now) *The Tempest.*

Julius Caesar and *Hamlet* I remember enjoying most though that may have been because I had seen them both on the stage. But there was nothing in my early girlhood, as I look back, a more undiluted pleasure than those outdoor readings, with no class-room restrictions, no elders to dull the edge of our zest, all of us so young and the glories of Shakespeare revealing themselves almost it seemed as our own discoveries.

The handful of boys who accompanied us, at least after the readings started, were "town boys," lads whose fathers preferred sending them away to preparatory school or college rather than to the Hill and who were home on holiday or perhaps to stay.

I think it was after Christmas in that year that I had begun to be more interested in "town boys" than cadets. Some of these boys already had entered business, generally with uncles or fathers in one of the big wholesale houses on Gay Street, or in the offices of the East Tennessee, Virginia and Georgia Railroad. Their main attraction for me was, I presume, that they appeared more sophisticated than the cadets, who, beside them, seemed now rather naïve.

In any case, and despite the fact that the same antagonism between collegians and non-collegians existed in Knoxville as in most college communities, town boys presently were mingling with my cadet callers. Soon I was going to dances at the Sans Souci Club[10] on Gay Street to which these town boys belonged. Their greater sophistication was, however, if she sensed it, no recommendation to Mama. If she had been distrustful of the cadets, she was even more distrustful of the new youths appearing on the scene. I was entirely too young, she insisted (though in the end she gave in), to be going to dances in town, however well chaperoned.

Among the town boys I had come to know was a Hu [*sic*] White, from some little place above Knoxville, his father a country merchant. Like so many ambitious youths up and down the great valley of East Tennessee, Hu had come to Knoxville to seek his fortune and secured a job with a wholesale clothing firm. In later years he became a rich lumberman in another Southern state and member of Congress. At the time, he was chiefly distinguished by being somewhat undersized, having a crop of tightly-curled light-brown hair, a surly mouth, a vulpine cast of countenance (as I see it now), no manners to speak of; by the fact that he dressed, though neatly, rather flashily, even wearing a cheap-looking ring or two. It is hard at this distance of time to see what in him could have attracted me and my infatuation with him, a species of Spring madness not uncommon in adolescents, in all probability would have passed almost as soon as it appeared but for favoring circumstances.

Recently a Dr. Herman Bayless, a Kentuckian, had come to Knoxville, its first physician of the modern type, wearing not a long black coat, as other physicians in Knoxville then, along with its preachers and lawyers, but a sack coat, like a business man's. Commandingly handsome and with genial, easy manners, he had become very popular and our own family doctor.[11] Just how it came about and at whose instigation I shall never know, but one day Mama took me in to the parlor to inform me what Dr. Bayless had told Papa concerning Hu and two of his constant companions who also were paying me some attention (sons of two prominent old families in Knoxville), that they were not young men Papa would wish a daughter of his to associate with. I was too stunned to inquire (though I surmised) what the charges were against them, but when Mama for some reason singled out Hu among this trio of young libertines, if that's what they were, and sternly forbade me to see him again, whatever charms he had held for me before instantly were enhanced ten-fold. Forbidden, he became completely irresistible.[12]

What I resented most was Mama's failure to trust me. These were the same young men the other girls went with and Mrs. Gaines—all the other girls' mothers, trusted their daughters. I thought of this hotly as I climbed the Clinch Street hill, over the uneven old brick pavements, every morning on my way to school, as I came home, in bed at night—constantly. Ever more burningly indignant, I even thought that by forcing me into intrigues (for which, ignorant though I was of myself, I realized I had no gift), Mama was corrupting my character! How could you hope to be trustworthy if people didn't trust you? And I remember, foolish as it seems now, but overwhelmingly serious then, that I thought perhaps I could find something from one of Emerson's essays to quote to her, some bit of the wisdom with which I was just getting acquainted since the new Riverside Edition of the *Complete Works of Ralph Waldo Emerson*, eleven volumes, recently had taken their place among our books—something to make her realize. . . .

My reading all this time more mature than my emotional affairs would suggest, I found Emersonian lines that shook me from head to foot, lifted me right out of the chair and I had an inkling, too, of what they meant:

> I am owner of the sphere,
> Of the seven stars and the solar year,

Of Caesar's hand, and Plato's brain,
Of Lord Christ's heart, and Shakespeare's strain.[13]

But no, they wouldn't do. I could never find the lines that quite seemed to fit the case. And had I found it, I knew in my heart I would disregard that high counsel of Emerson I had run across, "Always do what you are afraid to do."[14] I knew I would never find the moment when I would dare quote it to Mama. There were never any intimate moments between us. Mary—"the other girls," talked freely to their mothers, even discussed their beaux with them, but it would have been no easier for me to approach Mama on a matter of this sort than to ask Mrs. Bauer if she knew she looked like Queen Victoria.

As for Mrs. Bauer, she seemed to have washed her hands of me. She no longer called me in as I was passing to give me a wedge of Melton Mowbray pie she had saved, a piece of Scotch short-bread, or some other delectable morsel. She had seen me lately oftener than ever climbing the long steps to the Gaines' house. "Those nincompoops!" I could hear her snort. "Humph, no good will come of *that*!" I could feel her scorn. But it did not deter me. I would have to work out my own destiny.

At the Gaines', where girls in West End customarily met youths of their choice whom they were not permitted to meet at home, there was usually a little balcony vacant where, after dark, Hu and I could snatch a few minutes of secret talk. If no balcony was available there was a secluded corner at the back of the long Gaines' parlor, or in their library, its walls lined with those calf-bound volumes which none of the present generation of Gaines was ever moved to consult, and lighted only by the single gas jet, under its ruby globe, in the hall outside.

But a rendezvous at the Sans Souci Club was also possible. Hu did not dance. Perhaps there had been no opportunity to learn in the little town he came from. But he was always there on the night of a dance, among the stags. The club rooms, above a retail store, I've forgotten whose, and devoid of ornamentation of any sort, ran from the windows in front on Gay Street to a platform for the musicians at the rear. Opening off one side was the men's dressing-room, and opposite one for the girls, with a small watery looking-glass above the toilet-table improvised from a discarded packing-case, and with a few pine kitchen chairs where we could pile our wraps if the nails on the wall were full.

But characteristic of social functions in Knoxville at the time, a blend of elegance and crudity, if the club-rooms were crude, the dances there were not. Radiant in flower or ostrich-trimmed evening gowns, their bare shoulders gleaming, as the girls swirled through the dances, a shimmering shifting medley of delicate and brilliant color, the hall took on a truly resplendent air. There was a sense of éclat too, for the club was considered very exclusive, and there were always some older couples among the dancers who gave the dance dignity without robbing it of gayety. As I recall it, the cotillion (the german,[15] it was usually called then) was not danced at the Sans Souci Club till several years later, but with the caller roaring out above the violins his jovial, thunderous command, "Swing your partners! Hands all around!" for the lively square dances which alternated with the waltz and the polka, I remember no dances in after years in New York or Washington, in ball-rooms in Monte Carlo or Paris, from which I derived such boundless delight.

Naturally, however, my delight was intensified from the fact that Hu was present, looking on, and from a backward nod of his head as I whirled past, I understood that I was to slip outside, into the hall, when a dance was ended.

Flushed with heat and excitement, fanning myself feverishly, I would seat myself on one of the narrow wooden stair-steps, always covered with dust, which led up to the third story of the building and Hu would sit on the step below. It comes back to me as I write that I was always conscious first in these stolen moments of the strong scent of cardamom seeds (in vogue then to disguise the odor of liquor) which Hu exhaled, and that this scent, in some curious way, contributed to the slightly painful yet exquisite sense of guilt which pervaded me in these meetings. They were always very hurried, though. Either the violins, starting again, called me back to the next dance or some other couple wanted our place. Once, just as we heard others approaching and sprang from the steps, Hu seized and kissed me, my first kiss from a lad, and a slightly terrifying if ecstatic experience.

After the kiss, it was harder than ever to get Hu out of my mind and I felt more and more conscious of it when I was with Mama and Papa, as if they could look directly into my head and see there, as through glass, what had happened, so that on the day before Easter I was more than ever reluctant to join one of those long family drives in the surrey for which I no longer cared.

It was in April. We crossed the river and as always headed straight for the country, in the direction, as I remember it, of the Smokies,[16] though it was all so long ago I am not sure of that. I am perfectly sure, however, that I sat on the back seat with Mama, May between us, Harry beside Papa in front and Trix trotting behind or at the side of the horses. I can see, too, despite the unresponsive and rebellious mood I was in, the way the country looked that day; the patches of red earth, recently plowed; the blue spring daisies along the roadside, wild strawberries in bloom, papaw bushes hanging full of their garnet bells, the flush of red-bud along the edge of the woods, dogwood like drifts of snow through the forest, and around the stumps of giant trees which the loggers had cut years before, wild azaleas in all their early spring glory—rose and shell-pink, saffron and orange and blazing scarlet. I can remember the distant tinkle of cow-bells up some shadowy hollow we passed, and Papa and Mama, in a state of continuous if restrained, rapture, calling our attention to the weeping willows, fountains of green now, which here and there overhung some old stone spring-house roofed with moss, to cucumber trees along the creeks with their great snowy blossoms, and to the slow wheeling movements of hawks sailing overhead.

Dreamily conscious of the passing scene, Hu was ever before me, the way he looked that night in the hall at the Sans Souci Club, and I was only fully awakened to what was around me when on the homeward drive Harry noticed Trix was limping, and getting out found the pads of her feet worn to the quick and bleeding. Lifting her tenderly, he placed her below us, in the back of the surrey. May cried when she saw the old setter's feet and I lifted her head into my lap, buried my face on it and whispered, "Poor old Trix!" She seemed to me now the only creature in the whole world that I loved.

I remember that drive as no other in my life, though partly no doubt because it was the last, as a family, we would ever take together.

But there was another small happening, though it loomed large enough at the time, which helped preserve it in my memory.

It was growing dusk as we reached home. Uncle Pompey was waiting to put the horses in the stable, the house-girl already had lighted the gas and as we came into the house she took a large flat package from the seat on the hat-rack and handed it to me. "Miss Annie, dis heah come fer you whilst y'all was gone, Easter gif', I reckon, from one of yo' young mens."

My heart sank. I had a premonition there was something in the package that would cause trouble. I carried it into the sitting-room. Mama waited. Inside was an immense expensive-looking pale-blue satin padded sachet, heavily scented and a life-size dove painted on it with underneath in fancy lettering, *The Lord is Risen.*

"Whom is it from?" Mama asked.

My heart was beating furiously.

"I don't know," I said, adding truthfully, "There's no card."

Mama said nothing. She looked grave. And from that day the tension between us grew.

There were some lovely days nevertheless in the month of May that followed. The thing to look forward to now was the June hop on the Hill during commencement week. As the Thanksgiving hop had been the first I attended, so this would be my first June hop, and I believe even Mama was somewhat gratified when weeks beforehand one of the outstanding members of the graduating class asked to take me. At any rate she had a seamstress in the house days and days working on my dress, a white organdie or Swiss, its bouffant skirt a froth of narrow ruffles edged with real Valenciennes, dozens and dozens of yards of it whipped on by hand, and with a blue satin sash to girdle the waist and hang down behind in streamers.

I had never before had such a bewitching dress. After it was done and hung in the wardrobe in my room, covered with muslin to protect it from Knoxville's soot-laden air, I used to remove its covering stealthily at night after my little sister was asleep, put it on and looking at myself in the mirror in the bureau, my heart softened a little toward Mama.

But this happy time ended when I committed a sin. For the life of me, and rack my brain as I will, I can not remember what the sin was. Of course I knew at the time, but for at least the past sixty years I have not been able to recall the nature of it, only the smiting sentence I drew—now I could not go to the June hop.

If Papa had been at home, with his invincible good humor he might have induced Mama to temper justice with mercy. But Papa, immersed in business, flying back and forth across the Atlantic, was in England at the time, so the terms of the punishment stood. It must have been, as I think of it to-day, Mama had found out that I was still, in defiance of her authority, seeing Hu. But whatever it was, after she told me I could not go to the June hop, I felt the sun would never shine again.

However, in the course of a few days I rallied. A new idea struck me. This was years before I had ever heard of the poet Yeats, or almost anybody else had, but I decided that I would choose

> . . . the laughing lip,
> That will not turn from laughing
> Whatever rise or fall.[17]

I would brave it out. Pretend I didn't care, although I had hardly more than adopted this prideful attitude when another blow fell upon me.

An annual event in Knoxville was the Drummers' Picnic. It was to Knoxville what the annual Charity Ball was in that era to many cities in this country. Originated by Knoxville's traveling salesmen, it was always in the month of May and this year would be at Lake Ottosee. As the time approached, little else was talked about. There was always a merry-go-round, a tent where refreshments could be bought, a band, a pavilion for dancing and booths presided over, for "sweet charity's sake," by older and younger women of social prominence in Knoxville.

I had never been to a Drummers' Picnic. Mama had frowned upon them. The word "drummer" connoted something vulgar and rowdy to her. She had never realized, apparently, that the "drummers" sponsoring the Drummers' Picnic were often from very aristocratic families, that they were gentlemen, in the conventional sense, almost without exception. She had never realized that some of the best blood in the South flowed in the veins of many of them, men born during the Civil War and often when they were old enough to enter business with few opportunities open to them save to become traveling salesmen. But it was just another of those things about Knoxville which Mama would never, never, understand.

This year, though, I thought hopefully, perhaps it would be different. I was older. Maybe, too, Mama would feel I had been punished sufficiently; would want to make up to me a little for my terrible disappointment about the June hop. I thought best, however, not to broach the subject till the day came. It would give her less time to think. I would take her by storm, so to speak. But when on the morning of the picnic I mentioned going, she peremptorily refused even to consider such a thing and turned a deaf ear to all my pleading.

That day was one I shall never forget. I lay on the bed, sobbing convulsively at intervals through the long afternoon, picturing to myself all the fun Mary and the others were having. I had almost never cried during my childhood; it had become a legend in the family. Throughout my life I have seldom cried, cried outwardly. But now the flood gates were loosed. I would never forgive Mama as long as I lived. I was sure of that. I never wanted to see her again.

I see myself plainly, the pillow under my head drenched with tears. The room I was in was not my own, which must have been undergoing repairs of some sort. I was in one of our two guest-chambers in the Barnes house, both of which were occupied almost continuously by relatives or friends who would come with their mammoth Saratoga trunks (which I never dared watch the dray-men manoeuvre [*sic*] up our narrow twisting front stairs for fear the man above would lose his grip and the one below be crushed to death); guests who would stay for weeks, for months, according to the custom of the time, and with Mama and Papa never seeming to think any guest had stayed a day too long.

But at this particular time, as I lay crying my heart out, there seem to have been no guests in the house, and never had I been so unhappy. The only thing I could think of that I would like to do was die.

It was a sweltering afternoon, more like Midsummer than May. I recall that the thin lawn wrapper I had on was as wet from perspiration as my pillow from tears. It clung to my body, and as the supper hour approached, realizing I would be expected to appear, whatever state I was in, I got up, looked in the glass at my blurred red eyes, my swollen face, started downstairs to the bath-room, and it was on returning from a hasty bath that one of those trifling incidents occurred—hardly more than an instantaneous impression—which has stayed with me where a thousand more significant moments have been lost in the mists of time.

As I entered the guest-room, hurriedly closing the door behind me, I dropped off my wrapper and there confronting me in a pier-glass opposite was a figure that would not have startled me more had it been a ghost; a figure I had never seen before; my own completely naked body. In that prudish Victorian day, when we were afraid to look at the human anatomy, when women and girls of whatever age went in the ocean, a lake or river, fully clothed even to long thick cotton stockings, it was not only a shock, it was a revelation, to see in the pier-glass my own body, from head to toe, with the delicately roseate tints, lithe limbs, the firm unblemished flesh, gentle curves and clean lines of any normally-formed girl belonging to that half-world of adolescence when, not a child, she is yet not quite a woman. To my amazement the figure I beheld resembled nude figures, fabulous nymphs in bronze or marble, I had seen in art galleries my parents had taken me to in New York and Philadelphia, and stricken though I was, a pleasurable sensation shot through me.

Although this month of May had been on the whole a time of trial, there was one pleasure Mama had not forbidden. I could still go to the Hill on Friday afternoons to see Dress Parade. The parade ground lay to the right of the entrance gates, bounded on one side by Cumberland Street where little boys used to perch on the fence to watch the battalion, in full and gleaming equipment, headed by its band, march on to the field and go through maneuvres. There were no regular seats for spectators, but those who came, mostly young girls like myself, of "cadet age," sat on the ground which sloped down gradually from the Mess Hall above.[18]

I had been to many dress parades and the last one of this year was doubtless only marked out in my mind from all those before because of events shortly to follow, and because of the one and only experience of the sort I was ever to have—what I suppose may be regarded as an extra-sensory perception.

My brother Harry was a lieutenant in Company A and as his company wheeled and Harry, tall and slender, swung into view from the place where I was sitting on the hillside under a tree with other girls, I saw a funeral procession, superimposed on the view below me; a military funeral (a thing I had never seen then in actuality), the band with muffled drums going in front, the whole cadet battalion marching with measured steps down Gay Street, which was lined on both sides with silent people gathered along the curbs, the men with their hats off, gazing at the slow procession, and in the hearse, drawn by horses with black plumes on their heads and black tasselled nettings over their bodies, was Harry. I did not see Harry in the hearse, but it was as if I knew he was in the coffin, draped with a flag, which I could see through its glass sides.

I saw it plainly, although without the slightest feeling of shock, of grief or horror. It passed before me simply as something in a dream might, or some vagrant thought entirely unrelated to reality. In view of what happened a few days later I have rarely mentioned this experience to anyone. I can understand the skepticism with which it would be met by most people, while to me it remains as inexplicable as when it occurred.

But the days which followed likewise come back to me with great clarity. On Sunday evening was the Baccalaureate sermon, delivered as usual at Staub's Opera House, as the Hill had only its chapel, too small to hold all who would wish to attend.

It was the third of June and the Opera House was stifling, the men in the audience fanning themselves with palm-leaf fans, mopping their brows; the women wilted, and the sour-sweet sensuous perfume from all the magnolias with which the stage was banked almost overpowering.

I do not remember, of course, all the details of the evening, though I am certain it was not with my parents I went to the Baccalaureate sermon, for there is an impression of freedom associated with the occasion which lingers in my mind. True, as at Dress Parade, it was a mixed pleasure seeing in the Opera House all these cadets, unhappy reminders of the June hop to which I had looked forward so excitedly, and now only two nights off. Yet even so, I enjoyed some brief but merry conversations with cadets I knew among those on duty in the lobby or acting as ushers.

Harry also was one of the ushers. With very different temperaments, there had never been the ideal relationship between us that exists between some brothers and sisters. Perhaps I was too self-centered to look up to him as some girls to their older brothers. But we had very different tastes, too. Harry was one who accepted the prevailing thought around him without question. He had never stayed around as I had, more or less out of sight, drinking in conversations of my father with his friends on philosophic, religious, or political subjects. He had none of my own insatiate curiosity about books, my itch to know what was in them. The only books I had ever seen him take out of our book-shelves were *The Deerslayer, The Last of the Mohicans*, and some of Scott's novels. Yet for all that, we shared memories and knowledge shared by no one else in all this crowded Opera House. And never had I felt so close to him as when I saw him coming back up the aisle from seating some of the congregation, so tall and straight and handsome in his cadet uniform, with such youthful dignity. *This was my brother*! I was proud of him.

Harry would graduate next year. I could see him standing in the center of the stage, behind a similar bank of magnolias, delivering the farewell oration to his classmates seated behind him and to all the proud parents out in front; or if not the valedictory, at least the salutatory would fall to him.

I thought of the plans my parents had for Harry, as definite as those for me, that I should go to college, not merely to some "finishing school." After graduation, as they had always been a little uneasy about Harry's health (they had sent him one winter to live an outdoor life with the lumberjacks in one of my father's lumber camps), he was to have his *Wanderjahr*, to go to Europe, India, China, everywhere. Already my father had made arrangements with Mr. Olmquist, a Swedish accountant in his English office, a cultivated youngish man who spoke several languages and who would act on the tour as tutor to Harry as well as companion. Then, after the *Wanderjahr*, Harry was to enter Cornell, selected because of the interest he was showing in science and the fact that Cornell was taking the lead then, among American colleges, in attention to science.

But next morning all these serene and agreeable contemplations on Harry's future were swept away by an astonishing change in the pattern of our family life, a pattern that went back to our earliest memories.

Papa already had left for his office, and the last to come down I was alone in the dining-room with Mama. As I finished my strawberries and cream, my oatmeal, shad roe with bacon, scrambled eggs and muffins—the kind of breakfast we ate in those days—folded my napkin, inserted it in my napkin-ring, and hopped up from the table with "Excuse me, please," Mama, in her crisp white morning-dress, still behind the coffee-urn, detained me.

There was a strange look in her face. It was working a little and I sensed that whatever she had to tell me was not going to be easy for her to say. Immediately I was plunged into gloom. What had I done *now*?

Mama took another swallow of coffee. Her long slim fingers trembled, I noticed, as she lifted the cup. She did not look at me directly. "Annie," she said in a low voice, laboring to bring out the words, "—Annie, Harry wants us to have family prayers. We will start this morning." She got up from her chair. "Harry is waiting—and May—in the sitting-room."

I followed her. I was aghast. This was worse than anything I could possibly have imagined.

I sat down on the couch. Harry was sitting opposite, near the west window, his face grave and that sad book, the Bible, in his hands. He opened and read a chapter from it, though I could never remember afterwards what chapter it was. Mama, her head slightly bowed, looked down at the carpet as he read. Her face was dark and withdrawn, exactly as when she nibbled on the little square of bread in her gloved hand on Communion Sunday. My little sister's head was bowed, too, as if she hardly knew how to behave; her long fair curls hanging down, half covering her face. Oh, this was awful! Next, Harry would be "joining the Church." Family Prayers, at this late day! And when Papa and Mama had never had anything of the sort. Nothing so unnatural, so utterly alien to it, had ever happened before in our home with its many live wholesome interests, and in spite of Mama's strict discipline and my constant resentment of it in secret, no home could have been more cheerful than ours heretofore.

I was stunned, and when Harry, in the pious tone of a preacher or superintendent of Sunday School, asked us all to join him now in saying the Lord's Prayer, I felt as if the bottom of the world had dropped out.

Painfully embarrassed, I escaped from the room the instant we had said "Amen," ran upstairs to get a Latin grammar I had left there and was rushing out the front door, bound for the High School, where final examinations were starting this week, when Mama called me back and drawing me into the parlor, closed the door.

Her voice was soft now and there were tears in her eyes. "Annie," she said,

"Harry has talked it over with us and he has persuaded your father and me that we should allow you to go to the June hop to-morrow night."

I fairly gasped. "Oh, Mama! Oh, Mama!"

I wanted to cry. Even more, I wanted to throw my arms around Mama and hug her. But though Mama, I realized, was by no means of a cold nature and although while she had thwarted me in so many directions I had never for an instant doubted her love, yet there was a certain Victorian formality about her, at this stage of her life, in all her relations with her children. She had never, since I could remember, bestowed an impulsive caress on me, called me by an endearing name. So now, when a sudden great warmth welled up in me toward her, I was unable to express it openly.

All that unforgettable day I was seething with conflicting emotions. Dizzy with excitement, I could scarcely keep from dancing along the brick pavements, rough as they were, on the way to school. I was going to the June hop after all! But then the scene in the sitting-room would rise before me. How could I face having to go through "family prayers" every morning—that doleful proceeding I had dreaded at my grandfather's, abhorred at Mrs. Clotworthy's, that would take the joy out of a day before it started? Yet closely following this thought was one about Harry. For all my jubilant mood, I felt vaguely unhappy about him. How troubled he must have been (perhaps about all of us!) before he could have urged something so foreign to our household upon Mama and Papa.

In the afternoon, returning with other girls from school, I saw Harry coming in the distance, starting up the Clinch Street hill that we were going down. With him was Ben Pitman, a stocky, swarthy lad who had exhibited an almost dog-like devotion to Harry; one of the Pitmans who lived near us in West End and had sent me into fits of laughter when I was younger and watched them going by to church, Mrs. Pitman and her daughter without bustles when everyone else was wearing them.

Trix at their heels, it was evident Harry and Ben were on their way to the river where Harry kept his boat in a boat-house down below the bridge. Almost every afternoon, now that the weather was hot, he would row up the river and take a swim, though being subject to cramps, Mama had extracted a promise that he would never go swimming unless someone were with him.

We met in front of Em Parham's notorious establishment and Harry, lifting his cap quickly, as if in surprise when he saw I was among the girls he was passing, and his eyes lighting up, called out, "Hello, Sis!" His dark, wavy hair, when he lifted his cap, looked damp, I remember, and more curly than ever. The swift look that passed between us was like an electric current. I was trying to convey without words my gratitude to him and in his own look and tone of voice he was trying, it seemed, to convey something to me that he would never venture to put into more tangible form. I had never analyzed my feelings toward Harry, but for the first time I was conscious of love for him, or something akin to love. I was also acutely conscious of a sense of relief. Harry looked happy now, thoroughly alive. No trace was visible of that Harry of a few hours ago when we had sat awed and uncomfortable while he solemnly read the Bible to us.

Later, a little group of girls were gathered around me on one end of our long porch, the end in front of the parlor where we always gathered, leaving the other for Mama and Papa and their friends. Strangely, when so much else of that June day remains crystal clear, I can not recall who the girls were; only that they were rejoicing with me that I could go to the hop. They were waiting too—and made no bones about it—in the hope Harry would return while they were there. Maybe one of them could at last inveigle him into a flirtation.

Mama had gone up to the Pitmans, a block away, up the steep hill we faced at the Barnes house. Mr. Pitman was a native of Rhode Island, son of a sea captain and from a long line of sea captains; Mrs. Pitman a cousin of the well-known Lucy Stone, pioneer for women's rights. Among our neighbors in West End, the Pitmans, far less worldly than Papa and Mama, yet with sturdy New England traits, added to the neighborhood, as did the Bauers, their own distinctive flavor, one that my parents, with their catholic taste, were quick to appreciate.

With Mama gone, there was no one to restrain the gay chatter and wild outbursts of laughter on the porch. But supper time drew near and still Harry had not returned, though Papa appeared now, walking home from his office, which he preferred to driving. As he started to open the gate, a countrified-looking young man, clay on his boots, tearing up the street on horseback, checked his horse in front of the house, called out to my father by name, and leaning over from his saddle, said something to him.

I saw my father take a step backward on the sidewalk, staggeringly, then straighten himself and say a few words to the man, who whirled and rode off in the direction from which he had come.

Papa came up the few steps from the street. I ran down to meet him. His face was white.

"Where's Mama?" he asked, his eyes dazed, looking at me, yet not looking at me.

"What is it, Papa? What is it, Papa?" I asked, clinging to him in terror.

"Harry's drowned," he said simply, through dry lips.

Harry and Ben had tied the boat near the entrance to Island Home and swum across to the Cow and the Calf, two big rocks opposite that stood up out of the water. After resting, they started back. Some said the water was unusually cold that year for June. But however that was, Ben like most swimmers with no great skill made a good deal of noise in swimming. In his own account of what happened, Harry, far ahead, might have called for help some time before he heard the calls. At all events, with Harry helpless from cramps when Ben reached him, and Ben himself spent and unable to save them both, he had had to unloose Harry's arms from around his neck to save himself.

A great crowd had collected by the time Papa arrived at the point where Harry had gone down. Sometimes it was days before someone drowned in the broad swift-flowing Tennessee was found, and then found far below Knoxville. Sometimes they were not found. To spur the efforts of river-men among the crowd Papa offered five hundred dollars to the one who would recover Harry's body.

At home we waited, the house full of people; neighbors and others talking together in hushed tones. Cadets and professors from the Hill kept coming and going quietly. In the back yard Negroes had gathered in silent groups.

Mama was alone in her bed-room save for Mrs. Pitman. At first, when her knees had buckled under her and she had sunk to the ground, she had cried aloud in her anguish. But now she lay on the big walnut bed, staring in front of her, saying over and over, frenziedly: *"No, no, not Harry! Not Harry!"*

After it grew dark I could no longer stay in the house. I walked back and forth at the end of the porch where I had sat with the girls laughing and chattering. There was no moon. It was black outside. In the heavy night air the scent of the magnolias on the two big trees in front of the house was almost overpowering, as at the Opera House the night before—but how long ago that seemed!

The hours wore on. At last word came. Harry's body had been found under a raft, where it had drifted, and not far from where he had gone down.

The blinds half closed, Harry lay in his coffin in front of the black marble fireplace in the parlor. The room was stifling with the odor of tuberoses, jasmine, white lilies, magnolia blossoms and heliotrope. Heliotrope was the only colored flower ever to appear then at funerals or in a house where someone was dead. It was years yet till I would see at a funeral, and with a slight shock, some pink carnations.

Mama remained in her bed-room. Cadets who formed a guard of honor at the house ushered all who came into the parlor. If they were people I knew well, sometimes I would go with them and stand looking down at Harry on his tufted white satin bed. I had only seen one dead person before, Mary Leonard, a German Catholic nurse I had had as a child. Mama had taken me to see her where she lay in a dim room, a white marble figure, with tapers twinkling at her head and feet. The dead look so dead, it is commonly asserted. Mary Leonard had looked dead. But everyone who stood beside me looking down at Harry, in the flower of his manly youth, unwasted by illness, would turn away, weeping, to whisper incredulously, "Why, he doesn't look dead at all!" And so powerful an impression did this make on me that all my life since, until very lately, I have been visited by a dream that Harry, buried alive, in some mystifying way had freed himself from his grave and come back to us, to our overwhelming joy that was yet always coupled with a haunting uneasiness. How had it been where he was? But he would never say, in the dream. . . .

It was customary in those days in Knoxville, especially in hot weather, with the preservative arts of a later time unknown, or not generally practiced, to bury people the day following their deaths, in some cases less than twenty-four hours afterwards. But to Mama this haste, despite the obvious reason for it, was more than unseemly, it was barbarous. In her distraught state, she could not be brought even to consider such a thing, so there was the second long night for us to live through.

The second night was a torrid one. Upstairs I could not bear even the sheet over me. Down below in the quiet house cadets were tip-toeing back and forth, among them Jim Ramsey (captain of Harry's Company), who was to have taken me this very night to the June hop, cancelled now. On the dining-room table was an array of refreshments which our kind neighbors had set out for the cadets during their all-night vigil, and for the two undertaker's assistants, oldish, rather broken-looking men in long black coats who slipped into the parlor from time to time to bathe Harry's face and hands with some fluid they had.

Now and again the terrible sound of Mama sobbing would reach me from below through the open windows, and unable to sleep, the thing I could not stop thinking about was something that had happened only a few weeks before, when I had gone into Harry's bed-room one evening to borrow something, perhaps an eraser—I've forgotten what. Harry and I had always sparred and squabbled as even the most devoted of youthful brothers and sisters are wont to do, but he especially objected to my intruding when he was studying or doing experiments. His room, with all sorts of chemicals, retorts and so on ranged on the shelves that lined one wall, was as much a laboratory as a bed-chamber. Above all, he did not want me to disturb any of his chemical apparatus and if I approached the shelves would oust me from the room after a good-natured tussle. But this evening in our scuffling, to defend myself, I picked up from his study table a pen-holder holding a steel pen and jabbed him with it, making a long scratch on his cheek. He had put up his handkerchief to wipe off the drops of blood.

Neither of us had mentioned the incident since. But now in the night Harry's face was constantly before me with the red scratch standing out vividly on it. Though unintentionally, I had "brought the blood," a phrase that haunted me and made me deeply ashamed. It was still in my mind when early in the morning I went into the parlor to see Harry for the last time before the coffin was closed. But it was swept away with my first glance at him. His face had turned a greenish blue and was ominously dark in places. I knew now with tearing clearness that Harry had gone the way of all flesh. Harry was dead.

The graduates on the Hill had been given their diplomas in private. For the first time in its history there were no Commencement ceremonies at the University of Tennessee.

In front, the cadets marched in a body to the sound of muffled drums.

I sat in the closed carriage beside Mama, our faces covered with mourning veils. Papa was opposite with little May in her black dress.

Everything seemed unreal. But so enduringly were all the details of that June morning impressed on my youthful mind that thirty years after when my own only son, a naval aviator, had gone down with his plane, as the car in which I rode followed the caisson holding what remained of his broken body, draped with the flag, and led the way down the slope below the Unknown Soldier where he would lie among the thousands of quiet sleepers at Arlington[19]—in that hour of supreme sorrow, I was riding not alone through the leafy avenues of Arlington, with flowers dropping from planes overhead, in my ears the eerie unearthly beauty of Chopin's Funeral March—I was back again in the Knoxville of long ago, with Papa and Mama and little May in her black dress, as we passed slowly down Gay Street, along the curbs on both sides people standing, blacks and whites, the men with their heads uncovered, gazing at us sadly as we passed, as we crossed the viaduct over the railroad tracks, wound our way through the dull streets of North Knoxville and out Broadway toward Old Gray.[20]

NOTES

1. In 1826 trustees of East Tennessee College authorized the purchase of "Barbara Hill" (which had been named in honor of Governor William Blount's daughter Barbara); in 1828 the college moved into buildings constructed on "The Hill," which is still part of the campus of the University of Tennessee, Knoxville. Creekmore, *Tennessee,* 65; Rule, *Standard History of Knoxville,* 353; Rothrock, *French Broad-Holston Country,* 400–401. During the Civil War, this area was also referred to as "College Hill." Rule, 163; Rothrock, 130, 139, 140, 141.
2. A reference to Ayres Hall (1921), which took the place of three earlier buildings. South College (1871), although not one of the original buildings on the Hill, is the only one left that was there in the 1880s.
3. Charles William Dabney (1855–1945), UT president 1887–1904. Rothrock, 405–407.
4. During the 1920s and 1930s, Armstrong published numerous articles on business and labor management issues after having worked as personnel director at National City Company of New York City and assistant manager of industrial relations at Eastman Kodak Company in Rochester, N.Y.
5. Cooper D. Schmitt, M. A., was professor of mathematics. Rule, *History of Knoxville,* 377, 383.
6. According to Rothrock, Cary Fletcher Spence (1869–1943) distinguished himself as an athlete while attending the University of Tennessee. He rose to the rank of Captain in the Spanish-American War and was appointed a brigadier-general in 1922 after

commanding his regiment in France and Belgium from April 1, 1918 to May 20, 1919 during World War I. Rothrock, *French Broad-Holston Country,* 488.

7. Webb School in Middle Tennessee was founded by W. R. "Sawney" Webb in 1870 at Culleoka, Tennessee. His brother, John M. Webb, joined him three years later as a teacher at the school. In 1886 they moved their school to Bell Buckle, where it is still in operation. Sawney's grandson, William Robert Webb III (1919–2005), founded Webb School of Knoxville in 1955, using the school in Bell Buckle as a model. Robert Webb's father, Daniel Clary Webb (1881–1954), had come to Knoxville around 1907 to practice law in the office of a cousin, John Webb Green (1859–1957). Both were prominent Knoxville attorneys and also served as judges. For more information, see A. Jon Frere, "Webb School," in *The Tennessee Encyclopedia of History & Culture,* ed. Carroll Van West (Nashville: Tennessee Historical Society/Rutledge Hill Press, 1998), 1043; and, Ridley Willis II, "Webb, William R. 'Sawney,'" 1044. Online at < http://tennesseeencyclopedia.net/ > (viewed August 19, 2017). Jack Neely, *A Splendid Instinct: Robert Webb and the Founding of the Webb School of Knoxville* (Oak Ridge, Tenn.: Tellico Books, 2006), 22–29; Deaderick, 620–21; J.C. (Jim) Tumblin, "Judge John W. Green," in *Fountain City: People Who Made a Difference,* 93–98.
8. Thomas Babington Macaulay (1800–1859) said: "That honesty is the best policy is a maxim which we firmly believe to be generally correct, even with respect to the temporal interests of individuals; but, with respect to societies, the rule is subject to still fewer exceptions, and that for this reason, that the life of societies is longer than the life of individuals." T. Babington Macaulay, "Sir John Malcolm's Life of Lord Clive," in *Critical and Miscellaneous Essays,* Volume 3 (Philadelphia: Carey and Hart, 1841), 126–127.
9. Line from Sir Walter Scott's historical narrative poem M*armion: A Tale of Flodden Field* (1808), Canto vi, Stanza 17.
10. One of several dance clubs organized in Knoxville during the 1880s and early 1890s. "The Past and Present," *The Morning Tribune* (1895), reprinted in *Knoxville Bicentennial Yesteryear II,* Jim Miller, comp. (Knoxville Yesteryear Historical Society, [1976]), 27–28.
11. Dr. Herman G. Bayless practiced medicine in Knoxville from 1886 until 1890. Rule, *Standard History of Knoxville,* 515.
12. No information positively identifying Hu White has been found to date.
13. Ralph Waldo Emerson, "History," in *Essays* (New York: Thomas Nelson, [1925?]), [10].
14. Emerson, "Heroism," in *Essays,* 189.
15. See reference in footnote 10. This 1895 newspaper article discusses the german, among other popular dances of the time.
16. Great Smoky Mountains.
17. Lines from "The Green Helmet" by William Butler Yeats. Yeats, *The Green Helmet and Other Poems* (New York: Macmillan, 1912), 91.
18. The "parade ground" to which AWA refers (located near the southeast corner of Cumberland Avenue and present-day Phillip Fulmer Way) later became Wait Field, the first

athletic field on the University of Tennessee campus, used between 1909 and 1920 for football, baseball, marching band, and cadet drill teams. When Shields-Watkins Field (now surrounded by Neyland Stadium) replaced it in the early 1920s, it was converted into tennis courts. It is now the site of Walters Life Sciences Building. On October 11, 2019, Wait Field Campus Historical Marker was dedicated as part of the University of Tennessee's 225th anniversary celebration. Allen, *Knoxville Miscellany*, 124–25; "Campus Historical Marker Dedication for Wait Field," https://calendar.utk.edu/event/campus_historical-marker-dedication-_wait_field (viewed October 1, 2020).

19. Roger Franklin Armstrong, Lieutenant, United States Navy, died October 26, 1922. He is buried in Arlington National Cemetery, Section 3, Site 4637. Arlington National Cemetery Website: http://www.arlingtoncemetery.net/rfarmstrong.htm (viewed September 13, 2017).

20. A local newspaper article reported the details of Harry Wetzell's drowning and included information about him and his family. "A Watery Grave," *Knoxville Journal*, June 5, 1888, 5. Two days later, the death notice described how his fellow cadets attended the family at their home and led the "funeral train" to the cemetery. "Harry Wetzell's Funeral," *Knoxville Journal*, June 7, 1888, 6.

Chapter Ten

The Jolly Time

That summer after the first great shadow had fallen upon our family, Mama went to stay with one of her sisters. Papa had to return to England and I spent the summer with cousins who had a summer home on Lake Michigan, while the Barnes house was loaned to a young couple in Knoxville who during our absence would look after Trix, now doubly dear as "Harry's dog."

Sometimes that summer as I sat with the others watching the sun "drown" in Lake Michigan and then lingering on the porch as the twilight gathered, a sudden realization that Harry was gone, not to return, would sweep over me and involuntarily I would start sobbing. But in general it seemed as unreal now that he was dead as when taps had sounded over him after he was laid in Old Gray.

Most of the time I was the merriest of the merry and under my own supervision commenced doing my hair up on top of my head, thus announcing that I had taken another step in growing up.

All of us met in Cincinnati on the way home, Papa coming directly there from the ship after he landed, and the first thing Mama saw was the change in my hair. She smiled, though her eyes filled with tears. Her eyes were now seldom free from tears. She had wept so much that the doctor said she had injured them.

Papa had brought back ivy from both Kenilworth Castle and Melrose Abbey to plant on Harry's grave—a kind of thing people did in what seem to us now those sentimental days.

But coming back to the Barnes house was hard for all of us. It was September and every afternoon when the hour approached for cadets living in West End to be going by on their way home from the Hill we had to endure the sight of Trix at the side gate, waiting for Harry. The passing cadets would whistle to her, call her by name, but she would never join them, only wag her tail; still wait and wait for the one she was looking for till finally, abandoning her post, with a deep soughing breath, like a human sigh, she would settle down on the ground somewhere not too far away.

At every turn we were reminded of Harry, and Mama looked so sad it was harder to bear than anything else. Yet there was much to see to at this time. She had selected the college I was to go to, learned its entrance requirements and as some of the subjects were not taught in the Girls' High School was seeking a tutor for me. I would infinitely have preferred going to Miss Cary's in Baltimore—to any one of a number of "finishing schools" the girls I knew best were planning to go to. But now that Harry was gone, my parents, it was plain, were centering their hopes and ambitions on me, and there seemed no alternative to following their wishes.

For all she was carrying her usual responsibilities as capably as ever, Mama continued to be deeply depressed. Long, long afterwards she confided to me that there was a touch of morbidity in her make-up; dark moods, often inexplicable ones, she had had to fight from her youth on and only conquered completely in her old age. And now, this September, she was so unlike herself that in spite of my preoccupation with my own affairs her condition troubled me, so that I was not surprised when Papa announced that when he returned to England shortly he was taking Mama with him. A complete change of scene he thought would do her good. They would spend the autumn in Scotland, some time in London, some on the Continent. (The old 19th Century cure for all human ills—Europe!) They would not return till Spring and Aunt Allie would come to stay with my younger sister and me.

Just why Aunt Allie was chosen to come, I never quite understood. She was one of my father's sisters, unmarried, middle-aged, inclined to be fretful, and a trifle "queer" I had always thought. She was as different from Papa as brother and sister could possibly be.[1] I still remembered once in my childhood when Aunt Allie, visiting us, called my father's attention to the account of a theatre somewhere that had burned to the ground, remarking as she did so that it was "God's work." Next day my father called her attention to a church just destroyed by fire. Patting her on the shoulder affectionately, he inquired with a mischievous look, "And whose work was *this*, Alice?"

Well, Mama must be even worse than I had thought or Papa would have taken time to find someone else. But of one thing I was certain. Mama would never have consented to go abroad unless she had heard that Hu White was no longer in Knoxville. He had become a "commercial traveler" with headquarters in St. Louis, I believe it was. And reflecting on this, I wondered for the first time whether Mama's anxiety over Hu might have been due to fear that I might run away with him. Aunt Caroline, the most lovable of Papa's sisters, had eloped when she was no older than I, married a flashy young man who turned out a consummate rascal, even deserting her after they had a houseful of children.[2]

But Mama could have been spared further anxiety on this score had she only known all that there was to know.

One evening at the Gaines Hu had slipped a ring off my finger and on to one of his own, a bit of foolery that gave me no concern at the moment and none when, parting hurriedly, he failed to return it. The ring, however, happened to be valuable, a ruby encircled by pearls, and after Harry's death when I was leaving with the rest of the family for the summer and he still had not returned it, I was seized with panic. Suppose Mama should find out! I sent him a frantic message, though it was only at the last moment before the train started that one of his friends appeared and stealthily handed me a little package. Alone in my berth I unwrapped it, to find the ring but to my consternation another red stone, a cheap garnet, had been substituted for the ruby, a precious gem.

I never wore the ring again in Mama's presence. I almost never wore it again at all. I buried it at the bottom of my trinket-box, wanting no reminder of *L'Affaire Hu White*, ended once and forever.

I do not remember that I was in the least upset at the prospect of our parents going so far away and for so long. We had been accustomed always to quick decisions, to any or all of us going places and on short notice, and now almost at once a vista opened before me of limitless freedom. I was in high feather at the very thought. The keys of the kingdom were now to be placed in my hands. The kingdom was Knoxville, of which Aunt Allie was profoundly ignorant, but every foot of which was filled for me with potential adventure.

With all the hurry, however, of their getting off, Papa did not neglect to remind me to be considerate of Ben Pitman. He realized, apparently, that Ben, not one of my intimates, might not be too acceptable, dropping in as he did now every day. But Papa and Mama felt very tender toward Ben. No doubt they bore in their minds searing images of Harry in his desperate struggle with death pleading with Ben to save him. They knew that only Ben would ever know the true horror of those moments.

Mama, in leaving, was chiefly concerned that she had not been able to acquaint Aunt Allie with more of our neighbors. This, she said, would now be *my* responsibility and to make Aunt Allie as happy as possible in every respect.

I am visited by qualms even today when I think of the manner in which I discharged these responsibilities, although I lost no time in acquainting Aunt Allie with those of our neighbors I thought she would find most congenial. Never had I been so grateful for "good" Presbyterians and no farther away than across the street or around the corner. May and I would accompany her of course to church on Sunday morning and introduce her at Sunday School, but she would go with neighbors to Sunday evening church services, to prayer meeting on Wednesday night, and to the Ladies' Home and Foreign Missionary Society. This would make Aunt Allie happy and make me happy too.

What made me still happier was taking full charge of things even before Papa and Mama had boarded the *Umbria* of the old Cunard Line for Liverpool, and one of the last things they would have anticipated, for Aunt Allie had always been looked upon as something of a boss. I had heard it said that she ran over Grandmother and over her sisters as long as they were at home. But now, before she could assume any managerial prerogatives, I assumed them myself.

True, circumstances favored me. It was a bold move on Mama's part, but on the very eve of her departure she had employed a new cook, a white one, and even more ignorant than Aunt Allie of the way our house ordinarily was run—of regulations as rigid as the laws of the Medes and the Persians. But Becky had come with high recommendations and Mama felt it would be easier for Aunt Allie to deal with a white than a colored cook. Moreover Hester, Uncle Pompey, and Bonnie, the mulatto cook Becky was supplanting, all lived some distance away, and Mama thought there should be a servant "on the place" during her own and Papa's absence. Thus it was that Becky Melton came to be installed in the bleak, prison-like, hideous servant's room opening off our blue-walled, gloomy, hideous kitchen, and was to become my most active collaborator in the new regime.

A rosy, husky young mountain woman, her primitive instincts not yet perceptibly affected by a few years of town life, Becky was the nearest thing, in the shape of a woman, to a force of nature I had ever encountered or would again. She had married a son of Old Man Melton, almost as well known a figure in Knoxville's underworld as the town rat-catcher, Louis Ruckart.

Tall, stooped, with long white hair and dressed in a tattered soldier's uniform, Old Man Melton disdained begging on the street or among the swarm of beggars on Market Square. Calling at the front door of the best houses in town, he would ask for its mistress and when she appeared address her with great dignity: "Madame, I'm no beggar. I'm a veteran of the Mexican War and I would thank you if you can spare me a dollar or a little cold chicken," and amused by the old scamp's gall, few refused him one or the other and usually gave him both.

But Becky, married to a Melton, had found the family unsatisfactory. The son, like the father, had always been averse to work, so she had gone into domestic service, and although as far from humble as her father-in-law, and unaware of or refusing to recognize any differences in social rank, she had nonetheless built up an enviable reputation as honest, a hard worker, immaculately clean and an excellent cook. What more could Mama ask?

Becky, however, a very sociable being, could never have dreamed that Mama, unless for an occasional candy-pulling, did not allow her children in the kitchen and I had no intention of informing her of this fact, so now I began to visit her, watching her cook, joking and carrying on prolonged conversations with her, and presently, with the aid of Marian Harland's and Fanny Farmer's Cook Books and with Becky to clean up, I was cooking myself, making not only fondant and all sorts of "French Candies," but cakes, Charlotte Russe, salted almonds, and even chicken salad. I decided I had a flair for cooking. In any case never had I had such fun—creating all these delicacies, then helping devour my own creations.

Soon our grimy soot-stained dismal old kitchen, resounding with continual laughter, became the centre toward which Mary and the other girls, together with some of our beaux, gravitated the moment they entered the house.

Strongest of its attractions was Becky herself. Utterly unabashed by all these young town folks, with her quick wit, her spirited, astonishingly earthy sallies, expressed in the vernacular of the East Tennessee mountaineer, she was a source of unfailing amusement.

Becky, the fact is, taught me a good many things, and she added to my vocabulary. Preparing soup one day, as she picked bits of shell from the oysters, she exclaimed, "Phew! You-all can eat 'em if you're a mind to, but I ain't a-goin' to eat no critters with the guts in 'em."

"Guts" was not then a term heard in the best circles. To me it was a brand-new and arresting word, and with it still in mind at table that day, with guests present, suddenly I inquired, "Aunt Allie, what are 'guts'?"

Aunt Allie drew back in horror.

"It's not a word," she answered, after a pause, in a low voice, "you should ever use!"

But even Aunt Allie, spinsterish, almost painfully refined though she was, before long succumbed to Becky's ingenuous and lusty charm. In no time at all she was sharing with her some of her own prized recipes; showing her how to make spiced grapes, preserved crab-apples, jellied chicken molded in a special form, and Philadelphia scrapple.

To be sure from time to time all this familiarity with a servant—especially my own familiarity with one—gave Aunt Allie pause. Her Philadelphia notions of the social proprieties deeply ingrained, she would ask, her brow knit, "But Annie, do you think your mama would approve?" and I would reply promptly, recklessly, though all at once a trifle uneasy, "Oh, yes. Mama wouldn't care!"

All in all, however, Aunt Allie was proving a simpler problem than I had dared hope. She had interposed no objections when I proceeded to plan all our meals, presumably one of *her* functions, and seemed positively relieved when, taking her to market, I forged ahead, decided what we should buy, and bought it.

The Knoxville market as a matter of fact from the minute our carriage stopped at the back of the Second Presbyterian churchyard and little Negro boys came running to meet us and carry our baskets—with its surging Saturday crowds, wonderful array of comestibles and people buying live fowls to carry home by their feet, was as astonishing to her as was Becky.

The only thing that seemed to disturb Aunt Allie on these marketing trips was my extravagance. Chops, steaks, rib roasts—these of course were standard. But I was buying *turkeys*—turkeys not alone for holidays or Sunday but for any day in the week, and so *many* chickens! (Chicken salad had become daily fare.) But then I was buying Cuban pineapples too, whatever their price—anything at all that struck my fancy, once a whole dozen of costly shaddock, a novelty which had recently appeared (later called grape-fruit).

"Oh, everybody in Knoxville lives this way," I would assure Aunt Allie blithely, and there was at least a grain of truth in the statement. Many did.

But it was after we left the stalls in the Market House behind and started picking our way through stray dogs, beggars, marketers, and between the hucksters' wagons which helped block the narrow thoroughfare separating the Market House from Jim Anderson's[3] that Aunt Allie's near-sighted eyes behind her pince-nez began to wear a look of distinct discomfiture.

Jim Anderson's dark cluttered store was Knoxville's S. S. Pierce.[4] Here you would find the choicest dry groceries, tinned and bottled goods, in town. Here I would run riot; buying pickled oysters, Edam cheeses, bottle after bottle of the biggest olives I could find, box after box of Peek Frean's wafers, cans and cans of imported *Champignons* and *Petits Pois,* whose little French labels especially fascinated me—any epicurean items that caught my eye, and had I been acquainted at the time with *vol-au-vents* and Russian caviar and Jim Anderson been able to supply them, beyond question they would have been added to my order.

But now at last poor Aunt Allie, following me around meekly in her black dolman, her modest little black bonnet, would demur.

"Oh, Annie, we don't *need* such *expensive* food—just for *us*!"

And I would answer, "Why, Aunt Allie, Papa and Mama would *like* us to have whatever we want."

Certainly the money I was spending gave me no personal concern for never in my life had I heard my parents say of anything that they couldn't afford it. And when Aunt Allie and I ran out of money, all we had to do now was to go to Papa's offices on Gay Street, as he had arranged, and get more.

Money—it was something I never heard discussed at home, and never would, when it comes to that, not even in the hidden years ahead.

But this fling at high living was no mere matter of self-indulgence. As I was experiencing for the first time the joy of cooking, so I was having my initial experience in entertaining. Papa and Mama frequently entertained, in such restricted fashion as the Barnes house permitted. But all the time we had lived there, although I had often spent the night with other girls, none had spent the night with me, or even been asked for a meal. Ill at ease as I invariably was in Mama's presence when my young friends were around, I am not sure I would have desired it. In any event, now I was having girls constantly for meals, sumptuous meals; using our finest damask, the French Haviland decorated with butterflies, the Dresden dessert service, the pearl-handled knives and the gold after-dinner coffee spoons.

The whole mode of life in our house was, in a word, revolutionized. Mama would not have recognized her own home had she dropped in. I was making it over, to the best of my ability, in the image of Mary Gaines' home and of other Knoxville households where mothers resembling Mrs. Gaines in some degree kept in the background, slaving, if need be, from morning till night, far into the night, that their daughters might not miss the dazzling, if fleeting, gayety of belle-of-the-ball days *they* once had known.

Inspired by such examples, our parlor was now as lively as our kitchen and with the same wild shrieks of merriment coming from it that, coming from the Gaines' parlor, disturbing her sleep, so enraged Mrs. Bauer.

I was sixteen now. The lads who came were no longer largely from the Hill, their homes here and there in the state, or in other states. They belonged to Knoxville. They were the young men with whom I would associate through the rest of my youth, and they came and went, crossed the hall from the parlor to the sitting-room where someone seated at the piano would be playing and singing,

> After the ball is over,
> After the lights are dim,

or some other song to which no one was paying much if any attention—they moved back and forth with an air of being so completely at home, that Aunt Allie seemed to accept this constant stirring around, these mad gusts of laughter arising from one side of the house or the other, as a matter of course. She said to herself, perhaps, that this extraordinary frivolity was what she should have expected in Henry's house, "with *his* views!" For, Henry was a brother of whom she was inordinately proud, yet about whom, and whose "soul," she no doubt felt anxious at times.

But whatever her thoughts, Aunt Allie protested no more against these noisy evenings than against any other of the strange things she had witnessed since her arrival.

True, she was probably slightly dazed at the start, suddenly thrown into the midst of all these vivacious and anything but inarticulate young people. Notwithstanding that she was domineering by nature, she tended at first to be shy. But there was none of Mama's stately elegance about Aunt Allie, nothing to hold them at a distance, and soon the young men would seek her out where she was sitting apart with her tatting or crocheting. "We're *mighty* happy to have you here, Miss Allie," they would say in their warm friendly way. They would pay her compliments. Jim Fletcher—and a fine stroke of diplomacy it was—brought those superb bouquets from Mrs. O'Conner's green-houses, which heretofore he had brought to me, to Aunt Allie.

They won her. Knoxville won her. She was impressed by its great glistening magnolia trees, its early resplendent spring, by the Second Presbyterian Church, by all our kind neighbors, and by that magnificent show-place, Island Home, to which she had been taken, with other ladies, by no less a person than the Honorable Perez Dickinson himself, sitting beside him in the landau, at least on their return, and receiving from his own hand some of the celebrated Maréchal Niels.

Before that fall and winter and spring were over there would be more than enough for Aunt Allie to worry about. There would be conflict between us. But all the same she endeared herself to me by her delight in Knoxville. It was a bond between us. I could never bear to hear Knoxville disparaged and Aunt Allie, wholly unromantic though I considered her, yet seemed to have caught a gleam of that magic light which, for me, ever played over the town. To the end of her days, and she lived to be eighty, she spoke of her "happy" stay there. Its soot, the difficulty with me which developed, she seemed to have forgotten, and when she referred to Knoxville invariably her voice would suddenly become tender: "And all those lovely young men! What became of them? Tell me . . ."

Ben, she perhaps would not have classed as one of the "lovely" young men. He possessed none of those social graces, that flattering manner, common to Knoxville young men. I myself, I confess, took outrageous advantage of what seems to me now his touching eagerness, since Harry's death, to be of use to us. I had him fetching and carrying at a great rate, running endless errands. With no telephones then, there was always a message for him to deliver to someone. When the tutti-frutti ice-cream, or whatever it was, failed to arrive, it was Ben who could be counted upon to rush uptown to Peter Kern's[5] and bring it back. With his excessive good humor and unfailing readiness to joke, Ben contributed no little, the fact is, to the jollity of those disordered but honeyed days.

But while I gloried in my new-found freedom and in the blissful state of things I had contrived to create around me, nevertheless there were times when I suffered, if only momentarily, from twinges of conscience. I had so little time, it seemed, for studying, and I could never quite lose sight of the fact that this was the year I was preparing for college. But then would come letters from Mama and Papa, mostly from Papa, and my mind would be set at rest.

Mama was looking so much better, Papa wrote. She had loved their autumn days on Loch Lomond and Loch Katrine;[6] enjoyed the life in the English country houses in Cheshire and Herefordshire where they'd been visiting; she had found the ancient little Wood's Hotel, Furnival's Inn,[7] where Dickens wrote *Pickwick Papers* and where Papa always stayed when alone in London, very quaint and interesting, though they were stopping now, as his stationery indicated, at a hotel "more suitable for ladies," one in the fashionable West End. . . . They had had wonderful afternoons at the National Gallery and seen Irving and Ellen Terry in *The Merchant of Venice* and other plays. In Paris, there had been the Opera, the "divine Sarah,"[8] the Louvre, and "your Mama is having two dresses, which I suppose will be very fine, made by Worth."[9]

Clearly, there was no reason for further worry about Mama, and with every fresh reminder of the good times they were having I felt more comfortable about the one *I* was having.

But there were always wistful, slightly homesick touches, too, in Papa's letters:

"How May would enjoy a little two-wheeled pony-cart such as the Crouchley children [of the family they visited in Cheshire] drive around in. I think she must have one."

"How Annie would have enjoyed our visit to Gad's Hill, Dickens' home in Kent, where if the great master is no longer there (we placed flowers yesterday on his tomb in the Abbey), and the house not shown, yet your Mama and I had the privilege of listening to a nightingale as we strolled past the hedges in front of the place at twilight."

Often there was reference to a sailing or rowing match—to something "the dear boy always in our thoughts" would have enjoyed.

But there were also many references to happy years ahead, to the new house which Papa thought could be started this coming summer when he hoped not to be in England so much and could give it his attention. "Your Mama," he wrote, "has been very patient with the inconvenient old Barnes house, but never mind, it won't be long—" And then he would outline some of the features they were planning for the new house.

Sometimes, when I read passages of this sort in my father's letters, although my parents' return was still some distance off, it suddenly seemed imminent. I would resolve to start studying in earnest the next day. But I was caught in the web I had woven. It was difficult to extricate myself. And as the spring advanced, in addition to dances and the high-jinks at home there were surrey parties now to some nearby resort, and picnic parties on the river; all to be discussed beforehand, prepared for, and in the manner of young girls, talked over endlessly after the event. I was, the truth is, in a constant state of intoxication, not from drink but from sheer animal spirits, from a huge zest for living, and from that hurry which courses through the veins of youth. So my resolve would weaken, die completely.

There was a limit, however, to what I could put over on Aunt Allie, and once she realized the extent of my delinquency, she would warn me daily: "I'm going to tell your mother and father exactly how you've done!"

This jolly time was different from other times in more ways than one. It was not only that I hardly touched the piano from one music lesson to the next; that I frittered away my mornings, presumably devoted to Latin and to solving mathematical problems assigned me the day before by my tutor, Dr. Tuck. It was more than that. Heretofore, for several years past, I had lived in two equally joyful worlds; the real world and the world of books. Books like Hennell's *Inquiry into the Origin of Christianity*, Emerson's *Society and Solitude*, the works of Voltaire and Huxley (my more recent unorthodox delights), aroused in me intense excitement. They were part and parcel of my passionate secret life and I could have echoed a sentiment Thomas Wolfe was to express more than half a century later: "No one who has not known the adventure of great books knows what a good time is."[10]

But now was a time when I was living wholly in the real world. Books had no power to enthrall me. For all intents and purposes my education was at a standstill, save in one direction.

Mary, a year or so since, had prized out of the Gaines' cook all the information on the subject of sex—still recurrently of feverish interest to us—that she was likely to get from Aunt Melissa. A new source must be tapped and it was from the elemental Becky we learned more.

To Becky, there were no unmentionables, and hanging around her in the kitchen one late afternoon when Aunt Allie had not yet returned from the Missionary Society and Becky was cutting up a chicken, getting it ready to fry for supper, emboldened by her talk, as cheerful and uninhibited as the speech of that immortal old reprobate, the Wife of Bath,[11] Mary and I put some questions to her.

To Becky, there were not only no unmentionables, there was nothing in marriage that deserved reticence, so she gave us a frank and withal jovial account of her wedding night, but one so circumstantial, couched in such raw terms, that although we laughed heartily while we were with her, we came away thoroughly sobered.

"I vow," Mary said, in a subdued voice, when we reached a part of the back porch out of Becky's hearing, "I vow I'll never marry as long as I live!"

As I remember it, I took a similar vow. Becky's lusty realism had been too much for us. Never had Holy Matrimony seemed so unholy.

But the thing in those hectic, irresponsible days I look back upon with unalloyed pleasure, despite my disgraceful neglect of the lessons assigned me, was my afternoon hour or so with Dr. Tuck.

I have an impression that Dr. Tuck, a retired Presbyterian minister, had never had a pastorate in Knoxville. In any case I had never heard him preach, which was perhaps as well, for if his sermons were as dull as those I was accustomed to listening to, they would hardly have predisposed me in his favor.

Just where he came from and why he was living in Knoxville, I do not recall, if I ever knew. But he was living at the time on Walnut Street,[12] in an unpretentious frame house next door to Miss Betty Carter's boarding-house, and facing an unkempt vacant lot opposite, beyond which loomed the new and ornate *Vendome*, Knoxville's first apartment house and considered a definitely fashionable venture.

I became extremely familiar with this not altogether pleasing prospect through the many months when I sat beside Dr. Tuck at the table beneath the front windows of his book-lined study, trying, with his gentle aid, to solve some problem in advanced algebra, for which I had not the slightest gift, or blundering through a passage in Cicero's *Orations* or his *De Senectute* which I had failed to look at before leaving home, trusting I would be inspired, which I never was, to get through it when the time came without too much trouble.

For all my ineptitude, however, and general demoralization at the time, Dr.

Tuck was able to make a dead language come alive to me. Latin, to start with, was a study I had found more congenial than some others and when I was unable to grasp at sight the meaning of such a phrase, for example, as *Fortiter in res sed suaviter in modo*, and with a lively look in the old eyes behind the spectacles, wagging a finger at me, he would say, "Why, yes! Why, yes! Of course you understand. This refers, freely translated, to your father: 'Resolute in the conduct of his affairs but persuasive in his manner of dealing with his fellow men'"—then I would be enchanted.

Thus it was that, in spite of myself, Dr. Tuck led my lagging steps along the road I must travel if I were ever to enter college. He seemed never to despair of me entirely, though the thought must have crossed his mind more than once that I was anything but what we now call "college material." But observing me arrive at his house, often late, often with a lad or two accompanying me to his gate, to his very door, as we lingered, laughing and chattering together, he seemed to realize that there were strong and legitimate attractions competing with Latin and mathematics for my attention. All the same, thoroughly in favor of higher education for women, periodically he would applaud my "ambitious spirit," which, if it pleased me, at the same time made me feel more than a trifle guilty, knowing, as I did, that it was not of my own volition I was going to college.

It would be hard to imagine a figure less likely to capture the fancy of a girl of sixteen than Dr. Tuck. Aged, bent, slightly tottery, I can no longer, it is true, as with so many faces of that long past time, make out his features at all clearly. Nevertheless his shadowy image in a long black coat, shiny from wear, as he emerged through the folding-doors from the dining-room beyond, where he would retire from time to time, leaving me to solve some problem, if I could, by myself; the sort of youthful eagerness in his lined homely old face, aglow with goodness and kindness, intelligence and humor—with all lovely human traits, these will remain with me so long as memory itself remains. Of all my teachers, private or public, at grammar and high school, college, university, while I liked and respected many of them, Dr. Tuck, with Molly Hayes, stand by themselves as the two I loved.

But neither my love of Dr. Tuck nor his inexhaustible patience could save me. The day of reckoning was at hand. From the moment the cable came stating the date of Mama and Papa's sailing from Liverpool I had a sinking feeling, one that never left me.

My halcyon existence was over, when every day was a holiday, every evening resembled a party. I applied myself furiously now to my studies, but I could not escape the fact that already it was spring and I had nothing like covered the ground I was supposed to, which would mean inevitably that I must continue all summer going to Dr. Tuck.

The worst, however, was poor Aunt Allie. She had prodded me incessantly for weeks past, with negative results. Never had I known her so irritable, so peevish, while her face wore a more and more harassed expression as the day when she must make an accounting of her guardianship drew near.

It must have been late April, or possibly early May, when Papa and Mama reached Knoxville. I remember dreamily that apple trees around us in West End were in blossom and peoples' yards, vivid with tulips. But this was a year, when "the year was at spring," and I was too sick not alone at heart but actually in body, to be more than half alive to its enchantments.

The train from New York got into Knoxville early, so that Papa and Mama were home in time for breakfast. Mama looked more beautiful than ever in a little Parisian bonnet, without ties, the last word in chic. Her eyes were less sad, although they would not lose their sad look entirely for many, many years to come. She seemed pleased, though a bit regretful, to see how May had grown. Soon there would be no child in the house.

Papa started to his office directly he finished breakfast. Mama, at the table, continued to regard me thoughtfully.

"Annie, you're looking pale," Mama said. "Are you feeling all right?"

"Oh, yes!" I said, in as sprightly a tone as I could command.

"I hope," Mama said, "you've not been studying too hard."

A pang shot through me. But it was after breakfast the real ordeal began. My head was going round and round, my heart pounding. There was that feeling in my stomach. Would Aunt Allie tell or wouldn't she? Then when through a kind of roaring in my ears I heard her saying to Mama, "Linnie, will you come with me to the parlor?" and as the parlor door closed behind them, I started to feel as a prisoner at the bar must as he waits for the jury to emerge and announce the verdict. There could be of course but one verdict, but sentence would follow. Mingled with other emotions, I suffered now from some of that sense of exasperation expressed in Sherwood Anderson's story, "I'm a Fool."[13] Yes, I had been a fool, in addition to everything else.

But it was impossible to keep still. The time they were in the parlor seemed endless. I walked back and forth in the side yard, out of range of the parlor windows, and finally back to the kitchen, where I knew I would have succor, for the moment, if no more, in whole-hearted sympathy from Becky.

Becky was washing the breakfast dishes. "Law's a mercy, you're white as a corpse!" she greeted me as I appeared at the kitchen door. Then, as I started out again, wiping her hands on her apron, she followed me. "Honey," she said, "hit ain't no use you a-wearyin' yourself about hit." She slapped me playfully on the back. "Your mammy cain't do no more 'an kill ye!"

But for once I was in no mood for Becky's joking. Anyway, I might as well hear what I had to hear as soon as possible. Anything but this suspense. My legs trembling, I took up my stand in the doorway of the sitting-room, facing the door to the parlor across the hall, my hands gripping the door-facings.

I could hear the black marble clock on the sitting-room mantel behind me ticking away the awful minutes and the low rumble of talk in the parlor, although I was unable to distinguish any words until at length Mama's voice, raised and impatient, suddenly broke the stillness, "Yes, Alice! Yes, Alice!"

The parlor door opened. It was hard to tell whether Mama's or Aunt Allie's face was the deeper crimson.

Mama looked startled when she saw me confronting her, my face blanched, my hands lifted above me, clinging to the door jambs, in a posture suggesting one of the early Christian martyrs, prepared for burning. She smiled, a weak smile. After all, I was her offspring, however errant.

"Well, Annie," she said, "I suppose you'd like to see what I've brought you. Let's open the trunks," and she led the way back to her bed-room where the baggage-men had deposited them.

NOTES

1. Alice Wetzell (1852–1927) was almost ten years younger than her brother, who was born in 1843.
2. Caroline Wetzell (1849–1943) married George Davis Miles (1848–1920) in 1870. They had seven children together.
3. Jim Anderson Company, wholesale and retail grocers, 4 Market Square. *Knoxville City Directory,* 1893.
4. S. S. Pierce & Company, "importers and grocers," was established in 1831 by Samuel Stillman Pierce and was Boston's premiere place to shop for fancy foods and imported delicacies. Title page, *S.S. Pierce & Co. [Price List]* (Boston: S.S. Pierce & Co., 1886), Harvard Business School, Baker Library Web page: <http://id.lib.harvard.edu/aleph/007846778/catalog> (viewed November 1, 2017); "Laird of the Epicurean Manner," *Time,* June 23, 1967, 94.
5. Ice Cream Parlor at the corner of Prince (now Market) Street and Union Avenue near Market Square.
6. Lakes in the Scottish Highlands.
7. Wood's Hotel was a part of Furnival's Inn on its north side. Henry Benjamin Wheatley, *London, Past and Present: Its History, Associations, and Traditions* (London: J. Murray, 1891), vol. 2, 83–84.
8. French actress Sarah Bernhardt (1844–1923).
9. "House of Worth," fashion design firm founded by Charles Frederick Worth (1825–1895). Prominent during latter part of the nineteenth century.
10. Author Thomas Wolfe (1900–1938) was a friend and correspondent of Armstrong. It is possible that he made this remark to her in person. In September 1937 he stopped over for a few days at her home in Sullivan County, Tennessee, on his way from Asheville,

N.C., back to New York City. Ted Mitchell, *Thomas Wolfe: A Writer's Life,* rev. ed. (Raleigh: North Carolina Division of Archives and History, 1999), 73, 78–79. Anne W. Armstrong, "As I Saw Thomas Wolfe," *Arizona Quarterly* 2 (Spring 1946): 5–15.

11. Bawdy character in Chaucer's *Canterbury Tales*. After giving a long prologue about her own life and five husbands, she tells her fellow pilgrims "The Wife of Bath's Tale."
12. The Reverend Nathan F. Tuck lived at 143 Walnut, just across Union Street from Girls' High School which at that time occupied the northwest corner of Walnut where Knoxville's "Daylight Building" now stands. *Knoxville City Directory,* 1886–1889. In the 1885 Knoxville directory *only,* the first in which his name appears, he is listed as principal of Knoxville Female Seminary.
13. Sherwood Anderson (1876–1941), novelist and short-story writer, was an acquaintance of Armstrong in her adult life. His last home was in southwest Virginia near its border with northeast Tennessee, where Armstrong was living at the time she was writing her memoir. David McClellan, "A Personal Reminiscence," in Anne W. Armstrong, *This Day and Time* (1930; repr., Johnson City, Tenn.: Research Advisory Council, East Tennessee State University, 1958), xii.

Chapter Eleven

Summer of 1889

I think there could never have been a hotter summer in Knoxville than the summer of 1889. At sixteen, few things are of course of less moment than the weather. Even so, I retain an imperishable memory of sticky oppressive mornings when I sat hour after sweaty hour practicing the piano or upstairs in my bed-room toiling over Latin and algebra and geometry; of sweltering afternoons when, wet to the skin, I climbed the Clinch Street hills to and from lessons with Dr. Tuck, tormented by the thought of the other girls, going to "finishing schools," where no entrance examinations were required, and free to do what women and girls of Knoxville's gentry all did in summer, took off their clothes directly after the superabundant midday dinner, donned their nightgowns and lay on the bed till late afternoon when they made fresh toilettes for supper and the long leisurely evening on their own or someone's else porch. For all my envying them their freedom, however, I was experiencing a strong sense of relief. Neither my father nor mother ever mentioned to me the ruthless advantage I had taken of their absence. They might have reminded me—and this would have hurt—that they had trusted me and I had proved unworthy of trust. But they did nothing of the kind.

In any case, it was not with a contrite heart, not as the faithful climbing the Scala Sancta in Rome to wipe out their sins, that I climbed the hills of Clinch Street that torrid summer. If the true mark of *joie de vivre* is an unrepentant spirit, I possess it, for beyond doubt I would have done the same thing again had another such golden opportunity presented itself, and my collapse on the day of Papa and Mama's return was not rooted in a sense of guilt so much as in abject fear of the crushing price I might have to pay.

To tell the truth, that long stay abroad of theirs had been a sort of premature coming of age for me. However unconscious of it at the time, it had developed a sense of initiative; awakened latent instincts; fanned a spark that would not be too lightly blown out in time to come. Long years afterwards when in middle life I went into business and without previous business experience became an executive in an internationally known banking house in New York[1] (a story I told anonymously in the *Atlantic*, in "A Woman in Wall Street"),[2] it was nothing short of a minor miracle to Mama. To the day of her death, to her, as to most Victorian ladies, business—especially Big Business—was a profound mystery. She could hardly believe what had happened and expressed her amazement.

"But Mama," I reminded her, "I've had administrative experience in other lines, if not in business. And then," I laughed, "don't you remember that year you and Papa were abroad so long and I took complete charge of the Barnes house, bossing everybody, including bossy Aunt Allie? Wouldn't you say that showed I had the makings in me of a future executive?" And Mama laughed too.

But she did not laugh back in the summer of 1889.

All the same Mama was different that summer. She had replaced the irrepressible white Becky (whose informal ways and conversational powers she did not relish as I had) with our former cook, the quiet and mannerly Bonnie, and there were no more madcap goings-on in the kitchen now, none in the rest of the house. But this was to have been expected. The difference was in her relation to me. Not that any easy confidence was established between us. Nevertheless she was different. It may have been Harry's death combined with her long absence that made her less strict. It may have been a realization that I was older and would soon be going away for a long time myself. And it may have been that my father, the most adaptable of men himself, had persuaded her she must make more concessions to the environment in which I was growing up, more allowance for differing mores in different regions.

But whatever it was, she seemed willing now for me to have all the pleasure I could under circumstances for which, alas, I was responsible myself. Between work and play, never had I known days of such feverish activity. But if Mama offered no open encouragement to youths—gradually older ones—who called during hours I was free, at least I was less uncomfortable than heretofore when I sat in the parlor with them, or when a group of young people gathered after dark on our porch; while when a young man took me to the theatre—to the *Mikado*,[3] or whatever it might be—, or another on a surrey party, driving to Fountain Head, six or seven miles out of town, where we would have supper and later dance in the big airy dining-room of a rambling, rather shackly summer hotel there, flirt on the wide, dimly lighted verandahs that ran around three sides of it—Mama seemed almost pleased.[4]

It was only, that summer, when I went on the river that Mama could not conceal her anxiety. Since Harry was drowned she had no faith in the river. The very word filled her with dread. But to me, however foolhardily, utterly unafraid of the river or any other body of water, these were the best parties of all. There were no chaperones, for one thing, on these boating trips. Each girl would take a box supper for herself and her escort. We would meet at the boat-house on Front Street, under the bridge,[5] and with one or two couples to a boat row up the river to an appointed spot, usually Cave Springs, a fairly level stretch on the river's edge, strewn with mossy boulders, and with behind us a curtain of trumpet vines half-concealing the opening to the

Fountain Head Hotel, built in 1886. Later used by Holbrook Normal College to house female students.

cave and steep wooded bluffs that shut us in, as in a secret chamber, from all that lay beyond.[6] Here we would eat our supper and after the moon came up, float back to town in the moonlight, our voices ringing from bank to bank of the broad river as we sang more or less in unison whatever songs came into our heads.

There was only one feature of those river parties that marred my own pleasure. On the long walk with the boy who had taken me from the river back to West End, all the houses we passed would be sleeping, the streets deserted. In our house alone, as we neared it, we could see a light and whatever the hour, sometimes two in the morning, invariably through the semi-darkness could make out Mama, in a wrapper, pacing back and forth on our front porch. She would be in a state of extreme agitation and this would greatly embarrass me.

There were these embarrassments, but taking it all in all that crowded light-hearted summer was one of the happiest I would ever know.

As I look back, I am impressed, too, with the innocence of those golden days. A couple now and then on one of our outings would wander off by themselves for a while, but if there was plenty of foolery there was little wantonness. It was not that girls were more virtuous then, more chaste *au fond*. It was more that there were fewer opportunities for them to violate the moral and social code of the day. Obviously, the fact that girls did not drink then was a deterrent. Our mothers drank at formal dinner parties where in Knoxville, as elsewhere in that era, four or five wines were served. Men of all ages drank as a matter of course. I remember at dances at the Sans Souci Club not infrequently the boy who took you would be unable to bring you home. Nothing was easier to understand with fifty-one saloons in Knoxville and the "elegant barroom" of Schubert's Hotel only a step or two down the street from the club-rooms. When it occurred, some other young man brought you home. There was no fuss. You thought nothing of it. It was simply the custom of the day for young men to drink and young girls not to. But it must be acknowledged that there was another factor which helped sustain that age of innocence, so far as girls were concerned; the tacit understanding of the time and place that young men of social position, granted unlimited license when it came to drinking, were not by the same token expected to play sensuously upon a girl of their own class—not with the social risk involved, not (as you heard it a few years later put frankly) with a Crozier Street in town, an Em Parham's, with complacent Negro house-girls.

But be that as it may, in all honesty, not many of us, I believe, who were young girls then, while we might be plagued with curiosity about the whole subject of sex, yet living, as we were, for the moment, living still in a magical world, were much disturbed by thoughts of sinful secret courses some of the young men of our acquaintance might be pursuing.

One of the bright features of that last summer—as it proved to be—that we were to live in the Barnes house, was Mama's greater attention to my clothes. She had brought home from Europe beautiful summer silks and other lovely materials. Some of these she had had made up for me, so that for the first time I felt I had dresses as attractive as the other girls wore.

Not that I am able to recall at all clearly what any of these dresses looked like, only my satisfaction in them. I marvel at women who can describe costumes they wore a quarter—yes, a half a century ago; sleeves, passementerie, every frill and furbelow that adorned them. Dress, I conclude, was never one of my ruling passions. Certainly few dresses I wore in the past century can I see now in my mind's eye. But there was one in the time I am writing of I have not forgotten; a delicate beige, as we call the color to-day, a summer evening gown, batiste perhaps, that fell off the shoulders and had a bertha and flounces of English eyelet embroidery of the same tint. I felt that it was becoming and recall my joy in it, although a more probable reason for my remembering it is its association with a party at the Alexander A. Arthurs' to which I wore it and was taken by Don Waring, a family friend and almost, I think, of my father's age—a party that stands by itself in my Book of Days.

Don Waring. Alexander A. Arthur. What memories surge through me!

The Arthurs at the time had not been long in Knoxville. An English promoter, with his sandy hair and side-whiskers looking more Scotch than English, Mr. Arthur was given to wearing checks and other clothes a bit loud for that day, though made by Bond Street tailors. All the same you recognized him at first glance as a man of importance, albeit not without a suggestion also about him of self-importance.[7] With Mrs. Arthur a tall slender Englishwoman,[8] at once gracious and reserved, this traveled and sophisticated couple were regarded from the start as social acquisitions in Knoxville, which already had several English remittance men residing there, daring horsemen, fabulous drinkers, gentlemen of leisure—picturesque figures in the local scene to which the Arthurs would add further color.

During their year or so in Knoxville the Arthurs lived on Hill Street, that street with fine old homes and an aristocratic air, which followed the river and overlooked it. They had taken and converted to their own uses a former convent, a square old brick house painted white; like Island Home, Perez Dickinson's country house, a type of mansion known quaintly in the Deep South as a "raised cottage," deceptively modest from the outside but disclosing inside a series of nobly proportioned rooms, and in this case its most distinctive feature a gilded cross on top which the Arthurs retained.

The house stood on a corner, rather near the street, with many splendid old trees, great spreading magnolias, enormous crepe myrtles and other Southern shrubs growing luxuriantly in the grounds surrounding the house, sloping down deeply from one side of it and embracing in all a city block. Under the Arthurs, or any other occupancy, it was always, I thought, a jewel of a place.

Alexander A. Arthur, as he was always referred to—initial and all—either in deference or in derision by mocking spirits, was (so far as I have ever been able to understand) in something the same line as my father, although my father had in addition manufacturing interests in Michigan (where a town was named for him),[9] Minnesota, and North Carolina. But both engaged in bringing English capital to this country for investment in timber and mining properties in the South,[10] they often met in this country or in Manchester, heart of the rich English Midlands, and their chief source of English investors; so it was in the nature of a friendly gesture toward a business rival, I imagine, that when the Arthurs gave their first party in Knoxville I was invited, though no other girls of my age had been asked.

At any event, Papa was called out of town on the very eve of the party. Mama would not go without him, but when Don Waring, whose wife was soon to have a baby and unable to go, offered to take me, nothing could have delighted me more.

The Warings lived on White Avenue, the rear of their stable adjoining the rear of ours. Don was a cousin of the Charles Waring who lived opposite us on Clinch Street[11] and wore his monocle attached to the brim of his hat instead of screwed in his eye, and like him, was a civil engineer, though there the resemblance stopped. Born in Spain, his father an Irish gentleman, member of the British diplomatic corps at Madrid, his mother belonging to an impoverished branch of Spanish royalty, Don in early youth, an orphan now, had left Spain forever; gone to Ireland, acquired his degree at Trinity College, Dublin,[12] then came to this country to seek his fortune, where, after a prolonged bachelorhood in Knoxville, he had finally married a daughter of the rector of St. John's and settled down to family life.

And what a party the Arthurs' was! Japanese lanterns swung from the trees from one end of the grounds to the other and it was in their bewitching light we ate supper, a few at a table, under the trees; by their light we danced later in an old brick carriage-house which with rhododendron and laurel banked against its inner walls had been transformed into an arbor of a sort, a *plaisance*, with a celebrated orchestra brought from Cincinnati stationed there to play through the evening.

All this, at sixteen, was dazzling. It was the first time, too, I had eaten outdoors at a party, but this was a true *fête champêtre*, and with its romantic setting, soft magical lights, the dreamy entrancing strains of the violins coming to us through the intervening trees and shrubbery, it was the nearest thing to fairy land I could ever have imagined. Even the food was different and seemed celestial.

This party must have been, as I think of it now, in the month of May. I remember the scent of lilacs and mock orange blossoms in the night air and that there were strawberries, on each table a great luscious crimson mound of them from which you helped yourself, holding a berry by its stem to dip it into the little individual container of powdered sugar you found at your place, along with a silver holder bearing a card with your name on it.

But aside from the dancing with older men than I had heretofore, some of them superlative dancers I thought then (and still do), the cardinal feature of the evening for me was being accompanied by Don, more striking and distinguished than ever in his black and white evening attire, resplendent in tailcoat, and with his urbanity, poise, look of complete belonging, so mature, yet so debonair, so gay of spirit, that beside him most other men, young and old, seemed more or less drab and stodgy.

There is something else, however, connected with the Arthurs' party, and of quite different nature, that remains with me.

I had just finished a dance with Reuben Payne, one of the younger men who were there, and we stood in the wide open doorway of the pavilion to catch a light breeze that was blowing when Don appeared.

It was growing late, and mindful I daresay of his wife's condition and possible need of him, Don suggested that perhaps he and I should be seeking our host and hostess to bid them good night.

"Oh no, sir, don't take her away yet, Mr. Waring—not yet! She's not half through dancing." I can see Reuben's thin white hand as he laid it detainingly on Don's black sleeve. I can hear, as I waited breathlessly for Don's decision, Reuben's low hoarse voice, "Let me take Miss Annie home. Our carriage is here, waiting for me. I'll see her home safely, sir."

I knew Reuben well, though I always thought of him as belonging to Mary. With all Mary's beaux, she could never see anyone but Reuben and eventually married him. A little below medium height, of slight build, with his pallor, aquiline nose and receding chin, he was indifferent looking save for his great brown eyes with something understanding and tender in them not often found in youthful eyes. His movements were habitually languid as his voice was habitually hoarse, both no doubt indicative of tuberculosis, too often not recognized then in its earlier stages and from which he died while still a young man. But though he was markedly quiet and talked almost not at all, Reuben had his own appeal.[13]

We leaned back against the cushions of the Paynes' barouche, and its top up, the coachman high on the box, we were as secluded as in a little room by ourselves on the drive to West End. I was so tired that I offered no resistance when in the darkness Reuben slipped his arm around me and gently inclined my head till it rested against him.

We were silent through the long drive. There was a faint and exciting odor of cigarette smoke about Reuben and another scent—perhaps, I thought, of wine, of the champagne cup served at the party. Reuben held one of my hands in his, and as I rested wearily in his arms, for all the slightly frightening tremors that kept running through me, I was conscious of the most delicious sensation I had ever known. Surely earthly bliss could not go beyond this.

Reuben helped me from the carriage and up the steps as I held my long skirts in both hands to keep from tripping. At the door, he leaned over to kiss me.

Every fibre of my young being was urging me, almost beyond my power of resistance, to respond. But I drew back.

"It wouldn't be fair to Mary," I said.

However ridiculous, viewed from this distance of time, a code which permitted me to lie in Reuben's arms all the way home but forbade me to kiss him, yet such as it was, I proposed to abide by it.

Reuben laughed his little husky laugh, slowly withdrew his arm from around me, lifted one of my hands to his lips, held it for a moment, then carefully opened the door for me to enter the dark house.

"Good night, Miss Annie!" he said, in a voice even lower than his usual one, not to wake Mama, "Good night!" he whispered.

While all this time so far away and long ago tends to merge in my mind, it was not, I feel sure, the year Don Waring took me to the Arthurs' party, but a year or two before this I started to ride horse back under his instruction. The three accomplishments a young lady must have, if no others, in the '80s, were to play the piano, dance and ride, and as there was no professional riding master in Knoxville then, and my father in England so much of the time, he pressed Don into service.

I think Don accepted the office without much urging. He was very particular about my seat, position of my hands—a hundred details I have forgotten. But in general he treated me pretty much as if I were his age, and as Don was ageless, we could have the merriest sort of times together. On the evenings we were to go riding I would hurry into my black varnished boots, into the long black skirt of my habit (that death trap, if we were thrown, in the days when we rode side-saddle), into my tight-fitting basque buttoned up to the chin, my black derby, and would be waiting impatiently, crop in hand, at our side gate, where my horse was tied, when Don rode up, and got off his horse to help me mount.

It would be only moments then till we were out of town, could leave the macadamized pike and be on a dirt crossroads where, in what seems now that halcyon age, there would be no cars to encounter, seldom a buggy or even, at the hour, a farm-wagon.

It would be twilight when I went for my riding lesson and in a season when twilights were long; and although I never became an expert horse-woman, what little I learned about handling horses I learned from Don.

But riding to me meant no gentle amble, and it was wonderful fun when before we started back to town in the gathering dusk, Don would yield to my pleas, let me give my horse his head, and we would race down some stretch of road or woodsy lane, my long skirt billowing, hair unloosed and streaming, as I tore along so recklessly that but for the grace of God, as we like to say, was I saved from the end Fanny Kemble would have preferred for herself—to break her neck off a good horse at a full gallop.[14]

I like to dwell on these times with Don when he was still as high-spirited as I, a girl in her teens, for some very special things happened to Don. He was to be deeply wounded by life before he was through with it, or it with him.

I have long forgotten, if I ever knew, Don's Christian name, but because he was Spanish by birth and spoke with a Spanish accent, he came to be called Don in Knoxville, and it clung.[15]

He was a prime favorite socially during his bachelor years and particularly at the Meads, an Eastern family—from Pittsburgh as I recall it—with coal and marble interests in East Tennessee, and who lived in sober elegance and consummate comfort at the end of Hill Street where it broke off at the brink of the precipice below which, unseen, ran the spur of railroad that served the blast furnaces beyond.

On manorial lines, but set close to the ground, shielded by trees and shrubs and approached by a curving driveway, only the barest glimpse of the house itself could be caught from the street, a fact which contributed no doubt to the Meads' reputation for exclusiveness. It was generally understood at least that Mrs. Mead, an extremely proper though rather mannish woman (of the type we call horsy, though she was guiltless, I believe, of an special interest in horses), no less than her husband preferred the society of men, so that in the years before there was the Cumberland Club in Knoxville, the Meads' home became a center, virtually a club, for bachelors, particularly perennial ones, if they came from the East, were (preferably) graduates of Yale, and in any event, with impeccable pedigrees.[16]

On the basis of pedigree there could be little question that Don was eligible for membership in this coterie. It was known that he was a lineal descendant of Christopher Columbus, his mother a cousin of the contemporary Duke of Veragua, as also of the Princess Eulalia, aunt of Alfonso XIII, then King of Spain.

To be sure, in the Knoxville of the 19th Century, whatever may be true to-day, Knoxvillians were prouder of being descendants of James White, the town's founder, than they would have been of being descendants of Christopher Columbus, discoverer of America. There was greater prestige attached to being a cousin, however remote, of the McClungs, an influential Scotch-Irish family who had been among the early settlers of Knoxville, than a cousin of the Duke of Veragua y de la Vega and of Spanish royalty.

But Don's credentials satisfied the Meads, it appeared; satisfied them so well that, according to report, they never became reconciled to his marrying the daughter of a highly respected but impecunious clergyman and developing thereafter into an ideal family man, thereby robbing them, save on rare occasions, of his sparkling and distinguished presence.

I have an idea, although I can only guess at this, that it was not long after Don's marriage he made his fatal blunder. I knew in a vague way that something unfortunate had happened, because the Don Warings' fortunes had begun to decline soon after we first knew them. They had moved from a substantial home of many verandahs and generous grounds around it in the block beyond us on Clinch Street to the pleasant and homey though much less pretentious one on White Avenue. They had only one servant now and one horse. Don and his wife no longer drove around in the smart rubber-tired turnout I remembered them in earlier. But I would not know more till a day when we were traveling north from Knoxville on what is now the Southern Railway and along a river, probably the Holston. The train slowed down, then stopped, because of a "hot box," and at a point where we could see from the car windows on the opposite side of the river a single-span iron bridge resting lengthwise alongside the river on its high bank.

"Poor Don!" Mama said, gazing across the river at the abandoned bridge and shaking her head. "Poor Don!"

She explained then that Don, as engineer, had miscalculated the distance this bridge was to have spanned. The bridge, as ordered, was found too short and Don had never been able since to obtain an engineering assignment of any importance.

But in the days when I used to go riding with him and that spring when Don took me to the Arthurs' party, there was no mark on him, or none I detected, that he was a defeated man. He was still, at this time, I believe, buoyed up by the hope that he could outlive his mistake. He was not the first engineer to make one of a similar sort.

I first saw a change in Don a couple of summers later when I visited Don and Minnie in Middlesboro, Kentucky, in a coal mining region with other mineral resources, a town named for the iron city of the English Midlands and built by English capital—one of the enterprises promoted by Mr. Arthur (Colonel Arthur, by this time).

They were living in a raw new house, on a raw new street of deep red-clay gullies, with a couple of boards laid down for sidewalks, where there were any, and in an ugly, if beautifully situated, raw new town. But anxious, with such resources as the place offered, for me to have a good time, Don had arranged beforehand for some of the English remittance men who had flocked to Middlesboro (a few of them from Knoxville) as soon as the town was founded, to take me horseback riding and to dances at the swanky new hotel recently opened.

Charmed by the novel surroundings, riding and dancing, I had a gay time on that visit. Nevertheless I came away saddened.

The Warings' jerry-built house was barely furnished, though comfortable enough, and under Minnie's management had an air of refinement. But the first thing I had noticed on my arrival was not the house. It was Don. He seemed smaller. He had shrunk. His back was no longer so straight and gray showed in his thick jet-black hair. His charm of manner, however, was as great as ever. It was a delight to see him with his three little boys and his affectionate if whimsical way with "Min." Occasionally too, though reared a Catholic and now an Episcopalian, yet far from a sanctimonious man, there was a touch of the old deviltry as when he raced through grace at table, the briefest he knew, but which, brief or lengthy, Minnie insisted upon, *The Lord make us truly thankful for all we are about to receive* and then, with the roast in front of him and a roguish glint in his eye as he glanced at me would inquire in the same breath, "And which do you prefer, rare or medium?"

But some of the old buoyancy, the élan, some of the *grand seigneur* in Don, was gone, and it hurt me down deep inside.

There were other changes also. Capricious, impatient by nature, now and then he would flare up on some slight provocation and only Minnie's serene command of herself prevented a conflagration. Literal-minded, one would have said of Minnie, not subtle, anything but glamorous, yet stout-hearted and staunch, her feet on the ground, little Minnie treated Don as she treated her children, at once with indulgence and firmness. No woman, I am confident, ever dealt with a husband with both Latin and Celt in him with more skill. Accepting him as he was—and things as they were—with unalterable cheerfulness and bravery, hers, I should say, was no small soul.

When I next saw Don myself was some years after this. In '98, traveling home from the University of Chicago where I had been studying under John Dewey and other professors well known then, I stopped for a week-end with Don and Minnie in Lexington, Kentucky, where they were now living. They had recently moved there and I found them in a good, if somewhat run-down neighborhood near the heart of town, in an old red-brick house that reminded me of some on Church Street in Knoxville; the house a good deal out of repair yet with a welcoming air, for Minnie had been at work making a home out of it, a home not only for her own little family but for one or two of her younger brothers, all promising young men, who had found jobs in Lexington.

What Don's business or professional connections were there, if any, I never knew, but, as in Middlesboro, it was not the house he was in, but Don himself that struck me first, and if I had been saddened in Middlesboro, now I was almost unbearably moved by the change in him.

In Middlesboro, he was nervous, taut, rebelling against his fate, yet still hoping, I think, that in spite of everything he might escape it. Now he had accepted it. His exquisite courtesy, his courtliness, were the same, and he was not a whit less lovable than he had ever been. But this was merely a ghost of the Don I had once known. It was hard to think of this gentle soul as ever having been possessed of exuberant spirits; to identify him with the gay and eager presence of that cultivated man of the world who had so enchanted me in my teens. Knowing Don Waring and August Bauer remained among my most treasured memories. They had stimulated my imagination during my most impressionable years. August Bauer had given me some realization of the rich Germanic culture of which he was a product, and both he and Don, brought up within its framework, had given me the *feel* of the Old World; its traditions, pomp, glitter, its romance. They were, indeed, for me, the Old World incarnate.

There *are* no dull towns, I have long believed (speaking as of today), no matter how many prosaic persons may inhabit them—none essentially dull. All towns have in them interesting, exciting, inspiring persons. It is just a matter of discovery. And with all the other riches Knoxville furnished my youth, I had been lucky enough to know August Bauer and Don Waring.

But now Don was hardly more than one of what Cyril Connolly compassionately, if with cruel candor, calls "the unburied dead."[17] Few things had ever moved me so deeply. The truth is, I was not more deeply affected when I learned Don was dying in fact.

It was about the turn of the century, shortly before I left Knoxville for good. Heavily burdened at this time, restless, my mind in a state of great disquiet, I had lost touch, for the time, with the Warings, as with others whose friendship I prized. But one day someone brought me word that Don was in Knoxville; he had come back, at his own wish, to die there. Spain, Ireland—he had left them so long ago, and Knoxville might largely have forgotten him, but there he had been a man among men, a gentleman among gentlemen. A man must, after all, have a place he calls home, a place where he would wish to die. It was clear that Knoxville, to Don, was this place.

I hastened to the house on Asylum Street where Minnie had brought him, where they had taken rooms;[18] by strange chance the same house, the very same upstairs rooms, where the Thomas girls had once lived, in dire poverty, but with dignity, imagination, and style.

Minnie came to the door on my light knock. She stepped out into the broad bare hall that led to a back corner bed-room where Don lay. She smiled, though her eyes were swimming with tears—a luxury, after all the years, she allowed herself, now that Don could no longer see.

"I don't think," she prepared me, in a low voice, "that Don will know you. But I'm glad you came."

There was a frightful, all pervasive smell in the hall, no ordinary smell, an appalling stench.

"I think," Minnie said, "I should tell you about the smell before we go in. It's worse in the room. A rat died in the walls." She smiled again, resignedly, and shook her head. "It's mortifying, but there's nothing that can be done about it."

The room was a large square one, clean and orderly, but with the bleak and battered furnishings common to rented rooms of the class. But it was not the room I saw. I only remembered it afterwards. It was Don. His bed was in a corner that faced me as I entered, and he was not lying upon it, as I had expected, but sitting bolt upright, bolstered by pillows.

"He wants to be that way," Minnie whispered. "It's easier for him to breathe—"

But to my overwhelming astonishment it was the old Don I saw, the Don who had taken me to the Arthurs' party. In his end was his beginning.[19] With his short pointed black beard, long straight *mustachios*, his thick black hair, all meticulously trimmed, his face wore in dying, even more than in life, the grace and nobility of an ancient race, of an ancient aristocracy. Completely expressionless, its contours were more strikingly revealed, and stark black and white against his pillows, he was an El Greco indeed now. His face was the face, even to its bluish white, of the central figure in El Greco's masterpiece in Toledo, *The Burial of Count Orgaz*.[20] All it lacked of the 16th Century nobleman's was the white ruff encircling the Count's neck, and this was supplied in a degree by the long points in the collar of Don's white nightshirt, between which his short pointed black beard rested.

I sat down by the bed, placing my hand on his folded ones on the counterpane.

The stench of the dead rat was overpowering, almost beyond endurance, this hideous circumstance over which there was no control—this last, this supreme indignity, it flashed through me, that fate had reserved for Don.

"Don, it's Annie," I said. "It's Annie!"

I thought I saw a flicker of recognition in his face, but I was not sure. His black eyes, looking straight ahead, were unfathomable.

No pavane would be sounded for Don. And as I came away, filled with bitter sorrow, I thought, *Death of a Spanish Grandee on Asylum Street*—what irony!

But in this summer back in 1889 no cloud, or none of portentous proportions, as yet hung over Don; none over me. It was a summer of hard work, making up for that earlier shameless neglect of my studies, and of hard play—a summer of hurry and push, of confusion, commotion, rush—all things I loved, and never so many parties as now with all the girls I knew best going away to school this fall; to Nashville, Baltimore, Philadelphia, Cincinnati.

There were my fittings also to be sandwiched in. Mama had ordered a sealskin coat for me from New York, but my dresses were being made by Mr. Rollins (was that his name?), a man dressmaker, Knoxville's first, connected with Meek and Audes drygoods store on Gay Street. He was making me some beautiful dresses, all wool, or wool combined with silk or velvet (one with velvet sleeves, I remember), simple yet modish, a trifle too modish, I was to feel later at Mt. Holyoke where the girls, many from farms then, or villages, wore plainer dresses and ones I could see were better suited to the strong New England character of the institution.[21]

But I was disturbed by no such considerations in advance. It was the most tumultuous and the happiest summer I had known. There was only one thing that had been a disappointment, a disappointment at least to Mama and Papa. Early in July, just when they had hoped the new house could get under way, Papa had been called back to Manchester by the directors of the syndicate of which he was American manager. There was trouble of some sort at the English end of the line. Well, the house could certainly be started in September, Papa said, and for my part, heartless though it was in the face of their disappointment, I welcomed the delay, the longer the better so far as I was concerned. I always got a little tightening around my heart when I thought about coming back from college at the end of the year, and not to the Barnes house. It was hard for me to take even a polite interest in the elaborate plans for the new house when Papa and Mama were poring over the blue-prints spread out on the dining-room table. *I* wanted no new home. Lack of conveniences in the Barnes house had never inconvenienced *me*. I remembered a much finer home, but only as a dream now, as something in a previous incarnation, on another planet. The Barnes house was the only home I wanted myself and the very thought of having to leave it some day made me homesick for it, as though the thing I dreaded had already occurred.

By August 20th (and I have reason to remember the exact date) I had finished my studies under Dr. Tuck. As he walked to his front door with me when I was leaving he said with mock gravity, "Miss Mary Lyon founded Mt. Holyoke because, she contended, women have brains. Prove it my child! Pass your examinations." And then, patting me affectionately on my arm and with a mischievous smile in the old eyes behind the spectacles, "But I'm sure you will."

I was not so sure myself. But I had spent many a sweaty hour during the past months over my studies while the other girls were having fun. I had done my best. Now let come what may. There were only two weeks left at home and nothing was going to spoil them for me.

The day after I was through with Dr. Tuck, Papa returned from England, and the day after that, he was to go with many of Knoxville's prominent men on a day's observation tour over the new Knoxville, Cumberland Gap and Louisville Railway, which, begun in 1887, connected Knoxville with Middlesboro, a distance of some seventy miles, and ran through a rich agricultural and mining region. As the first trip over the new railroad it was important in Knoxville's history and there was to be a banquet to celebrate the event when the guests, directors and other stockholders, reached Middlesboro.

It was always an event in our household when Papa came back from England. This time he had brought me a ring (for my next birthday, he said) that he had got in Paris. The gold of the ring was designed to look like a buckle, with a diamond set in the buckle. Mama was pleased, but thought I was too young to wear a diamond. I should put it away for awhile. But Papa laughed and said, "Nonsense! The diamond is not large."

I was wild with joy over the ring, but it was more than any presents he brought which always recharged the house with something akin to electricity when Papa came home. We had as yet hardly seen him, however, this morning when he was hastening to get off on the trip to Middlesboro (patting and feeling into his pockets to make sure he had with him what he would want) and it may have been for this reason that as he said a hurried good-bye I saw him afresh, not merely as Papa, but as an individual, and for the first time somewhat objectively.

I can not to-day see my father's face. Even when I look at photographs of him I can not see it, save perhaps for one, a *carte de visite* of a youth of sixteen or so, in uniform, taken during the Civil War. In this I seem to discern the kind of person he was going to be. But he had blue eyes, I know; a strong, though not unduly prominent nose, a cleft in his chin, and the general coloring of the blondish line of people from which he came.

As he reappears to me now on that morning of August 22, 1889, he is standing in the sitting-room, May clinging to his hand, a tall broad-shouldered man of easy movements. He is wearing new light-gray tweeds made by a London tailor. His face is tanned from his recent voyage. Somehow you can detect a spirit of unconquerable buoyancy, a hint too—but perhaps these are the same—of the unconquerable adventurer in him. You would know, I think, when you looked at him, that although he was a business man he was also an outdoors man, a man for forests and streams, an ardent sportsman. You might suspect that he was a man of many

Papa (H. B. Wetzell).

and highly varied tastes, loving the world of art and letters and science as well as the world of nature. And you would be pretty sure, in any case, that he was one to extract joy out of existence, existence on almost any terms.

But much of all this very likely I read into him now, knowing that it was so. What he was, in all probability, to casual observers then, was a man at the top of his manly strength and vigor, and young for his age, if they knew it—forty-three.

What concerns of my own I was busy about that day do not survive in my memory. It is all a blank from my father's leaving the house that morning until late in the afternoon when my cousin Merrill, a lad around fifteen who was spending the summer with us[22] and had been down-town—or up-town, as we called it—knocking around in my father's offices, at Peter Kern's Ice Cream Parlor and elsewhere, to entertain himself, came streaking through the front gate and up the steps, his freckled face ashy.

"There's been a terrible accident, Aunt Linnie, on the new railroad!" he called out even before he reached my mother where she was sitting on the porch.

Mama dropped the needlework in her hands. "Your Uncle Henry—?" breathing hard, she was able to ask.

"I don't know," Merrill panted. "It was at Flat Creek. The train was on a trestle. The cars went down into the creek. Nobody knows much. But they're bringing them back. On flat cars. A lot of them hurt. Some killed, I guess."

Mama did not scream. She did not burst into sobs or sink to the floor. She only shook, her whole body. Her long discipline of sorrow had started with Harry's death.

People began running up and down Clinch Street now, shouting to one another; stopping, but only for an instant, at our gate.

It was raining. It had been raining off and on all day and after dark it rained hard. Nobody could find out anything exactly. There were no telephones then. No telegraph line had yet been built along the new railroad. The news of the accident was dribbling into Knoxville bit by bit. All that was known for certain was that nearly all the fifty or sixty men aboard the train, the outstanding men of the town, had been injured, some killed.

Men now began coming to our house, gathering on the porch. It was a black night, still raining. At last word came that they were bringing my father home.

Mama preserved her outward calm. I can see the lights in the house, the darkness and rain outside, as the men with muddy feet carried the stretcher from the porch through the open French windows into the sitting-room, carefully lowering it onto the floor.

No doctor was with the men who bore the stretcher. All over town they were calling for doctors. There were not enough.

I followed Mama into the sitting-room and knelt down beside Papa. His new tweed suit had been cut off of him, probably in extricating him from the wreck. It lay in strips, soaked with rain, across his body. Many of his teeth had been knocked out or broken and his mouth kept filling with blood, so that a man, a stranger, squatting beside the stretcher on the other side, kept sponging Papa's mouth out, to prevent his choking.

If only a doctor would come!

Finally our own physician, Dr. Bayless, then another, a surgeon, came and we went from the room so that the doctors could make their examination.

All night long we kept going back and forth to the sitting-room. My father was conscious and in great agony, it seemed. One of the men, another stranger, whispered to me in the hall that they thought my father's back was broken.

The doctors stayed on. About three in the morning someone told us that they thought my father might live—his heart was strong—and that a telegram had been sent to Cincinnati for a surgical bed to be sent down, one that would be suspended from the ceiling by pulleys. Meantime, until it arrived, he must not be moved, although before daylight two men nurses had been installed.

There was no hospital in Knoxville then. There were no professional nurses. It was years yet before I would see in Knoxville a nurse in crisp white uniform and cap, its first trained nurse and a sensation. But no professional nurse that ever lived could have brought more comfort, become more endeared to us, than James

Morrison, who had been a nurse all through the War in the Confederate Army, a minister at one time in the Methodist Church, later had run the Mess Hall on the Hill, and now came forward voluntarily to take chief charge of my father, the most seriously injured of all those who had survived the wreck, unless Ed Barker, a young man who lived next door in the house below us on Clinch Street, whose leg had had to be amputated and who, like Papa, hung between life and death.

Mama and Papa's huge elaborate bed with its panels of walnut burl and diamond-shaped ebony insets with daffodils carved on them had been taken down and sent into storage. Mama slept now in what had been Harry's room. In the middle of the downstairs bed-room back of the sitting-room Papa lay on the narrow surgical bed that hung from the ceiling.

The least vibration of the floor hurt him but from time to time I would take off my shoes and tiptoe into the room.

It was hard to make myself look at his face. But there had been no concussion and despite his continuous and terrible suffering and the fact that he could only make signs, he was perfectly aware, as he had been from the hour he was brought home, of what was going on around him. His eyes looked more blue than I had known before that they were. I would touch his hand or kiss him lightly on the cheek and slip out again.

At the rear of the bed-room was a window opening on to the back porch. Ordinarily, for privacy, its outside blinds were kept closed. But in these hot humid days at the end of August, to catch any air that might be stirring, the slats in the blinds were left open and sometimes when I slipped into the room, I would catch sight of black eyes peering between the slats; eyes, outside the range of Papa's vision and belonging to friends of Bonnie, Hester, or Uncle Pompey, unable to restrain their curiosity. How in the world would a bed like that look and a man at the point of death lying on it?

There were Negroes now, silent and respectful, but whom I did not know, in the kitchen, on the back porch, or under the grape arbor, whenever I ventured in that direction. The whole house, in fact, as I relive those days, seems to have been full of people, known and unknown, coming and going, talking in subdued tones or whispers.

Outside, the street at first had been tan-barked[23] and then roped off, so that no vehicles could pass, and there was the same oppressive quiet in the neighborhood as when Harry lay in the parlor.

Mama, in perfect control of herself, moved around, seeing to everything, but I think it was in those days her face took on the "still" look it would wear for many years.

Each day seemed endless. Would Papa live or die? I could not conceive of a world, a world of any solidity, of which Papa was not a part. But death was so unreal—until it came, and when it came, I had found out, it was more unreal than ever.

It was on one of these long sultry afternoons when I was in this dazed state that I was alone in the parlor and wandering idly to the bay-window stood looking out toward the Barkers' house below us, wondering vaguely whether if Papa died I would go off to school just the same (all the other girls had already gone) or whether, if he *didn't* die, I would go. It didn't seem to matter much either way.

But as my eyes rested, almost unseeingly, on the Barkers' house, on a level a little below ours but not far away, my attention was arrested by some movement at the window in their parlor, which had been converted into a bed-room when Ed had been brought home the night of the wreck.

The outside blinds of the window had been thrown open and someone was taking down the heavy white lace curtains that hung in front of it.

Almost every street in town had someone on it who had been injured or died from the wreck. It was the greatest disaster Knoxville had ever known and there were few cases sadder than that of Ed Barker, a tall upstanding, good-looking and very popular young business man who was engaged to be married to Miss Lily Simmonds, a lovely girl who lived on Fort Sanders, an older sister of the Rob Simmonds with whom I had gone to the Hallowe'en party on Bell Avenue (so long ago, it seemed now) and one of the younger set to which I belonged.

Ed had rebelled against the doctors amputating his leg, but Miss Lily had told him she would marry him just the same. Now, rumors were, that the doctors feared they would have to amputate the other leg and Miss Lily had come and assured him on her knees that in that case *still* she would marry him.

I could see plainly now, with the window open and curtains down, into the Barkers' parlor. I did not notice particularly when a long table, like a kitchen table, was placed in front of the window. Absorbed in my own thoughts I walked away a little, but when I returned and looked down at the Barkers, I saw, in one horrified glance, what the doctors were doing. They wore no smocks, masks, gloves—none of the paraphernalia of a present-day surgical operation. One of the doctors was in his long black coat, and one of the others, his shirt-sleeves rolled above the elbow, was severing Ed's leg, high on the thigh.

Ed died at dawn next day. Papa of course was not told of this. He was not told that one of his most esteemed friends, Judge Andrews, had died, touching him, as they lay side by side in the rain on the open freight car that brought them back from Flat Creek.[24]

But he was conscious that the days were passing and before long was able to make the doctors understand it was time, past time, for me to leave for College. Never before in the least concerned whether or not his children entered school when it opened, nothing would do now but that I should start for college without further delay, and the doctors, after consultation, decided the effect on him might be worse if I stayed than if I left.

Of course I would have to make the long journey alone now, manage the change in New York by myself, another in Springfield, and still another at Smith's Ferry, from train to stage-coach. I was not in the least daunted, however, by this prospect. I had just been through the shattering experience of witnessing an amputation, in addition to the strain of seeing my father's terrible condition. Nevertheless I would have started around the world alone, without an instant's hesitation, had there seemed a reason for it and it had been proposed.

A piercing thought ran through me all the same that I might hardly reach my destination till I was called back home. But I must not dwell on this thought. Papa had asked for watermelon and joked with the doctors. These were good signs, everyone said. Then at the depot, as we still called a railway station, though the other girls were gone, the boys would be there. Two or three of them would get on the train and ride with me as far as Morristown. Dr. Bayless, handsome and jovial, equal to any occasion, was sure to be there, and some of the firm that handled Papa's legal affairs. It would be nice to be surrounded by all these people when the train pulled in. I would hardly realize I was leaving. . . .

But at sixteen it is a glory just to be alive. Everything is bound to turn out all right and I was highly excited as I watched Mama hastily packing my trunk with the dresses Mr. Rollins had made, the sealskin coat.

There was only a little weakening, a little sickness, somewhere inside me, as I came out the front door, with the carriage at the gate. This, I realized, was no ordinary goodbye I was saying. I did not realize, however, that never again would there be the bright magic of those days, those years, in the Barnes house; that the Knoxville I would know hereafter would be a different Knoxville. I did not know—no one had heard yet—of the failure of the great Midlands [i.e., Midland] Bank in England, which in its crash would spell financial ruin for English investors, nor that Papa, struck down at almost the same hour, when his scattered American interests needed consolidation and expert direction, had also been ruined financially by this bank failure in far-away England.[25] I did not dream that the sumptuous new home on Fort Sanders, which I had not cared to consider, would now never be built, nor have the slightest prescience that the wreck at Flat Creek would profoundly affect my whole future life, and as I came down the steps of the Barnes house on that September afternoon in 1889, in my traveling dress, carrying proudly my little new traveling bag of alligator leather, if I failed to see that the Barnes house in our modern parlance was a point of no return, even less I saw that, for me, it was as well a point of departure.

NOTES

1. National City Company of New York. National City Bank of New York, *A Short History of the National City Bank of New York* (New York: National City Bank, 1918); National City Bank of New York, *The Work of Number Eight,* rev. ed. (New York: National City Bank, 1921). Armstrong's position was "employment manager for women" during 1918 and 1919.
2. [Anne W. Armstrong], "A Woman in Wall Street / by One," *Atlantic Monthly*, vol. 136, no. 2 (August 1925): 145–158.
3. Comic operetta by Gilbert and Sullivan.
4. Renamed Fountain City in 1890, Fountain Head was once a popular resort with numerous springs, a park, and the hotel, which opened in 1886. The town was annexed by the City of Knoxville in 1962. Rothrock, *French Broad-Holston Country,* 340–344.
5. Knoxville's Gay Street Bridge was the only one crossing the Holston (now called the Tennessee) River at the time Armstrong was describing. Front Street, running parallel to and just above the river, had formed the southern boundary of the original town as it was laid out in 1792. Rule, *Standard History,* 88, 302–303. When a wooden bridge was constructed in 1880, it joined Gay Street up the river bank at the level of Hill Street, leaving Front Street under the bridge. Creekmore, *Knoxville,* 115, 119. A few disconnected blocks of Front Street still remain between present-day Hill Avenue and the river.
6. Cave Springs, at the base of a bluff about a mile from where the Holston and French Broad Rivers come together to form the Tennessee, is now part of Ijams Nature Center, a wildlife sanctuary in south Knoxville. The cave, called Maude Moore's Cave, can be seen from the park's River Trail boardwalk. It was gated in 1997 as a safety precaution and to protect wildlife. Paul James, *Ijams Nature Center*, Images of America (Charleston, SC: Arcadia Publishing, 2010), 106; Ijams Web site, "River Boardwalk," http://ijams.org/river-boardwalk/ (viewed January 17, 2018).
7. Alexander Alan Arthur (1846–1912) was Scottish, having been born in Glasgow, although his family immigrated to Canada when he was a child. He joined the 104th Highland Regiment in Scotland in 1867 and was involved in the timber business in Sweden before coming to Boston in the 1870s. Wilma Dykeman described him as: "The epitome of elegance in his Prince Albert coat, his fashionable hat, sideburns, and lord mayor air." *Kentucky Encyclopedia,* ed. John E. Kleber, Lowell Hayes Harrison, and Thomas Dionysius Clark (Lexington: University Press of Kentucky, 2015), s.v. "Arthur, Alexander Alan" (accessed January 15, 2018, ProQuest Ebook Central); Wilma Dykeman, *The French Broad,* Rivers of America (New York: Rinehart, 1955), 167.
8. Mrs. Arthur, the former Nellie Goodwyn (or Goodwin), was not from England but Lowell, Mass. *Kentucky Encyclopedia,* s.v. "Arthur, Alexander Alan" (accessed January 15, 2018); Dykeman, *The French Broad,* 168.

9. A Michigan Historical Marker, erected in 1989, shows the location of the Village of Wetzell, in Mancelona Township, Antrim County, where in 1881 "the Wetzell brothers" laid out the town and opened a sawmill. It is now a ghost town. Larry Wakefield, "Wetzell: Broom Handles and a Bank Robbery," in *Ghost Towns of Michigan*, (W. Bloomfield, Mich.: Northmont Publ., 1994), 30–34; Registered Site L1618, Michigan Historical Marker Web Site, http://www.michmarkers.com/pages/L1618.htm (viewed November 29, 2017).

10. Alexander A. Arthur was among foreign investors who, exploiting the South after Reconstruction, "bought and cut timberlands, set up land companies, financed railroads, and extracted [Tennessee's] coal and iron." After his developments in Cocke County (the Scottish Carolina Timber and Land Company) were flooded in 1886, Arthur came to Knoxville, where he led a group of foreign investors called the American Association, Ltd., in building a railroad to Middlesboro, Kentucky (including the first tunnel through Cumberland Mountain) in hopes of making Middlesboro "the Pittsburgh of the South." Ann Toplovich, "Conservation," in *The Tennessee Encyclopedia of History & Culture*, ed. Carroll Van West (Nashville: Tennessee Historical Society, Rutledge Hill Press, 1998), 221. Wilma Dykeman devotes an entire chapter, based on interviews with Arthur's widow, to describing Alexander A. Arthur the man, his timber operation in Cocke County, and its impact on the town of Newport. Dykeman, *The French Broad*, 166–177, 347. Arthur is listed in Knoxville city directories, beginning in 1887 through 1890, with various business affiliations including the following: general manager of the American Association, Ltd. of London (with capital of $1,200,000); general manager of the Knoxville, Cumberland Gap, and Louisville (KCG&L) Railroad Company; vice-president of Cumberland Gap Construction Company; general manager, Middlesborough Town Company; and, in 1889, president of the Knoxville Chamber of Commerce. *Knoxville City Directory* (1887–1890). In 1887, A. A. Arthur and Henry B. Wetzell were among a group of men who obtained a charter for the Knoxville Belt Railway Company, with a projected twelve-mile line to eventually encircle the city. Rule, 299–300.

11. Knoxville city directories list "Don" Waring as Charles H. Waring, civil engineer (1887), and assistant engineer, Knoxville, Cumberland Gap, and Louisville Railroad (1888–1889), residing at 410 White Avenue (northeast corner of John). The residence of his cousin, Charles Waring, civil engineer, surveyor, and abstractor of titles, was 410 Clinch. *Knoxville City Directory* (1887–1890); Andrew Morrison, *Knoxville, Tennessee,* 39–40.

12. Rule mentions a Charles Waring, C.E., of the University of Dublin, appointed as instructor of drawing at East Tennessee University in 1872. Rule, *Standard History,* 364.

13. Reuben Saunders Payne and Mary Towns Gaines were married Oct. 6, 1896. He died June 30, 1900, at the age of 28. She died May 31, 1922.

14. Fanny Kemble (1809–1893), English actress and author, wrote ". . . and [I] have always thought that the death I should prefer would be to break my neck off the back of my

horse at a full gallop on a fine day." Frances Anne Kemble, *Journal of a Residence on a Georgian Plantation in 1838–1839* (London: Longman, Green, Longman, Roberts, & Green, 1863), 19.

15. See note 11 above.
16. Industrialist William S. Mead (1833–1908) and his wife, both natives of New York City, came to Knoxville in 1873. His business interests included the Knoxville Iron Company, Brookside Cotton Mills, and Republic Marble Company. In addition, he was a director of Third National Bank, one of the original trustees of Lawson McGhee Library, had a large personal library, and "was considered a connoisseur of the arts and wine." The Mead residence was at 832 W. Hill Avenue. Deaderick, 573; Rule, 210, 216, 259, 544.
17. Cyril Connolly (1903–1974), English critic, essayist, and editor. Armstrong is probably alluding to his book *The Unquiet Grave*, published under the pseudonym Palinurus. [Cyril Connolly], *The Unquiet Grave* (New York: Harper & Brothers, 1945).
18. Charles H. Waring, 644 Asylum Ave. *Knoxville City Directory, 1901.* The next year's directory lists Minnie Waring, widow Charles H., 502 Henley. *Knoxville City Directory, 1902.*
19. Allusion to: "In my end is my beginning," motto of Mary, Queen of Scots (1542–1587). Also, much later, a line in T.S. Eliot's long poem, *Four Quartets* (1936–1942).
20. Famous work by El Greco (1541–1614), Spanish painter of Greek origin. Born Kyriakos Theotoco-poulos on the island of Crete.
21. Mount Holyoke Female Seminary was founded in 1837 in South Hadley, Massachusetts. At the time Annie Wetzell entered the school in 1889, it was called Mount Holyoke Seminary and College. Today, Mount Holyoke College is a women's liberal arts college. Mount Holyoke Web site, https://www.mtholyoke.edu/ (viewed January 10, 2018).
22. Merrill L. Wetzell (1875–1901) was the son of Henry B. Wetzell's brother, Daniel M. Wetzell (1841–1909) and his wife, Mary Hammond Yoder Wetzell (1846–1938). *U.S. Census*, 1880; *Find a Grave*, database and images, citing Oakhill Cemetery, Grand Rapids, Kent Co., Mich., https://www.findagrave.com, (viewed August 5, 2020).
23. Covered with the crushed bark of a tree rich in the tannin used in converting hides to leather.
24. News about the Flat Creek train disaster filled the pages of Knoxville newspapers for several days following the accident, listing the dead and the injured, their conditions, and other details about the accident. *Knoxville (TN) Daily Journal*, August 23, 1889; *Knoxville (TN) Journal*, August 23, 24, 1889. Rule lists among the dead and injured Judge George Andrews, H. B. Wetzell, Ed Barker, and Alexander A. Arthur, promoter and general manager of the new railroad. Rule, *Standard History of Knoxville, Tennessee*, 294. For other accounts of the accident see: Jack Neely, "The Flat Creek Horror" in *From the Shadow Side, and Other Stories of Knoxville, Tennessee* (Oak Ridge, Tenn.: Tellico Books, 2003), 15–18; Allen R. Coggins, *Tennessee Tragedies : Natural, Techno-*

logical, and Societal Disasters in the Volunteer State (Knoxville: University of Tennessee Press, 2011), 159–160; "The Flat Gap Horror," in *Ansearchin' News: The Tennessee Genealogical Magazine*, 47, no. 3 (Fall 2000), 3–7, http://www.tngs.org/Ansearchin-News (viewed January 15, 2016).

25. Midland Bank was founded in 1836 in Birmingham (England) as the Birmingham and Midland Bank. According to *The Routledge Companion to British History*, "It began its policy of branch multiplication and predation in 1888" and acquired the Central Bank of London in 1891. "Midland Bank," in *The Companion to British History, Routledge*, by Charles Arnold-Baker. 2nd ed. (Routledge, 2001), http://proxy.lib.utk.edu:90/login?url=http://search.credoreference.com/content/entry/routcbh/midland_bank/0?institutionId=680 (viewed December 18, 2017). According to *Britannica,* it merged with the Central Bank of London in 1891 after absorbing several banks in the Midlands. *Britannica Academic*, s.v. "Midland Bank PLC," http://academic.eb.com.proxy.lib.utk.edu:90/levels/collegiate/article/Midland-Bank-PLC/52579 (viewed December 18, 2017). No record of an 1889 failure of the Midland Bank was found; however, some sources refer to a failure of Baring Brothers Bank of England in 1890. Charles B. Roberts, "The Building of Middlesborough," *The Filson Club History Quarterly* 7, no. 1 (January 1933): 18–33; reprinted in Henry H. Fuson, *History of Bell County, Kentucky* (New York: Hobson, 1947), 2:559–587; *Britannica Academic*, s.v. " Baring family," (accessed February 12, 2018).

PART TWO

Chapter Twelve

Highland Avenue

Someone has said (was it George Moore?) that the rise and fall of a family is as interesting as the rise and fall of a nation; but to the family involved I doubt if it appears, especially the fall, and certainly at the time, in this light.[1] In the case of my own family, I became only very gradually aware of what had happened. My full awakening was when I came home at the end of my second year in college to face the reality that though still in West End we no longer lived in the same neighborhood.

Though so close, only two blocks above Clinch, Highland Avenue was a street I had not previously even walked through. Viewed objectively, it was probably a pleasanter street than Clinch. Around many of the homes on it, none of them pretentious, in their large, sometimes unkempt yards were remnants of earlier apple and pear and cherry orchards when what was Highland Avenue only a few years before had been out in the country. Now a street-car, drawn by mules, ran along it. It was, it must be owned, from the start, an eminently respectable street and its respectability had been heightened by a private school, the first in Knoxville, preparing boys for college, which had just been built and whose raw ugly new red-brick buildings confronted me as I reached the house, facing them, where I would find my own family.[2]

I could not of course see Highland Avenue objectively myself. But it is a very curious thing about towns. The part of one with which you are first acquainted, particularly if your life there has been on the whole extremely happy, is the one from which you continue to orient yourself, with other parts continuing, even for years and years, to remain more or less foreign terrain. It is undoubtedly true at least that when the hack which brought me from the depot landed me in front of a brown frame house on a corner of Highland Avenue, and only a short walk from the Barnes house, I could hardly have felt more strange had I been set down on the Virgin Islands or in Cairo, Egypt.

As I took in the almost treeless yard, the small porch at one side, in front on which someone had trained moon vines to give it a little privacy, there rose before me achingly the great magnolias which had shadowed and softened the front of the Barnes house, the porch extending clear across its front and on which twenty people could sit without crowding; its French windows and little balustraded balconies; the crepe myrtles and all the tangle of old shrubs, planted years before, in its yard. It was the baldness, the soulless newness, of this place which hurt me. There was something else about it that hurt me also. But then—as I stood for a second at the gate—a memory of long ago flashed through me.

I was a little girl, not more than four or five. I had driven with my mother to the outskirts of the city where we then lived. It was a humble neighborhood where we stopped. A bookkeeper for my father lived there. He was sick and Mama had come with fruit and a bottle of port. The house was tiny although its yard was neat and prettily planted with flower-beds; portulaca and lady's-slipper. Our own home was a large one then and with quite lordly grounds. I was not sure that Mama and I were exactly where we ought to be and must have made some remark to this effect, for as we went up a short walk to its small latticed porch Mama leaned over and said in a low voice: "Fine people do not *need* to live in fine houses."

I never forgot the rebuke. The memory of it was a steadying hand laid on me now. But it flooded me with shame, too. After all, inside this house, whose front door at this early hour was still closed, were Mama and Papa and May. Then, whatever revulsion of feeling I had suffered on first sight of the house, mingled with other emotions was the pure joy of being back in Knoxville. When from the car window as we approached town my eyes lighted on the deep rich red of a clay bank alongside the train, I had been caught up in a warm glow of delight. Even the mud of East Tennessee was beautiful to me!

The house itself, one of three of similar style which made up that block on Highland Avenue, was considerably better-looking as a matter of fact than most houses being built then for rent in Knoxville.

Once inside, a feeling, a feeling almost wholly pleasurable, invaded me. The house had none of the old-fashioned charm I had found in the Barnes house; but in its good-sized parlor which opened off one side of the square front hall were the old familiar pieces, some of them at any rate. (Others Mama, incapable of selling things and with no room for them now, had started at this time to give away.) At the windows were the same lace curtains, with their crimson plush lambrequins, which had always hung in our parlor; the same ebony cabinet with the white marble Cupids and Hebe; the same Persian rug in front of the fire-place; the same ebony chairs with their gold inlay, though the satin brocade with which they were covered beginning to show wear. In the dining-room was the same massive ornate dining-room furniture dwarfing the room itself as it had the dining-room in the Barnes house. In the front bedroom, above the parlor, was the mammoth walnut bed with its burl panels, ebony insets with their carved daffodils, the huge marble-topped matching pieces—superlative achievement of contemporary Grand Rapids art. And blessedly, here on Highland Avenue, as on Clinch Street, there was a fire-place for an open fire in every room.

Mary "May" Wetzell.

Yes, this was home, I decided, after a glance around—home despite the unfamiliar and obtrusive golden-oak woodwork, fussy mantels, the little squares of glass in various crude colors bordering a window on the landing where the stairway turned. Yes, yes, I was home!

I was home: Yet perhaps when I saw the girls, when the young men I liked best started coming, things would seem more natural. It would be easier to accept Papa as he was now, and Mama, very quiet as she moved about with so many things to do, things she had never done before. Even May was startlingly altered. She was no longer "little May." Her pretty face, framed in its soft wavy light-brown hair, kept its shy look, but she had suddenly sprung up into a tall slender girl, taller than I, and was going to High School.

Neither Papa nor Mama indicated by a single word that there had been any change in our circumstances. But everything was different. Even Trix was gone, "Harry's dog." Trix had died from poison a neighbor who disliked dogs had set out. Bonnie, our mulatto cook, was gone; faithful black Hester with her six fingers—Hester, who had been with us so long; and Uncle Pompey, for there were no horses now. There was only Magnolia, a jet black Negress who had been our laundress and still was, and a half-grown colored girl to help in the kitchen, where for the first time in my life I saw, with a start, Mama bending over a stove, though stately even in the simple wash-dress she was wearing.

The only things that were the same were Papa's and Mama's intense interest in what was going on in the world, both in this country and abroad, and their enjoyment of books. I remember that when I came home Mama was reading Du Maurier's *Peter Ibbetson*,[3] out that year, and with its enchanting illustrations by the author; while Papa was engrossed in John Fiske's latest volume.[4]

Books meant more to them than ever now that Papa was an invalid and Mama spent her evenings reading or playing bezique[5] with Papa when his unending discomfort was too great to permit of the sustained attention his own more serious reading called for.

It was Papa that was hardest to get used to. That fall, two years ago, when they had brought him home from the wreck at Flat Creek, they had said his back was broken. Since then he had been taken again and again to New York. His injuries were more than to the spine. There had been operation after operation and by the finest surgeons of the day. Finally the doctors had got him on his feet, though it went through me like a knife when I saw him walking with two canes and in a shambling fashion. I thought for a moment I could not look at him. Recently, however, at his insistence, he had dispensed with his nurses and was being taken once in a while down to his offices, though they were no longer in their expensive location on Gay Street.

But the change in Papa hardest to bear was in his face. Its youthful look had disappeared. The marks of his unremitting suffering were on it. Only his laugh was the same; and his eyes, as alert as ever, as quick to catch the slightest humorous suggestion, and with the spark in them of the man, racked by pain, wiped out financially, but who will not be conquered.

Of course Papa was not penniless. He and Mama no longer, it is true, pored over blueprints. They had little hope now that the sumptuous new home they had planned would ever be built. But obviously there was still enough for us to live on in a restricted way, and I have never entirely understood what brought about my father's business collapse; while even less, I believe, did Mama ever understand it. Papa had never made the slightest effort to make his complex business operations clear to Mama, and, intelligent woman though she was, I am not sure he could have, had he tried.

But one thing Mama and I *did* understand. Papa was no longer American manager of the English syndicate he had interested in investments in timber and mining properties in the South. The syndicate itself was no longer in being.

I had seen Papa designated as "capitalist" in the list in the *Knoxville Journal* of the injured and killed in the Flat Creek wreck. But it was years and years after this that I learned of the failure of the Great Midlands Bank in England which had ruined the English investors, and what I make out to-day is that with my father struck down at almost the same hour when the Midlands Bank closed its doors (regarded heretofore as solid as the Bank of England) and when his directing hand was needed to consolidate his widely scattered interests, his own ruin was inevitable, especially when for months afterwards the doctors insisted no business problems be brought him.

But now, whether money entered into the matter or not, and while it had been intended I should complete four years of college, there was no mention of my going back.

I was not sorrowful over this. I had not been too happy at Mount Holyoke. It was not the magnificent institution it became later under Miss Mary Wool[l]ey.[6] Some of the austerity of Mary Lyon[7] still lingered. It is recorded that Emily Dickinson, whose poetry was to rank her in time as perhaps the greatest of all women poets, wept a good deal during her attendance there; wept when she was supposed to be in her closet engaged in prayer. A circumstance that beset her Mount Holyoke life was that she was not a "professing Christian." The group that had not "professed Christ" was constantly harried in Miss Lyon's anxiety to "save souls." Emily was one of those classed as "Impenitents," and prayed over at special meetings.

Forty years later[8] when I entered Mount Holyoke some of this ardor to save souls had slackened. Yet prayer meetings were still held every evening in "Silent Hour" and you were expected to attend them or to be praying in your own room.

I did not weep, as had Emily; neither did I pray during the hour officially designated for the purpose. I could have been properly classified as one of the "Impenitents" had they still been known by this name. After one evening prayer-meeting held in the private sitting-room of Miss Barden, grim head of the department of mathematics, with the depressing atmosphere that prevailed, I never went to one again, and only attended the half-hour in chapel every morning because it was compulsory, a service conducted by Miss Anna Edwards, a descendant of Jonathan Edwards,[9] and one who might easily have been the author herself of his famous sermon, "Sinners In The Hands Of An Angry God."

What I disliked most, however, was the service which followed our simple and wholesome supper of bread and milk, apple-sauce or some sort of canned fruit. While we were still chattering at our respective tables an ominous silence would start stealing over the room, and every voice would be stilled as we turned our chairs, unavoidably with a great clatter, toward the piano, facing the room at its entrance, and then with one of the teachers seated there and in the dim light of the oil lamps we would sing:

> Abide with me: fast falls the eventide;
> The darkness deepens; Lord with me abide,[10]

of all hymns best calculated to increase my homesickness, unless another frequently sung at this hour:

> Lead kindly Light, amidst the enriching glow,
> The night is dark and I am far, far from home.[11]

Then I yearned for the cheerful surroundings in which I had been brought up, would be filled with longing for Knoxville. My homesickness became almost more than I could bear.

Most of the girls, I think, did not react so unhappily as I to the hymns. They had been brought up in hymn-singing families. My room-mate my freshman year was from a family of missionaries. She had never been in a theatre, gone to a dance. Few of the girls had tasted the worldly gayeties I had. None, I imagine, had conceived my own early distaste for the usual evangelical hymn-singing as I had heard it at church and in Sunday School. It was not, either, that I was absolutely insensitive to sacred music, for I could be lifted even then into ecstasy by Handel's *Joy to the World! The Lord is come!* and one of the high points of my life was when later for the first time I listened in the Church of Saint Eustache in Paris on Good Friday to Bach's *Passion according to the Gospel of Saint Matthew*.[12]

But I was also subject during my freshman year to an experience related to religion which I was not likely to forget.

One morning we were detained after chapel for the taking of a census to determine the quota of each church denomination represented in the student body.

"All members of the Congregational Church please rise!" Miss Edwards directed. A goodly number of girls rose. Then she called for members of the Baptist, Presbyterian, Methodist Church and so on to rise and be counted. Finally, after a short silence, and in a subdued voice, as if reluctant even to suggest of such a thing: "If there are any girls who belong to *no* church, please rise."

Alone, among more than four hundred girls, and conscious of the girls in the pews near me eyeing me askance, I stood up.

I not only stood up, I sprang up. I stood larger than was strictly necessary for the teachers beside Miss Edwards to jot down the figure 1 under the category to which I belonged. I felt a certain pride along with my designation. Papa, I felt, was standing beside me—Papa, who belonged to no church, because he could subscribe to the doctrines of none, but who could say *he* was not a Christian?[13]

I do not know whether after this revelation of my true status I was prayed over, as had been that earlier "Impenitent," Emily Dickinson; but, if so, I am glad, though so far separated in point of time, to have been in such extraordinarily good company. In any event, the census-taking that morning in chapel was not conducive to increasing my love for my Alma Mater.

Nevertheless, despite my rebellion, secret or open, against some of its features, there was much in Mount Holyoke I found congenial. New England itself was an experience—one an American can ill afford to miss. It was not the South. It did not possess the South's romantic appeal. But its charm was equally distinctive. I refuse to admit indeed that anyone could have derived more unalloyed joy than I from the college surroundings: the village street on which it faced arched over by its great elms; the tidy white cottages in the village, along with a few gambrel-roofed mansions, but houses, great or small, alike with lilac bushes in their dooryards more luxuriant than any lilacs I had seen before; the orchards ruddy with apples in the fall; the oldness of things, as American oldness goes; the tranquility; the feeling at once of coziness and of Peace and Plenty inspired by this New England scene—by the whole lovely Connecticut River Valley, so little disfigured as yet, even its factory towns with their somber tones seeming to fit with perfect propriety into the seemly half-rural New England of the day. I loved it all—loved it with my eyes, my senses, my mind.

I loved, too, hours spent in Williston Hall[14] on the campus. There in the Art Gallery, filled mostly with reproductions of classic sculpture, famous Madonnas and other masterpieces of religious art, were two gigantic landscapes by Albert Bierstadt, first artist, with his scenes of the high Sierras, to awaken Americans, no less than Europeans, to the soaring grandeur and solitude of our wild Western mountains.[15]

I would only stay when I had the gallery to myself, but that was nearly always; and seating myself on a bench I would lose myself in Bierstadt's grandiose conceptions of America. They would produce in me the same feeling of exaltation evoked later by Wagner's grandiose *Die Walküre* and *Götterdämmerung*.

But another source of enjoyment was the course of illustrated lectures given by Professor Goodyear,[16] formerly curator of the Metropolitan Museum of Art. Under him I became excited about such things as caryatides, flying buttresses, the frescoes in the Sistine Chapel; while, as a sophisticated and polished man of the world, with his cultured, beautifully modulated voice, his cosmopolitan air, and smoking his fine Havana cigars in defiance of all faculty rules, he was as exotic a figure as could well be imagined in an environment still strongly tinctured with Puritanism, and as diverting himself as were his lectures.

I found excitement also in an entirely different direction, in the Biological Laboratory. I found no more delight, it is true, in dissecting an earthworm or in studying the movements of an amoeba under the microscope than I had in high school in tearing apart a flower to discover its genus. But when I spied Darwin's *Origin of Species* and *The Descent of Man* in a collection of books attached to the laboratory, and still considered dangerous works, I read them ravenously. It is difficult in the 1950s to picture what fires this great pioneer in scientific thinking lit in the young of that day, when the Theory of Evolution was as fresh and stirring a subject as nuclear fission now.

Pursuing, however, only such subjects as I found irresistible, I was, I must admit, as unconscientious a student, viewed from the academic standpoint, as I had been in high school or under Dr. Tuck.

I cut classes remorselessly and availed myself of "snap courses"—readily detected then as now—; among them Mineralogy, entirely remote from any interest I had or ever would have, and, of all subjects, considering my aversion to hymns—Hymnology!

There was one teacher, though, Miss Bowers,[17] whose classes I never cut. She was dying of consumption, as we continued to call tuberculosis, and I can see her vividly, a frail bent little old lady in black, always wearing a short crocheted cape around her shoulders, often a spot of bright color in each of her sunken cheeks, but her dark eyes in their hollows full of fire, yet with a joyous expression. She used to go around after midday dinner to all the tables in the dining-room and dip up every spoonful of blood she could find in the platter from which a rare roast of beef or steak had been served, gathering it into a bowl to drink later, as a cure, advocated then, for consumption.

She was also set apart from the other teachers—all spinsters—in the girls' minds, from the fact that the young man to whom she was betrothed had been killed in the Civil War, and in her sitting-room his picture in an oval walnut frame had ivy trained around it.

It is not alone these personal attributes, however, which make Miss Bowers stand out in my mind now. Purely as a teacher, I had known none so inspiring. I had Chaucer under her and Shakespeare, along with other Elizabethan dramatists, and her own consuming delight—even when broken by fits of coughing—in these immortals to whom she had devoted a life-time of study must have been transmitted in some degree to every girl who ever sat in her class-room. She made "the spacious time of Great Elizabeth"[18] come alive as if it were yesterday, and I owe an incalculable debt to Mount Holyoke, if for nothing else, for hours with Miss Bowers—and for its library.

I would begin to be happy as soon as I pushed open the heavy doors of the corridor which led from the main building to this vaulted chamber of many alcoves, with its thousands upon thousands of books and stack-rooms beyond. I had known before only private libraries, and all these shelves, where there was no light fiction, no "best-sellers" (unheard of then, or by any such term), yet offered a rich and limitless field for exploration. Much of my time there was spent simply in browsing: taking down volume after volume for hasty or lengthier examination. I sampled Kant's *Critique of Pure Reason*, Fichte, Schelling, Hegel—all manner of heavy obscure, difficult philosophic writers beyond my comprehension, but from whom I got *something,* or fancied I did at the time. Just to be immersed in the perfect quiet of this sanctuary, only a few other living beings, wide distances apart, anywhere near, but with the smell of books in my nostrils, and surrounded by all the great spirits of the present and past, was boundless bliss. Seated at one of its long oaken tables, I read hour after hour, willfully deaf to the clanging of gongs that announced change of classes—read, among other things I remember, not only Goethe's *The Sorrows of Werther*, whose sentimental hero had led so many romantic youths in the previous century to take their own lives, but his *Wilhelm Meister*, even his *Elective Affinities*, a work I should dislike to be forced to re-read to-day.

It would be entirely false, however, to represent myself at Mount Holyoke as a typical book-worm. My flagrant neglect of my regular studies left me plenty of time outside my adventures with strange books for lighter pleasures. Together with two or three intimates, girls from the South, and a few bold spirits from the Middle West, I tasted the forbidden delight of dancing. With someone playing waltz music very softly at the piano, on evenings when enough moonlight came through the windows, we would dance with each other in the unlighted "gym." We would make "Vassar fudge"[19] in our rooms, also forbidden. Reclining lazily in each other's beds we would spend an untold amount of time in exuberant, foolish, happy talk, seldom touching on our studies, usually about the places we came from and people there, including our beaux, letters from whom we read aloud to each other. From these never-ending conversations centering on our home towns, I became convinced that Knoxville was an infinitely more exciting place than any of the places the other girls came from, and I believe I even convinced some of the others that this was true.

But now Mount Holyoke, with what I had loved and what I had hated there, was behind me, forever it appeared; and for all the dark shadows in the background, my broken father, my mother never complaining yet with her somber eyes, yet at once—as if I had not been away—little Negro boys on horseback were riding up to the gate with notes from this one or that, asking to take me to a dance, on a Surrey drive with another couple—whatever it was. Almost at once there were young men in the parlor in the evening when nothing else was on.

The young men who came were older now. There were no cadets among them. There *were* no cadets. The military department on "the Hill" had been discontinued on the happy assumption that this country henceforth would be perpetually at peace.

Young men who came now were reading law, or had gone into their father's or an uncle's business. Some had been at college in the North. I myself during holidays in Boston or New York had seen Julia Marlowe[20] in *Pygmalion and Galatea*, Richard Mansfield in Clyde Fitch's new tragi-comedy, *Beau Brummell*;[21] heard the comic opera star Lillian Russell,[22] with her hour-glass figure and fabulous beauty—which for two generations made her an American household name. I had gone to an after-theatre party at Delmonico's, for the first time sipped champagne; listened to the Boston Symphony Orchestra, very young then, in Symphony Hall in Boston; and, most momentous of all, heard George Kennan, coming on to the lecture platform in the convict garb, limbs naked, of a Siberian exile, iron clamps around his ankles, and the clanking of the chains he dragged a sound which sent shivers down my spine. This was the George Kennan who, after traveling thousands of miles in Siberia, now was touring America, attracting the attention of the whole world as he exposed the Czarist system of political exile in Siberia, those cruelties under Czarist Russia which aroused people then as do tales to-day of Russian Communist barbarities.[23]

We were all a little more knowledgeable now, a little more sophisticated, and there was never any lack of things to talk about. When I read the other day of a young Yale man hunting around for the bar at a debutante party with the complaint: "All you can do at a debutante party is talk, and *who wants to talk*?" I could not but reflect that in the '90s, as in the '80s, one of the chief diversions of young people—or certainly this was so in the South—was to talk.

And if the talk was not brilliant, yet soon our parlor was as full of laughter as ever it had been in the Barnes house. Surprising soon, Highland Avenue began to seem home.

Altogether it was a gay summer and hardly marred even by Papa's condition, for whatever his suffering and private anxieties he managed always to appear cheerful, while Mama put nothing in the way of my having as good a time as I could.

In the previous year, during my summer vacation, and near its end, at Cave Springs, our usual destination for picnic supper when we went on a boating-party, I had met Bob Armstrong, son of the Armstrongs whose home was Bleak House, overlooking their plantation on Kingston Pike; the Bob Armstrong who had spent five years with the Sioux, this dare-devil I had first laid eyes on years before as he entered his parents' pew in the Second Presbyterian Church. Bob was older than the other young men at the party but instantly he and I seemed to have much in common.

But that same summer I had met, also for the first time, a young man I shall call Theodore De Groot.[24] He was from New York, descendant of one of the Dutch families who early dominated the island of Manhattan and the farm of De Groot's ancestors covering a large part of what is now the City of New York.

A graduate of Yale and of the Yale Law School, De Groot had only very recently come to Knoxville to enter the law firm of Charles Seymour, a crusty old bachelor but able lawyer, from a distinguished Connecticut family of governors, clergymen, scholars; a graduate of the Yale Law School himself and always on the lookout for recent graduates who showed promise.[25]

Some young man brought Theodore with him on the last evening, as it happened, before I returned to college. The room was full, girls and young men, and we were having a last lively get-together when Theodore was brought into the parlor and introduced.

A well-built young man, he was slightly aloof, much more formal and dressed more punctiliously than young men in Knoxville dressed. His nose was long, though well shaped, his mouth full-lipped and sensual, though I think I hardly noticed this at the time. I was not drawn to him and believe he would have made little impression of any sort except for his unusually deep and sonorous voice, and the low tone and rather intimate fashion in which he addressed me directly, the few times he did.

I was greatly surprised then when after returning to college I received from him a handsome edition of *L'Abbé Constantin* by the French novelist, Ludovic Halévy, popular then. The book interested me as little as its sender, though I wrote him a note of thanks. Next he sent me Amiel's *Journal*, another curious choice I thought, and again I wrote my thanks, though this time I must have indulged in some flippancy, for in his lengthy reply he remonstrated with me. He had expected me, he implied, to be more serious-minded.

"What cheek!" I exclaimed, as I read his letter aloud to my room-mate. "Who does he think he is, anyway?" This was certainly one young man I had no desire to see again.

But now in my first September on Highland Avenue, one evening I was expecting Bob Armstrong. We were to go to a home in West End where there was always a gay crowd on the porch in the evening. (I seldom went to the Gaines anymore. I seemed to have outgrown that stage of my life, though Mary and I remained good friends.) Bob had not been quite sure he could come. There were house-guests at Bleak House. But on the chance he might, I dressed more carefully than usual and when I heard the gate click went to the front door, held out my hands, and before I made out clearly in the darkness who the man approaching was, called out: "So, Bob, you got here after all!"

"It's not Bob!" an answer came back in the deep voice of Theodore De Groot.

He stepped up on the porch and we sat down in the two chairs behind the moon vines. I kept hoping Bob would come, but he failed to appear.

Mr. De Groot (as I called him) said he had spent most of his time since he saw me last in making trips down into Polk County,[26] Tennessee's Copper Basin, where companies operating mines and refineries were clients of Charles Seymour—trips in the interest of other clients, all over the mountain country around Knoxville. He had not been impressed, it was evident, with the beauty of the region, only with the discomforts he had encountered. It was equally clear he had not found the mountain people interesting, only uncouth.

He was a snob, I said to myself. He referred to various plain people he had dealt with as belonging to "the great unwashed."[27] Nevertheless, on this second meeting, in a way he impressed me. He was the first young man definitely an intellectual I had known and I suppose I was flattered when he said I was the one girl he had met in Knoxville whom he cared to call on again. But I was far more shocked than flattered when, on leaving, as we stood at the porch step, he peered into my eyes and said in his deep masterful voice: "I suppose you might as well know that you are the girl I am going to marry."

Something like a shiver had run through me at the moment. Why, I didn't *like* the man. Didn't even *know* him! But from then on Theodore De Groot kept coming. I seemed to have no control over his coming.

He kept giving me books, and always deluxe editions, one of them a new translation of Goethe's *Faust*; and when there was no one else present would read me some article he considered important in the current *North American Review* he brought with him.

Long afterwards, Bob Armstrong insisted naggishly that De Groot's interest for me—so far as there was one—sprang from the fact that he wore spats, carried a cane, had gone to Yale, and read the *North American Review*!

In any case, Theodore De Groot was making more and more acquaintances now. He had the faculty, when he cared to exert it, of making friends, though those he made in Knoxville were always men who had gone to Eastern colleges. Southern colleges and universities, he averred, were nothing more than High Schools. As for "Southern Gentlemen," a term he used facetiously, he made it plain he had only contempt for their "code," at the same time throwing out dark hints that wild oats he had sown himself at Yale had been on a higher plane, one on which New York chorus girls—not "mulatto wenches"—figured.

I resented these coarse insinuations; resented his sneers at "Southern Gentlemen." Resented hotly his whole attitude toward the South. Moreover, although he was an aristocratic and distinguished [man, I felt] a slight physical repugnance in his presence. I was always glad when others were present.

All this time Bob was coming often too. Frequently they met in our parlor and from the start I was conscious of the instinctive dislike the two men felt for one another. Theodore would become almost completely silent after Bob arrived. I think he resented (perhaps secretly envied) the extreme courtliness and gallantry of Bob's manner. But Bob, with a savoir-faire nothing could faze, if Theodore was unwilling to talk, would carry on a spirited conversation with me alone, and with his bold humor and interest in people, high or low, be even more amusing than ordinarily.

It was in November that Theodore, leaving his office early one afternoon, asked me to take a walk in the country with him. No one walked in the country then for pleasure, no one *I* knew. Hikes were unheard of. I was not too eager to go but we walked out the pike a couple of miles and turning into a lane which led down to the river stopped and rested our arms on a rail fence below which was a corn field, the shocks not yet removed, and below the field the river.

It was a heavenly day, neither hot nor cold, and everything lightly veiled by the Indian Summer haze. It was nice, after all, to be in the country on such a day. I was dreamily conscious of an all-enveloping sense of well-being and not too conscious of Theodore's nearness until suddenly he laid his hand on mine.

"Annie," he said, in that deep voice of his that had in it an almost hypnotic quality, "I am going to speak to your father to-morrow. I want to ask his permission—"

"Permission—" I stopped him. "Permission for what?"

"Permission for you to marry me."

"Oh, no, no!" I fairly gasped and I withdrew my hand. "Papa would be horrified!"

"Permission at least for us to be engaged."

"But I don't *want* to be engaged," I protested. "I don't want to settle down with just one person. There are so many other—"

"Other what?" Theodore interrupted with sudden sternness.

"So many other people," I faltered. "So many people I like—and like to be with."

Theodore suddenly buried his face in his hands. After a silence, a sound like a sob escaped him. There was a stricken look in his deeply flushed face when at last he lifted it. His eyes were swimming with tears.

"How can it be possible," he said in a choking voice, "that when *you* are all that is necessary for me, others are necessary for you?"

All his arrogance had fallen away from him. He seemed like a little boy who had been deeply wounded—this young man who had been so sure of himself before, so supercilious. And he was so terribly serious. I felt sorry for him, yet his words that first night on the porch came back to me now with fresh and frightening force.

Meantime, although there was constant discomfort in my mind in regard to Theodore, I continued to have a gay time.

I had become used to the situation at home. Our household machinery ran as smoothly as it had always done. Mama called on me for no assistance. And the meals, which she cooked herself, seemed as good, as varied, as ever. It is a painful thing for me to reflect on now, but I do not believe it ever crossed my mind, at the time, that in my parents' changed circumstances, Papa a permanent invalid, I had any responsibility in the way of lightening their burdens. An idea of lightening them financially would have seemed to me fantastic. With my enormous youthful zest for life, I lived only from day to day, extracting every drop of joy I could from each day as it passed.

Of course there would be no coming-out party for me now, but few girls in Knoxville had formal coming-out parties then, and there was too much else of a pleasurable nature for this to matter.

There were the races I went to with Bob, who, after the races, would drive me cross-country home to Bleak House for supper. That electric spark I had felt—still a little girl with braids down my back—at first sight of Bob in church, that flash of pleasure, tingle in my veins, he could still call forth the moment he appeared.

Even Mechanicsville, which we must drive through on the way to the race-track, a section of town where workmen lived in respectable but drab little houses, took on a certain glamour when I sat beside Bob, behind the spirited horses he handled with his light sure touch.[28]

Then there were plays at Staub's Theatre (as we were beginning to call the Opera House). Above all there was dancing. Neither Bob nor Theodore danced, but this did not prevent my going to dances. We were dancing the cotillion now at the Sans Souci Club and cotillion favors—tiny fans, crystal vinaigrettes, all manner of pretty tinselly trifles, dangled from around the mirror in my bed-room.

There were elaborate afternoon teas and luncheons, given even by girls of my own age who lived in great Victorian mansions like the Woodruffs' in West End—elaborate luncheons of many courses, served with the utmost elegance. I have always doubted, in fact, if anywhere else in the South, even in Charleston, there was a more elegant and sophisticated social life in that era than in Knoxville; with its essentially Southern culture, devoted to the art of living richly and joyfully; a society still dominated by an aristocracy of blood; one which a *nouveau riche* might labor hard to enter, yet not be accepted, while some of its most admired and influential members had little money.

But how could I ever pay back all these social obligations? I do not remember, the truth is, that this troubled me in the least. I probably thought—if I gave it a thought—that but for the disaster at Flat Creek and Papa's ruin, I should be giving parties too. As it was, I enjoyed whole-heartedly those others gave. The golden years of my girlhood, in spite of everything, were not yet past.

Most splendid of all was the Hallowe'en party given by Colonel Dickinson at Island Home. In my early teens there had been the Hallowe'en party engineered by the Thomas girls, with their fertile imaginations. We had fought our way in the darkness through dusty, overgrown, brambley paths into the ancient basement kitchen of the deserted old mansion on Bell Avenue. It was no more fun, but now I was going grandly in a closed carriage, my escort Rush Strong, a traveled man of the world, president of a bank, a bachelor who squired the latest girls to take their place in the social whirl as well as those who had been out several seasons.[29]

The mile-long avenue from the porter's lodge at Island Home was lighted all the way by Japanese lanterns strung through the trees. Every room in the mansion was glowing in the light of innumerable wax tapers. All the traditional rites of Hallowe'en were performed, but everyone was in full evening dress; there was a magnificent midnight supper, champagne, an orchestra to dance by, and the hospitable old Colonel in his glory.

House parties, too, at this time were beginning to be a feature of our social life. This meant jolly week-ends at country-houses in various little towns not far from Knoxville. Harriman was one of them.[30] Like Middlesboro, Kentucky, it was one of the brand-new towns springing up in a New South that offered new business opportunities; its streets still unpaved, but surrounded by beautiful hilly country.

Harriman, however, was unique. It had been brought into existence through the efforts of General Clinton D. Fisk, recently the Prohibition Party's candidate for President of the United States, and by the Women's Christian Temperance Union.[31] Seat of the American Temperance University (long since defunct), Harriman was to be a model of morality and sobriety, with a householder forfeiting the deed to his property should "intoxicating liquors" be discovered on his premises.

One of the early temperance experiments in this country and well publicized, socially-prominent families with bibulous members flocked to Harriman from New York, Philadelphia, and Boston before the little town's first dust was laid. Half a century before Alcohol[ics] Anonymous came into being, here was a possible solution for their common problem. They built houses in Queen Anne style that would not have looked out of place in Tuxedo[32] and, except for serving wines, established as nearly as possible the type of social life to which they had been accustomed.

There were no English remittance men here, as in Middlesboro, but the thing which gave Harriman its special flavor was the style in which these Eastern families lived in a town carved out of a raw countryside almost over night. I went to card parties in some of their luxurious homes,[33] to rather mixed dances in the town's one little hotel, and had glorious riding on blooded horses accompanied by young men in the smartest of riding togs.

But it is not the gay house-parties, the horseback riding with young swells, the cotillions—it was a social observance in this long past time which I look back upon now with most pleasure.

It was the custom then for ladies whose homes lent themselves to large scale entertaining to keep open house on New Year's Day from early afternoon till midnight or later.

No invitations were issued but the papers announced who would receive and what young ladies would assist them. Only men called, men of all ages, coming alone, or perhaps three or four, if they were older men, sharing the same livery carriage as they made their rounds.

On New Year's Day of this year I was one of the girls asked to assist. The house was darkened, but the lamps burning softly under their huge, delicately-tinted, silken shades, the radiance from the open fires, and all of us who received in shimmering evening dress, combined to give it a festal air. Then the gentlemen began to arrive in their frock coats and top hats, and more and more of them as the afternoon wore on and night approached.

Sooner or later all the pillars of Knoxville society appeared, but many who came were men never seen at any other social function throughout the year; many of them, though in formal clothes, more than a little seedy. Some of the older ones were both stone deaf and tottery. Nevertheless, one and all they were happy, glowingly happy, for one day in the year at least.

Already definitely mellowed by the time they reached homes in West End, the manners of these gentlemen of the Old School, the Old South, were now gallant beyond description. What compliments they paid! Never had the "Southland" produced "young ladies" more beautiful, more bewitching! They quoted poetry to us, laughed, joked, did everything but burst into song. And how they enjoyed the strong hot rum punch from an enormous punch bowl frequently refilled. How they enjoyed the cold turkey, Smithfield ham, the smoked tongue, the great rounds of cold spiced beef, the oysters, the cheeses!

It was *their* day. Especially it was the day of those, once men of some importance, now fallen on lean days; or of others, men of gentle birth but too sensitive to have made much headway in the New South. And it was these gentlemen we were expected, as assistants to the hostess, to welcome a little more warmly, more effusively, than any of the rest; the ones to whom we were to give the major part of our attention, and, as the rooms began to steam, if one or another of them seemed a trifle unsteady, to give him, inconspicuously, a bit of aid as he plowed his way through the crowd in coming or going, or once more in the direction of the punch bowl.

But stumbling a little though some might, they were all so happy, with their deep bows, their jovial "Happy New Years!" to right and left. The whole house, open to any who cared to come, seemed pervaded with such a feeling of love, love for everyone—love, or whatever it was—, as I had never known before. And there was something about it that moved my heart. Something so beautiful it made me want to cry.

Some time that winter Aunt Sarah, Mama's sister, came. She was a stately woman, like Mama, in a day of "stately" women, though less reserved, and where Mama was a decided brunette Aunt Sarah had a wealth of reddish gold hair coiled around her head, blue eyes, and features, if pleasing, yet not so finely-cut as Mama's. She was an artist, I don't know how good, but she painted not only china but landscapes much admired, and had converted one of the rooms in her home into a studio where she taught painting.

It was a joy to have Aunt Sarah with us. Having no children of her own, she lavished affection on her nieces and nephews and seemed to understand them better than did their parents.

It was a joy also for Aunt Sarah to come to Knoxville, where she had visited several times. She loved the South and all its ways, good or bad. She used to say she didn't see how once you had known the South you could ever be content anywhere else.

She came early that winter, in November, I think it was, and I have an idea it was an appeal from Mama that brought her, for Aunt Sarah could do anything with clothes, or with almost anything she turned her hand to; whereas Mama, though a fine needle-woman, would never have attempted to make pretty, inexpensive evening dresses for me, such as Mrs. Gaines made for her girls, though with so many dances, I could not go on wearing the few I had over and over all winter.

Aunt Sarah raked through closets and trunks, rummaged through all the boxes in which Mama, for all she was not of a saving nature, had saved lengths of uncut silk and satin, bolts of ribbon, ostrich-feather trimming, lace and artificial flowers. Aunt Sarah was in her element as she designed and draped on me one evening dress after another; all with the demi-trains we wore then, and one made from a discarded pink tea-gown of Mama's and transformed till it bore no resemblance whatever to the original garment.

But there was an incident connected with these dresses which I have never been able to forget.

On the evening I was going to a dance Theodore would always come after I was dressed and before my escort arrived. He always seemed moody at such times, partly perhaps because I was always full of excitement, keyed higher than usual in anticipation of what was ahead.

This evening I was wearing for the first time one of Aunt Sarah's creations, of white tulle with an underdress and sash of pale yellow satin and the low cut bodice edged around the top with little satin primroses to match the sash and my yellow satin slippers. Papa, Mama, Aunt Sarah, all had passed on my appearance before I went into the parlor where Theodore was waiting.

Theodore never paid compliments, but this time he took one long look at me and his face turned a deep purple. It was livid with anger. I had never seen him look like this and I could see he was trying to master himself as he said deliberately, his full lower lip quivering, though with an air of authority: "Go upstairs and take that dress off! It's entirely too low."

I was indignant. How did he dare talk as if I were his property? But the doorbell rang, announcing my escort, and I was saved from making an answer.

I was not saved, though, from fright, and the fear that gripped me now was not fear of Theodore De Groot. It was fear of myself. Why did I stand such things? What was it about this man who was repellent yet at the same time exerted some sort of influence that made it impossible for me to say I never wanted to see him again? I didn't know what it was. I don't know today, or am not at all certain. But I was more and more troubled, my mind now in a state of constant ferment.

Things were like this when Donna came. It must have been in February. I know that by this time Bob was not coming so often because he was sure to find Theodore in the parlor when he arrived and they had reached a stage of antagonism where they sat on opposite sides of me in front of the fire and no longer made any pretense of recognizing each other's presence. Theodore sulked. Bob did most of the talking, but he would always leave first. In spite of his reputation for wildness and the savage life he had led with the Sioux, Bob was tender-hearted. He could not bear to see my anxiety when the clock showed it was nearing ten, for Mama insisted my callers, even Mr. Rush Strong, [almost] as old as Papa,[34] must not stay later than this hour. But I seldom, in fact, saw Bob alone now except when he drove me home to supper at Bleak House. And I welcomed Donna's coming. Maybe it would ease the situation, for I would have to give more time to her and of necessity less to Theodore.

For Mama, it must have been a sore trial to have a guest in the house that winter, unless Aunt Sarah. But when Donna, who had never been South before, wrote, suggesting the visit, Mama agreed there was nothing to do but ask her to come.

I had come to know Donna at the resort on Lake Michigan where I went that summer after Harry was drowned and ever since, as girls do, we had corresponded with each other.

Donna belonged to a family of considerable importance and with a very handsome home. The house we lived in ourselves now left much to be desired. However, she proved an easy guest, fitting into things as they were, and finding much in Knoxville to interest and amuse her. Then, while any formal entertaining was out of the question, Mama would ask various young people for supper each Sunday. She would have Bonnie come to prepare and serve the supper, and with minced Saddle-rock oysters baked in their shells, chicken salad—all sorts of good things, and the table shining and sparkling with the fine damask, silver, cut glass—all the nice things we still had, I would have the illusion for a few merry hours that nothing had happened and we were as well off as ever.

Petite and pretty, Donna had no end of attractive dresses and was a good dancer. Though she talked little, she was a gifted listener, could say things with her eyes, and met all the men's sallies and stories with a delightful little chuckling, highly appreciative laugh, so that as a visiting girl she had no lack of attention.

Even Theodore made himself, during Donna's visit, more agreeable than usual. He was not so moody. The fact that Bob was in New York at the time may have had some bearing on it.

Bob, tired of idling, of simply playing the gentleman, was growing restless again. With no professional training and no need for him on the plantation now that the Armstrongs were selling off more and more of their land as the town began to extend into the country, he was looking around for a business opening somewhere.

True, whenever Theodore could get me alone for a moment, he would insist I leave Donna to entertain the callers and come with him into the small sitting-room at the back of the hall on the other side of the house, so we could be by ourselves for awhile.

Donna, however, had begged me never to leave her alone with "all those men." She enjoyed them thoroughly, enjoyed the humorous and flattering things they said, but coming from a larger city, with its more formal pattern of social life, she was not used to so many. She was sure, too, there must be more men in the South than elsewhere, or at least that they paid more attention to girls.

For me, it was lovely to have this jolly crowd and all the laughter once again in our parlor. Lately, not only Bob but other young men had not been coming so often.

Loveliest of all, though, to me, were evenings when Papa would join us. It was not merely deference to age, or even compassion for his infirmities, that made the younger men, springing to their feet, welcome him as they did when he opened the door into the parlor. It was the spirit of youth still in him they recognized, for all his ravaged face, plowed with suffering. It was the radiance he generated, the unconquerable lightness of heart with which he entered into whatever we were discussing. They remembered the stalwart man he had been once. But what they saw now was the innate fortitude and invincibility of the human spirit rising above a maimed and broken body, and I can still feel the tearing joy that went through me as I saw him surrounded by my young friends; never seeking to dominate the conversation, but in his way of telling even the simplest thing magnetizing his hearers as I had seen him since I could remember anything at all.

What Donna, in after years, seemed to remember best about Knoxville were the serenades the young men gave us, along with the other girls, and a custom then in the South like open house on New Year's Day.

We would perhaps already be asleep and wakened some time around midnight by harmonious men's voices floating through our bedroom windows up from the ground below where the men stood.

Usually a quartette, they sang without instruments and softly, not to arouse the neighborhood. You were not supposed to go to the window, speak to the serenaders or betray any awareness of their bodily existence as their voices in the midnight stillness stole up to you in:

> Drink to me only with thine eyes,
> And I will pledge with mine.[35]

The young men sang well. Some of them had belonged to college glee clubs. Never, I thought, had men's voices sounded so endearing and I can smell now exactly the way the night air smelled on those mild soot-impregnated winter nights in Knoxville; can hear across the long years the tones of their blended young-men's voices as they ended always with the same song, though singing slowly, more softly than ever now, and dying down to a whisper:

Good night, ladies, Good night, ladies,
Good night, ladies! We're going to leave you now.[36]

Donna was married soon after her visit to Knoxville. She went to England to live and lived there the rest of her life, with her town house in London, and a villa at Hampton Court, once David Garrick's,[37] where she spent part of the year.

When I would see her in England in later years Donna could remember, as I could not, what all the songs were the men sang. There was one of them, however, I had not forgotten, or its effect on me, the *Eton Boat Song*,[38] and to this day when occasionally I hear it:

Jolly boating weather, And a hay harvest breeze,
Blade on the feather, Shade off the trees,

with Theodore De Groot's rich deep-toned voice clearly distinguishable among those of the other unseen singers, it brings back to me with a certain excitement, painfully, and as nothing else, the *feel* of that time, at once anguished, joyful, full of a vague alarm and confusion.

There were the serenades Donna remembered, and something else, less romantic—the street-cars in Knoxville, especially the one which ran past our house on Highland Avenue. The driver would stop on a signal from any lady living along the line; give her time to adjust her hat and veil, even to change her dress, before she emerged from her house to board the car. After she had finished her marketing on the Square, if she wished to shop elsewhere and placed her basket in his charge, he would deposit it on her front porch as he passed her house. Some mornings he would be hopping off his car, delivering heaped-up market baskets, along his whole route, and all this without charge and the greatest good humor, as one might accommodate a close friend or near neighbor.

But what Donna relished most in her recollection of Knoxville street-cars was when a driver would get off his car, leaving the passengers inside, and walk along outside, dusting the car off with a feather-duster as it moved slowly up the street at a pace set by the mules.

"Where else," Donna would say, sitting in her villa and rocking with laughter, "could you see such a sight?"

But at the time there were things in Knoxville which gave Donna, easily amused, no such delight—things that had we not both been so young and as yet scarcely begun to take life seriously, would probably have prevented her from getting much, if any, enjoyment out of the visit.

She conveyed to me my first knowledge of what others were saying about Theodore De Groot. Every time she was alone with one of the young men I had known from my early teens, he would say, "Miss Donna, for God's sake don't let Miss Annie marry De Groot!"

Donna gave me my first knowledge, too, of how worried Mama and Papa were. Neither of them had ever said a word to me in criticism of Theodore. They feared, I imagine, as I look back, that any criticism on their part might only strengthen whatever attraction it was he had for me. (Perhaps they remembered *l'affaire Hu*!) They had nothing specifically against him, Mama told Donna; only that he came far too often, stayed too late, and was monopolizing me. They were filled with anxiety.

Whether I laughed off these things Donna told me, or how I met them, I can not recall. Only the salient points of that troubled time remain in my mind. I recall, however, that under my surface gaiety, I was secretly becoming more and more disturbed and made no less so when one Sunday shortly after Donna left Theodore induced me to take a walk with him—not in the country this time, but in West End. There was something, he said mysteriously, he wanted to show me; and, to my utter surprise, when we reached a section of West End lying behind the University grounds, between "The Hill" and the river, mostly laid out in building-lots but not yet built upon save for a few commonplace little dwellings that had long been there, he stopped and pointed to the vacant treeless lot beside us.

Thrusting his arm through mine, his voice husky, "This is the lot," he said, "I've bought. This is where I'll build our house."

I was speechless. I looked around me, and sensing, I suppose, at least one thought in my mind, he added, "This will be a very desirable residential section of Knoxville a few years from now."

He was right in his prediction, as time proved. But with Sunday afternoon a depressing time at best, never had my spirits dropped so low. To start with, there was nowhere I should dislike to live more than in this vicinity. It was not even Knoxville to me—it might as well have been the plains of Nebraska. But infinitely more disturbing was the feeling that Theodore was obsessed, that he would never give up, and that I was being swept along in spite of myself, to some destination that had no relation to any future I had ever pictured for myself. I would marry eventually of course. But I wanted to tell Theodore straight off, once and for all, that I could not marry *him*—ever! But again his face had taken on the look it had had in the country that afternoon. It was deeply flushed. His eyes were misty and I could feel his arm, still hooked in mine, shaking. I could not tell him, and things drifted along.

Some time in March Miss Kate Ogden called at our house. I was not at home but on my return Mama told me the purpose of her call.

Miss Ogden had opened that year a private school for girls in one of a row of three or four modern houses on Main Street. Tall, narrow, citified-looking structures with partly shingled walls and only a small area between them and the street, they were considered quite fashionable additions to Knoxville.[39]

The mellowed red-brick buildings of the old East Tennessee Female Institute, where that dynamic educator, Mrs. Lizzie Crozier French, had conducted of recent years her "School for Young Ladies and Children," and which had stood on Main Street since before the Civil War, were now torn down; so Miss Ogden, who had imported her teachers from the East, was getting most of Mrs. French's former pupils, girls with parents still unwilling to send their daughters to Public Schools.

I had gone to school myself to Miss Ogden. She had taught English in the Girls' High School. Belonging to a cultivated, highly respected English family, she was a stoutish middle-aged woman with a beaming florid face and rather fussy manners. I had neither liked nor disliked her; but then, with a few outstanding exceptions, teachers, like preachers, had always seemed to me a separate part of, if not a little outside, the human race; so I had never given a thought to her opinion of me and was astounded when Mama said Miss Ogden wanted me to take the place for the rest of the school year of a teacher from Boston who had proved unsatisfactory and who, the truth was, she had fired, though Miss Ogden would never have used so unrefined an expression.

Mama put Miss Ogden's proposition to me without comment. Miss Ogden wanted me to teach Latin, it would only be for a few months, and she would pay me forty-five dollars a month.

The last thing I had ever thought I would do was teach. I had not the remotest idea *how* to teach, having never observed the methods, if they *had* methods, of those who taught me. But the forty-five dollars had a tempting sound.

There were many little things I needed and wanted, and the time had come when I hesitated to ask Mama and Papa for money. Then there was the ever present, ever more pressing, problem of Theodore which, it flashed through me, I would have less time to think about if I accepted Miss Ogden's offer. I decided almost at once to do so and assumed the position next day.

Teaching, in the beginning, save for having to get up while I was still heavy with sleep the morning after a dance, I found easier than I had expected. The surroundings were pleasant; [the] girls well-bred; so recently out of college, I had no trouble with my classes in Latin; and Miss Ogden interfered with me in no way; never, in fact, entering the room where I was teaching the whole time I was with her, which, as things turned out, was fortunate both for Miss Ogden and for me.

I had only been in the school a few days when she told me—what she had not mentioned before—that in addition to Latin she wished me to teach advanced arithmetic, as my predecessor had done, to the girls who were graduating this year. She considered it important, she said, that they go out with a sound knowledge, not only of the simple problems in arithmetic they had had in lower grades, but of "Higher Arithmetic," as she called it.

I was flabbergasted. The very term, "Higher Arithmetic," struck terror to my heart. Lower arithmetic had been torture, and what would I do with "Higher Arithmetic," which I had never heard of before, and only too wretchedly conscious of my mental incapacity in the whole field of mathematics, and how I had flunked outright or only got through by the skin of my teeth algebra, geometry, and trigonometry? But I took the text-book she handed me, carried it home, and between my social engagements endeavored to do some of the problems in its opening section, though I found I could not, to save my soul, solve a single one of them. It would have been as easy for me to read Sanskrit.

When the morning came for me to teach my first class in Higher Arithmetic I was in a state of panic. But I glanced around the sunny, cheerful, third-floor classroom, met the questioning gaze, the shining faces, of the mischievous-looking young girls before me, and suddenly had an inspiration. There, in the front row, sat Jean Crawford.

Jean's father, Colonel Crawford, had been commandant of cadets when they still had military training on "The Hill." Now he was professor of mathematics.[40] Having a mathematical father, Jean would be sure to know how to solve all these problems. I assigned the first one, giving the class a certain amount of time to work it, then asked Jean to do the example on the black-board and to explain it, step by step, so that any girls who had failed to get the right answer might now understand it; meantime giving my own undivided attention to her operations in an effort to understand them myself.

This became my daily pedagogic procedure, varying my approach to it slightly from day to day so it might not be too obvious who in the room was most in need of instruction.

Sometimes I would see the light, if still somewhat dimly, by the time Jean had finished her first explanation. If not, I would say:

"Are there any girls in the room who *still* do not understand this example?"

Happily for me, a number of hands would usually go up. Then I would ask Jean to go over the example once again, point by point, till I could finally (if at all) grasp it myself, while Jean, a bright, lively girl, appeared to quite enjoy her importance in acting as my assistant.

Whether Jean or any of the others ever suspected how dense I was on the subject, I do not know. What I know is that gratitude has never ceased to well up in my heart when I think of this pupil who saved me from open disgrace.

Secretly, at the time, after my system seemed to work, I considered it a great joke that Jean Crawford should be teaching for me (unconsciously, I hoped) my class on Higher Arithmetic.

It was impossible, however, for me to regard as a joke something else connected with this brief interlude when I was a member of Miss Ogden's staff.

Perhaps to reassure her patrons, should there be any question of my fitness to teach (all the other teachers were much older), soon after I took the position Miss Ogden asked me to get letters of endorsement from my professors at Mount Holyoke. She based, I imagine, any confidence she had in me herself on the fact that I was the first girl in Knoxville (except Miss Mary Temple long before) to go North to college.

Strangely enough, I applied for these testimonials with no misgivings. I realized I had been no "ideal student," yet my college teachers would probably find something of a complimentary nature they could say. And several did, so that I was able with some pride to show their letters to Papa and Mama before turning them over to Miss Ogden.

But then came an answer from Miss Bardwell, stern head of the department of mathematics at Mount Holyoke and when I read Miss Bardwell's letter I felt the deepest sense of shame I had felt thus far in my life.

Miss Bardwell made no effort to spare me. Without mincing words, she stated it would be impossible for her to recommend me for any teaching position whatsoever. I had been, so far as her own experience went, a most unconscientious and completely unsatisfactory student.

Needless to say, Miss Ogden did not see the letter. I burned it in the fireplace in my bed-room, my cheeks almost as hot as the flames which consumed its single damning sheet.

I found it was no momentary prick of conscience either that I must suffer. I could not banish from my mind thoughts of the sorrow Miss Bardwell's letter would have caused my parents had they seen it. Filled with remorse, it was a joyful moment then when I received my first pay check—the first money I had earned—and hastened to spend it on some beautiful and expensive wool and silk material for a dress for Mama, while for Papa I bought a handsome leather-bound edition of Carlyle's *Hero and Hero Worship*.[41] Now I could feel a trifle less guilty in their presence.

What happened when I received my next month's check was less joyful. Pulling the bills I had brought home out of my purse, I displayed them proudly, but when I went upstairs to my bed-room, Mama followed, closing the door behind her, and her face grave.

"Annie," she said, "could you let me have fifteen dollars of it—for the housekeeping?"

Oh, I thought, why hadn't I saved Mama this embarrassment and offered the money before she had to ask? But in the same instant I perceived, in a blinding flash, how poor we must be now, or Mama could never have brought herself to do so.

Even so, however, I was not unduly downcast. With the resiliency of youth, consumed by youthful desires for gaiety and excitement, I was still able, save at intervals, to forget these painful moments and to believe, just as I had when in the Barnes house misfortune first overtook us, that through some miracle or other, things were bound to turn out all right. Such a successful man as Papa had been, surely he would recoup some of his losses sooner or later. . . .

I was wrapped in this dream one Sunday morning when Mama and I were walking to church together. I had ceased going to Sunday School but went to church with Mama now that Papa was unable to go. Church, I think, with Mama, was more than anything else a social convention she had followed all her life, a habit she hesitated to break.

At all events, as we started up the Clinch Street hill Mama, who had been silent since we left home, suddenly said in a low voice: "Your father was shocked when Mr. De Groot came to him yesterday and asked his permission to marry you."

When I did not answer, Mama said: "Your father told him that was a matter for you to decide."

I could see that Mama was laboring under strong feeling, but I still said nothing. With the reticence that had always been between us, I had never been able to discuss with her any of my girlish affairs, least of all my mixed-up and troubled relations with Theodore De Groot. How could I hope to make her understand what I didn't understand myself?

As, still silent, we climbed the hill, a Victoria passed us, then carriage after carriage. It was Easter Sunday, but more people anyway drove to church now than in former years. They seemed to have overcome their scruples about taking their horses out on "the Sabbath."

"Remember, Annie," Mama said at last, "if you marry Theodore De Groot, you will never ride in your own carriage."

It was the most startling thing I had ever heard her say. Mama was high-spirited, ambitious, with worldly and luxurious tastes which she was no longer able to indulge; but neither she nor my father had ever appeared to be mercenary. The possession or absence of wealth was the last criterion by which they seemed to judge people.

The words were out of character for Mama. Worry, I thought, must have wrung them from her. Something I had heard her say long before in defense of Aunt Margaret, one of her sisters who had had a hard life and became querulous and bitter, came back to me now.

"Iron has entered your Aunt Margaret's soul," Mama had said.

Had "iron," I wondered, entered Mama's soul too, to change her so?

Was it that things which money, money alone, could give and that she no longer looked forward to herself, she wanted now for her children? Was she trying to make me see what it would mean to marry a young lawyer just starting to practice and who must slave for ten years, as the saying was, before he could support a family properly?

Well, whatever it was, one thing was clear, her terrible anxiety—and her distrust on whatever grounds of Theodore De Groot

NOTES

1. George Moore (1852–1933) was an Irish novelist, playwright, poet, and critic (see in Part 1, Chapter 7). Armstrong may have been thinking of sociologist Carle C. Zimmerman who, in his 1947 book *Family and Civilization*, drew comparisons between the rise and fall of different types of families and the rise and fall of civilizations.
2. The University School, also called the Baker-Himel School, was established in Knoxville in 1889 by Lewis M. G. Baker and Charles M. Himel, both of the University of Virginia, who had been invited by local citizens to come to Knoxville to start the school. It met in a rented building on Main Street while the three-story structure to which Armstrong refers was being built. This building was destroyed by fire on March 23, 1893. Rule, 396.
3. Novel by George du Maurier (1834–1896).
4. John Fiske (1842–1901), U.S. philosopher and historian.
5. A card game similar to pinochle but using 64 cards.
6. Mary Woolley (1863–1947) was president of Mount Holyoke College from 1901–1937.
7. Mary Lyon (1797–1849) founded Mount Holyoke Female Seminary in 1837; the name was changed to Mount Holyoke College in 1893.
8. Emily Dickinson attended Mount Holyoke Female Seminary during the 1847/48 academic year. Emily Dickinson Museum Website, http://www.emilydickinsonmuseum.org/node/134 (viewed October 30, 2018). Armstrong was a student at Mount Holyoke during 1889/90 and 1890/91.
9. Anna C. Edwards was associate principal and teacher of Theism and Christian Evidences, and of Ancient Literature at Mt. Holyoke. Annual Catalogue of the Mt. Holyoke Seminary in South Hadley, Massachusetts, 1889–90 (Published by the Seminary and College, 1890), GoogleBooks https://books.google.com/books?id=NS04AAAAMAAJ&printsec=frontcover#v=onepage&q=1889–90&f=false (viewed November 1, 2018); Jonathan Edwards (1703–1758) was an American clergyman and theologian.
10. Words by Henry F. Lyte (1793–1847); music by William H. Monk (1823–1889).
11. Words by Cardinal John Henry Newman (1801–1890); music by John B. Dykes (1823–1876).
12. Sacred oratorio written in 1727 by Johann Sebastian Bach (BWV 244).
13. Although Henry B. Wetzell had belonged to no church, his funeral service was conducted by the Reverend Dr. R. R. Sutherland, pastor of Second Presbyterian Church, assisted by the Reverend Dr. J. H. Frazee of Pilgrim Congregational Church. Dr. Sutherland "bore testimony to the manly traits so conspicuous in Mr. Wetzell's life," and Dr. Frazee, who, according to the report, had known Mr. Wetzell more intimately

than anyone other than his family, "bore touching testimony to his noble manly character." "Funeral of Henry B. Wetzell," *Knoxville Journal*, September 13, 1894.

14. Williston Hall, built in 1876, was used for natural history and art classes. It burned to the ground December 22, 1917. Mount Holyoke website, https://www.mtholyoke.edu/~dalbino/williston.html (viewed October 31, 2018).
15. Albert Bierstadt (1830–1902) was a German-born American artist known for his paintings of the American West. He was associated with the Hudson River School and White Mountain art, which took it name from nineteenth-century paintings of the White Mountains of New Hampshire.
16. William Henry Goodyear of New York City, lecturer in the history and philosophy of art, Annual Catalogue of the Mt. Holyoke Seminary in South Hadley, Massachusetts, 1889–90, Google Books https://books.google.com/books?id=NSo4AAAAMAAJ&printsec=frontcover#v=onepage&q=1889–90&f=false (viewed November 1, 2018).
17. Ellen Priscilla Bowers taught English literature at Mount Holyoke Seminary and College from 1861 to 1904. Mt. Holyoke website, https://www.mtholyoke.edu/~dalbino/women6/bowers.html; Annual Catalogue of Mt. Holyoke Seminary and College, 1889–90, Google Books (viewed November 1, 2018).
18. Line from "A Dream of Fair Women," by Alfred, Lord Tennyson (1809–1892), alluding to the literary renaissance during the reign of Queen Elizabeth I.
19. Supposedly, Vassar College girls made fudge in their dorm rooms at night using spirit lights or gas from a gaslight as documented in a letter written by a Class of 1892 alumna. Elizabeth Randolph, "Fudge Mania," in special "EAT" issue, Darra Goldstein, ed., *Vassar Alumnae/i Quarterly*, Spring/Summer 2013 http://vq.vassar.edu/issues/2013/02/vassar-yesterday/ (viewed November 2, 2018).
20. Stage name of English-born American actress Sarah Frances Frost (1866–1950).
21. Play written by U.S. playwright (William) Clyde Fitch (1865–1909) for the actor Richard Mansfield. Max J. Herzberg, *et al. The Reader's Encyclopedia of American Literature.* (New York: Thomas Y. Crowell, 1962), 338.
22. Stage name of American soprano Helen Louise Leonard (1861–1922).
23. Journalist, traveler, author, and lecturer George Kennan (1845–1924) traveled extensively in and wrote about Siberia, where he investigated the Russian prison and exile system. Not to be confused with George F. Kennan, U.S. author and diplomat born in 1904. American Biographical Archive (ABA) https://wbis.degruyter.com/biographic-document/A239045 (viewed October 6, 2018).
24. It is unclear how or why Armstrong chose this name for the man who would play such a decisive role in this story of her life.
25. Charles Seymour [no middle initial] appears in various Knoxville City Directories (from 1889 until 1909) as a lawyer with offices on Gay Street. The 1891 directory lists Seymour & Waldron [De Groot], lawyers, at 124 Gay Street. Born December 20, 1843, the son of Elizabeth Day and Nathan Perkins Seymour; died April 25, 1913, in

Knoxville. Thomas Day Seymour, *The Family of the Rev. Jeremiah Day of New Preston to January 1, 1900: A Genealogical Appendix to The Chronicles of the Day Family* (Tuttle, Morehouse &Taylor Company, 1900). 20. Google Books: https://books.google.com/books?id=S15GAAAAMAAJ&dq=%22Thomas+Day+Seymour%22&source=gbs_navlinks_s; "Alumni Notes," *Western Reserve University Bulletin*, 17, no. 7 (November 1914): 183 https://books.google.com/books?id=kdFDAQAAMAAJ&pg=PA183&lpg=PA183&dq=charles+seymour+knoxville+tn&source=bl&ots=UikqOwMwSG&sig=yR8AkrqkIrUwKAhE80VzFKdMjJs&hl=en&sa=X&ved=2ahUKEwj15-SQpsveAhVMUt8KHRXXClE4ChDoATAGegQIABAB (viewed online November 5, 2018).

26. In southeastern Tennessee.
27. Expression that came into use mid-19th century when the upper classes began taking pride in bathing and the lower classes did not have the facilities to do so. Attributed to English statesman Henry Peter, Lord Brougham (1778–1868). Bergen Evans, *Dictionary of Quotations*. 518.
28. The city's only race track was in the Burlington area of east Knoxville. It was owned by Calvin F. "Cal" Johnson (1844–1925), who had been born a slave in Knox County but became a wealthy black businessman after emancipation. Although Johnson's chief business enterprise was "The Poplar Log," a saloon on the corner of Vine and Gay, he owned other real estate and a number of thoroughbred horses. The site of his race track is now a residential neighborhood called Speedway Circle. Rothrock, 321–22; Deaderick, 41, 642; Creekmore, 131, 148. Mechanicsville was a working and middle class community which had grown up on the northwest edges of Knoxville. It was annexed and became part of the city on January 1, 1883. Deaderick, 32, 42, 84.
29. Benjamin Rush Strong (1847–1915), son of Sophronia and Joseph Churchill Strong, Jr., was president of East Tennessee National Bank from June 1892 until June 1894. He was also a director of the Mechanics National Bank, organized in 1882. Two scrapbooks in the Special Collections Library at the University of Tennessee, Knoxville, document the travels of Rush Strong, which he frequently wrote about in local newspapers. Strong bequeathed money to the University of Tennessee for the construction of a women's dormitory to be named in memory of his mother. Sophronia Strong Hall, whose cafeteria was known affectionately as "Sophie's," housed women students from 1925 until 2008. The building underwent extensive renovation and expansion beginning in 2014 to convert it for classroom and laboratory use. It reopened in 2017. Rule, 254, 255; Benjamin Rush Strong Scrapbook, MS.1124, University of Tennessee Libraries, Knoxville, Special Collections.
30. Armstrong would later live in Harriman and, in 1908, was instrumental in obtaining a $10,000 grant from the Andrew Carnegie Foundation to build a Carnegie Library (which still exists) in Harriman. Walter T. Pulliam, *Harriman: The Town That Temperance Built* (Walter T. Pulliam, 1978), 248–49.

31. It was actually Frederick Gates, a businessman and real estate developer, who had the idea of building a town based on temperance and prohibition. He, along with friends and associates, founded the East Tennessee Land Company in 1889 and named General Fisk, the Prohibition Party's presidential candidate in 1888, as president chiefly because of his prominence in the Prohibition Party. The company purchased several thousand acres of land in Roane County which it auctioned off as building lots in 1891 to establish the town. Harriman was named for Civil War General Walter Harriman who, while camping in the area with his regiment, had remarked that it would be a good site for a town. General Harriman's son, Walter C. Harriman, was managing director of the East Tennessee Land Company. Pulliam, 19–23, 63–64.
32. Tuxedo Park, an exclusive village in southeastern New York, was built in 1886 as a retreat for the rich. The tuxedo or dinner jacket for small dinner parties was introduced there. "Tuxedo Park," *The Hutchinson Unabridged Encyclopedia with Atlas and Weather Guide*, edited by Helicon (Helicon, 2018), https://search.credoreference.com/content/entry/heliconhe/tuxedo_park/0?institutionId=680 (viewed October 25, 2018); Julia Lawlor, "If You're Thinking of Living in/ Tuxedo Park, N.Y.," *New York Times (1923-Current File)*, Jun 18, 2000, https://login.proxy.lib.utk.edu:443/login?url=https://search-proquest-com.proxy.lib.utk.edu/docview/91329239?accountid=14766 (accessed October 25, 2018).
33. The Cornstalk Heights Historical Community Organization (CHHCO) was created in 1990 to preserve Harriman's historic homes, and the Historic District is listed on the National Register of Historic Places. Until recently, Christmas tours of the homes were conducted every year during a weekend in December. Cornstalk Heights Historic Community Web page, www.cornstalkheights.org/ (viewed September 28, 2018).
34. Henry Wetzell was born in 1843 or 1844 (based on census records and his reported age when he died in 1894); Rush Strong was born in 1847.
35. Words from a love poem by seventeenth-century English poet Ben Jonson, sung to an old English air.
36. Traditional, lyricist and composer unknown.
37. David Garrick (1717–1779), important English actor and theater manager who did much to revive the popularity of Shakespeare during his career. Benét, *Reader's Encyclopedia*, 383.
38. Not the school song, but still sung at Eton College (England), which has a long boating tradition. Words by William Johnson Cory, music by Captain Algernon H. Drummond, both alumni of the school. First performed June 4, 1863. Eton College web site, "The Eton Boating Song," https://www.etoncollege.com/BoatingSong.aspx (viewed October 26, 2018).
39. "Miss Ogden's School" was in the Institute Building on West Main Street at the corner of Henley. *Knoxville City Directory, 1890.*
40. Colonel Samuel B. Crawford may have taught mathematics while an instructor in the

preparatory department at the University of Tennessee in 1877, but most of his time there was as professor of military science and commandant of cadets. Rule, 364, 365, 366, 370, 371. In addition, Crawford served as Chairman of the Faculty during 1886/87. ("From 1883 to 1887 while the University of Tennessee was without a president the 'Chairman of the Faculty' carried out the responsibilities of the president.") Chairman of the Faculty Papers, AR.0257, University of Tennessee Libraries, Knoxville, Special Collections.

41. *On Heroes, Hero-worship, and the Heroic in History* (1841), by Scottish-born English essayist and historian Thomas Carlyle (1795–1881).

Chapter Thirteen

Bleak House and Drury Paine Armstrong

When I told Theodore I would not be home in the evening, that I was driving out to Bleak House with Bob Armstrong, he would lift his eyebrows, give a slight shrug, say nothing, but the blood would rush to his face, I would know he was angry, and I would be frightened.

But once I was seated beside Bob, behind his high-stepping horses, my fright would leave. It was impossible to be afraid now, for Bob was afraid of nothing, not even of bolts of lightning. Throughout his life he liked nothing better than to be in the very heart of a violent storm. To him, none of the elements, the manifestations of nature, were evil. And as chivalrous as he was daring, it was the adventurer in him that appealed to me most.

But even the name, Armstrong, had come to be invested for me with a distinctive charm. I had seen the Armstrong coat of arms, an armed arm grasping an uprooted tree, with underneath *Invictus Maneo*, and one day asked about it.

"The Armstrongs," Bob laughed, "were sheep robbers on the Scottish Border —a fine bunch of thieves!"

Then he told me of an ancient King of Scotland who, having his horse killed under him in battle and being remounted by his armor-bearer, had rewarded him with lands on the Border and to perpetuate the memory of the service—"for Fairbairn took the King by the thigh and set him on his saddle"—gave him the appellation Armstrong and assigned him for a crest an armed hand and arm.[1]

But there was also, it seemed, a ballad sung along the Scottish and English border in the sixteenth century celebrating an Armstrong, a bold outlaw, who in some foray, "[though] runn through the faire boddee," yet rallied his followers:

> Saying, Fight on, my merry men all,
> And see that none of you be taine;
> For I will stand by and bleed but awhile,
> And then will I come and fight againe.[2]

And once I heard this ballad and knew the meaning of their crest, the tall, fair-haired, rangy and red-blooded Bob Armstrong of Bleak House became the living embodiment to me of these for[e]bears of his in the remote and misty past.

ARMSTRONG FAMILY TREE

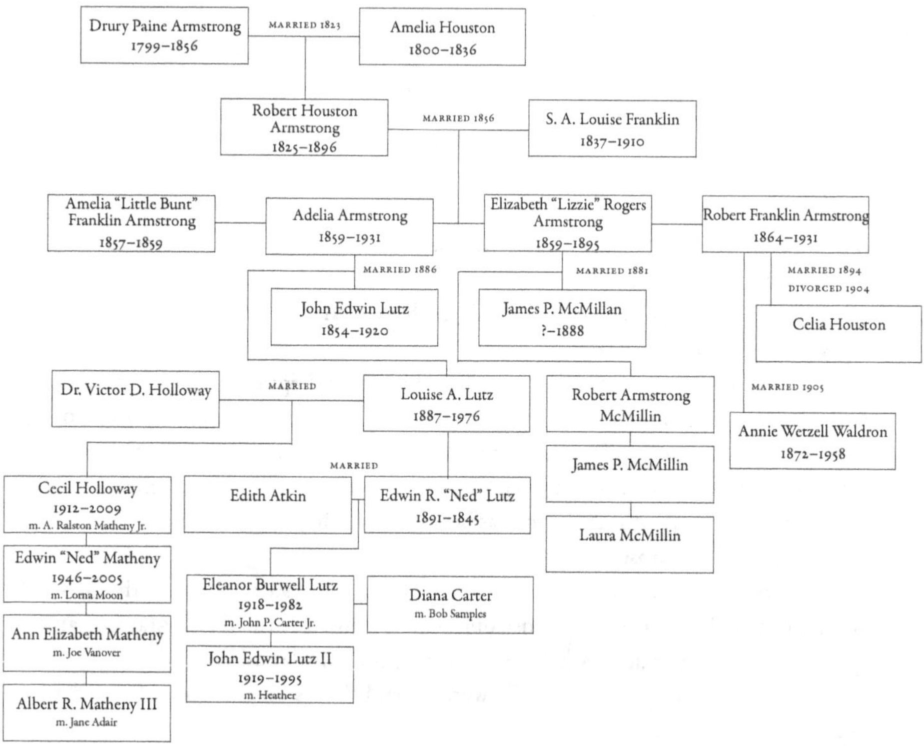

I was not the only girl of course that Bob drove home to supper, and for the definite purpose, it may have been, that his parents should know them better. I am sure I was not the only one, either, to whom he made love. In a day when flattery softened the whole Southern way of life, he would never have failed to pay extravagant compliments and make love to any girl he found in the least attractive—make love, that is, within the bounds society in the time and place imposed on all save engaged couples. There was gossip, too, that Bob's mother had her heart set on his winning one of the five Woodruff sisters whose patrician beauty and superlative graciousness were to become a Knoxville legend; whose father was one of its "merchant princes" and home the imposing Victorian mansion facing the grounds of the University;[3] whereas my own father's fortune had been swept away and we lived in a commonplace rented house on Highland Avenue.

But none of these considerations marred my pleasure in going to Bleak House. Notwithstanding that Bob was the most fascinating man I knew, I had never pictured him to myself as a husband, anymore than that shadowy first Armstrong who had taken the King by the thigh and set him on his saddle.

The truth is (and of this I am certain), all that gay yet troubled year I dwelt on the future, including marriage, as little as possible. I refused to peer into what was ahead. More and more I lived only in the day, the hour, the moment, and as I drove out the pike with Bob I would enter a realm of enchantment as soon as we reached the plantation home of his grandfather, Drury Paine Armstrong, planter, banker, man of affairs, and the place known then, from its position on the river, as Crescent Bend.[4]

Drury Paine Armstrong had long been dead at this time and the fine old red-brick house built in 1823,[5] in post-Colonial style and its bricks made by his slaves, was in the possession now, with what acres remained to it, of Marcellus Mur[a]t Armstrong, Bob's "Uncle Whack," his father's brother.

Set some distance back from the pike and amidst huge oaks, the house, as we passed it at dusk, would look a little gloomy and the whole place rather run-down. Bob would explain that Uncle Whack was no sort of manager, but devoted to fox hunting and similar pursuits. Bob always spoke of him, however, with the greatest affection and indulgence, despite the fact he had let the valuable plantation he had inherited go all but to rack and ruin. It was plain that Uncle Whack appealed to the sporting side of Bob's nature as strongly as his father to another side, and that the most fun he had had when he was growing up was with Uncle Whack and his boys.

I loved to hear Bob tell of his childhood on the two adjoining plantations; his uncle's and his father's, embracing islands in the river and all of what today is a fine residential section of Knoxville.

Crescent Bend.

Bob's education had been of the most desultory, in large part directed by himself, and gained almost wholly, as he represented it, from dusty stacks of old magazines and papers which had been regularly deposited in the tower at Bleak House from the time the house was built in 1851,[6] and among which, before he reached his teens, he would spend whole days, safe from intrusion; while later he drew heavily on the family library below, although to the end of his days, for all that he looked upon his years with the Sioux as the most vital and worthwhile experience in his life, he never quite ceased feeling remorse that he had not prepared himself for Princeton, and gone there, as his father wished. Even so, however, he was more widely read, especially in the classics, than any other of the young men I knew then, whatever their education. I remember in this connection that a book he gave me at the time was *The Meditations of Marcus Aurelius*.

But what delighted me most were Bob's accounts of his life in childhood when, as a young savage—his mother, a woman who could not live out of society, occupied with her social activities; his father absorbed in painting, music, books; his twin sisters years older—his only playmates were the children of ex-slaves who continued to work for the Armstrongs, living in slave quarters still intact and that extended in a row down the slope that ran from the back of Bleak House to the river. Bob would form these small darkies into a company, himself chief over them all, leader in all their exploits; and Tom Sawyer had nothing on Bob Armstrong when it came to a boyhood on a broad, deep, swift, and magnificent river. His completely untrammeled childhood was the happiest, he was convinced, a boy had ever known.

Born during the War, he remembered freed black men on their plantation singing with gusto, *I'd rather be a nigger [th]'an a pore white man*. He remembered another song that was sung during the uneasy fearsome Reconstruction days, when the Ku Klux Klan were riding, or some other form of night patrol was abroad. Now, in the safe '80s, all these reminders of the War, its evil aftermath, and of a glamorous social order gone, not so long before, but gone forever, were thrilling. They would become more so as time went on and they came more and more to take on a semi-mythical character.

But nothing, in the time of which I write, was more alluring to me than Bleak House itself each time I came in sight of it. Here was a noble ante-bellum mansion shadowed, but not smothered, by the great trees against which it was set; with the ivy that half veiled its brick walls, brick made by slaves on the plantation, and the huge box which led to its entrance, properly restrained. Here was a house that was cherished—you knew at a glance—by its owners.

Its name, for one thing, lent it romantic interest, associated in one's mind as it was with Dickens' *Bleak House*, in a period when Dickens was still widely, all but universally, read.

The house was of course, in the '80s and '90s, as later, to most people, chiefly of

Bleak House (ca. 1895).

interest from the fact that the Confederate General James A. Longstreet had made it his headquarters during the siege of Knoxville in the War; also because from Bleak House General Sanders, in command of the Union forces and a conspicuous target on his white horse, had been mortally wounded by a sharpshooter concealed within the walls of Bleak House.[7]

But for me, in those long past days, it was less its historic interest than the parties, the balls, unsurpassed in splendor in the whole region and for which Bleak House was famous—it was its atmosphere of worldly sophistication combined with culture, along with all the traditions that still clung to the slave-holding class in the South, which gave it most of its witchery.

Both the portly genial white-haired old Colonel Armstrong and his saucy, black-eyed, sparkling wife would come out to the broad entrance hall at Bleak House to meet me when Bob had handed over the horses to a waiting Negro and we entered the front door. Whatever their ambitions for their only son, they could not have given me a heartier welcome. But there was nothing stiff, nothing stuffy, about the Armstrongs. Always I felt at home with them and could enjoy to the full a supper which even for a single guest at Bleak House would wear a gala air; with wine decanters on the table, the Sérres plates, food more lavish and delicious, I thought then, than there could be anywhere else in the world.

After supper at Bleak House we would stay for a while, and around a log fire, if it was chilly, in the sitting room. Like all the rooms in the house it was spacious and high-ceilinged, but with its inviting chairs, crimson damask curtains, Chinese screens to ward off draughts, it had a feeling not alone of comfort but of informality, even intimacy; so that the talk here as at supper was as lively as if we all belonged to the same generation.

Sooner or later, however, Bob would find an excuse to lead me across the hall and into the formal drawing room, and this room extending almost the length of the house (the ball room above it of equal proportions), with its prism chandeliers, gilt cornices, its oval marble-topped tables, ornate sofas and chairs—all its lush Victorian pieces, never failed to impress me deeply. There was the square rosewood piano, transported from Baltimore by wagon before a railroad had entered East Tennessee, in its satiny case Minié balls embedded, as in the walls of this room; while in marked contrast were acquisitions of a later period: two gigantic Chinese vases that stood one at either end of the white marble mantel; huge paintings in heavy gilt frames, copies of works in Munich or Dresden which, in the taste of "the Elegant Eighties," Mrs. Armstrong had brought back from Europe, together with a robust nude white marble figure mounted on a mythological beast—a reproduction of Dannecker's celebrated "Ariadne"[8]—and standing on a revolving pedestal in a front corner of the room.

But while I looked upon all these marvels with romantic reverence, it was nothing [compared] to my delight when the old Colonel would join us and suggest, in his gallant way, that Bob perhaps had had me long enough; that there were books I would enjoy seeing, too.

The library was back of the drawing room, but opened off a transverse hall between them, and connected with no other room. Although it had the same lofty ceiling as the rest, it was the only room in Bleak House of moderate size and its situation plainly intended to promote privacy. But for all its seclusion and sober book-lined walls, it was anything but gloomy. There was its glowing open fire in winter and in warm weather its French windows opening on a private porch (the Armstrongs called it "gallery") at the rear and overlooking the river. The most hospitable man imaginable, yet when the Colonel wanted to be alone, here was his sanctum. And when the old Colonel ushered me into this room, I felt no higher honor could be paid me. I was being inducted now into the fellowship of all true book lovers.

Bob would seem pleased when his father took me to the library. He would leave us there alone. He teased me about my partiality for his father: "If you would just *once* use the tone of voice to me that you do to Father, give me *one* look of the sort you give him—!"

But Bob adored his father as much as he admired—though not adored—his handsome ambitious mother. In later years he recognized that but for his mother's innate prudence underneath a sharp and dazzling personality, Bleak House and their plantation, with his father as easy-going as his Uncle Whack, might well have gone the way of Crescent Bend. He realized then that it was *her* shrewdness which not only had conserved her own inherited fortune[9] but preserved and enhanced the value of Bleak House and the lands that went with it; moreover, that he and his sisters, blinded by their father's lovableness, owed more to their mother than once they had been inclined to admit.

For me, in the days I am writing of, the old Colonel, with his culture, urbanity, poise, united to the deep underlying humanness and kindness that were in him, was Bob's ideal—as indeed, whatever waywardness in his own life, he never ceased to be—of "the good man."

For me, with his chivalric and distinguished air, his great dignity yet entirely approachable, with the profound compliments he would pay—out of sheer compassion and tender-heartedness if nothing else—to the most unlikely-looking recipients, there was not a little in him of Thackeray's Colonel Newcome.[10] And when the old Colonel led me to this room, none too orderly but unmistakably his, seated me in one of the pleasantly worn old leather chairs, I felt no greater honor could have been paid me. White marble busts of Caesar and other illustrious ancients ranged around on top of the book-cases; on an easel an unfinished landscape he had been working on; his flute on the mantel; a great brass-mounted globe standing by the French windows; and books all around us. We were shut in, it seemed to me then, in a happy country all our own.

[The fact that one of my baptismal names was Audubon had always seemed to interest the old Colonel and I recall clearly that][11] the first book he ever showed me was Audubon's *Birds of America*, with the original Elephant Folio engravings and their incomparably beautiful paintings of birds, a work he treasured, I believe, more than any other he possessed.

But equally of interest to me were rows on rows of leather-bound eighteenth century volumes that had once belonged to the Colonel's father. True to the immutable law of the Old South that a gentleman should be a scholar, Drury Paine Armstrong had been something more than planter, banker, man of affairs. A hundred years ago he had accumulated a private library large for his, or any, day.[12] Here was a Knoxville library, consistently expanded, which, when much of it would pass at no distant day to Bob, would have been in the same family for four generations, not too usual in our young country.

Of all the books this library contained, though, I believe that, save for Audubon's *Birds of America*, the old Colonel's favorite was a first edition of Prescott's *History of the Conquest of Mexico and Peru*. The old Colonel's glowing account of this work, in two bulky volumes of fine print, induced me to read it, and where before I had only been interested in European history, I was amazed now at the warmth and color and drama to be found in the history of our Western Hemisphere.[13]

But the old Colonel was wholly responsive—very flattering to a young girl—

when I mentioned any of my own enthusiasms among books, and so completely did he put me at my ease that I could talk to him without the least self-consciousness. Hours with the old Colonel were indeed among the most magical I spent in a house whose very bricks and mortar held magic in them for me.

It was not many years after this that the old Colonel, stricken with an obscure but fatal malady, had his bed moved into the library. There at his bedside, Bob, who lived in New York now, sat long nights in lonely vigil, in bitter sorrow, eating his heart out, as many a son before him, going over and over in his mind all the ways in which he felt he had disappointed his father.

But the old Colonel was at peace. He was dying as he wished, his beloved books where he could put out his hand and touch them, his flute on the night-table, easel and palette within range of his eyes and with a turn of his head a long view under trees—some of which, rare species, he had planted as saplings—all the way to the river: for the hodge-podge of ostentatious gardens developed by a subsequent owner of Bleak House at the cost of untold thousands; gardens leading one into another, English, Italian, Japanese, with a boxwood maze, with their grottos, marble balustrades, belvedere, their stone lanterns, miniature bridge, Japanese tea-house—all manner of exotic, elaborate, artificial effects, none of all this existed then.[14]

There were merely some well-tended though unpretentious flower-beds and old-fashioned shrubs near the house, and the Colonel's dimming eyes could rest unobstructed on an open grassy space between the old barns of the plantation and the old brick slave-quarters down below, and catch glimpses below them of the glinting willow-fringed Tennessee.

So whatever Bob's grief and remorse, the old Colonel died blessedly, as he had lived.[15]

[At this point in her narrative Anne Armstrong included "A Trip to Texas," her version of a journal "the old Colonel" kept as a young man while traveling to and from the Southwest as part of a three-man government commission sent to treat with the Indians (Comanche) on the border of the United States and Mexico. The "Private Journal of Robert Houston Armstrong," which he kept between November 1850 and September 1851, is available in the McClung Collection of Knox County Public Library and in Special Collections at the University of Tennessee Libraries in Knoxville.]

When the Robert Armstrong I was to know best,[16] my husband, was young, absorbed in his own adventures, five years, starting when he was seventeen, and shortly after the battle of the Little Big Horn, with the Sioux Indians in Dakota Territory, followed by a quite different, if equally exciting year in Paris, it is doubtful whether he had much interest in this journal his father kept as a young man, if indeed he even had access to it. But when his father was long dead, and his own youth past, he got a good deal of amusement out of its naïveté, its superlatives, multitudinous exclamation points, its underlinings, used as prodigally as Queen Victoria in her early diaries and later voluminous correspondence.

He would laugh at his father's cautious youthful behavior, so different from his own, and marvel that his father had been so easily shocked. "Father narrowly escaped becoming an insufferable prig," I remember him saying once. But what amused him most was the extreme susceptibility of his father to feminine charm which the journal revealed, and the flowery language in which he expressed it: the raven hair, lily skin, the sparkling eyes; the angelic beauty of one, mischievous loveliness of another; while Mexican girls he observed, unseen himself, bathing in the River Leon, "when they emerged, veiled almost to their knees in their long black hair, were so indescribably beautiful that no wonder Venus is represented as rising from the sea!"

It was easy enough to poke fun at all this in later years, but what his only son never forgot was the respect, the downright reverence, for women which the old Colonel never lost. His father could not bear to say of a woman, in the journal (or outside it), anything uncomplimentary. If she were not beautiful, he must at least set her down as "amiable and unaffected"; grant her intelligence or, at least, "dignity." Even for the "fancy girls" at the Masquerade Ball in New Orleans he had compassionate words. Under their makeup and tawdry finery he saw them haggard, discerned the misery of their lives, "and what a misnomer to call them ladies of pleasure!"

What his son never forgot was that to the end of his days his father kept a certain innocence in his heart, as he kept his sense of wonder at the beauty of the world. And it was all this in him, I imagine, that reminded me of Thackeray's Colonel Newcome when as a young girl I first knew the old Colonel at Bleak House, his historic plantation home, headquarters of the Confederate General James Longstreet during the Civil War, and with Minié balls embedded in its walls.

As a rule when I went to Bleak House I left my wraps in the huge downstairs bedroom, back of the sitting room, which Colonel and Mrs. Armstrong occupied, and with old mahogany furniture, inherited pieces, which ante-dated the Age of Black Walnut.

Whether she wanted me for Bob's wife or not, Mrs. Armstrong was as cordial as the old Colonel. She would go with me when I was placing my wraps on her four-poster and always contrive that then or later she and I have a little visit by ourselves, as I had with the Colonel.

I was not afraid of her, as many were. I had only heard of her barbed tongue; never felt it. She lacked the great human warmth of the old Colonel, but she had some of the same electric attraction for me that Bob had; was full of fire and a touch of gamin still in her.

Then there was the aura of any great lady of society in her heyday. She was the foremost hostess in Knoxville, the one who gave its grandest parties. Besides, although people were afraid of her, she was immensely popular at this time, especially with duller matrons whose lives were brightened by her indiscretions, her witty and wicked tongue.

In these little visits alone with her, Mrs. Armstrong would always have something to show me of a sort to interest a young girl; pour out the contents of her jewel-cases, in one of which she kept pieces she no longer wore; among them, I remember, a set of garnets—necklace, bracelets, earrings—and an immense broach made from the hair, various shades, of her children when they were infants.[17]

"This was little Bunt's," she said, as she pointed to the flaxen hair, intricately set in gold, which formed one of the branches of the broach, and her voice softer than I had heard it before, or would again. Little Bunt had died when she was four or five.[18]

But I never felt I could express freely my admiration for anything Mrs. Armstrong showed me for fear she would insist on giving it to me. Even so, she seldom let me leave Bleak House without some remembrance of the evening. Once it was a chunky copy, bound in blue and gold, of Spenser's *The Faerie Queen* which had belonged to her as a young girl; for, with all her frivolity, she was a discriminating reader and like the other members of the family delighted in good books, good pictures, good music.

To me, in those days, she seemed happy. With Bleak House so rich in interest, its surface life so brilliant, I could not imagine that underneath ran dark currents; that despite her vivacity, her amusing talk, even now she was making life in Bleak House all but unbearable, especially for her daughters, gentle, like their father; and with Bob only faring better because he had more of her in him. She could strike sparks out of him—which she enjoyed—and he pursued his own courses, undeterred by her gibes.

It was the old Colonel who suffered most. How could he have seen in the dazzling Louise[19] Franklin, motherless, undisciplined, a madcap, an heiress, who at sixteen came from Cocke County to taste the gayeties of Knoxville,[20] directly after he had returned from his Western journey, and swept him off his feet—how could he have seen in her the latent virago?

I have an idea he never ceased to be dazzled by her. But there could have been no greater sorrow in his life than when he must listen to her tirades.

"Oh, Mammy, Mammy!" he would protest sadly, helplessly.

After the old Colonel died, she became ever more restless, more bitter. Some of the bitterness may have derived from jealousy—resentment of the almost worshipful regard in which her children held their father. But however that may be, some balance he had supplied was gone now. She could still afford to entertain in the grand manner, but she ceased to entertain at all. The old Colonel had been needed, it seemed, to give Bleak House parties the flair that had made them famous. The great days of Bleak House were over, she saw. Too many rival hostesses had sprung up, among them (bitterest pill of all to swallow) one of her own daughters, in her handsome place, Westwood, hardly more than a stone's throw away.[21]

Bleak House became a burden to her. She could not live in it any more. She was haunted there, Bob said long afterwards, by wounding things she had said to a beloved sister of his, now dead.[22] In her widowed solitude its walls gave back to her things she had said.

She began to spend winters in Florida, summers at summer resorts, and to rent Bleak House, at a purely nominal rent, to various individuals; one of whom, a university professor, a widower with small children, turned it over to slatternly servants, and when he departed, leaving it in wretched condition, took with him (with admirable taste, it must be admitted) Audubon's valuable *Birds of America* and the great globe which had stood by the French windows in the library.

In her last years, broken in body, perverse, difficult in the extreme, at odds (whatever appearances might be kept up) with most of her descendants, she lived in a little none-too-elegant "family hotel" in Knoxville,[23] assuaging her endless boredom as best she could by playing cards and gossiping with old cronies or with new acquaintances who, with the rigid caste system still prevailing in Knoxville and pioneer stock at the top, had not yet been able to establish social positions and thought it worth while to court the little old lady with the bowed back, flashing black eyes, the retorts that made them laugh even as they winced.

But these last bored and unutterably unhappy years of hers were in the distant future. In the days when I first knew her, while she dazzled me as so many others, she would often say something which sharply arrested my attention and stuck in my mind.

One evening at Bleak House when there were others there the subject of slavery came up. Now, in the late '80s, while dissolution of the Union had been unthinkable to the old Colonel, he continued to believe in slavery. He had been good to his own slaves; hence reasoned it was a system that could be administered humanely and should never have been abolished.

It was in the course of this discussion that the Emancipation Proclamation was mentioned and Mrs. Armstrong laughed—that impish laugh, the diablerie in it, I hear now.

"So far as the Emancipation Proclamation is concerned, I was the one on this plantation," she declared, "who was emancipated—not the slaves!"

And she went on to give a lively account of her responsibilities in slavery days; teaching young Negro girls to sew, do fine needlework, fine cookery and laundering, to nurse children or the sick—training them in a dozen domestic branches, whereas no one, she said, bothered to train them now, not knowing how long they could keep them.

It must have been, however, that in the old days, as later, she possessed the gift of keeping servants satisfied, for all of them at Bleak House, when I knew it, were former Armstrong slaves—or their children—who had remained with the family from choice. Mrs. Armstrong had a way of bewitching them, you could see. She was exciting. She kept them, as she did everybody else, stirred up. Whatever outrageous things "Miss Lou" might do or say, when they spoke to or of her, there was always a mixture in their voices of keen amusement, pride, and high respect.

But it was long after both the Colonel and Mrs. Armstrong were dead that the Armstrong "Slave Book" came into my possession, a small book, 6 x 4, of a sort in which household accounts might be kept, and considerably battered by the time it reached me.

Undoubtedly many slave-holding families kept "Slave Books," for slaves were valuable property and various matters pertaining to them needed to be recorded, though this is the only one I have ever seen or known of.

Written heavily in a quill pen by Drury Paine Armstrong, it starts in January, 1823, and is continued after his death in 1856 by his daughter-in-law, the mistress of Bleak House, whose husband had inherited some of the Crescent Bend slaves to add to his own.

It is noteworthy, I think, that nearly all the deaths of slaves recorded, whether of young or of old, unless by accident, were from "decay of the lungs," as tuberculosis is variously termed in the book.

But I have often wondered if there was not a special significance in its final entry, made by Mrs. Armstrong, in the delicate chirography characteristic of ladies of the period, though utterly inexpressive of her own vigorous personality:

Born, "General Lee," son of Dan and Eliza, 26th day of January 1863.

Mrs. Armstrong was feeling good when she made that entry. Sportively, she put quotation marks—the only ones in the book—around the name she had given the new black baby. Only a few days before,[24] Lincoln had issued his first Emancipation Proclamation.

"Humph!" I can hear her say, as with saucy defiance she names for Robert E. Lee this last slave—as it proved—that would be born on their plantation. "Humph! Proclamation or no Proclamation, with Lee we're bound to win!"

Many things went to make up the spell under which Bleak House held me. All the romance, the glamour, I had found in Knoxville and which had dominated my youthful imagination from that first day when I gazed out the windows of old Schubert's Hotel at the steep, shadowy, narrow street I could see opposite, plunging down the hill at the side of Staub's Opera House, were distilled now in this house with a past. It became indeed, in a sense, mine, and would remain so—whatever hands it might pass into—so long as I lived.

But there was one evening at Bleak House which stands out from all the rest. It was coming spring now, for I recall I had started teaching at Miss Ogden's. It was the last time I would go to Bleak House with Bob—the last time during my girlhood—and he proposed taking me upstairs where in the hall, hung around on the walls, was his Indian collection.

I remember as we stood at the foot of the broad curving stairway Mrs. Armstrong's objecting: "Oh, Annie doesn't want to see all that trash. Just dust collectors. Some day I'm goin' to burn 'em all up."

And I remember Bob flashing back, good-humoredly, yet with a hint of something else in his voice: "Yes, and she's capable of it, too! Once when Father was on a trip she had a bonfire made of newspapers and magazines that had been accumulating in the tower for fifty years. Father and I never *have* forgiven her."

"Yes?" Mrs. Armstrong said. She laughed her impish laugh, and Bob and I proceeded up the stairs.

On the landing, half way up, we paused to look at a huge steel engraving in a massive walnut frame which hung there. The picture was called "The Coming of Age."[25] On the steps of an Elizabethan manor house a handsome, lordly-looking young man was standing, his parents behind him, and at his feet, thronging the courtyard he faced, retainers who had assembled to do honor to the occasion through offerings of fruit and flowers and game, and an oldster among them reading an address to this son and heir of the nobleman to whom they paid fief.

"I used to stop here on my way downstairs every morning of my life," Bob said, "when I was a kid. I pictured my own coming of age as something like this. But when I *did* come of age, I was out in Dakota hunting buffalo with the Sioux!"

He had never before spoken to me of his years with the Sioux. He would discuss the new plays, books, refer to Louis Martin's, Rector's and other restaurants, fashionable then, which he frequented in New York; would talk perhaps of his life in Paris and enthusiastically of French food; relate some amusing incident that had occurred when he was bicycling in England and Scotland, talk of his life as a little boy on the plantation—talk of a hundred things, but never a word of Dakota.

But now when I saw the great collection of Indian trophies displayed in the upper hall at Bleak House, a few of which I had seen in store windows on Gay Street when Bob first came home from the West—vivid, colorful reminders of the exciting life he had shared only a few years before, I saw why his mother, fearful that Dakota and the Sioux were still in his blood, had spoken flippantly, slightingly, of the collection. I saw also, for all his worldly sophistication, a different Bob Armstrong.

As he explained an Indian painting, stretched at length on one wall, depicting some mysterious Indian ritual and given him by the Sioux, though the work of a Kiowa, a rare artist, whom the Sioux had taken captive—as he explained Indian superstitions, customs, the weapons, utensils—things around us they had used and worn, and as he answered my many questions, there was a seriousness in his voice I had not heard heretofore.

He went into his bed-room and brought back a small pocket note-book he had kept during his years at the Cheyenne River Agency.

We sat down on a sofa underneath the Indian painting. He let me look through the book, opening the door—admitting me to a chamber in his life into which I had not even peeped before.

Stamped on the corner of the note-book was:

DEPARTMENT OF THE INTERIOR
U.S. INDIAN SERVICE

How unreal to me, but vibrantly alive to Bob, were the names in it: Bear with Black Body, Hunts the Enemy, Turning Heart, Fears Nothing, Drops at a Distance, Swelled Rump, Walking Crane, Tall Prairie Chicken, Running Rattler, Swift Bird, Brings Plenty, White Wolf.

Written in pencil in an unformed boyish hand were bare brief accounts of the writer's day by day life.

It seems incredible to me now that a mere stripling, new to the country, Bob had been sent on a trip up the Missouri and Moreau Rivers, alone save for an Indian boy as interpreter, when he had not yet learned (as he soon did) to speak the Sioux language—a trip into unknown territory where, without landmarks on the boundless prairie, they were lost several times—moreover, into a region many of whose Indians had fought in the Battle of Little Big Horn and were threatening fresh trouble.

Incredible, that along with issuing supplies to the Indians, measuring fields, helping break up inflammatory Indian dances forbidden by the U.S. Government, this tenderfoot from Tennessee, still in his teens, held council at various Indian camps; decided disputed Indian claims.

But everywhere, it was evident, Bob made friends.

"Stayed all day at Four Bears. Roped wild colts and helped him break them. Luckily, did not get thrown."

"April 16. Helped High Hawk brand cattle all day. Spent the night in his teepee."

And if it was often dangerous business he was sent on, yet in the course of his official duties he always managed to have fun with the Indians, as he entered heartily into their pursuits.

Fun, also, sometimes, it appeared, outside the line of duty. One memo read: "Must explain to Agent about trip to Pierre and my pulling off my boots in a saloon and other behavior reported to him."

But whether we laughed together or were sober, Bob was different this evening. Along with greater seriousness, I detected greater restlessness in him than usual.

During the drive back to town he confided that Knoxville was beginning to pall on him.

"I'm not going to settle down here," he said. "That's a dead sure thing."

He had seen something of the world now, and a tame humdrum business life in Knoxville was the last thing he was willing to consider.

We lingered a few moments on the small front porch when we reached the house on Highland Avenue, enveloped in darkness. There was only the delicate thin curve of the new moon in the sky. It was a balmy night, the smell of spring already in the air.

"Annie," Bob said, "I haven't told them yet at home, and I'll see you again, but I'm going away. To Mexico, I think. Maybe Peru."

He took my hands in his.

"It may be some time," he said, "before you hear from me if I go into the interior of those countries. But I'll be back. You'll wait for me, won't you?"

"Yes," I said.

I knew now, if I hadn't before, that this was the man, fearless, frank, gay and reckless and witty—the man out of all the world I wanted to marry.

My heart was beating fast. I was flooded with happiness, though a sickening fear shot through me. How could I tell Theodore—when the time came I must?

Bob held my hands tightly in his. He made no attempt to kiss me.

"Yes," I had said, and there was no further pledge between us.

NOTES

1. Mark Anthony Lower, *The Book of English Surnames* (Baxter & Sons, 1839), 51.
2. "Johnie Armstrong," Ballad No. 169, Stanza 16, in Helen Child Sargent and George Lyman Kittredge, eds., *English and Scottish Popular Ballads* (Boston: Houghton, Mifflin, 1932), 414.
3. Rothrock confirms that merchant and civic leader W. W. Woodruff (1840–1926) and his wife had five daughters, in addition to one son. Woodruff built his elegant brick mansion in the 1870s. The estate where it stood was bounded by Cumberland Avenue, White Avenue, 14th Street and 15th Street. The Woodruff property is now part of the University of Tennessee campus and the site of Hoskins Library. The Carriage House, damaged by fire in 2002, is all that remains of the original estate. It stands at the corner of White Avenue and 14th (now James Agee) Street. Rothrock, 507. University of Tennessee Campus Heritage Plan, http://isse.utk.edu/cpc/pdf/CampusHeritagePlanFinal.pdf (viewed January 3, 2019).
4. Drury P. Armstrong named his 600-acre gentleman's farm "Crescent Bend" for its "commanding view of a majestic crescent bend of the Holston River, now called the

Tennessee River." Crescent Bend House & Gardens website, http://www.crescentbend.com/ (viewed December 10, 2018).

5. Anne Armstrong may have used this date because Rothrock wrote: "In 1823, Drury P. Armstrong married . . . and established a home upon his large plantation west of Knoxville." Most sources say the house was built between 1832 and 1834. The Crescent Bend website states that Drury Armstrong and his family moved in on October 7, 1834. Today his home, which has been restored, is known as the Armstrong-Lockett House and is a house museum. Rothrock, 369; Deaderick, 416; Crescent Bend House & Gardens website, http://www.crescentbend.com/ (viewed December 10, 2018).
6. Here again the date is in dispute. The house itself was a wedding present for Robert H. Armstrong and Louise Franklin, who were married December 9, 1856. The land was the gift of his father, and the house was built by her father's slaves, who even made the bricks in a kiln on the property. Most sources place construction of the house between 1854 and 1858; Charles Dickens novel *Bleak House,* for which it was reportedly named, was published in 1852. The house was owned by the Armstrongs until 1906. Two other families lived there before Knoxville Chapter 89 of the United Daughters of the Confederacy (UDC) purchased Bleak House in 1959 and named it Confederate Memorial Hall. It was placed on the National Register of Historic Places in 1984. Deaderick, 417; Creekmore, *Tennessee,* 86; Knoxville Bleak House website, https://www.bleakhouseknoxville.org/ (viewed January 11, 2019).
7. Confederate General James Longstreet made Bleak House his headquarters beginning probably on November 17. After his forces' defeat in the battle of Fort Sanders on November 29, he withdrew from Knoxville, retreating to the northeast on the night of December 4/5, 1863. During the siege, Longstreet confined Mrs. Armstrong and her children to one bedroom on the second floor (Colonel Armstrong apparently was not at home at the time, but his whereabouts are unknown). Following the Blue and Gray Reunion in Knoxville, October, 8–9, 1890, when veterans from both sides, including General Longstreet, visited the Armstrong home, a newspaper account describes the shot that had killed General Sanders, the tower from which sharpshooters had fired, the answering "prettiest shot of the war" that hit the front wall of the house, and other damage still visible in the house. Digby G. Seymour, *Divided Loyalties: Fort Sanders and the Civil War in East Tennessee,* 2nd ed. rev. (Knoxville: East Tennessee Historical Society, 1982), 138–146; *Knoxville Journal,* October 10, 1890.
8. *Ariadne on the Panther* (1816), by German sculptor Johann Heinrich von Dannecker (1758–1841).
9. When Louisa Franklin Armstrong was twenty-one years of age, her personal estate value was listed as $12,000. Her husband's personal estate value was listed as $18,000, although he also had real estate valued at $25,000. *U.S. Census, 1860.*
10. "A prominent character in *The Newcomes* [by William Makepeace Thackeray (1811–1863)], distinguished for moral beauty of his life." Frederic Taber Cooper, comp., "Fa-

mous Characters in Poetry and Prose," in "A Reference Library" supplement, *Webster's Home, School and Office Dictionary* (Baltimore, Md.: L. & M. Ottenheimer, 1929), [no page number].

11. Anne Audubon (née Wetzell) Armstrong crossed out this part of the sentence in her manuscript.
12. In its biographical sketch about him, *The French Broad – Holston Country* takes note of Drury P. Armstrong's "large and well selected library." Mary Utopia Rothrock, editor of the book, was a librarian, and the biographical section was the work of Laura E. Luttrell, also a librarian. Rothrock, viii, 370.
13. American historian William H. Prescott (1796–1859) was author of the two-volume work *History of the Conquest of Mexico* (1843) and *History of the Conquest of Peru* (1847).
14. For a discussion of this and other ornamental gardens in Knoxville during the early twentieth century, see: W. R. McNabb, "Italian Villas of East Tennessee: The Formal Garden Revival Movement in Knoxville," East Tennessee Historical Society, *Publications* 61 (1989): 16–28, 19 (Bleak House).
15. Robert Houston Armstrong, born March 16, 1825, died at his home on May 13, 1896. "Col. Armstrong Died Yesterday Evening at Six O'clock," *Knoxville Journal*, May 14, 1896; Find A Grave website, https://www.findagrave.com/memorial/41419489/robert-houston-armstrong (viewed January 12, 2019).
16. Robert Franklin Armstrong (1864–1931).
17. The Armstrong children were Amelia Franklin, born in 1857; twins, Elizabeth Rogers (Lizzie) and Ann Adelia, born 1859; Robert Franklin, born 1864.
18. Amelia, "Little Bunt," died July 25, 1859, so she was two years of age or less at the time of her death (the month of her birth is unknown). Find a Grave database and images, https://www.findagrave.com/memorial/68026506/amelia-franklin-armstrong (viewed 12/10/18).
19. Editor's Note: Louise Franklin Armstrong is referred to sometimes as "Louise" and sometimes as "Louisa," even at times in the same source. A descendant told me that her given name was usually always written "Louise" but that most family members called her "Louisa" when speaking of her.
20. Louise Franklin, born February 19, 1837, in Cocke County, Tennessee, was not yet ten years old when her mother, Elizabeth Rogers Franklin, died April 22, 1846. Her father, Lawson D. Franklin, was a landowner, cattle farmer, and slave trader who owned thousands of acres of land. "A large portion of the land eventually owned by Lawson D. Franklin lay along the Old French Broad River, now Douglas Lake, between Newport and Morristown, one tract being some twenty miles in length from Cocke County, through Jefferson County and into Hamblen County. The geographical center of this tract was located in Leadvale, Tennessee." Goodspeed's *History of Tennessee* states that Franklin established Leadvale (in Jefferson County near White Pine) in 1848 when he

built a store and a home for his family there; his house is now listed on the National Register of Historic Places. Franklin had other business interests in the area and was reported to be Tennessee's first millionaire. Howard Hill, *The Herbert Walters Story* (Morristown, Tenn.: Morristown Printing Co., 1963–1966), 11, 12, 23. *Goodspeed's History of Tennessee: Containing Historical and Biographical Sketches of Thirty East Tennessee Counties*. Repr. from Goodspeed's *History of Tennessee* (1887). (Nashville: Charles and Randy Elder, 1972), 863. In the 1850 census, Louisa and her sister Jane (b. 1834) were living in Knoxville in the household of James C. Luttrell and his wife Eliza. Luttrell was postmaster of Knoxville from 1849–1853 and served as mayor in 1854 and again from 1859 to 1868. Jane Franklin married Dr. John M. Boyd, "Knoxville's beloved physician" (see Part 1, Chapter 2). Another sister, Caroline Elizabeth (b. 1832) married William Montgomery, president of Carson-Newman College in Jefferson City. U.S. Census Bureau, *1850 Census*, 97; Rule, 124, 125; Rothrock, 440–441.

21. Adelia Armstrong married John Edwin Lutz in 1886. They lived with her parents until their home, Westwood, was completed in 1890 on land given them by her father. Westwood, on the opposite side of Kingston Pike about 0.3 mile from Bleak House, has been on the National Register of Historic Places since 1984. Armstrong family members lived in Westwood until 2014, when it was purchased and restored to serve as the headquarters for Knox Heritage. "Historic Westwood," Knox Heritage website, http://knoxheritage.org/westwood/ (viewed January 14, 2019).
22. Undoubtedly referring to Adelia's twin, Elizabeth (Lizzie), who married James P. McMillan in 1881 and moved to Chattanooga. They had three children, one of whom died young. Lizzie's husband died in 1888, and she died in 1895.
23. Knoxville City directories list Mrs. Louise F. Armstrong at Hotel Cumberland (1903, 1904, 1905) and Oxford Hotel (1908). Bleak House was sold in 1906, and the 1910 U.S. Census lists her as a boarder in the household of Mary M. Sevier, 1403 White Avenue. Mrs. Armstrong died June 21, 1910.
24. On January 1, 1863. He had issued a preliminary proclamation September 22, 1862.
25. Title of the work is actually *Coming of Age in the Olden Time,* by English painter William Powell Frith (1819–1909).

Chapter Fourteen

Whiskey Row

Now it was evening. It was not late, but already at the end of September dark came early and outside the car window was nothing but darkness and drizzly rain. We passed through no towns, passed not a single house from which a light shone. Only darkness.

The coach, dimly lighted and smoky, was filled with rough-looking, mostly bearded men—loggers and miners. At one end was a stove and from time to time Theodore would get up, join the men near the stove, then return to his seat beside me and lapse again into silence. This was the way he had been since we left Seattle. There were many questions I was aching to ask, but I kept silent too. Was he worried, or what?

I kept my eyes on the rain-splattered car window, hoping against hope to make out something through it, but never had darkness seemed so dark. I can feel it now.

I had often seen Theodore moody, but I could not fathom his present mood. He should have been happy and at least a little excited. . . .

What sort of place had he found for us to live in? His letters, though expressing passionate love, had never given the least hint.

This man beside me was my husband, but I knew him even less than that evening a year ago when, almost a complete stranger, he had frightened me by saying I was the girl he intended to marry.

We were traveling on the little spur of railroad that ran from Seattle to Snohomish, where Theodore had opened a law office, hung out his shingle. Now and then I glanced at him sideways. He seemed not so much sunk in gloom, as completely withdrawn.

He had been this way from the evening, a few days before, when he came down from Snohomish to meet me at Seattle, at the end of my long journey across the continent to join him.

Sitting beside him now, I was still painfully conscious of my impression as he came hurrying across the station platform when he saw me appear among the other passengers getting off the train. It was raining then too—it seemed that here it rained, a sort of drizzle, most of the time, and Theodore was wearing his mackintosh and the broad-brimmed black hat lawyers, young or old, wore then, with their black suits and long coats, to lend them dignity, I suppose.

My first thought was how thin, almost gaunt, he looked, as if he had not had enough to eat. It made his nose stand out more prominently. Perhaps he had taken all the money he could scrape together to fit out his office and a place for us to live, and I was filled, instantaneously, as he approached, with the old feeling of slight physical repugnance he created in me, mingled with a sense of pity. But my heart fell when he met me with so little show of emotion. In spite of everything, I had had a joyful trip all the four or five days from Chicago to Seattle. I was bursting with things to tell him but Theodore did not wish to hear any of it, it seemed. By the time we reached the cheap little hotel in downtown Seattle where he took me for the night he was in one of the moods I remembered too well. Even in the privacy of the hotel bed-room he did not seem very glad to see me, and I remember feeling it was almost immoral to go to bed with such a stranger.

Next day we went to friends of his, a young couple Theodore had never spoken of before, but the husband a classmate of his at Yale; in the lumber business now and apparently from a wealthy family, for their home on Queen Anne Hill was much more elegant than young couples usually live in.

The luxurious guest suite Theodore and I occupied looked out on Lake Washington, with a back-drop of the high Cascades and snow-capped Mount Rainier. Beautifully situated and with its steep streets, I fell in love at once with Seattle and when our host said that, like Rome, Seattle was built on seven hills, I could hardly keep from bursting out, "Like Knoxville, too!" But Theodore's face would grow dark whenever I mentioned Knoxville, Papa and Mama, or my old friends—all I had left behind. I must not speak of Knoxville now. I must not even *think* of it—more than I could help. . . .

We stayed a couple of days with the Simpsons, if that was their name, and one evening they took us to a play. Seattle was very young then and the play was given in a rough barn-like hall, though the audience, I recall, was well-dressed and prosperous-looking.

I have forgotten what the play was, but what I have reason to remember is that as we came out I heard someone call my name, and pushing through the crowd behind us was Bessie Sligh, a beautiful curly-headed girl I had met the same summer I met Donna, at the summer resort on Lake Michigan.

Bessie introduced her husband, Don Davenport, from Montana, though they were living now in Seattle.

When Don took my hand he said: "Annie, I'm the ugliest man you've ever met, but also the most fascinating!"

We all laughed and there was such good humour in his voice, if deviltry in his eye, that even Theodore did not seem to resent this bold and familiar remark.

When Don heard we were to be at Snohomish he said he was often there on business and would be looking in on us before long.

Now as I sat in the train, with Theodore silent beside me, I knew that already I was looking forward to Don's coming. He had extremely irregular features and a strangely marred face, but he was magnetic. If not in the least handsome, he was attractive. I had almost never before felt lonely, but it made me feel a trifle less so to realize that Bessie, whom I had known in the past, and Don, whom I liked the moment I met him, would not be far away, only forty miles or so, in Seattle.

How, anyway, I asked myself miserably, had I ever come to marry Theodore De Groot? But I would never be quite clear about that. And sitting in the dirty, crowded, jolting little train, impenetrable blackness outside, bound for some place I knew almost nothing about, and with no one to talk to, my thoughts inevitably flew to Bob Armstrong.

I had told myself again and again in the past months that this was the subject above all others I must not dwell upon. But I could not help going over in my mind now every detail of our last meeting.

It was very soon after the night when Bob brought me home from Bleak House and in leaving told me he was going away before long—the night he drew a promise from me.

Our last meeting was on an evening when Theodore and I were sitting in front of a fire in our parlor on Highland Avenue, for the early spring evenings were still often chilly. It was growing late and I was hoping Theodore would leave, when the door-bell rang. As it happened, Mama was in the hall, on her way upstairs. She opened the front door, and it was Bob.

Mama, I think, had always been somewhat distrustful of Bob. It was his manner, his extreme gallantry, I imagine, which made her doubt his sincerity.

But now she led him into the little sitting room at the back of the hall, and then opening the door into the parlor, said she wanted to see me.

I closed the parlor door behind me as I came out, but only because I thought it was some private matter she wanted to see me about. Perhaps Papa was worse; without telling me, she has sent for the doctor; and the ring was his. But she motioned toward the sitting room and Bob was standing there, in front of the couch by the windows.

"Annie," he said, "I've only got a minute, but I had to see you."

He explained he was leaving sooner than he had expected, but a man he had known in Paris, a man with interests in Mexico was passing through Knoxville, en route there, next morning, and he had decided to go with him.

Bob took something from his vest pocket, a plain gold ring. "I had no time," he said, "after I decided to go, to get a ring for you, but I picked this up from Delia's dressing-table—she'll never miss it. Dele's an artist, you know, her head in the clouds. She wouldn't care anyway—she never wears it."

It was his sister's wedding-ring, with *Adelia* engraved inside. He slipped it on my finger.

"Don't take it off," he said. "When I come back I'll replace it with a more appropriate one. But I couldn't go till I staked out my claim. Remember, *Wiwita*," he said (*Wiwita* was Sioux Indian for "my own"), "—remember that one of your little fingers means more to me than the whole body of any other woman in the world."

"Have a good time," he said, then, nodding toward the parlor, "but for God's sake, whatever you do, don't see so much of De Groot!"

He kissed me then, for the first time, and many times, and with a few more hurried and whispered words, was gone.

I went back to the parlor, my face flushed, I suppose, but hiding my hand with the ring on as best I could, without seeming to do so. Nevertheless Theodore caught a glimpse of another ring than the one I usually wore, set with a diamond, the one my father brought me from Paris when I was sixteen.

Theodore seized my hand, roughly pulled the ring Bob had placed there off my finger and without a word thrust it into his own vest pocket.

I remember my sickening feeling of helplessness as he did so. I am confident I was, in general, anything but a spiritless girl. But what could I do or say, without hurting him too terribly, that would rid me of Theodore? And did I *want* to rid myself of him once and for all? He was the first and only young man I considered an intellectual that I had known. I would like to see him sometimes. And to ask my sick father, a constant sufferer, to *order* Theodore never to come to our house again was out of the question. I couldn't mix Papa up in such a matter. This was *my* affair. I would have to manage it myself. As for revealing to Theodore my relation to Bob, that was even more out of the question. I had seen enough of Theodore's temper not to risk rousing it further—not at any rate till Bob came back. Bob would be behind me then. He could take care of the situation....

All I could hope for was that something would happen to deliver me from what seemed, inexplicably, my bondage to Theodore. But Mama was planning I should spend the coming summer—and summer was not far off—away from Knoxville, with Aunt Sarah. That might solve the problem.

In the days that followed Theodore kept coming as usual. Bob was gone now and save for an occasional dance one of them took me to, a play or concert, I saw less and less of young men who had previously paid me attention. At last Theodore had me virtually to himself and never had I known him so agreeable; in what for him, inclined to be morose, were such high spirits.

For me it was a singular time. Since the days when cadets began calling on me in the Barnes house, there had been boys, young men, coming and going constantly in our house. Mama had come to accept this as a matter of course; even, I think, to be somewhat gratified by it.

I was lonely now. Although I often saw Ida, Ella, Margaret—girls I had gone to school with and with whom I remained on the best of terms, yet I had no real girl chum, no confidante. To tell the truth, I had had none since Mary Gaines in my early teens. And when I *did* see my girl friends now, they told me that everyone thought I was engaged to Mr. De Groot, as they called him.

Engagements were not announced then in Knoxville. A girl wanted to have all the beaux, the gaiety, she could till at least her trousseau was started, or even her wedding invitations issued. But when I denied to the other girls that I was engaged to Theodore, I could see they did not believe me; so this being true, and Theodore more companionable than formerly, all that remained, I thought, was to get such enjoyment as I could from being with him.

Spring, when it really started, as always in the South, came fast. The evenings were warm enough now so that when Theodore suggested we walk up to Fort Sanders, with its wide spaces under the open sky, it was a change I welcomed after the hot sticky day in one of Miss Ogden's class-rooms.

Twilights were longer. Theodore would bring a book, we would make ourselves comfortable, half reclining, on the grassy slopes of the old fortifications, and with almost no one ever passing he would read aloud while the light lasted.

One evening he brought with him a book he had recently acquired, a new, and I believe the first unexpurgated, edition of Walt Whitman's *Leaves of Grass*, the poet's recent death[1] having focused fresh attention on this work.

Whitman was still little more than a name to me. I knew of him vaguely as a rebel against convention and had heard whispers that most public libraries did not permit his poems on their shelves. Certainly I had not found *Leaves of Grass* in the library at Mount Holyoke. But Theodore was well acquainted with the work, and always attracted myself to any book considered "dangerous," I was eager now to hear what clearly Theodore was eager to have me.

I shall never know just how much guile went into Theodore's introduction of me to *Leaves of Grass*. But beyond a doubt had he started with "Children of Adam"[2] I would have found these poems of passionate sexual love as shocking, revoltingly carnal, as did the majority of Whitman's contemporaries. For all the normal curiosity about sex I had carried over from childhood into adolescence and still retained, I was not in the slightest degree prepared for such startling realism—for a poet who insisted not only on the infinite importance of sexuality, but that sexual intercourse was a proper subject for poetry.

But, Theodore did not start with "Children of Adam." He acquainted me first with "When Lilacs Last in the Dooryard Bloom'd" (not yet in all the anthologies).

Previously he had read me in our parlor at home closely reasoned, more or less dry articles in the *North American Review*, articles I often found boring. But now, under the boundless sky, in the dying light, when he read this long poem in memory of the martyred Lincoln, he read with a deep though restrained feeling, a dramatic power, I had never suspected in him.

I had been aware from the first—uncomfortably aware—of the richness of his deep virile voice. It had a compulsive quality and in it, I recognized confusedly, lay such influence over me as he exerted. But now when in a subdued voice he chanted, more than read, those last vibrant lines of the poem:

> For the sweetest, wisest soul of all my days and lands [—and this for
> his dear sake,]
> Lilac and star and bird twined with the chant of my soul,
> There in the fragrant pines and the cedars dusk and dim,[3]

the chant seemed mystically to unite Theodore and myself, and in our shared rush of feeling for the moment to make us one.

As Theodore read, even as in the poem, the fragrance of pines—the pines on Fort Sanders—, and the fragrance from a clump of shadowy cedars, "dusk and dim," were wafted to us. As in the poem, a solitary thrush sounded its liquid notes, its good-night song; a great star appeared in the West.

I was lifted out of myself.[4] I hardly knew where I was, for Whitman himself was there with us in the dying day. And Lincoln was there, a Lincoln mightier in stature than I had discerned before.

But Theodore also all at once had assumed greater stature. His lips slightly parted, eyes alight, in his face with its dominant nose, voluptuous mouth with the full pouting lower lip, its fine brow, the brow of a thinker, I saw for the first time what seemed a look of nobility.

One evening he read "Out of the Cradle Endlessly Rocking," that long, infinitely touching poem of the "Two feather'd guests from Alabama, two together"[5] and of the mourning of the male bird when his mate disappeared from the nest; and I could not keep back the tears as he read, albeit not unaware that Theodore was making the poem applicable to ourselves, foreshadowing his own possible desolation, in the impassioned stress he laid in his deep low voice on the refrain.

Seeing me agitated as he had not before, with consummate skill he led me on now to "Starting from Paumanok," rendering as only he could, it seemed then, its closing ecstatic lines. This was wild music for my uninitiated ears, and in another twilight hour I was to hear "To a Common Prostitute," with its superbly audacious, divinely compassionate: "Not till the sun excludes you do I exclude you."[6] Never had I known such a feeling of exultation. Yet there were warnings too:

> Who is he that would become my follower[?]
> [Who would sign himself a candidate for my affections?]
> The way is suspicious, the result uncertain, perhaps destructive.[7]

By this time, however, my interest in *Leaves of Grass* had reached fever pitch. I must go on—go on at any cost. I must know all that was in this book.

Whitman was opening up a new and infinitely expanded world, and it was Theodore who was leading me into this world.

Theodore was still on sure ground, too, when he began to familiarize me not only with Whitman, the humanitarian, but to the Whitman who had gone still further than Emerson in throwing overboard church and dogma, with the religion that remained to him of the kind that can make immediate passage from man to God; who insisted that no one had ever yet been half devout enough in his worship of the sacredness of man.

Although a devout Episcopalian in all outward observances, Theodore was as unorthodox as I in his general views on religion; as ready to accept "the restorer"—as William James called Whitman— "of the eternal natural religion—the religion of healthy-mindedness."[8]

Here, then, Theodore and I were rapport to an extent I had scarcely recognized heretofore.

But Whitman all in all was proving, in truth, the most disturbing experience I had known. Moreover, it is not to be wondered at that a girl still in her teens should have been overwhelmed by one of the most perceptive and prophetic minds in modern history. It would be some years till I read Bucke's famed biography of Whitman. I had never heard then of "cosmic consciousness."[9] But for some years past I had been moving away from the concept of a dualistic universe, groping my way toward the idea that there is but *one* life, *one* substance, and the Whitman who now took complete possession of me was the one Theodore's voice brought me—the Whitman of the line which burst on me like a thunderclap, leaving me breathless:

> Nothing, not God, is greater to one than one's self is.[10]

Through all these tender spring twilights, however, I was being conditioned, whether premeditatedly or not, for what was to follow.

By the end of May, it was almost time for Miss Ogden's School to close, for me to leave for Aunt Sarah's. The days were as hot as in deep summer and the evenings, even on Fort Sanders, I remember, had become languorous, before Theodore finally ventured to acquaint me with "Children of Adam," that unprecedented challenge to Victorian ethics and the genteel age.

I was to know now the Whitman who proclaimed copulation no more rank than death, man as divine about the loins as about the temples. I was to hear earthy words, expressions, I had never heard before; be confronted with burning images at once sickening, terrifying, almost unbearably exciting.

When I think back now on that time and my dense ignorance of my own nature, I can not but recall also, well known though it is to-day, that there was *no* open discussion then of sex. Furthermore, I had read no erotica whatever, and if I had devoured Dickens, Thackeray, and George Eliot, while there was much "love" in them, sex might scarcely have existed so far as any light they threw on the subject. Decent young women—if not, indeed, *all* women—were presumed to have no sex promptings. Only men harbored animal instincts, with women their more or less willing victims. Sex, to the children of my generation, so far as we were able to penetrate the mysteries of this adult realm, was a thing to snicker over. It continued to be a thing to me that could only be whispered about.

But now, all at once, the revolutionary Whitman began to influence my ideas on sex as Renan[11] and Emerson earlier my ideas on religion.

It was vastly more, however, than an intellectual adventure I was embarked on now. As Theodore read "From Pent-Up Aching Rivers"—his deep voice deeper, more tense, than ever—, "I Sing the Body Electric," "A Woman Waits for Me," and at last "One Hour to Madness and Joy," it was not my brain, it was my blood, that caught fire.

As we lingered now on the solitary heights of Fort Sanders until the stars came out, I could no longer think clearly for the throbbing in my veins. I was inebriate—drunk on something more potent than wine. Dimly, shudderingly, I perceived that Theodore, though I continued to dislike more than like him, was gaining ascendency over me. Would a day come, an hour, when I could no longer resist him?

It was early morning, not yet fully light, when I reached Chicago. I had to change cars here for the little town, two or three hours away, where Aunt Sarah lived.

Still dressing in my berth as the train, slowing up, entered the city, I raised my shade. We were passing street after street, that extended endlessly, lost in the distance, their rows of new-looking brick houses of some pale deadish tone and all exactly alike.

For some reason the look of these streets in the wan half-light, no one yet abroad on them, was a sight that engraved itself on my soul, as the Spanish say. I could never forget it. Never recall it without a slight shudder. In its desolateness it bore an outer semblance to my inner state of mind.

I seemed to have lost my bearings. All the old landmarks were gone. Even the figure of Bob had become blurred. Bob was somewhere in the interior of Mexico. No letters from him had reached me lately; none since Theodore and I had started going up to Fort Sanders in the evenings . . . .

Bewildered, uncertain about everything, I felt utterly alone. Adrift. I had left home in a dazed state and as I gazed out the car window at these monotonous, dimly discerned, sad rows of houses on the outskirts of a strange city, I wondered distractedly what was ahead.

But a measure of healing awaited me at Aunt Sarah's. Her old-fashioned modest white house stood on an elm-shaded street that might have been in New England. Planted in the midst of rolling prairie, the little town with its many stately homes, its invariably neat cottages, its white church steeples, had, in fact, been founded by New Englanders and bore their unerasable mark.

Uncle Henry was jolly; golden-haired Aunt Sarah's spirit warm and understanding—big, like her big beautiful body. There was a pervasive sense of happiness in their home, and hiding from them, from everyone, the turbulent sense of uneasiness that filled me, for a few days I knew something that, momentarily, was almost peace.

I would wander around and look at Aunt Sarah's paintings, mostly landscapes, though in the fashion of the day she had painted the broad canvas frames of her mirrors; morning glories twined around me, I recall, and on another woodbine in autumn hues, some of its scarlet tendrils trailing down on to the glass itself.

I would wander around in her unpretentious back yard, with its towering lilac bushes, in full bloom now, in early June; its glowing peonies, gay hollyhocks, and along a board fence at one side a row of rhubarb plants, horse-radish, parsley, a bed of asparagus—everything growing rankly in the deep rich black Illinois soil; and the yard sloping down to a little rustic bridge at its lower end, over a creek that ran through this part of town.

Sometimes I crossed the bridge to a meadow beyond and watched idly the bumblebees sipping from rosy clover blossoms amidst the long grass there. Anything not to *think*.

Aunt Sarah put no questions to me. But I looked tired, she thought, and she persuaded me to go to bed early and lie late in the morning these first days I was with her.

Miserable though I was, it was pleasant to lie in the deep, soft, big bed in Aunt Sarah's white-walled downstairs spare-room. The fragrance of the lilacs came through the open windows and the first sound in the morning was the clanging of bells from a near-by Catholic church calling the faithful to early mass. To me this was exotic and fascinating, if somewhat discordant, music, though for Aunt Sarah fraught with sinister suggestions. Dear Protestant, Presbyterian Aunt Sarah, tolerant of all human kind except Catholics.

It was a week or so after I came, as I lay in bed one morning with the sharp insistent clangor of the Catholic bells in my ears, that I also heard the door-bell ring, and after a pause Theodore's deep disturbing voice in the front hall.

So he had come—followed me!—for all there had not been a word between us of such a thing. But then I had not seen him alone a single time since our last evening on Fort Sanders. Mama had taken care of that! There had been the final hectic days at Miss Ogden's, the shopping and packing; and Mama, for the first time, had seen to it that others should be with me when Theodore came, and for as long as he stayed.

Now, as I heard his voice, a shiver of excitement ran through me, though whether from dread or delight I could hardly have said.

Theodore had reached town late the evening before and gone to a hotel for the night. Uncle Henry and Aunt Sarah received him cordially. Impressed by his voice, Uncle Henry wished he might have him in the church choir he directed. Aunt Sarah, to whom Theodore had put himself out to be agreeable during her visit in Knoxville the fall before, listened receptively when he told her he came to deliver an invitation from his sister, a young widow who lived in Chicago, near Lincoln Park. He was in Chicago, he said, on legal business, and his sister had asked him to bring me back with him, to be her guest for the few remaining days he would be there.

I have no memory of Theodore's and my train trip to Chicago. It is a total blank in my mind. What I remember is our boarding a street-car when we got to the city; after what seemed a lengthy trip getting off in an attractive suburban neighborhood, walking down a shady street and Theodore stopping before the gate of a refined-looking house with Boston ivy half covering its brown shingled walls and next it a small stone church.

"What a pretty place!" I said. "Is this your sister's?"

"No," Theodore said. "We'll go there later. This is a rectory. The rector will marry us." He felt in his coat. "I have the license."[12]

I had lost all will of my own, it seemed, and whatever Theodore said, I did. But just as I have no memory of our train trip to Chicago, so none remains of my sensations at this crucial moment. I only recall, as in the dimmest of dreams, standing up with Theodore in the rector's study, with the rector's wife and a housemaid as smiling witnesses, and my astonishment when Theodore drew from his vest pocket the identical plain gold ring Bob Armstrong had placed on my finger only a few weeks ago, telling me not to take it off, and which Theodore had forcibly removed. Now I was being wedded, ironically, with a ring Bob had provided. But everything at the time was unreal, like death, and this no more than anything else.

From the rectory we went to the Hyde Park Hotel, only a few blocks away, where Theodore appeared to have reserved a room.

Our room overlooked Lake Michigan and when I woke early next morning and looked out from our bed on its boundless gray waters, with not a sail—a craft of any kind, not even a tug-boat in sight, I was seized with the same feeling of forlornness, homelessness, I had known a week or so before when I looked out from the moving train at the city's empty streets at this hour. Only now, in addition, my numbness in recent days was beginning to give way to a sharp sense of sorrow. Theodore asleep beside me, as I gazed out at the featureless, cheerless, illimitable waste of the great lake that stretched before my eyes, I pictured to myself the suffering, the profound humiliation my secret marriage, when they knew of it, would bring to Mama and Papa, already so heavily burdened from other causes. No bride, I believe, ever woke more sorrowfully from her bridal night.

Next morning we went to Theodore's sister's on Chicago's North Side. She knew of our marriage, though understood that no one else was to know for the present. Plenty of time to disclose it, and nothing I wished so much to postpone as that terrible moment!

I went back alone to Aunt Sarah's, carrying, feverishly, my heavy secret with me.

I was fated, however, not to reveal the marriage myself. Aunt Sarah had written Mama of my going to Chicago with Theodore, and Papa, instantly suspicious, wired Chicago. Had a marriage license been issued there in the name of Theodore and myself? Informed that there had, he wrote Aunt Sarah, insisting she make the fact public.

Aunt Sarah did not show me Papa's letter, though she told me what she felt she must—I would not hear again from him or Mama, he said, nor did they wish to hear from me.

I can never forget the unending night that followed. Papa's letter had plunged me into utter darkness. I had brought eternal disgrace on my parents, broken their hearts. I would never know another happy day as long as I lived....

In the morning there was a telegram from Theodore. In a couple of days he would be with me.

When he arrived, it was to tell me he already had left Knoxville for good; was on his way to a new little town in the Far West which he had learned might be a good place for a young lawyer to make a start on his own, and he would send for me as soon as he could.

There was at least something now, if nothing very definite, for me to look forward to. But in retrospect, my mind dwells on how excruciating all this must have been for Aunt Sarah. Under suspicion of having supported me in my wayward course, it had caused a breach between her and Mama, sisters heretofore unusually close to one another. Then, though far less reserved, she was as conventional as Mama, and I realize to-day if I did not then, what it must have meant to her in her own environment—a woman of queenly dignity, but apparently upholding me in what in effect was a runaway marriage.

But whatever she suffered on my account, she never reproached me. Throughout that long summer, entirely cut off, as I was, from my family, my young friends—for none of them wrote me—, Aunt Sarah seemed bent only on keeping me occupied as pleasantly as she could. She gave small parties in my honor, as if my marriage had been of the most regular. She taught me to make bread. She interested me in preparing the linens traditionally provided by the bride's family. Ready-made sheets and pillow-cases could not be bought then, so she provided the linen, and although I was never deft with a needle, she had me make them —had me making, too, all sorts of humble domestic necessities, such as dish-towels and dust-cloths.

Theodore wrote daily, burning love letters, though he gave me little idea of Snohomish save to say that one side of its wide unpaved main street, called Whiskey Row, was an unbroken line of saloons, and once, jestingly, that I would be one of only two respectable women in the town—the doctor's wife and myself!

None of this, however, dismayed me. It would be a rough life, but it would be exciting. It would be an adventure. It was the only thing in the future I had to hold to, and I held to it tight. Hemstitching pillow-cases, as the days went on I began to know a certain content. Something was always gnawing on me. Even so, I pictured to myself more and more happily the first little home of my own, even if only a shack on a side street . . . .

When at last money for my ticket came from Theodore, Aunt Sarah spent days preparing delicacies for the big basket of lunch that must last me almost a week. She went with me as far as Chicago to put me on my train; at the moment of parting her eyes brimming with tears, but whispering cheerful encouraging words in my ear, holding me close in a last warm embrace.

When Theodore and I got off at Snohomish it was not late, but so dark that as I stepped down on to the rain-soaked wooden platform I could hardly make out the outlines of the dimly-lighted little depot in front of us.

It was still drizzling. Theodore carrying our bags, we started across a long broad stretch of rough muddy ground and then, Theodore ahead, felt more than saw our way as we clambered up a slippery bank and toward Whiskey Row, a few of whose scattered lights appeared now, and as we drew closer, at its far end, some distance away, the wavering glow of red lights visible through the rain.

"What are those red lights for?" I asked innocently, and to break the silence, pressing on me almost unendurably by this time.

"That's the red light district," Theodore's muffled voice drifted back to me. "Nothing but whore houses at that end of town."

At last we reached the sidewalk—a couple of long boards laid lengthwise—where Whiskey Row began. Light gleamed smokily, though rather rosily, from a big window in the first building we came to, and on its window, emblazoned in large fanciful letters: THE BROKEN HEART SALOON.

It was, I noticed, a two-story building, and just beyond the big window in the saloon Theodore turned up some steep narrow pitch-black stairs, while I stumbled up them behind him. In the cramped space at the top, he fumbled for a key in his pocket, unlocked a door, entered a dark front room, found a small oil lamp and lighted it.

I gave a quick glance around. Theodore still said nothing, but this was obviously his office. There was a little round iron stove in a rear corner, facing me, wood on the floor beside it, a few straight-back chairs, a plain deal table that apparently served as a desk, and shelves along one wall holding his law books.

Carrying the lamp, he led the way through a door near the stove to the room behind, where I saw before me a cheap pine bedstead, bureau and washstand, and between two windows at the back a sort of cupboard he had contrived out of a couple of small packing cases, its open shelves displaying some heavy white china dishes, an iron skillet and a few other cooking utensils.

So this was the home I had come to—one room over the Broken Heart Saloon! My first impulse was to burst out crying. But not from disappointment. Not from resentment. Theodore was strange. I couldn't understand him at all. But he had done his best—and his best was so pitiful! It was that that made me want to cry.

Through the windows I could hear the loud sound of rushing water. It filled the room. Theodore threw up one of the windows and pointed down to a swift narrow river directly below, a few glints of light falling on its dark turbid surface from a window in the rear of the saloon underneath us.

"The Pilchuck," Theodore said. "Indian for 'Bad Water.'" Then he laughed, though not mirthfully; more, it seemed, from embarrassment. "They tell great tales here," he said. "The backs of all the saloons on Whiskey Row open on it, and when a man gets killed in one of them in a brawl, they just pitch his body into the Pilchuck."

I looked around.

"Everything looks so clean and neat," I said, and it did. The bare pine floor had been carefully swept and even the bed, with its white spread, looked as if a woman had made it.

I took off my damp hat and coat and hung them on some nails I saw on the wall, although I noticed as I was doing so that Theodore had not removed his own hat or rain-coat.

"Aren't you going to stay a while?" I asked, uneasily, though mustering a playful tone.

Theodore said he would have to be off. He looked at his watch. "I'm late now."

It was important, he said, for him to make all the acquaintances he could, so he had joined an amateur dramatic group in town and was taking one of the principal parts in a play they were rehearsing to-night.

"Oh, let me go with you!" I begged. "I can't stay here—*alone*!"

"No," he told me, emphatically, "you can't go. *No*!" when in my fright I continued to beg him. And then it happened.

I do not remember feeling any pain at the moment, only a blinding flash as though a bolt of lightning had struck me. What I remember was gradually becoming conscious of my surroundings, as if I were coming out of sleep. I was lying on the bed. My head was throbbing. There was a wet towel across my forehead and severe pain in one spot where the towel rested. Theodore was on his knees beside the bed, bending over me, his face deeply flushed and quivering. In a broken voice he was imploring me to forgive him, kissing my hands, lips, my throat and bare shoulders—for he had partially undressed me—, calling me by endearing names, making love to me with utter abandon.

I was aware now that there had been a blow on my head. But my feeling was one of relief. Now Theodore would not leave me . . . .

He had never been like this before. He was all but mad with excitement. But when his ardor had somewhat spent itself and he had known gratification, to my horror I realized that he was putting on his rain-coat—going to leave me after all! And with these raucous cries, this terrifying uproar from wild drunken men in the saloon below, coming up through the floor and thin walls!

Now, however, I did not beg to go with him. If he had knocked me unconscious this time, next time he might kill me. I lay quietly on the bed as Theodore went out the door, the wet towel pressing more and more painfully on a great lump that had formed on my forehead.

I was facing life in reality now, learning early—earlier than many—to accept the tragedy of human existence along with its joy. Stunned by Theodore's brutality, I was incapable, it is true, of thinking clearly. I had heard of men among very low people beating their wives. But I could not have conceived of such behavior in the class to which Theodore and I belonged. My own father and mother no doubt had their private differences, but I had never in my life heard so much as an uncivil remark pass between them. It crossed my mind that for all his normal behavior ordinarily Theodore might be insane. Well, whatever lay behind his cruelty, I was not completely crushed. My will to live, to survive, was still strong. I do not think it occurred to me for an instant to leave him. (Where would I go?) I had always suspected Theodore was possessed of a savage temper, and I had aroused it by opposing his will; therefore I must not oppose his will. I must move warily from now on . . . .

The challenge immediately before me was to make a home out of this back room over a saloon. Fortunately, the effort to do so took all my time, strength, and ingenuity.

The chief problem was meals for two healthy young people who—as I look back on it—had hardly yet attained their full growth.

The last spike in the Great Northern Railroad would not be driven till the following spring and Snohomish was a center for construction crews working on it. The Monte Cristo Silver Mines were also only a short distance away and there were twenty logging camps in the immediate vicinity. This meant heavy demand for such food as a raw new town in a largely undeveloped region could supply, and prices for food exorbitant. Moreover, as I soon knew, Theodore thus far had not had a single client, and his money fast dwindling.

Before I came, Theodore had been eating here and there in the roystering back room of one saloon and another, in company with miners, lumber-jacks, railroad workers—toughs of every variety, and women from the red-light district always among them. But now I must cook our meals myself and on a diminutive oil stove atop the little cupboard Theodore had devised.

The only meat and grocery store, a one-story frame structure with a false front, was obliquely opposite the Broken Heart Saloon. Like the saloon, it was the first building you came to on its own side of the street. It was where the town began when you climbed up from the railroad track and depot at the bottom of the chasm below; and I can see myself, as if it were someone else, picking my way in a sea of mud across the wide waste of Whiskey Row when I went to the store.

I can still feel my consternation on finding eggs sixty-cents a dozen and storage eggs shipped from the East at that, when in Knoxville the freshest of eggs sold at ten.

I can see, as something in a motion picture of years ago, Theodore and myself sitting down to our first meal on Whiskey Row. It was in his office. He had removed the inkstand and other paraphernalia from the table he used as desk, and I had spread over it a pretty lunch-cloth from the linens in my trunk.

The meal had taken me a long time to prepare. I had made a sort of compote out of apples for our dessert. Then I had boiled potatoes and when they were done, as only one thing could be cooked at a time, wrapped the sauce pan in towels to keep the potatoes hot while I cooked the main dish—creamed chipped beef.

Before we sat down Theodore had warned me that if we heard a step on the stairs it might be a client and we must whisk everything off the table and into the bedroom. This gave me the feeling of a friendly little conspiracy between us, and although the bulge on my forehead was badly discolored now and constantly painful, yet in spite of everything it seemed rather jolly to be sitting down together to the first meal I had ever cooked myself.

I had chosen dried beef because it was the cheapest meat the butcher had to offer and the dish looked appetizing as I set it before us. But with my first taste I realized the beef should have been soaked before adding it to the sauce. I was seized with fright. The meal was ruined! What would Theodore do?

To my infinite relief, Theodore took the failure good-naturedly. Briny or not, we ate every morsel of it, and Theodore even praised my cleverness, as he called it, in keeping one dish hot while another cooked.

What I marvel at, sixty years after, is that we kept well on the diet, day after day, week after week, we were limited to. As time went on I made of course fewer blunders. Occasionally Theodore was able to buy venison from some lumber-jack, as deer abounded in the surrounding forests. This made a welcome change, as did brook trout from a stream a little outside town, and equally plentiful and cheap. But I recall clearly that never did we have fresh vegetables, and none of the green stuff now considered essential. We lived on oatmeal, cocoa, potatoes and apples, and on stale baker's bread toasted over the embers in the little stove in Theodore's office.

It took as much time to keep the room clean and neat where we cooked, slept, dressed and bathed as to prepare our meals. But clean and neat it must be. Theodore was the most immaculate of men. He had stood out in Knoxville because he was always extremely well groomed when good grooming was not so common among men as today. Whether pleasing him in this way might help save me from further brutality, I did not know. But I must overlook nothing.

We had no dish-pan, not even a tin basin, only the bowl to the toilet-set on our wash-stand to hold water in. No bucket, and early and late, when I was not preparing meals, I would be carrying the heavy white china pitcher of the toilet-set down the dark steep stairs to the street and around the corner of the saloon to a narrow shackly walk-way along its side, perched on high wooden props and threatening to give way with every step I took, but which led to a pump and a little beyond to a privy built over the river.

Nearly always it would be raining. Looking neither to right nor left, I would carry my pitcher past the rough-necks of every description invariably gathered near the corner of the saloon. Often there would be fighting and always cursing. I would try not to, but could not help catching glimpses of bloodied faces. I would hear oaths and obscenity that left me nothing to learn long years afterward. Not once, however, did these drunken ruffians accost me. In the midst of a brawl they would push each other back to make way for me as I passed with my empty or filled pitcher.

Once upstairs I would resume washing dishes, clothes, scrubbing the floor, whatever it was, and throwing the dirty water—slops of every sort, out the window, into the muddy evil-smelling Pilchuck down below, the only place I had to dispose of waste.

Never at any time did Theodore carry up a drop of the water that must meet all our needs—offer to help in any way. It was not that he was lazy. He was out every day, trying to add to his acquaintance in the hope of sooner or later getting his law practice started. But he seemed oblivious to the fact that a young slender girl, not overly robust, and brought up in refined surroundings, was doing heavy unaccustomed work and under frontier conditions. He seemed not in the least concerned. And I did not demur, for I could not understand to save me, especially since I never opposed him now in anything, what produced the brutal attacks which still went on.

Theodore's sudden violence stemmed, it seemed, from the most insignificant causes—if they *were* the causes. He no longer struck me on the head. Sometimes with one blow he knocked me to the floor, and if I could not get up would lift and carry me to the bed, while he poured forth burning expressions of his love for me. More often he struck me in the face, and then seemed to derive intense pleasure from tenderly wiping the blood from my broken lips. His face at such times wore an expression of ecstasy, almost exaltation, and would be accompanied by evidence of high erotic excitement.

The last thing I could have imagined was that lust and cruelty could be closely linked. I did not dream that I had married a sadist. I had never heard of the Marquis de Sade; never heard the word "sadist."[13] I barely knew there was such a thing as sexual perversion, to say nothing of a pathological condition where men obsessed with an impulse to subdue, even destroy, the object of their desire, could only know amorous satisfaction after working themselves into an artificial state of anger by inflicting torture on the desired one.

I did not understand at all—did not even attempt to understand, the terrible things that were happening to me. I only knew I wanted to live, if I could. Knew I had made my bed, and in the old vulgar phrase, must lie in it.

It would seem impossible that there could be any joy in life under such circumstances. My old world was gone—the world of Knoxville. But if it was gone, I must make a new one, whatever the hidden horrors of my strange private life.

No one wrote me now—no one save Aunt Sarah, but when her letters came, my heart sang as I carried my heavy pitcher back and forth through the staggering cursing crew outside the saloon. When she sent me table silver, cut glass, a dainty Wedgwood tea-set, incongruous though they were in our crude quarters, yet they filled me with all the delight any bride could know from wedding gifts.

Then there were evenings that, for all my constant uneasiness as to what might follow, on the whole were pleasant. We would sit in Theodore's office. I would wear a long silk tea-gown of primrose yellow which Aunt Sarah had made me and high-heeled red slippers Theodore bought me during the brief stay in Chicago after our marriage. Theodore liked to see me dressed this way, especially in the red slippers.

The room, with a fire in the little wood-stove, was comfortable. Theodore, one side our small oil lamp, would be reading the Seattle paper; I, darning or mending. I could not read any more. My mind would not follow . . . .

Theodore never, then or later, said anything uncomplimentary to me. There was no bickering. And never, never, did I make any reference to his brutality, though never for an instant was it absent from my thoughts. But now for a couple of hours I felt safe. Knew a certain content for the time being.

I took keen interest, too, in our novel environment, in all that was going on around us in this raw and roaring mining town. [When] we went fishing, with salmon eggs for bait, we followed a trail through the woods to the trout stream. There were rainbow trout and black spotted trout and silver trout, but I don't remember catching many, if any, fish myself. What stays with me is the look and feel and damp delicious aromatic smell of the magnificent forest; our parting ferns higher than our waists as we made our way under giant hemlocks and cedars and pines, through a green twilight that yet was not gloomy, and then coming quite suddenly to a break in the woods and there before us was the sparkling little trout-stream.

I think it was at this time I first began to pay any particular attention to mosses and lichens, to the minute exquisite ground-vines which spring from the loam of deep woods, to look closely at forest growths in their infinite variety—at this time became more alert to the beauties of nature and began to find in them some of that enduring joy which had so enriched the lives of my parents under any and all circumstances. I recall clearly, at any rate, that in this small opening, with its glints of sunshine, amidst the evergreen forests around Snohomish where we went fishing I felt happy, regardless of anything that had gone before or would come after . . . .

In time I saw the play whose rehearsal Theodore had gone to the evening of my arrival on Whiskey Row—that evening of deathless memory.

Ironically, the name of the play (one I have never heard of since) was *The Knobs of Tennessee*—that Tennessee for which, deep inside, I yearned night and day, at times to the point of physical pain.

It was played in a barn-like hall packed to suffocation with men, Theodore in black wig and whiskers taking the part—not too well, I thought—of a sheriff in some lawless mountain region. A lurid melodrama, fortunately it suggested no Tennessee I knew. But it is all very blurred in my mind at this late day.[14]

What is less blurred is an evening when we went to Everett, a thriving mining and lumber center, a seaport, not far from Snohomish. In this fall of '92 Benjamin Harrison was running for President in a red-hot campaign against Grover Cleveland.

Theodore was slated to speak for Harrison at a political rally and we made the trip between Snohomish and Everett by river in a little stern-wheeler.

A black night, not a star in the sky, we sat out on deck as the steamer wound its way around curve after curve in the narrow river, shut in on both sides by dense forests down to the water's edge.

I haven't the faintest remembrance of Theodore's speech in behalf of Benjamin Harrison, while the place where he spoke no longer takes even shadowy shape in my mind.

What I still see are those dense dark forests which walled us in as we sat on deck, close together for warmth, in the chilly night air. I see the black forests lighted briefly by a fire in front of some teepee as we came in sight of one and another small Indian encampment.

What I remember with perfect clarity is that the sight of these Indian fires and teepees brought Bob Armstrong back as nothing else since I had left that world to which he, and once I, had belonged.

These were not the fine stalwart Indians of the Plains Bob had known in Dakota. They were Siwash,[15] canoe Indians, undersized and resembling Japanese. But they were Indians. Indians would be forever associated in my mind with Bob, and I thought of him achingly now. How could I have been faithless to the one man I loved or ever had wanted to marry? How could I have treated my parents as I had?

Yet I did not for an instant regard Theodore's terrible cruelty to me as punishment. The mixture in him of good and fiendish evil was completely beyond my comprehension. But I did not view it as a visitation. After all, how could I have behaved other than I had? I had been the play of forces stronger than myself. Caught in a trap—one of those traps life sets for youth—, thereafter there had seemed no course but the one I had followed.

Thinking of it all, here on the dark river that wound through the Washington forests, agonies of regret, of homesick longing, surged through me. But I was not weighed down by a sense of guilt. If those I had made suffer understood—understood everything (though they never would!) —they would forgive everything.

It was a happy moment for me when Don turned up. At once he was entirely at home and made us feel that living over a saloon on Whiskey Row in Snohomish, though he was obviously a prosperous man himself, was an adventure he envied us. This was the real West we were getting a taste of —the West of "The Luck of Roaring Camp" and "The Outcasts of Poker Flat."[16] Under the influence of Don's lively imagination, his witty magnetizing talk, our two rooms furnished with only the bare necessities, devoid of even the commonest comforts, took on something close to a romantic air.

I have forgotten what Don's business was (something, I think, to do with land and titles) but whatever it was, it would keep him busy all day. He had learned, however, that in the evening there was to be a miners' dance. This was something I must not miss. I would be perfectly safe in his hands and he was going to take me to it, he insisted.

I could hardly contain my excitement and waited nervously to hear what Theodore would say. Theodore did not dance because of an accident in early boyhood which, while not observable in his walk, had slightly stiffened one of his knees. But he offered no objection now to my going with Don.

The dance was held in the parlor, opening off the lobby, of the one hotel in town, near Whiskey Row but on a side street. The women there, all from the red-light district, were dressed gaudily though decently and if some of the men who remained in the lobby were somewhat tipsy, yet there were no fights—nothing unseemly occurred.

As I think of it now, again I am in that hot steamy hotel parlor, Don piloting me skillfully through the dense crowd of dancers. Don himself was not only a born mixer (he seemed to know most of the miners and some, I suspected, of their girls) but a beautiful dancer. Never had I danced under such miserable conditions, but never had I known such ecstatic joy in dancing—if only it could go on forever!

It was after midnight when Don and I climbed the steep black stairs from the street and opened the door to Theodore's office.

Theodore was reading and smoking his pipe. He seemed in a good humor and urged Don to remain with us till his train back to Seattle left at three in the morning.

Don was a capital story-teller and never had I heard Theodore laugh so heartily as at some of Don's escapades at the University of Michigan, from which he was finally fired, returning to Montana, where his father, owner of a big ranch, a man of some importance, gave him a job at twenty-five dollars a month for sitting—according to Don—on top of one of his barns and ringing a bell when he saw a cyclone coming.

It was the way Don told things. I laughed as hard as Theodore—laughed till I cried, and we both fairly clung to him when he got up to leave, with just time to catch his train if he ran.

We had had such fun sitting there after midnight in the hard straight chairs in Theodore's office! Theodore had been at his best. Surely things would be better . . .

Theodore closed the door after Don, and as I turned to say something to him on the way back to our bedroom to undress, he came toward me, suddenly stopped and without a word spat full in my face.

I was stunned. Had he been jealous of Don? Secretly resentful, all the while he was laughing, of the good time Don and I had had at the dance? But I was too shocked to speculate more than momentarily on what had prompted him to go to such a shameful and disgusting length.

Now, for the first time, I felt despair. Things would *never* be better. What should I do? Where could I go? Dizzily, unceasingly, these questions, as the days went on, whirled round and round in my head.

I found no answers. But at least I could retain some shred of what little human dignity remained to me. No one should know the degradation to which I had sunk.

It was after Don's visit—and on a day, I remember, when I felt even more hopeless than usual—that Theodore brought three young Englishmen up to our rooms. They were new acquaintances of his, having only recently come down from the neighboring British Columbia to take jobs as accountants with one of the big lumbering concerns operating around Snohomish.

They were not in the least like the remittance-men I had known in Knoxville and Middlesboro, Kentucky—sportsmen, hard drinkers, swells, idlers.

These young men were from somewhere in the West of England—I've forgotten the county—, one of them son of a parson, and they had come to America, not to idle, but for the commercial opportunities it had to offer.

They were fresh-skinned, clear-eyed, middle-class young Englishmen, with cheerful countenances, completely unspoiled, educated, though not University men, and soon they were dropping in, one or all, almost every afternoon or evening. Theodore, too, seemed thoroughly to enjoy these young Englishmen. As we only possessed four chairs he found a box for an extra seat, though they all appeared to like equally well sitting cross-legged on the floor.

One afternoon they suggested walking up a hill opposite us, along which streets were being laid out and houses built, and from the top of which they promised a fine view at sunset, but only at that hour, when the daily drizzle ceased, mists disappeared, the air cleared, and in the distance Mount Rainier could be seen, towering above the serrated ridges of the Olympics in the west.

When for the first time I climbed this steep hill, stood with the four men and saw, many miles away, but rising above the billowy clouds which veiled its base, the snowy rounded summit of Mount Rainier, and now bathed in the rosy light of the setting sun, I could understand why, to the Japanese, Fujiyama was a sacred mountain. Surely mortal eye could never look upon a more celestial sight! It lifted me, for the time, out of my despair, and into a heaven of delight.

After this I made a daily pilgrimage to the top of the hill not to miss the unearthly beauty of Mount Rainier at sunset.

Sometimes only the young Englishmen were with me, and all day long I looked forward to this hour. But it was not alone the sublime sight that awaited me which had restored to a certain extent my desire to go on living. Partly it was the camaraderie with these young Englishmen. They were not Southern men. They did not say those pretty, extravagant, flattering things which made me feel so good. But sincerity shone out of their clear direct eyes; they were friendly and kindly. When I was alone with them I would talk about Knoxville and they would talk about England, tell me about their homes and families there. I no longer felt so lost.

And Theodore must have discovered he could exercise more restraint—at least more caution, since these wholesome and fine, if unpretentious, English lads had become our constant companions. His brutality was less frequent, less extreme.

A night came, however, when the demon which possessed him at such times found vent, as earlier without warning and accompanied by no words, but in savage blows, and on this occasion I was more troubled as to what I should say next day when our young English friends came than by the blows themselves.

As usual, late in the afternoon, one of them came running up the stairs, while the others waited below, for me to join them in our walk, and when he knocked lightly at the office door and then came in, I emerged from the bedroom.

"My word!" burst from him as he stared at my swollen and discolored eye, bruised cheek, cut and swollen lips. "Whatever in the world has happened to you?"

"It was those steps," I said. "I always knew I'd stumble some day—"

"My word!" he said again, his fresh young face suddenly growing very red.

"It's a shame, a bloody shame," he began stammeringly, "your having to carry—"

But then he stopped himself and looked at me hard. Somehow I felt he knew I had lied.

Anyway, from that time on, though it was several days till I was presentable enough to go with them up the hill at the sunset hour, yet there was hardly a day when one of these young Englishmen did not show me some small special attention. One of them brought some of the choice tea his mother had sent from England; another, oranges just received at the store. I don't remember all the things, though I recall the ferns they brought from the woods to deck our bare rooms, little oddities they had found among forest growths and thought might interest me, and what touched me most, his own well-worn copy of Wordsworth which one of them brought as a gift, unaware that I could not read now, not even Wordsworth, one of the poets I loved best. . . . But just the same I felt these modest young men were standing by, trying to help me in such ways as they could.

As Christmas approached, they were resolved that we must celebrate it together, and traditionally, at least to the extent of plum duff, as they called plum pudding. One of them declared he knew how to make it. They provided the ingredients: flour, raisins, currants, suet, spices—everything, and entered into all our preparations with the utmost zest. Then when Christmas Eve arrived, after we had seeded all the raisins, cut up the suet, mixed, stirred—finally poured the pudding into its bag and set it to boil in a pot of water over the oil burner in our bedroom, the five of us sat down in Theodore's office alternately to play poker and sing.

The tiny oil stove frequently needed refilling, the pot replenishing with water, and it was three or four o'clock Christmas morning before the pudding was pronounced done. But all through the night, between rounds of poker, we sang every song that any of us could think of.

Theodore, who had sung in the Yale Glee Club, with his deep, rich, sonorous voice, contributed not a little to the revelry, while one of the English lads, who had served in the British Navy, could himself furnish an endless variety of lively chanties he had learned from the sailors. We had nothing whatever to drink. Nevertheless, at times we were able to drown out with our own din the thunderous Christmas yells and uproar from the Broken Heart Saloon underneath. It was a merrier, happier, time than I had thought ever to know again.

Then, on Christmas Day, after a few hours sleep, as luck would have it Theodore found at the post office a letter which meant more to us than any Christmas gift. It was from a man named Morton, president of a bank in Fargo, North

Dakota. Private banks were still common then in this country, at least in the West. Mr. Morton wanted a young lawyer who would give his whole time to the legal affairs of the Morton Bank. He had written the Yale Law School and they had recommended Theodore. The salary Mr. Morton offered, though I am no longer sure of the amount, seemed at the time quite princely both to Theodore and myself, especially when during the months (*years*, it seems, as I look back on it) we had lived on Whiskey Row Theodore had had but one client, a man whose will he wrote and who paid him five dollars, an amount we promptly invested in a feast—all the good things to eat we could find at the store.

But now we were down to practically our last cent. Fargo, a place of which neither of us knew anything, even by repute, loomed ahead as deliverance. We sold everything save Theodore's law books and what would go in our trunks, and somehow or other scraped enough together to buy tickets to Fargo on the Canadian Pacific Railroad.

Again hope stirred within me. In a different environment Theodore might be different, and at least I would be more than a thousand miles nearer Knoxville, still the center of my own universe.

NOTES

1. On March 26, 1892.
2. Title which Whitman gave to a group of sixteen poems on the body, physical love, and procreation.
3. Walt Whitman, "When Lilacs Last in the Dooryard Bloom'd," section 16, lines 20–22. All quotations of Whitman's verse have been verified in the "Inclusive Edition" of *Leaves of Grass* edited by Emory Holloway "from the text of the edition authorized and editorially supervised by his literary executors, Richard Maurice Bucke, Thomas B. Harned, and Horace L. Traubel." Included in this edition are Variorum Readings, by Oscar Lovell Trigg, PhD, which document changes Whitman made to the text over the years. Walt Whitman, *Leaves of Grass,* Emory Holloway, ed. (Garden City, N.Y.: Doubleday, 1926), 282, t.p., 540–671.
4. Armstrong recounted this experience at Fort Sanders in an interview with Carl Edward Campbell on June 27, 1956, in Abingdon, Virginia. Her reaction, as she describes it here, was also recorded by Campbell. Carl Edward Campbell, "The Knoxville Walt Whitman Fellowship," (master's thesis, University of Tennessee, 1956), 22–23.
5. Whitman, "Out of the Cradle Endlessly Rocking," line 26; Holloway, 209.
6. Whitman, "To a Common Prostitute," line 2; Holloway, 323.
7. Whitman, "Whoever You Are Holding Me Now in Hand," lines 5–7; Holloway, 97.
8. "The Religion of Healthy-Mindedness" is the title of Lectures IV and V of the Gifford Lectures on Natural Religion, which William James delivered at the University of

Edinburgh in 1901–1902. What James said was, "... many persons to-day regard Walt Whitman as the restorer of the eternal natural religion." William James, *The Varieties of Religious Experience: A Study in Human Nature* (London: Longmans, Green, 1902), 78, 85.

9. In 1883, Dr. Richard Maurice Bucke (1837–1902), a Canadian psychiatrist who became close friends with Walt Whitman, published the first Whitman biography, *Walt Whitman* (cited above). A philosopher and mystic, Bucke also wrote *Cosmic Consciousness: A Study in the Evolution of the Human Mind* (1901), which introduced the radical ideas to which Armstrong refers. Additionally, Bucke served as one of Whitman's three literary executors. Artem Lozynsky, ed., *Richard Maurice Bucke, Medical Mystic: Letters of Dr. Bucke to Walt Whitman and His Friends* (Detroit: Wayne State University Press, 1977), 9,10; Harold Jaffe, *Richard Maurice Bucke's Walt Whitman, edited, with an introduction and variant readings* (PhD diss., New York University, 1968), i.
10. Whitman, "Song of Myself," section 48, line 3; Holloway, 73.
11. French writer Ernest Renan (1823–1892). See Part 1, Chapter 8 for Armstrong's discussion of the impact his *La Vie de Jésus* (1863) had on her ideas about religion.
12. According to newspaper reports, a marriage license was issued for "Leonard Waldron (23) and Annie Wetzell (20)" on June 28, 1892. In reality, Annie Wetzell was only nineteen and would not turn twenty until September 20 that year. *Chicago Daily Tribune*, June 29, 1892, 3; *Daily Inter Ocean* (Chicago), June 29, 1892, 7.
13. Comte Donatien Alphonse François de Sade, known as Marquis de Sade (1740–1814). French novelist whose works graphically depicted rituals of sexual perversion and cruelty, and from whose name the terms *sadist* and *sadism* are derived.
14. It seems obvious that Armstrong is referring to *The Gilded Age*, a novel written by Mark Twain in collaboration with Charles Dudley Warner, when she remembers "the knobs of Tennessee." Chapter One begins with a description of "some lawless mountain region" in a district called "The Knobs of East Tennessee" (shortened to "the Knobs of Tennessee" by the end of the chapter). Twain and Warner had applied for dramatic copyright even before the book was published in 1873. When they learned that someone else had dramatized *The Gilded Age* and staged a production in San Francisco in April 1874, Twain invoked copyright and wrote his own play adapted from the novel, calling it *Colonel Sellers*, which was produced beginning in September 1874. It seems entirely possible that some dramatic version of *The Gilded Age* was still being produced in the West during the time of which Armstrong was writing. She could be confused about the title, or someone could have re-titled the play that her husband appeared in. At any rate, there *is* a part for a sheriff in the cast of characters in Mark Twain's play. Mark Twain and Charles Dudley Warner, *The Gilded Age* (New York: Harper & Row, 1873); Thomas Schirer, *Mark Twain and the Theatre* (Nürnberg: Carl, 1984), 41–48; Jerry Thomason, Tom Quirk, introduction to "Col. Sellers: A Drama In Five Acts by Saml L. Clemens," *The Missouri Review*, 18, no. 3, (1995): 111–112, https://muse.jhu.edu/ (viewed February 14, 2019).

15. A North American Indian of the northern Pacific coast (*derogatory*). Origin: Chinook Jargon, from Canadian French *sauvage* 'wild.' Oxford Dictionaries Online, https://en.oxforddictionaries.com/definition/Siwash (viewed February 13, 2019)
16. Short stories by American writer Bret Harte (1836–1902) about a gold-mining camp and frontier life.

Chapter Fifteen

Fargo

It was early in January when we reached Fargo, where the thermometer that day had registered 42° below zero.

We had had, to be sure, a slight foretaste of what was in store when a few hours earlier the train stopped for half an hour or so at Winnipeg, Manitoba, giving us a chance to walk up its main street and limber up a bit after our long train trip.

It was mid-afternoon and on this brief walk in Winnipeg my first sensation was of being blinded by the dazzling light of the sun on the snow. But then the ferocious cold began to strike through my thin coat. Tears froze on my face as they fell. My eyelashes froze. People walking past us were muffled in furs and with great fur caps pulled down over their ears. Those who sped by in sleighs were covered up to their chins with buffalo robes.

How could people live, I wondered, resentfully, to say nothing of appearing healthy and content, in such horrible cold as this? I thought I should freeze to death before we got back to the train.

The trip, however, except for the painful stop in Winnipeg had been pleasant. Traveling through British Columbia, with the magnificent scenery of the Canadian Rockies unrolling before us in all the snowy splendor of mid-winter, I had been transported to another world. I had stored up memories of a glory I could draw upon as long as I lived.

But during the whole journey there were lesser pleasures, too. We were traveling tourist, sitting all day on hard slatted seats that lacked even a vestige of upholstery, though I do not recall that we minded this in the least. Then it was almost like a picnic when with our fellow passengers in the tourist-car we boiled coffee on a big iron stove, provided for this purpose at one end of our coach, or heated other food out of the big lunch-baskets or boxes we all carried with us.

I suppose there must have been a diner on the train, but if so, with our purse as flat as it was, it is a certainty that Theodore and I could not have patronized one. At all events, I do not recall feeling humiliated in traveling, for first time, second class. It was just another adventure, and I was filled with fresh hope, the more so that Theodore had been in an extremely amiable mood since we left Snohomish. For one thing—though perhaps only through force of circumstances—, there had been none of the blows I had come to live in such constant dread of. On the train

I felt safe. And besides, although I was not sure, I believed I was pregnant. If this were true it might—who knew? —work a profound change in Theodore, whose cruelty continued to be as deep a mystery to me as ever. If he drank heavily, I could have understood. But he seldom drank at all, and never to excess. Well, whatever the cause, the very thought that the greatest of all miracles was perhaps about to be wrought within my own body added a new and happy excitement now to my every waking moment.

The hack took us directly from the depot in Fargo to Mrs. Shepherd's, where Theodore's new employer had reserved board for us till we had time to find a house.

It was night when we arrived and as it happened every room in Mrs. Shepherd's old-fashioned rather roomy white frame house was full.

A pretty white-haired woman, a motherly soul, Mrs. Shepherd arranged for us to spend the night next door. She would have a room for us, she said, in a day or so at latest.

That first night in Fargo remains as vivid in my mind as the brief walk in Winnipeg. Mrs. Shepherd's neighbor, a Swede who spoke broken English, put us in the only spare space she had just then; in her attic, where snow had sifted through and lay on the floor in little windrows here and there and we could touch the rafters overhead from our bed.

She gave us many quilts, but the cold, terrible though it was even under the weight of all the covers, was not the worst problem I faced that night. Theodore had developed a severe cold in the course of our journey, one probably aggravated by our walk in Winnipeg when, after the overheated train, he, too, in spite of the heavy Ulster he wore, had been severely chilled. At any rate, now he was burning with fever, and as the night wore on talked deliriously.

Here we were, in a miserable attic-room, in a strange town, in a town where Theodore had not yet even met his employer, and where he was seriously—perhaps dangerously, ill. *If he should die, what would I do?* In my distraction, even the freezing cold became a minor evil, though I remember how I clung close to Theodore's burning body, to get what warmth from it I could.

Here we were, knowing no one, with less than five dollars left, a month to go before Theodore would receive anything from the Morton Bank, and heaven only knew what was ahead!

Almost crazed with anxiety, I think that rarely through my long life have I lived through a night of such horror.

But in the morning Theodore's fever had abated. With the resiliency of youth he was soon up and around. Within a couple of days we were occupying a comfortable room at Mrs. Shepherd's, sitting down at table with agreeable people, largely young men, and to good substantial food, while Mrs. Shepherd was taking me under her wing as if I were a daughter, or granddaughter, returned after a long absence.

First of all, she insisted it would be impossible for me to get along with only my light-weight coat, sufficient for the mild winters around Puget Sound, but never for North Dakota with its lengthy sub-arctic winter still mostly before us! What I must do was wear one of her own two sealskin coats; the one, she said, she had grown a little too stout for, but just right for me, and which would cover me from head to foot.

But all the people we met now were friendly. Some of them came and took me for long sleigh rides; miles and miles with nothing but snow, snow, snow, as far as the eye could reach, and only a small homestead now and then, long distances apart, to break the flat, endless, mercilessly glittering white waste, which kept my eyes going black on me and made it easy to believe stories I was hearing of people who went permanently blind from over-exposure to the glare of the sun on the snow during a Dakota winter.

A newcomer, how could I refuse an invitation to go on a sleigh ride? Yet agonizingly cold as I always was, even in the sealskin coat, a buffalo robe tucked around me, I was only happy when at last we turned back toward town.

Just the same, miserable or not, I was learning things on these sleigh rides: learning of the vast golden wheat fields that would cover this limitless Dakota prairie when summer came; hearing, for the first time, of *No. 1 hard wheat*; that Dakota was its greatest producer in the world, and that it was making fortunes for some men, among them for private bankers, like Mr. Morton, who made loans to the farmers.

Along with the sleigh rides were other attentions. Almost at once, we had invitations from family connections of Mr. Morton and from others of the socially prominent in town. Social gayety in Fargo at the time took the form mainly of dances—the form I loved best, though after one or two, warned by Theodore's dark looks when I mentioned going to the next one, I made excuses and we went to no more.

My disappointment did not last long, however. Other interests were coming to the fore. I knew now for a practical certainty that I was pregnant and surprisingly soon we had found a house.

The house although the last one on the street, beyond which stretched the boundless treeless prairie, was nevertheless in a neighborhood which did not have the raw look one expected in a town no older than Fargo. On it lived old settlers who, as they prospered, had built themselves comfortable substantial homes.

The cottage we were able to rent belonged to people who, with a growing family, had outgrown it and built a larger house next door. But they still had a sentimental attachment to the cottage, their first home; kept it in good condition and left behind in it enough of their old furniture so that, luckily, we had to buy none.

Painted a light gray, a short flight of steps led up to a small square porch in front and another short flight to a similar porch at one side. There were double parlors, with a small bedroom opening off the front parlor and a larger one off the back parlor, where the base-burner stood, and which we used, as the family before us, both as sitting and dining room.

It was a cheery little house, with plenty of sunshine streaming in through the heavy double windows made necessary by Dakota winters, and with always a rosy glow through the little mica panes in the base-burner. After our one room over the Broken Heart Saloon, it seemed all but heaven.

There was a harrowing experience, however, for me to live through before we could start housekeeping in the new surroundings. We had no money, and Theodore was unwilling to ask Mr. Morton for an advance or to write his father, a retired business man in New York, for funds that would tide us over until he received his first month's salary. Instead, the morning we moved into the cottage he told me I should go to the grocery and butcher shops nearest us and ask for credit.

I was dismayed. How could I ever go out and ask strange men in a strange town to trust us till we could pay? Surely this was a matter, if ever there was one, for Theodore to attend to. But I was more terrified of opposing Theodore than of any ordeal he might propose, and just as I can see myself, as if it were someone else, picking my steps across the muddy waste of Whiskey Row on the way to the sole grocery store in Snohomish, so I can still feel my cheeks burning, heart pounding, as I entered a little butcher shop in Fargo that I had never before laid eyes on.

There were no customers in the shop when I entered, for which I was thankful.

"What would you like, young lady?" the ruddy, round-faced butcher asked politely when I found it almost impossible, after one or two starts, to state what I had come for. "What would you like this morning?"

But when at last, in my embarrassment, I summoned courage to explain our situation, the butcher agreed at once to give us the credit I asked for. I went out of the store carrying a small roast of beef and greatly strengthened for my approach to the grocer, who gave me credit, however, with equal promptness and politeness.

That butcher, that grocer, in Fargo, North Dakota, dead and gone so long ago, but how they still glow in my memory!

For a while I felt that my hope of things being different, better, in Fargo were going to be fulfilled. With Theodore extremely busy, absorbed now in legal problems, new to him, connected with private banking, there were fewer "incidents."

Like a combat soldier, though, never in these days in Fargo, as never in Snohomish, did I look far ahead. I lived only from hour to hour, at most from day to day, immersing myself in new housekeeping problems as Theodore in problems confronting him at Morton's Bank.

It was a joy to have a pump and a sink in a real kitchen, instead of carrying every drop of water we used from some distance away and in full sight of a crowd of ribald drunks; a joy to have a real stove now, an iron range.

Aunt Sarah sent me *Fanny* [i.e., Fannie] *Farmer's Cook Book* and I was learning how to cook more than the few dishes I had been able to achieve on the little single-flame oil-stove on Whiskey Row. Soon I was setting out meals on the drop-leaf table in the sitting room that won high praise from Theodore, who seemed proud to bring home with him for midday dinner or supper various young men he found congenial among our new acquaintances.

We would be lively and jolly on these occasions, Theodore at his best, and as amused as I, seemingly, in recalling it afterwards, when one of the young men, not knowing I was pregnant, insisted on engaging me for his partner when tennis started, after the snow disappeared.

Exactly this way Theodore had been when our young English friends were with us in Snohomish, invariably gay and agreeable, although at times like this I marveled more than ever that he could have two such utterly different sides to his nature, and the one hidden from all but me—*what it was!* In the midst, in fact, of our merriment when others were present, in Fargo now, as in Snohomish, there would flash through me, frighteningly, the memory of that night Don brought me home from the miners' dance, Theodore laughing and joking with us both—and then the sequel.

It was not till February we knew what a blizzard really was. It began some time during the morning, appearing at first an ordinary snow-storm, but with the wind suddenly gaining hurricane force, the blinding snow whirling more and more furiously. By noon all I could see outside was a dense curtain of snow against the heavy outer storm-windows, impenetrable, yet its flakes perceptibly in mad motion and from moment to moment shifting direction. Inside, there was an eerie, awesome light, and alone in the house I was numb with fright.

There were still no telephones then, no one to turn to, and no one on earth, surely, could find his way through this inferno of snow that had been raging for hours.

Dinner time came and went. *Would this blizzard ever end?* Cattle—people, lost their lives, I knew, in blizzards—buried under mountains of snow.

At last I believed I heard muffled sounds from the side-porch and when I opened the door, afraid to do so, yet afraid not to, along with a violent blast of snow Theodore plunged across the threshold, too exhausted longer to stand, even speak, his face swollen beyond recognition, a deep purplish red, and a tell-tale dead-white patch on either cheek.

We had not been long in Dakota, but long enough to know what to do, and kneeling, I scooped up snow that had blown in and lay on the carpet and packed it against his frozen cheeks.

Theodore had been hours fighting the blizzard foot by foot, feeling for fences, hitching-posts—any guide; had lost his way again and again; was utterly spent from his long and terrible struggle against the storm, and I felt deep concern and pity for him.

Strangely, though I never loved Theodore, I never hated him, and it was this pity which welled up in me from time to time that complicated still further the almost hopelessly confused feeling I had had about him from the beginning.

It was pity, far more intense, I was to feel for him shortly again, though from a quite different cause. It was on Sunday, and late in the afternoon. All day Theodore had been working on a bill favorable to the Morton interests which Mr. Morton had asked him to prepare. The time was short now. The bill must be presented within the next day or so to the State legislature, then in session.

I could tell that Theodore was worried. He had only eaten a bite or so of dinner and kept consulting one or another of his law books, which he kept at home, on some book-shelves in the front parlor.

When it was time to light the lamps he was still bent over the papers before him, stopping occasionally to rest his head on his clenched hand and plainly lost in thought.

At length I went to the kitchen to build up the fire there and put the tea-kettle on. But as I came back into the sitting room to set the table for supper I saw Theodore with his head buried in his hands and heard sobs that he was trying to stifle.

"Oh, Theodore, what *is* it?" Putting down the dishes I was carrying, I ran to him.

But he kept on sobbing, his whole strong young-man's body convulsed. It was a good while before he lifted his head, and I shall never be able to blot from my mind the image of his face at this instant, with its dominant nose, noble brow, sensuous mouth, weak chin, and tears streaming down it, as he explained brokenly that he had had no training or experience, either in law school or since, that fitted him to prepare the bill he was expected to, and he was sure the one he had written would not fill the requirements.

I had seen Theodore agitated before, but now all his self-confidence, overweening pride, his arrogance, were gone. He was just a humbled human being, facing defeat, possibly disgrace.

He was no longer the masterly man of whom I lived in deadly dread. He was a little boy, suffering more than he could bear. And seeing him thus, I could forgive, if not understand, his brutality. My heart softened toward him, and in a time to come, with all that was to happen, while I could not explain to others what was beyond my own comprehension, yet I never entirely lost this strain of tenderness in my feeling for him.

Now, in February, I was beginning to feel wretched in the early morning with various ills common to pregnancy. It seemed all but impossible to get out of bed when it was time to go to the kitchen, and shaking with cold, build the fire there and start breakfast.

Everything that could freeze would be frozen in the icy kitchen. My roughened, raw-looking, skinned hands were constantly painful, my knuckles perpetually broken and bleeding, from taking out ashes, handling coal, breaking ice on the rain-water barrel in a corner. Never, however, had Theodore offered to help me. He would lie in bed till breakfast was ready.

But there came a morning when I felt much worse than usual. This time I *could* not get up, I thought, and much as I feared to, I *must* ask Theodore if he would not build the kitchen fire.

Theodore refused to answer. Then, in desperation, I begged him to do so, just this once, and his answer, without a word, was to thrust me out of bed so violently that it was torture finally to lift myself from the floor.

That morning something changed in me. I think it was even as the back of my head struck the floor from the force of his blows, in that dazed moment, that I had a clear vision of unending cruelty stretching ahead of me. If Theodore could act this way when I was pregnant, it would be no better when the baby came. There was only one escape.

Among Theodore's law books in the front parlor was one with the title *Criminal Jurisprudence,* and some time during that morning I read about poisons, and decided on the one I would take. Bruised and aching, I could not go to the drug-store at once, but there were a few other preparations, anyway, that I wished to make.

Although I had been an avid reader from almost as soon as I could read at all, never since my marriage had I been able to read a book. As soon as I opened one, my awful situation opened before me. I was unable to follow even the simplest narrative, to say nothing of concentrating on more serious reading. From the time of Theodore's first fiendish attack, I had found that my only salvation—if there was one—was to work, work, work, with my hands, to the limit of bodily endurance; then would come a measure of relief in rest or sleep. But now I turned to one of the few books, outside of Theodore's law books, that we possessed, a work I had not touched, unless to dust, since those fateful spring evenings on Fort Sanders—so long, long ago they seemed—when Theodore had introduced me to it, Whitman's *Leaves of Grass.*

But it was not Whitman, the revolutionist, the social radical, the "dangerous" writer, so fascinating to me then, that I sought now. Not Whitman, the great humanitarian, nor yet the sensuous Whitman whose magnificently imaginative love poems had done their worst for me. The Whitman I sought now was the Whitman who had written "Whispers of Heavenly Death."[1]

Sitting beside the base-burner, the little house half buried in snow, wrapped in silence, I read:

. . . I will show that nothing can happen more beautiful than death,[2]
And to die is different from what anyone supposed, and luckier.[3]

I read "To One Shortly to Die," with its final soaring line:

I do not commiserate, I congratulate you.[4]

And as I read, I felt soothed and happy. Healing came.

Papa and Mama would not know why I had killed myself—that it was because I could no longer endure the horror of my existence. But when I was dead, they would forgive all the suffering I had caused them.

For the next day or so I lived in a sort of trance, buoyed up, possessed of what seemed superhuman strength. Now, at last, I knew what I should do . . . .

When I asked the druggist for the poison, he raised no objections. Nothing was easier in those days than to secure from almost any pharmacist the deadliest of poisons.

It was a terribly cold morning, even for Fargo. I remember as I left the drugstore looking at the thermometer outside—40° below, almost as low as the day we arrived there.

But the cold—nothing—could deter me now, and my feet in their cumbersome arctics fairly flew.

On the way home I stopped at a little shop, scarcely more than a hole in the wall, where we often bought a loaf of homemade Boston Brown Bread and a pot of steaming Boston Baked Beans to carry with us. Theodore was especially fond of them for Saturday night supper. I bought some now. I would put them in the warmer on the range, so he should not be left without any cooked food in the house.

Breathless when I reached there, I started further preparations at once. I wanted everything completed before Theodore returned for dinner.

I am fully aware, I believe, of the tricks memory plays, but I am as sure as I ever was of anything in my life that I did not know a moment of faltering or fear as I placed on Theodore's pillow, beside mine, the volume of Whitman, open to pages on which I had marked:

> Come lovely and soothing death,
> . . . .
> . . . the soul turning to thee, O vast and well-veil'd death,
> . . . the body, gratefully snuggling [*sic*] close to thee.[5]

I undressed, put on my night-gown; with a pervasive sense of comfort, deep relief, I poured out some of the colorless liquid that was to end my suffering, and lay down on the side of the bed on which I always slept.

* * *

When I began to regain consciousness from what seemed a sleep so sound I still could not struggle out of it, everything in the hushed room seemed dark and hazy. I was bewildered and at first conscious only of bodily sensations. I was cold all over and numb. My tongue was stiff. I could not move it. Then slowly I realized there were fingers on my pulse, firm masculine fingers. Someone was lifting my eye-lids, peering into my half-seeing eyes. A hand was moving over my body, a head pressed against my abdomen . . . .

Now things grew a trifle less dreamy. There was a man sitting beside me, a man standing behind him, and farther away another man, pacing the floor. All at once it became clear that the man in the chair at my side was Dr. Darrow, a "family doctor" I had consulted when I first was convinced I was pregnant. The man standing, looking down at me, younger and sandy-haired, I recognized as a Dr. Campbell, and the man walking back and forth between the bed and the dimly discerned front window—Theodore.

With this I knew all—that the doctors were trying to save my life, and with the realization came the blackest feeling I had ever known—utter despair.

But the doctors kept on working. They were talking to me in low and kindly but firm tones, and when at last I could open my stiff lips to protest passionately, "I don't *want* to live!" I heard Dr. Darrow, his fingers still on my pulse, though his voice coming as from a distance, "Oh, yes, my dear child, you *do*, and you must cooperate, for we want to save, too, that other little life that is going to bring you great happiness!"

Then they insisted on using a stomach pump, in doing all sorts of repulsive and agonizing things; asking me to help them do the last thing in the world I wanted done—help me survive.

It was some days before I was able to be out of bed. I never knew whether the doctors, or anyone else, suspected it was Theodore who had driven me to this desperate attempt to take my own life. The doctors perhaps, either consciously or unconsciously, had made it easier for Theodore by suggesting that morbid conduct was not unusual during pregnancy; I don't know. I only know that after the doctors left Theodore, weeping, knelt by the bed, and smothering me in caresses, poured forth his love in more flaming words than ever before, though he expressed no remorse, no responsibility for my act, one he never referred to afterwards. It was as if it had not been.

I only know that from this day forward friends seem to rise up all around me. Mrs. Osgood, next door, who owned the cottage we lived in, came and nursed me. She saw to it that Theodore had all his meals until I was able to prepare them once more. Mrs. Campbell, the young doctor's wife whom I had only known casually before and who was pregnant herself, her first baby due shortly, came every day, wading through the snow, however deep; bringing one day a chocolate cake she had made especially for me, and useful things of all sorts, including a pattern for baby slips, which she thought I might like to get started on. This radiant creature, a handsome brunette, several years older than I, was a graduate of Wellesley, I learned now. We soon found we had many interests in common, and while I never confided to her the nature of my married life, yet she became a cherished friend.

But for all these manifestations of neighborly friendliness, I continued to be deeply depressed. I had muffed my chance of delivering myself from a future in which I no longer had any faith. I had taken an overdose of poison—it was the overdose that had foiled my attempt. When, where, and by what means, could I make another? I feared I did not have the courage to use a revolver, even if I knew where to obtain one. As for the unborn child inside me, it seemed less than ever a solution, if even a reality. However cheerful I might seem to others, alone I knew only black hours, terrible inner turmoil.

Then one day, it must have been in March, I sat down beside the base-burner to rest a little before going on with the morning housework. It was snowing, had been snowing steadily for an hour or so. Suddenly I felt something moving vigorously within me—like a small foot, or maybe hand, pushing against the outer wall of my body, and in that instant the baby inside me became *mine—my child* that never again could I risk killing! From that hour, I felt I could face anything. Henceforth my one thought was to preserve from harm this little being within me.

As it proved, although I was ever on the alert not to provoke, in any way I could foresee, fresh brutality on Theodore's part, I knew some weeks of relative peace of mind.

I wrote Aunt Sarah. She responded warmly, assuring me she would come to Fargo to be with me when the baby was born; so that at once, although the event was still months ahead, I began to get the small bedroom off the front parlor ready for Aunt Sarah's coming.

But Aunt Sarah had written also to my parents, telling them I was expecting a baby in September, and promptly came letters from them with no reproaches, but overflowing with affection, and soon beautiful linens from Mama's still large store of such things, and shortly exquisite little baby dresses she had made for me.

Once more it became a rich and satisfying experience merely to be alive, on any terms. Joyous by nature, my vehement love of life reasserted itself and one morning in April when I heard the jubilant notes of a whole flock of robins that had arrived overnight and were hopping around in our small front yard, nothing I would ever hear again, not even Brahms' great First C Minor Concerto, would sound so sweet, so confident and triumphant, as this chorus of robins announcing that the awful winter was past—Spring had come.

There was tragedy in life—perhaps inseparable from it—but what glory too!

By the first of June patches of snow could still be seen on narrow sunless spaces between buildings on the main street in Fargo. There had been days and days when the wind blew ferociously, unceasingly, all day long. There was bottomless mud everywhere. But for all these unpleasant conditions, spring came fast, once it started.

People now were all making gardens in their back yards. To my surprise, Theodore suggested we have a garden, too. To my greater surprise, he spaded up himself a strip on either side of the narrow board walk that led from our back door to the outhouses beyond, and together we sowed seeds; lettuce and radishes, beets and carrots and peas. Neither of us knew a thing about gardening, but we had fun watching the seeds come up and grow like magic, although unaware that we should have mixed ashes with the too fertile black Dakota soil, so that the radishes sprang up into luxuriant little trees, with nothing underneath, and everything else in our garden likewise went to tops.

But my greatest and most joyous surprise came when Papa wrote to Theodore saying that, with Knoxville growing as it was, he believed there was as good a chance for a young lawyer there as anywhere else; that if he chose to consider such a thing he could use the office Papa still maintained opposite the Custom House in Knoxville, though seldom used himself; and that nothing would give him and my mother more pleasure than to have us near.

I had not supposed that Theodore, under any circumstances, would ever consider going back to Knoxville, but from the moment he read Papa's letter he spoke of it as a possibility.

Then one of the most unexpected of happenings forced a decision from him.

Afterwards a rumor circulated that [the] owners of a "racket store" in Fargo (forerunner of the later five-and-ten cent stores), losing money, had set fire to their own property in order to profit by the insurance on it. But whatever the source of the fire, along with the "racket store" most of Fargo was burned to the ground, every building on the main street gutted or completely destroyed, and much of the residential part of the town wiped out. Only the section where we lived escaped, as the wind was not blowing in that direction.

It was mid-morning when prolonged and insistent whistles and bells made me first aware of what was happening. Then people began streaking by on foot out toward the open prairie, and carrying with them the few possessions they had been able to snatch from their burning homes. Two-horse wagons dashed by, loaded with household furnishings, and driven furiously by women standing up in the wagon-box—all the men were fighting fire—and headed also for the limitless prairie beyond us.

Unable to stay indoors, not knowing what to do, and in no immediate danger myself, though my heart pounding, I remained in our front yard, where I could at least exchange a few words over the fence with some of those who were fleeing wildly from the burning town. One old woman screamed at me: "You're in the family way—get in the house for Lord's sake! Do you want a birth-mark on your child's face? Don't look at the fire!"

But how could I help looking at the fire, this compelling, if horrifying, spectacle of a town—a nice, neatly-laid-out little prairie town—being destroyed, the whole sky above it a deep, sinister, infernal red?

It was dusk when Theodore returned from hours of helping salvage whatever could be salvaged from the burning buildings on Main Street. He was black as a chimney-sweep from head to foot, his clothes singed in places and ruined, his face ashy where you could see the skin between streaks of soot and grime.

"Well, the Morton Bank's gone too," he said, as he sank wearily into the nearest chair. "Now it's Knoxville."

NOTES

1. A Whitman poem (1868) and also a group title first used by Whitman in 1871. Holloway, 369, 654.
2. Whitman, "Starting from Paumanok," Section 12, line 14; Holloway, 19.
3. Whitman, "Song of Myself," Section 6, line 32; Holloway, 30.
4. Whitman, "To One Shortly to Die," line 15; Holloway, 376.
5. Whitman, "When Lilacs Last in the Dooryard Bloom'd," Section 14, lines 28, 50–51; Holloway, 280. Whitman's poem reads "nestling" instead of "snuggling" in line 51.

Chapter Sixteen
Highland Avenue Again

When late in August once more I saw before me the brown frame house I had first seen two years ago on coming home from college, it had none of the look it had worn then, at first glance, in my snobbish young eyes.

In the two years since, I had lived through a great deal. Now even the moon vines, which still shielded the small front porch from view, and which I had considered hopelessly commonplace—every aspect of the house looked lovely to me and dear beyond words.

Inside, I no longer found the golden-oak woodwork garish, the fussy oak over-mantel in the parlor offensive. Mama and Papa had lived here long enough to create the atmosphere of comfort, refinement, of quiet elegance, they always created around them; and with books everywhere, the etchings and engravings on the wall I had known from childhood, there was something in the house, despite its unpretentiousness, more congenial to my own spirit than I had realized before.

Papa had not altered much. His face, no longer youthful and with its lines of suffering, tore at my heart. I would never get used to it, but he was able to walk now with the aid of only one cane. Though Mama's beautiful clean-cut face was sad in repose, she was invariably cheerful, outwardly at least, and for all her luxury-loving nature and long years in the past of easy and extravagant living, she still, in their changed circumstances, never uttered a word of complaint.

Together, in fact, they had made for themselves, within present limitations, a new and by no means dull life. Papa was the moving spirit in a small club of thoughtful men and women who met weekly in their parlor to discuss books, ideas, and world affairs. If they never went out, friends flocked to them; and the more doubtless when they had borne with dignity their tragic disappointment in my marrying as I had.

It was May who surprised me most. Her pretty face, in its frame of soft, wavy, light-brown hair, retained its touch of shyness, but she no longer in any sense was "little May." This fall, the first year women had been admitted to "the Hill," she would enter the University.

One evening during the past winter, in the time when my name was not mentioned in the house, May, at the piano, had started playing Chopin's Moonlight Sonata, which I had often played, when suddenly she burst into tears and fled from the parlor. Mama told me of this in that first momentous letter from her which broke the long silence between us. And now May, as Papa and Mama, welcomed me home with as comforting warmth as any errant member of a family could ever know.

My old girl friends came to see me at once, and every fresh proof that I had not lost my place among them filled me with joy. Then it was sheer ecstasy just to be back again in Knoxville, with its familiar sights, sounds, smells. Even to be wakened in the morning by the aged Negro cook next door beating biscuits for breakfast, her low wailing voice in r[h]ythmic accompaniment to the pounding of her rolling-pin as she sang one of those mournful songs that came out of slave times—to look out on the mule-drawn street-car moving, in the same leisurely fashion as of old, up and down Highland Avenue and past our door—even these things added to my sense of security.

I was back now where nothing could harm me, where Theodore would not *dare*, I said to myself over and over, attempt any brutality, as he had recently, during our weeks in Chicago.

This was the summer of the World's Columbian Exposition in Chicago,[1] four hundredth anniversary of the discovery of America, and I was delighted when Theodore proposed that on our way to Knoxville we stop in Chicago with his sister Lottie, the one we had stayed with briefly after our marriage, and who lived now on the South Side of Chicago and very accessible to the Fair Grounds.

I had a dress made at Marshall Field's, the first good dress I had had in a long time, a blue suit with a jacket that somewhat concealed my now bulging figure and in which I could feel comfortable when we met old Yale friends of Theodore as well as some of my own college friends visiting the Fair. We went there with them, had jolly times. A good deal of my old vivacity returned. I was not afraid, for the time, to be myself. Things looked so hopeful now, and there was the added interest and excitement of the Fair itself, with its gleaming white classic buildings on the Lake front, like some dream of ancient Greece. I spent happy hours, with a group of our friends or alone with Theodore, wandering among its collections of great paintings, or gazing at the exhibits, many of them marvels of beauty, especially those of Modern Germany, greatest revelation of the Fair to most of its visitors.

I can not remember what led to the act which broke the spell of these few wondrous weeks. As always before, there was no quarreling, no wounding words had preceded it. There was only the act, without warning, like a freak flash of lightning out of season.

What comes back to me dreamily is lying in bed afterwards in the guest-room at Lottie's. The doctor had been there. What seemed labor pains had started almost immediately after Theodore struck me. In a sudden instinctive move to protect my body, I had fallen. The doctor, after examining not only my body but bruised face, and asking gravely a few pointed questions—which I evaded answering—, had warned I must lie in bed, be extremely quiet, for several days.

I remember that aghast as I was at Theodore's renewed savagery—the act of a madman, when I was so near my hour, and in his sister's home!—yet not for an instant did I think of trying again to put an end to myself. I must save the baby at any cost—do what I could to avoid its coming prematurely.

There remains also, as a glowing piece of fire among the embers of my long past, the figure of Lottie, a strikingly handsome if rather tragic-looking woman in heavy widow's mourning, her long black silk and crepe skirts rustling, crackling faintly, as she stole into the room where I lay, after the doctor left and Theodore had gone out on some real or pretended errand.

It was night, the gas in the room turned low. Lottie knelt by the bed and took my hand in hers, wetting it with her tears.

She did not need to be told. She knew from the first what had occurred.

"And to think, Annie," she sobbed, "he was the dearest little boy!"

Lottie sat on the bed beside me now, holding my hand.

"I've feared," Lottie said, "ever since he grew up, something like this! He's so like his father—my step-father, you know—in his looks, his disposition, and his father treated my mother the same way. That's why she lives in the West, and he in New York. Then I suppose," she went on, still crying, "we all spoiled him. You see we were so much older, my sister and I, and he was an only son—a child really of his parents' old age—, a darling, and so smart, but very wilful, [*sic*] and always allowed to have his own way.[2]

Perhaps now, it struck me, though far from reassuringly so far as the future was concerned, I had at last a clue, in his inheritance and overindulged childhood, to Theodore's strange Satanic behavior.

Lottie left me a moment and came back with a photograph of Theodore as a child. She turned up the gas so I could see it better—the face of a little boy about ten or eleven, sweet, thoughtful, winsome, a trifle wistful.

I asked Lottie to let me have the photograph and she gave it to me. "Psychology" was not the household word then it is to-day. But it crossed my mind that maybe in time I could figure out what, as he grew up, turned this little boy with his sensitive, intelligent, appealing face into the man, possessed of a devil, I knew in private.

Anyway, more than ever my only hope lay now in getting back to Knoxville. Theodore left for New York to borrow funds, if possible, from his father, for the start in Knoxville, but it was arranged I should travel south with a woman, a good friend of my parents, a neighbor in West End, who was visiting the Fair.

At two in the morning the baby was born in the good-sized front bedroom upstairs which my parents had turned over to Theodore and me, moving themselves into a smaller bedroom—born in their massive ornate walnut bed with its burl panels, its carved daffodils.

All that September night,[3] from early evening, I had struggled, with Theodore somewhere downstairs; Papa outside, in the dark, crippling back and forth, back and forth, in the back yard, though my screams reaching him even there.

All night long Mama, with drawn face, came and went in the room where I was suffering tortures I thought would never end.

A tall, fat, unprepossessing old Negress in a blowzy white cap, the "monthly nurse" (as we called the nurses then who were engaged in advance for such events) gave a little flaccid assistance now and then to Dr. Hood, trying to shorten my labor.

I had wanted Dr. Bayless, younger, more modern, than other outstanding doctors in Knoxville. Theodore, however, for reasons of his own, had insisted I have old Dr. Hood, who lived up the street, in the next block, one of my father's physicians who could be depended upon to come at any hour of the night or day, and for whom, as a matter of fact, we all felt esteem and affection.[4]

But whoever the doctor, I was far from brave, I must confess; not like women I'd heard of, held up as an example (Mama among them!) who had borne all their children without an anesthetic and with scarcely a sound escaping them.

In my case, I felt no shame in extracting beforehand a rather reluctant promise from Dr. Hood that when I asked for it he would let me have chloroform, and true to his promise, when my pains reached a point more horrible, I thought, than any human being could endure and survive, he took a small bottle out of his shabby old doctor's bag and was bringing it to the bed for me to sniff when all at once I changed my mind. I was frightened now at the thought of losing consciousness.

"No, no, Doctor!" I waved him away. "But oh, Mama, how could you love any of us if you had to suffer like this?"

"There, there!" the doctor soothed me as my pains, nearing the final convulsions, grew more and more agonizing. "There, there! Just a few minutes now and you'll have a fine baby!"

"But I don't *want* it!" I cried out franticly [*sic*]. "I *hate* it! Don't *show* it to me when it's born!"

And then, after some terrible throes, when it seemed as though forces of unearthly power and cruelty outside myself were tearing my body limb from limb, there came an instant of relief and in the same instant the lusty cry of a new-born infant rose in the room—a more glorious sound than I had ever conceived of, or would know again. It was as if the very gates of heaven had swung wide open in the midnight sky above that brown frame house on Highland Avenue, and in this celestial radiance all the angels—those angels I didn't believe in—were singing in chorus, rejoicing with me that I had borne a child, a son.

With sudden strength I sat straight up in bed.

"Oh, give it to me!" I cried, beside myself with joy. "It's *my* baby! Let me see it!"

The whole world was changed now, but my head fell forward. I had fainted.

The fat old nurse dozed in an arm-chair by the side window. Everyone else had gone to bed. It was wonderfully still in the house. Weary but wide awake, I kept opening up a baby's blanket wrapped around the small bundle beside me in the big bed, gazing at the rosy, slightly swollen, little face inside. I wished that even the old Negro nurse, asleep though she was, was out of the room. I wanted to be all alone with this treasure. I thrust my finger into his little pink curled-up hand and he gripped it hard with his tiny fingers. Why, only a few hours old, this was a miracle, and it was the happiest night, I may say truthfully, in my whole life!

Theodore seemed very happy over the baby too. He had bounded up the stairs, like any other young father, when he heard its first cry, and he was as impressed as I when early that morning he thrust his own finger into its tiny fist and the little fingers clung to his.

Theodore had barely reached Knoxville before the baby was born, only a day or so before. His father had sent with him the christening robe, a long elaborate dress adorned with countless puffs, fine tucks, rows upon rows of narrow "real" lace insertions.

My pleasure in the christening robe had been a little dampened, though, by things Theodore told me about his days in New York. Apparently they had not been spent entirely with his father. He had had a gay time, and with a touch of glee in his deep voice, a gleam in his eye, he hinted broadly that his relations with the chorus girls he had seen and taken around were not of any innocent nature.

I recall clearly, however, that this did not arouse jealousy in me. I saw it with the eyes of my mind, not of my heart or senses. What I felt was resentment. Whatever follies he might have committed in New York, how could he be so coarse-minded as to reveal them to me at this time? Was it just another form of cruelty—as on the night when he spat in my face?

But I put away thoughts of this kind so far as I could. The baby was here now, and with it lying beside me in the big walnut bed, I spent some blissful days.

It was a week after the baby was born that the nurse went home for the first time. She was not the nurse Mama had tried to get, considered the best of her class in Knoxville, but already engaged for the time specified. This one was slatternly, lazy, and unlike most Negroes, old or young, none too good-natured, but she had performed certain services and her first week's pay was due.

On this Sunday afternoon friends had taken my parents on one of those long drives in the country they loved so well, but Theodore would be in the house, and May, should the baby or I need attention.

It was customary then to keep a "monthly nurse" at least two weeks. That morning she had reminded me her pay was due and that she needed it, which I didn't doubt, for like most colored women of her age she had a large family of children at home in "Niggertown" which she had to support in some fashion or other.

After the nurse had spoken to me, I asked Theodore, when she was not in the room, to pay her, but he put me off and when I urged him, I saw the blood rise in his cheeks. I had known before that Theodore was not inclined to pay bills promptly, even when he had the money for them. But in the afternoon, when the nurse left in a sullen mood, her heavy lips stuck out, I felt I had no choice but again to try to persuade Theodore to pay her. Otherwise, Papa would have to.

I was sitting up, bolstered by pillows, as I talked to Theodore in a low tone, the baby asleep, and Theodore standing beside the bed. He said he was going up town to get some cigars.

In my anxiety, I talked, if not vehemently, very earnestly. I may have been crying, I'm not sure. But suddenly Theodore struck me full in the face, then hastened downstairs and out of the front gate.

I must have cried out when he struck me, for hardly had he disappeared than May rushed into the room and with one horrified look in my direction poured water into the bowl on the washstand, and her own young face blanched, wiped the blood tenderly, with trembling hands, off mine.

My parents knew now what I had tried to conceal from them—forever, I had hoped.

The weeks that followed, where they are not completely blotted out of my mind, are blurred almost beyond my power of bringing them back. But through the thick curtain that seems to have been wrapped around me, protectively, at this time, I became aware of a few facts; not only had Theodore not slept in the house that night, he had not entered it since, although Papa had had a leather couch and armchair moved into his office, so that Theodore could sleep there if he chose to, as well as continue to use it for his office. Where Theodore took his meals during this period, and how much knowledge there was outside the family of what had happened, I never knew.

I was in a dazed state, both as to the present and future. Mama—I'm clear about that—did not discuss the situation with me then, or ever. And strangely, though Papa must have had talks with me, I can not visualize us talking together in any room in the house, or remember anything we said. The only thing I am positive about is that although I admitted that Theodore's demonic attack on me while I was still in bed was not the first, I did not disclose any particulars of previous attacks. After all, Theodore was my husband. I thought of marriage as a permanent institution. My only attempt to escape from it, through death, had been unsuccessful. Divorce, as a means of escape, was the last thing that would have entered my head. I had never known a divorced person, never known *of* one in Knoxville, and only seen one, long ago, in my childhood, driving in a phaeton along the beach at Long Branch, New Jersey; a pretty, fashionably-dressed, though rather sad-looking young woman, a child in her lap, and sitting beside her important-looking father. Pointed out to me by an older child as "divorced," I thought of her principally as a curiosity, as someone set apart, like nuns in their black robes and great caps, from other people.

No, it was not divorce I gave any thought to. Whatever had happened, Theodore continued to be my husband. A certain sense of loyalty, pride perhaps, made me want others, even my family, not to think worse of him than they must.

But if I did not think of divorce, Papa did. As I would learn later, he had consulted lawyers immediately after the incident that had opened my parents' eyes and appalled them as nothing before in their lives.

None of my girl friends, who had rushed to see me as soon as they knew I was home, came now. In virtual seclusion, I devoted all my attention to the baby. Weighing him on the scales in the kitchen, he showed little or no gain, and his face no longer was rosy. Perhaps because of worry, I had been unable to go on nursing him, but I went on preparing dairy or canned milk for him after one formula or another as the doctor prescribed, although while he seldom cried, he still did not grow.

One night I brought him downstairs when he whimpered, heated his bottle in the kitchen and carried him into what formerly had been the dining room but now converted into a sitting room.

It was very late and was raining. Everyone else in the house was in bed. I sat down with the baby across my knees in front of the coal fire in the grate, still glowing. I felt extremely discouraged about the baby's condition, more downcast than ever before. What would I do if this baby—the one thing I clung to more tenaciously than life itself—if *he* should die? My tears fell on his face, and feeling them, he looked up directly into my eyes, a little smile curling around his lips. The smile cut my heart. I bent over, showering kisses on his downy head, on his pitifully wizened little face, beginning to look like an old man's. But as I did so, the stillness in the room, save for the faint crackling of the coal fire, was broken by a light tap on the window near me.

I looked out and saw Theodore's face, red and wet, peering through the rain-splattered window. He tapped lightly again and motioned to me to raise the window. I felt the slight physical repugnance I always felt on seeing him again after a lapse of even a few days, but simultaneously I felt sorry for him, standing there in the dark, rain-drenched, and looking in at us. I realized instantly that he still had a stronghold on me. But I was afraid, actually terrified, lest he be discovered there. I shook my head and motioned him to go.

"Go away! Go away!" I said, making the words with my lips, without sound.

It was the only time during those weeks I saw Theodore, but from then on he managed to get notes to me. He would send them by Bonnie, who still worked for Mama off and on and who would pass them to me secretly. In them, Theodore begged me to come back to him. I was his wife, he wrote, and would never be anything else. These notes touched me.

Theodore was persistent, and late in November, I think it was, he had a talk with Papa. He had rented a little house out near Bell Avenue. It was ready now for his wife and child, whom he did not propose, he made it plain, to give up without a fight.

I can not recall a single thing about my rejoining him. Apparently I played no part in the proceedings. I haven't even the most shadowy recollection of how it was all arranged, though as I think of it now I am acutely aware, if I was not at the time, of the anguish Papa and Mama must have suffered when they saw a little girl, as they no doubt still thought of me, and a baby grown as dear to them as their own had been—saw these two hapless young beings leave the safe refuge of their home, to be at the mercy now of a man in whom they had lost the last shred of what small faith they had ever had in him. What sleepless nights they must have known, thinking of me so far away—farther away it must have seemed, with their new knowledge, than Fargo or Snohomish—, almost at the end of the Bell Avenue street-car line, on the outskirts of town, beyond even the old part of town known as East Knoxville.

NOTES

1. The Chicago World's Fair of 1893.
2. Leonard Waldron's parents, Leonard A. Waldron and Cordelia Clark (née Griffith), were married May 17, 1868, in Muskegon, Michigan. Their son, Leonard Truman Waldron, was born March 24, 1869, and baptized August 14, 1869, at St. Paul's Episcopal Church in Muskegon. His mother's two daughters by her previous marriage to Horace J. Clark were Estelle (or Estella), born ca. 1858, and Lottie (or Lotta), born ca. 1861. Muskegon County (Muskegon, Michigan) Genealogical Society Databases, http://genealogymuskegon.licentia.biz/Databases/databases.htm (viewed April 30, 2019); U.S. Census, 1870, 1860.
3. Her baby was born September 8, 1893.
4. Dr. Samuel P. Hood, born in 1834 at Newport in Cocke County, Tennessee, studied medicine in Knoxville under Dr. Beriah Frazier and also attended Nashville Medical College but did not graduate. After serving as a surgeon with the Tennessee Confederate Cavalry during the Civil War, Dr. Hood practiced medicine in Jefferson County, Tennessee, until 1885, at which time he moved his practice to Knoxville. Dr. Herman G. Bayless, a Kentucky native born in 1854, was a graduate of Ohio Medical College, Cincinnati, Ohio. He practiced medicine, beginning in 1878, in Ohio, Kentucky, and abroad before locating in Knoxville in 1886. Rule, 508–09, 515.

Chapter Seventeen

A Little House Near Bell Avenue

The little white frame house had nothing to distinguish it from thousands like it you could find then in any part of the United States. There was not the slightest touch of the picturesque about it, nor did it have the substantial appearance of the cottage we had lived in in Fargo. There were five smallish rooms, a small porch back and front, a whitewashed picket fence. I remember, on first sight of it, no trees, shrubs—surrounding greenery of any sort, although there was a weather-beaten dilapidated cow-shed in the rear and beside it a hen-house.

Distinctly a cheap, poor-folks sort of house, the rutted red-clay road leading to it from the street-car line[1] (about the distance of an average city block) was hardly more than a lane; there were no houses for a considerable stretch beyond us and we faced fields, sloping downward, that were used for pasture.

The little house was on high ground and commanded a view below, in the distance, of Knoxville and its spires. However, not only was it isolated but, counting out Whiskey Row, never before had I lived in so undesirable a locality. It was neither town nor country and the very name "Bell Avenue," since I first knew it, had stood for all that was rundown and disreputable.[2]

There was, however, one redeeming feature in the location. Oddly enough, Papa, before the accident which crippled him for life, had been one of a group of men who believed that this high-lying section on the border of town could be developed into a desirable residential district. Papa had largely financed the venture, one which bore his name.[3] Streets were laid out, lots staked off, at least on paper, and to encourage builders of the type they sought, the investors had built, on what might be called the "corner" where we got off the street-car on the way to our own little place, a pretentious brick and frame residence of a style fashionable in the era.

By the time I joined Theodore in this remote district, the project, which still bore Papa's name, and in which undoubtedly he had sunk a good deal of money, had been recognized as a failure. No one else had been tempted to build a fine house in the new "Addition," though the handsome house already built was now occupied by another investor, Hugh Lawson McClung, a lawyer of prominence, inherited wealth, of unimpeachable social standing, and who had lately married my close friend and one-time school-mate, Ella, half his age, and regarded one of the beauties of the day in Knoxville.[4]

Living, Theodore and I and the baby, in our humble little home on the outskirts of town, there was a certain reassurance, I suppose, in the thought that the McClungs were near. It made this remote region at least respectable.

But, looking back, I don't think this was much of a consideration in my mind at the time. Strange as it seems, even to me, reflecting on it, I was genuinely happy to be in a little house of our own once more. I could not get away from the fact that I was married to Theodore, and what would I do if we were to separate permanently? More than ever, I realized I could not go back to Papa, broken as he was, for him to support. Then, just as I had never known a woman who had been divorced, so I had never known, personally, a girl—a white girl—who earned her own living, and in the farthest reaches of my imagination had never pictured doing so myself.

Yes, if it were a possible thing, I must go on living with Theodore. It was several weeks after I tried to put an end to myself in Fargo before Theodore again was brutal, so whatever the compulsion upon him at times, it was evident he had some degree of control over his satanic impulses, and this recent temporary separation from him might make him more cautious, if nothing else.

This was the course of reasoning with which I stilled my fears. Moreover, whatever my other interests then or later, I was definitely domestic. I liked to cook good meals that Theodore enjoyed and praised. I took pleasure in arranging the furniture Theodore had bought together with other, better pieces my parents had taken out of storage for us to use. Mama and Papa had handed over also my own books, quite a collection, so that the little house, inside, began to wear, in its modest way, a rather attractive air, or so I fancied. I was not ashamed, at any rate, to receive in it old friends with far greater possessions and living in "elegant" surroundings. In no time at all, this cheap little house was home to me.

But I was mainly absorbed, of course, in the baby. At last he was thriving. We had found the right food. He was no longer like a wizened little old man. His cheeks had lost their pallor, were filling out. This in itself gave me fresh heart. We had no crib, so he spent his nights as his days in a high, ornate, rather cumbersome baby-carriage, such as were used then, and given us by West End friends who had no further use for it. I would wheel him room to room as my housework took me, and he would sit up in the baby carriage, noticing things now, cooing, still almost never crying. A continual source of wonder to me, I had never dreamed there could be such utter sweetness as I found in this baby—and he was mine!

There were evenings, though, for all my content with the little house and the baby, when a wild wave of homesickness would sweep me. After supper, when the baby was asleep, Theodore reading, I would go out to the small front porch and stand looking off at the lights of Knoxville down below, one here and there, clustered more closely in the heart of town, and strung intermittently up the hills of West End beyond. Then I would be sick with longing.

Spread before me in the darkness, this darkness sprinkled with far off lights, was the world to which I had once belonged; the world I had lost—that gay world in which parties, splendid wedding receptions, plays at Staub's Opera House, dances, balls, cotillions, were still going on—a world so near now, and yet farther away, it seemed, than Fargo or Snohomish.

On evenings like these, inevitably I would think of Bob, of Bleak House. Living in New York now, Bob came home only occasionally for a few days visit. How different life with Bob would have been. For all my efforts to shut it out, this thought gnawed at my heart.

I had seen him only once since my return to Knoxville. It was during the weeks Theodore was not allowed to come to the house on Highland Avenue, though I believe few, if any, of my friends knew as yet the true state of affairs, what had actually happened, for Papa had revealed this only to his lawyers.

Mama had secured a young mulatto girl to wheel the baby out in his carriage every afternoon and sometimes I went along, though always then leading the way to back streets, in the direction of Mechanicsville, where there was little chance of meeting anyone I knew.

On this particular afternoon, however, for some reason or other, we took a different direction. Where we were bound I don't know, but we crossed the viaduct on Clinch Street and were climbing the hill ahead, toward Gay, when on the corner just beyond Em Parham's notorious establishment, though opposite it, I realized that the man in tweeds coming down the hill on the other side of the street was Bob. He often walked the four or five miles out to Bleak House, I knew, in preference to driving or riding.

Apparently Bob recognized me at the same instant I recognized him, and my heart began beating fast when I saw that with his easy familiar stride, and quickening his step as he drew nearer, he was cutting across the street diagonally to the point we had reached, next the small red-brick church that stood there.

Bob gave a swift sidelong glance at the baby in his carriage, then fixed his eyes on mine. He made no attempt to touch me, even to shake hands.

"Are you happy, Annie?" he asked, in a low shaken voice.

"Oh, yes! Oh, yes!" I said, pointing to the baby.

He glanced again at the baby, then brought his gaze back to me.

"Yes, of course, of course!" he said, but a look of slight suspicion in his eyes. He shook his head, grasped my hands in his, then quickly released them, and without another word went on down the hill.

On these wild winter evenings, alone on the little front porch, when I looked off into the darkness that was sprinkled with the lights of Knoxville, I would relive this brief encounter with Bob. Did he resent my treatment of him? Did he still love me, as his eyes, voice, his hard quick grip of my hands in his, seemed to show? But

I did not dare dwell on such thoughts. I would go back into the house, tiptoe into our bedroom where the baby was asleep in his carriage, kiss him on his cheek, soft as a rose petal, though lightly, not to wake him, then resume my place on the other side of the lamp from Theodore and pick up my work-basket again. Blessedly, inept though I was with a needle, there was always, in those hours of yearning, of terrible emotional unrest, plenty of darning and mending that must be done.

For all our isolation, however, old friends found us. Even old beaux, few of them married as yet. On Sunday afternoons we would have more callers than chairs, and although I was always a trifle nervous, ever on guard, yet I would be exhilarated by the presence of these young men I liked so much and had known so long, and our little sitting-room with its heterogeneous and none too lavish furnishings would rock with laughter as the parlor on Highland Avenue once had done. After all, one and all, we were still very young.

These Sunday callers naturally were Southern men. They belonged to Knoxville's most prominent old families. Theodore invariably treated them cordially, but what he liked better was to have for supper the few Northern men he knew in Knoxville, young men who had gone to Yale or other Eastern colleges and whom he found now, as before our marriage, more congenial.

Bonnie would come to help me. Like most Negroes, Bonnie loved an intrigue. She had relished carrying notes secretly from Theodore to me during the weeks we were separated, and now that we had this little house out near Bell Avenue she seemed to feel a strong tie to us. But for her, we might not have been here! She would walk the enormous distance from her shack in Niggertown, could always be depended upon to be on hand when I wanted her, do up the baby's dresses beautifully in the morning, work for hours preparing some of the old Knoxville favorites—chicken salad, scalloped oysters, cold smoked tongue, wafer-thin, beaten biscuits, charlotte russe or ambrosia, and a glistening iced layer-cake; then don white cap and apron, wait on table, and get home finally to her no-'count husband and houseful of children at heaven knows what hour.

There was one Sunday afternoon we had very special visitors: Margaret and Charlton, just returned from Havana, a farther distance than most bridal couples in Knoxville ventured then on their honeymoons.

I can see how Margaret looked as I met them at the front door; her black hat with both plumes and aigrette, her dotted veil, a cluster of fresh violets nestling in the sables she wore, a slender crescent of diamonds at her throat, and emitting the expensive fragrance of Roger & Gallet's *Vera Violetta;* her refined sensitive face not beautiful, her lips too thin, but attractive nevertheless, and her whole person, her air, the very quintessence of elegance and chic in the Gay Nineties, as people like to call them now, though more grim than gay for some who lived through them.

I can see Charlton too; almost disturbingly handsome, debonair, very much alive, not quite trustworthy one might suspect, but thoroughly charming and with a laugh few could resist.

When they had been there only a short while Margaret said she wanted to see the baby, so I took her into the bedroom where the baby was asleep. I sensed at once, though, that what she really wanted was to see me alone.

"How did you like Havana?" I asked lightly, to hide a slight self-consciousness when I had closed the door behind us.

Margaret sat down on the bed and I sat beside her. The chairs were all in the other room.

"Oh, Cuba, Florida—they were interesting," Margaret said. "It wasn't that," she said in a low tense voice, "—it was *marriage!* Oh, Annie, I would never have married if I'd known what it's like!"

She went on then to divulge, whisperingly, that her whole six weeks honeymoon had been a horror. "If that's what marriage is," she said, "I hate it! I loathe it! It's disgusting!"

I saw that Margaret was deeply disturbed and that she had come to me, married longer, for comfort, advice, understanding—I didn't know what, though, distressed as she was, I must offer something.

"Oh, Margaret, it isn't disgusting," I whispered, "unless you look at it that way!"

I was prompted, inwardly, I remember, to quote Walt Whitman to the effect that man is as divine about the loins as about the brow. Whitman might have been my own undoing, changed the whole course of my life, and for the worse, but just the same I had learned things from him, things I would like to pass on to Margaret.

But Margaret, I suspected, had never even heard of Whitman. I was certain she had not become acquainted with *Leaves of Grass* at Miss Cary's Select School for Young Ladies in Baltimore, and in her father's handsome home on Main Street where, while there was a billiard room, a great stained-glass window on the stair-landing, there were few books. No, Whitman's name would carry no weight with Margaret. Besides, we had only a few moments before we must rejoin the men, whose hearty masculine laughter came to us in spurts through the thin door between the two rooms. All I could think of to tell her was that her view, I thought, of the marital relationship as "disgusting" was unwholesome, and she must try to look at it differently.

I remember also that I wanted to ask her, though didn't dare go quite this length, that if the marriage relationship was so distasteful to her, wouldn't Charlton, with whom she was madly in love, sooner or later seek some woman who found it less repellent?

I often thought of this talk with Margaret afterwards. I thought of it ten years later, on another Sunday afternoon, when I stood looking down at Margaret's still body, after she had put a bullet through her head. Why had she done it? Everyone was asking. Perhaps my own guess was as good as another's . . . .

I may have been a trifle flattered at the time that Margaret, reserved, extremely reticent by nature, and only just returned from her honeymoon, had passed up all her other girl friends and come out to this cheap little cottage in the wasteland to make her unhappy revelation to me.

I recall, however, no such reaction on my part. What struck me at the moment with such force I couldn't forget it was that Margaret, who seemed to have everything, was carrying her heavy secret even as I mine, with the horror of my own private life very different from hers, yet never absent from my mind.

It was gratifying, in any case, considering our isolation, to have so many old friends come to see us, some of them men who as boys from "the Hill" had started coming to see me in the Barnes house, in those giddy, utterly irresponsible years—ages ago they seemed—when I was growing up.

But what meant more to me than anything else were visits from Mama and Papa. It tore at my heart, yet all the same filled me with joy when I spied them coming from the street-car, Papa hobbling along on the rough path to our gate, and a little black boy behind them carrying a big heaped-up market-basket.

They would come in the morning or early afternoon when there was less chance of encountering Theodore. They treated him with punctilious politeness whenever they met him, but it was plain that although they would put no obstacle in the way of my continuing to live with Theodore, if it proved possible, nevertheless they preferred not to see him.

It was plain, too, that they feared we were not getting enough to eat, for Theodore, barely started in his private practice, was earning almost nothing as yet and I had been able to manage suppers for his special friends only through what Papa and Mama brought and gifts from Bonnie—sweet potatoes she claimed she had raised herself, apples, pears, and grapes she said grew on her own place, and often cocoanuts, which I felt a little anxious about. She couldn't have raised the cocoanuts. She had either bought or stolen them.

But I felt a little anxious, too, when I unloaded the basket Papa and Mama brought, with its rib roast of beef, celery, cranberries, oysters or a dressed fowl, fresh eggs, butter—all sorts of things. Food was still plentiful and cheap in Knoxville. Even so, I knew they were sharing now not from any superabundance. More likely they were stinting themselves to make sure I should at least not be suffering from hunger.

For the first time in my life now I began to be conscious of a profound and unique affection for both my parents, for my own family, and to feel a faith in them that nothing could shake. They had become the one absolutely stable force in the universe so far as I was concerned.

One morning, in my longing to see them even between their weekly visits, I decided to take the baby and surprise them. I had not been in their house since I had left it to rejoin Theodore, three or four months before.

I could not go all the way by street-car, for I had only a nickel, the rest of the little we had having gone the day before into Theodore's favorite Havanas, and I knew I did not have the strength to wheel the baby in his heavy carriage the long distance—miles it was—, so the only solution was to carry him till I reached the corner of Clinch and Gay where I could take the street-car that ran out Highland Avenue.

I started out by a bumpy cross-country road and by the time I reached the pavement on East Clinch I was almost completely exhausted. My arms ached unbearably. My body seemed to have lost its last ounce of strength. I had never carried the baby before save for short distances inside the house. I had not realized his weight till now when he became heavier and heavier with every step I took. Only my desperate homesickness kept me going on and on.

Worn out, however, though I was, when I reached what was known as East Knoxville, the quiet loveliness of this part of town where the first settlers had built,[5] struck me as never before. Fashion and wealth had more and more moved toward the University, built the great Victorian mansions in West End, but this older part of town was, naturally, its most beautiful part.

Too far from my start now to turn back, I dragged and stumbled along the uneven old brick sidewalk, shifting the baby from side to side of my body to carry him at all. I passed one dignified old square red-brick house after another, set high above the street, box bushes leading up to the front porch, in their deep yards old trees that were just coming into leaf.

At one of these places, when I could not force myself a foot further, I sank down on a lower step of the long flight leading up from the sidewalk. The Van Gilders, I knew, lived in this delightful well-tended old place.[6] I didn't know them, but they wouldn't mind, I was sure, my sitting here for a while on their steps, the baby in my lap. The baby had never whimpered once; he was enjoying the trip.

It was a beautiful spring day, probably in late March. I remember that jonquils were blooming in the Van Gilders' yard and flowering quince bushes here and there a blaze of scarlet. But the sun was hot. Still in my winter clothes and with all the extra exertion, I was wet to the skin. Now and then an old colored man passed me and took off his battered hat respectfully. I wondered, almost in terror, whether I would be able to carry the baby another foot. But weak as I was, somehow or other I managed to muster sufficient strength to resume my journey, though when at length I reached the Highland Avenue street-car, the walrus-moustached good-natured driver had almost to lift me, as well as the baby, into one of the long seats that faced each other inside.

My strength revived, however, with the glad cries that greeted us when, without ringing, I opened the front door of that brown frame house which only a few years earlier I had felt, deep down in me, a little ashamed of living in; while never had a room looked so attractive as the one into which they drew us, to take off my wraps and the baby's cap and coat.

With incredible clarity, I can see this room, more than sixty years after, as it looked at that moment; the sofa in one corner, with a knitted afghan in Roman stripes lying across its lower end; the comfortable if slightly worn chairs; the felt-topped library table with its books and magazines that were being read; on the walls the series of French engravings in their ebony frames, and the small fire-place in front of which I sat that night, the baby across my knees, fearing he would die, my tears raining down on his wizened little face, and then the tap on the window and Theodore outside, in the rain, looking in. . . .

The searing memory of that night flashed through me as I took off my hat and coat, but for all that I loved the room, permeated now by the spirit of my parents. I was inexpressibly weary, but here, for the time, I was absolutely safe.

The truth is I still lived on the razor's edge. Though I had grown increasingly wary, yet I never knew at what instant one of Theodore's blows, like lightning, would strike me, and I was always extremely uneasy after our last caller left on Sunday. Excited by the presence of these young men I had known so long, I might have been too much my old self. Then, being Southern, they would pay, if quite openly, just such extravagant compliments to me as to every other girl or woman they knew. But more than once as Theodore listened to this flattery, I would catch a dark look momentarily cloud his face, see his eyes narrow. Would I have to pay later for the present jolly time? Above all, I dreaded the approach of bed-time, for it was then, in the past, I was in greatest danger, with his blows at this hour inevitably followed by almost equally violent love-making. . . .

But for all my constant fear of him, and my wariness, there had been a change in my state of mind since I came back to Theodore after our separation. During those dazed weeks at home, when I had been more or less in seclusion and full of uncertainty, most of the few talks Papa had with me regarding my situation made little impression. But Papa's talk on the eve of my leaving to rejoin Theodore had left its mark.

There were legal aspects of my case which Papa explained. I could not get a divorce from Theodore unless I left him immediately after one of his acts of brutality. Otherwise, in the eyes of the law, I would be condoning the offense and have no redress. What I must do, he said, if there was another brutal attack, was go at once to Mr. McClung, one of his lawyers who would be near,[7] and who would bring me, with the baby, back to Highland Avenue.

I was shocked, and a little resentful, at Papa's assumption that if Theodore gave further provocation there was no alternative for me but divorce, though when I demurred, Papa became more agitated than I had ever known him. Both his voice and his hands shook.

"But, Annie, he will kill you," Papa pled with me. "He has already killed your spirit, if not your body! He will destroy you utterly if you continue to submit to such degradation."

As time went on I kept thinking more and more about this last talk Papa had had with me alone. I hoped fervently that the Satanic side of Theodore would not again assert itself. It was not that I clung to him, except for a certain purely carnal attraction he had for me. It was simply that I still could not picture to myself how I could live—and now with the baby—if I *left* Theodore. When I tried to picture such a thing, there was only confusion, chaos, in my mind, which seemed to whirl round and round, or went completely blank.

Nevertheless, little by little, a definite resolution took form within me. I began to stiffen inwardly, if not outwardly. Should Theodore strike me again, I would leave him.

Meantime, whatever my hopes and fears, spring had come in earnest. Forsythia bushes along the fence which I had hardly noticed before burst into golden bloom. Unexpected flowers and plants sprang up in the neglected yard around us; snowdrops, grape hyacinths, Johnny-jump-ups, even lilies of some sort, and peonies. It delighted me to make these little discoveries.

Then late one afternoon a countryman came driving a Jersey cow up the road and around to the cow-shed in our back yard. Theodore had accepted the cow from a client, a small farmer, in lieu of the cash he could not pay. Another day, as payment under similar circumstances, some hens and a rooster, Plymouth Rocks, were brought from the country and installed in our hen-house.

The cow was fresh and a man who would milk her, for part of the milk, was found not far away, so now we had not only new-laid eggs every day but an abundance of milk and cream.

What surprised and pleased me (as when he had spaded the ground for our little garden in Fargo) was that Theodore, city born and bred, and always with a rather contemptuous attitude toward country folk or ways, should take such interest and pride in these new possessions of ours. I even dared to tease him a little over how much more interest he took in the cows and chickens than in the baby, whom he had never taken in his lap since it was born, never done the least thing for, whose existence, in fact, he scarcely recognized.

I felt no particular concern, however, about his indifference to the baby. I had heard it was not unusual for men to be indifferent to their children as infants, only interested in them after they showed some intelligence, and yet would make good fathers.

But I welcomed any sign whatever of the more normal sides of Theodore's nature. His interest in the cows and chickens cheered me, as did even the fact that, kissing me goodbye at the front door on leaving for his office in the morning, often when he reached the gate, if he saw me still standing in the doorway, he would come back to kiss me again, over and over, like any other young husband, I imagined.

Save for Theodore's shameless selfishness, which I had come to accept as something I could probably do little or nothing about, things seemed for the most part to be going along pretty well.

I did not worry in the least about having no spring coat or Easter hat—no new clothes at all. Plenty of young couples everywhere had started with little, and later became prosperous.

I seldom dwelt any more, or not achingly, on the fact that I alone, among all my old friends, had no part in the social gaieties of Knoxville. With my insatiable love of life, I was making the best, with a vengeance, of what little we had, and when we were able to hire for a dollar a week a nice, pretty, clean young white girl from a poor but respectable family over the hill beyond us to help me in the morning and wheel the baby out in his buggy in the afternoon, I felt that perhaps already we had started on the upgrade.

Things were like this when one day, early in June, a Negro boy on horseback rode up with a note from Reuben Payne, the same rather frail Reuben, with his perpetually husky voice, for whom I felt genuine affection, and who ultimately would marry Mary Gaines.

Reuben wrote that his mother had gone to Nashville, to be gone several weeks; that while she was away no one would be using the carriage. Couldn't their coachman come for me every afternoon, take the baby and me for a drive, wherever I wanted to go?

I and the baby in the Payne's barouche—the vision rose before me! What lovelier thing could happen? But on second thought, I told the boy I couldn't give him an answer straight off; for him to come back next morning. I would have, of course, to show the note to Theodore. There was nothing in its wording (to "Dear Miss Annie," and "From your friend Reuben") he could possibly take exception to. All the same, how would he react to Reuben's proposal?

My blood at fever heat, I thought of nothing else all that evening, but could not screw my courage to a point where I could mention the note to Theodore. Better wait till morning. It would be safer then. What I *did* mention, casually, though rashly, as I realized later, was that the young girl working for us had wheeled the baby farther that afternoon, been gone with him longer, than I thought best, and I was going to speak to her about it.

When morning came, I at last showed Theodore the note as he was dressing. I had slipped a wrapper over my nightgown but left my hair down my back in braids till I could make the fire in the kitchen and start breakfast.

"Look what wonderful outings Reuben Payne proposes for me and the baby!" I said, in a jaunty tone to cover my fright, though in the same instant it shot through me that probably, after all, I should have shown him the note the evening before. I had made a mistake!

Theodore read the note without a word, his face expressionless, and placed it back on the mantel in our bedroom from where I had taken it.

I began to have a feeling now of suffocation, but the baby was awake and crowing and I wheeled him into the sitting-room on my way to the kitchen. While I was there, the young girl who helped me came and I sent her to set the breakfast table in our small dining-room, but as I started to grind the coffee in the coffee-mill, I heard a scream and when I reached the dining-room the girl was crouching under the dining-table with Theodore kicking her viciously, one kick after another. I had never seen such an awful sight. It tore me to pieces.

"Stop, Theodore, stop!" I cried at the top of my voice and then he turned on me, dealing me blow after blow, on my face—anywhere, in an absolute frenzy, as if all his pent-up demonic urges of weeks past were finding vent now.

But somehow or other—I shall never know how—I broke away from him, fled from the house and ran toward the McClungs.

A Negro maid in black uniform and fancy white cap and apron answered my ring at the McClungs' front door. I can see that Negro maid as if it were yesterday, aghast at the sight of me, disheveled, only half dressed as I was, and blood streaming down my face; see her suppressing an outcry and leading me to the dining-room where the McClungs were at breakfast.

I can see Mr. McClung, facing me as I appeared in the doorway of the dining-room; see him in his long black broadcloth lawyer's coat, rising quickly from the table, standing behind it, clutching the white damask napkin he was using, holding it against him, and his face as white as the napkin.

I can see him, after he had gone back with me to our little house, standing, a man of great dignity, in our sitting room, grasping the handle of the baby carriage as he prepared to take the baby and me away from Theodore, and Theodore himself facing this eminent member of the Knoxville bar, staring at him; Theodore speechless, his own face whiter than death and as immobile.

Even in that terrible moment there was something pitiful about Theodore, something I could never forget.

NOTES

1. Presumably the Mabry Street, Bell Avenue & Hardee Street Railway. Rule, 304; Deaderick, 217.
2. Although Armstrong never mentions the street name, she and her husband lived at 116 Cruze Street near its intersection with Bell Avenue (now McCalla). Knoxville YWCA's Phyllis Wheatley Center is located at 124 South Cruze Street, probably near where

Armstrong lived in 1893/94. At that time, Bell Avenue was a continuation of Hardee (now Jackson Avenue). It ran east from First Creek to the city limits and formed the dividing line between the northeast and southeast sections of that part of town. Today, the continuation of Jackson Avenue east of Central is called McCalla Avenue. *Knoxville City Directory*, 1893; Knoxville, Knox County, Knoxville Utilities Board Geographic Information System (KGIS) website, https://www.kgis.org/KGISMaps/Map.htm (viewed May 31, 2019); Ronald R. Allen, *Knoxville Miscellany: People, Places and Events in Old Knoxville* (Knoxville: R. Allen, 2008), 145,158.

3. Although Sanborn maps of Knoxville at that time do not show a "Wetzell Addition," a large advertisement placed by H. B. Wetzell & Co. shows the lay-out of twenty-five numbered building lots between Bell Avenue and Mabry Street, bounded on one side by Cruze Street. *Knoxville Daily Journal*, June 1, 1889. Another Wetzell & Co. advertisement states: "We will exchange very desirable Knoxville property for good timber and coal lands!" *Knoxville Daily Journal*, August 22, 1889, 7.
4. Hugh (sometimes "Hu") Lawson McClung, Jr. (1858–1936) practiced law in Knoxville from 1879 until 1908. He married Ella L. Gibbins December 15, 1892. During the time of which Armstrong is writing, they were living at 2118 Bell Avenue. Rothrock, 447; J. C. (Jim) Tumblin, *Fountain City: People Who Made a Difference* (Knoxville: Celtic Cat, 2016), 83–86; *Knoxville, Tennessee, City Directory, 1895*. For more about Armstrong's school friends Ella and Margaret (also mentioned in this chapter), see Part I, Chapter Four, "The Barton Building and The Lost Cause."
5. East Knoxville was a suburb farther east than the original town of Knoxville. Allen, *Knoxville Miscellany*, 113–14. According to the Historical Overview in a report prepared for the City of Knoxville: "One of the first new cities to incorporate outside of Knoxville was East Knoxville. People who lived to the east of the Old City petitioned the State Legislature and on February 22, 1856, became the City of East Knoxville. This new city included East Clinch Avenue, East Church, East Cumberland, East Hill, East Main, Willow and their cross streets. The town was bounded by Bertrand Street on the east, Central on the west, Linden Avenue on the north, and the river on the south. The City of Knoxville annexed East Knoxville in 1869." Thomason and Associates, Preservation Planners, "Knoxville Historic Resources Survey Update, Knoxville, Knox County, Tennessee" (September 2016), https://thomasonandassociates.com/wp-content/uploads/2018/08/knoxville-historic-resources-survey-report.pdf (viewed May 24, 2019).
6. John Somers Van Gilder (1825–1902) moved to Knoxville in 1851 and became influential as a manufacturer, banker, and mayor. The family home was on East Clinch Avenue. Rothrock, 499–500.
7. Hugh L. McClung, as noted above, lived on Bell Avenue near its intersection with Cruze Street.

Chapter Eighteen

Death of a Capitalist

All that summer I lived in a state of bewilderment. But Papa was not bewildered. There was something he must do. I must have a divorce and he must see that I had it, for it was obvious I was too dazed, too inert, too bereft of all will, to take the necessary steps myself.

Now that I was back in the house on Highland Avenue, with Papa and Mama again in their good-sized bedroom over the parlor, May in the room once mine, the baby and I were given the small bedroom on the other side of the house. But no room could be too small for me now. I wanted to hide. I would see no one, not even the closest of my old friends. I would not even go downstairs at hours when I might encounter someone outside the family. My suit for divorce was set for late August and through all the intervening weeks I remained more dead than alive; sharply conscious only of a feeling of humiliation, a sense of shame, as the time approached for my private affairs to be aired in court—become the talk of the town.

In a house full of books and with ample leisure, I was unable to read. All I could do was think, think, think, in a dull hopeless way. It was now, in fact, as it had been ever since my marriage to Theodore. Passionate reader though I had been before, always with him I was too apprehensive to be able to concentrate on books of any significance, and now even less was I able to. What was ahead? My marriage had perished. What lines could my shattered life possibly take in future? I seemed to be lost, to be groping my way through a thick fog that would never end.

My one interest was in the baby as I saw him develop day by day; my one solace that he was worth all the suffering I had known or ever could. On this I was clear. After dark I would carry him down to the back yard where, unseen, I would walk around with him in my arms. I would pick a blossom off the four-o'clocks which grew along the back fence and fit it, like a cap, on the end of his snubby nose, where, through suction, he could retain it, to his great glee.

Papa never talked to me about my divorce. There was no need to. All the preliminaries were in his hands or those of his lawyers. But when he saw me sitting hour after hour, if the baby were asleep, looking down apathetically into the side street where nothing passed except at rare intervals a horse and buggy or a countryman with a wagonful of peaches or watermelons he was taking to market, then he would try to amuse me. He would urge me to write.

Though I had no belief that I could write, and no desire to, yet Papa evidently believed I could. Mama had told me that when I sent home from Mount Holyoke our college publication containing a review by me of Olive Schreiner's *Story of an African Farm*,[1] Papa's eyes, as he read it, had been full of tears. He had seen in it a promise that I might become one of the things he probably desired most for me—an "author."

To please him, then, I tried to write. I can see myself—one of the few distinct pictures I retain in my mind of this secluded, shrouded, sad summer—sitting in that small upstairs bedroom in the house on Highland Avenue with a pad on my knee, a pencil in my hand, the baby playing with some little toy on the bed beside me. But ideas, words, would not come; images would not form. I tore up sheet after sheet of paper. I simply could not write. There was no use trying.

Meantime, at his desk in the little sitting-room beneath me for hours on end every day Papa continued his own writing, whatever his physical pain, often torture. He was contributing to the *North American Review* and to other periodicals, English and American, some of them trade journals, such as the *Manufacturers Record* and the *Southern Lumberman*, of which he was an editor; writing on Forest Conservation long before Gifford Pinchot's name became synonymous with the subject. It was during this time he had the gratification of being asked to write on American Forests for the Ninth Edition of the *Encyclopaedia Britannica*. His writing was, indeed, now his chief source of income and sufficient to support us in comfort, if not in luxury.

But Papa, for all his unremitting bodily suffering and concern over me, none the less, seemed better than for years past. Never, in fact, since we had lived in the Barnes house, before the train wreck which had broken his body beyond repair and simultaneously robbed him of his fortune, had I seen him so alive, so intensely alert, filled, at moments, with what seemed his old buoyant boyish unconquerable spirit.

For one thing, there was his joy in the baby—a child in the house, and his grandchild. But more than that, he had before him now the possibility of financial recovery. He was in touch with Dutch investors. I could see the old light in his eye when letters came from Rotterdam. The English investors in timber and mining properties in the Southern mountain region had been ruined, and he with them, by the failure of the great Midlands Bank in England. But there was plenty of money in Holland waiting for similar investments. Already he had sent trusted men out into the mountains of North Carolina, Kentucky, and Tennessee to report on tracts of timber, garnet, mica, and other mines. He was planning (and this I heard with astonishment) shortly to go himself into the mountains, to secure options on some of these properties.

In spite of everything, Papa was elated this summer. I could not hide it from myself.

It was not alone, however, his vision of recovered fortune that filled him with this new life, new enthusiasm. Even then I realized that part of it was due to his determination to deliver me from something he considered worse than death and that now he felt was all but accomplished—only a matter of weeks.

It was some time during this summer I learned of Bob Armstrong's engagement to a rich girl in the East, an heiress, whom he was soon to marry.

I heard the news with strange calm. From time to time afterwards there would be a dull ache at my heart when I thought of Bob. But this ache merged with my whole state of dull wordless misery. One wound more or less hardly mattered. I myself would live in the shadows henceforth. Bob's life and mine would probably never touch again and all that was certain was that I must go through with the dreaded ordeal of my divorce, the horror of its publicity, and after that face a future for which I had no plans, and saw only as a dark disordered waste stretching ahead of me interminably.

The sole pleasurable memory I have of that summer when, crushed by all that had happened and was to happen, I stayed so closely indoors and in my own room, oddly enough is connected with the couple which had been so great a source at once of amusement and inspiration to me in my early teens—Sophie and August Bauer.

The Bauers lived now in a house they had built on the leafy side street I looked down on from my bedroom window and only two doors away. A frame house, painted gray, it was much more substantial-looking than the one they had rented from the Widow Gaines on Clinch Street.

In the late afternoon often I would take the baby, steal around the corner, and join Mrs. Bauer at the back of her house where I was sure to find her at this hour sitting in the shade of one of those apple trees that were remnants of old orchards in this part of town.

Mrs. Bauer would be in a spotless print dress, its long flowing skirt somewhat disguising the lines of her short ample figure, and its neat turned-over collar fastened with the same mosaic brooch depicting the Roman Coliseum [*sic*] that I remembered her always wearing. In her rather scant gray hair, parted severely in the middle to form smooth bands, there was still never a hair astray.

She would be mending or darning perhaps when we arrived, her work-basket at her feet, but more often reading a newspaper, though seldom the *Knoxville Journal*, in which she continued to have little faith, but usually the *New York Tribune* or the *London Times*.

Without fussing over us, nevertheless in her own fashion she seemed unmistakably glad to see me when I appeared with the baby, and though far from a tactful person in general, she never indicated there was anything different in my situation from that of the usual young mother with her first child.

She would bring out a quilt and spread it over the grass for the baby to sit on, then take me on a tour of her little domain. There were her flower beds, which she worked in every morning before the sun was too high; long narrow colorful rows of old-fashioned annuals or perennials—bachelor buttons, love-in-a-mist, mignotte [i.e., mignonette], stocks, larkspurs, velvety wallflowers, French marigolds—planted along the outer sides of a grape arbor which ran, a mossy brick walk underneath, almost the length of the deep lot. There was her treasured herb garden here, too, as on Clinch Street.

Sometimes, leading the way with that majestic gait she had managed to achieve despite her squat figure, she would take me through the kitchen into the house. With her customary thrift, she had rented its second floor to another couple. Her daughter Marie married now and living in Chicago, there was plenty of room below for herself and Mr. Bauer, and their combined dining and sitting room took me back instantly to their former one—the same neatly racked newspapers, American, English, German; the same sofa, across its foot the Scotch plaid blanket presented to August by Queen Victoria; hanging above it the same immense engraving of a scene centering around the German hero Wallenstein.

From all these familiar furnishings, this familiar atmosphere, I derived, temporarily, if only half consciously, a kind of reassurance. If my own world had gone to pieces, this small orderly world Sophie and August Bauer had created around themselves (quite oblivious to loftier ambitions their neighbors or others might entertain)—this world persisted; and the Bauers' back yard, where, screened from the street, the baby and I sat with Mrs. Bauer as the shadows lengthened on those summer afternoons, became for me a little green paradise. Safely enclosed within its cool green sweet-scented verdurous walls, my troubles seem[ed] to melt away. I would go home refreshed.

There is another memory, though, of this time, I would more willingly lose than any other I possess. It was Sunday afternoon and not long before the date set for my divorce proceedings. Mama was in the parlor with friends who had called, Papa in their bedroom above, resting. I am not quite sure how it all was, but apparently from the bedroom windows Papa caught sight of Theodore coming up the street and nearing our gate.

Immediately after I left him—on the presumption that should he gain access to me, he might exert his former influence and persuade me to return to him—an injunction had been issued prohibiting Theodore from entering our premises on Highland Avenue.

This was the first time he had presumed to defy the injunction. From my own room I became suddenly aware that something was happening when Papa, a sharp note in his voice such as I had never heard before, called down from the upstairs hall, "Don't let him in!"

Dropping the baby on to the bed, I ran to my door. Papa already had started down the stairs in his slow crippled fashion so painful to look at. I saw him stop on the landing at the turn of the stairs and glance out the diamond-shaped window there with its border of crudely-colored glass squares. Almost at the same instant I noted with horror that in his right hand, shaking visibly, he was clutching his revolver. So he would kill Theodore before he would let him in! He would commit murder—! Papa, of all men!

Rooted to the floor, too shocked, too terrified, to move, I heard the muffled voices of both Papa and Theodore at the front door; then I was conscious of Theodore's leaving, and after that of dead silence below.

But once more, shortly after this I was to see Papa—ordinarily the most self-controlled of men—moved out of himself in his determination to save me, not only from Theodore, but from myself.

One morning as I sat in my small room, crowded by the big bed, Papa came in with a paper for me to sign. It was necessary no doubt—though I did not perceive its full significance then—that I indicate by my own signature that the divorce action was voluntary on my part. But while I still had no desire to return to Theodore, yet I shrank, however irrationally, from taking this irrevocable step.

I was convinced that my life was ruined and now I was being asked to place the final seal on its ruin. I refused to sign the paper. I burst into tears and cried as I had never cried before. I could not stop crying and simultaneously a feeling almost of hatred arose in me toward Papa, who was urging me to do this thing against which my whole being rebelled.

Whether Papa had anticipated this resistance on my part I do not know, but when I sank to the floor, knelt by the bed, my face buried on it, one convulsive sob after another rending my body, Papa knelt and wept with me. His arm around me, slowly, sorrowfully, patiently, he brought me at last to a point where I would sign my name to the document he had brought.

When the morning arrived for my case to be heard, before we left for the courthouse Papa told me that my lawyers were not asking for alimony, a matter, however, that I had not given a thought to myself. He explained that it might be difficult for Theodore, just starting in private practice, to pay alimony for some time to come, and in any case he would look after me and the baby and I was not to worry about the future. Things, he said, were coming his way now, once again.

It is all very much like an unhappy dream to me today, and with a dream's haziness and incoherence, but the hearing must have been held, not in the open courtroom, but privately; for I remember no one in the lofty, oak-paneled, book-lined, rather cluttered judge's chamber save those directly concerned with the suit.

I sat in a chair between Papa and Mama on one side and on my other Dr. Ringgold, rector of St. John's,[2] who had come to our house the evening before, offering to be present, and whose flowing white beard and clerical garb lent even greater solemnity to the proceedings than their unusual and serious nature already provided.

Facing us were my counsel, three of Knoxville's ablest and most highly respected lawyers; and separated from them by a considerable space, though facing us also, in a chair near the tall dusty windows of the chamber, was Theodore, who would plead his own case.

I had not seen Theodore since the morning I left him. He looked thin, very pale, with an almost waxy look, and his prominent nose more prominent than ever. I remember that as I glanced at him, avoiding his eyes, I felt more sorry for him than anything else. It was almost as if we were taking advantage of him, all alone as he was. This was not the madman who had knocked me unconscious more than once, whose blows again and again had brought blood. It was the young husband in Fargo, North Dakota, who had broken down and sobbed when he was unable—too inexperienced—to prepare for the Morton Bank the bill they wanted presented to the state legislature.

In his deep voice, in a low tone, Theodore denied categorically all the charges against him. What defense, if any, he made, I can not recall, any more than I can recall what my lawyers said, except when one of them stated that Theodore had gained his power over me through hypnotism, and this stuck in my mind because I doubted that it was true. I am confident, however, that none of them suggested, if even suspected, that Theodore's monstrous behavior was pathological, far less that it was a form of sexual perversion, a fact I did not recognize myself till years later when, looking back, piecing this and that together, I realized that his wish to inflict bodily pain on me, his blind and senseless violence, arising as a rule from the most insignificant causes or none at all, had been closely linked with sexual desire and gratification.

Mercifully, however, time has blotted out of my mind any clear recollection of what I suffered in the hours immediately following my divorce, when I was now that anomalous being, a divorced person (the term divorcée, with its frivolous connotations, had not then come into common use in this country).

Mercifully, too, my parents shielded me from knowing what a sensation the divorce had created. It was only long afterwards I learned of an editorial which the *Knoxville Journal* carried the morning after it was granted. Such cruelty as this suit for divorce revealed, the paper commented, perpetrated by a man of the defendant's class, well born, a gentleman to all outward appearances, not addicted to drink, and highly educated, was unique, utterly inexplicable, and had profoundly shocked the whole community.[3]

But Papa and Mama were concerned not alone with shielding me now. They must help me, as unobtrusively as possible, build a new life for myself. Believing I should have a complete change of scene for awhile, they suggested I take the baby and visit our friends, the Dames, in Harriman, only a few hours away, and the little new town where I had spent gay week-ends during my girlhood.

The Dames had formerly lived in Knoxville. A cultivated, warm-hearted couple who had lost all their own children—"blue babies"—as infants, they were drawn to young people, as young people to them, and had shown more than ordinary interest in me from the time when I used to pass their red-brick house on Clinch Street on my way to and from Dr. Tuck, and would often stop for a chat with them.[4]

The Dames' comfortable and hospitable home, a picturesque "Queen Anne" house with a wooded ridge rising behind it, seemed more attractive to me than ever. Soon I was laughing whole-heartedly at Mrs. Dame's stories (she was one of the few really gifted raconteurs I have ever known among my own sex); I was entering without self-consciousness into the general lively and jolly talk when, the baby in bed, we gathered in the moonlight on the Dames' spacious front porch and young people dropped in, some of them young men I had danced and gone horseback riding with only a few years before.

How pleasant it all was! I could be myself again, and without fear! A great load seemed to have been lifted off me.

But this happy interlude was not to last long. After a few days I was summoned back to Knoxville. Somewhere up in the mountains of North Carolina where Papa had gone as soon as my divorce was granted, he had been taken desperately ill and brought home.

An ominous hush in the house struck a chill to my heart the moment I entered the front door, and Mama did not hide from me what the doctors said—that Papa, in his condition, should never have attempted the trip to North Carolina and had at most only a short time to live. She had telegraphed Aunt Sarah, asking her to come, and Mr. Morrison, one of his nurses in the first years after he was hurt, was with him again.

I carried the baby up to the bedroom where Papa lay in the huge carved walnut bed—the bed in which the baby had been born, from which I had weakly tried to rise on that Sunday afternoon when I was imploring Theodore to pay the nurse, and then he had struck me. . . .

Papa was propped up against the pillows. It seemed impossible he could have changed so much in a few days! A terrible pain shot through me. I saw for myself now that Papa was dying.

With a feeble movement he put out one of his big hands, so full of character, and let it rest on the baby's silky blond head. But his heavy eyes did not light up, his plain strong face was not illumined by that smile which the very sight of the baby heretofore had called forth. His eyes closed wearily, and I saw that I could not show him, as I had been eager to, that the baby could take a few steps now by himself.

Aunt Sarah came. The doctors were in and out at all hours; both slovenly, old-fashioned, good Dr. Hood, our neighbor in the next block, and black-coated, black-bearded, portly Dr. Deaderick, solemn, exuding importance, generally considered then Knoxville's leading, if not most beloved, physician. Day and night, sandy-haired, rheumy-eyed, stooped Mr. Morrison watched over Papa, cared for him as devotedly as he always had. Mama, her dark eyes sadder than ever, but tearless, slipped silently in and out of the sick-room and at the front door was a constant stream of callers, inquiring of Papa's condition, and bringing with them every imaginable delicacy, even whole meals, beautifully prepared, for the rest of us, to save us effort.

Never were there more thoughtful, more wonderful, friends than in Knoxville at times like this. And never did a man die more agonizingly than Papa. He was dying of cancer (perhaps induced by the fearful injuries he had sustained in the railroad wreck), though it was thirty years after before I learned the true cause of his death, following Mama's from the same dread disease, when in examining papers among her effects I came upon a certificate dated 1894, and signed by Dr. Hood.

All these years, it was plain, Mama had known, but under the influence of an attitude prevalent in the 19th Century and by no means entirely relinquished today—that cancer is a sort of disgrace—, she had never confided even to my sister or myself what she knew. The very word, "cancer," was one, I remember, she never uttered except in a whisper.

Whether Papa himself, suffering at the end from internal hemorrhages, knew they were due to cancer, I can not of course be sure, but I think it probable he had known his true condition for some time past, and realizing he had only a short time to live, it was for this reason, disregarding his pain-racked body, he had worked so unremittingly in those last weeks of his life, first of all to secure my divorce, then to push through, as he hoped, a final business deal that would yield a substantial amount for the four of us he would leave behind.

On the Sunday before he died, as so often with those near death, he became more and more restless, finally insisting he must sit in an armchair that was across the room, near a window.

When he had been placed there Mama and I returned to the room. I can still see him. I relive the moment at this instant. It was an overcast, close, depressing day, though now, in early September, with no chill in the air. In his white nightshirt, a light covering over his knees, he looked far more deathly than in bed. He was too weak to speak more than a word or two at a time, but looking directly at us, with an expression almost of supplication in his sunken eyes, as though he were begging our understanding and indulgence, he brought out slowly, and with an effort, "I have tried so hard, but I can't try any more—"

"Yes, Papa," I wanted to cry out, "We know! We know!"

For five years, without a murmur of complaint against the fate which had overtaken him when still a young man and at the height of his business career, without a trace of bitterness, with an undaunted spirit, with a courage that put fresh courage into other men—for five years he had fought, but he could fight no longer. . . .

The men lifted him back into bed. He did not ask again to be moved, but his unceasing suffering became ever more terrible.

Dusk came and I went down to draw some water from a cistern in the back yard, a few steps below the house. Dr. Hood followed me. "Daughter," he said, gently, gravely, "your father is dying. I think I may tell you," he said, "that I was a surgeon in the Confederate army all through the late war and never have I seen greater suffering than your father's, but I believe he will soon be released. I think the end will come during the night."

But the end did not come that night. He was dying all the next day, the next night. Only on Tuesday morning did the end come.

Through all these dragging anguishing hours Mama and I, save for a moment or so, did not leave the room, even to eat or sleep. He might go—and we not be there!

Through it all, Mama remained composed, dry-eyed, as if the past few years, with what they had brought to our family of disaster and tragedy, had drained her of all the tears she would ever have to shed. But if Mama remained composed, I became continually more uncontrolled. How could the doctors *let* Papa suffer so? And once, when they were having a consultation in the hall, outside the bedroom door, I burst in on them: "Oh, doctors, give him something—*something* that will make him suffer less!"

I shall never forget the look Dr. Deaderick bent on me when it seemed my very heart was being torn out of my body—a stern, disapproving look, tinged with disgust, as if I had offered an affront to his professional dignity. It was borne in upon me in that instant that he expected decorum even in the presence of death, perhaps especially then. But tender-hearted Dr. Hood, his hand on my arm, tried to calm me, to soothe me. "We're doing all we can, daughter! To give him anything more might bring death immediately."

"Then *give* it to him!" I begged, completely beside myself. "*Give* it to him! *Bring* death! That's what he longs for! What everyone who loves him longs for—to see his sufferings end!"

But the doctors were adamant. They would do no more than they had, and through their refusal I was converted instantaneously to a belief, one I have never lost, in "mercy killing," as we call it today. Had I had the means at my disposal, undoubtedly I would have brought death to my father myself, and gladly taken whatever the consequences. Why should they let this torture Papa was suffering go *on* and *on* and *on*?

At times he would say it was like flames; that he was burning up. Yet when they placed his hands and feet in ice water, the fire devouring him did not cease; it raged on, more fiercely than ever.

But it was more than his suffering which was crazing me. Did he know [illegible]—did Papa *know*, how much we had loved him always, trusted and honored him? Did he know how we *felt* about him?

I turned to Mama, entreating her to tell him—tell him *now*, before it was too late! But Mama understood, better than I, that with his life fast ebbing, we must not put additional strain upon him. "He knows, Annie," she quieted me, in a low voice. "He knows!"

Through all that last night Papa was perfectly conscious, holding his own fingers on his pulse, even on the last one to be felt, in the groin.

As his pulse grew weaker, though his agony no less, he would say, "It can't be long now!" Again, "It can't be more than twenty minutes—"

Once he said, "I shall soon see Harry!" (Dear Papa! Whatever orthodox beliefs he had discarded, he had retained his belief in an orthodox heaven).

Toward the end he begged Mama not to get an expensive coffin. "There will be so little—you'll need it all."

Sometime during the night he had said, "I'll go with the dawn, as day breaks," and so it was, with the faint, far-off, eerie sound of cocks crowing somewhere, and the first streaks of light in the sky. Propped up against the pillows, all at once his haggard unshaven face was suffused with a singular, indescribable radiance. It was transfigured before our eyes, filled with a strange unearthly beauty. Then the radiance passed. His chin dropped to his breast. The dawn, for him, had come at last.[5]

Long years after that night—indeed until after I had reached middle life, I was still haunted with the memory of my father's death. It remained before me with scarifying vividness. I could see his big wasted figure propped up in the huge walnut bed. His last piteous heart-breaking words continued to sound in my ears. All that was finest in life and human character had been embodied for me in my father, and that he should have died as he had! I could never get away, it seemed, from the thought of it, while at the time, my mind, I believe, would have given way had I not been almost at once confronted with the problem not only of supporting myself but others.

Even so, the night after Papa's death I experienced extreme mental confusion. Although worn out physically, I could not sleep, and as the night wore on became more and more excited and confused. The accumulated tension of several years—my marrying a man I did not love and had never wanted to marry, my life with him, the strain of my divorce, and now Papa's slow and excruciating death—all this finally was taking toll. I could not think consecutively. [Everything seemed whirling round and round in my head.[6]] It was the most terrifying sensation I have ever known. I was quite sure I was going mad and beseeched Mama and Aunt Sarah not to let me be taken to Lyon's View, the state asylum for the insane, a few miles from

Knoxville, and where I had seen, from outside, inmates standing against the iron bars at their windows.[7]

I shall never forget the horror of that night. But I was young, my body healthy, and when day came I was able to consider matters that must be attended to.

There were the clothes. Papa had disapproved of mourning. He considered it a barbarous custom that long since should have been abandoned. Nevertheless, the custom of wearing heavy mourning was still so general that not to wear it would make us too conspicuous, cause talk, and seem a disrespect to Papa's memory; so Mama put on her widow's veil and May and I the lighter mourning I would wear for the next year.

Another custom universally observed then was that there should be only white or purple flowers at a funeral, and I recall the slight shock I felt when I went into the parlor where Papa was lying in his coffin and there among the white roses, heliotrope, the white lilies, the tuberoses with their deadly sweet, suffocating odour, was a sheaf of long-stemmed pink roses someone had sent—the first bright-hued flowers I had ever seen at a funeral.

Strangely, though I remember such an inconsequential thing as the pink roses, I retain not even a vestige of remembrance of Papa's burial beside Harry in Old Gray. What comes back to me, little dimmed by time, is my high excitement again, as during the night—my wild fears, as the hour drew near for the services at home, lest Dr. Sutherland, pastor of the Second Presbyterian Church, should take occasion, as he had at the funeral of another man, a man of some prominence, who had recently died in Knoxville, to deplore the fact that the man had not been "a member of the Church," and therefore not a Christian.

Nothing like that should be said about Papa—the best Christian I had ever known! I resolved to stand right up, there in the parlor, and stop him, regardless of how scandalized Mama and everyone else would be, should Dr. Sutherland start saying any such thing.

Fortunately, he said nothing of the kind, and when frail saintly old Dr. Frazee, pastor of the Congregational Church in Knoxville and one of Papa's close friends, followed Dr. Sutherland, and through the thick black veil which enveloped me I heard him saying in a moved voice, "Here was a man who fought from beginning to end in the late War, fought in many of its engagements, but who fought his hardest battles here in our midst in the past few years—fought them with as superb fortitude, bore his great wounds as valiantly, I dare affirm, as any man has ever done in war or peace"—when I heard these words, for the first time in days my troubled and rebellious heart knew some ease.[8]

After Papa's death, we never again referred, even among ourselves, to his last ghastly hours; for all that we talked about him freely, brought him constantly into our conversations, as though he were no farther away than in the next room.

Once, soon after his death, we visited Old Gray, to put flowers on his grave, but we did not go again. If we did not discuss it, yet we knew that Papa, the most vital, the least morbid, of men, would understand it was not that we were forgetting him; it was because we were determined to keep him alive among us, and not think of him as dead.

Foremost help in those days was the baby. He was saying a few words now, as well as taking a few steps. An unfailing source of delight and amusement, he would draw smiles, even laughs, from us, and without our feeling a sense of guilt. Then gracious, serene, capable Aunt Sarah was a strong support, too, as we started re-adjusting to a new way of life. The rift that had come between her and Mama at the time of my marriage was healed, and it was plain that the two sisters had never meant so much to one another.

A few days after the funeral we learned what there was for us to go on for the present—one paid-up insurance policy for twelve-hundred dollars. (The rest of his policies had lapsed.) This was Papa's estate—Papa, who in his thirties had been rated a millionaire, a promoter (as I suppose he would be called today), a business adventurer who had made and lost fortunes, who had come to Knoxville a "capitalist," who had, in truth, brought much capital, both English and American, into the rapidly developing Southern mountain region, but who, in dying, had left behind for his family twelve hundred dollars.

There were, as a matter of fact, along with the insurance policy in his safety box at the bank, stocks in various mining and other companies which one day—and not far distant—would have yielded us more than a comfortable living. But hardly a year after his death Mama, in her ignorance of business and failing to get legal advice, parted with this whole packet of securities for a hundred dollars or so, persuaded by one of Papa's former business associates that they were hardly worth even that, though as an accommodation he was glad to take them off her hands.

Mama, however, did not seem dismayed at the small amount we had to start on. If she was worried, she did not betray it. High-spirited and impatient by nature, she had become very quiet and under the impact of our many misfortunes very patient. Extravagant also by nature, and luxury-loving, yet neither in these days, nor subsequently, did she ever complain, ever express anxiety as to how we would get along. Her whole nature seemed, indeed, to have undergone transformation, and if she was quieter than once, she was not gloomy, and, like Papa, not in the least embittered. Life was this way or that, and you must meet it as best you could.

To me, who had handled little money, the twelve-hundred dollars, immediately available, seemed a considerable sum, though, at that, I must have felt a certain anxiety as to what we should do when it was exhausted, for when a few days after Papa's death, one of Dr. Hood's children brought a bill from him for two hundred and fifty-dollars, I remember that I was more than disturbed, I was keenly hurt by what seemed to me an indelicate action, though Mama warmly defended Dr. Hood. He had waited a long time, she said; had a large family, needed the money. She sent him a check at once; also paid immediately the funeral and other bills that were due. Whatever else was ahead of us, at least we should not be harassed by duns.

It was during these first days of readjustment that one afternoon at home, in the parlor, we had the baby christened and given the name of Roger, since I was unwilling he should bear longer a name I had never liked, and of a father he would never know.[9]

It was after the christening, probably early in October, that I woke up to the fact, albeit with no reminder from Mama, that before long I should *have* to start earning money in some way or other. Other people, apparently, had already been giving this some thought, for that evening at the cistern, after Dr. Hood had come to tell me that Papa was dying; suddenly Mrs. Bauer appeared, sailing briskly toward me from around the corner of the house and not wasting a moment till she informed me, in an undertone, that there was a vacancy in the Public Schools she thought I might fill, if I applied for it.

I had long been acquainted with Mrs. Bauer's managing nature and I recognized, I trust, her good intentions, but there was nothing I could have resented more than such a suggestion at such a time.

Moreover, the last thing I would consider was teaching. My brief light-hearted fling at teaching at Miss Ogden's fashionable private school before I was married was something altogether different, and I was too familiar with the dowdy tired-faced Public School teachers of Knoxville to entertain for an instant the idea of becoming one of them. If I *had* to start before long on the unknown road of self-support, at least I would not consider *that*!

Now, in October, I was even more of this mind. I was coming at last a little more alive than at any time since I left Theodore. Once again my imagination was beginning to work. There were stirrings within me. Surely there must be something I could do which would be less prosaic than teaching.

It was in this mood I started scanning a column headed Female Help Wanted in the *Knoxville Journal* and came upon an advertisement for "general agents" wanted by some publishing house—or it may have been merely a distributing concern. In any event, you would travel and employ agents to sell books the company handled.

In correspondence with the company I learned you must pay them twenty-five dollars for your appointment as a "general agent," but would receive a commission of five dollars for every agent you appointed yourself.

Nothing, it seemed to me, could be more interesting than to travel to places you had never been in before, and the five dollars you would receive from every agent would insure your earning a good amount, even if you *did* pay your own traveling expenses. It was not in the least, either, I convinced myself, like being an ordinary "book agent," the kind of pest refused admittance to many houses where he called, including our own. No, I would not be selling books myself, and this would be, whatever else, a dignified way of earning a living. Of course I would have to leave Roger, but I did not dare dwell overmuch on that. Mama would look after him as well as I could, or better, and I would come home often.

When I explained the whole proposition to Mama, and with more enthusiasm, I dare say, than she had seen me show in a long time, she listened attentively, made no comment, but straightway put on her little black crêpe bonnet, with its flowing widow's veil, its snowy ruche forming a peak above her sad beautiful face, and went down to talk it over with the president of the East Tennessee Bank, and for whose judgment she knew Papa had had much respect.

On her return I could detect that the president of the bank had not been too favorably impressed with the idea, but by this time I was so on fire with it that whatever her own misgivings Mama kept them to herself, feeling, I presume, that any proposal on my part which showed initiative, after my long deadness, should not be discouraged. At any rate, she gave me without apparent reluctance the twenty-five dollars I must pay to the company and enough money besides to pay for my traveling expenses until I could take care of them out of my earnings. She even saw to it that, although I was all in black, the clothes I would start out with should be as becoming as possible.

The whole project, as I view it today, was such a palpable fraud, that it is hard for me to see how I could ever have been taken in by it, notwithstanding the fact that I was as ignorant as Mama of the ways of the business world. I have conveyed a little, however, I believe, of my actual feelings at the time in my first novel, *The Seas Of God*, written twenty-five years after,[10] and in which among its heroine's experiences I give an almost literal account of my own as I journeyed from one little town to another in lower East Tennessee (the territory the company assigned me), tramping endless weary miles in my endeavor to find agents who would sell the *History of Famous Women* and the *Imperial Galaxy of Poetry and Art*.[11]

At the end of ten days of as arduous effort as I have ever put forth, I had not been able to persuade a single person to go out and try to sell the two bulky ornate volumes which I lugged, as samples, around with me. I had not appointed a single agent; realized I never would, and, most alarming, that my money for traveling expenses was almost exhausted.

I had had adventures to be sure, though of a far from attractive, and sometimes frightening, character. At Sweetwater, the first little town on my itinerary, the impertinent desk-clerk at the hotel where I stopped for the night had practically forced his way into my room under the pretext of seeing it was in order, and, once there, suddenly seized and kissed me.

When I repulsed him furiously and blazed out at him, "I thought a business woman would be respected anywhere!" he came back at me with mingled anger and scorn, "You're a picture of a business woman, *you* are!"

But for all these unhappy experiences I could not go back—not yet, and report to Mama my utter failure.

I counted my money. There was just enough to get me to Atlanta where my cousin Jenny[12] and her husband, Arthur, a young couple with their first baby, were living.

Leaving the *History of Famous Women* and the *Imperial Galaxy of Poetry and Art* behind on a bench in the railway station, I caught a train headed for Atlanta. There Jenny and Arthur welcomed me warmly, quickly making room for me in their cramped quarters. Arthur, especially, found my recent misadventures highly amusing. He roared with laughter over them. He brought me to look at them less seriously myself and not to feel that the end of the world had come because I had been completely unsuccessful in this first "business" venture, so that by the time I reached the house on Highland Avenue I was able to make even Mama laugh over some of my experiences as a "general agent."

Thinking of those weeks, almost buried in time now, I marvel, considering the uncertainty of our future, that the atmosphere of our home remained prevailingly cheerful. There must have been in all of us, I think, at least a grain of that spirit which had animated Papa—we were not to be too easily downed as a family.

Of course there was Roger, who had become the center of our family life—Roger, who, more than ever I felt was worth every bit of pain, suffering, sorrow, I had been through or ever would be; who was running around everywhere, his antics a constant source of diversion, and upon whom, to my surprise and delight, Mama was lavishing the tenderest expressions, all those outward signs of devotion which she had never bestowed on her children, or in any such form.

But notwithstanding this normal family life, I continued to shrink from seeing friends of my own age, separated from me now, I could not cease feeling, by an all but impassible gulf; although I remember my distinct pleasure when Mrs. Lizzie Crozier French came to see me one afternoon.

I had admired Mrs. French from my first knowledge of her, because of her striking courage in standing out against much of the religious bigotry of which Knoxville was then a stronghold—and for aught I know still is. She was no longer principal of the East Tennessee Female Institute, which had passed into other hands, but alive in every fibre of her sturdy little body, she now taught private classes in "elocution" in her old red-brick house on Cumberland Street, her chief models of oratorical splendor Shakespeare and Victor Hugo.

Forthright, never effusive, yet a warm-hearted responsive human being, on this afternoon she talked with me about books and authors. She did not indicate in even the slightest degree that there was anything unusual in my present status or situation, but as if I were someone who would naturally be interested in subjects of absorbing interest and importance to her, especially in Victor Hugo as a great humanitarian; and while her call was not long, it was long enough for her to reopen windows for me on to that broader world to which I had once aspired to belong; it restored some of my self-respect, made me feel less a branded creature.

All this time, however, since my return from Atlanta, I still had not the faintest notion of what I was going to do to earn a living; but one day, shortly after Christmas, Mama gave me my first intimation of efforts some of her church friends had been making; and what they had found was a position for May as governess with a well-to-do farmer's family—Presbyterians, as would have been expected—somewhere up around Morristown, a small town north[east[13]] of Knoxville. As there was no school near, May would live with them and teach their three or four small children.

This news came to me as a shock. With five years difference in our ages—a considerable difference at that time in our lives—, although there had never been any hostility between us, not even the usual sisterly bickering, yet we had never been in each other's confidence. With friends of her own age, May was living in a world of her own, her inner life as completely hidden from me as mine from her. But now a slender, none-too-strong girl of seventeen, her face retaining a trace of the shyness it had shown in childhood, she was going out into the unknown—! The thought was sickening.

May had, of course, graduated from High School, had a year at the University, but I could not believe she was any more eager to teach than I. Furthermore, it would take far more courage for *her* to go out among strangers to earn a living than for me, who had never been timid when it came to meeting people I had never seen before.

All at once I was flooded with remorse. It swept through me that I had never realized before, as I should have, that May had not enjoyed such gayety as I had known in *my* girlhood, had been deprived of much that I had had. All the years of her own growing-up had been clouded, not alone through the change in our family fortunes, but she had shared my parents' tragic disappointment, their sense of family disgrace, when I had married against their will and secretly. She had suffered with them much that I knew of, much no doubt that I would never know. May, at whatever cost to herself, when I was far away, had been their one real comfort. And now she was going away to earn her living, and I, at home, making no further efforts to earn mine! The thought shamed me.

It not only shamed, it put some fight in me. Somehow or other I got hold of a book on shorthand and started to teach myself from it.

Stenography, as a job for a young woman, was still in the '90s, at least in Knoxville, looked at askance. With the intimate association with a man, her employer, which it required, it was not considered proper for a "nice" girl—if even "safe."

Aware, however, as I was, of all this, yet I had heard also that young women stenographers were more and more in demand, and from the moment May went forth from the house on Highland Avenue and I caught the stricken look in Mama's eyes as she bade her goodbye at the front door, though with cheerful and encouraging words, I set myself to studying shorthand in dead earnest. "Little May," as I still thought of her, should not be the only one of us earning something!

Except for brief stops to attend to Roger or play with him, I studied day and night. Almost every waking moment I devoted to the toughest subject I had ever tackled. As soon as I had even halfway learned the symbols, I had Mama dictating to me, to test my progress. But although I was beginning to fear I would never get anywhere with it, however hard I tried, yet I had not relaxed my efforts, and on the whole was less unhappy than for a long time past, and in a vague way more hopeful, so that I was not altogether surprised, and not resentful, as I would have been earlier, when one afternoon late in January Mama came to tell me that Mr. Jesse Rayl was downstairs in the parlor and would like to see me.

Mr. Rayl's call, I sensed instantly, could mean only one thing. A man of means who lived in one of the fine old red-brick houses on Main Street, a staunch Presbyterian and highly esteemed, Mr. Rayl was also a member of the Board of Education of the Public Schools.[14]

It was a cold dismal day and almost supper time. There was a fire in the parlor grate and as I entered the room, rather dusky except for the ruddy glow from the fire, Mr. Rayl, a small, wiry, gray-headed man with a short pointed gray beard, sprang from the arm-chair where he was sitting, met and shook hands with me cordially.

What he had to tell me was that they needed a teacher at the Bell House. An old square red-brick building, not far from the river and Gay Street, the Bell House, originally an inn, had been a hospital during the "late War," and was now one of the two public schools for boys in Knoxville, the Bell House used for those in its lower grades.[15]

Located in the toughest part of town, only a block away from the notorious Crozier Street, a solid line of saloons and houses of ill fame, the boys who went to the Bell House were well known as incorrigibles. No woman had ever taught them, and now, it seemed, the boys in the third grade there had "run off" three male teachers in succession. This was the "opening" which Mr. Rayl offered me, though he explained in the most kind-hearted manner that if I couldn't manage them, it would not go against my record, whereas if I could, it would lead to a much better position for me.

This was the first time that anyone officially—and only Mrs. Bauer, unofficially—had ever suggested my teaching in the Public Schools, but by this time I had come to the full realization that the only genteel thing a young woman in Knoxville could do to earn a living was teaching, unless clerking in a dry goods store, and that between the two, teaching, if not desirable, at least was less undesirable.

The salary, Mr. Rayl said, would be thirty dollars a month, and I accepted the position, with the understanding I would assume it a week hence—accepted without even consulting Mama. The truth is, I could now see no alternative.

As for the salary, thirty dollars did not seem to me a beggarly sum. It was the rate at which all Public School teachers started then in Knoxville, at least in the primary and grammar grades, and I would not have expected more. Even so, however, for Mama it posed a fresh problem. She had to face the fact that the insurance money could not last much longer. May, though her living was provided for, was earning as governess only three or four dollars a week, and with our rent on Highland Avenue thirty dollars a month, and my salary thirty, clearly the next thing to do was to find a cheaper house. This she found, with the aid of friends, and within the week we had moved to that vague hinterland—the last place I should have chosen to live in and the very thought of which had always depressed me—North Knoxville.

NOTES

1. A. Wetzell, "The Work of Olive Schreiner," *The Mount Holyoke* 1, no. 1 (June 1891): 1–3.
2. Dr. Samuel S. Ringgold was rector of St. John's Episcopal Church from 1887 until 1907, when he was named Rector Emeritus.
3. The day following the court hearing, on August 22, 1894, the *Knoxville Journal* reported that a decree of absolute divorce had been granted in the case of Annie A. Waldron (née Wetzell) vs. Leonard T. Waldron, but a search of the newspaper found no editorial such as mentioned by Armstrong. "Chancery Business," *Knoxville Journal*, August 23, 1894. However, the day after the original suit was filed in Chancery Court, an article under the headline "A Sensational Divorce Bill" stated that "the wife of Leonard Waldron, a young attorney of this city . . . alleges, among other things, cruel and inhuman treatment." "A Sensational Divorce Bill: Mrs. Waldron, Née Wetzel[l], Asks Release From Her Husband," *Knoxville Journal*, June 9, 1894.
4. Melvin L Dame and his wife, Ella, lived on West Clinch in Knoxville before moving to Harriman when East Tennessee Furniture [Factory] Company, of which Dame was secretary and manager, was recruited, along with other industries, to move to the new town of Harriman. Dame bought a lot on Unaka Street during Harriman's Great Land Sale in February 1890; however, the couple was living on Margrave Street in 1891 when Dame was elected chairman of the first Board of School Directors for Harriman. He held other public offices, and he and Mrs. Dame became influential members of the community. By 1900, Dame owned the East Tennessee Furniture Factory plant and converted it to the M. L. Dame Mantel Company. Knoxville City Directory, 1898, 1890; Pulliam, *Harriman*, 17, 184, 495, 498.

5. Henry B. Wetzell died at 5:30 a.m. September 11, 1894, at the age of 51. "Knoxville's Loss," *Knoxville Journal*, September 12, 1894. Readers who are familiar with *The Seas Of God* will notice marked similarities between Anne Armstrong's account of her father's death and her description of Lydia's father's death in the novel.
6. Armstrong had marked through this sentence in her manuscript.
7. Eastern State Hospital for the Insane opened in 1886 at Lyons View in West Knox County. It was closed in 2013.
8. Henry B. Wetzell's funeral service was conducted by the Reverend Dr. R. R. Sutherland, pastor of Second Presbyterian Church, assisted by the Reverend Dr. J. H. Frazee of Pilgrim Congregational Church. Dr. Sutherland "bore testimony to the manly traits so conspicuous in Mr. Wetzell's life," and Dr. Frazee, who, according to the newspaper report, had known Mr. Wetzell more intimately than anyone other than his family, "bore touching testimony to his noble manly character." "Funeral of Henry B. Wetzell," *Knoxville Journal*, September 13, 1894.
9. What name the baby was first given is not known. Knoxville City Health Department birth records list only an "unnamed male Waldron," born September 8, 1893, to Leonard and Anna W. Waldron. Knox County Archives, e-mail message to editor, July 15, 2019. Up until this point in her narrative, AWA refers to him only as "the baby" or "it." According to church records, baby "Roger Waldron," born September 8, 1893, was baptized "in private" on September 21, 1894, by the Reverend Samuel Ringgold. Parents listed as Leonard and Annie Waldron. No record of a previous baptismal name was found. Parish Register, St. John's Episcopal Church, entry no. 196. It should be noted that, although Armstrong changed the baby's given name, she retained his father's surname. In fact, she kept "Waldron" as her surname also. According to the divorce decree, "at her own request she is not restored to her maiden name." Case File, No. 6098 *Annie A. Waldron v. Leonard T. Waldron* (Knox Co., Tenn., Chancery Court 1894).
10. *The Seas Of God* was published anonymously in 1915 by Hearst's International Library Company. Armstrong revealed her identity when the book was published the next year in Great Britain by Mills and Boon.
11. The first book is more than likely *Famous Women of History: Containing Nearly Three Thousand Brief Biographies and Over One Thousand Female Pseudonyms*, by William Hardcastle Browne (Philadelphia: Arnold and Company, 1895), 434 pages. The second, *The Imperial Galaxy of Poetry and Art: A Peerless Cluster of the Choicest Productions of the World's Masters in Literature and Art . . .* "Selected by a Large Staff of Literary Experts" (Philadelphia: Hubbard Bros., 1890), 543 pages.
12. Jenny was the daughter of Daniel M. Wetzell, the brother of AWA's father. Her husband was Arthur Williams.
13. Marked out in manuscript.
14. Jesse Addison Rayl (1825–1897) was "one of the founders and always a strong friend of the public schools in Knoxville." In addition to helping secure money (through the first

tax levy for public schools), he was a member of the first Knoxville Board of Education, remained a member for twenty-three years, and served as president for ten years. He was involved in a number of business ventures in Knoxville, was a ruling elder in First Presbyterian Church for forty years, and served on the board of directors of the Associated Charities of Knoxville, a benevolent organization. Rayl Elementary School on Park Avenue (now Magnolia) was built in the late 1890s and named in his honor. Rule, 413; Rothrock, 303; Deaderick, 238–39, 242, 245, 343.

15. The Bell House, at the southwest corner of East Main and State Street, was originally a hotel. It opened as a Knoxville public school in September 1872. Rule, 403. The space where it stood is now occupied by the Riverview Tower BB&T Building, a bank and office complex.

Chapter Nineteen
North Knoxville

The double house into one side of which we moved was on Third Avenue, I believe it was, though I'm no longer sure of the name of this street. A faded yellow, the house had a sort of slapped-in-the-face look, as its tall broadish front was all windows. The entrance to each division being at the side, through a good-sized old-fashioned porch, such as you saw in the country then, only a step above the ground.

A picket fence separated the shallow bare front yard from the street, while next us, on our open side, and all too near, was a sprawling, exceedingly ugly house whose noisy family we were quickly made aware of through its owner and occupant, a slatternly middle-aged widow, at all hours of the day yelling at the top of her lungs to her son, a boy in his early teens, "Young man, if you don't behave yourself, I'm goin' to send you to Bell Buckle!"—that school famed for its teaching of the classics, equally for its floggings, and generally looked upon as a sort of reform school.

Never before had we had a near neighbor of this class and I reflected sadly that if our family had come down a notch in moving from the Barnes house to Highland Avenue, beyond a doubt it had come down another in moving to this house in North Knoxville. But you couldn't have everything for fifteen dollars a month, and the street itself, along which ran a streetcar, one no longer drawn by mules, but electrified, was lined with trees and not painfully raw-looking for all it was in this newer part of town. Some handsome homes had, in fact, been built on it, the handsomest directly opposite us, home of the Presbyterian friends who had found the house with its cheaper rent for Mama; while just beyond them lived other friends of ours, the McAdoos, than whom, whatever else might be said about this extraordinary family with strains of both cavalier and pioneer blood in its veins, yet no one could deny there was none more cultivated or aristocratic in Knoxville.[1]

So however commonplace our new home, however uncouth our next-door neighbors, I could take comfort in the fact that the neighborhood as a whole was a genteel one. Besides, the house, three stories high, had more room than the one we had left, and Mama was able to rent two sizable adjoining rooms on its second floor to a couple who would do light-housekeeping there, and their rent add a little to our alarmingly small income.

Then, although Mama had given away some of our more massive pieces of furniture, enough remained to give the smallish, detached, square front parlor downstairs that air of elegance I felt our parlor had always worn. She succeeded, too, in making the larger room, back of the parlor, separated from it by a narrow hall, and which we would use as dining- and sitting-room, not only comfortable, but attractive, in spite of its discouraging outlook on the unkempt side yard of our neighbors next-door. None the less, it must have been, as I look back, a sore blow to Mama's pride when, to make ends meet, she must have "roomers" in her home.

The "roomers," recent arrivals in Knoxville from somewhere in the Middle West, stated at once, not vauntingly, but as a thing they should tell us, that they were Seventh Day Adventists, a sect of which we knew little, though considered, so far as we did, more than a little peculiar. But with their frank, cheerful, rosy faces, in their simple old-fashioned clothes, they were so immaculate in appearance, so disarming in their manner, that Mama had only hesitated a moment or so when they applied for the rooms.

With a short fair square-cut beard, always in a well-brushed black suit, the man may have been a minister, or perhaps they were both missionaries seeking converts to their particular faith. In any event, they made no attempt to convert us, and though no one, as I recall it, ever came to see them, they were out a good deal of the time about whatever their business was. In their rooms, which they kept as spotless as themselves, they were always quiet, though always quick to give help when occasion suggested help might be acceptable.

Reminiscently, I believe it was the presence in the house of these two kind and capable Seventh Day Adventists which made it possible for me to undertake the hardest test to which my powers of endurance and ingenuity have ever been put—what was to prove my ordeal by fire.

From the day they settled into their rooms they showed deep interest in little flaxen-haired, blue-eyed Roger. They romped with him, contrived toys for him out of kindling wood or anything at hand, read and sung to him, from time to time fed him some of the wholesome dishes which, as vegetarians, they prepared for themselves. They bandaged his cut finger or chubby skinned knee, ministered to all his childish ills, including measles and a sudden attack of membraneous [*sic*] croup one night when Mama and I were panic-struck lest he choke to death before the doctor arrived. Both of them, as a matter of fact, had had considerable experience in healing and nursing, as well as a knowledge of dietetics. But best of all, at their own insistence they looked after him when Mama must go to market or on some other essential errand; so that whatever lay ahead of me, it was with a free mind, so far as Roger was concerned, I could start out the minute I finished breakfast for the Bell House, dreadfully afraid I'd be late, for school began at eight, teachers were docked a dollar if not on time, and it was a long walk, two or three miles at least.

I wonder today why I didn't take the streetcar. Was it because it didn't run at the right hours and anyway wouldn't have taken me the whole distance? But whatever the reason—and more likely than anything else it was because we couldn't afford even car-fare—I always walked every step of the way, in fair weather or when it was raining torrents; often, in my first weeks of teaching, not fully light when I left home in the morning, dusk when I returned in late afternoon.

I always went the same way; along Third Avenue for a good many blocks, then striking off obliquely in the direction of the wooden viaduct which spanned a broad grimy expanse of railroad tracks, with engines always shifting back and forth, and half hidden by smoke the soot-stained passenger-depot and freight-sheds in the murky depths underneath.

After I crossed the viaduct, I would leave Gay for State Street, below and parallel with it, where I would meet few people at this hour, but pass the dead-looking backs of Gay Street store-buildings on one side; on the other, the century-old First Presbyterian Church, with its Greek portico and its old burying-ground[2] in which were the graves both of William Blount, first "Governor of the Territory South of the River Ohio," and of James White, founder of Knoxville. But I had no eyes at this hour—or at any hour in those days—for old churches, appealing though I once might have found them—none for historic sites, for landmarks of any sort. As I hurried along, nearing the Bell House now, and almost running, I was always completely absorbed in the one thought that had filled me since I left home: *What shall I try today?*

But it was my first day at the Bell House which naturally remains with me more vividly than any other. There were about forty boys in the front corner room on the second floor which the janitor informed me was mine; boys mostly around ten or eleven, though among them one great loutish youth of fifteen, still in knee breeches, and who appeared to be a ring leader in all the devilment that started as soon as they had marched into the room at the sound of a gong somewhere and seated themselves behind the double desks where apparently they were supposed to sit.

Not a word of suggestion or advice had been given me beforehand by Prof. Andes,[3] principal of the school, a good-looking, pleasant-mannered young man whom I had met, a few minutes before, and for the first time, as I was taking off my hat and coat and hanging them up in the hall—not a word from him or anyone else. It was up to me, it seemed, to survive or to go down in ignominious defeat before these hoodlums, as my three predecessors had done.

A second gong sounded. I stood on the small platform in the front of the room, near its door into the hall, and faced the boys, nearly all of them shabbily dressed, some of them anything but clean. In my hand I held a book, *Biblical Selections*, which I had found on the desk beside me, and I opened it at the Psalms, intending to read one of them and follow it with the Lord's Prayer, repeated in unison, the

Map of downtown Knoxville (from Pill's New Map of Knoxville, Tenn., and Suburbs, 1895).

usual opening exercises, I knew, in the public schools, but before I had finished reading the first verse in the Psalm my voice was drowned out by whistling and catcalls.

I started once more. This time one of the boys landed a savage punch on his seat-mate's nose, which began bleeding; the other boys sprang from their seats, blows started to fly in one direction and another as the boys took sides in the fracas, and what I faced now was pandemonium.

I asked the boys to be seated again. Some instinct prompted me not to raise my voice as I did so. I asked a second and third time, if in a little more decisive tone, yet no louder. But the boys continued to pay no attention, so I continued to stand and look at them, silent now and my face as expressionless as I could make it. Scared though I was, I was getting interested, too. What would happen next? Surely, I thought, they must have *some* curiosity about the first feminine teacher ever in charge of this or any other boys' room in the Knoxville schools. Sooner or later they would stop long enough in their stalking around the room, scuffling, shooting marbles, firing at each other erasers and sticks of chalk they took from under the blackboards—long enough at least to look me over, size me up.

But they evinced no curiosity about me whatever. Not one of them threw me so much as a glance. So I went on standing or sitting, alternately, but fearfully conscious all the while that directly under us was the office of Prof. Ruth, Superintendent of Schools,[4] a rigid disciplinarian, an ogre not only to every school child but to every school teacher in town. As the din went on, my heart began to pound. Known as Rufus the Red, from his bristling auburn beard and fiery temper, Prof. Ruth at any moment might rush up the stairs, burst into the room, take a hand himself, and above everything, I didn't want *that!* This was *my* challenge. *I* must meet it!

The horrors of that first day at Bell House were such that I have never wished to recall them too clearly. They remain a good deal of a jumble in my mind. All the same, I *do* remember that at length I abandoned any idea of reading a Psalm, saying the Lord's Prayer, or even attempting a roll-call. I just sat now and waited, silently watching the boys, observing their looks, little by little getting from them, one after another—not without some resistance on their part—their names, and fixing them in my mind by pencilled [*sic*] notes. "Willy, the big one. Clyde, neat. Pete, red hair. Walter, lame. Harry, dancing black eyes."

I remember, too, trying, when the morning already was far spent, to start a geography lesson, and when a boy here and there showed slight signs of wanting to hear what I was saying but other boys started making various crude and deafening noises, that I did not reprove them, I simply stopped and waited until there was comparative quiet before I went on.

By the time a gong announced that school was over for that day, disheartening, maddening, though the day had been, yet I could tell that the fun of these young rascals in baiting a new teacher who did not storm at them, did not appear even to notice their riotous behavior, unless by silence, had lost some of its gusto, was not so much fun after all.

What I had hit upon, by purest chance, long before Gandhi had become a world figure, long before I ever heard of him, was his method of "passive resistance." In charge of the room before I came these boys had known only some stooped, seedy, gray-faced, tired-looking, bloodless oldish man, such as taught boys then in the lower grades, laying about him with a stout hickory stick, and when they ganged up on him beaten to his knees.

To pit my own slight physical strength against this demoralized roomful of boys I realized at once would be ridiculous. But the method of handling them which, in my desperation, I decided upon during the first moment of our encounter, had at least the virtue of novelty. What's more, it worked, and through it ultimately I was able to attain—unbelievable as it may seem—a school-room that was a model of order and at times so quiet I could hear the ticking of the big round clock on the wall.

This state of things, it needs hardly be said, was not achieved in a day. It was days and days before I could conduct a lesson not interrupted by the shooting of paper-wads, of boys talking out loud or scraping their feet on the floor, if nothing worse; still longer before I was able to arouse in them any real interest in their studies. Moreover, once aroused, I realized this interest must be maintained. I could not rest on my oars. I must never relax my vigilance in dealing with these half-grown rowdies, so alert themselves, so experienced and devilishly resourceful in mischief-making.

It was this I constantly thought of while I was walking to school each day, and one dark drizzly morning as I was hastening across the long Gay Street viaduct, barely conscious of the gloomy chasm of railroad tracks yawning underneath, of locomotives puffing and snorting below, it suddenly occurred to me—I remember the moment perfectly—that I might try reading to the boys during the last period in the afternoon whenever their conduct in the preceding hours had been a bit better than usual and seemed to warrant recognition.

This course proved successful beyond my brightest hopes. I was touched when I observed how intently the boys listened to *Robinson Crusoe* and *Swiss Family Robinson*, works not one of them has ever heard of before, or to stories I told them, stories I dug out of Oliver Optic[5] and other boys' books that had belonged to my brother Harry.

I don't think, in point of fact, I was ever completely discouraged, ever despaired, while I was being put through this rugged test at the Bell House, or save, at most, for a few moments in the course of that first tumultuous, awful morning there. I had no time for discouragement. Too much was at stake. I was engaged in what loomed before me as little short of a life and death struggle. Every fibre of my still very young being was concentrated on it. I was responsible now not only for my own and Mama's bodily support, but for Roger's. My course was clear, mind undivided; and as I came and went to the Bell House, often weary on the homeward way almost to the point of utter exhaustion, yet, happily, I had lost the sense of humiliation, if not actual disgrace, over my strange new status as a divorced person, a feeling which only a few months before had all but obsessed me. I had also ceased to think, except fleetingly, of Theodore. All the horrors of my life with him seemed, for the time, blotted out. In my heart and soul concentration on present necessities, in my new-found iron determination to overcome all obstacles in my path, insuperable though they might have appeared at the outset, even thoughts of Bob, the one man I had truly loved, seldom crossed my mind. Still less did I suffer from envy of old friends who continued prominent in social affairs from which, through force of circumstances, I was now, and perhaps forever, shut out. But never before, the truth is, had existence had such point.

Such point, and such joy! Every morning, as winter dawns gave way and it grew light earlier, Roger, his dimpled hand hotly clasped in mine, would run along beside me for a couple of blocks on my way to school. Already we were great chums.

Always on the same corner I would bend down, and his arms tight around my neck, kiss him goodbye. Often, after we parted, I would run back a few steps to kiss his sweet, clean, rosy face again, to look once more into his dewy eyes, shining into mine, and even after this second parting and I had started on, irresistibly I would turn, and there he would be, still standing on the spot where I had left him, little tufts of his fair hair pushing out all around his forehead from under the red knitted cap he wore, gazing after me, smiling a little wistfully. But now something would close around my heart and hurt me sharply, although, inextricably mixed with this pain was such happiness as I had never known before.

Some mornings, as we made our brief blissful journey together, instead of holding my hand, Roger would be pushing a little red wheelbarrow ahead of him, and then, after we parted, I would keep looking back as long as I could see him, the dangling peak of his red cap bobbing up and down as he trudged along toward home on his sturdy little legs, the wheelbarrow before him. But whatever my last sight of him had been, however absorbed I was in the pressures of the moment, yet all day long in the dusty school-room my inner eye would be fixed on this glowing early morning vision of Roger in his red cap. It was this that fed me.

It was this, I believe, that made for quicker understanding on my part than I might otherwise have had of these guttersnipes in the Bell House—and guttersnipes they were. Through Roger, all boys of any age, anywhere, had become of interest.

But be that as it may, it is certain that from the first day I knew them, despite their outrageous behavior at the start, I began to like these boys. Of course this may have been, partly at least, because I had not entirely forgotten what an unconscientious pupil *I* had been—what a natural rebel against authority. I may have discerned in them, if in exaggerated form, yet something of myself, something that made us kin.

In any event, I could not fail to realize that I was having contact now with the lowest strata of Knoxville's population, with boys who had had little, or no, chance to be anything else than what they were. With the river only a block or so below the Bell House, some of them came from tough families who lived in dilapidated houses along the river-front, piecing out a precarious existence by rat-catching, promoting cock fights and other illicit sports, by begging and thieving. Others were from Crozier Street, as near the Bell House, in another direction, as the river, and a solid line of brothels and saloons—Knoxville's "bad street." The first thing, in fact, I learned about the origin of any of these boys was that Harry, with his merry black eyes, a slim handsome lad in long pants, had been born and never lived anywhere else than in the house of ill fame of which his mother was madam.

But these, such as they were, were *my* boys, and shortly a friendship grew up between us, though this is not to say that with the friendship all my problems and perplexities vanished.

When it came to individual boys, for a good while any sudden outbreak of disorder, in whatever quarter, could usually be traced to Harry, who, along with his smiling guileless face, was sly. So I changed his seat to one directly under my eye and from then on, while we frequently exchanged glances, mine of warning, his of mischievous understanding, now he no longer disturbed the peace which in general prevailed.

Seeing this handsome good-natured little fellow at such close range, it would have been hard to convince me that, in spite of his devilish air, there was anything vicious in Harry, yet only a few years later he robbed Old Man Melton, the town's most gentlemanly beggar, of his pension from the Mexican War which he had just cashed, murdered the old man, threw his body into one of the sluggish creeks that ran through this part of town, and at sixteen was sentenced to life imprisonment in the state penitentiary at Nashville.

But if Harry, destined to be a lifer, is as plain to me today as when he sat directly under my eye, there was another boy in the room who would make an even deeper impression. It was the tall, loutish Willy who, I soon learned, had been in this same third grade room for years, incapable of advancing, and much of the work even in this grade beyond his comprehension.

Like Harry, Willy was amiable, and there was nothing in him that seemed really evil. Nevertheless he became my hardest problem. He would break into almost any recitation with guffaws that distracted the attention of the other boys, or with loud foolish remarks that set them tittering. No reprimand, no keeping after school, had the slightest effect, and at last I sought the advice of the principal.

"There is only one thing," Mr. Andes said, "that Willy understands, and that is whipping."

Corporal punishment was, of course, not only practised [*sic*] in Knoxville but common at the time in schools throughout this country. For all that, however, Mr. Andes' suggestion gave me a sinking feeling.

"But *I* can't whip him," I protested, as Mr. Andes and I talked together in the hall, with Willy in the room where I had told him to remain after the other boys were dismissed. Willy had been even more exasperating than usual all that day.

"Well, I can whip him *for* you," Mr. Andes said. "I've whipped him before, but he will never respect your authority, he will never behave any better, unless you whip him yourself."

Seldom in my life, I believe, has my heart gone more out me than at this instant. But I could see that what Mr. Andes said was probably true.

"When," I asked, in a hushed and horrified voice, "shall I whip him?"

"Now," Mr. Andes said, softly but firmly. He opened the door to my room. "Willy," he called, "come out here. Your teacher is not going to stand any more of your bad behavior." He brought a whip from his office and left me alone with Willy.

"Willy, stand in that corner," I said.

Willy meekly took his place in the corner, his back to the wall.

I was trembling. I realized that this big ungainly fellow, his small head towering above mine, could, if he chose, easily overpower me, though it was not this—or not this entirely, which made me tremble, made my knees weak. It was the thought of the thing I was about to do, against which every instinct in me revolted. But I grasped the whip as resolutely as my shaking hand permitted and whipped him across his long bony shanks in their coarse wrinkled gray stockings that were half coming down, exposing his knobby knees. I lashed him again and again, with all my strength, in this close proximity sickeningly aware of the fetid smell which escaped his great overgrown, undernourished, unclean body, and from his shabby clothes, seldom changed. But Willy made no attempt to resist me. He stood perfectly still, only making a little whimpering sound when the whip cut into his bare flesh, and all of the time a surprised, hurt look on his face, and in his eyes the dumb, timidly-beseeching expression I have seen only in dog's eyes—and in Willy's.

Never again, after I whipped him, did Willy cause any trouble. He became the quietest, the best boy in the room, even walking on tiptoe, if gawkily, in his clumsy worn-out shoes, across the school-room floor; always seeking some little way to serve or please me; asking to stay after school so he could erase the blackboards for me, and as spring advanced bringing me each morning a handful of more or less wilted flowers he had picked up somewhere.

But in all the years since, I have never quite been able to get Willy out of my mind. Long after my days at the Bell House, at the Prado in Madrid, as I gazed at those masterpieces of Velázquez, portraits of El Bobo and El Nino, dwarf jesters at the court of Philip IV, with their dim-witted, gently-pleading faces, I quailed before them. I was looking at Willy. I felt on my own flesh the lashes long ago I had laid on Willy's.

It was near the close of school, final examinations had started, when something happened which preserved in my memory still another of the boys at the Bell House.

Clyde had stood out from the first among the other boys because he was the smallest of them, and the neatest, his hair always carefully brushed. No instigator of trouble, he had been simply a follower, though inclined to be inattentive, and often as I passed up and down the aisles to see what the boys were doing with the examples in arithmetic I had given them, and found Clyde dreamily looking into space or idly drawing pictures, I would rap him sharply across the knuckles with the ruler I carried, to bring him back to his work.

On an afternoon in late May, as he was running across the street to reach home, he fell and was trampled to death by the horses of a heavy truck that was passing. It was rare, almost unknown, in those days, for children, even children playing in the street, to be killed by a vehicle of any sort, and little Clyde's sudden and terrible death, only a few minutes after school had been dismissed, made a deep impression, especially on his school-mates.

The day of the funeral I went with the boys, strangely slicked-up and sober-faced, to Clyde's home, too small for us all during the funeral services, so I took my place with the boys outside in the yard, and I shall never forget that when the coffin holding Clyde's small mutilated body was carried past us to the waiting hearse, the thought that ran through me was of the times when, impatiently, I had rapped him sharply across the knuckles, though it was I who winced now, just as years later it was I who would feel the sting of the whip I had used on Willy.

But whatever regrets troubled me on the sad afternoon of Clyde's funeral, from that hour a strong tie bound the other boys and myself together.

All these weeks, however, all these months, that I had been at the Bell House, though I had frequently consulted with Mr. Andes after school, not once had either he or Prof. Ruth ever visited my room. Perhaps they thought best to leave me entirely to my own devices. In any event, while I had noticed it, I had given no particular consideration to this lack of attention, not even wondering whether it augured well or ill for my future. In those driven days at the Bell House, with the incessant pressure of the present, I had as little time for indulging in dreams of the future as for dwelling on the past. At most, I expected I would probably be continued in my present position; so that nothing could have surprised me more when early one morning, during the last days of school, as I was dressing, Mama appeared at the door of my bedroom, breathless from climbing two steep flights of stairs faster than usual, her face flushed, her eyes flooded with tears.

"Look, Annie, look!" and she held out the morning paper, where I read that the Board of Education, in making assignments for the coming year, had appointed me teacher of English in the Girls High School, and at a salary almost double what I had been drawing.

I could hardly believe my eyes!

But I had barely taken in this joyful news when I learned, to my dismay, that even after appointment, a teacher, through some recent regulation, could not assume a position in the High School until she had passed examinations on all subjects taught there, and that such examinations were given by Prof. Ruth.

True, I had only been out of school four years, but I had lived through much in those years. I felt they had erased from my mind all I had learned either at college or high school. The only examinations I did not dread were in English and Ancient History—probably I could get through them. As for Latin, although it had been one of my favorite subjects, this was a different matter, at least when the examiner was Prof. Ruth, with his reputation as a classical scholar. Worst of all, though, would be geometry, which like all other branches of mathematics I detested and in which I had been conspicuously weak.

However, I would not be examined till late August, and with fresh heart in me from the recognition of my work at the Bell House, I started at once gathering together my old text-books, and buckled to.

All that long hot summer, when usually I was wet to the skin by noon, and with its sweltering nights when even a sheet was too much cover, I bent for hours on end over studies which once I had been so casual about, but now must master.

Looking back, it seems to me I worked harder that summer than any other I have known, although it was not without its alleviations. It was pleasant after supper, somewhat cooler then, to sit in the semi-darkness of our broad side-porch, with friends dropping in and time at this end of the day to romp with Roger, strong-willed but constitutionally happy, so that it was fun even to put him to bed.

Furthermore, there was what, for me, was a momentous experience that summer; close association with the McAdoos, living, as they were now, only across the street. It was the beginning of my intimate acquaintance with Laura (named for Petrarch's Laura), that radiant creature who had fired my imagination way back in the days when I was going to school in the Barton Building and Laura would pass through our room on the way to her own, leaving a trail of incandescent light in her wake, a young goddess, as I looked upon her—and still was inclined to.

In those earlier days, the McAdoos were living in the plain square old white frame house which was near the river and in romantic proximity to the tavern where Louis Philippe of France, in exile, had stopped on his "wilderness journey"; Laura's father a professor at the University; her mother, to eke out his small salary, keeping boarders, although from all accounts hers was no ordinary boarding-house, with even its simplest dishes served with dignity, with its table-talk never allowed to degenerate into the usual local petty gossip, and with Mrs. McAdoo herself rising every morning at four that she might have some hours for reading Shakespeare, Corneille, Racine, or Moliere, before the heavy duties of her day caught her.

In the years since, the McAdoos had lived, for a while, in the Union Bank building on Main Street, which had been converted into a private residence; a noble structure in the Greek Revival style, with four massive Corinthian columns supporting its classic pediment; its entrance, directly from the street, through a broad portico with stone balustrades and flagged floor; its austere outlines softened by tall waving trees that partly shadowed it on either side—to me, with its lofty rooms, the only residence that ever seemed worthy of this distinguished family.[6]

But if their present home, built for his parents by their son, the William Gibbs McAdoo, a New York attorney who would one day be Secretary of the Treasury of the United States and marry a daughter of President Wilson[7]—if this gray frame house, of a type common in the '90s, was far from imposing, yet doubtless it was more convenient and comfortable than their previous ones. Moreover, inside at least, despite its scanty, rather shabby furnishings, it preserved some of that atmosphere inseparable from any house the McAdoos lived in.

When, late in the afternoon, as a brief respite from study, I would cross the street to see Laura, she would take me into their shuttered, dim and coolish, if airless, library, lined from floor to ceiling with books, and I would think of the first time I had been in the room, a year or so before. I would see Laura's father, a tall, stooped, very frail old man who, with his snowy hair and whiskers, looked, as was often remarked, like the poet Longfellow—see him tottering into the room in his slippers and dressing-gown, in vague search of some volume or other. I would hear Laura's tender, "Let me help you, Pappa!"—as if his fine mind were still intact.

Pappa was lying in Old Gray now,[8] but upstairs, invariably, whatever the heat, Mrs. McAdoo, her own intellectual vigor unimpaired, would be stitching away on organdy or Swiss dresses, whipping on by hand their yards upon yards of lace or embroidery trimming; dresses that were always for Laura, youngest of seven, still unmarried, and with her regal beauty, air at once imperious and gracious, her brilliant mind, a source of more pride to her mother than, for all her selfless devotion to her other children, she could quite hide.

Once in a while now, as a special self-indulgence, I would spend almost all afternoon with Laura, and then we would sit on their shady side-porch, dense honeysuckle vines shielding us both from the street and the eyes of neighbours, and in turn read aloud Maeterlinck's *The Sightless*,[9] his *Pelléas and Mélisande*, and other of his early plays, with their delicate fantasy, mystery, their melancholy tone; plays still new at the time, and considered somewhat baffling even by readers attracted to them.

But if some of our reading was melancholy in tone on these midsummer afternoons when most of that North Knoxville neighborhood was drowsing, our talk in general was anything but that. Laura, along with her swiftly alternating moods, grave and gay, had one of the most spontaneous, one of the merriest, of laughs; while for me it was the first time since I had felt the terrible compulsion to marry Theodore that I had laughed unrestrainedly. Some tension in me at last was broken, and Laura and I laughed together as much as we read or talked.

The thing, however, that brought us closest together was our mutual interest in the work of Walt Whitman—Whitman, one of the strong shaping influences of my own life; Whitman, who had, in fact, whether for ultimate good or ill, changed its course, and who still had little recognition in this country, notwithstanding he had already won a place, internationally, as an outstanding poet of the New World; so that Laura and I, reading to each other from his *Leaves of Grass*, stirred and fused by our common acceptance of this social radical, sexual radical, radical in democracy, too American for Americans slavishly following European cultural patterns, felt all the excitement of fellow conspirators in our opposition to the respectable, orthodox ideas held, as we well knew, by most of our acquaintances in Knoxville, or anywhere else.

Except Theodore, Laura was the first person with whom I had ever discussed this revolutionary poet. But Laura's world was expanding in more directions, and much faster, than mine. She was away from Knoxville a good deal now; visiting cousins in Georgia, where she needed all these elaborate white dresses her mother made her (she was in "light mourning" at the time). It was in Georgia she met an Italian count, a social lion of the hour, and who, dazzled, I suppose, by Laura's commanding beauty, her supreme aplomb, made mad love and proposed to her, although when he came to Knoxville and spent a week-end in her home, his ardor cooled, a contretemps which Laura, while not averse to becoming a countess, nevertheless laughed over in her usual merry fashion after the count departed, obviously seeking a more substantial lot than was promised by the McAdoos' modest ménage.

It was, though, Laura's experiences in New York, where she visited her brother Will at his home in the suburbs, or stayed in the city, boarding somewhere, that made the most vivid impression on me.

In New York, where she was having treatment by a celebrated specialist for some digestive disorder (for all her appearance of superb health, she was never strong), somehow or other Laura had been drawn into the circle of aesthetes that flocked around Parisian-born William Ordway Partridge, noted sculptor, who was making portrait-busts of many of the bigwigs of the day, and with frequent exhibitions of his work in this country and abroad.

Here, in this circle of cosmopolitan, highly-sophisticated artists and intellectuals, Laura found a milieu that was completely congenial, and some of whose color and fascination she was able to pass on to me, together with an impression that Partridge himself had become of more than ordinary interest to her, as she to him;

though, for all that, when a year or so later a story went the rounds in Knoxville that Laura had posed for this sculptor "in the altogether," I doubted it; just as I was to doubt subsequent stories about her when I had grown to understand better and better the deep-seated anti-intellectual tradition in American life, which inevitably would make a family like the McAdoos suspect, and *facile princeps*, in almost any American community, for gossip of a more or less scandalous nature.

But whether stories about Laura, first and last, were true or false, I have known, personally, few more stimulating persons, and I can say, without reservations, that she enriched my life.

I like, too, to recall the friendship which developed, during that summer in North Knoxville, between Laura's mother and mine, who previously had known each other only slightly, but now almost every evening, sooner or later, would have a visit together, just by themselves, on our shadowy porch.

A tall gaunt woman, always in the plainest of black, with her cavernous eyes and deep croaking voice, Mrs. McAdoo suggested the Tragic Muse more forcibly than did the famed Mrs. Siddons in her portrait by Sir Joshua Reynolds.[10] She possessed, however, a strong sense of humor and there was as much mirth in her hoarse chuckling laugh as in her daughter Laura's silvery-toned, merrier one.

But for all her sense of the comic, her chuckling laugh, Mrs. McAdoo was, in truth, a woman of many sorrows, and one who still carried heavy burdens. Now over sixty, she worked as hard as any slave ever had on her father's great plantation on one of the Sea Islands of Georgia where she had been born and grown up; yet she refused to be defeated, to be embittered, even to lose her great natural dignity.

Though born to luxury, her father, a general in the Confederate Army, had been ruined by the War, so that she had early known deprivation, even biting poverty.[11] She had written several novels, well received at the time; contributed to various periodicals;[12] finally kept boarders to help support her growing family; and now, in her age, at last with a home of her own, she had taken into it two little boys to bring up, children of a son by her first marriage, a son who had become what today we call a chronic alcoholic, then simply, and perhaps less charitably, a drunkard—in any case, a social outcast, who, so her closest neighbors reported, was often seen at dusk skulking around to his mother's back door for food; reporting also, with some indignation, that it was Mrs. McAdoo who did all the work that was done in her home—that it was she who carried in the heavy buckets of coal which kept the fires in the house going, carried them even upstairs to the bedrooms of Laura and her older sister Carrie, who, to all appearances, never lifted a finger themselves in the way of domestic labor.

It is doubtful, however, if Mrs. McAdoo herself felt any indignation at this state of things. One of those incredibly unselfish Southern mothers of her generation, in straightened circumstances she was chiefly concerned, like Mary Gaines' mother, that her daughters should not miss social triumphs of a sort *she* had known in her youth, before the old social order in the South was swept away. If there was any finery, it must be for her still unmarried daughters; if red and roughened hands, it must be her own, not theirs.

At all events, she was keenly enjoying the little boys, five and seven, she was bringing up. Frequently, in the evening, when Mama and Mrs. McAdoo were visiting on our dusky porch, their laughter, though subdued, would reach me inside, where I was studying, and I suspected they were laughing over some comical sayings or doings of Mrs. McAdoo's little grandsons.

But Mama likewise had a lively little grandson in her care. The two women had, in fact, not a little in common. Both were widows; both had known in their lives sharp reversal of fortune; both had lost a promising young son through drowning, Mrs. McAdoo within the past year. Then, if Mrs. McAdoo must carry on her heart a living son for whom she had cherished great hopes, but now a drunkard, Mama had known the mortification of my secret marriage and its recent sensational sequel in the divorce court. Yes, beyond a doubt, it was a world of wordless sympathy which forged, during that summer, a lasting bond between these two essentially reserved and proud women.

But there was still another of the astonishing McAdoos we came to know at this time. Carrie would often come in the evening, if quite sure she would find neither her mother nor Laura on our porch.

Tall, slender, patrician-looking, Carrie was yet not the outstanding beauty her sisters were. It was not this, however, which marked her out signally from the other members of her family. Endowed with the same exceptional intelligence that all the McAdoos possessed, her own interests, judged by her conversation, were wholly frivolous.

Carrie's ruling passion had become "pretty clothes," and on these evening visits she was always talking about the costumes, describing them in minute detail, she was going to have as soon as she could save enough out of her niggardly salary from teaching school, a profession no teacher could ever have hated more, notwithstanding that she was known not only as an excellent teacher but a popular one.

When Carrie was not talking about clothes, she was poking fun at the intellectual pretensions, as she made them appear, of her brothers and sisters; sparing none, though reserving her deadliest satire for Laura, who read easily in any number of languages, and of whom obviously she was extremely jealous, though jealous, one could guess, not so much on the score of Laura's scholarly attainments as because Laura's suitors were mature and eligible men, whereas Carrie—a Blanche DuBois,[13] frustrated and piteous, as I see her now—had had to fall back on the attentions, such as they were (never paid openly and usually taking the form of buggy rides after dark), of young boys many years her junior.

Exceedingly witty and a matchless mimic, what I remember best was Carrie's hilarious account of their weekend visit from the Italian count, whose abrupt end to his courtship of Laura it was plain she relished wickedly.

But although Mama and I might laugh irresistibly at some of Carrie's stories caricaturing her family, we always felt disloyal in even listening to them and would welcome the arrival while she was with us of any other visitor, especially when, as often happened, it was Mrs. Percy of Greenville, Mississippi, spending the summer with her daughter, who had married a Knoxville man and was living in the next house beyond the McAdoos.[14]

Mrs. Percy was the unforgettable "Mur" of Will Percy's *Lanterns on the Levee*, his grandmother who, left on the plantation while her husband in the Confederate Army was away fighting the War, had raised her little brood single-handed and managed the thousand-acre plantation besides; "Mur," Will Percy's first chum, whom he pictured "always dressed in black," . . . "[her] figure ample, moving splendidly and slowly like an ocean steamer, with back of her silver-white pompadour a small widow's bonnet from which hung a widow's veil to her waist." Exactly so we saw "Mur" too, and coming to know this rare, stout-hearted, lovely woman, could understand what he wrote when "Mur" was no more: "[. . .] one night as she was sleeping she died, [. . . and] I have never been so close to any living creature since."[15]

Sometimes that summer May would come for over Sunday from up in the country where she was governess in the well-to-do farmer's family. She seldom spoke of her life with them, at least to me, so that, intensely occupied with my own affairs, I had, and still have, only the dimmest notion of what it was like. I remember, though, how wrapped up in little Roger she was when she came home; how he clung to her when she started to leave and would stand at the gate looking after her wistfully as when I parted with him myself in the morning on my way to school. And remembering how loath he was to be separated from any part of that small world which gave him his sense of security, how he would call after her in a tone which still pierces me, "Come back, Auntie May! Come back!"—remembering this, reliving my memorable experiences at the Bell House and in association with the McAdoos, recalling the lovable Mrs. Percy—thinking of all this, it seems as if we must have lived for years in North Knoxville, though in reality it was merely a matter of months until we were back in West End, and like exiles returning from a foreign land, so overjoyed to be there that I, for one, could have knelt and kissed the very ground on which stood the modest old-fashioned house on White Avenue into which we moved now.

NOTES

1. The McAdoos lived at 729 North Third Avenue. *Knoxville City Directory,* 1894, 1895. The father, William Gibbs McAdoo (1820–1894), had been a lawyer and Attorney General in Knoxville and a lawyer in Milledgeville, Georgia, before joining the faculty of East Tennessee University (now the University of Tennessee) in 1877, teaching English and history. In addition to publishing articles and essays, he was co-author of a textbook, *Elementary Geology of Tennessee* (1875); he and his wife, Mary Faith Floyd, co-edited a literary journal, the *Southern Head-light,* which had a brief existence in 1885. Rothrock, 443–44. It was through the efforts of the McAdoos' son, William Gibbs McAdoo Jr. (1863–1941), that Knoxville streetcars were electrified.
2. Knoxville's First Presbyterian Church, founded in 1792, is still where it stood then, on State Street in the block between Church and Clinch, with the graveyard adjoining.
3. James A. Andes, principal, Bell House school. "Only a Few Changes: Nearly All the Old Teachers in the City Schools Re-elected," *Knoxville Journal,* June 7, 1895. In the *Standard History of Knoxville,* Andes is listed as principal of John Sevier School from 1892–1899. Rule, 406.
4. Albert Ruth was superintendent of Knoxville City Schools 1881–97, 1902–06. Deaderick, 243, 652.
5. Pen name of William Taylor Adams (1822–1897), who wrote a number of book series for boys.
6. A painting by Russell Briscoe depicts the Union Bank building much as Armstrong describes it. On the south side of Main between Market and Walnut streets, it was torn down in the 1920s. Deaderick, see plate following p. 370.
7. William Gibbs McAdoo Jr. (1863–1941) returned to Knoxville with his family in 1877 while still a teenager. After attending the University of Tennessee, he moved to Chattanooga where he studied law and was admitted to the bar in 1885. Seeking to electrify Knoxville's streetcars, he raised the funds to buy Knoxville Street Railway Company and inaugurated the city's first electric streetcar line on May 1, 1890. However, his new company failed and went into receivership in 1892. A long and bitter battle in the courts and on Knoxville's streets ensued, erupting on March 1, 1897 in a violent confrontation known as "the battle of Depot Street," in which McAdoo took part and was arrested even though he had moved to New York City in 1892 to practice law there. Timothy P. Ezzell, "McAdoo, William Gibbs," in *Tennessee Encyclopedia of History & Culture,* ed. Carroll Van West, 580; Philip M. Chase, "William Gibbs McAdoo: The Last Progressive (1863–1941)," 44, 45, 48–49 (PhD diss., University of Southern California, 2008), http://digitallibrary.usc.edu/cdm/ref/collection/p15799coll127/id/140194 (viewed August 23, 2019); Rule, 305–307; Rothrock, 443, 444. For a detailed account of the Knoxville electric streetcar wars, see Deaderick, 217–227.

8. The elder William Gibbs McAdoo died August 24, 1894. "Death of a Noted Man: Professor William G. McAdoo Died . . . Yesterday Forenoon," *Knoxville Journal*, August 25, 1894.
9. Also known as *The Blind*. Translation of *Les Aveugles*.
10. "Sarah Siddons as the Tragic Muse," a 1784 oil painting of English actress Sarah Siddons (1755–1831) by the English painter Sir Joshua Reynolds (1723–1792).
11. Armstrong is either confused or misspoke here. It was Mrs. McAdoo's *husband* who was an officer (a captain, not a general) in the Confederate army, and whose family was impoverished by the War. McAdoo had moved his family from Knoxville to Georgia in 1862, living first in Marietta, where their son, William Gibbs McAdoo, Jr., was born, and then in Milledgeville. The McAdoos did not return to Knoxville for thirteen years, partly due to threats against the father, who was charged with treason. W. Todd Groce, *Mountain Rebels: East Tennessee Confederates and the Civil War, 1860–1870* (Knoxville: University of Tennessee Press, 1999), 14, 132, 149; Robert Tracy McKenzie, *Lincolnites and Rebels: A Divided Town in the American Civil War* (New York: Oxford University Press, 2006), 50–52, 208–09. W. G. McAdoo's brother, John David McAdoo (1824–1883), *was* a general in the Civil War. Bruce S. Allardice, "McAdoo, John David," in *Handbook of Texas* Online, http://www.tshaonline.org/handbook/online/articles/fmc01 (viewed August 27, 2019); "John David McAdoo (1824–1883)," in *Justices of Texas 1836–1986* (online), Tarlton Law Library, University of Texas at Austin, http://tarltonapps.law.utexas.edu/justices/profile/view/67 (viewed August 27, 2019). Mrs. McAdoo's father, Charles Rinaldo Floyd (1797–1845), had been a brigadier general in the Georgia militia, known for removing the Seminoles from the Okefenokee Swamp, and her grandfather, John Floyd (1769–1839), had been a general in the War of 1812. Megan K. Nelson, "Charles Rinaldo Floyd (1797–1845)," in *New Georgia Encyclopedia* (online), https://www.georgiaencyclopedia.org/articles/history-archaeology/charles-rinaldo-floyd-1797–1845 (viewed August 21, 2019). Diaries, correspondence, and other materials relating to the McAdoo and Floyd families are held in Special Collections at the University of Tennessee and at the Library of Congress.
12. Mrs. McAdoo (1832–1913) wrote under her maiden name, Mary Faith Floyd. Her novels include *The Nereid* (Macon, Georgia: J. W. Burke & Co., 1871) and *Eagle Bend* (published in serial form in the *Savannah (GA) Weekly News* in 1883). *Antethusia* may be an alternate title for the latter, or possibly the title of a different work. Mrs. McAdoo also contributed the chapters on "Journalism" and "Literature" to Goodspeed's *History of Tennessee* (1887). Her first husband was Randolph Gillis McDonald, who died in 1854; she married William Gibbs McAdoo in 1857. Mr. McAdoo had also been married previously and had two daughters by his first wife, Anna Cleopatria Horsley, who died in 1853. Among his grandchildren from this union were the Knoxville artists Anna Catherine "Kate" Wiley and Eleanor "Nell" McAdoo Wiley and UT librarian Edwin Wiley. Rothrock, 442–43 (NB: the biographical entry in Rothrock contains an incor-

rect year of death); Deaderick, 448, 621-22; "McAdoo, Mary Faith Floyd," in *Marquis Who Was Who in America 1607–1984*, edited by Marquis Who's Who. Marquis Who's Who LLC, 2009, (online, viewed August 7, 2019); "McAdoo, Mary Faith Floyd," in *Library of Southern Literature,* ed. Edwin Anderson Alderman . . . [et al.] (New Orleans: Martin and Hoyt, 1910), 15:269.

13. Character in the Tennessee Williams play *A Streetcar Named Desire*.
14. Mrs. Percy's daughter, Lady Percy (1866–1937), married Charles J. McKinney, Jr. (1862–1918). In 1895 their home was at 733 North Third Ave. *Find-A-Grave*: Nancy Irwin "Nana" Armstrong Percy; U.S. Census, 1880; Knoxville City Directory, 1895.
15. William Alexander Percy, *Lanterns on the Levee: Recollections of a Planter's Son* (New York: Knopf, 1941); reprinted with an introduction by Walker Percy (Baton Rouge: Louisiana State University Press, 1973), quotations from p. 31, 32, 34. The exact wording on p. 32 is: "Mur's figure was ample and she moved splendidly and serenely like an ocean liner. Back of her silver white pompadour she wore a small widow's bonnet, from which hung a widow's veil to her waist." Born Nancy Irwin Armstrong (1835-1897), Mrs. Percy was also sometimes called "Nana" or "Nannie." Her grandson, William Alexander "Will" Percy (1885–1942) of Greenville, Mississippi, became a decorated World War I veteran, lawyer, plantation owner, and poet. He adopted and reared fourteen-year-old Walker Percy and his two younger brothers (the sons of his cousin LeRoy Percy) after they were left orphans.

Chapter Twenty

White Avenue

This modest old-fashioned house (in which, as it turned out, I was to spend more years than in any other, save one, in the course of my long highly-varied existence) had a sort of story-book air about it, as I see it now. A gabled story-and-a-half white cottage, it stood on a corner, a short pebbled walk leading from the gate up to the small front porch over whose latticed trellises clambered a luxuriant Maréchal Niel.

This glorious rose alone, with its heavy golden heads and incomparable fragrance, would have invested the house with charm, but beds of gay old-fashioned perennials bordered not only the pebbled walk in front but one which ran along the side of the house. There were flowers, in fact, or flowering shrubs—crepe myrtle, snowballs, mock orange, lilac bushes—everywhere in the yard; a tangle of honeysuckle here and there overhung the white picket fence around the place; and best of all, behind the house were sprawling old apple trees and a flagged walk which led to a grape arbor and the partially concealed out-houses at the end of the arbor.

It was perhaps, though, the cozy, homey look of this small white house, embowered in greenery that had been planted long ago, which drew me to it from the first hour I knew it was to be our home; drew me the more powerfully in its striking contrast to the barrack-like naked-looking front, the bare yard, of the house in North Knoxville which we were leaving so joyfully.

Beyond a doubt, however, the strongest appeal the new home had for all of us was its location. Our side-gate was hardly more than a stone's throw now from our side-gate at the Barnes house, a house on which I, at least, would always look back nostalgically, for all the tragedy mingled with happiness during the crucial years we lived there. Moreover, on White Avenue, we were only a block from the gates, down below, of the University, while directly opposite us lived its most popular professor, Prof. Schmidt [i.e., Schmitt],[1] and beyond the Schmidts' lately-built Queen Anne house stretched the Woodruffs' rose garden, at the rear of their huge Victorian mansion, with its great fountain, its extensive grounds, facing the University.[2] Once more, through an incredible stroke of luck, all around us were old acquaintances, old friends, old neighbors, familiar houses, familiar streets—at every turn old associations, and I could have wept for pure joy. In as true a sense as we were ever to know, we had come home!

It was some such feeling, I suppose, which more than anything else colored my initial impression (one I have never completely lost) when I knew we would live in this little house: for the sober truth is, I had rushed past it hundreds of times in the hectic days of my gay girlhood, and it was invested then with none of the idyllic charm I found in it now. It was simply then a small white house with a cluttered yard, a house from which old Dr. Rogers [i.e., Rodgers], with his long straggly brown beard and head shaking with palsy, would often be starting out in his high shackley buggy, behind his decrepit horse, on the round of calls he still made; a house where old Mrs. Rogers, with her bleached face and hunched back, would be forever pottering around among her flowers. I would remember vaguely, perhaps, as I passed, having heard that the Rogers built the house when they were bride and groom. But now they were both dead, and a daughter of theirs had rented it to us.[3]

Part, however, of the glow of happiness connected in my mind with our moving into this house derived, I am sure, from the fact that only shortly before I had passed the dreaded examinations for which I had been preparing so feverishly all summer; passed them, to my amazement, creditably enough to win a wintry smile of approval from Prof. Ruth, the only time, incidentally, I ever saw a smile on the red face of this choleric little man. I had demonstrated that I could, with Mama's careful management, support her, myself, and Roger, at least in simple comfort and refined surroundings, and a new and brighter era seemed opening before us.

Oddly, I haven't the faintest recollection of our actual moving from North Knoxville back to West End. I can not even recall just when we moved, although it must have been suddenly, and before the opening of school in September, for in the farthest reach of my memory of teaching at the Girls High School, we are already snugly settled in the little white house on White Avenue, and I am climbing the hills of Clinch Street on my way to and from the High School, as years before when I had been a pupil there.

What puzzles me still more is, how did we learn this little house on White Avenue was for rent, and at only two dollars more a month than we had been paying? I believe that it must have been through some of our Presbyterian friends in West End,[4] as it was Presbyterian friends in North Knoxville who had found the house for us there with its low rent.

Thinking of it today, I realize also that although I had found the religious services of the Second Presbyterian Church and Sunday School, from my first knowledge of them, far from inspiring, in fact intolerably boring, nevertheless I must acknowledge that in all our lean struggling years in Knoxville following my father's fatal accident, it was members of the Second Presbyterian Church who were always the first to offer help, in whatever form, when we seemed to need help, and invariably with such grace and delicacy as would give the smallest possible wound to our pride. It was they, I must admit further, while I might find them prosy, yet they who seemed ever aware of our plight; who always, unostentatiously, were, in a way, looking after us.

But however it was we came to move into this little house, my memory of it, outside and in, remains of the happiest.

It opened into a square front hall, at the back a stairway, with a sharp turn half way up, leading to the small chambers above; at the right a parlor with the only open fire-place in the house, heated otherwise, so far as it was, formerly by a stove or two, now by a small furnace lately installed in the cellar. But we seldom used the parlor. The room we really lived in, the heart of the house, the center of my most poignant memories of it, was across the hall, a room in which there was not a great deal of space, yet enough for our piano, for the ebony cabinet surmounted by the white marble cupids, holding the white marble Hebe—displaying all the treasured *objets d'art* which had survived so many moves; space enough for our library table, for comfortable chairs upholstered in warm-toned, if slightly worn, velvet, and a sofa in one corner next the door where you stepped down, a considerable step, into the long, narrow, low-ceiled, not-too-light dining-room, where our old French engravings in their ebony frames now hung on the walls; and off the dining-room, at the right, Mama's good-sized bedroom, into which had fitted, without crowding, her massive ornate walnut bed and its massive matching pieces, the bedroom's one window looking out on the street that ran at the side of the house, and its outside door leading through a flagged porch straight into the straggling old apple trees in the back yard.

The house had no bathroom, a feature seldom found then in Knoxville houses as old as this, but I do not remember that we were particularly upset when we found there was none, or were ever particularly incommoded by the lack of one. After all, at the time, Her Majesty, Queen Victoria, without a single bathroom in Windsor Castle, was bathing very much as we bathed; using a china bowl and pitcher, with the aid of extra hot water in some sort of container, and contriving somehow or other to keep about as clean, I believe, as in earlier and later years when the amenities were all at our disposal.

In any event, we were not disposed to cavil at any defects in this new home in West End and we rejoiced in all its pleasant features. This bedroom of Mama's, for example, well shaded, with its outside door, and so near the ground, was the coolest room in the house in summer, warm in winter, and, for Mama, still more important, conveniently near the rough old kitchen, back of the dining-room, where she would spend much of her time.

In this connection, I should like to record that it has taken me a large part of my life—I have had to arrive, indeed, almost at my present age, before I could evaluate at all properly the kind of woman Mama was. In our childhood and early youth, through her great reserve with us, through her impatience with all her children, especially with me, the most openly resistant of them, she was overshadowed in our minds and imaginations—yes, and in our hearts, by our brilliant and dynamic father, whose achievements in the outside world we were early aware of, a man intensely alive and at the same time of more serene mind than Mama; more indulgent and laughter-loving; furthermore, possessed of that philosophic spirit which would carry him through not only financial ruin but years of intense physical suffering without damage to his essentially sweet nature.

But Mama, also high-spirited, though hot-tempered, inclined to be selfish, and with the touch of morbidity in her make-up, had much to fight in *her* nature. She was one of those people, it seems plain now, whose character proves strongest in adversity. Here she was, a beautiful woman in early middle life, taking on all the humblest household duties once performed for her by servants, and although her face, in repose, still wore its sad look, yet never uttering a word of complaint. Here, on White Avenue, she had the crudest kitchen she had ever known or could have imagined, hardly more than a shed, intended only for Negroes to work in, but here she cooked all our meals, excellent ones, and without exception daintily served. Efficient in whatever she undertook, she had in fact become an excellent cook—she, who once had heartily disliked cooking and seldom entered a kitchen unless to give an order; and what is more amazing (as I view it today), she never failed, whatever she did, to look as immaculate, as dignified, as much the Victorian lady, in the simple print dresses she wore about her housework as in elaborate dresses made for her in days past by Worth.

What mattered most to me, however, at the time, was that under adversity, she had grown, paradoxically, ever more cheerful; and if she never complained now, never burdened me, at the end of my own exhausting day, with domestic problems, but solved them herself, so also she kept to herself any problems she had—and she had them—with vigorous strong-willed little Roger, during my absence, and was as unfailingly patient with him as impatient with her own children when they were young.

In any event, if it was the Seventh Day Adventists in our house in North Knoxville who, through their kindly spirit and experience, freed my mind and thus helped me survive my grilling early days at the Bell House, it was Mama, above everyone and everything else, who helped me when I began teaching at the Girls High School.

I had developed, to be sure, a certain self-confidence through my hard-won success at the Bell House. I was heart and soul determined to succeed in this new position, too. But there were problems here, if entirely different, scarcely less taxing than those at the Bell House; also the same crushing fatigue to endure in the beginning.

Though the walk to school was not so long now, yet much of it, going or coming, was uphill; then there were always things I must attend to before school started, so that I must leave home as early as ever, while other matters would hold me in the school-room after school, till finally I must make way for the janitor, arriving, in the course of his rounds, with broom, dust-pan, and feather duster. Often it was almost supper-time when I reached White Avenue, with still ahead long hours of preparation for the classes I would teach next day.

At the time, not only Rhetoric but English and American Literature, the branches under me, were still taught almost solely from text-books, with pupils expected to repeat literally their accounts of authors, whether John Greenleaf Whittier, Shakespeare, or William Makepeace Thackeray, and with little or no attempt to acquaint them at first hand with an author's work, so that to conduct classes, without reference myself, while I was doing so, to the textbooks, I was obliged to memorize many of their pages the evening before, in addition frequently having to grade papers I had brought home.

After supper, and a romp with Roger, two years old now, I would be so worn out that I would sink down onto the sofa in the sitting-room for a brief rest before starting the evening's study and other school work which would keep me up till long past midnight.

At once I would fall into a deep sleep, although I was so afraid I might oversleep, I would always say, as I lay down: "Mama, now be *sure* to wake me exactly at half-past seven!"

Seeing me fallen into this sleep of utter exhaustion, nothing, I imagine, could ever have been much harder for Mama than to wake me when the time came, and once I heard her saying, "Annie! Annie!" but was not yet fully awake when I became aware that she was kneeling on the floor beside the sofa.

She placed her hands on mine and I saw now that tears were rolling down her face.

"Oh, Annie," she said, in a choking voice, "if I had known how few years of good times you would have, I would never have been so strict! Forgive me, darling!"

It was the first time Mama had ever called me by an endearing name—a moment so strange, so piteous, so stabbing, I could never forget it.

In the morning, on my way to school, I was always conscious of a sense of relief when I had passed the Aults without seeing them up and about. When we lived in the Barnes house, they were across the street; now directly behind us, with only an alley between. But they were usually at breakfast at this hour, so couldn't detain me.

This affable, complacent, cautious, well-to-do, elderly couple were exactly the same as when we had lived near them before; Mrs. Ault still selling her magnolias, where everyone else *gave* theirs away; still inviting callers to make a tour with her of her rose garden, then giving them at parting a single blossom, already shedding its petals, from among her hundreds.

In the afternoon, while the weather was warm, I could seldom escape them. Unless it were raining, they would be on their side-porch, only a few feet back from the street, placidly rocking, each with a palm-leaf fan and fanning themselves or shooing away an occasional fly. They would cease rocking as I drew near their gate and, leaning from their rockers, insist I should stop and visit with them.

Laden with books and papers, I would try to be polite, though filled with secret resentment not unmixed with twinges of guilt, as Mama often urged me: "Annie, *do* stop on the Aults' porch for a few minutes sometime. Mrs. Ault is always asking me why you don't. I think she's a little hurt."

"But, Mama," I would protest, "I'm always so tired, ready to drop, when I'm on my way home, and anyway I just can't stand their simple-minded boring talk."

"Yes, Annie, yes," Mama would say with an understanding smile, "but they're old, and they're neighbors—humor them once in a while."

I don't remember, however, that I ever did. I had no time for the Aults or for anyone else who seemed to stand in the way of what I was undertaking at present. I must put into it, just as I had during the fateful months I taught at the Bell House, every ounce of my strength, every waking moment, save for the far too few I had for Roger. I had no time, either, now as then, for dwelling on the past.

Twice daily, on the way to and from school, I passed the side-gate, across the street, at the Barnes house, where once Trix every afternoon, her paws on top, would wait quiveringly for Harry's whistle as he returned from the Hill. But I was hardly conscious, passing the gate now, of its existence. So it was, too, as I passed in front of the Barnes house, with its great magnolias, one on either side, shadowing the front porch. Other people, people we did not know, were living in the Barnes house, and I no longer saw in my mind Harry's body being brought home from the river when we lived there; Papa being carried on a stretcher through the open French windows into the sitting-room after the wreck at Flat Creek; my coming down its steps for the last time, carrying proudly my new little satchel of alligator leather, as I started North to college.

Only six years had passed since then, but everything had changed. The Barnes house had become only a house to me, as had the house, further down Clinch, where the Bauers lived when we first knew them. Even the big old Gaines house opposite the Bauers, once overflowing with life and gayety, from which, at night, issued those mad shrieks of laughter which so enraged the more sober-minded of the Gaines' neighbors—even this, the Gaines gone and turned into a rooming-house, evoked in me no emotion, no disturbing sense of the past. I gave it, I am confident, not a thought as I hurried by it in early morning or late afternoon. I was dwelling now, not in the past, but in the present; on every step of my way to and from school absorbed in the fresh problems confronting me.

It would be long, long years before I recognized that being a teacher, like being a ballerina or a nun, is a dedication, or it is nothing. Nevertheless, quite unconsciously, I was animated, I believe, by the *spirit* of dedication, when I entered the profession of teaching, for all it was one I had been plunged into through force of circumstances, almost in desperation, and only a year before looked upon as unbearably drab. No stone, at any rate, must be left unturned if I were to succeed in it. And how whole-hearted I was in my determination to do so, I realize when I recall my violent reaction when young men I knew, and who were still unmarried, began calling again or inviting me to go places with them.

We were still in North Knoxville when one evening, sitting on the porch and with others there, the streetcar stopped in front of our house and most unexpectedly a young man came through the gate, a young man whom I had known since I first went to dances, on surrey and boating parties with boys. Member of one of Knoxville's prominent families, son of one of my father's lawyers, he had continued to pay me attention almost up to the time of my marriage to Theodore.

Seldom have I been more embarrassed than when this young man stepped up onto the porch and I saw in the dusky light who it was.

I asked him into the parlor, I remember, and then after a few moments, as it was an unusually close evening, he suggested it might be cooler outside and that we take a walk.

We strolled around the nearby dimly-lighted streets, now and then sitting down on a stone wall as we came to one in front of a dark house, and all of the while he was talking earnestly, in a low, fervent voice, trying to persuade me to marry him.

It was not the first time he had asked me to marry him. Gentle, quiet, sincere, I liked him and always had; but it is not too much to say that I was horrified at his suggestion. The day when a woman, or man, was divorced as often or not, or more often, simply in order to marry someone else, had not yet arrived: and now, in the '90s, that he, or anyone else, should think I wanted to marry again, seemed to cheapen, to degrade, me—all but an insult. It was the last thing in the world, I told him, that I would consider.

Soon after this, other young men I knew, and who were still unmarried, if I met them anywhere by chance, would greet me in the old friendly, chivalrous, flattering way, which reassured me and warmed my heart, I confess, though when they asked to take me to a play at Staub's Theatre, to a concert perhaps, or a lecture, I shrank from the very thought of appearing with any of them in public; and this notwithstanding that not once in the years since I had been divorced (nor afterwards), was I ever made to feel there was even the slightest stigma on me because of it.

Even so, however, I was still acutely, painfully, conscious myself of my unusual status, so that for all my love of gayety and gay companions, I was more comfortable in declining these proffered attentions than I would have been in accepting them. My life, perforce, was utterly different now from that of my old intimates; and such satisfactions as I could find henceforth I must find in the new life I had started on. In my singleness of purpose, it was almost as if I had taken the veil.

It is possible, for all I did not perceive it then, that I accepted without rebellion, even welcomed, what I assumed would be a vastly less colorful life than I had once dreamed of, because of a subconscious sense of guilt. From buried depths within me may have come vague suggestions now that this was a penance for my wilful [*sic*] defiance of my parents in marrying Theodore, my callous disregard, virtual desertion, of them when they needed me most—expiation for all the suffering and humiliation I had brought upon them: and this regardless of the fact that in my conscious mind I always justified myself, convinced myself that step by step I had been in the grip of forces beyond my power of resistance, and could not have done other than I had.

But whatever my complex feelings at the time, I was sustained then and through seven years that followed, not alone by my unquenchable love of life and the intense interest in teaching congenial subjects which I developed, but by my constant and ever-growing joy in Roger.

I do not know what he might have thought about it in his own maturity, but I do not believe that any little boy ever had a happier childhood than Roger's on White Avenue. He had the big back yard to play in all the year around; a small red wagon to succeed the little red wheelbarrow, a wagon which he could load with leaves in autumn, or with whatever treasures he had unearthed in the course of his day; he had a playmate of his own age, Woodruff Meek, grandson of the Woodruffs[5] who lived in the great Victorian mansion obliquely opposite us—"Wooshy," as Roger called him, with whom he could fight, exchange childish blows, bites, and scratches, without imperiling their relationship; by the time he was three or four he had, not a stuffed Teddy Bear, but a live pup to adore, a stray of unknown breed. Then, if he had no toys bought in stores, of the sort heaped upon children nowadays in such profusion that often, in their satiety, they get more pleasure in smashing them to bits than in playing with them—if he made his own toy out of scraps of rubbish he picked up here and there, yet left to himself most of the day while I was at school and Mama occupied indoors, he was also busy learning about spiders and their webs; about ants, beetles, bumblebees, butterflies and other insects with which his own special sphere abounded; about snails, the fat slugs whose slimy iridescent trails he found each morning on the flagstones at the rear of Mama's bedroom. He had responsibilities, too, from time to time: once as a sentinel to stand at the side-gate and warn the postman not to shove any mail through the slit in our postbox beside the gate, because a pair of wrens were building a nest inside it.

During these first years on White Avenue, the only thing, in fact, that was ever given him of any consequence (aside from the priceless boon of plenty of wholesome neglect which he was enjoying) was a gift from our old friend, the wealthy bachelor, Rush Strong—a Christmas tree, together with all the gold and silver and vari-colored glittering baubles to hang on it. We set it up in the parlor, the first Christmas tree Roger had ever seen, and a thing to remember was his dancing delight when we permitted him to light all the little wax candles he could reach, and then his childish rapture, touched with awe, when the whole tree burst into fairy-like bewitching bloom. Every evening he was almost beside himself as the time approached for him to light its candles again; although with equal vividness comes back to me his passionate grief when, the holidays over, one morning he came upon the tree, stripped of all its glory, lying out in the alley for some drayman to cart away with other refuse. He could not understand how anything that had been so beautiful could ever be abandoned. It was his first heart-break. He was inconsolable.

But there is still another memory of these first Christmases on White Avenue, one all *too* vivid, which remains with me. By this time Roger must have been four or five, and Sunday mornings our neighbor, Mrs. Woodruff, would stop in her Victoria to take him, along with "Wooshy," her grandson, to Sunday School in the Baptist church on Gay Street which the Woodruffs attended.

At Christmas time, Roger came home from Sunday School one Sunday morning bursting with excitement. The superintendent had told them they must all come to the Christmas entertainment for the Sunday School a few evenings hence.

I hoped he would forget about it before the evening arrived. I hated to give up a single evening of my brief Christmas vacation, only a week. However prescribed my day by day life in the school-room, this was a chance, if for nothing else, to dip into some of the books always tempting me; books, new or old, but unconnected with my teaching, and the one way I had now, I felt, of enlarging my world. Then, to take Roger on this long trip at night, walking both ways, as we would have to, down to the Baptist church on Gay Street for a Sunday School "entertainment" that would be anything but entertaining for me, was a sacrifice I was unwilling to make.

Roger, however, had not forgotten. He could talk of nothing else but the "entertainment," a word he had difficulty in pronouncing, but whose sound evidently impressed him, and when the evening for it came, sensing my resistance, he begged me harder than ever—his arms around my neck, beseeched me, to take him to it, and, when I refused, cried until I thought he would never stop.

At last, though, I quieted him sufficiently to get him into his little nightshirt, to have him, still sobbing, say his "Now I lay me," but once in bed, as I started to tuck him in, he lifted himself on his knees, and, facing me, his tear-stained face red and swollen, threw out his arms imploringly, to make one last plea.

"But, Mother," he cried, "he *told* us to come! He *told* us to come!"

In his mind, besides his terrible disappointment, was clearly a sense that he was betraying a trust, failing to do something that had been expected of him.

I was deaf to this final appeal, as to his earlier ones, but to the end of my days I shall never cease to hear the sound of his voice, see his face, as he made it. Of all the sins I have committed, I consider it the most unforgivable. Years afterwards I was still bearing the burden of it on my conscience, and when Roger had left childhood far behind and was in command of the destroyer *Walker* in the Pacific Fleet,[6] one day I confessed this to him.

He burst out laughing. "Why, Mother," he said, "I don't remember a thing about it!"

But if his childish sorrows had long since faded from his mind, if not from mine, I think he must have always retained many pleasurable memories of this little world of his on White Avenue, the first world, in all probability, he would be able, as a man, to recall. Perhaps he could still see the country wagons loaded with watermelons that in late summer would lumber by on their way to Market Square; see himself, as soon as he spied one, running into the house for a nickel, the price in those days for a heavier melon than he could carry, so that the driver would good-naturedly climb down from the wagon-seat and carry it for him to the house. Perhaps he could see, mistily, himself and Wooshy, many a hot afternoon, enjoying a watermelon feast, all by themselves, under the apple trees in our back yard.

But whatever he would forget or remember, I do not think he ever felt a shadow over him in those years when he was very young—ever missed having a father.

Although I did not reveal to him until he was sixteen or older, the reason for our divorce, yet I told him soon after we moved to White Avenue that he *had* a father, his father living in New York and I in Knoxville because that seemed best, and he accepted this brief equivocal explanation without evincing any interest in it. Never subsequently, moreover, did he make any inquiries about his father, a thing that now and then made me a trifle uneasy. It seemed uncanny. Did he understand, without anyone telling him, that here was a subject he had better not explore?

In any event, if he showed no curiosity about a father whom he never saw and did not remember, nevertheless, from the time he was very young, he showed curiosity in endless other directions, and almost from infancy manifested an adventurous spirit, the spirit that would take him ultimately into naval aviation[7] while it was still in the experimental stage, in the early '20s, those days of "flying coffins," when even Navy planes were sometimes far from safe. Danger always attracted—seemed, in fact, irresistible to him.

In this connection, an afternoon stands out among so much I can not recover. Callers were with us in our sitting-room on White Avenue when suddenly above the buzz of conversation I caught the sound of water running in the kitchen.

Going to investigate, as there was no one else in the house or yard except Roger, and he was too small to reach the faucets, I found him standing on a chair in front of the sink, holding one of his chubby hands, from which the blood was streaming, under the water he had turned on.

His usually rosy face was pale, but he turned it to me beamingly.

"I cutted myself," he explained, "but I didn't cry."

"I was brave!" he added triumphantly, though I saw he was badly scared.

Picking him up, I carried him into the sitting-room, laid him on the sofa, and when the folded sheets we laid under his hand were quickly soaked with blood, sent posthaste for the doctor.

What he had done, we found, was deliberately to break a bottle, cut himself, and refrain from crying, in order to prove his courage; a result, no doubt, of our frequently encouraging him, after some trifling hurt, with "You're brave, aren't you? *You* don't cry!"

The doctor started at once—none too soon—on the delicate business of tying together the ends of a severed artery, the main artery leading to the hand.

During this operation Roger made no sound, but when it was over, too weak to sit up, but in the doctor's lap, his tousled blond head resting against the doctor's shoulder, he cast his eyes up at the rest of us, standing around anxiously.

A wan smile crossed his ghostly little face. "The doctor hurted, too," he said, "but I didn't cry, did I?"

He was never, so long as he lived, to "cry," the truth is, when he was "hurted," and he knew, I dare say, first and last, as many hurts, however well he might hide them, as most of us do.

My chief worry about him, then, even when he was very young, was not that he might be cowardly, but that he might develop the savage temper his father had shown. Knowing so little about heredity, and nothing at all as yet about the nature of his father's brutal outbursts, I was haunted by a fear that this might be a taint in the blood which would carry on from generation to generation.

Despite my unceasing watchfulness, however, I never saw him exhibit more temper than any other small boy I had opportunity to observe. His little storms were soon over, and he never harbored resentment, never sulked; although this is far from saying that he was a saintly child. More than ordinarily energetic, highly imaginative as well as highly investigative, he was perpetually doing forbidden things, needing discipline, and I did not hesitate frequently to spank him soundly, when he would arouse all the near neighbors by his yells for mercy—outcries that would indicate he was being murdered, although a few moments later he would be his usual sunny self.

The sporting fashion in which, in general, he took punishment remains with me most clearly through one particular incident.

He was keenly interested in boys who went to the University, and, living at home, constantly passed our house on their way to and from "the Hill."

Before he was five, a sturdy tow-headed blue-eyed youngster, chock-full of mischief, he had struck up an acquaintance with any number of University students, "my friends," as he called them; and the first thing we knew, out of sight for a moment, he would have gone alone to "the Hill," finding his way around the campus with no trouble at all apparently, and up to his "friends'" rooms in one dormitory or another, where he had rare times, it seemed, though he was never explicit about them.

But presently, when he had slipped off on one of these independent excursions and not returned by suppertime, we knew something must be done. Even if one of us went to "the Hill" to fetch him, we would not know which way to turn, not knowing even the names of his "friends," as he did not know them himself; so that finally I told him if he went again I would have to punish him severely.

For a short while after this, he contented himself by watching for his "friends" at the hours when they passed, and with brief jolly conversations with them over the side-fence. But then the old urge became too strong, and one evening he had disappeared, supper was over, it was growing dusk, and still he had not returned.

Quite confident where he was, and more exasperated than alarmed, I was starting out the front door on the way to "the Hill" when I heard him whistling, as he neared our corner, coming up the slope from the gates of the University.

I stood stark still. He kept on whistling as he came jauntily through our gate, but when he met my irate eye, bent on him from the porch, he stopped whistling, though still with a saucy gleam in his eye, and called out gayly, "Well, Mother, I went, and now you can punish me!"

What could you do with a boy like that? What I *did* do, I can not recall. What I vaguely remember is that this was his last visit by himself to "the Hill," although this may have been because it was about this time he started to school himself.

Through some special dispensation on the part of the Board of Education, I was allowed to enter him when he was five, a year younger than the required age, in the primary grade of the school on Highland Avenue where May had gone, and only two blocks away, on the hill above us.[8] I had been moved to secure this permission because I had so little time for him myself, and he was so filled with gusto that he was getting to be a little more than Mama, with all her patience, could handle; for, besides everything else, he had recently acquired an imaginary playmate, "Rob Seeps," even more real to him than Wooshy, and on whom he conveniently blamed all his own mischievous misdeeds.

But school for him at five proved the happiest of solutions. He loved it from the first day, and was so enamored of his first teacher that I almost felt a pang of jealousy when, putting him to bed one evening, he confided, "Mother, when I shut my eyes at night, I can see sweet Miss Alice!"

There were times, however, when he proved too much even for sweet Miss Alice,[9] or until she hit upon the expedient, when he was getting out of hand, of sending him to run around the block, and thus wear off some of his excess energy. Friends of ours who lived near the school would be much amused, seeing him at almost any hour in the morning charging at full steam around and around the block, past their houses.

But if he was filled to overflowing with *joie de vivre* and could wear out almost any normal adult through the demands of his boundless energy, yet he could be the quietest, most attentive and responsive listener when another side of his nature was appealed to.

It was about this time, in fact earlier, when he was only three or four, I began telling him stories, whenever I could manage a quiet half-hour with him. He was such a rapt listener that he would sit without a single wriggle for an unbelievable length of time if only I would go on telling him stories from *Tanglewood Tales*.[10] Greek myths, stories from classic mythology, appealed to him more than any other at this age; while later there were wonderful times for both of us when I read him from Kipling's recently published *Jungle Books*;[11] and still later when I would simplify sections of works for adults and tell them to him; such as the doings of David Copperfield[12] as a child, his visits with [Clara] Peggot[t]y, his faithful nurse, to her brother Daniel, the fisherman, in his snug and most fascinating of dwelling places, once a boat, on the beach at Yarmouth.

To my unutterable joy, Roger would catch, not only the broadest, but even the slightest, suggestion of humor in the stories I read or told him, though on the other hand would be so deeply affected by the sufferings either of animals or humans in these stories, that, curled up beside me in a big chair, he would swallow hard, sometimes turn away his face to hide his tears, yet invariably beg me to read or tell him over again their sad parts, as for instance the death of David Copperfield's mother, so that again he could have the luxury of indulging, if surreptitiously, his childish grief over these sad happenings.

A manly little fellow, if ever there was one, this was the kind of hurt, hurt to others, especially to animals, the only kind, he ever cried over.

So long ago, those years on White Avenue tend to merge in my memory; therefore I can not be sure, but believe it was the first year we lived there that a young cousin from Tullahoma, in Middle Tennessee, came to live with us while he attended the University. One of eleven sons, his father, a prosperous manufacturer, a pompous but good man, and thoroughly orthodox—though notwithstanding this he had been a great admirer of Papa—, when this first son of his was ready for college, he wanted him to live in the family my father had left behind, rather than on "the Hill."

We called him M. R., as his own family did, although on "the Hill," where he became a popular football player, he was known as Black Mike, from his swarthy complexion and shock of jet-black hair. A powerfully-built youth, somewhat inarticulate and quiet in his manner, he fitted easily into our household, as did his brother, a year or so younger and called J. D., who joined him the next fall;[13] the brothers then occupying together an upstairs bedroom on the opposite side of the house from mine, both chambers, with their low ceilings, sloping walls, and each with only one small window, almost unbearably torrid in summer, though comfortable enough the rest of the year.

I think these youths were never much of a problem to Mama. Brought up in a large family, they made no special demands but took things as they found them; and, in any case, Mama had learned, in the course of the past few years, with the many adjustments she had had to make, to take things easier; learned what was essential, what could be let go, while still preserving reasonably-well her long-established domestic standards. She could tolerate a little dust now, even some disorder; had grown constantly more comfortable to live with.

At all events, if these two young students did not add, as I remember it, any particular interest to the life of our small family on White Avenue, they never disturbed it, and one of the greatest surprises of my life came years later when I learned that their life with us had made a lasting impression on at least one of them.

Traveling on the Southern Railway from New York to New Orleans, I noticed across the aisle from me a dignified, impressive-looking man, his extremely black hair streaked with gray, and something about him strangely familiar. Can it be possible, it flashed through me, that this is my cousin, M. R. Campbell, whom I had not seen for nearly thirty years?

At the same instant, it turned out, he was asking himself a similar question about me; so that soon we were sitting together and had hours of talk before he left the train at some point where he must change cars. He was the president now of the company his father, now dead, once had headed.[14] But, naturally, our talk was mostly about the days when he had lived with us on White Avenue. My life since then had been vastly more varied than his, and he remembered all sorts of little incidents I had completely forgotten, among them many amusing ones involving Roger, still a very little boy when he had known him last, now lying in Arlington.[15]

The thing that amazed me, though, was when he said: "You know when I first became a member of your family, I was terribly shocked at the freedom of talk at your table. I had never known anything even remotely resembling it—the way you discussed politics, religion, books, current events, with the greatest candor, expressing all kinds of ideas I had never heard of before. But the end result," and he laughed, "while *you* might consider me a mossback today, in my own town I am considered a dangerous radical!"

What surprised me most, however, was that in those early days of my teaching, when I was always so exhausted at meal-time, I had spirit enough left to discuss anything at all of the sort he indicated. I would not have supposed, had I given it a thought in the crowded intervening years, that our table-talk in the little house on White Avenue, retained, as M. R. suggested, some of the liveliness, the savor, Papa had given it as long as he lived.

Thinking of those days when the Campbell boys boarded with us, I recall that after they came we were able to afford some one to help regularly in the kitchen, though the one helper who reappears to me is "Half-wit Mary," as I called a story I wrote about her in after years for *Munsey's Magazine*, I believe it was—a "poor white" at once dim-witted and incredibly shrewd, more than a match for us on occasion, but clean and good-natured, so that Mama's life was easier from then on.[16]

Dwelling now on our years on White Avenue, what drifts back to me for the most part is pleasant; yet among its joys, no small ones, stands out one of the saddest things that ever happened to us; another tragedy, another step downward, it struck me achingly at the time, in the fall of a family once affluent—part of that endless aftermath of the railroad wreck at Flat Creek.

It was during our first year on White Avenue that May came home from wherever it was she had been acting as governess. Piecing one shred and another of hazy memory together, I think she must have decided to try to find something to do in Knoxville, something more to her taste, and certainly not less remunerative, for thus far she had earned hardly more than her bare living, not even enough for her clothes when they needed renewing, and of course with nothing whatever to contribute to the family budget, although I am confident that none of this had ever been discussed among us, the least money-minded of families.

At home now, I recall her flying in and out the front door with one or another of her intimate girl friends, or with young men who were taking her places, usually youths she had known at the University. I remember also that the grate fire in the parlor was lighted now in the evening, as she often had young men calling on her. But where she was going when she went out, what she was thinking, what her problems were—all this was a mystery to me, one I did not seek to probe.

It was not that there was any hostility, even the slightest, between us. But the five years difference in our ages seemed to have become a wider gap than ever; so that she never confided to me (with enough on my shoulders as it was, she may have thought) any of her dreams, her disappointments—far less the plan she was making secretly.

Then, one evening, when, as usual, I was in the sitting-room, studying, preparing for the next day at school, when Mama had gone to a neighbour's, and May had gone somewhere, though, as was always the case, I had not inquired where, Mama came home to find, when she opened the front door, a note that had evidently been pushed under it from outside and was lying on the floor. Mama brought it into the sitting-room, read it, and, with an anguished cry, sank to the sofa, covering her face with her hands, her whole body shaking convulsively.

There were only two or three lines: *I can not stand Annie's tired face another day. I am going away—to find something, I don't know what. –May.*

Never since Harry was drowned had I seen Mama so prostrated. *This could not be!* We did not even know where May had gone; but we knew now what she had suffered when she was flying back and forth with her young friends, how she must have brooded.

It was days before we knew she had gone to St. Louis, was with old acquaintances of ours for the time being, and had found a small acting part, she wrote, in a summer theatre there.

But in my whole life, and I think in Mama's, never was there a more terrible night than the one when May left us—May, still in her teens, frail, gentle, shy, born to be protected and gone to breast alone the great unknown outside world!

This was a shock, a blow, we felt that night, from which we would never recover; a thing, too, of so intimate a nature we would never be able to discuss it with others, but must lock it in our own hearts.

NOTES

1. Cooper D. Schmitt was professor of mathematics at the University of Tennessee. Rule, 377, 383; U.S. Bureau of the Census. *Twelfth Census of the United States: 1900*.
2. The Woodruff estate, mentioned earlier in Part 2, Chapter 2, was bounded by White Avenue, 14th Street, Cumberland Avenue, and 15th Street (now James Agee Street). Today the University of Tennessee's Hoskins Library building occupies the site where it was located.
3. Dr. James Rodgers (1818–1898) and his wife, Rosannah, were married in 1843. Although Mrs. Rodgers died in 1890, her husband did not die until 1898. At the time that Armstrong and her mother rented their house, Dr. Rodgers was living with a daughter, Anna, and her husband, Edward G. Oates, whose home was nearby on White Avenue. Rule, 507; Rothrock, 476; *United States Federal Census*, 1880, 1900; *Knoxville City Directory*, 1895; "Mortuary Notice," *Knoxville Journal*, April 3, 1890.
4. Dr. and Mrs. Rodgers were longtime members of Second Presbyterian Church, where he served first as a deacon, beginning in 1847, and then as an elder from 1872 until his death. Rule, 507; Rothrock, 476.
5. William Woodruff Meek was born November 12, 1892, the son of Daisy Woodruff Meek (1869–1945) and William Monroe Meek (1866–1901). Like Roger, he would go into the U.S. Navy, retiring as a captain. Following his death on December 5, 1967, "Wooshy" joined Roger in Arlington National Cemetery. *U.S. Federal Census*, 1900; *Find A Grave*, database and images, https://www.findagrave.com (accessed September 28, 2019). (Incidentally, another Woodruff daughter, Lutie, married Edward Terry Sanford, who was named to the United States Supreme Court in 1923 and served until his death in 1930. *U.S. Federal Census*, 1910; Rothrock, 480–481; Deaderick, 45, 443.)
6. No record was found relating Roger to service on the *Walker*, although Roger was commissioned a lieutenant in the U.S. Navy on June 29, 1917, following his graduation from the U.S. Naval Academy. *Walker I (Destroyer No. 163)* arrived in southern California on August 8, 1919, conducting local operations off the west coast until late that year, after which she was assigned to the Reserve Destroyer Flotilla. USNA (U.S. Naval Academy) Virtual Memorial Hall (Online database), https://usnamemorialhall.org/index.php/ROGER_F._ARMSTRONG,_LT,_USN (viewed September 21, 2019);

Naval History and Heritage Command (Online), s.v., "Walker I (Destroyer No. 163)," https://www.history.navy.mil/research/histories/ship-histories/danfs/w/walker-i.html (viewed September 21, 2019).

7. Roger received the designation "Naval Aviator" in 1920.
8. Highland Avenue School (also listed as West Knoxville Public School) was on the south side of Highland Avenue, with Fifth Street to the east. Bridge Avenue ran behind the school, which was three or four (counting Bridge) blocks from where they lived on White Avenue. *Sanborn Fire Insurance Map from Knoxville, Knox County, Tennessee.* Sanborn Map Company, Mar, 1890. Map. https://www.loc.gov/item/sanborn08331_002/ (viewed September 30, 2019).
9. Miss Alice Haws, teacher, Highland Avenue School. *Knoxville City Directory*, 1890; *Twenty-Eighth Annual Report of the Knoxville City Schools, 1898–1899* (Knoxville: Ogden Bros., 1900), 7.
10. By Nathaniel Hawthorne; a children's book (1853) retelling six Greek myths.
11. Two volumes of animal stories for children; published 1894–1895.
12. Autobiographical novel (1849–1850) by Charles Dickens.
13. Michael Ransom Campbell (1877–1948) and John Daniel Campbell (1879–1943), sons of Michael Ross Campbell (1840–1916), whose mother was a Wetzell from Lycoming County, Pennsylvania, as was Armstrong's father, Henry B. Wetzell, although exactly how they were related is not known at this time. Her cousins' father had come to Tullahoma (in Coffee County, Tennessee) in the 1860s. *United States Census*, 1900; *Find A Grave*, database and images, https://www.findagrave.com, (accessed September 24, 2019).
14. The father founded M. R. Campbell, Inc., in 1870 as a hub and spoke factory in Tullahoma. Later, the company began making wooden parts for carriages and buggy shafts, and in the 1920s manufactured baseball bats, golf shafts, and other sporting goods made from wood. Although the company ceased operation in 1935, its baseball bats are now collector items. Find A Grave, database and images, https://www.findagrave.com, (accessed September 24, 2019); "M.R. Campbell Inc. Tullahoma Tenn. Baseball Bats," Key-Man Collectibles online database, http://keymancollectibles.com/bats/m.r.campbell baseballbat.htm, (viewed Sept. 24, 2019); W. J. Davidson, "1929 History of Tullahoma," *N. C. & ST. L. RY. News Item* 11, no. 5 (May 15, 1929), reprinted in *Tullahoma Time-Table* (publication of the Historic Preservation Society of Tullahoma), ed. Angela B. Arnold (October 1985), excerpts online at: http://drbobyoung.net/Dad%20Website/Mayor%20Davidson%20Tullahoma/EXCERPTS%20FROM%20MAYOR%20DAVIDSON'S%201929%20HISTORY%20OF%20TULLAHOMA.htm (viewed September 25, 2019).
15. Roger was killed October 26, 1922, along with a fellow naval officer, when the plane they were testing crashed at Hampton Roads Naval Air Station.
16. "Half-Wit Mary's Lover: A Short Story" was published under the by-line Anne W. Armstrong in *The Cavalier* 15, no. 1 (April 27, 1912): 90–96. *The Cavalier* was issued weekly, at that time, by the Frank A. Munsey Company of New York.

Girls' High School. Art Work of Knoxville, 1895.

Chapter Twenty-One
Girls High School

What later was the Knoxville High School was still known, when I taught there, as the Girls' High School, as boys and girls continued to be taught separately in the lower grades, and a mere sprinkling of boys attended high school. Families with sons of high school age, if they could afford it, usually sent them to Bell Buckle, to Sweetwater Military Institute in lower East Tennessee, or to Colonel Bingham's Military School in North Carolina.

The building itself went up in flames more than a quarter of a century ago,[1] but in my mind's eye it remains a rather handsome structure of light-colored brick, fancied up a bit with marble trim, and with none of the grim, forbidding, prison-like aspect of most public school buildings of the day.

It is certain, at any rate, that I never drew near its side entrance on Union Street (the one I used), in all the hundreds of mornings I approached it, with any feeling of depression. Moreover, because my memory of them is wholly agreeable, I believe I never failed to find pleasure in the last two blocks of my walk to school. Climbing the Clinch Street hill, when I reached Locust I would turn the corner and for a short block Locust was bordered on one side by Peter Staub's place—the Peter Staub who had built Staub's Opera House in 1871, a theatre that for more than two generations greatly contributed to cultural life in Knoxville, the Peter Staub who had been U. S. consul at St. Gall, Switzerland, who was an ideal citizen, keenly interested in civic and educational affairs, and whose home was a rambling two-story white house, with a balustraded, vine-wreathed gallery above and one below on its side that faced the deep, gently sloping, somewhat informal, yet beautifully cared for grounds, extending all the way down to Clinch. Perhaps it was only so in my imagination, but I fancied then that the Staubs' picturesque home resembled a genuine Swiss chalet.[2]

Sometimes I would see Peter Staub himself at this early hour in the morning when I was on my way to school. A tall, erect man of sturdy build and with a great shock of curly snow-white hair—to me, easily the most distinguished-looking man in Knoxville, unless old Colonel Armstrong, Bob's father—he would be walking around among his shrubs and flowers, examining them, but never too occupied to lift his great curly white head, give me a genial smile, a few cordial words, as I passed.

Opposite the Staubs' was the imposing gabled brick or stone mansion, a dark gray, of Charles McGhee, closely connected both by birth and marriage with Knoxville's oldest and most prominent families, and president, at the time, of the East Tennessee, Virginia, and Georgia Railroad. The house, though the last word in late-Victorian elegance of the less plush, the more restrained, order, always wore a shut-up, gloomy, inhospitable air, and not once did I ever see Colonel McGhee walking around in his grounds as I passed through this quiet, leafy, lovely, short stretch of Locust Street. He spent much of his time now in New York, but even had he been at home and in his grounds, an aloof, self-important man—or so he appeared—it is safe to say he would never have had a glance for, never have accorded to a young teacher, hastening by on her way to the G.H.S., the genial smile, the few words, which regularly warmed my heart when the Hon. Peter Staub noted my passing.[3]

But, for all that the McGhees' house year in and out looked uninhabited and somewhat like a stately tomb, I was able to enjoy to the full the McGhee grounds, open to my view;[4] even to take ecstatic joy in them on dewy spring mornings when they were an enchantment of dogwood, redbud, and other early-blossoming trees and shrubs. And when I had left the Staub and McGhee places behind, and turned the corner into Union Street, there was still something to enjoy, in the fine, dignified, old red-brick homes along my way clear to the point where the school-yard began.[5]

All in all, though the G.H.S. was only a block from Market Square, and two from Gay, yet I approached it through what was still one of Knoxville's best neighborhoods, and this gave me, it is probable, unconscious of it though I may have been then, a feeling of gentility, so far as my new position was concerned; a feeling that would have been harder to come by at the Bell House, situated, as it was, in the lowest, the most disreputable, part of town. If this was the life—school-teaching—destiny had woven for me, at all events now I was more at home in my surroundings, they were more congenial.

As at the Bell House, my first day at the G.H.S., if it lacked the horrifying features which confronted me there, none the less, stands out, an unfading memory, among all the other days of my seven years at the high school.

The ninth grade room, which I would preside over, was a large well-lighted corner room at the rear of the building, on its third floor. And what, at this moment, I see before me from my small platform near its entrance from the hall, is some sixty boys and girls, less than a fourth of them boys; clean, well-dressed, polite—anything but hoodlums.

These were to be my special charges, although from time to time I would go to other class-rooms in teaching "Rhetoric" and "Literature" (not lumped together then under the general head of "English") to less or more advanced classes. But this was *my* room, the one for whose general tone I was responsible. And as I took in for the first time the faces of my young charges, with several dull, even dead-looking ones among them, but for the most part fresh, rosy, eager, I recall that I regretted I was going to have to teach them Rhetoric, although I hoped to make it less boring than I had found it at their age. When it came to Literature, I recall clearly the flash of joy which shot through me. What fun I would have teaching them Literature (at least as I proposed to teach it!) A new fire had been lighted in me, and from my first hour at the G.H.S. I was convinced I could make the subject vastly more vital than it had been when I was a pupil in this self-same school, so long ago it seemed, albeit only a few years before.

True, I sensed instantly that I must demonstrate I could maintain order in this roomful of teen-agers before I could get anywhere in teaching. This, however, was to prove the least of my problems, though this is not to say that there *was* no such problem in the higher, as in the lower, grades the building housed.[6]

There was but one teacher then at the G.H.S. who had attended Normal School, Miss Amanda Stoltzfus, the able and extremely efficient teacher who presided over the tenth (and highest) grade room, in the front of the building, on the same floor as my own, and whose uncompromising, drill-master bearing—whose every movement, was what I can best describe as "teacherly." With "teacher" written all over her, as might have been expected she maintained at all times in her own room perfect order. Even in the school-yard, her appearance there, holding on her hip a big brass bell with which to marshal the pupils back from recess, was enough to quell any incipient turbulence, and although first and last I respected her (in time even had affection for her), yet I could not think of a woman, or of a teacher for that matter, I should less wish to be like.

But women teachers in the public schools of Knoxville by and large were seldom recruited then, as Miss Stoltzfus had been, on the basis of their fitness for teaching. The truth is, they were chosen almost solely on the basis of their gentility coupled with their needs. Almost without exception they were of good family, and to some extent the Knoxville public schools of the period served as an asylum, an infirmary of sorts, for more or less indigent gentlewomen.

Thus it was that a tall, heavy-set elderly woman who shall be nameless remained for I don't know how many years in the Knoxville high school. None too amiable even under favoring circumstances, at the hours when she was in charge of a classroom connecting my own with the tenth grade room, regularly every day her voice would come booming through the closed door between us as she stormed at her pupils in impotent rage, stamping her substantial foot on the floor as she did so: "I *will* have order! I *will* have order!"

Besides this teacher, there were two others in the high school in my time, teachers of mathematics, both mature, highly intelligent women, well qualified to teach their subjects, but neither of them capable of securing enough quiet in which to teach it with any satisfaction. A room where they taught, when they left it at the end of the day, was the despair of Mr. Joy, the janitor, from the paper strewn from end to end of it, the chalk wars and other unseemly doings that had gone on there.

One of these mathematic[s] teachers was Annie Riley Hale, a widow, and mother of Ruth Hale (later wife of Heywood Broun).[7] We were good friends both then and afterwards, as long as Mrs. Hale lived.

Nevertheless, when school turned out each day, Mrs. Hale would take out some of her indignation, her hot resentment, on me. Red-faced, worn out, how was it, she would ask, that *I* (young enough, incidentally, to be her daughter) could have such order, and she none? Then one day after school she told me, a little spitefully, I fear, that she thought there was something I ought to know—that it was through *sarcasm* I held my own pupils in line. She knew this because she had overheard comments to this effect when she was walking home behind some of them one afternoon.

Sarcasm! Rarely have I received a more painful shock. I had come to feel deep interest in the boys and girls under me, to have real affection for many of them. When I liked *them* so much, could it be, I asked myself anxiously, that they did not like *me*?

Mrs. Hale's wounding words continued for a long time to rankle. Dwelling on them today, I think it quite possible that I *was* sarcastic at times, perhaps frequently, at least with pupils who had failed to prepare their lessons. But, if so, I absolve myself of all guilt on this score, if not on some others. Only a very few years older than they, utterly untrained in the art of teaching, with the task, no small one, of holding attention and getting results from a large overcrowded room of restless, very-much-alive adolescents (presently more than seventy of them), almost anything, as in love and war, I think now, should have been considered fair.

In any event, the real secret, I believe, if there was one, of how I maintained as good order as Miss Stoltzfus, with her Normal School training, was that I adopted from the start the identical method which had worked at the Bell House. If there was whispering, the slightest interruption, the least untoward noise, when I was speaking or someone reciting, I stopped proceedings, stood or sat still, completely silent, and waited until absolute quiet again prevailed. Here in the high school, I learned also how to meet another almost daily occurrence. If anything happened in the room that set pupils tittering, I encouraged them to laugh outright. I laughed with them, laughed as long as *they* seemed inclined to.

Instinctively, I felt that laughter was a vent these adolescents needed much and often, and I doubt if ever a school-room resounded with more than mine at the G.H.S., though permitted, invariably it soon died down.

Perhaps frequent and hearty laughter in the school-room is common at the present day. I don't know. I only know that it was not common in the days when I had been a high school pupil.

On that very first day at the G.H.S., I started what was then an unorthodox method of teaching "Literature." I asked my pupils each to write a list of books they liked best among those they had read; a list of those they had liked only moderately, another of those they had not liked at all. In order to insure honesty, I told them not to sign their papers. These lists were, of course, merely an effort on my part to learn something of their tastes before we began our actual study of books and authors.

The lists, when handed in, shocked me. Almost none of these boys and girls were acquainted with any of the works of Dickens, Thackeray, and George Eliot, which I had revelled in at their age. But what truly startled me was to find that the one classic with which they were familiar, and foremost favorite on the boys' lists (easily distinguishable by their handwriting), was *Salammbô*, Flaubert's historical romance, with its blood-curdling sickening accounts of barbaric cruelties, piled-up horrors, its lurid realism unparalled up to that time in the entire field of fiction. It offered, I suppose, some of the same sort of excitement today's youth seek in "Westerns."

At any rate, this preliminary survey showed me that if I were to arouse interest in some of the glories of both English and American Literature to which, plainly, they had not yet been awakened, I could not confine myself to Burke's *On Conciliation with the [American] Colonies*, Hawthorne's *The House of the Seven Gables*, Milton's "L'Allegro" and "Il Penseroso," and the rest of those "English Requirements" recently adopted by the Knoxville high school along with all the other high schools in the land, and which many a man in later years confessed had destroyed for a lifetime any budding interest he might have had in reading.

To be sure, I would have to devote part of our time to these "English Requirements." I had no choice, as I had no choice when it came to the textbooks then in use. But bent on making English Requirements, if teach them I must, as palatable as possible, I found, to my astonishment, on re-reading some of them at least, such delight that in coming now, in our course, to "L'Allegro," for example, and never before so captured by the charm of this pastoral idyl, with the very breath of 17th Century rural England in its merry, earthy lines, I was determined to make my pupils, too, love this poem. In my ardor, my missionary zeal, I recall going the length of saying to them: "And remember, if you don't like Milton, there's still nothing the matter with Milton!"

Perhaps this was a sample of that sarcasm Annie Riley Hale had informed me was alienating my pupils. And it is true that in my new-found joy in trying to pass on to these receptive young minds some of the intense pleasure I had derived myself from this writer or that, I was quite willing to browbeat, to bully them, if I thought it would help, into loving my own literary loves.

Later, in any case, I would have much more scope for exercising this pressure as we came to the lives and works of some of my own long-time favorites outside the English Requirements.

It was very soon, however, that I started something else. I told pupils they need no longer memorize word for word accounts of authors in their textbooks. Simply to give the sense of the account would be enough. I wanted them to spend less time on memorizing, more in reading the works themselves. Unbelievable as it may seem, this, in the '90s, was an almost revolutionary change in the method of teaching high school English. And I made this drastic change without consulting one of such few authorities as were presumed to be over me. I could not forget how deadly dull "Literature" (no less than Rhetoric) had been for me in high school, how alive and exciting it had been at college, and with or without authority I was going to make this change.[8]

I had undergone a transformation, the fact is, almost overnight when I stepped into my new position. All but instantaneously I had recovered a certain self-confidence I possessed as a child, in my teens—and up to the time, indeed, of my disastrous marriage. I was embarked now on a venture where I felt I knew (or certainly to a greater degree than the boys and girls under me) my way around. It would be many, many years before I realized that I was by nature an aggressive, an adventurous, human being. But some of the boldness, the initiative, I had shown, in however ridiculous a fashion, in taking over the management of the Barnes house that winter Papa and Mama were abroad, and with poor Aunt Allie nominally in charge, was beginning to reassert itself.

This, it must be owned, was easier for me because here, as at the Bell House, no one gave me any instruction whatever as to how I was to teach or govern.

The principal, Prof. White,[9] called Billy White (except in his presence), was a middle-aged bachelor, Irish, an attendant of the Church of the Immaculate Conception, and in his severe black garb, with his soft swift tread, his preoccupied air, as he rushed about the building in the discharge of his various duties, he always suggested to me a Catholic priest who had somehow strayed into the field of secular education; while with the stubble of black hair standing straight up on his bullet-shaped head and the curious movement of his mouth, as if he were constantly on the point of wanting to say something, but lacked the courage to bring it out, he was a figure of fun, it must be owned, to teachers no less than pupils at the G.H.S.

Morbidly shy, he would shoot noiselessly in and out of my room a dozen times a day, muttering a few words which I could seldom catch as he left on my desk a slip of paper containing a new regulation, to which, unless it suited me, I paid not the slightest attention; or leaving a magazine, for he was a University graduate, an avid reader himself, and in the magazine he left would always be some serious article marked for my attention, and one seldom connected, incidentally, and rather flatteringly, I felt, with the subject of education.

An honest and thoroughly good-natured, if abysmally irresolute, man, you could not possibly dislike him, and I suffer a few pricks of conscience even today when I recall how consistently I flouted what might have been called his orders; how I rode rough-shod over him when some matter of school government of which I did not approve came up for discussion. Even so, however, Billy White and I remained, through some seven years of close association, on the best of terms, be it said to his honor, if not to mine.

I was here then, as at the Bell House, almost completely on my own, when it came to the experiments I was undertaking. Here, however, Prof. Ruth, who had never visited my room at the Bell House, did occasionally appear.

When Carrie McAdoo, teaching on the first floor, would spy Prof. Ruth's buggy drawing up in front of the building, she would always, as for years past, send that scribbled line—*The devil is coming! Beware!*—around to all the other teachers, so they might have their rooms in apple-pie order before this dread little man arrived. Her message, however, would sometimes not reach me, two floors above, in time to be of use, and I have an undying memory of a day when in my own room we were in the midst of Swedish Ling exercises (a system of gymnastic exercises without apparatus then in favor), which we went through with daily, windows flung open, for ten minutes or so. At the moment, I was on my platform, directing the exercises through my own movements, and my arms extended above my head, when I became aware of a fixed stare in the eyes of all my pupils, standing in the aisles facing me, and realized that what they were staring at could be no other than the fiery little man with the jutting auburn beard, that "Holy Terror," the superintendent of schools,[10] who had opened the door to the room in his habitual manner, without a sound.

Without seeming conscious of his presence, I went through all the customary exercises of heads, arms, legs, and when they were finished and I turned to meet him where he was still standing in the open doorway, he gave me, if not a smile, at least an unmistakable nod of approval.

"That's the way," he said jerkily, in his brisk decisive manner, "Ling should be given. I'm going to send other teachers to your room to observe you give them."

The truth is, I had always enjoyed these Ling exercises myself, found them refreshing, slightly exhilarating, and with a faint suggestion in their movements of the joy I had once found in dancing. Furthermore, I had studied carefully the charts in my book on Swedish Ling, to make them as perfect as I could. But I believe that in all my years of teaching I never appreciated any compliment more than these few words of praise from one of the sternest, most irascible and exacting of men.

There was another gratification, however, that belongs to my teaching years, both the earlier and later ones.

School began at eight, for teachers (still docked a dollar even if only a minute late, with Billy White, his big silver watch in hand, at the door where we entered the building, so there should be no mistake), and let out at two, with a half-hour for lunch at noon.

During this luncheon period, high school teachers and some from grammar grades would gather in a school-room on the first floor, empty of children now, and eat the lunches we had brought from home.

Molly Hayes would be in the group; also Rosebud McClanahan,[11] that staunch little Scotch-Irish Presbyterian who on sultry Sunday evenings used to pass our house when we lived on Clinch Street, her partially-paralyzed mother dragging on her arm as they made their way to the wide-open, more airy spaces on Fort Sanders.

Most of the teachers in the group were middle-aged or elderly spinsters. Only I had been married, though one of them, about my age, had been in the same Sunday School class with me. But all of them, young or old, had been teaching at the G.H.S. before I came, some of them from the first day its doors opened. Miss Stoltzfus alone, for some reason I can't recall, was never among us.

We used to have a good time together; never talking of school matters during this brief period of relaxation, and sometimes arguing over such ridiculous questions as one raised by Miss Rosebud: "Could God make a banana grow at the North Pole?" with Miss Rosebud vigorously supporting the affirmative; I, as vigorously, the negative.

Even, however, when our discussions were of this ticklish nature, they were always jolly, and what meant most to me was the attitude toward me of the other teachers. None of them ever exhibited even the slightest tinge of resentment that I had been placed in a higher position and at a higher salary than they, with their years of experience. They seemed, indeed, proud of my rapid advance; so that whatever else I had to contend with it was not my fellow teachers—or not yet, not for some years, when an old acquaintance of mine, formerly a lady of leisure, would join our forces.

But there was another support I had in these first and hardest years at the G.H.S. One day, when Roger was not more than four or five, he came by himself all the way from White Avenue with a message from Mama, I've forgotten what, but which evidently she considered urgent.

It was Friday, and the last period in the day. Various pupils were reciting passages I had given them to memorize (according to an immemorial Friday afternoon custom in the Knoxville High School) from Byron, Keats, Shelley, or some other poet.

Motioning Roger to sit down on the edge of my platform, where he could wait for me till school was out, he listened intently to the recitations going on.

The pupils were always amused and apparently delighted when Roger appeared. It was something novel, something very human, perhaps they felt, this presence in the school-room of a very little boy, child of their teacher. In any event, his ordinarily mischievous blue eyes were very sober now, and I thought I detected a shade of wistfulness crossing his face.

"Roger," I asked, "would you like to say something, too? Would *you* like to tell a story?"

"Yes," he said, gravely.

I left the platform, seating myself at an unoccupied desk among the pupils.

Roger stepped up on the platform. Facing the whole room, he told a story I had told him at bedtime a few evenings before, the story of Phaëton, son of Phoebus, the sun, when he undertook to drive his father's chariot, upset, and would have set the entire world afire had not Zeus, king of the gods, transfixed him with a thunderbolt.

Roger told the story without the least self-consciousness, though with a few embellishments, to my surprise; even a few improvised gestures with hands that had not yet lost their dimples. And as I listened to his piping childish voice, gazed at this little rosy-faced, flaxen-haired youngster standing there before us, I thought my heart would burst. How could anything so utterly sweet ever have happened to me—that this little boy should be *mine*? Why, this was the very flower and fruit of life. More than ever I thought now how worth while all I had gone through in my short and terrible marriage, if it had yielded me this!

Occasionally, if Mama was prevented from preparing my lunch before I left home, some time during the morning Roger would bring it to me. Opening the door from the hall tentatively, he would thrust his head in first, an impish light in his eyes; then march up to the platform and hand me the small basket he had brought, and each time, at this sudden sight of him, I felt the same rush of joy, the same glow of infinite happiness, I had felt when he told the story of Phaëton.

Yes, it was Roger, together with my growing absorption in teaching, which kept me happy then—as happy, I suspect, as I had ever been, or would be.

All these seven years when I was a teacher, both the earlier and later ones tending to merge in my mind now, I am not at all sure just when this or that happened. But I am practically certain it was my second winter at the G.H.S. when one extremely cold morning I stopped to stand above a large register in the hall, on the first floor, to warm my feet, before climbing the two long flights to my room.

As I approached the register, I noticed that a couple of other teachers were huddled over it, talking in subdued tones, noticed that they stopped talking when they saw me coming, and that Prof. White, standing near them, an open newspaper in his hand, started away as I drew closer, then abruptly turned back, and even more embarrassed than usual, asked me: "Have you seen the morning paper?"

"Why, no!" I said.

I imagine we did not take a paper at home at this time. We still were having to count the pennies very carefully. But I took the one Prof. White offered me, pointing, as he did so, to a telegraphic item from Columbus, Ohio, on its front page.

The item, dated the day before, stated that my sister had been married at an Army post there to a lieutenant in the Regular Army, son of a then well-known Cavalry general.[12]

I was dumfounded. It was a moment of such mortification time would never blot it out. But pulling myself together, I laughed. I took the news as if I had expected it, known all along what was to happen; when, as a matter of fact, I had never heard before of this young man who apparently was now my brother-in-law.

It was a year since the sad night when May left home, leaving behind, slipped under the front door, the few lines which had never ceased to burn like coals of living fire in my brain. We had heard from her all through the year, and she always wrote cheerfully, if without details, though Mama and I both knew she would never disclose to us any hardships she might be meeting; never add, if she could help it, to our natural anxiety about her. Then, we had felt deeply, besides all else, the manner of her going away. It was a subject we had never discussed even with our closest friends. We were as reluctant to mention even her name, as no doubt Papa and Mama had been to mention mine, when I had gone away myself and, to their shame and sorrow, secretly married the last man in the world they would have had me marry.

But now, when the first edge of my shock had worn off, when I had recovered a little from the blow to my pride at hearing the news as I had, I became conscious of a distinct sense of relief. It was the best thing, it occurred to me all at once, that had happened in our family since the decline in its fortunes had set in. May, at least, would be taken care of from now on. We wouldn't have to worry about her any longer. She had married a young man with a profession, and from a "good family." Henceforth she would be secure. What we should do was rejoice, and rejoice we did, in our hearts. Now we could talk openly about May, and that, I suppose, was our greatest relief of all.

Very soon May's young husband would sail for Manila, and soon thereafter she would join him—start on her long years, some forty of them, of "following the flag" in far-flung Army Posts; in the Philippines, Alaska, Hawaii—at home or abroad, wherever the U.S. flag went.

But this first year of May's marriage, while she waited for a transport to carry her, with a few other Army wives, to the Orient, she spent much of her time with us in the little house on White Avenue.

It was a happy time; happiest of all, perhaps, for Roger, wildly joyful in recovering the "Auntie May" who had mysteriously disappeared, but whom he had not forgotten.

It may be because this *was* a happy time that I remember all the more clearly an experience which, inconsequential though it might seem, was to influence my life in no small degree for several years to come.

For all that I still had invitations to them, I no longer went to parties. Most of my former intimates were married by this time, with homes of their own, and young married couples in that day seldom went, as before their marriage, to cotillions or other dances. Their social life took the form now of ladies' luncheons and teas, and, with cocktail parties not yet in vogue, if even originated, of formal dinner parties and evening receptions, if both men and women were to be present. I had neither time nor clothes now for such affairs. Moreover, I had not been to a function of this sort since my divorce—in fact since my marriage, and as I had come to think they were not for me, I thought, I believe, little about them.

As usual, therefore, I sent my regrets, along with Mama's, when invitations came to a large wedding reception to be given in West End. With only the immediate family to be present at the ceremony, the reception would follow. But in this case, the bride's mother would not accept my regrets. In the midst of all her preparations for the wedding, she took time to come down to White Avenue from the hill above where she lived and insist that I should be there. She was a gentle, unpretentious, sweet-spirited, sincere woman, and finally I succumbed to her urging, when Mama, too, urged me to go.

At this distance of time I cannot recall whether, when the evening came, I shrank from going to the reception, or looked forward to it. What I shall remember as long as I remember anything is how I felt after I got there.

Home of a big, breezy, rather countrified-looking but exceedingly friendly man who had made a fortune in wholesale groceries, the house was a handsome, recently-built, red-brick mansion, lights streaming from every window of its three storeys [*sic*] as I approached it, on foot, alone, while carriage after carriage was drawing up under its *porte-cochère*.

When a maid had taken care of my coat and the scarf I had worn over my head, I found myself one of a long procession of guests seeking to pay their respects to the bridal party and then surging on through the crowded, flower-decked rooms beyond; the men all in tails—full evening attire, the women, without exception, décolleté, jeweled, in shimmering silks and satins, gold or silver slippers; and I in the best I possessed, and good of its sort no doubt—a high-necked, long-sleeved winter dress of some dark shade, and in high buttoned black shoes.

It seems, as I think of it now, that I, or certainly Mama, should have realized what was in store for me. But however that may be, I could not have felt more out of place had I been a soot-grimed chimney-sweep suddenly set down in the midst of this glittering throng.

It did not help, either, that there was hardly a man or woman among them, young or old, whom I did not know personally, or who had been associates of my parents in their own prosperous days. It did not help when one after another, in flattering terms, they expressed pleasure at seeing me there. But never did kindness so hurt. Never have I spent so bitter an evening. I remember how hard it was to swallow even a bite of the elaborate wedding supper, of the chicken salad, minced oysters, to nibble at a slice of the frosted wedding cake, when someone had shown me into the dining-room with its resplendent bridal table, someone else had considerately come and sat beside me.

A Gertrude Stein under any and all circumstances might rise above the consideration of dress. It is a quality of noble souls. But I was not a Gertrude Stein. Not a noble soul. I was just a very young woman brought up in conventional surroundings, but who in these lean days was struggling principally to survive.

Through the long hours of that night after I returned home, my heart literally ached. Oh, how *could* I have dreamed that it would be otherwise than it had been? A Cinderella without the crystal slippers, the fairy finery, to give me at least a passing triumph, I had gone to this party, as I had come away, in the drabbest of garments, conspicuously, grotesquely, out of place!

But one thing, in my misery that night, I resolved upon before dawn crept dismally through the window of my small sloping-roofed upstairs bedroom—never again would I expose myself to what seemed to me, though I blamed only myself, an indignity.

That night was a turning point. Despite my natural love of gaiety, I would *not* be one of those poor-in-worldly-goods, obsequious, slightly ridiculous hangers-on of society, of which, even in the Knoxville of my day, I had seen too many. I would work out an independent existence. From now on, my pleasures would be such as I could encompass within the present conditions of my life.

One of these pleasures, one that had no obverse side, I found in recourse to books. From the day after this wedding reception I led what might be called a dualistic life; half in the work-a-day teaching world and simple pleasures at home; half in the enchanted realm created for me by great writers both of the past and present.

This was the era when Robert Louis Stevenson was at the height of his popularity. Everyone who could be said to read at all was reading not only his *Treasure Island*, *Kidnapped*, his charming *A Child's Garden of Verses*, but many were reading his *Virginibus Puerisque* and other collections of his informal and irresistible essays. For a while I lived part of my twenty-four-hour day in far off Samoa. I mourned Stevenson's recent death as if it had been the death of a beloved personal friend; followed along with the natives the "Road of the Loving Hearts" which they had built to his grave. Thrilled with tales of his adventurous life, and scarce though money was, I bought a photograph of this frail yet dauntless man, had it framed, and hung it on the wall of our sitting room.

Part of my time, a little later, I lived in Wessex, that dewy English countryside which Thomas Hardy through his *Return of the Native* and *Tess of the D'Urbervilles* had made as real to me—nay, far more real, than the country round about Knoxville.

I remember well, too, the night I started to read another work by this great master of English letters, the first to revolt against the Victorian tradition in fiction—*Jude, the Obscure*.

It was a Friday night. Mama and little Roger long asleep, the house still, curled up in a chair in the sitting room I read this tragedy of the poor youth who so longed to partake of some of the fruits of scholastic learning that he would climb up to the roof of a shed in his native village from which he could glimpse, mistily, afar off, the spires and towers of Oxford, that goal he had set for himself, that star he would steer by, only in the end to go down in defeat.

I read straight through till morning, I remember; until I heard the early hucksters from the country beginning to lumber by on their way to Market Square. With its compassion, its portrayal of the courage of the human spirit as it moved toward its doom, no novel had ever affected me so deeply, or ever was to. Not even Hardy's "pessimism" dimmed the work for me, as already I had accepted tragedy as an integral, an inescapable, part of human existence, whatever its joys; and I added Hardy now to the lengthening row on our sitting-room wall—photographs of authors who had become my closest and most inspiring associates.

But there was Kipling, too, in this period, to add a new and quite different kind of excitement to the society in which, unseen, I was now moving.

No odium had as yet, or would for some time to come, attach itself to his name as a glorifier of British Imperialism. With a clear conscience we could revel in his *Jungle Books*, still coming out; in his *Plain Tales from the Hills*, his *Light That Failed*; could thrill to his *Barrack-Room Ballads* when Tommy Atkins was becoming a household word; when "Gungha Din" [*sic*] was a favorite recitation and when in Knoxville parlors, "In the gloaming, oh, my darling," or "Just a song at twilight, when the lights are dim [i.e., low]," were being replaced by "Come you back, you British soldier, come you back to Mandalay," or by the virile and booming strains of "Danny Deever." Yes, every generation has its outstanding thrills, and Kipling then was one of ours. Above all else, he was giving us the flavor, some of the *feel*, of the Orient, so far as it was reflected in his strikingly-novel verses and tales of British soldiers in the British colonies.

Then besides Hardy and Kipling in that day there was the Pre-Raphaelite Brotherhood: poets and painters, with their mysticism and fantasy, their richness and vividness of detail, to feed our imaginations in a new and again quite different direction, among them Dante Gabriel Rossetti with his "The Blessed Damozel," and I remember, though money was still scarce, nevertheless ordering from Boston a Copley print of Rossetti's painting of *The Blessed Damozel* to hang, as well as the row of photographed authors, on a wall in our sitting room, thereby displacing, a little to Mama's concern, an old steel engraving which had previously hung there.

Most exotic of all the literary tastes of the day was, however, *The Rubáiyát of Omar Khayyám*. Though this 12th Century poem had been published in the Fitzgerald translation several decades earlier, yet only now, in the '90s, was it coming into popular circulation, and one stanza in particular in this sensuous, if symbolic, poem of Persia's golden age delighted me, as many others, with what we then considered its daring:

> *A Book of Verses underneath the Bough,*
> *A Jug of Wine, a Loaf of Bread—and Thou*
> *Beside me singing in the Wilderness—*
> *Oh, Wilderness were Paradise enow!*[13]

But it was not only fiction and poetry which fed my inner fires now. It was at this time I first read Herbert Spencer's *First Principles of Synthetic Philosophy* which I pored over with the same intense interest as at college over Darwin and Huxley.[14]

All in all, it was a rich time. If my external existence seemed to others bounded at one end by the little house on White Avenue, at the other by the G.H.S. and my daily beat back and forth between them, my inner world knew at least no geographical limits.

Many of the books, however, that were feeding my inner fires were not in our own library, though it was a considerably larger collection, I have reason to believe, than the average Knoxville home contained then, and, furthermore, for all our moves from rented house to rented house, Mama had never discarded a single volume, whatever else she had to discard in order to make room for our books.

But new books were constantly coming out, books I heard of, which excited my interest, and which I could only hope to see, at least in the near future, if I could find them at the Lawson McGhee library.

Although it was only at this time I began to visit it, this public library and reading room had come into being ten years before. A gift from the Colonel McGhee whose imposing, gloomy-looking home I passed every day on my way to and from school, and a memorial to his daughter Lawson who had died a short time before, it occupied the second storey [*sic*] of a building on the corner of Gay and Vine Streets.[15]

Prior to its opening, one of Knoxville's all too few civic-minded citizens had stated publicly: "We support twenty-one saloons in Knoxville [a conservative estimate]. It remains to be seen whether we can support one library."[16]

The *Knoxville Journal* at the same time advised its readers that the library would be open until ten o'clock and would be "an elegant place for young men to spend their evenings profitably."

Lawson McGhee Library reading room (1886 or 1887).

I do not remember, I confess, in my countless visits to this library, ever seeing many young men, or any at all of my own acquaintance, spending an evening in this profitable fashion. But, for me, the Lawson McGhee Library furnished more solid enjoyment, at any rate of its kind, than I could find then anywhere else.

It would be Friday evening, directly after supper, when I started on my regular weekly trip to the library, usually alone, and my joy would begin when I commenced climbing the broad flight of stairs leading up to it from Vine Street; while all my weariness from the day in the school-room and the long walk from home would fall away the instant I set my foot inside the long and lofty but plain chamber which housed the library.

Its librarian, in my day, was Miss Mary Nelson, of blessed memory, sister of Frank Nelson, for long years Knoxville's most distinguished musician.[17] Miss Mary would welcome me as warmly as though she were hostess at a party in her own home, and with very few others there, I would browse around blissfully among the library stacks in the rear, often for a couple of hours, dipping into one volume after another that aroused my curiosity, and departing at the closing hour with as many books as I could carry.

Some of the glow, in fact, from my visit to the library would still be with me when I stopped down below at a little fruit-stand on the Vine Street side of the building, to buy a few dates there, or roasted chestnuts, to take home to Roger, and for a few minutes chat with the vendor himself, an Italian, squat, dark, dirty, but always smiling, and who bore the glorious name of Fiorenzi [*sic*] Rebori![18]

Next to my evenings at the library, my greatest pleasure, of a kindred sort,

Lizzie Crozier French (ca. 1890).

throughout my teaching years, was the Ossoli Circle, a woman's "literary club" founded by Mrs. Lizzie Crozier French, whom I continue to regard today as Knoxville's Citizen No. 1 for the duration of her adult life.

A highly-charged spirit, a woman with a social conscience, Mrs. French, from one of Knoxville's "old" and eminent families, was generally considered a crackpot; a crackpot because she was an early advocate of woman suffrage; because she was a leader in the movement to oust the saloons—grown to fifty-one by the turn of the century—in which men in the Queen City of the Mountains, as Knoxville called itself, continued to drink most of the liquor they provided. A crackpot, in sum, because of the many innovations she introduced, or proposed, for the betterment of Knoxville's civic life; although, as a matter of fact, she probably had as sound and sane a mind as the town ever produced.

Founding the Ossoli Circle in 1884, and naming it in honor of Margaret Fuller Ossoli, one of the outstanding feminists of her time, it was the first woman's club in this country, or so Ossoli has steadfastly maintained, notwithstanding that a number of other woman's clubs in the country have made an identical claim, so that I shall not press the point.[19]

In any event, Ossoli was founded by Mrs. French with the avowed object of "stimulating intellectual growth and moral development."[20]

It met on Monday afternoons, for some years in private homes, though later—and while I was still a member—in the Woman's Building which it built and owned.

I joined myself in 1904,[21] or so I have recently read in a published article about Ossoli, though I was previously very hazy about the date, and can only account for my joining the club in that particular year, when my divorce had just been granted and I shrank from all social contacts, on the ground that Mrs. French, a positive person and no sentimentalist, but with a warm heart in her stout little body, recognized that I could only be drawn by fresh interests out of the Slough of Despond into which I had sunk.

The youngest member when I joined, I soon became rather prominent in the club, was on its program committee year after year, and looked forward the whole week to its meeting.[22]

Though it was as soon as I could get there from school, I would invariably be late, and after the business part of the program, which I detested, was over (I have consistently throughout my life avoided the mechanics of any of the many organizations to which I have belonged), and the literary part had just begun.

I remember what a happy yet sad feeling would flash through me as I entered and spied Mama, also a member, sitting, somewhere among the rows of women, her quiet beautiful face framed in its widow's bonnet and veil. Her face would light up if our eyes met and somehow through this exchange of glances in the midst of others not tied to us by blood we would seem closer to each other than at any other time.

I know that much fun has been poked at the woman's literary club. I have done some of it myself. Ossoli, in the years I knew it, was no marked exception. We would "cover' Locke's *Essay Concerning Human Understanding* and *Trilby*,[23] the latest sensation in fiction, on the same afternoon.

But for all that, I think Ossoli, from its beginning, fulfilled to some extent its founder's object of "stimulating intellectual growth." Many and many a member, I am confident, read more widely and seriously because of Ossoli.

For myself, I have rarely experienced more rewarding hours than when I read *Walden* for the first time, then *The Maine Woods* and all the rest of Thoreau, this eccentric, extremely individualistic writer, with his profound love of nature, his streak of mysticism, and to whom I had not been drawn previously, but now read thoughtfully in order to present him to the best of my ability before the Ossoli Circle, and, incidentally, expanding my own world, at the same time, in yet another direction.

As the years went on Ossoli became more and more ambitious in its programs and as near as I can guess it was during my last year in Knoxville that part of our attention that season was devoted to sociology, the then new science of human society.

It was Lucy Crozier, sister of Ossoli's founder, a brilliant, electric person, traveled, more worldly-wise, more sophisticated, than Mrs. French, but an intellectual, as we would call her now, and very *avant-garde* in that day—Miss Lucy, who had suggested this subject, one only lately being taught in our universities.

Miss Lucy proposed that I was the member who should discuss the subject under the heading of "Static and Dynamic Sociology."

I demurred.

"Why, Miss Lucy," I protested, "the ladies won't want to hear a paper on sociology. They would be bored to death!"

Miss Lucy laughed gaily. "It will do 'em good," she said, "just to hear the words you use."

But if the weekly meeting of Ossoli during its season was, at the time, one of the high spots in my life, and if there were the golden evening hours at home when I read books of my own choosing, it was, more than anything else—and I am quite sure of this today—the exalted experience of teaching which helped preserve in me my vehement love of living, helped restore that lightness of heart, perhaps constitutional, but which had been dimmed for awhile, if not lost, when, after my wrecked marriage, I had had to face life on so strange a new front.

It was in my second, or possibly third year at the G.H.S., when Miss Stoltzfus left to take a more important position somewhere else, and I was promoted to her previous post, in charge of the 10th grade room, at a salary of seventy-two dollars a month, the top salary then in the Knoxville schools, except for principals,[24] and considered high in the days when even an instructor at the University of Tennessee got less than a $1000 a year.

From now on Mama and I felt less cramped so far as money was concerned. It is true that the Hon. Sam Heiskell, mayor of Knoxville for thirteen years and strongly opposed to high school education at public expense, from time to time would try to get the salaries of high school teachers reduced. At least once he succeeded, my own cut at the time from fifty-two dollars to fifty a month. Usually, however, the City Council overruled him, so that after I reached seventy-two dollars, my salary stayed at what the mayor termed "a preposterous figure."

But if my anxiety on this score grew less and less during my last four or five years at the G.H.S., also I taught with ever increasing zest. While life at no time in these years seemed to me prosaic, humdrum, far less drab, yet now the days became wondrously alive as I sought to fire my pupils with some of the enthusiasm I felt myself for various authors.

Among poets, the boys and girls themselves, I discovered, were far more attracted to Byron than to any other poet, living or dead. It amounted to adoration. By and large, Byron was still the idol of 19th Century youth. To them he was a glorious creature, and from my own reading I could add to their limited knowledge of this idol such details of his romantic life and death, of the wildness, evil, and debauchery which had helped build his fame, as I thought suitable for class-room consumption.

As an antidote to Byron, however, I led them along as fast as I could to another great poet among the early leaders of Romanticism in England, one I thought (though I was careful to drop no hint of this) might be a more wholesome influence—William Wordsworth, with his worship of nature, humanitarianism, interest in the lives and speech of lowly people.

School children were not so familiar then as now with his lyrics on daffodils, skylarks, and violets half-hidden under mossy stones. It was a fresh field to work on, and I started with these lyrics, then had my pupils read, or read to them, everything from "I Wandered Lonely as a Cloud" and "The Idiot Boy," to "Intimations of Immortality" and his matchless sonnet, "Composed [up]on Westminster Bridge," and evoked by his sight of London at dawn.

From all the vast variety of Wordsworth's poems, I did not exclude, either, some of the so-called "silly" ones, which would give these young beings in front of me something to laugh at; for the first article in my credo as a teacher, if I had one, continued to be, that the school-room must never be stuffy. There must be touches of humor in every recitation period; and Wordsworth, the man, with his overweening egotism and other traits bordering on the ridiculous, supplied a comic element more easily than did the dashing, flamboyant Lord Byron.

All of the time, though, whatever the "silliness" of some of his poems, whatever his personal weaknesses, I tried to make it clear that Wordsworth remained one of the chief glories of English poetry.

All this time, too, re-reading Wordsworth with infinitely intensified pleasure as I endeavored to make these responsive adolescents feel the splendor of his finest work—all the time I was dwelling myself in Grasmere Vale, living in Wordsworth's country, that beautiful lake country of northern England, with its hilly pastures, stone cottages, mists and tumbling streams, until it became as familiar to me as Hardy's Wessex.

But now we came in our study to the Victorian age, and to Tennyson, its most representative poet, immensely popular then, and for special attention I chose his *Idylls of the King*.

I don't know who reads Tennyson now, in the heyday of T. S. Eliot and other disillusioned, frustrated, super-sophisticated, more or less obscure poets, wont to speak contemptuously of Tennyson's idealism, of his limitless hope for the erring human race; denouncing him for sentimentality, insipidity, and over-ornateness.

I don't know whether there are people, fairly literate people, left in the world today who read simple understandable poetry like Tennyson's.

I don't know, indeed, how long his *Idylls of the King*, whose grandeur and pathos, whose indestructible beauty (or so it seemed to me) I wanted to impress on my pupils—how long these *Idylls* lived in their youthful, often eager, minds. But I know what they meant to me at this time. They were filled with enchantment. Moreover, another corner of England became mine—Cornwall, Somerset, all the country of that shadowy British warrior of the 6th Century, King Arthur, of his Round Table, and in the midst of a woodland paradise "the dim rich city of Camelot."

Twelve *Idylls*, too many for high school consideration, so I chose those I thought best suited to the stage of development of my pupils, though at home read them all, as it happened, for the first time, and I think the hour, late at night, when, alone in our sitting room on White Avenue, I read *Guinevere*, will never fade from my memory. Never had a poem so stirred my pulses as this story of the guilty passion of Queen Guinevere, "the fairest under heaven," and Sir Lancelot, King Arthur's warrior "whom he loved and honored most"—Guinevere who had married Arthur when "the world was white with May," and when her adulterous relationship to Lancelot was revealed to the king, had fled through the mists of autumn to the "holy house" at Almesbury, there to become a nun.

It may be because I was so starved for romance now in my own life, that I lived vicariously in that flesh and blood passion of Lancelot for Guinevere, Guinevere for Lancelot. But no poem had ever so stirred my pulses, and in after years when again and again I would be in England, one autumn I made a pilgrimage to the Arthurian country, stayed in the ancient village of Glastonbury, the abode in British fable of Arthur, and the legendary burial place of both King Arthur and Queen Guinevere. One misty evening I drove slowly over the self-same road along which Queen Guinevere had fled. I lived once more in that magical midnight hour of a long past night on White Avenue in Knoxville, when I was still so young, and this Idyll of Guinevere had set my heart beating tumultuously, brought a sensation of choking to my throat.

But in these years at the G.H.S. when my only traveling, or traveling to storied lands, was by reading, it was not alone through poetry I hoped to expand the world of my pupils no less than my own. There were prose writers, too, with whom we journeyed together. There was Thomas Carlyle, who opened up a different Scotland then the Scotland of Scott or Burns, on which we had dwelt briefly in previous studies; Carlyle, who also brought us a quite different London than the London of Dickens we would riot in later.

I realized from the start that Carlyle's famous *History of the French Revolution*[25] was too lengthy for these youthful students to tackle, and that his *Sartor Resartus*, which had aroused such a storm of protest when it appeared, was too savage, too violent, too full of heavy Germanic expressions, for them to read with understanding and pleasure; so I read to them a few of its more lucid passages, and written tenderly, as Carlyle always wrote of the Scottish peasant life from which he sprang. For the rest of his work, I recommended to them his somewhat more temperate *Heroes and Hero Worship*,[26] loaning my own copy to those who exhibited interest in it; and concentrating on the man himself. One of the most arresting, most picturesque figures of the Victorian age, here was a writer, if not his *writing*, to whom we might well give attention, and if to Thomas Carlyle, inevitably to his wife, Jane Welsh Carlyle.

Now, as I write, in the middle of the 20th century, a whole spate of new books about this most remarkable couple in literary history are pouring off the press. The Carlyles, it seems, are being rediscovered. But these new books have little to offer that I did not find more than sixty years ago in Froude's biography of Carlyle, published in the '80s, a sensation of the day, one of the prized books in our family library; or in the *Letters of Jane Welsh Carlyle*, a paper-bound copy of which I had got hold of in some way I don't recall, and beyond the peradventure of a doubt the gayest, wittiest, most sparkling collection of letters ever produced by a woman, or by a man, when it comes to that.

I would pore over one or another of these works night after night to all hours; then next day convey to the class all the flavor I could of the life together of these two geniuses. . . . I was bewitched by the life history of this extraordinary couple: Carlyle from a frugal peasant family who lived in two or three rooms, an uncouth, fantastically awkward youth, introduced by a friend, a school-master, into the elegant drawing-room at Haddington, near Edinburgh, where, in her distinguished father's home he would meet Jane Welsh, "the Flower of Haddington," not beautiful, but *belle laide*, with her own brilliant mind, a wit of wits, a belle of belles, of whom it was said that "every man who spoke to her for five minutes felt bound to propose."

I remember mornings in the school-room when I could hardly wait till I finished the roll call, read some verses from *Biblical Selections*, and we had said in unison the Lord's Prayer, so impatient was I to bring to the class fresh lights I had gleaned overnight on this endlessly fascinating pair.

There was their five years' courtship when Jane defended this gauche peasant against her family, against all her intimates, as a man who had all the elements she deemed essential in a husband—"a warm true heart to love me, a towering intellect to command me, and a spirit of fire to be the quickening starlight of my life."

There were her trials when, in the earlier years of their marriage, they lived at Craigenputtock, a farm Jane had inherited, on the desolate Scottish moors . . . .

There was the long period after they had gone to London, taken a house on Cheyne Walk, Chelsea, a house in which they would live the rest of their turbulent lives together . . . .

Then there was also the finer side of this man who seemed to inspire in any company a feeling almost equally of love and terror—a side which I thought I should impress on these impressionable young beings sitting in front of me . . . .

On the other hand, I did not gloss over the last sombre [*sic*] chapter in this life drama of the Carlyles; the fifteen conscience-stricken years he lived after Jane's death, tortured unremittingly by memories of his ruthlessly selfish treatment of his [wife] . . . .

But whatever aspects of this extraordinary couple we considered, it seemed to me we never had had such good, such exhilarating, times together, the class and I, as during our study of Thomas and Jane Carlyle and my own intense interest in them had not grown dim when in after years I was making a pilgrimage to Tennyson's Arthurian country, I made one also to the house in London, by this time a national shrine, but the self-same house, with the self-same furnishings I knew so well—that house in which Jane, with more patience than she was born with, had protected a husband who made heavy weather of his work and life . . . .

I saw it all again, though with moist eyes in this later time, I confess. For me, with all its touching momentoes [i.e., mementos] of the life lived there, this was no museum. It was a house the Carlyles had left only the day before.

After Thomas and Jane Carlyle, there was no other writer I thought would not be anti-climax—none save Charles Dickens, and I arranged my English course each year so that Dickens would follow the Carlyles.

In recent years there have been some damaging revelations in regard to Dickens, the man. But in the '90s we knew him only as the immortal creator of characters who wrung more mingled tears and laughter from his readers than any other novelist before or since. We didn't talk condescendingly then about his melodrama; we revelled in it. His deathless characters had been familiar in our own, as in many another American household, for as long as I could remember, and I could never forget a story I heard in my childhood of a man in Virginia who was dying but begged the doctor to keep him alive at least until he read the next number of *Harper's Magazine*, in which *Bleak House* was running as a serial.

For Dickens' personal life, I had my pupils (though they read, first and last, many of his novels before the year was out) concentrate on *David Copperfield*, to a considerable extent autobiographical, my own favorite among his works, as it was, Dickens admitted, the one among them which in his "heart of hearts" he himself loved best.

To this I added, however, from my own reading of John Forster's *Life of Dickens*, other views of him, including a picture of Dickens walking the streets of London all night long, weeping, in an agony of grief, after he had written of the death of Little Nell in *The Old Curiosity Shop*, so real to him was this brain-child of his: and a passage, no less memorable, where Forster tells of Dickens, a little boy of nine, a few musty crusts in his pocket, trudging all the way up to London, where he would seek his fortune, along with the rest of his improvident, poverty-stricken family headed by his airy, highfalutin father, the imperishable original of Micawber; though pausing in his weary walk through a Kentish road to peek through the gates at an ivy-clad mansion, known as Gadshill [sometimes, Gad's Hill] Place, which he vowed, on the spot, would be his, if ever he became a rich man.

Few things seemed more like a fairy tale to me than that Dickens actually did this when he became rich and world-renowned: though looking back today, in my eighties, on my own life, it seems hardly less fabulous that within a decade of the time when I was teaching these boys and girls at the G.H.S., I would become, through the happiest of accidents, acquainted with living descendants of Charles Dickens; be entertained time and again at the London home of his granddaughter, born Sydney Dickens,[27] wife of Thomas Whinney, a London architect; taken by the Whinneys on an all-day excursion to this very Gadshill Place, no longer in the Dickens family, but owned now by a retired East Indian judge; visit with them the very inn in nearby Rochester which "Grandpappa" (as Sydney referred, always with something of a shock to me, to her illustrious forbearer) had made famous through the adventures in this inn of that naïve, benevolent, elderly gent, Samuel Pickwick, and the doings there of Sam Weller, center of comic interest in *Pickwick Papers*.

A thing also I could never have imagined in my teaching years—no, not in my wildest dreams, was that through this chance but soon firmly-established friendship with the descendants of Charles Dickens, I would one day be taking his great-grandchildren, as my guests, to a Christmas pantomime at the famed, centuries-old Drury Lane Theatre in London.

But if all this, "in my stars," was hidden from me then, nonetheless I could hardly have had, I think, a happier, more rollicking time with my pupils than when each year we lived for a while in Dickens' world.

One year I decided that Commencement exercises should be enlivened by more than the customary, pretty tame proceedings. I worked out for members of the graduating class a series of scenes, in costume, from Dickens. They gave the scene from *Oliver Twist* where the half-starved Oliver, starting his career in the workhouse, commits the unspeakable crime of asking for more gruel; a scene from *The Old Curiosity Shop* in which not only Little Nell, its heroine, appears, but that dirty, smart, extremely flowery young man, Dick Swiveller; gave, among other scenes I can't remember, one from *Martin Chuzzlewit*, featuring the drink-sodden, disreputable, monthly nurse, "Sairey" [Sarah] Gamp, complete with her great bonnet, bulky cotton umbrella, the bottle of "stimulant" to which she was addicted, and her perpetual references to the mythical "Mrs. Harris," to whom she attributed all her own weaknesses.[28]

From the laughter it evoked from the packed house at Staub's Theatre that evening, I could only conclude that the performance had been something of a triumph—certainly one to warm my heart as an amateur theatrical producer. But also it left me in a state of collapse.

It was the first time I had ever organized and managed any such project. There had been weeks of preparation for this ambitious venture, while I was carrying the usual overload of duties in the school-room, and then this wind-up in mid-June came when the normal Knoxville summer of semi-tropical heat already had set in.

I remember perfectly what happened when it was all over and with Mama and little Roger I went, for a few weeks of economical change, to the farm, a few miles from Knoxville, of some Presbyterian acquaintances, an elderly blue-nosed couple, well-to-do, but who starved us almost as mercilessly as Oliver Twist had been at the workhouse.

It was the day after Commencement, late afternoon, when we arrived there and were shown into a good-sized downstairs bedroom containing two large, early Victorian walnut beds.

Mama took Roger out for a short walk down the little lane which led to a spring-house while we were waiting for a supper more frugal than we could possibly have anticipated, but nothing mattered to me now but—*Rest!*

I sank down on to one of the big walnut beds, and lay there, motionless, looking through the windows into the lovely glow, as it seemed—after the heat and glare of town—of tall, gently-waving, incredibly green trees, and I thought I could lie there, in this cool and quiet, forever! After all my labors, at last I could relax. I have never known a more heavenly sensation.

Recalling these overburdened years, it comes to me that one of the things which eased them for me was the absence of friction between Mama and myself. We never indulged in "scenes." It was not a family habit. Perhaps an occasional scene might have relieved some of the tension between us in earlier as later years. But now, when we lived on White Avenue, I recall but one spirited difference between us—a quarrel, not to put too fine a point upon it.

It was Sunday. Roger, around seven then, although I had never tried to dissuade him from going to Sunday School, had found it boring at an even tenderer [*sic*] age than I had. On this Sunday morning he begged not to go, and I was not for forcing him to, while Mama, despite the fact she had grown increasingly unorthodox, continued to attend Sunday morning church services, and felt—from the standpoint of the conventional, if no other—that Roger should be *made* to attend Sunday School.

Just which of us prevailed after an argument which reached heated and painful, even bitter words—what its outcome, has sunk past recovery from my mind. What I retain is an impression of the wonderful harmony which prevailed, in general, between Mama and myself throughout this whole period in our lives.

Mama continued to solve alone all her domestic problems, as well as those with Roger in my absence, never imposing them on me, though *her* heart, too, must have been eased, seeing me again happy, light-hearted, and never, never, buried in bleak moods.

Another thing that comes to me now, and with a certain astonishment, is the few days I lost from teaching in these years. Anything but robust, weighing not over a hundred pounds, and with intermittent attacks of asthma, which I had had from childhood, and from which sometimes I would sit up in bed almost the night through, gasping for breath, yet when daylight came somehow I would gather together strength enough to start to school.

There came a time, though, when sheer will-power was of no avail. My birthday was in late September, and that evening, to celebrate the occasion Mama had set the supper table with our best "company" damask, china, silver, decked it with flowers, and prepared my favorite dishes; but when I took my place at the table, suddenly I found I could not sit up a moment longer. All day in the school-room I had felt dreadfully ill, but now, burning with fever, trembling all over, I bowed my head on the table, and losing all control, began crying, to Mama's bewilderment, as she had never seen me cry before.

It did not take the doctor long to determine what the trouble was—typhoid fever.

It was the year of the Spanish-American War. In Knoxville, in the summer and fall, there were always many cases then of this dread disease, so often fatal. But this fall it had become epidemic, with more than seventy-five cases in West End, whose water supply, separate from that of the rest of the city, had been polluted due to the situation of Camp Poland, on a height near Knoxville, where more than nine thousand men were stationed, many of them ill, or dying, with typhoid, and with the hospital's sewage draining directly into the stream below which furnished West End its water.[29]

In a couple of days Roger also came down with typhoid and Mama had two of us to nurse, Roger in her downstairs bedroom, I in the parlor, where a bed had been placed, and her only help kind women in the neighborhood, one of whom every afternoon, foregoing her usual siesta—for the weather was still sweltering—would come in her crisp percale wrapper, sit at Roger's or my bedside, fan us with a big palm-leaf fan, or bathe our fever-parched faces and hands from time to time with cold water.

As soon as my fever had broken, shaky though I was, my one thought was to get back to school. I was losing my pay every day I was absent. And how would we ever make it, with next summer's long summer vacation to take into account, when for almost three months I would not earn a cent? I remember that one fall, later than this, when I started back to school in September, neither Mama nor I had enough left to dare buy so much as a postage stamp until I got my first salary check, so I went a month without answering a single letter, even one or two that seemed rather urgent.

Viewed financially, teaching was unquestionably a precarious occupation in those days; so, for all the doctor's protest that I was not yet able to return to school, I did so.

I had to pay, however, for not heeding the doctor's advice. More and more tired as the days went on, in the following February, one afternoon as I stood at the blackboard, a stick of chalk in my hand—I see it plainly—suddenly I sank to the floor, unconscious.

This was a different sort of illness, and more alarming, than any Mama had dealt with heretofore. She had a bed brought again down to the parlor, and there I lay, silent, except to ask her to take all the pictures down from the walls, remove everything from the room save the barest necessities, and refusing to see anyone who came except, reluctantly, the doctor.

I was deeply depressed, though I could not focus my thoughts sufficiently to recognize the cause of my depression. I lay there day after day, without pain, my mind almost a blank. To think at all seemed almost beyond me. This illness was, I suppose, if not purely psychotic, at least as mental as physical, and a result of extreme nervous exhaustion.[30]

When at last I began once more to show some interest in life, Mama told me of a thing that had happened during my illness. One of our Ossoli friends, a beautiful and queenly woman, a native of Kentucky who had known hard days once in her own life, but who lived now in one of the three or four turreted, Mansard-roofed, sumptuous Victorian mansions in Knoxville—she had come with a gift of fifty dollars, offering it with all the worldly and truly spiritual grace with which she was possessed, as a little help, perhaps, she said, now that my salary had once more been cut off through illness.

Grateful as we were, however, and sorely as we needed the money, I do not know whether, in our pride, Mama or I suffered more in accepting this gift. *Charity*—how terribly it hurts the first time we must accept it!

But how dark these days had been for Mama was borne in upon me when I was definitely convalescent. One evening, usually so self-contained, she told me, in a low voice: "Annie, I had made up my mind that if you died I would take Roger in my arms and jump into the river."

May in the far-away Philippines—and far away they were then—on the other side of the world, with me dead, and with her own innate distrust of making a living for herself and Roger—in her desperation, this was the only solution that had presented itself. But I knew then that Mama had carried as heavy a stone on her heart, as ever I on mine.

NOTES

1. The building burned in 1924 and was replaced in 1927 by the Daylight Building (501–507 Union Avenue), which has been used as retail and office space over the years, including offices of the Tennessee Valley Authority from around 1934 until the early 1980s, and today houses a local bookstore, restaurant, and other shops. KnoxHeritage. *Historic Downtown Knoxville Walking Tour* [brochure] (Knoxville: KnoxHeritage,

2013), #43 (http://knoxheritage.org/our-work/neighborhood-tours/historic-downtown-knoxville-walking-tour/daylight-building/ (viewed January 20, 2020); Deaderick, 249.

2. Armstrong would have turned left (north) onto Locust from Clinch; Staub's home would have been on her right. Sadly, Peter Staub's place—the house and "beautifully cared for grounds" that she describes—are no longer there. The space is now occupied by Locust Street Parking Garage. Peter Staub (1827–1904), an immigrant from Switzerland, came to Knoxville in 1856 and set up a tailor shop. Investing his earnings in real estate, he became an important business, civic, and cultural leader. He served twice as mayor of Knoxville and was appointed U.S. Consul to Switzerland in 1885. Staub's Opera House, on the southeast corner of Gay Street and Cumberland Avenue, opened in the fall of 1872. Rothrock 146–47, 489–90; Deaderick, 38, 463–465.

3. Despite all the negative comments that Armstrong makes about him, Charles McClung McGhee (1828–1907) was an important leader in the growth and development of Knoxville following the Civil War. Additionally, he was a philanthropist, giving money to establish St. John's (Episcopal) Orphanage and to build a library building in memory of his daughter. Rule, 542; Rothrock, 243–44; 447–48; Deaderick, 42, 417; Creekmore, 137–38. William Joseph MacArthur, Jr., wrote a doctoral dissertation on "Charles McClung McGhee, Southern Financier." It is available in Special Collections at the University of Tennessee and online at < William Joseph MacArthur, Jr., "Charles McClung McGhee, Southern Financier," PhD diss., University of Tennessee, 1975, https://trace.tennessee.edu/utk_graddiss/2652 (viewed November 29, 2019). MacArthur served for several years as manager of the McClung Historical Collection (part of the Knox County Public Library System), which grew out of the donation of the personal library of Calvin Morgan McClung, who was married to McGhee's daughter Annie. Rothrock, 249, 445–46.

4. The McGhee house is still standing, but has been greatly altered. It serves today as a Masonic Temple and is directly in front across the street as one drives out the exit on the west side of Locust Street Parking Garage.

5. Girls' High School, built in 1886, was on Walnut Street at the corner of Union Avenue. In 1911 it became the Boyd School (for seventh grade students) and later Boyd Junior High School. Rule, 404, 407; Deaderick, 242–49.

6. In addition to the high school grades, G.H.S. provided classrooms for grades three through seven, attended mostly by girls. High school, at that time, consisted of only three years (eighth, ninth, and tenth grades). Rule, 404; *Twenty-eighth Annual Report of the Knoxville City Schools, 1898–99* (Knoxville: Ogden Bros., 1900), 115.

7. Ruth Hale, who was born in Rogersville, began her career as a newspaperwoman in Washington, D.C. at the age of eighteen. An outspoken feminist, she was a proponent of women's suffrage and co-founder and first president of the Lucy Stone League, which fought for a woman's right to retain her maiden name following marriage. She married

Heywood Broun, also a journalist, in 1917, but continued to call herself Miss Ruth Hale. Her mother, Annie Riley Hale, was equally vocal in her opposition to feminism, declaring that a woman's place was in the home. Mrs. Hale traveled around east Tennessee giving speeches against women's rights and published letters expressing her opinions on race problems and economic policies in various newspapers (including the *New York Times*). Mrs. Hale later lived in New York and in Pasadena, California, where she ran for a senate seat in 1932. "Ruth Hale Is Dead," *New York Times* (September 19, 1934), 19. Richard O'Connor, *Heywood Broun: A Biography* (New York: Putnam's, 1975), 45.

8. As "Supervisor of Literature" at Girls' High School in 1898/99, Armstrong wrote a detailed and passionate report, addressed to J. H. McCallie, superintendent of the Knoxville City Schools, about changes she had implemented based on her belief that, rather than being taught *about* literature, students should learn by reading the classic works of literature themselves. Her letter, signed "Annie Wetzell Waldron" as she was known at the time, is included in the annual report for that school year. *Twenty-eighth Annual Report of the Knoxville City Schools, 1898–99* (Knoxville: Ogden Bros., 1900), [75]-78.
9. W. T. White. Rule, 407; *Twenty-eighth Annual Report of the Knoxville City Schools, 1898–99* (Knoxville: Ogden Bros., 1900), [3].
10. Albert Ruth was superintendent of schools from 1881 to 1897. Rule, 405.
11. Miss Norma R. McClanahan. *Twenty-eighth Annual Report of the Knoxville City Schools, 1898–99* (Knoxville: Ogden Bros., 1900); *Knoxville City Directory*, 1897, 1898, 1900.
12. Armstrong's sister Mary (whom she most often refers to as May) was married to Leon L. Roach on February 27, 1899, in Franklin, Ohio. "Ohio, County Marriages, 1789–2013," database with images, FamilySearch (https://familysearch.org/ark:/61903/1:1:XZKR-Q45 : 8 December 2014).
13. *The Rubáiyát of Omar Khayyám,* stanza 12, translated by Edward Fitzgerald.
14. Spencer (1820–1903) was an English philosopher and social scientist. *First Principles* was the first volume of his 10-volume *System of Synthetic Philosophy* (published 1886–1900).
15. Lawson McGhee Library (on the northeast corner of Gay and Vine) opened on October 28, 1886. The book collection from a previous Knoxville public library, organized by stockholders and often in debt, was consolidated into the new library, named for May Lawson (McGhee) Williams, who was only 23 when she died in 1883 a few weeks after giving birth. The three-story building, which cost $50,000, was designed so that library operations could be supported by money raised from leasing the first floor for business. The third floor, with an auditorium that could seat 500 people, was used as a lecture hall. Rule, 541–42; Rothrock, 242–46; Deaderick, 44; Lance Coleman, "Library History Lives Here," *Knoxville News-Sentinel*, November 5, 2011.
16. Attributed to O. P. Temple, president of library stockholders in 1880; quotation from the *Knoxville Tribune* (March 11, 1880). Rothrock, 243. The bracketed comment is Armstrong's.

17. Mary M. Nelson became librarian of Lawson McGhee Library on July 1, 1896. Rule, 542; Rothrock, 244, 246. For an interesting tale and description of Miss Nelson, see Laura Still, *A Haunted History of Knoxville* (Asheville, N.C.: Stony River Media, 2014), 36–39. Frank Nelson was organist and choir master of St. John's Episcopal Church in Knoxville for fifty years, and "was recognized as one of the leading musicians of the southeast." Rothrock, 295.
18. Long-time tenant Fiorenzo E. Rebori bought the library building at auction in 1915. Although he died in 1946 and his descendants sold the building in 1999, it is still referred to in Knoxville as the Rebori Building. The current owners use the second and third floors as their private residence and lease the first floor to Nouveau Classics Contemporary Furniture and Interior Design. KnoxHeritage. *Historic Downtown Knoxville Walking Tour* brochure, (Knoxville: KnoxHeritage, 2013), #2; online at http://knoxheritage.org/our-work/neighborhood-tours/historic-downtown-knoxville-walking-tour/lawson-mcghee-library-rebori-building/ (viewed November 27, 2019); Jack Neely, *Historic Knoxville* (Knoxville: Knoxville History Project, 2018), 60; Lance Coleman, "Library History Lives Here," *Knoxville News Sentinel*, November 5, 2011.
19. The Ossoli Circle was founded on Friday, November 20, 1885 (not 1884), when Lizzie Crozier French invited about a dozen women to meet that afternoon at the old Knoxville Female Institute to organize a literary society. The name "Ossoli Circle" was chosen December 7. Sadie Boyd Saxton and Elizabeth Skaggs Bowman, *Highlights of Ossoli Circle's History, 1885–1960*, 7–8. The Ossoli Circle remains a prominent women's organization in Knoxville and has had its own club house at 2511 Kingston Pike since 1933. It still claims to be the oldest federated club in the South. Deaderick, 441.
20. From Article II of the Ossoli Circle Constitution.
21. Armstrong undoubtedly means 1894.
22. "Miss Annie Wetzell" is listed as secretary in the Yearbook for Ossoli's eighth season (1892–93), but she had probably been elected to that position during the year before her July 1, 1892, marriage. Her name is not in the 1893–94 Yearbook, but in 1894–95 "Mrs. Leonard Waldron" is listed as a member of the Prospectus Committee and as giving a program in February. Beginning with the 1895–96 Yearbook, "Mrs. Annie Waldron" is listed as an active member. In 1896–97 she again served on the Prospectus Committee. *Year Book of the Ossoli Circle, Knoxville, Tennessee*, 1892–1897.
23. George du Maurier's 1894 novel.
24. Average salary paid principals for the 1898/99 school year was $850; teachers, $456.81. At $72 per month, Armstrong would have earned $648 for the nine-month school year. *Twenty-eighth Annual Report of the Knoxville City Schools, 1898–99* (Knoxville: Ogden Bros., 1900), [23].
25. *The French Revolution* (1837), a history in three parts.
26. *On Heroes, Hero-Worship, and the Heroic in History* (1841).
27. Daughter of Charles Dickens, Jr.

28. "An Evening with Charles Dickens" was included on the program for closing exercises, held June 9, 1898, at Staub's Theatre, for the 1897/98 school year. *Twenty-seventh Annual Report of the Knoxville City Schools, 1897–98* (Knoxville: Ogden Bros., 1899), 47–48.
29. The first site of this encampment, originally called Camp Wilder, had been east of Knoxville. On June 29, 1898, it was moved to the Lonsdale addition, "near the Southern railway shops," and, following the August 7, 1898, death of Brigadier General J. S. Poland, was renamed Camp Poland by Brigadier General McKee, who visited Knoxville looking for a "more healthful location" for his troops, then at Chickamauga. By September 1, nine regiments (nearly 9,000 men) were encamped there. The Division hospital at Fort Poland remained in operation until February 1899. Rule, 187–88, 190; *Knoxville Sentinel*, June 29, 1898; Colin F. Baxter, "Spanish-American War," in *Tennessee Encyclopedia of History & Culture*, ed. Carroll Van West (Nashville: Tennessee Historical Society / Rutledge Hill Press, 1998), 871–873.
30. Although first thought to be meningitis, her illness (which occurred in January rather than February) was called "nervous prostration, coupled with brain complications." Under "Personal Mention," *Knoxville Sentinel*, January 21, 1899, 5.

Chapter Twenty-Two

High Days and Holidays

The summer when we spent a few weeks at the only place we could afford, on the farm, a few miles from Knoxville, of the stern gaunt elderly blue-Presbyterian couple who all but starved us, serving us at supper, as at other meals, after an endless grace before meat, only there was no meat, unless some slabs of half-cooked bacon, skimmed milk, and warmed-over potatoes among the few other miserably-cooked and always unappetizing dishes—these weeks, nevertheless, I recall with a good deal of pleasure.

The farm was within easy walking distance of the "Dummy" line, a steam railroad which ran between Knoxville and the then summer resort of Fountain Head, where I had gone to dances in my girlhood.[1] The walk to the Dummy was along a path through the lush meadow below the old but very decent white farm-house, and over a little foot-bridge, spanning a slender, sparkling stream edged with watercress, and being gay-hearted by nature, just as I became more than usually happy the moment I began to mount the stairs which led to the Lawson-McGhee library, so now I would feel more than usually joyful as soon as I took my seat in the one coach of the Dummy line on my way to town, to bring back with me a fresh supply of library books, the only purpose that could tempt me to leave, even for a few hours, the fresh clean air and beautiful peaceful country all around us at the farm.

We could never, indeed, have found a more restful spot, if we hadn't been perpetually hungry, though I was able to surmount even the misery of gnawing hunger when I saw Roger's overflowing delight in surroundings different from any he had known before.

Early every evening, but after dark, he would light a little toy lantern we had bought him, and carrying his lantern, careful to make no noise, but quivering with childish excitement, walk between Mama and me down the lane toward the spring-house, where, without fail, he would have the bewitching sight of three solemn baby owls, perched in a row, close together, on one of the high limbs of a tall cedar.

It was a nightly adventure too, for him, when he went to bed alone, but with a bottle he had filled with fireflies, and which, set on the walnut bureau near him, gave off a fitful magic light for him to go to sleep by.

For myself, I was almost reconciled to our half-starved state when each evening, as daylight was fading and mist beginning to gather over the meadow below, an unseen blackbird, somewhere near, would whistle repeatedly across the meadow to another blackbird, which would answer with the same sweet, slightly wistful notes.

But there was also my satisfaction in being able to indulge freely now, and at leisure, my own tastes in books; great ones sometimes, but whether or not, books unsuitable for high school students.

In the previous summer, our only diversion had been a ride once in a while in the open streetcar, with its crosswise breezy seats, out to that small artificial sheet of water, Lake Ottosee, where Roger had the fun of swinging under the trees in one of swings of this little amusement park;[2] or occasionally, on unbearably hot evenings, to "cool off," taking him with us simply for the long street car ride back and forth to Lake Ottosee—this same amusement park where the Drummers' Picnic had once been held, that annual affair for charity which, to my passionate grief and undying resentment (as I felt in my early teens) Mama would not allow me, among all the girls I knew, to attend; although a thing, now that there was no hostility between us, seemed something that had happened in a long buried past, and a past that had hardly belonged to me.

But during that summer spent entirely at home, and when streetcar rides were our only outings, I had become acquainted with George Meredith, whose novels, still coming out, and though considered obscure, were then at the height of their popularity.

I read nearly all of them; getting almost as sharp relish out of *The Egoist* as later out of Butler's *The Way of All Flesh*, although attempting recently to reread *The Egoist*, I could only force myself to plow through its first few pages. Even Meredith's *The Ordeal of Richard Feverel*, now ranked as a classic, on rereading it after more than half a century, for all its psychological interest, but with its affected style, transparently-contrived situations, its ostentatious display of learning, no longer held me.

In those weeks at the farm, however, I steeped in a writer who would never grow stale, not for me—Balzac.

I became so absorbed in his *Comédie Humaine*, opening up to me the vast domain of French provincial, as well as Parisian life, that in order to keep Roger, excessively active, quiet enough for me to read Balzac without undue interruptions, I would place myself at one end of a hammock swung under the trees in the small front yard at the farm house, and place Roger at the other end, where he would remain absolutely silent, apparently spell-bound, while I read aloud everything from *Père Goriot*, the poignant *Curé of Tours*, *Eugénie Grandet*, with its incomparable portrayal, in her father, of a type of French greed and domestic tyranny, to *La Cousine Bette*, and (in its English title) *Splendors and Miseries of a Courtesan's Life* [i.e., *Splendeurs et misères des courtisanes*, translated *The Splendors and Miseries of Courtesans*].

Roger would listen hour after hour, never moving, speaking, or falling asleep. Being no more at the time than four or five, it is impossible to say what he got out of these highly sophisticated adult works. Perhaps it was only the sound of my voice, running on and on, which lulled him into this unnatural, if wide-eyed, passivity; though the fact remains that years later, when he became entangled in a temporary but costly infatuation with one of the show girls at the Winter Garden in New York, an affair which gave me no little concern, he chided me laughingly: "Well, Mother, what would you expect when you read *The Duchess of Langeais* to me when I was practically in my cradle?"

It was in 1897, the second summer after I started teaching, that Nashville was celebrating Tennessee's 100th anniversary as a state by a Centennial Exposition.

I had not been away from Knoxville and its environs, except for my brief stay in the little nearby town of Harriman, when I was called home because Papa was dying—not since I came back with Theodore from the West. But now when Cad Finch, a classmate at Mt. Holyoke, a girl from Cairo, Illinois, whom I had found more congenial than most of my college associates, but had hardly heard from in the interim, wrote and urged me to join her in Nashville, where we could have a few days together and at the same time visit the Exposition, I was seized with a strong desire to go.

Mama also was anxious I should. The whole trouble was money. Even with reduced railroad rates, the trip would cost no less than twenty-five dollars, a sum we could not possibly spare if we were to get through on what we had saved for my long summer vacation.

Of course there were friends from whom we could borrow, but we had never bared our personal finances to any of them, and were not ready to now.

It was within two or three weeks of school's close for the summer that Cad's letter came, and I was still racking my brain as to how I might raise the necessary amount for the trip when one afternoon, the pupils all gone, as I was tidying my desk preparatory to leaving myself, Mr. Joy, the janitor,[3] entered with his broom, feather duster—all the usual paraphernalia, to take over as soon as I was out of the way, and suddenly I had an inspiration.

Judging by appearance, there was no more unlikely source of monetary aid than Mr. Joy. A short misshapen old Irishman with as thick a brogue as if he had only left his native Cork the day before, in his dust-colored work-clothes and brogans, his scant, straggly gray hair full of dust, his worn pock-marked face deeply grooved with it, a rubber device over his broad and enormous nose to prevent his breathing in any more than he must, he looked as if he were *made* of dust. Moreover, he was perpetually grousing, muttering "Holy Mother!" and other imprecations against the "outhrageous" conditions of the rooms he had to clean; forever threatening, "Wan day I'm goin' to get me a bether job!"

For all this, however, he had been with the schools for years, grown hoary-headed in their service, was thoroughly dependable, accommodating, if looked upon as a joke yet well-liked by both teachers and school children, and, according to hints I had heard, had accumulated, without a family, quite a little property. It was something else, though, that gave me the courage to speak to him now—I had always suspected that within his grotesque dust-laden body a warm Irish heart was beating.

I explained my situation.

"Mr. Joy, would you be willing to lend me the money? I'll pay you back, fast as I can, after school starts again in the fall."

"Ay, shure, an' I will," he said without an instant's hesitation. "Yis, shure, I will, an' meself, proud to!"

So I had my trip to Nashville.

This trip, so eagerly looked forward to, turned out something of a disappointment.

July heat in Nashville proved no less sweltering than in Knoxville. We were wet to the skin from daylight to dark, dark to daylight. Then the boarding-house whose address I had secured before leaving home, while respectable enough, was grossly overcrowded, our suffocating first-floor room, though large, was noisy, dirty, never attended to, its lumpy bed wretched—altogether anything but desirable.

The Exposition itself was especially disappointing both to Cad and myself. With no comparable setting here, for all its full-sized plaster replica of the Parthenon in Athens,[4] it paled before the glorious vision we retained in our minds of that dream "White City" beside Lake Michigan at the Chicago World's Fair four years ago. Its exhibits, too, suffered in comparison. We found none of them particularly arresting. But perhaps my own greatest disappointment, loath though I was to admit it even to myself, and beyond my power then to analyze, was Cad.

Still unmarried and a teacher herself, Cad had the same quick mind, the same pretty face, I remembered. Her low laugh was as delightful as ever. But where she was plump before and inclined to be untidy, now she was downright slovenly and definitely fat. Furthermore, while we still were sufficiently congenial to have good times together, yet some impalpable veil seemed to have dropped between us during the six years since I had seen her last. Perhaps it was because she had been leading a relatively care-free life during these years, while I had gone through things (things I never discussed) which had altered my sense of values. In any event, she was no longer one I would have gone to great pains, and at some sacrifice, to meet again.

All the same, Cad's sense of adventure, which had attracted me to her in college, was not dead, nor mine, it appeared, for it accounts for an experience we shared now, one neither of us was likely to forget.

Here in Nashville, though on a scale much more modest (if "modest" may be used in this connection), was what had been in Chicago the outstanding sensation, of its nature, at the World's Fair—its Streets of Cairo, introducing more or less openly to this young country the age-old lascivious *Danse du Ventre*.

As Cad and I were leaving the Exposition grounds one evening shortly after dark, and by a slightly out-of-the-way passage we had not discovered before, we came upon flaming banners proclaiming that what we were actually in was the Streets of Cairo and approaching the pavilion, with its spieler out in front, where this scandalous dance was being shown.

Consumed by curiosity, and losing our heads, we bought tickets and went in.

We took seats, not too far forward, among the gathering, all men, mostly rough-looking men, and in what, as I recall it, was a tent, and dimly lighted, save for the small stage.

The dance had already started. Two scantily-clad girls in Egyptian costume, and with bare bellies, were going through the suggestive gyrations characteristic of the dance, but apparently were not putting their hearts into it, for the red-faced manager of the show now began imploring the men, all craning their necks, "Warm 'em up, boys, for God's sake! The girls can't give you no show without you help 'em!" Whereupon the men, some of them staggering to their feet, began with obscene gestures and hoarse yells to "warm up" the jaded, not very young dancers, who followed with the more and more frenzied movements which would induce an orgasm.

Cad and I were aghast. We were almost equally disgusted, horrified, frightened. Frantic to get out of a far more bestial place than we could possibly have imagined, we were afraid to move or call attention to ourselves in any way, lest some of the more intoxicated of the men might accost us.

None of them did. But as we were coming out of the tent, I suffered another instant of sickening terror. Hundreds of Knoxville people were attending the Exposition.[5] Suppose I should come face to face with Prof. Ruth, passing by on his way to one of the less dubious "entertainments" the Exposition offered!

But if there had been disappointments, nevertheless, when I think back, I know that I returned from Nashville with a distinct upsurge of spirit. It had been a complete change, somehow or other I had been recharged, and never had the little house on White Avenue looked so good, so truly home, as when I saw it again after this few-days absence. Never had I known a sweeter moment than when Roger, playing under the apple trees in the back yard, caught sight of the hack I had taken from the depot rounding our corner, raced to the front gate, leaped into my arms, and I hugged him to my heart.

I made no mention of disappointments. Having me back again, Roger hung on my every word, and easily amused, when I gave him exaggerated accounts of comical little occurrences on the trip, he insisted on my repeating them over and over. Telling him exuberantly of my sensations, on a first ride on a roller-coaster, he would roll gleefully on the floor. To Mama and our close neighbours, I was able to give enthusiastic accounts of all I had seen—all except that extension to my education, of which I breathed not a word—seeing the hoochie-coochie!

And if this was the last, as well as first, time I ever visited Nashville, it was not the last time I would visit Middle Tennessee. From the time when those cousins on Papa's side, the Campbell boys from Tullahoma, came to board with us while they were attending the University, our relations with the whole family grew closer, and the next summer after the Nashville Exposition I visited them for a week or two.[6]

They lived in the biggest house in town, as befitted the size of the family, with its eleven sons and one daughter, besides a bachelor uncle and an attractive unmarried aunt who made their home with them. The immense frame house, with a verandah, bordered by fancy machine-carving, which extended all the way across its broad front, was furnished inside, if adequately, in a casual commonplace fashion, although its easy-going, informal, agreeable atmosphere made up for any lack of elegance in its fittings.

To sit down to midday dinner with its heaped-up platters of ham, chicken, roasting ears—all kinds of good country food, and with thirteen males, ranging from the bachelor uncle, the long-bearded patriarchal father, and sons home from college for vacation to the youngest in his high-chair, and then with another male, the white-coated, good-natured black man who waited at table, was, to say the least, an experience.

Most impressive of all, though, was that the older sons, disciplining the younger, through a mixture of sternness and kindness, allowing none to talk at meals unless he was old enough to have been away to prep school, if not to college, there was never any confusion, never have I seen better-behaved boys, and never at meals, nor at any time, did there seem to be a boy too many around.

The flat country around Tullahoma, with its stretches of scrub pine, had none of the beauty and picturesqueness found almost anywhere in East Tennessee. But there were beauty spots and places of interest not far away, and the members of the family were tireless in their efforts to make me have a good time: Mrs. Campbell taking me to Monteagle, a nearby resort where dwellers in the Deep South had been summering since antebellum days; then on up to Sewanee, seat of the University of the South, with its superb site, its theological seminary, and other Episcopal influences so all-pervasive on that secluded, forest-rimmed height that even the hack drivers who drove us around, pointing out the sights, when they spoke in their rich deep tones seemed to be chanting from one of the services in the Episcopal prayer-book.

It was in a more profane surrounding, however—at a ball park on the outskirts of Tullahoma, something happened which would influence my life, if not permanently, yet up to the day I left Knoxville not to return.

I had no interest then, or ever, in baseball, but being a guest, made no objection to whatever sort of outing my friendly hosts suggested. As we were coming away from the game, a tall, unusually handsome, blondish young man, around thirty I would have guessed, began making his way through the crowd and obviously toward us.

He recognized me before I recognized him. "It's Annie, little Annie!" he exclaimed, with a slight stutter, grasping both my hands in his, and then I knew it was Jim Ramsey.

Jim Ramsey had been Captain of Company A to which Harry belonged at the University. They had been close friends. As one of a cadet guard over Harry's body as it lay in the parlor at the Barnes house, he had spent two nights in our home. With his tact, engaging manners, his deep sympathy, it had given us a tender feeling for him that would never die. But I had quite lost sight of him in the years since. I had never known, in fact, where he came from, and never would have save for this chance meeting at the ball game, which he had come to Tullahoma to see from the neighboring McMinnville, a small farming and manufacturing center and his home town.

Jim went home with us to the hospitable Campbells for supper and lingered afterwards. Extremely witty, his slight stutter seemed to enhance, rather than detract from, his amusing talk.

After he had gone, the Campbells told me something about him. Jim had been connected with one of the important banks in Nashville, and a social leader; but through drink had lost out and returned to McMinnville, where his crabbed eccentric old father was one of its wealthiest and most influential citizens; where he had rehabilitated himself to the extent that he was now cashier in a bank there (of which his father was president), though never, apparently, had felt strong enough to return to the gay and much more congenial circles in which he had moved at the State capitol.[7]

Jim kept coming over to Tullahoma every day as long as my visit lasted. Presently, in the evening, we would be left alone, with what I surmised was the Campbells' connivance, on their dusky front porch, and inevitably, being a typical Southern gentleman of the period, he began making love to me.

That same year, during my Christmas holidays, I visited in Tullahoma again. This time it was for the express purpose of speaking one evening at the Campbells' home, on the invitation of Mrs. Campbell and her sister, before guests they would assemble there, and on a subject of my own choosing.

I chose Rostand's *Cyrano de Bergerac*, whose première in Paris had been an outstanding event in the theatrical world during the past year, was still of fresh interest, and which I had recently discussed before Ossoli.

When the evening came, the Campbells' big barely-furnished parlor was crowded to its limit, and among the audience was Jim Ramsey, who had come from McMinnville for the occasion.

Reciting or reading from its scenes, I felt from the start, from their rapt faces, alternate bursts of laughter and tear-filled eyes, that I had my audience with me. But it was only at the end, when these Tullahoma men and women, still wiping their eyes, crowded around me, overwhelmed me with praise, that I tasted success of a sort I had not known heretofore. My presentation of the play had been a triumph, if a small one, yet a triumph, as I could not doubt when, after the others had gone, Jim Ramsey remained to make far more ardent love to me, seeing me in a new light, than the summer before.

As a result, a correspondence sprang up between us, gradually growing more and more lover-like; and in the next few years after this meeting at Christmas time assumed the shape of an engagement, not formulated in so many words, yet carrying the assumption that after Jim had established himself a little more firmly in McMinnville—sooner or later, we would be married.

Nevertheless, for all this, and witty, with no small charm, lovable though he was, I do not believe that I was ever "in love" with Jim Ramsey. It would have been impossible for him to sweep me off my feet. But it was nice to have a man in my life again, especially as no one in Knoxville—no one but Mama knew of it. Nice to have someone making love to me once more—a sop to my vanity, if nothing else. Then it was pleasant to reach home after my day in school and find waiting for me on the table in the hall a letter postmarked McMinnville. It was nice to have a photograph of this photogenic man on the bureau in my small, sloping-roofed, upstairs bedroom, even if I never let it be seen below-stairs.

What Mama thought about these letters, this photograph, I can only conjecture. Not once did she mention them. Having been a friend of Harry, Mama was naturally predisposed in Jim Ramsey's favor as an individual. When it came to my marrying again, she must have had her anxious hours. With May in the far-off Philippines, what would become of *her* if I should remarry?

By the following summer, however, the summer of '99,[8] I was far more excited over the prospect of going to the University of Chicago for a summer of study than about Jim Ramsey.

It was Miss Lucy Crozier, the dynamic sister of the dynamic Mrs. Lizzie Crozier French, who had planted the idea in my head. She had spent a summer herself at the University of Chicago,[9] and another in research and study in England, at the Bodleian Library in Oxford—Oxford, the nearest thing to an earthly paradise Miss Lucy, with her cultivated tastes and passion for knowledge, could conceive of, although she assured me that, next to Oxford, there was no place where I could spend a more fruitful vacation than at the recently-founded University of Chicago, with as distinguished and brilliant a faculty as had ever been assembled in this country.

As fate would have it, that spring I unexpectedly fell heir, on the death of a bachelor uncle, to a small legacy. This set me on fire. Why not invest it in what seemed to me the best of all possible ways—in my further development as a teacher?

Mama and Roger traveled with me as far as Chicago, then on to Aunt Sarah's, a few hours away, where they would spend the summer, while I settled down at Foster Hall, one of the women's dormitories on the campus, and started to study in earnest.

There would be no disappointments at Chicago. It far exceeded my expectations. To start with, my associates at Foster Hall, though I saw little of them save at meal time, were wholly congenial. Coming from every state in the Union, all were teachers, and with one or two exceptions considerably older than I; some preoccupied, others lively and responsive, but all women who had fallen in love with learning.

In that summer of ['98], revolutionary, all but intoxicating, ideas were in the very air you breathed on the campus. Such an atmosphere satisfied a craving always in me. Long before Dr. Robert Hutchins had stated that the purpose of higher education was not to settle, but unsettle, the mind—back in those days of Dr. Harper, its first president, you felt this was the spirit animating the new university which had sprung up on the prairies of America and through Rockefeller millions grown so soon to gigantic proportions.

I say no disappointments, but, looking back, I must admit that among its famous professors, I got least from the most famous (even then) of them all—that grand pioneer in advocating education for a new social order, John Dewey, head of its department of philosophy, psychology, and pedagogy.

Amusing stories about Dr. Dewey and his unconventional, uninhibited family were rife on the campus. But feeling that this summer was, for me, the chance of a lifetime, I was looking for more than amusement; and when each morning he would appear before the large class in which I was enrolled, his socks flapping around his ankles, sagging and shuffling as he walked back and forth across the rostrum, as if too deep in thought to mind where he was going, lecturing in a distracted manner, crumpling his notes into a ball and gazing into space, apparently simply thinking out loud, I could find nothing whatever to jot down in my note-book.

It would be a long time before I realized what Dr. Dewey was trying to do in these disconcerting lectures of his—trying, not to think *for* us, but to induce us to do some thinking for ourselves. But if, due to my own limitations, I got little from this mild and drawling man, who at ninety would still be the nation's most noted philosopher, I had rich compensation under other of the university's professors.

By all odds the one from whom I got most was Dr. Oscar Lovell Triggs, one of the leading Whitman authorities of the day. It was not Whitman, however, that I studied under Triggs, but Shakespeare and Browning. The manner, under his guidance, of studying a Shakespearean play was a marked advance over the relatively superficial method of studying Shakespeare at college; though, for me, Browning under Dr. Triggs that summer was an adventure of the mind beside which every other paled.[10]

The first poem of Browning Dr. Triggs (the most popular professor on the campus) read to his overflowing class was "My Last Duchess." Short but sturdy, grayish-toned, quiet-mannered, anything but striking in appearance, Dr. Triggs read with a sort of subdued passion. Like most poets of a high order, Browning was far more moving when read, and read well, than on the printed page, and it is no exaggeration to say that his first reading of Browning, amidst an unprecedented class-room stillness, was an event in my young life. I was transported. I was not in Chicago; I was in Italy, in Ferrara. Not in the 19th century, but in the great age of the Italian Renaissance, with all its wickedness, all its glory.

Awakened earlier at college, through lantern slides and the stirring lectures there of our professor in the History of Art, to some of the glories, major and minor, of the Italian Renaissance, these masters, through Browning, and under the inspiration of Dr. Triggs, became living figures now in their "fair town of Florence." Browning's dramatic monologue "Fra Lippo Lippi," his "Andrea del Sarto"—these poems (so familiar to us today) brought me, for the first time, what seemed the very breath of a glorious age when Raphael and Michelangelo were "pricked on by popes and kings."

In the poet's "Old Pictures in Florence," I came to know Florence itself, and more than Florence—Tuscany; while presently through other of his poems, to know, pervasively, this "land of lands," the Italy of wild tulips, buttercups, sunflowers, as glowing on Browning's pages as on any canvas of Van Gogh. Browning and Italy, inextricably bound up with each other, were, in truth, the gifts above price which I brought back with me from that summer in Chicago.

But if Browning that summer in Chicago added a new country, one of transcendent interest, unparalleled loveliness, to the world in which I lived inwardly, he did something more.

I was anything now but the spiritless slip of a girl of five years ago, when barely recovered from the brutalities of my brief married life, when all I had been born and brought to had been swept away forever, as it seemed, through my father's death and financial ruin, I had faced the realities of human existence, with my grilling initiation at the Bell House. If I wore no feather in my cap, yet I held my head high once more—I had won a respected place in the life of Knoxville. Even so, however, there remained no doubt chinks in my armor, and though in our present super-sophisticated day, cynics may sneer at their naïveté, I found strong reinforcement to my natural buoyancy of spirit in poems like Browning's "Saul," where David, the young shepherd, voices, "Oh, the wild joys of living...," and in "Pippa Passes," with the ragged little girl from the silk mills singing:

The year's at the spring
And day's at the morn;
God's in His heaven—
All's right with the world!

But there was another sort of spell, and a powerful one, which Browning, this lover's poet if ever there was one, cast over me through his love poems.

In '9[8], and for long afterwards, even up to the day of *The Barretts of Wimpole Street*,[11] Robert and Elizabeth Browning were still the world's ideal wedded lovers, and when I read his inspired tribute to his dead wife in dedicating to her *The Ring and the Book*, when I read in "By the Fireside" of that "perfect wife"—when I read in poem after poem of "the warmth and light and bliss" of earthly love between man and woman, a love of soul and mind and body; and even when what might be called Browning's nature poems (so different from Wordsworth's) were all infused with earthy and human passion, and for all their delicacy, so personal, so burning, the sensations I had known a few years before in reading Tennyson's *Idylls of the King* were nothing to the quickening of my pulses now, the pounding of my heart.

I am unable to anatomize at this late day, if I ever was, the change which began to take place in my inner being after I read the love poems by Robert Browning. That change would work slowly, though ultimately revolutionize both my inner and outer life. A side of my nature which in the struggling years immediately behind me I had kept steadily in abeyance now reasserted itself. I was never again to know quite the same ease of mind I had known in the preceding years. And for the time being, both in Chicago and after my return home, I found far deeper emotional and sensuous satisfaction in the poetry of Browning than in the unremarkable love letters which continued to come to me weekly from Jim Ramsey.

But there were a few memorable occasions that summer outside the most intensive studying I had ever done. One was when Jane Addams, whom I met through a mutual friend, invited me to spend a week-end at Hull House, the famous settlement-house in Chicago, modeled on Toynbee Hall in London, but the first social experiment of the sort in this country.

A decaying mansion, now in the heart of Chicago's worst slums, it was the most interesting, the most astonishing, place I had ever visited.

What stands out most vividly, however, in my memory of Hull House is gentle Miss Addams herself, moving tranquilly among all these intensively-alive and vocal young disciples of hers, and with her quiet sad face (though she was by no means devoid of a sense of humor), her tender compassionate eyes, looked upon by the children, even the adults, of the surrounding slums, whether of the Greek Orthodox or Roman Catholic faith, almost as on the Holy Mother herself.

With almost equal vividness, however, comes back to me the repercussions of this visit to Hull House on my return to the campus. Nothing could my mature, scholarly, socially-conscious associates at Foster Hall have envied me more than being a guest of Jane Addams, a name to conjure with then, and only recently returned from Russia and her visit to Tolstoi [*sic*] at his estate near Moscow, Yasnaya Polyana.

Nothing unless—being women and human—when shortly thereafter Dr. Triggs asked me to dine with him at the university's club-house for faculty members. It brought to the surface a thwarted frivolous streak in their sober natures. They were as excited as I, or more so, over this invitation. What would he be like, this campus idol, in personal contact with him? They were much concerned too, I remember, and it seems a little pitiful in retrospect (both as regards them and myself) as to what I should wear, on this important occasion, out of my extremely limited wardrobe. They were even eager, afterwards, to know in detail what we had had for dinner!

The dinner, the truth is, though better than those at Foster Hall, and while I probably dressed it up a bit in telling them of it, was nothing much out of the ordinary, save for the gala touch of wine which Dr. Triggs picked from the club's wine list.

What I did *not* report to these fine women—just as I had not reported to Mama my disappointments in my visit to the Centennial Exposition at Nashville—was that I had not been so entirely comfortable as I allowed them to suppose when seated across from this quiet-mannered popular professor at one of the small tables in the club's dining-room.

Courteous, kindly, but reserved, Dr. Triggs had none of the innate courtliness, none of the flattering small talk, I had been accustomed to from Southern men. Nothing easier for me, throughout my life, than to talk to almost anyone, anywhere; but now, for the first time within my memory, I was at a loss to know what to say.

I was not exactly embarrassed, either, but a bit overawed, I presume, by Triggs' reputation, and more than anything else, even though no Knoxville eyes were upon me, because not since my divorce had I been alone with a man in public.

I only began to be natural when in the course of the dinner he mentioned Laura McAdoo, my close friend, the most brilliant woman I had ever known, and whom, it seemed, he had become acquainted with not long before in New York. I could see that he was deeply interested in her (it was to Laura, no doubt, I owed this invitation to dinner), and here was a subject on which I could let myself go, talk spontaneously and with enthusiasm.

It was not long afterwards that Laura became engaged to Dr. Triggs, and in the course of the year ahead, under very different circumstances, I would come to feel at home with this grave, thoughtful, socially unspectacular, but mentally magnetic, quick-blooded man to whom, to this day, I feel I owe much.

One immediate result of the summer at Chicago was that I formed that fall a small private class for the study of Browning, holding it in our sitting room at home when I returned from school in the afternoon. I *must* pass on to others some of the new fires which had been kindled in me. Then, too, I had in mind the extra money I could earn in this way, for already I was hoping for another productive vacation, and if I could possibly manage it, spend my next summer in New England, visiting literary shrines, of which there were many more there than anywhere else in the country.

My private class was composed in part of youngish women of leisure from New York or elsewhere in the East, who more or less regularly wintered in Knoxville because of its milder climate; in part of Knoxville "young ladies" who had graduated from public or private school, but wanted to go on with the study of English literature.

It may seem faintly—even highly, ridiculous today that one should receive money for endeavoring to make Browning's poems clearer. But Browning, it has to be remembered, was just coming into vogue then, becoming a literary fashion, and women who wanted to understand his poetry were probably not radically different from women today who want to be able to read understandingly, or at least pretend to, James Joyce, or Kierkegaard, say.

How much of permanent value this private class in Browning got out of my teaching, I can not say. I only know that I derived no little delight from it myself, aside from the very moderate pay; although it occurs to me as I write these lines that I must have grown considerably more vigorous in body by this time, or I would never have been able, after my arduous day in the school-room, to stand the strain of this extra effort, into which I threw myself with great gusto.

But coming back thoroughly refreshed from that fruitful season in the sun at Chicago, though Browning was not yet, I realized, for high school students, I brought to my teaching of them a heightened ardor along with greatly increased self-confidence.

It was this same fall that Dr. Triggs came to Knoxville to pay his formal suit to Laura, and a dinner was given in honor of the newly-betrothed couple by Mr. and Mrs. Calvin McClung in their modern red-brick mansion whose grounds, on Locust Street, adjoined those of Mrs. McClung's father, the Col. McGhee whose imposing and gloomy home I passed daily on my way to and from school.[12]

A friendly, unpretentious, scholarly man, Cal McClung (as he was known) was almost the only male member of that old, wealthy, socially-prominent Knoxville family of McClungs ever distinguished for his cultural interests, public spirit, and independent thinking, and the Cal McClungs' home was different in atmosphere from any other, equally sumptuous, in the Knoxville of the period.[13]

The dinner was served, I am sure, with all the elegance one would have expected in a McClung home, and with food on which the town plumed itself and its many gourmets would have put their stamp of approval. But save for a hopelessly blurred impression of a table sparkling with cut glass to which ten or a dozen of us sat down under the soft glow of candles in branched silver candelabra, I have no recollection whatever of the dinner itself.

What remains with me is an unfading impression of the evening afterwards in the McClungs' book-lined crimson-curtained library. Nothing like this had I known before, known anywhere. The guests had been chosen from Knoxville's small *avant-garde*—devotees, moreover, one and all, of Walt Whitman; and this in a day when it took almost unbelievable courage to endorse Whitman's free speech, or even to avow an acquaintance with what was considered his scandalous work; a day when Miss Lucy Crozier, taking *Leaves of Grass* from the Lawson-McGhee Library, had been urged by Miss Mary Nelson, the librarian, albeit with a twinkle in her eye, "Miss Lucy, *do* let me wrap it up before you carry it through Gay Street," and Miss Lucy, refusing to have the book concealed, had quipped, "Oh, anyone in *this* town who sees it will only think it's an agricultural work!"

Miss Lucy herself was of course present at the dinner, and besides Dr. Triggs and Laura, tall beautiful Laura, with her superb carriage, looking like a princess in white lace, white roses in her dusky hair (Dr. Triggs, if the truth be told, appearing, beside her, a midget), though her face still wan from a lengthy and critical illness. Then there was Ed Wiley, head librarian at the university; Junius Parker, a rising young lawyer, late of North Carolina, surprisingly soon to be chief counsel for the American Tobacco Company and live in New York; some others I can't recall, but dominant in the group Mrs. J. K. Otley [i.e., Ottley] of Atlanta, an outstanding social leader as also an intellectual, and one of the organizers a few years later of the Association of Southern Women to Prevent Lynching.[14]

On this unique and to me glorious evening, we talked of nothing but Whitman. This group was, in fact, the nucleus of one of the Whitman Fellowships, to foster appreciation of this revolutionary poet, beginning to form now here and there all over the United States and Canada.[15]

It seems odd, looking back, that it was not Dr. Triggs, a foremost authority on Whitman, it was Mrs. Ot[t]ley who read from the poet that evening, pointing up our talk as we passed from one phase of his work to another.

But a woman of dazzling social charm, as well as scintillating mind, not even Dr. Triggs could have read with more telling effect passages from Whitman which in Mrs. Ot[t]ley's low, controlled, yet vibrant voice will never cease to reverberate in my mind; as she chanted, more than read (like Theodore, long ago in those fateful twilights on Fort Sanders!), from Whitman's "Song of Myself."

Here was sublime reassurance and in a form I could accept. As these winged words fell on my ears amidst the tense hush of the McClungs' library, I felt we had been tuning in (as we say today) on the Universe. I came away in such an exultant, rapturous mood as I have rarely known.

Some time that winter, early in February as nearly as I can guess, Laura sent a note, asking if I would come over the following evening and go with her to the train. She was leaving for Chicago, to be married privately there to Dr. Triggs by a Congregational minister, a friend of his.[16] For some reason I do not recall "Mamma" would not be able to see her off, and poor frustrated Carrie was out of the question, for while dwelling under the same roof, she and Laura no longer spoke to each other.

It was the dreariest of evenings, and I sensed Laura's depression, in spite of her occasional merry laugh. The train as usual was late, and I can see us, in a drizzle of rain, waiting for it, below the gloomy grimy old "depot," and close to the railroad tracks.

Laura did not explain—though I thought I could guess—the reason for her marriage in Chicago, instead of at home. She was wearing a dark red winter suit which her mother had made for her the winter before, and a bit ill-fitting, as she had lost in recent months some of the curves in her rather voluptuous figure. Her face was sallow. I had never seen her less attractive, and in her dark, heavy-lidded eyes was a suggestion, for the first time, of the tragic look in her mother's eyes. In Laura's eyes that evening I thought I saw foreshadowed (or did I read this into them later?) the doom to which she would move, for all her subsequent triumphs in Paris, but with the cause of her death there, while still a young woman, never determined—whether suicide or murder.[17]

In any case, now at the moment of parting with her, it came over me sadly that it was not for love Laura on this dismal winter evening was starting off alone for Chicago, but as a solution. With Dr. Triggs' fame, an established position awaited her, and in a congenial environment.

When spring came that year, I saw that with the extra money I had earned from my Browning class, together with what was left of my uncle's small legacy, I should be able, after all, to spend my approaching long vacation in New England.

It was the summer of 1900. Mama would take Roger with her to a sister of hers who lived on a big farm in Nebraska, which would be an ideal summer for him, nearly seven now, and showing a stronger and stronger resistance to being fenced in. I would make my headquarters with a college friend in Massachusetts while visiting literary shrines, although stopping on my way north for a few days with Laura and Dr. Triggs at Bayhead,[18] on Barnegat Bay, an inexpensive Jersey seaside resort where they were spending a couple of weeks.

The days with this far from ordinary couple were as stimulating as any I had known at Chicago. They had just come from a week-end with John Burroughs at his rustic retreat, Slabsides, in the Hudson River Valley, where they were able to stand its crudeness and considerable discomfort, including verminous attacks, when their reward was companionship with a man who, besides having played an important part in the whole American romantic movement to further emotional interest in nature and science, had written *Whitman, a Study*, and been a personal friend of the poet.

The three of us would spend all day long loafing on the sand in the front of the flimsy, unpainted summer hotel, where we ate poor meals, slept in poor beds, but here on the beach indulged in the most exhilarating of talk.

In a burst of confidence, when we were alone together, Laura told me that her brothers and their wives in New York had tried to dissuade her from marrying Dr. Triggs. They had more grandiose ambitions for her; had even resorted to the deadliness of ridicule, she reported laughingly. "Why, Laura, do you think his little arms can reach up around your neck?"

But Laura appeared to have no regrets. Certainly her beauty had not suffered. Though still a little wan, with slight hollows in her cheeks, never had it been more commanding, and never had I seen her in what seemed higher spirits. It was plain she already had made an outstanding place for herself at the university, with her intimates the most eminent men on the faculty, among them Lester Ward, author of *Static and Dynamic Sociology*.

At Bayhead, they were both on fire from their reading of Thornton [i.e., Thorstein] Veblen's just published *The Theory of the Leisure Class*, which would shake the world with its challenge to established social and economic institutions. A magnificent thinker, Veblen himself was now a professor at Chicago, this grimly whimsical man, "a stick of dynamite wrapped up to look like a stick of candy"—as a man a tragic failure, but as an economist, philosopher, and writer, no one denies, I suppose, one of the shining triumphs of the age.

On fire themselves, it is not strange that they set me on fire too, so that Veblen was to become, after Whitman, perhaps the strongest influence on my future thinking—on my entire social outlook.

Sometimes in the midst of our talk Laura would get up, shake some of the sand off her and run back and forth on the beach, at the edge of the breaking waves. Her hair unloosed, with her tall lithe Olympian figure, she seemed one of the swift-footed Greek maidens in Atalanta's Race, celebrated by William Morris in his *Earthly Paradise*, and by Swinburne in *Atalanta in Calydon*.

I would watch Dr. Triggs' eyes as they followed her, eyes full of adoration touched with awe. I felt reassured. After all the venomous gossip about her in her hometown, in a larger world of scholars and thinkers, Laura had come into her own. This marriage, I decided, was perhaps the most fortunate she could have made. Little did I foresee its bitter dissolution a few years later in England, Dr. Triggs a visiting professor at Oxford, Laura leaving him to marry shortly thereafter a French scientist of note, and to live the rest of her life in Paris.[19] But now, when I left this little Jersey seaside resort, I carried away happy thoughts of them.

Of all the literary shrines I visited that summer, Concord afforded me the most pleasure. The *Little Women* house, now open to visitors, was exactly as I had imagined it in my childhood when I had pored over the works of Louisa May Alcott, dearest of all my childish loves (as for millions of other children, both American and foreign). Jo, Beth, Meg, Amy were all there, and immeasurably more real than I found them decades later in the movie made from this juvenile classic. Then across the road from the *Little Women* house was the plain square white frame house where Emerson, the Alcotts' beloved Transcendentalist neighbor, had lived and died, written essays and poems destined for immortality, or so at least we did not doubt then; while a short distance beyond on the same road was "Wayside," home of Hawthorne after he had attained fame and fortune, a more modern and pretentious house, and with no suggestion of an earlier storied New England, though in the Old Manse, over-clambered by ivy, where this solitary, shy, sensitive genius had lived in his beginning days as an author and written *Mosses from an Old Manse*, I found all the charm I was looking for in the most famous village in America; and with close by the Old Manse, in a leafy approach to the Concord River, Daniel Chester French's statue of the *Minute Man*, to call up Emerson's thrilling lines:

> *Here once the embattled farmers stood,*
> *And fired the shot heard 'round the world.*

But I could not of course leave Concord without a trip to Walden's Pond. Its immediate surroundings not yet spoiled by later generations of tourists, even so it was anything but the sequestered sylvan spot I had pictured in reading Thoreau's *Walden*. The small muddy pond scantily screened from view by sparse, rather mean trees, it was tame to the last degree in comparison with our great forests, wild mountain scenery, in East Tennessee.

In Salem, however, even more closely associated with Hawthorne than Concord, and with its stately old three-story white mansions built by captains of merchantmen who had sailed the Seven Seas, brought back to fill them priceless treasures from the Orient from ports on every continent, there was all the atmosphere I had hoped for; and my only let-down, ironically, Salem's most celebrated relic, the repellent, hodgepodge, bare-walled frame dwelling, unsoftened by verdure, crowding the corner where it stood, close to the street, and lacking even the grace to look ancient, but which had inspired his *The House of Seven Gables*; the novel which in time would bore multitudes of school-children forced to read the English Requirements and make them suspicious forever after of classics in general.

Unexpectedly, though, it was at fashionable Marblehead, on the North Shore of Massachusetts, with all its ornate, often palatial summer homes, I had one of the most rewarding experiences of the summer, for Marblehead was the scene of Whittier's "Skipper Ireson's Ride."

From way back when in the sitting room in the Barnes house Harry had recited Whittier's "Snowbound," memorizing portions of it for the "literary society" to which he belonged, I had loved this "Winter Idyll," so evocative of early New England, of its bygone "simple life and country ways." Bits of it had stayed in my mind—with its Quaker family and wayfarers caught in the storm, shut in from the whirling world outside, but content to let "the north-wind roar, a hard dull bitterness of cold," as snug inside they sat around the great log fire, telling stories, the mother turning her spinning-wheel.

All I found most appealing in old New England was instilled for me in "Snowbound." But Whittier's "Skipper Ireson's Ride," with no such tranquil tone, had also captured my youthful imagination, and now as I followed my guide up a narrow rocky road in the poor dilapidated fishermen's quarter of fashionable Marblehead I could see, as if I had been there,

> *Old Floyd Ireson, for his hard heart*
> *Tarred and feathered and carried in a cart.*

I could see the "wrinkled scolds with hands on hips," their shaking fists—hear their shouts, the "conch-shells blowing and fish-horns' twang" as they sang over and over in hoarse and furious voices:

> *"Here's Flud Oirson, fur his horrd horrt,*
> *Torr'd an' futherr'd an' corr'd in a corrt*
> *By the women o' Morble'ead!"*

—Floyd Ireson who had sailed away from a sinking ship, to leave their husbands, sons, lovers, sink or swim, be lost at sea, buried "fathoms deep."

No other spot in New England with literary associations—not even the *Little Women* house—was so revitalized by my visit to it.

All in all, if less fruitful than the summer at Chicago, yet this vacation, too, had filled me with fresh enthusiasm. I went back to teach my classes in American Literature at the G.H.S. with renewed ardor.

As these two years of my life in Knoxville come back to me, they are far more confused than the previous ones. I am not at all sure of the order in time of the small or more momentous events that marked them. But it was, I believe, not the fall after my summer in New England, but in the preceding autumn, [that] Mrs.

Westwood (1892).

Lutz, older sister of Bob Armstrong, gave a large evening reception, in her handsome new home on Kingston Pike, opposite Bleak House.[20]

Mama and I were invited. I had been to no evening party since the wedding reception, of painful memory, four or five years before, when I alone was not in evening dress. But at this party there were to be guests of all ages and drawn, I understood, not only from Mrs. Lutz's social intimates but from church acquaintances. I had been assured that evening dress would not be necessary, and Mrs. Lutz would not take no—Mama and I must be there.

A queenly woman and graciousness itself, Mrs. Lutz was also an artist, an outstanding one in the Knoxville of that day. Tall, of ample figure and with a certain yielding softness, a florid blonde, "a perfect Armstrong," as people said, she closely resembled Bob and had some of the same fascination for me he had possessed from the time when I wore pigtails down my back. Moreover, she had more than once written me appreciative beautiful notes after some meeting at Ossoli in which I had taken part; so now I finally decided to go, and as I started with Mama for the party, which I knew, in the Armstrong tradition, would be a grand affair, however informal Mrs. Lutz sought to make it seem, I was troubled by no, or only the faintest, misgivings.

The house was crowded for all its various reception-rooms and the great studio, extending from one end of the house, open to the rafters high overhead, its walls hung with Mrs. Lutz's paintings, and over the massive oak fire-place facing its entrance Raphael's *Madonna della Sedia*, a copy of which she had made from the original in the Pitti Gallery in Florence.

The studio was thronged too, and as I left Mama with some of her old friends

Adelia Armstrong Lutz (ca. 1888).

and made my way into this room of which I had heard much and was eager to see, suddenly I came face to face with Bob.

Something closed tight around my heart, seemed to snap in my brain. For an instant everything went black. No one I could have been more astonished to see. Bob was living in New York and I did not know he had come down especially for this house-warming at Westwood. I had not seen him since our brief unhappy encounter when Roger was only a few weeks old and I was climbing the Clinch Street hill with the young Negro nurse-girl beside me wheeling Roger in his baby-carriage.[21]

Looking me straight in the eyes, but as if he, too, were seeing a ghost, Bob exclaimed, "Annie!" Then, grasping my hand, he led me back through the throng of other guests to a corner where we could be slightly more private.

Time was annihilated. My heart was beating fast. It was as though Bob and I had been alone together only the evening before. Save for his strong athletic figure being a little more filled out, he was unchanged; with the same lordly bearing that yet was without a trace of pomposity, the same chivalrous manner, the same magnetic presence, and the same protective air, at once manly and infinitely tender, such as I had known in no other man.

"It's strange," I said, "to be here. I don't go to evening parties any more."

"Yes, I know," he said. "I know all about you—from Delia and others. I'm proud of you, little woman!"

But this was verging on dangerous ground. I spoke of his sister's paintings, most of which, including her later impressionistic ones, I had not seen before.

"Oh, yes," he said, "Delia is a real artist. She should be in some cosmopolitan art-center where her work would get the recognition it deserves. But you can't see her paintings tonight, Annie, not in this crowd. Some day I'm going to bring you here and you can see them properly. You know," he added, in a lower voice, "I'm coming back to Knoxville to live."

This struck me like a clap of thunder. Was I more terrified or enraptured at the thought?

Our talk inevitably became more personal.

"Do you remember, Bob, a book you gave me once, *The Meditations of Marcus Aurelius*? I've often needed it since!" I laughed, though my heart was pounding almost unbearably now.

"Yes, yes—I remember everything!" he said, and then in a still lower voice, holding my eyes with his, "*Wiwita*" (using his old name for me, Sioux Indian for "my own"), "you know that day I ran into you on the Clinch Street hill with your baby? You looked just a child yourself, and I wanted to pick you up, baby and all, and carry you off to the ends of the earth. I wish I had!"

I can not remember anything else we said. I can not remember how we were drawn out of the corner where Bob and I stood against one of the low book-cases, filled with books and art portfolios, which ran around the studio, under the paintings. I can not remember leaving the party with Mama. I was in a trance. All these years past I had shut Bob out of my mind so far as I could, and now he was back. But now he was married, though forgetting everything else, I had not had the courtesy, I remembered afterwards, to ask after his wife, in New York.[22]

For a fleeting tremulous magic moment a new heaven and a new earth had opened up before me only to be plunged into a new darkness. But from Bob's and my meeting at the party at Westwood dated, as I see it now, though did not then, my dissatisfaction with my life as a teacher, the restlessness which took root in me and would grow and grow.

NOTES

1. The Dummy Line, called that because it was not a real train but had only a steam engine, was built by the Fountain Head Railway Company and put into service in 1890. It could make the trip to and from Knoxville without turning around.
2. Now Chilhowee Park.
3. William Joy (occasionally Joye) is listed in numerous sources as janitor at Girls High School.
4. As AWA states, the replica of the Parthenon created for the 1897 Tennessee Centennial Exposition in Nashville was made of plaster. It deteriorated over time, and in 1920 the city, often called "The Athens of the South," decided to turn its Parthenon into a

permanent structure. It is now the only exact-size replica of the original temple in Athens, Greece, in the world. Wesley Paine, "The Parthenon," in *The Tennessee Encyclopedia of History & Culture*, ed. Carroll Van West (Nashville: Tennessee Historical Society/ Rutledge Hill Press, 1998), 721.

5. On "Knoxville Day" at the Centennial Exposition, the featured soloist was renowned Knoxville singer and composer Mrs. John Lamar Meek (née Mary Fleming), who had also represented Tennessee at the Chicago World's Fair in 1893. She later wrote the words and music for the University of Tennessee Alma Mater. Through the efforts of local women's organizations, the Knoxville Building that had been constructed for the Tennessee exposition was dismantled and re-erected as the Woman's Building on Main Street in Knoxville. Creekmore, *Knoxville*, 126; Rothrock, 454–55.
6. This visit probably did *not* occur the year after the Nashville trip, as will be detailed later.
7. James C. "Jim" Ramsey, Jr., was born in June 1868 and graduated from the University of Tennessee in 1888. He was working for Fourth National Bank of Nashville in 1895, and also worked for American National Bank in Nashville. Later he was cashier of First National Bank of Manchester, Tennessee, and was listed in the 1900 census as a boarder in Coffee County (in which are both the towns of Manchester and Tullahoma). Jim Ramsey died March 5, 1903, and is buried in Riverside Cemetery, McMinnville. When his father, J. C. Ramsey, Sr., died in July 1903, a special report to the Nashville newspaper referred to him as "one of McMinnville's leading financial men for many years." *U.S. Census*, 1880, 1900; *Southern Standard* (McMinnville, Tenn.), June 9, 1888; *Kappa Alpha Journal* 12, no. 5 (August 1895), (https://books.google.com: viewed March 17, 2020); *Annual Report of the Comptroller of the Currency for 1902*, Vol. 2 (Washington: GPO, 1902), 1324 (https://books.google.com: viewed March 17, 2020); *Nashville American*, March 6, 1903; Find A Grave database and images (https://www.findagrave.com/memorial/88669196: viewed March 17, 2020); *Nashville Banner*, July 15, 1903.
8. "Annie Wetzell Waldron" studied at the University of Chicago during the summer of 1898 (not 1899). University of Chicago. [Seventh] *Annual Register*, July 1898-July 1899 (Chicago: University of Chicago Press, 1899), 487, https://babel.hathitrust.org (viewed March 20, 2020). In Part I, Chapter 11 [p. 202], she herself says: "In '98, traveling home from the University of Chicago where I had been studying . . ."
9. Lucy Graham Crozier was a student at Chicago during summer quarter 1897. University of Chicago. *Annual Register*, July 1897-July 1898 (Chicago: University of Chicago Press, 1898), 443, https://babel.hathitrust.org (viewed March 20, 2020).
10. Oscar Lovell Triggs (1865–1930) graduated from the University of Minnesota and, after studying abroad, received his PhD from the University of Chicago in 1895. He was author of *Browning and Whitman: A Study in Democracy* (London: S. Sonnenschein; New York: Macmillan, 1893) and edited *Selections from the Prose and Poetry of Walt Whitman* (Boston: Small, Maynard & Co., 1898). He also edited Volume 3 of *The Complete Writings of Walt Whitman* (New York: Putnam, 1902, 10 vols.), for which he

compiled and arranged the variorum readings of *Leaves of Grass*. Patricia J. Tyrer, "Oscar Lovell Triggs," and Arthur Golden, "*Leaves of Grass*, Variorum Edition," in *Walt Whitman: an Encyclopedia*, ed. J. R. LeMaster, Donald D. Kummings (New York: Garland, 1998), 381–83, 746.

11. A 1930 play by Rudolf Besier.
12. Mrs. McClung was McGhee's daughter Annie. The McClung home was south of McGhee's, on land occupied today by Knoxville's Downtown YMCA. Annie McGhee McClung died in 1898. Rothrock, 445–46; Deaderick, 566.
13. Calvin Morgan McClung (1855–1919) earned A.B. and M.A. degrees from East Tennessee University (now the University of Tennessee) and also earned a degree from Yale. A merchant (with Cowan, McClung and Company, and later president of C. M. McClung and Company), he was greatly interested in local/regional history and genealogy, and amassed an outstanding collection of historical and manuscript materials which, donated by his second wife, Barbara Adair McClung, after his death, became the nucleus of the McClung Historical Collection of the Knox County Public Library. Rothrock, 445–46; Deaderick, 40, 44, 412, 565–66; Creekmore, 135–36.
14. The Association of Southern Women for the Prevention of Lynching was founded in Atlanta in 1930 by Jesse Daniel Ames and twenty-six other women. Christine Lunardini, *What Every American Should Know About Women's History* (Holbrook, MA: Bob Adams, Inc., 1994), 223–24. However, Mrs. John King Ottley (1869–1940), née Passie Fenton McCabe, was much better known as a leader in the Atlanta Woman's Club and the Georgia Federation of Woman's Clubs. She worked to secure ratification of the suffrage amendment and was appointed a Democratic Executive Committeewoman from Georgia. The *Woman's Who's Who of America* noted her years of work promoting "social betterment movements" in her state. John William Leonard, ed., *Woman's Who's Who of America, 1914–1915: A Biographical Dictionary of Contemporary Women of the United States and Canada* (New York: American Commonwealth Co., 1914), 615; Jane Cunningham Croly, *The History of the Woman's Club Movement in America* (New York: Henry G. Allen & Co., 1898), 357–58, 360, 364, 366; *Literary Digest,* 65, no. 9 (May 29, 1920), 70.
15. The Knoxville branch of the International Fellowship began in the summer of 1895. *Walt Whitman Fellowship Papers,* Third Year, no. 3 (July 1896): 8–9; *Conservator* 6, no. 7 (September 1895): 107–08. Among its members were James Walter "Jim" Young of Clinton (son of Judge David K. Young), president; Edwin Wiley, librarian at the University of Tennessee, secretary; Ed Cummings, a writer for the *Knoxville Tribune,* treasurer, and Mary Louise Davis, librarian at Lawson McGhee from 1892–1896. *Walt Whitman Fellowship Papers,* Second Year, no. 11 (Feb. 1896): 43–45. The group proposed a series of lectures, and in 1897 Dr. Triggs came to Knoxville to speak on Whitman. "At Lawson-McGhee Library: Dr. Triggs, of Chicago, Will Lecture Tonight," *Knoxville Journal,* May 10, 1897, 5; "Whitman Admirers Pleased with a Lecture by Dr. Trigg[s], of Chicago," *Knoxville Journal,* May 11, 1897, 3. The dinner party given by the McClungs

was on Tuesday evening, May 11, 1897, and on Thursday Triggs presented a program on Robert Browning in the parlor of Miss Lucy Crozier's home. "Woman's Interests and the Social Side," *Knoxville Sentinel*, May 12, 1897; "Lecture on Browning," *Knoxville Journal*, May 13, 1897, 6. Carl Edward Campbell, who wrote a master's thesis on the Knoxville Whitman Fellowship, interviewed AWA on June 27, 1956, in Abingdon, Virginia, about her involvement with the group and quotes her account of her "conversion" to Whitman while reading his poetry on Fort Sanders "with the young man that I married first." He also quotes verbatim the section of Armstrong's memoir in which she describes the dinner and evening spent discussing Whitman at the McClungs' home. Carl Edward Campbell, "The Knoxville Walt Whitman Fellowship" (master's thesis, University of Tennessee, Knoxville, 1956), 22–23, 31–34. *N.B.*: The McClung Historical Collection holds a copy of Triggs' *Selections from the Prose and Poetry of Walt Whitman* with the signature "C. M. McClung, Dec. 5, 1904," on the flyleaf. A 1904 copy of *Leaves of Grass* has "Barbara A. McClung / Oct. 1906" handwritten on the flyleaf.

16. Laura McAdoo and Oscar Lovell Triggs were married January 6, 1899, in Chicago. FamilySearch database (viewed February 24, 2020).
17. Laura died December 17, 1911. "Find a Grave Index," database, FamilySearch (viewed February 24, 2020).
18. Or Bay Head.
19. Laura and Triggs were divorced August 24, 1907; she then married Dr. Pierre-Julian Gagey. Dr. Triggs had been dismissed from the University of Chicago faculty in February 1904 after much negative publicity about him and his controversial views appeared in the *Chicago Tribune* and other newspapers. "Triggs of Free Love Fame Is Again Married," Special Dispatch to the *Call* (Dateline: Chicago, April 10), *San Francisco Call*, April 11, 1908.
20. There are several discrepancies in this chapter regarding when things happened. Triggs' visit to Knoxville was in 1897, *before* AWA studied at the University of Chicago in 1898. Furthermore, she seems confused about exactly when Laura and Triggs married (which *was* in 1899). At this time, no evidence has been found which establishes what year she visited her relatives in Tullahoma and ran into Jim Ramsey. However, a newspaper "Personal" in spring 1900 mentions that she would spend the summer on the coast of Maine. *Knoxville Sentinel*, April 14, 1900, 5. Mrs. Lutz may have given a party at her home during the fall of 1899 or 1900, but it *could not* have been the Westwood house-warming party to which AWA refers a few paragraphs later when she encounters Bob Armstrong.
21. Westwood was built in 1890, and the house-warming party occurred on New Year's Eve, December 31, 1890— *before* AWA married in 1892 and *before* Roger was born in 1893. Articles about the party appeared in the Knoxville *Daily Journal* on Thursday, January 1, and on Friday, January 2, 1891, and in the *Knoxville Tribune* on January 2, 1891. See also Still, *Haunted History of Knoxville*, 192.
22. Robert F. Armstrong married Celia Houston of Pennsylvania on October 24, 1894.

Chapter Twenty-Three

Miss Hilton's

A perfectly plain square frame house, painted a light gray, and with the porch across its front opening directly on the street, Miss Hilton's boarding-house, close to the heart of town, was two short blocks in one direction from the Girls High School, and on the other, a side of the house separated only by an alley from the rear of St. John's Episcopal Church.[1]

Miss Hilton had come from Wilmington, North Carolina, where, reportedly, she had kept its best boarding-house, and now, in Knoxville, an erect spare spinster approaching fifty, completely lady-like, yet a thoroughly likable human being, in the course of a year or so established hers as one of the best of the four or five first-class boarding-houses still at the time in the immediate neighborhood. Furthermore her patronage already was considered the most select of them all, both as to those who merely came in for meals and those who roomed with her.

It was to this boarding-house I came on my return from the summer vacation in New England, although it is only through the most resolute searching of my memory, confessedly far more foggy than about the preceding years, that I am able to fix the fall of 1900 as the time I went to Miss Hilton's.

But I am perfectly clear on one point. When I first stayed there, I was alone. Mama and Roger, after their summer on the farm in Nebraska (when Roger learned to milk, "helped" the thrashers and was permitted to sit with them at dinner, a proud privilege when aged seven), had gone to Aunt Sarah's for some months and did not join me at Miss Hilton's until Christmas-time, or it may have been later.

In either case, this means that it must have been at the beginning of the preceding summer we gave up the little house on White Avenue and sent our furniture into storage. As I think about it now, it amazes me that I retain not even a dream-like remembrance of our preparations for making this crucial change, or what led to our making it. I can only conjecture that Mama, a by no means unperceptive person, had sensed the beginning of my restlessness, some more or less covert change in me, and anticipated my re-marriage, though we never discussed the subject, realized a break would come in any event in the not distant future, and was feeling her way by degrees toward a time when in all probability she would have to make her home with one of her sisters.

There was certainly no friction between us preliminary to breaking up a home

Saint John's Episcopal Church. Art Work of Knoxville, 1895.

that on the whole had been a happy one for us both, for friction would have left its permanent mark on my mind. We must have come to this decision by mutual and amicable agreement, and for reasons, if lost to me now, which seemed desirable then. Perhaps we thought we could live more cheaply by boarding and that Mama would have less work. I do not know. What I know is, looking back, that it was at this time Mama's face began to take on the withdrawn look it had worn in the first years after Papa's fatal accident and financial ruin. And with the less cheerful, often sad, look on Mama's face, some of the old reticence between us, as in my girlhood, began also to build up again. As I see, indeed, the whole picture now, my heart heavy with regret and remorse, this must have been a period of ever-deepening anxiety for Mama; and no less hard for her to bear with outward dignity than for me my own secretly more and more disturbed state of mind.

It was probably through Edmée Boynton that when we broke up our home on White Avenue we came to live for the next year or two at Miss Hilton's where Edmée was living, instead of at one of the other boarding-houses in the vicinity.

Edmée was teacher of Latin at the G.H.S., with the room she presided over on the same floor as mine. Four or five years my junior, Edmée was a unique individual, at once an unusually successful and popular teacher and one of Knoxville's outstanding belles during the Gay Nineties. From a family of the highest social standing and a granddaughter of "Parson" Brownlow, Tennessee's famous and fiery governor during its bitter Reconstruction days, she had inherited from her celebrated grandfather, if not his vitriolic tongue, his superior mind, and along with it, from whatever source, such an eager and radiant spirit as I have rarely known.[2]

I had been attracted to Edmée, with her bright sweet face, her bubbling laugh, when we were both very young, she a mere child; and she became one of my chief joys when, vivacious and sunny, she joined our predominantly sober, and in some part drab, staff at the high school; dividing her energies and charms between the pupils she taught by day and her beaux—the more less gilded youth of the town—at night. Seeing her in party array, all-a-flutter, as she went forth from Miss Hilton's evening after evening to a ball or other gala affair, I relived (and I hope I am truthful when I say without envy, but with wholehearted joy in *her* joy) some of the gaiety and excitement of my own girlhood, after all not so many years behind me.

But Edmée was not only a belle; she was a natural-born and unusually talented teacher. She could make Virgil, even Caesar, palatable—absorbingly alive in fact, and to the most recalcitrant of pupils. What's more, for all her beaux and the whirl of social gaiety in which she was nightly immersed, she was ambitious to improve herself constantly, and in every possible way, as a teacher. The summer directly behind us which I had spent in New England, seeking first-hand impressions which I hoped might enrich my teaching of American literature, Edmée had spent at Cornell, taking the latest courses there in the teaching of Latin; and, incidentally, so novel then was this procedure that the two of us were, I believe, the first teachers in the Knoxville schools to go away to one university or another for a summer of study.

But there was another tie between us, and in addition to the one that grew inevitably out of our having many mutual acquaintances in the Knoxville "society" of the day; some of the same young men, still unmarried, who had called on me, taken me to dances, parties, the theatre, now were among Edmée's beaux. But the additional tie to which I refer derived from the fact that both Edmée and I at this time were beginning to take an interest in something more than purely local events—in national, and to a certain extent, international affairs. We both read one or more periodicals, such as *Harper's Weekly*, dealing with this larger sphere.

Descended from a conspicuously political-minded family (one that would send future members to Congress) I dare say this was an interest bound to show itself in Edmée sooner or later. But however that may be, at the time she was my only feminine acquaintance who had ever manifested even the slightest interest in matters of this kind; as the brilliant Laura McAdoo had been the first to share my enthusiasm for Whitman and other writers not yet generally accepted.

In the September when I first came to Miss Hilton's, Edmée's mother (like Mama, a widow), as well as my own, was absent, probably visiting one of her married daughters living at a distance, or a son studying medicine at Johns Hopkins.[3]

Edmée and I, each alone in a big barely-furnished square upstairs bedroom, would open the door between our rooms and talk back and forth incessantly every morning as we were dressing. This period, brief though it was, provided both of us a feast of merriment with which to start our day. We would shout with laughter over some ludicrous happening at school the day before; laugh to tears, and mercilessly I fear, over Billy White, our conscientious but perpetually embarrassed principal at the GHS; laugh at frailties and foibles of some, I own, of our most intimate friends: laugh at all sorts of absurdities, foolishness, nonsense—laugh at nothing at all.

Almost invariably, however, there would be a break in our laughter before we went down to breakfast; a few minutes when we would discuss articles we both, for all our pressed lives, somehow or other found time to read; articles concerned with the vast world of which Knoxville and its doings were only one of the minutest parts.

In Edmée's gay and eager presence, with her keen sense of fun, yet underlying seriousness, I had found my most congenial feminine friend up to this time, not even excepting Laura; and despite the fact that more and more I was rebelling inwardly at what I had come to feel was the narrowness of my life, nonetheless these weeks when Edmée and I, each alone, lived with only a wall, a door, between us were on the whole the happiest I had known since my girlhood—certainly the most lighthearted I would know during the rest of my days in Knoxville.

For one thing, I had shed, for the time being, responsibilities I had been carrying for more than five years. Never, in those years, had I felt so care free as, all at once, now. True, there were moments when I suffered sharp pangs of homesickness for Roger. Always he was at the back of my mind. I suspected he, too, might at times be homesick for me, with the bond between us close as it was; though always I reassured myself with the thought that in Mama's charge he was having the best of all possible care, and that with his happy and adventurous nature his childish days were full. He would not be miserable for long.

At Miss Hilton's, I continued to have a private class after school, holding it in my bedroom there, though the class drawn now wholly from girls who had graduated or at least been under me at the GHS and who wanted to go on with the study of English and American classics. By this time I was sufficiently experienced as a teacher to carry the extra work without feeling its weight. Then, too, with my shorter walk now to and from school I had more time. But by now I was able also to indulge in more outside activities than in the years before when, aside from other reasons, I lacked strength for anything besides teaching.

At the insistence of Mrs. French, the town's most progressive citizen, I attended the meetings and had been made one of the directors of the local branch of the Women's Educational and Industrial Union, founded in 1877 as an early part of the feminist movement in this country, and one of its purposes to discover opportunities and new occupations for women.

In Knoxville, it was concerned solely then with social welfare, for which, heaven knows, there was plenty of need, and its efforts chiefly directed toward furnishing aid to indigent families temporarily unable, through illness or other cause, to support themselves.[4]

Save for myself, all the members of the Women's Educational and Industrial Union were the town's social leaders, for it was getting to be the fashion in Knoxville as elsewhere for "society-women" to concern themselves, at least in a modest, if organized, way, with the condition of some of the less fortunate in the community. Even Miss Mary Temple, with an innate distaste, I was convinced, for this new thing called "social service," had been unable to resist the influence of the dynamic Mrs. French and became one of our members.

In this connection there was an incident which conveys, I believe, as truly as could any other, the prevailing social atmosphere of the Knoxville of the '90s. At one of our meetings it was suggested by Miss Temple that we should allot for the relief of the particular indigent family under consideration a dollar and a quarter a week.

When some faint protests were heard over the smallness of this amount, Miss Temple drew herself up, and with obvious resentment that her judgment should have been questioned, with an air of finality, declared: "They should be able to live *opulently* on a dollar and a quarter a week!"

When she stressed the word "opulently," drawling it out syllable by syllable to its full length, I observed that some of the ladies present with difficulty restrained their smiles, although none of them would have dreamed of laughing. To laugh openly at Miss Temple would have been little short of *lèse-majesté*. But while not a few of the members were women of social grace, no less than of social influence, wealth, and generous inclinations, nevertheless all were reluctant to take issue with Miss Temple when she expressed herself in her characteristically regal manner. Only Mrs. French had the hardihood to oppose her and in the end won over the rest of the ladies to a less niggardly allotment for the family in question.

But it was not alone my being a member of the Women's Educational and Industrial Union, nor the increasingly prominent part I played in Ossoli, which had widened my life in the past year or so. I went now to elaborate ladies' luncheons, in case of close old friends sometimes given on Saturday especially so I could be there. I went to afternoon teas, and friends with victorias would take me, whenever I had time, on long drives out Kingston Pike, following the windings of the river, and still the loveliest drive leading out of town.

Altogether my life had much more variety now, and during these first months at Miss Hilton's, I revelled [*sic*] in a feeling of freedom such as I had never known in the little house on White Avenue, where my life had been tightly tied up with Mama and Roger. No longer so acutely sensitive about having been divorced, in Miss

Hilton's sitting-room I could pass an evening, untroubled by self-consciousness, with the two unmarried young men who, alone or together, often called on me.

To be sure these young men were not looked upon by me, nor, I was sure, by anyone else, as beaux. Neither of them was regarded as eligible. Neither, so far as I can recall, did anything in the way of earning a living. But they were among the extremely limited local circle of what we thought of as literary sophisticates. A sort of literary camaraderie united the three of us. Both the young men were devotées of Whitman, and one of them, Jim Young, had collected more than two hundred works, in various languages, on Whitman for the library of his wealthy father, Judge Young, whose fine old riverside home, Eagle Bend, not far from Knoxville, was situated picturesquely on one of the tributaries of the Tennessee River (the whole region, in its close proximity to the later Oak Ridge, now transformed beyond recognition).[5]

As erratic and generally irresponsible a young man as I have ever met, Jim and I would spend long evenings in Miss Hilton's commonplace though sufficiently comfortable sitting-room, discussing Whitman, Walter Pater, to whom Jim, a literary epicure, had introduced me, or some other writer.

Jim would write me long and witty letters between his frequent visits to town. Invariably he would sign them, "Yours of the acute and honorable minority, Jim Young."

There were those who said Jim was cracked, due to an injury to his skull in a horse and sulky runaway accident a couple of years before, and he had, I knew, a silver plate in the back of his head. But cracked or not, I thoroughly enjoyed my evenings with him.[6]

There was something, however, I relished far less. I had acquired in the past year or so what I suppose I must call a lover, an importunate and unwelcome one in the person of a reporter for the *Knoxville Journal* named Henry Warnack.

A loose-jointed stooping youth with a high-pitched squeaking voice, habitually grubby hands, ink-rimmed finger-nails, and far from immaculate linen, Henry came from some little town, or it may have been a farm, in lower East Tennessee,[7] and out of what was unmistakably a most unusual family: one whose members performed Shakespeare's plays in a little theatre of their own contrivance within their home.

I am not sure how I came to know Henry. To the best of my remembrance he just came out to our little house on White Avenue and introduced himself. In any event, he soon, like a loving waif dog, attached himself to me, and soon I was impressed by the burning spirit housed in that frail body, and by his wide reading which included an astonishing familiarity with the controversial *Leaves of Grass*.

I even made efforts through correspondence to get him admitted to Harvard and was encouraged by Harvard's response: "It is written in the books of Harvard University that no man shall be debarred through lack of means."

Henry, however, though he wept when I read him the letter, felt he could not avail himself of an opportunity he craved above all others. It might be arranged for him to go through Harvard, but there remained the large, now fatherless, family to which he belonged[8] and which he helped support through his job as crack reporter on the *Knoxville Journal*, and through going literally ragged and almost starving himself—he could not expect Harvard to take this responsibility off his hands.

Henry was ever a youth who tugged at my heart-strings. Just the same, he became a great annoyance, a veritable pest, when each morning on White Avenue, when we went to look for the morning paper, we would find, shoved under the front door, a missive from Henry, addressed to me as *Annie Audubon*, my baptismal name, which he had taken a fancy to, and often in the form of a poem, though in whatever form expressing his love for me in the most flaming terms.

I tried to laugh him out of this love-making. Used crude terms. Did not spare him. Called it "moony." But ridicule proved of no avail. Henry's daily notes became more and more tempestuous, and after I went to Miss Hilton's, where apparently he did not feel at liberty to present himself (perhaps because he was so shabby and it was different when I was at home), and where he could not deliver his notes in the former fashion, one day he appeared at the door of my room in the high school, called me into the hall, and was so distraught, so violent in his protestation of love, I rebuked him sharply. Indignant—furious, that he should have had the presumption to force himself on me during school hours, I told him I never wanted to lay eyes upon him again, to which he replied with a stricken look: "You will have to suffer a great deal, Annie Audubon, before you understand what others suffer"—a prophecy, I may add, which would be fulfilled.

But I was to see Henry once again after this low-toned but stormy scene outside my school-room door. While interviewing some visiting celebrity at his hotel, Henry was seized with a hemorrhage, found to be suffering from advanced tuberculosis, through the assistance of fellow-employees on the paper for which he worked was leaving for Denver, and the evening before he left ventured to come to Miss Hilton's to say goodbye to me.

Now he was as dignified as I could have wished. I was shocked at his old-young face, ghastly in its pallor, his hollow eyes. All at once deeply disturbed at the thought of his starting out in this condition to a part of the country of which he knew nothing, "But Henry," I protested, "you don't know a single soul in Denver!"

"Oh, yes," he said, a winning smile suddenly lighting his wan unshaven face, "I have a hundred friends waiting for me there!"

And so it turned out. Henry grew better, and through new friends to whom he had endeared himself found, farther afield, in Los Angeles, a much better newspaper job than he had held heretofore; shortly after was married there—quite as in a fairy tale—to an heiress, lived with her in her palace (one of the show-places then of Southern California), and before he died in early middle-life had become one of the best known newspaper men on the Pacific Coast.[9]

I had had, of course, in the high school, the same experience that probably every teacher as young as I has in the course of teaching adolescent youths: some of them falling in love with their teacher; a lad's first love almost universally some one older, frequently much older, than himself; and which Dickens immortalized in *David Copperfield*, with David's first love "the elder Miss Larkins."

I learned to know its early signs: boys too anxious to stay after school to help me; trying to win my favor through unnaturally good behavior; gifts, bashfully presented, of fruit, flowers, and once an old and valuable volume which I surmised the giver had purloined from his parents' or grandparents' library. In its last stage, there would be a note slipped in between papers on my desk where I would be certain to find it when I went through them later.

Most of these cases of calf love, as we somewhat cruelly call it, were easily handled; usually ignored, or otherwise ended without too much embarrassment to the youth so afflicted. But one of the lads who believed he was in love with me became even more troublesome than Henry Warnack.

I shall call him Joe, as this was not his name, and eventually he became one of Knoxville's well-known lawyers.

Joe would fix his eyes on me, during either a study or recitation period, with an almost hypnotic gaze, and apparently oblivious to the rest of his surroundings. After this, as I had anticipated with dread, began to appear among the papers on my desk pencilled [*sic*] notes on tablet paper, sometimes lengthy letters, as fervent love letters as I think could ever have been written, and never any, I am confident, more fearfully and wonderfully misspelled. At last they turned into brief and desperate epistles, Joe threatening to kill himself unless I assured him that I returned his love.

Now I was genuinely alarmed. No knowing what an adolescent was capable of! But fortunately I was rescued by the Spanish-American War, Joe enlisting on the first call, leaving us, I was pleased to see, in high spirits (possibly dreaming of becoming a hero, thereby softening my hard heart); Miss Stoltzfus presenting him at the moment of his departure with a Bible; I, with a Spelling Book, which I suggested he might study at off hours in camp, notwithstanding that time and again he had brashly assured me he did not need to know how to spell. As soon as he got through school he would have a stenographer. She could spell for him. I confess, however, that when I presented him with a parting gift so unsentimental in character that I hoped it would crush any latent fancies about me he might still harbor, and he took it from my hands with a rather blank look, I felt a slight twinge of conscience. After all, Joe was starting off to War!

But all these ticklish experiences, at once amusing, annoying, sometimes a trifle touching, and so common to young or youngish teachers of a feminine type, I should not set down now except that in a belated self-examination of a young person once myself, they provide perhaps one small link in the whole chain of circumstances which led to the restiveness that first, in any marked degree, took possession of me about the time I went to Miss Hilton's.

Of course my growing dissatisfaction was due in large part to my growing perception that within the restrictions imposed upon a school teacher's life I could not possibly hope for that deeper exploration of life which I hungered for. Moreover, about this time I was beginning to reflect uneasily on my age. A couple of years more and I would be thirty. The very word had a dead sound. Thirty was an age beyond which I could not imagine anything happening to me of a romantic nature and romance, I see clearly today, was at base what I was more and more yearning for—not necessarily marriage, of which my own experience had been so terrible a one, but romance. Much of my reading for years past had intensified this yearning; and besides everything else, no doubt some of my father's innately adventurous spirit was beginning to stir more pressingly now in my own blood.

In any event, these protestations of love—throughout my teaching years—from lads in their later teens, however vexatious, however comic, I found them, yet had served to keep in my mind that I was more than a teacher, I was a woman. Very likely weekly letters from Jim Ramsey, urging lately that we meet in the not distant future and set a date for our marriage, also helped keep me aware not only that I was a woman, but with all a woman's normal longings for a life which would include a man—if not Jim Ramsey, some other; a man I could love, and be loved by, without measure, love vehemently, love elementally; for I was facing now the dilemma of being human, and while I would never lose completely my sense of the enchantment of living, it was no longer so rich and satisfying an experience merely to be alive.

But I can not hide from myself, or can not at this late day, what was doubtless the most deep-seated source of my growing restlessness—the meeting with Bob Armstrong at the party at Westwood, his sister's home, the year before.

Try as I might to stifle the memory of those few excruciating moments when we had been together—tell myself, as I did, it was vain to feed myself on dreams of what now could never be, nevertheless, wherever I was, whatever I was doing, the disturbing figure of Bob kept appearing before me.

In the dead of night I would hear his voice, as that evening at Westwood, in a moment of terrifying glory— hear him call me by his old Sioux Indian name for me, "*Wiwita!*"

After Mama and Roger came, Miss Hilton gave us a large front corner room with two beds, and I do not remember that, with my being away most of the day and Roger started back to the school he had gone to before in West End, we ever felt uncomfortably crowded. I do not recall either that we felt any particular concern when our only bathing facilities here, as on White Avenue, consisted of a heavy china bowl and pitcher on a marble-topped wash-stand, supplemented by a daily can of hot water from the kitchen below; the uninviting bath-room at Miss Hilton's, like most of those in Knoxville even as late as the turn of the century, where one existed at all, located in the most inconvenient of places, downstairs, opening off an ell that extended at the back of the house; unheated, its rusty tin tub unconnected with hot water, and hardly used even by the most vigorous of the boarders except in midsummer.

But Mama had long since ceased to demur at such primitive arrangements, and while in earlier affluent years she could never have envisaged living in a boarding-house, she fitted into Miss Hilton's without any observable jar. She was thankful, I think, in her heart, in finding a refined atmosphere at Miss Hilton's; for however straightened our circumstances in the years directly behind us, we had never lived grubbily. Mama had always managed to maintain, through all our change of houses, in whatever, wherever, was our home, an air of refinement.

At Miss Hilton's, a set of rooms on the first floor ("suite" would imply more elegance than it suggested) was occupied by a Col. and Mrs. Terry. The Terrys, like so many prominent Knoxvillians, were natives of New England, and from distinguished New England families. They had had their own handsome home in Knoxville, entertained there with great dignity. They were not impoverished. They had sought Miss Hilton's because they were old; the Colonel, stone deaf, retired now from his law practice; and Mrs. Terry, obese, crippled with rheumatism, though still the "great lady," no longer able to carry the responsibility of their former large home; so that to live at Miss Hilton's without care, and with the Cumberland Club, Knoxville's gentleman's club, only a block away, where the Colonel could bury himself in newspapers, talk to, if not hear, some of his old associates, and reënforce [*sic*] himself through long afternoons with some of the cheer provided by the Cumberland Club's superior cellar—in a word, Miss Hilton's seemed the only solution if the Terrys were to end their days in a town where, it is true, they had a most limited acquaintance, yet had lived so long, so exclusively, they did not know how to live anywhere else.

Another couple, among those in the neighborhood, who came for meals, were also New Englanders, though rather recently transplanted, a Dr. and Mrs. Boies. A retired Presbyterian minister, nearing eighty, Dr. Boies was as deaf as Col. Terry, but able to read lips to a certain extent, and the eyes behind his spectacles so lively and responsive, it was possible to carry on a conversation with him. Mrs. Boies, almost as old as her husband, but as slender and graceful as a young girl, her step as light, always dressed in black, but black in infinite variety, in exquisite taste, and with her definitely worldly charm, was one of the most attractive women of her age, at least from the physical standpoint, I have ever known.

A cousin of Mrs. Terry, these two "great ladies" added in themselves no little elegance to the atmosphere at Miss Hilton's; as well as no little amusement for the other boarders with their lady-like, though lively tiffs at table from time to time. Rivals from their long past youth in New England, and all but octogenarians now, they both retained a certain coquetry. They were still competing, it was evident, for first place in the obvious admiration they called forth. "Etiquette" was all but an article of religion with both of them, and when they differed, as they often did, on some point, vital to them, of social usage (for instance, as to where the teaspoon should be placed in drinking from your cup of tea), their repartee was something not to miss; with Mrs. Terry, whose mind was not fatty, if her body was, invariably, in her soft-spoken cultivated voice, having the last word, sometimes in the form of a delicious quip, slightly spiced with malice.

There were also a couple of youngish doctors with their wives who came for meals, as well as an elderly physician no longer practicing (another New Englander, brother of Mrs. Boies), a bachelor who had an apartment somewhere near, dignified and reserved, though unfailingly courteous. Then there was Edmée and her mother; and altogether, when the dozen or so of us sat down to the one long table in Miss Hilton's dining-room, where there was never a surfeit, but always a sufficiency of well-cooked, well-served, varied and frequently delicious food, where there was cheerful and pleasant, though never boisterous, conversation, it was almost as if we were in a private home where the guests had been carefully selected—something the atmosphere of European pensions here and there that later I would know.

As I had expected, Mama found this tone of extreme gentility at Miss Hilton's congenial.

The question was, how would Roger fit into a house where he would be the only child, and there had been none before him?

Roger quickly answered this for himself. While his blue eyes were always brimming with mischief and he was not bashful, yet he was not forward, never saucy, never spoke at table, save to Mama or me, unless spoken to, and soon he became the human center of a house of adults, most of them elderly where not definitely aged. Seven years old, coming and going his own self-reliant way, living his own imaginative childish life, he proved the catalyst which bound all the boarders more closely together. Even Col. Terry, who seldom recognized the existence of any of the rest of us except by a courtly bow, could not resist patting Roger on his fair tousled head whenever their paths met.

Probably I am not a reliable chronicler when it comes to Roger. Memories of him at this stage of his life glow and bubble. The sun streams through them all. To be sure he was naughty now and again. I recall spanking him so soundly for some childish misdemeanor—I have long forgotten what—that Mama and May (home from the Philippines on a visit) rebelled at my severity. Nonetheless, I am sure no child ever brought more brightness into a house largely of old people.

Certainly I had none of the problems with him such as today send so many

Roger as a child.

parents to a psychiatrist. The only tendency in him that ever gave me pause was the indomitable spirit he exhibited almost from the time he could walk and talk.

In connection with this there was one of his childish exploits during our second winter at Miss Hilton's which none who knew of it would forget.

Admiral Dewey, hero of the Battle of Manila Bay in the Spanish-American War, had come to Knoxville in the course of what I presume was a national tour and an evening reception was planned for him at the Imperial Hotel (later the Farragut), a reception to which the general public was invited.[10]

Nothing else was talked about. The evening came. Roger already at this tender age was filled to the brim with the immemorial conception of War as glorious, and personified now in the person of the greatest American hero of the time. He begged me to take him to the reception.

Realizing the tremendous crowd that would gather for the occasion, and the endless wait we would have in the long line (doubtless stretching out on to Gay Street) of those who wished to shake hands with the Admiral, I refused. But when I did so, never had I seen Roger so wrought up since in his early childhood when I had been unwilling to take him to the Sunday School Christmas entertainment on which he had set his heart.

Now, as then, he plead [*sic*] with me passionately: "But, Mother, they said *everyone* could come!"

Finally, however, I got him sufficiently quieted so I could tuck him in bed in the back bedroom he and I were occupying then, though I was somewhat troubled in conscience, for while he had stopped pleading, I could still hear an occasional smothered sob as I prepared to leave.

Next morning I was relieved to see that his face bore no traces of his grief of the night before. To my surprise, he was his usual blithe self. Whistling as he put on his shoes, he was positively jaunty. How quickly, I thought to myself, children get over their griefs and disappointments! But, to my utter amazement, the first man I met on my way to school that morning, an old acquaintance, greeted me with a broad smile.

"Well," he chuckled, "so you sent your young son, I noticed, to represent you last evening at the reception for Admiral Dewey!" and he went on to say that Roger was the only child there, that Dewey had patted him on the head and seemed to have more to say to him than to anyone else he had observed among the crowd presented to the Admiral.

What had happened, as I remembered then, was that after putting Roger to bed, I had gone downstairs to read quietly till my own bed-time. What I was soon to learn was that with me safe below Roger had got out of bed, dressed himself, climbed out of a back window in our bedroom on to a porch-roof below, slid down a drain-pipe to the ground, and for the first time in his life alone in the streets at night, gone by himself to the hotel.

Whether this adventure was on sudden impulse or considered awhile before he undertook it, I shall never know. I was in no mood to inquire, much less to punish him. It was no act of disobedience, for I had not forbidden something I never dreamed could occur. The truth is, I secretly gloried in the independence, the daring and enterprise, he had shown.

Thinking of it now, long, long after, how strange it seems that only a few fleeting years would pass and Roger would be marching, as one of the whole corps of midshipmen at Annapolis, in the cortege accompanying Admiral Dewey's body to its final resting-place in Arlington. Stranger still, but a few years more and he himself would be borne to his own long resting-place among all those quiet sleepers in beautiful Arlington, and not far from that of the nation's great hero he had sought, at some risk, to do honor to as a small boy.

It was the first winter we were at Miss Hilton's May came home from the Philippines, to Roger's wild delight. Now he had close to him all his family!

May had brought him from that far-off other side of the world, still so unknown to most Americans, a little model of a native's hut—all manner of exotic toys and Oriental curiosities.

She had brought with her the mingled scent of sandal-wood and ylang-ylang, in all her garments, and, more elusively, something different in herself from the person she had been before.

In the years May had been away she had come to know San Francisco in her wait there for the Army transport that would carry her to Manila. Irresistibly, she had lingered there on her return; found it, as have countless others, the most fascinating of cities—above all, the gate to the Orient—not only to the Philippines, but to China, Japan, India, and which henceforth, to the end of her days, would exert an even more potent influence over her mind and thinking than Europe and European culture on my own; eventually leading her to an intense interest in Oriental religions and to becoming herself a dedicated Theosophist.

She had known in these years a vast variety of experiences; experiences of which she had given us only vague impressions, not to alarm us unduly, in her letters home, absorbingly interesting though they had been. She had known shocking, almost unbelievable, discomforts, to say nothing of actual dangers. If she had come from another planet, May could hardly have brought us stranger tales.

But the thing that worried us was her health. Life in the Philippines, however exciting, had taken its toll. Never had she looked so frail. A doctor Mama induced her to see insisted she must be built up before she risked the tropics again. Nevertheless, she was planning to return to the Philippines after a few months at most.

It was plain enough for me to see, even then, that after her life in the Army, there was nothing in Knoxville, outside her own family, of any interest to May. Knoxville had never had for her the romantic appeal it had for me. Memories of her girlhood there, even more shadowed than mine by our family misfortunes when she was growing up, could only be, in general, far from happy ones. Moreover, such intimates as she had had were scattered now; mostly married, or living elsewhere. I could see that after the first joy of our family reunion, for all her devotion to little Roger, she was restless, eager to be off again.

But if May was restless, from almost the moment she arrived at Miss Hilton's, my own restlessness increased. In contrast to the way May's world had expanded, my own seemed to shrink more and more. I thought now of what courage it had taken for May, less aggressive by nature than I, to leave us that night on White Avenue, leaving behind for Mama and me only that brief note which had almost broken our hearts, but that had given her a vastly more colorful existence than mine would ever be if I remained where I was.

I thought of a line in one of Shaw's plays: "The people who get on in this world are the people who get up and look for the circumstances they want, and if they can't find them, make them." If May could accomplish this, so could I, and my resolve grew stronger than ever to escape, somehow or other, from what had come to seem my own meager life. It became a thought that burned like a flame within me from then on; now higher, now lower, but incessantly.

As the only one to whom I would dare confide such a thought, I ventured one day to express it to May. I remember the exact spot where I did so. She and I had been to a dressmaker, then the best in Knoxville, where May was having a couple of dresses made. We were walking along Church Street on our way back to Miss Hilton's. It was midway of the block. I can see the very row of attached red-brick houses we were passing. When I mentioned briefly, as casually as possible, even with a slight laugh, my own growing dissatisfaction with my life as a school-teacher, May gave me a quick look but made no reply in words.

I remember I was a little chilled by this lack of response, though I would realize in time what a shock my confession must have been. I had had some success as a teacher and made a certain place for myself in the life of the town. May had probably taken comfort in the presumption that Mama and Roger and I were securely anchored in a safe harbor. No doubt flashing through her at the moment was what *she* had faced (bravely hidden from us then and forever) during the first year or so when she was "making the circumstances" which would deliver her from the limitations of her life in Knoxville. She would not have me go through what *she* had gone through. She was frightened at the very thought. But however that may have been, never again did I confess, or so much as hint at, to anyone, my own state of inner turmoil.

When there was more delay than she had anticipated in getting an Army transport to take her back to Manila, and the summer heat in Knoxville had become worse, she said, than in the Philippines, the four of us went to Fountain Head, where in its rickety old summer-hotel we had large bare rooms that were comparatively cool, and with its long broad porches and tree-shaded grounds plenty of space in which Roger could exercise the normal animal spirits of a small boy.

With my own unrest, I must have become somewhat on edge by this time; for at Fountain Head May and I had the first difference—one of the few serious differences—that ever arose between us. I recognize now that I was the one at fault. I felt if I were more free I might more easily effect what was now becoming almost an obsession; and failing to take into account that without Mama and her care of Roger I could never have achieved even what I had, I suggested to May that she take a larger share of the responsibility for Mama.

There was no scene, but when May obviously resented my suggestion, a breach opened between us which left a bitter memory and would take several years to heal; though not deter me from the course I was determined on.

It was some time during this same summer I made a brief visit to my old friends, the Dames, in Harriman, and for the express purpose of meeting Jim Ramsey there, less embarrassing than having him come to Knoxville, where still no one save Mama knew of the relationship between us. Jim stayed only a few days, the guest also of the Dames in their hospitable home. With his fine appearance, courtly manners, and quick wit, the Dames were much pleased with him.

Jim and I spent most of the day wandering around in the woodsy ridge that rose behind the Dames' home, lingering now and then in some sequestered spot to talk over our plans, such as they were. Jim was incomparably more ardent now than ever before, far more urgent. He thought we should be married without further delay, while I insisted I must teach another year and we could be married the following summer.

Jim seemed now my only escape from my present life. Settling down in a small market town in Middle Tennessee, for all that his eccentric old father was its wealthiest and most influential citizen, had little appeal. I had begun, however, to feed myself on dreams, among others, of the pleasure of having a home I could furnish and preside over as my own creation, after years spent in the school-room.

What made me increasingly hesitant to take the actual step of marrying him was that while I enjoyed Jim in his rôle of lover during these languorous summer days, he was losing some of whatever attraction he had had for me in previous meetings. More or less unconsciously I was, I suppose, contrasting him in my mind with a very different sort of man; one with an incomparably wider exposure to life, far richer background—a man not less courtly, less witty, but of an immeasurably more virile and adventurous type.

In the end, it was settled that I should teach another year, with Jim coming to Knoxville at Christmas time, and we would be married at the end of the school year.

As it happened, it was either that fall (or it may have been the previous fall), that Bob Armstrong and his wife came back from New York to make their home in Knoxville. Nothing, at this hour, seems more extraordinary to me than that I have not even the faintest remembrance of what could not have failed to be a most disturbing event. What I see now is Bob in his customary tweeds, which he wore, as all his clothes, casually but with an air of distinction, passing Miss Hilton's as he returned from the Cumberland Club where with other *bon viveurs* he had been lunching on the Lucullan food the club was famous for, or had whiled away the afternoon with poker, Scotch and soda, and was on his way home to the modern substantial red-brick house he had bought on Cumberland Street, and hardly more than around the corner from Miss Hilton's.[11]

At once Bob and his wife had been swept into the social rounds of the town's most exclusive circle of younger married couples; often he was away on short trips to a racing center here or there; and when at home, if not at the Cumberland Club, on the golf course, the first in Knoxville, not yet with a clubhouse, but which Bob, an enthusiastic golfer, helped develop.

In his completely worldly and largely idle life, when he first returned he seemed infinitely farther away than when he had been in New York.

Perhaps, I thought, this was best. But inevitably we soon met and presently I was often having supper on Sunday evenings in his nearby home, furnished primarily for comfort, but with the many pieces Bob had brought from Bleak House or gathered on his travels in foreign countries, giving it an atmosphere that suggested no home I had known before.

His wife, Celia, a dignified young matron, always dressed with quiet elegance, usually in black, talking little, completely lacking in animation, somewhat impenetrable even when you knew her best, yet invariably met me when I was invited to their home with the utmost graciousness. What impressed me most forcibly, however, when I began to see them together, was her markedly indulgent, unpossessive attitude toward Bob, allowing him, it was obvious, to go pretty much his own capricious way without interference, even with some encouragement: though I was struck simultaneously with what a strangely ill-matched pair they seemed; Bob with his big-hearted frank manner, captivating uninhibited way of talking, his fine mind; Celia, extremely reserved ordinarily and her mental limitations all too plain.

Nevertheless I found myself at once quite at ease with them both, as with the other guests who were present at these Sunday suppers. With the best cook in town, Bob's tradition of fine food and drink behind him, and vintage wines always served, these were rare feasts to me, in addition to more sophisticated and amusing conversation around their handsomely appointed supper-table than I heard at Miss Hilton's, or anywhere else in those days.

But despite the merriment on these Sunday evenings, I soon saw that Celia, for all her reserve, had *her* problems. I also saw that Bob was openly as restless as I secretly. With his many-sided nature, the purely time-killing life he was leading as a defense against boredom, with no stimulus any longer, it appeared, from the world of books, art, culture in any form, no stimulus from discussions of anything whatever of a serious nature—how could such a life, I asked myself, ever satisfy Bob Armstrong?

Shortly, on Sunday, or whenever I was free, Celia would be coming to Miss Hilton's and up to my room. "Annie, come go home with me. Bob's in a bad humor, and you're the only one who can get him out of it."

But before this came about, or soon thereafter, Bob came to know Roger and opened up in a new era in Roger's life, if not indeed in his own.

Bob was the first man who had ever taken a strong personal interest in Roger, and now from a window in the Cumberland Club, if he spied Roger on his way back from school to Miss Hilton's, he would leave the club, catch up with him and take him along to his own home. There for hours on end he would entertain him: showing him books, such as Stanley's *Through the Dark Continent*, with its exciting illustrations; but still more exciting, tell him hair-raising stories of his own life among the Sioux, of buffalo hunts; would dance, for Roger's benefit, Indian dances; let out, for Roger's sole delectation—though sometimes to the consternation of a passerby on the street—an Indian war-whoop. He taught Roger to speak some words in the Sioux language; showed him the fringed and beaded buckskin suit he had worn among the Sioux, the six-shooter in its scabbard and the hunting-knife he carried thrust in his belt; explained to his young visitor the significance of a ghost-cloth, of Indian paintings, and of many other trophies in the immense collection he had brought back from Dakota Territory; always sending him home before supper-time at Miss Hilton's, proudly carrying with him some Indian trophy, now his own, which "Uncle Bob" had given him.

Proudest of all Roger was, I think, of now having an "Uncle Bob," when never before had he had an uncle, or only one in the far-away Philippines whom he had never even seen. Some of the hunger, if he ever had it (I do not know) for a father must now have been satisfied. Bob had completely won his heart. Roger had at last what he may have supposed all fathers were more or less like, although he could not have believed all fathers were quite such heroes as "Uncle Bob"—Uncle Bob, who feared nothing (or nothing Roger had cognizance of) and who henceforth, in his little-boy mind, took precedence, in his hierarchy of heroes, even over the great Admiral Dewey; while Bob, on his part, was knowing, it was plain, assuagement of some of his hunger for the children he had never had, nor was likely to.

The closest possible tie grew up between the two (one never to be broken while they both lived), and nothing could have given me more deep-down joy than this relationship between the little boy dearer to me than all else on earth and the man whose image I had carried hauntingly in my mind from that evening long ago on Highland Avenue when Bob came to say goodbye before starting to Mexico and for the first time made known to me fully, and in no uncertain terms, his love for me.

Even so, however, I was not blinded to the fact that there were dangers, explosive elements, in the situation. It was drawing Bob and me ever closer together. If, through circumstances, Bob and I were alone together for even a few minutes the air would become electric; I would become extremely uneasy; and when he insisted, as any gentleman would, on walking back with me to Miss Hilton's, short distance though it was, if it were after dark, I would be on tenterhooks.

My fears were not without foundation. One evening as Bob bade me goodnight in the dusk of Miss Hilton's porch, the street below deserted, suddenly he drew me into his arms and started saying what, if I had longed to hear, I dreaded more.

"No, Bob, no, *no*!" I stopped him, almost in terror. "Never do anything—say anything, like this again!"

But my dominating desire now to break away from my life as a teacher, though intensified by it, did not, after all, spring from this torturing, if rapturous, moment with Bob in the dusk of Miss Hilton's porch.

Nor did it derive from any repugnance to teaching in itself. To the last day I taught, I think I may say with perfect honesty, I taught with enthusiasm. During my years at the GHS, even in the last feverish ones, teaching had never seemed to me a prosaic occupation. Living, as I did, in my off hours, almost entirely in the enchanted world of books, I came into the class-room each morning still living in this world and eager to bring, if I could, some of the beauty, the magic light which played upon it, to my pupils. The truth is, I loved teaching.

Moreover, I had had no little encouragement. I had been made Supervisor of English in all the Knoxville public schools, if with no extra pay, a mark of distinction. Then there had been a change in Superintendents from Prof. Ruth, summarily dismissed when the Board of Education finally realized to what extent this martinet was hated and feared by both teachers and pupils throughout the school system. His successor, portly Prof. McCallie, if of no comparable scholarship, was genial, considerate, cooperated with me in whatever I undertook—altogether, so far as he was able, made teaching easier and more agreeable.

Incidentally, and ironically, the dismissal of that fiery little man, Prof. Ruth, after years of conscientious service, while it afforded a measure of relief to all the teachers who had been subject to his despotic rule gave us at last a touching glimpse of him as a human being.

One evening, shortly before he left the town in which he had spent most of his life, a small group of us who taught at the GHS went to the pleasant white-frame, tree-shaded house in West End where he and his family lived, bringing with us a parting remembrance for him. With a few choking words, his eyes full of tears, he accepted the gift we had brought, and before we left[,] handed me privately an envelope in which was a letter of recommendation of me as a teacher. "In case," he said, in a quiet voice, "it might some day be useful to you, for you will go further—"

Besides better conditions now for teaching, there had been, too, in the past year or so, more diversions, and more recognition of me as an individual apart from school. I had seen *Midsummer Night's Dream*, the first time I had been to a play in Staub's Theatre since my ill-fated marriage, now growing dimmer. Rush Strong, the wealthy bachelor and traveled man of the world who had paid me some attention in my girlhood, had taken me to hear the then popular lecturer on literary subjects, Hamilton Wright Mabie; and, more memorably, to a formal dinner of only a dozen or so given in honor of a group of visiting New York men prominent in various fields and interested in the growing development of the "New South"; among them Felix Adler, philosopher and founder of the Ethical Culture movement, and Adolph Ochs, father of the modern *New York Times*. More than this, Mr. Strong had arranged that next me at the dinner, on the other side from himself, should sit Adolph Ochs, in his early forties then, in the full flush of his success as publisher of what already was rated the most influential newspaper in the United States. Short and stocky, but with his leonine head, his strong handsome Jewish face illumined by remarkably alive and responsive eyes, he was an extraordinarily impressive figure—at once full of fun, kindly, dynamic, dictatorial, with the air of a conqueror—by all odds the most magnetic man I had ever met.[12]

. . . But if there was more variety now in my outside life, and teaching in some respects easier, on the other hand it had been made unutterably less agreeable through the addition of another subject, or subjects, to the congenial ones I had taught heretofore.

I was never certain on whose authority, but someone had decided, and very properly, that more science than elementary botany should be taught in the high school. The new subjects were physics and mechanics, combined in a weighty textbook which later I discovered had never been intended for high school, but only for university students, and I was the one selected to teach from this, to me, abstruse work.

This was the most exasperating, the most abominable, experience I knew throughout my teaching years. To start with, I was already overburdened, some of my classes in English numbering more than seventy pupils. Then, as Supervisor of English in the schools, I must at short intervals visit other buildings and confer with the teachers there. How I ever carried such an inhuman load I can not conceive today. But worst of all, no branches of education could have been more repugnant to me. I was abysmally unfitted to teach them, being, for one thing, a mechanical moron, if ever there was one.

However, there was no use rebelling against the Board of Education or whoever was responsible for this torture I must undergo. So I resorted to the same devious expedient I had made use of when, just out of college, at Miss Ogden's Private School for Young Ladies, I was given, in addition to Latin, "higher arithmetic" to teach, and had resorted to the talents of Maria Crawford,[13] smartest girl in the class, to save my face. Now it was the adolescent boys in my room who, under such cover as I could devise, took over; made clear to everybody but me such matters as what was generated by the revolution of a parabola on its axis, and who had no end of fun in experimenting with the electric equipment I was furnished, including a galvanic battery which threw off sparks, and the very sight of which upset me.

But not even with the enthusiastic assistance of the boys could I have got away with this teaching by proxy. It was Prof. Charles Perkins, professor of physics at the University, who saved my face this time, so far as it was saved. A spare New Englander with a peculiar gait, sparse whiskers, a strong "Yankee" accent, and a high-pitched voice which frequently broke into a giggle, he yet, if he had little dignity and no what we call "personality," had that finer thing, character. Few men are so enshrined in my memory. A family friend, when he knew through me, confidentially, the difficulties I was encountering, he would come in the evening to White

Avenue, where we were still living when I first started teaching these odious subjects, and explain what I could not have understood otherwise, especially in regard to the nature of electricity, so far as it had been penetrated in that long past day. Furthermore, from time to time he would have me bring my whole large class to "the Hill," where in his own class-room and laboratory he would give them demonstrations and other competent instruction.[14]

But there were things not so directly connected with teaching itself that each in its degree contributed to what now was becoming my state of wild unrest. One of them, perhaps absurdly, was the Teachers Meetings I must attend.

Robbing us of one of our precious Saturdays, the meetings were always held on that day and always, to my inconvenience, in the room I presided over; for I must see to it beforehand that it was a model of order and neatness, no half-hidden, half-eaten apples to offend their nostrils, or other refuse in the desks at which the teachers would sit. By this time, however, I had large framed photographs of Cologne Cathedral and other imposing classic structures hung on the walls above my blackboards, so that it was probably more inviting than most public school-rooms of the day.

In any case, the papers read at these meeting, with little discussion of any of them, and no spirited discussion—the whole program, was insufferably boring. The thing, though, which affected me most adversely was the sight of the men teachers of grammar grades who were present. There they sat, gray-faced, dull-eyed, with hunched backs, and in their seedy clothes—grossly underpaid, men with families, and burnt out in middle life, if there had ever been a spark of life in them. No more depressing sight, no more pitiful male of the species, could I imagine. And they came to symbolize for me the limitations of the teacher's life. The glory of life, would it escape me, too, if I went on teaching as they had year after year after year? Don't wait, something said to me peremptorily, until you also may shut yourself out forever from an enormous realm of human happiness. Don't wait too long for new experience to come to you. Go out and search for it! You are young yet, compared to them. Live, live all you can! Live before it's too late!

But there were impressions of a different sort, and even less directly connected with teaching, which affected me at the time quite as powerfully.

One evening Mr. and Mrs. Joel Tyler invited teachers who had under them, or formerly had had, their teen-age twins,[15] to have supper and spend the evening at their home; among them, of those I remember, that jolly saint Molly Hayes, Miss Stoltzfus, a little stiff (still the teacher), but amiable, Miss Rosebud McClanahan, doing her stout little best to be at ease, Edmée and myself.

It was the Tylers who bought the house in West End where previously lived the beautiful and notorious Mrs. Hamilton when she left for no knew where.[16]

A superior couple, at once highly cultivated and warmly human (their grandson in later years—son of one of their twins—the well known litterateur, James

Agee, poet and composer of the symphony *Knoxville, 1914*),[17] the Tylers had removed from the house the stigma it had borne during Mrs. Hamilton's occupancy, and an evening with them was bound to be a more than ordinarily pleasant one.

Thus it turned out. Regardless of this, however, during the course of the evening, and with a strong feeling of revulsion, it came to me that school teachers were thought of—and even by people as enlightened as the Tylers—as a segregated class, and more comfortable by themselves than when others of different interests were asked to meet with them.

No doubt such an inference on my part was more or less unwarranted. The Tylers, quite naturally, in wishing to honor their children's teachers had invited those they assumed would be congenial. And so they were—up to a certain point. Most of them I felt genuine affection for. But nothing could mark more plainly than my reaction to this occasion the progress of the fire now burning within me. Tormented by an overwhelming urge to break away once and for all from the school teacher's life, I could no longer think as rationally as I might have once.

Not the least, either, of the factors contributing to my present unrest was the nature of my Sunday afternoons after we had gone to Miss Hilton's.

This was the time I wanted to devote especially to Roger. With no yard now for him to play in, wasn't there some way in which we could get away from our bedroom there and for a few hours have a complete change of scene, a little amusement if possible? But where could we go? What could we do? There were no movies then. Street-car rides, except in summer, were far from tempting. There was only left a walk for us to take together.

Sometimes, after we had started out, we would stop at Margaret and Charlton's, now with her parents in their big ornate red-brick house on Main Street. There we were sure to be received cordially. Margaret had remained, through the years, for all her barbed tongue, one of my most loyal, thoughtful, and generous friends, bringing me back when she went to that Europe I so craved to see myself exquisite trifles in tortoise and gold, fine gloves and silk stockings from Italy, perfume and lingerie from Paris.

But Charlton would be at home and buried in Sunday papers. It was a time of relaxation for them both. Whatever their cordiality, I always felt that Roger and I were intruders in their, or any other, home on Sunday afternoon.

Soon I stopped making calls anywhere. Driven, as the only alternative, toward Gay Street, Roger and I would walk down it to the long bridge over the river (now lost forever in the placid waters of the man-made Fort Loudoun Lake),[18] where I hoped Roger would find something diverting in the great river below us.

We would walk the whole length of the bridge, but on Sunday afternoon there seemed to be little or no river traffic. The river would be as dull as Gay Street through which we had just come, hardly a soul on the street, the indigo-blue shades

MISS EDMEE BOYNTON

MRS. C. E. M'TEER

MRS. ANNIE WETZELL WALDRON

MRS. ANNIE HALE

MISS M. A. HAYES

Teachers at Girls' High School. From *The Voice* (May 1902), p. 8. Dedicated by the Class of 1902 to their teachers. Annie Wetzell Waldron taught with and mentions each one of these teachers somewhere in her memoir.

in the windows of all the business houses drawn down to the sills—as lifeless as in a city of the dead, the awful pall of Knoxville's blue-nosed Sunday settled upon it exactly as it had been when I first knew it, and the dreariest of sights.

An awful depression would overcome me, notwithstanding that my cheery little companion would seem unaffected, never cease his lively talk. But, for me, never would he and I seem so alone, so homeless, so separate from the town where we lived and must shortly go back to. Of all my memories of Knoxville, this is, beyond comparison, the most painful.

It took more, however, than all these vagrant depressions, unsettling revulsions of feeling, to forge in me an iron determination to end my life, at whatever cost, in the place which for the rest of my conscious existence would live vividly in my mind.

It was an astonishing development in my own school-room which furnished the last fagot for the fire within me. From my start at the GHS I had always felt my pupils were in harmony with me. There had never been the least sign of rebellion. Then this last year a robust, full-bosomed, high-spirited girl began to show marked hostility toward me. She would come into the room in the morning, her head tossing, throw me an impudent look, and as the day went on meet my remarks or directions, her eyebrows lifted, and with a sneering sidewise smile for the benefit of the lads who sat near her, previously, to all appearances, devoted to me, but who now began to be as impertinent as they dared. Soon it was evident that this girl was the leader of what I now had to deal with—a small, but by no means inconsequential, disloyal minority, one that, few though they were, poisoned every recitation and to a certain extent the whole school day.

It preyed on my mind. For some time it was a mystery to me. The girl was bright, always well prepared in her lessons, there had never been the slightest difficulty between us. How could she possibly have anything against me? An only child, from one of Knoxville's old and influential families, her mother and I had always been on the friendliest of terms; while her aunt, an able woman with whom I had for years worked closely in Ossoli, now taught history at the high school, the room she presided over directly across the hall from mine.

The girl's aunt had only very recently come to the high school. Her home was one of the large, dignified, oldish red-brick houses on Main Street. But her husband had recently suffered reverses. Many years older than I, I admired the woman's pluck when, at her age, she assumed an arduous position in order to help out in this family crisis. What's more, as I was the only high school teacher she had had more than the most casual acquaintance with before, I welcomed her warmly when she joined us. I could not forget the wonderful support the other teachers at the GHS had given me when, so much less experienced, I became one of them.

I was greatly disturbed, though trying not to show it, by what was happening, and only through other teachers, and a few outsiders, did I get a clue to its source.

The newcomer among us had strong influence, they reported, over this particular niece, always hanging around her aunt, as I had noticed, at noontime and after school; but more significant, her aunt was most discontented, it seemed—a fact she had made no secret of—at having to teach history, when she thought she should have been given my own job of teaching English and American literature, for which she considered herself, apparently, better qualified than I, anyway preferred to teach.

I was more disturbed than ever now, but the matter did not clear up entirely until some time later in the year.

One winter evening, shortly before supper-time, Miss Hilton sent a Negro maid up to my bedroom to say that Major McCroskey was downstairs and wished to see me. Although I could not guess what he wanted to see me about, I felt no apprehension. He had been Chairman of the Board of Education as long as I had been connected with the schools.[19] A quiet-mannered, never effusive man, nevertheless he had always seemed thoroughly friendly whenever he and I met.

Short, broad-shouldered, heavy-set, with gray hair and a stubby gray beard, he rose and shook hands with me when I entered the sitting-room, fortunately with no one else there, and moved his chair close to mine.

Apologizing for coming at this hour, he said in a grave low voice: "There is something I wanted to tell you before someone else might." He then explained that there had been strong pressure upon the Board of Education to remove me from the schools on the ground that my "lack of religion" made me unfit to teach.

No charge that could possibly have been made could have so amazed me. I was all at sea. I had never discussed religion in any form or fashion before my pupils. I had taken genuine pleasure in reading to them each morning one of the beautiful Psalms of David from our *Book of Biblical Selections*; joined them reverently when in unison we repeated the Lord's Prayer. What's more, I had never discussed my views on religion with anyone, not even Mama. True, I seldom went to church: partly because I was usually obliged to spend my Sunday mornings on the immense amount of paper work inseparable from teaching and which I often had no time for during the week; partly because the sermons I heard, when I *did* go, were almost without exception far from inspiring.

I stared at Major McCroskey blankly. I was stunned. But when the full force of what he had said suddenly sank into me, I thought I was going to faint, and my face must have turned white, for he went on quickly to reassure me.

He had no hesitation, he said, in telling me who had brought this accusation before the Board, and brought all the political influence to bear he could on men outside the Board. It was an alderman, whose wife was the teacher seeking my own position at the GHS.

"I only wanted to tell you," Major McCroskey said, as he had before, "so you wouldn't learn about it from someone else," and as he rose to leave, placing his hand on my arm: "Daughter, your position is in no danger whatsoever. So long as you want it, it's as strong as Gibraltar!"

How kind he had been! I can see that evening so well. When I went to the front door with him it was starting to snow. My heart was still beating fast, but I was filled with gratitude. But for this man's loyalty and that of the rest of the Board, I would have lost a job in which I had taken no little pride. I would have faced a disaster as great as any I had known!

Oddly, shocked though I was, my blood did not boil at the thought of this fellow teacher's treachery, if that was the name for it. It was just one of those aberrations in human behavior you must be prepared for and sustain, if you met them, to the best of your ability. But Major McCroskey's revelation had given me something to think about indeed! It threw light on several recent incidents.

Not long before I had been asked by the program committee of Ossoli to give a paper on Darwin's *Origin of Species*. It would be years yet before the famous Scopes trial in Tennessee resulted in sustaining a state law forbidding the teaching within its borders of the Darwinian theory of evolution, and Darwinism, in its entirety, is no longer tenable today. But then, as a presumed threat to orthodox religion, many people, among them members of Ossoli, were curious to know more about this theory than merely that man was descended from monkey, as it was commonly summed up.

Knowing the bitter controversy that had raged about the explosive subject I was to handle, I prepared my paper with the utmost care, and with as much objectivity as possible.

To my gratification, the paper seemed extremely well received, and one member, Mrs. Boies, the great lady and charming person, who took her dinners with us at Miss Hilton's, was so enthusiastic she asked me to let her show the paper to the present incumbent of the Second Presbyterian Church, Dr. Robert Bachman, whose uninspiring interminable sermons from time to time I had sat through myself.

Wife of a retired Presbyterian minister, whether any cunning entered into this action of Mrs. Boies, I have never been able to decide in my own mind. With a "finishing school" education, and none too knowledgeable, she may have been entirely sincere in her apparent approbation of the paper. In any event, when she handed it back, with it was a letter Dr. Bachman had written her, with some flattering references to my "cleverness," as he chose to put it, as a writer, but ending with a warning that "this young woman should be reminded that God is still spelled with a large 'G' and nature with a small 'n.'"

This had given me some slight pause, though more amusement; but another incident, following closely, did not amuse me.

Becoming aware about this time of how ignorant I was of the Bible, I had decided to join the Sunday School class of the Hon. Joshua Caldwell at St. John's, next to Miss Hilton's, and to attend it every Sunday I possibly could.

The Hon. Joshua Caldwell was a man I heartily disliked. A leading member of the Knoxville bar, a popular speaker on public occasions, I had seen much of him first and last. Tall, lean, dyspeptic-looking and with an arrogant bearing, it was impossible to escape the impression that he had a very exalted opinion of himself, while his smile reminded me of what, freely rendered, Caesar said of Cassius: "Seldom he smiles, and as if to mock himself that he did smile." But he had founded the Irving Club, composed of university professors, lawyers, clergymen, and a few carefully chosen business men. Its permanent president, and always meeting in his own home, he dominated, in his long day, the male intellectuals of Knoxville, became their unofficial high priest—in short, a sort of local Henry Adams. With contempt for any intellectual pretensions in women, he had once given us a talk at Ossoli in which he deplored the direction in which our programs were tending. We should go back, he said, to *Evangeline*, and works more suitable for women.[20]

But enjoying great prestige, he had the reputation also, whether earned or not, of being Knoxville's finest Biblical scholar. So, refusing to allow my dislike of him to stand in the way, I found myself one Sunday morning in his Bible class at St. John's, among two pews full of genteel, timorous-looking, oldish, unmarried young women.

The lesson for the day was drawn from the Book of Leviticus, and our teacher, to my disappointment, dwelt exclusively on the laws, or collection of laws, it contains. It was as absolutely drained of color, as dull, as Sunday School lessons I remembered in Sunday School at the Second Presbyterian Church when I had fidgeted under those two good and gracious women who taught us there.

Toward the end, however, of this Bible lesson, and in what I judged—from the downcast embarrassed looks of the others in the class—was a departure from our teacher's usual procedure, he launched into a veritable tirade on women who were "free thinkers."

"*Women*," he exclaimed acidly, "who owe everything they have today to Christianity!"

This was a statement I was not disposed to dispute. But when I saw, what no one could fail to, that his harangue was directed pointedly at me, and at me only, and that I was learning nothing which really enriched my knowledge of the Bible, I resolved on the spot that if this was the first time I had attended the Sunday School class of the Hon. Joshua Caldwell, it was also the last.

Now, however, in the stillness of the night after Major McCroskey's call, I began to put one thing and another together.

From my early teens I had been aware of the amount of religious bigotry in

Knoxville. I knew that my father, although a regular church attendant before his back was broken, did not "belong" to the church. I had never ceased to smart when I recalled the position in which I had been placed at Mt. Holyoke when alone, among four hundred girls under questioning, I had stood up and put myself on record as not "belonging" to any church. But now, it seemed, I was being called in the town where I had grown up—and by how many I could not guess—an "infidel," an "atheist"—one of those names with which the illiterate, the semi-literate, even the fairly literate, tarred those who did not conform to the usual pattern of membership in and regular attendance at some church.

From this hour, I made my definite plans. Cowardly though it may have been, and unfair to the man I had in mind, yet I saw no other certain channel through which I could free myself from an environment that was becoming more unpleasant than pleasant, and where there were perhaps further pitfalls in store for me—in sheer desperation I must marry Jim Ramsey, and no more shilly-shallying about it.

From this hour, I must see as little as possible of Bob and Celia, particularly of Bob. Roger might go, but I must not, to their house, if I could avoid it. Nothing must swerve me from my main purpose.

I started having my wedding-clothes made, little by little, as I could afford. Though I have no remembrance of talking them over with Mama, I must have done so, for she set to work now making my lingerie, things that still could not be bought ready-made. I do not believe she ever touched a sewing-machine in her life, but she made me also dainty white blouses, with lace insertion in them, and with her fine needlework, the nicest I had ever had. Her beautiful face more withdrawn than ever, I can see her working on them when I came home from school each day. She even made me a few pretty dresses, white or in delicate color, that I would need, in my new life, for summer wear; and when spring came I had the first tailor suit I had ever owned, made by the dressmaker who had made such attractive dresses for May when she had come home from the Philippines to visit us.

A few weeks before school closed I took the irrevocable step—sent in my resignation to the Board of Education.[21] From this, everyone knew, or surmised, that I was leaving my position to be married. All this time, however, I did not admit it—to the best of my memory, not even to Edmée, in whom I had complete confidence. I had grown as reserved, as reticent, when it came to my personal affairs, as after my divorce, which, with the circumstances that led to it, it took me half a century to be able to discuss at all freely.

The only person who appeared to suspect what continued to be, in spite of everything, my unsettled state of mind, was Mrs. French, with her usual perceptiveness. One evening shortly before I left she asked me to come down to her big old-fashioned red-brick house on Cumberland Street, center of more liberal, thought-provoking talk than I had ever heard anywhere else in Knoxville.

After talking about a number of other things she said that if by any chance I should decide later I wanted to come back, she would like me to help her establish, here in her own home, another private day school. She thought there was room for a more progressive private school for girls than the one already existing in town, and impressed on me that her offer would be open so long as I wished to consider it. There was no one, she said, she would rather have associated with her.[22]

Mrs. French was not a person who indulged in flattery. This was a great deal for her to say, and when she spoke as she did, I was pierced with a sudden feeling of homesickness—homesickness for the place I had not yet left, the only town I had ever really known (or ever would). Bound up with it were all my loveliest, as all my most anguishing, memories. After all, not only Mrs. French, but how many, many people in Knoxville had been good to me!

But my sense of life as an adventure never left me. It sustained me in moments like this when otherwise I might have wavered.

The June day came. It was a Saturday. I had kept the exact day of my leaving as secret as everything else. I could stand no goodbyes.

The plan was, I should take the day train to Chattanooga, Jim Ramsey to join me there for the week-end. Mama would remain behind, keeping Roger till Monday, when she would put him on the train and he would travel alone to Chattanooga. From there he and I would go to Atlanta to spend a few weeks with my Atlanta cousins, while Mama would go to one of her sisters for an indefinite stay. The wedding, with only the family present, was to be at May's home later in the summer when she returned from her second and shorter stay in the Philippines and her husband's new station would be Fort McPherson, just outside Atlanta.

It was toward evening when I reached Chattanooga and took a hack (still in universal use) for the Reed House. I signed the hotel's register and had just turned away from the desk when I saw Jim Ramsey coming toward me from across the lobby.

My heart sank when I saw at once that he had been drinking. A man who had destroyed his earlier fine prospects through drink, it gave me a sickening sensation to find him in his present condition.

We only talked a little that evening, but next day, carrying a lunch with us, took the Incline which shoots straight up the steep face of Lookout Mountain, and where we would be by ourselves in one of the wooded stretches on top.

The day was sweltering even at this height, and we were not too comfortable sitting on the ground. What was more discouraging, Jim had been drinking again, and though in the course of the day its effects seem[ed] to wear off, he remained somewhat irritable, something I had never seen in him before.

To my dismay, however, in all the discussion of our future plans he failed to say a word about Roger. I had never assumed anything else than that Roger would live with us after our marriage. There was no man in the world for whom I would give up Roger, or only for brief periods. I gave Jim several openings in the hope that sooner or later he would assure me that of course Roger would be with us.

No such assurance came and, thinking for the time being it might be better, I switched our talk to more impersonal matters. In the course of it, apropos of what I have long forgotten, Jim made some damning remark about "niggers" in general.

The Negro problem was not then, at the turn of the century, a live, far less a burning, issue in the South. It was still in a more or less slumbering state. The Negroes were still very largely staying in what was considered "their place." That a Negro should aspire to a college education was an idea too fantastic even to be thought of, and the later outraged challenge: "Would you want *your* daughter to marry a nigger?" had not yet been sounded, at least in my ears.

The truth is, I had heretofore had only the mildest interest in the subject. Only recently, through some of my reading and an occasional comment from Mrs. French, with her keen sense of social justice, had I given it any serious thought at all.

But now when Jim spoke of the whole race so abusively, already stung by his failure to mention Roger as a member of the home we were planning to have, when he denied that Negroes were entitled to any education whatever, or capable racially of any progress, I was aroused to defend them.

At this, normally gallant, if utterly unreconstructed, though he was, Jim became so angry that I made another and fateful decision. Even leaving aside his having resumed drinking, I could never live with a man whose mind was so feudal.

That evening, as we sat in a sequestered corner of the lobby, Jim in another half-hour to take his train for home, I broke our engagement.

I was now completely adrift. But few sights have ever been so heavenly to me as Roger next day, leaning from the rear platform of the train from Knoxville as it arrived, his eyes alight, his whole little-boy body reflecting his unbounded joy and relief when he saw me hastening toward him.

In Atlanta, he had four children, none far from his own age, to play with all day long. Unaware of my own predicament, he had some weeks of unalloyed happiness.

At the time, Arthur's salary was only sufficient to meet the family's essential needs. Their cottage was small and crowded. But they converted their sitting-room into a bedroom for Roger and me, and never for an instant through these weeks did they make either of us feel anything but the most welcome of guests.

It was to Arthur and Jenny[23] I had gone when my first venture in trying to earn a living as a traveling "General Agent" for a cheap and unreliable book-publishing concern had turned out an ignominious failure. It was they who refused to take this failure too seriously; through their cheerfulness and humor had put fresh heart in me and given me courage to go home and confess my failure to Mama. And it was to them I opened up now, without reservation, my present situation.

A day or so after I arrived, letters began coming to me from Jim Ramsey imploring me to reconsider my decision; the last one, when I refused to do so, ending with a sentimental phrase which for some reason has stuck in my head: "I shall never wander again in the garden of love!"

But I was through with Jim Ramsey. I could, of course, return to Knoxville. Along with Jim's letters had come one from Mrs. French, confirming her earlier offer in writing and offering me a considerably higher salary than I had received in the high school.

But, equally, I was firm in my resolution not to return to Knoxville. I had parted with Knoxville. I did not realize then I would never part with Knoxville. In time to come, on soft sooty winter days in London, its smell—in Southern Spain, a certain scent I would catch, a mere whiff, and again I was under the old spell of Knoxville. Even today, in my eighties, as I write these lines, living in a little town in the Virginia Highlands,[24] when I walk on its mossy brick sidewalks, laid a century ago and sunken in spots, I am climbing again the old brick pavements I climbed on my way to school in my early teens. For an exquisitely painful instant I am not remembering, I am breathing the same air, amidst the same beloved surroundings which would haunt me forever. *I am actually there.*

But now in Atlanta, I had no inclination for such remembering, reliving, the past. Nor could I read, even had I been in a quieter home. My mind was in too much of a ferment. I had but one thought. I must find something to do, something that would support myself and Roger. After years of incessant work, I could not be idle. Nothing could irk me more. Besides, I could not much longer take advantage of my cousins' generosity.

When they found how in earnest I was, immediately they sought to help me. Why not apply for a position in the Atlanta schools? They knew personally a woman, a member of their church, who was also a member of the Board of Education.

I went to see this woman, whose name, as so many, has slipped me. She gave me encouragement. There was no vacancy, but sure to be one before long, for a substitute if nothing else, but which might easily lead to a permanent position.

Why wasn't this a solution? I was buoyed up. My money, however, was almost gone, a thing that worried me. If this position materialized, as it promised to, there would yet be some weeks till I drew my first pay.

But all at once I thought of May. She and Leon would soon be here, in their new quarters at Fort McPherson. What a God-send! Roger and I could stay with them until I could earn enough for us to be by ourselves somewhere.

On my first visit to Fort McPherson I was charmed. May and Leon were already settled in their attractive quarters, one side of a double three-story red-brick house with ample room, and Mama's massive furniture, shipped from Knoxville, more in scale and appropriate than it had seemed in all our years there, gave their large lofty rooms a handsome look.

I told May of my prospects. Though she did not commit herself, she appeared pleased that Roger and I were to be so near.

It was getting by this time toward the end of August. One late afternoon, driving in from the post in an army wagon, May came to my cousins' house. For a few minutes she and I were alone, and while she did not say so in so many words, she made it plain that while she would love to have us, Leon, a most devoted husband, nevertheless was not disposed to take into their home other members of her family.

This was a hard blow, although I felt no resentment toward May. Left to herself, I knew she would not have hesitated a moment to have Roger and myself, at this juncture, with them.

My pride, however, was too great for me to do anything but acquiesce quietly in the decision she had brought. But now I must think of something else!

Through long tossing hot August nights, I thought and thought. At what moment I do not know, it occurred to me to go to a great and unknown city. May herself had gone to an unknown city and there had opened up to her the fuller life she now enjoyed. From time immemorial, dauntless spirits had sought London, Paris, New York—all great cities, to find in them a richer fulfillment than they could have hoped for otherwise. I did not forget that there were wrecks, too, tragic victims, of such adventures. But that was nothing to dwell on now. In great cities there were vastly more opportunities. I was young, healthy, energetic, imaginative. Surely I could find something to do there, and it might turn out for me also the most fortuitous step I had ever taken.

When I revealed to my cousins this new decision, they were shocked beyond measure. But nothing would turn me now from what I proposed.

On the evening I was to leave, May came, and more agitated than I had ever seen her, gave me such bills as she could spare from her housekeeping money and a beautiful black lace scarf she had brought from the Philippines. In a pinch, I might sell it—it should bring a good price. But what meant more, she promised to keep Roger with her till I had a place for him. In her hands, he would be safe.

Arthur and Jenny went with me to the train, Arthur following me into it, and when the train had already started to move, tears streaming down his face, pressed into my hand a bill he could ill afford to give.

What, it occurs to me now, would I have done without this bill from Arthur? The ticket for my long journey had taken all the rest of the money I had, and when I reached my destination, Arthur's bill was enough to pay for a couple of days at a hotel until I could get my bearings. But I would be safe, as well as Roger, whatever happened.

Dressing for the train, I had fastened around my neck a thread-like gold chain

I would wear henceforth underneath my dress. On it I had hung a gold locket set with a turquoise, a trinket saved from my childhood, and inside the locket fitted the face of little flaxen-haired Roger, taken at two or three, and which I had cut from a small snapshot. I had never known a moment of sharper anguish, but this was my amulet, my St. Christopher's medal, to preserve me from all harm.

NOTES

1. Miss Anna (or Annie) R. Hilton's boarding house was at 708 Walnut Street. *Knoxville City Directory*, 1900, 1901, 1902.
2. Edmée Boynton (1876–1967) was the youngest child of Sue Brownlow Sawyers (daughter of William G. Brownlow) and Dr. Daniel T. Boynton, whom she married after the death of her first husband. Boynton had come to Knoxville during the Civil War as surgeon of the 104th Ohio Infantry and was appointed pension agent at Knoxville in 1869. Edmée (often listed as Edna) married Louis D. Huntoon (1869–1947), Professor of Mining and Metallurgy at Yale University, on October 7, 1903, and lived the rest of her life in Connecticut and New York. Rule, 521; *US Census*, 1880, 1900, 1940; *Men of 1914* (online), s.v. Huntoon, Louis Doremus, https://books.google.com (viewed June 4, 2020); "Mrs. Huntoon, Teacher, Dies, *Knoxville News-Sentinel*, May 6, 1967, 8.
3. Edmée's father died in 1887. Her mother's other children were Lillie Sawyers (by her first husband, Dr. James H. Sawyers, d.1857), who married the Reverend Samuel Long and lived in Abingdon, Virginia; and (by Boynton): Lucile (Mrs. Clarence A. Benscoter), Chattanooga; Ilia (Mrs. Franklin Pierce Swindler), Salt Lake, Utah; and Dr. Emerson Boynton, later of Mountville, Pennsylvania. Zella Armstrong, *Notable Southern Families* (Chattanooga: Lookout Press, 1918), vol. 1, 92.
4. The Women's Educational and Industrial Union (WEIU), a social service and educational agency, was founded in 1877 in Boston, Massachusetts, to promote the advancement of women. Lizzie Crozier French organized the Knoxville chapter in 1890. Among the various projects it supported were Mount Rest Home, a residence for elderly women with insufficient funds or family to care for them, and the Knox County Industrial School, which became John Tarleton Institute. Since 2016, "Economic Mobility Pathways" (EMPath) of Boston, which evolved after the Women's Union merged with Crittenton, Inc. in 2006, is carrying on its legacy of helping women and families. Rule, 580; Rothrock, 304–06; Deaderick, 342, 344; EMPath Web site, empathways .org/about/our-history (viewed May 25, 2020).
5. Judge David K. Young, Sr. acquired, in 1865, the plantation home and its approximately one thousand acres of land in the Eagle Bend of Clinch River near the town of Clinton, in Anderson County. Three generations of the family lived there before the Tennessee Valley Authority (TVA) purchased a large portion of the land, including the house. A few years later, U. S. Army engineers chose nearby parts of Anderson

and Roane counties for the "secret city" of Oak Ridge, where huge war production plants were built as part of the Manhattan Project during World War II. Katherine B. Hoskins, *Anderson County*, Tennessee County History Series (Memphis: Memphis State University Press, 1979), 90, 91, 92, 98–99.

6. James Walter "Jim" Young (mentioned earlier as founder of the Knoxville Whitman Fellowship) was born at Eagle Bend in 1868. He became interested in literature—Whitman in particular—while attending the University of the South in Sewanee, Tenn. Later, while studying law at the University of Tennessee, he edited a monthly literary magazine. After graduating in 1891, he went to New York to pursue a writing career and worked for the *New York Sun*. Upon returning to Tennessee, he practiced law with his father although he continued writing for magazines and newspapers. He published two critical essays in the *Sewanee Review* (1899, 1902) and contributed articles and reports to the *Whitman Fellowship Papers* and to the *Conservator*, a journal founded to promote Whitman and his works. A popular after-dinner speaker, he also lectured widely on Whitman and other literary subjects. Jim Young died at Eagle Bend in 1908. Campbell, [13]-14, 40–43; Bar Association of Tennessee, *Proceedings of the Annual Session of the Bar Association of Tennessee* 28 (1909): 146–47 (online), Googlebooks.com (viewed May 26, 2020). The accident to which AWA refers occurred in 1889. "Young Is All Right," *Knoxville Daily Journal*, April 16, 1889, 5.
7. Henry was born Oct. 1, 1877, in Campbell County, Tenn., but his family was living in Loudon County by the time AWA knew him in Knoxville. *Who's Who in the Pacific Southwest* (Los Angeles: Times-Mirror, 1913), www.sfgenealogy.org/caldatanook/tagdata/5-who/318.htm (viewed April 22, 2020); *U. S. Census*, 1900. His ink-stained hands were probably due to working as a pressman for the *Knoxville Journal and Tribune* before becoming a reporter.
8. Eleven children were born to Henry's parents although only eight survived childhood. Contrary to what AWA says, the father did not die until years later. *U.S. Census*, 1900, 1910; "Death Comes to Him in Old Home State," *Los Angeles Times*, May 6, 1921 (online), ProQuest Historical Newspapers, (viewed May 28, 2020).
9. Henry C. Warnack (sometimes Warnick) had a life every bit as unusual as AWA's. His middle name seems to have been Christian, but, as time went on, he used "Christeen" instead. After leaving Knoxville, he was a reporter on the *Colorado Springs Gazette* and the *Rocky Mountain News* (Denver). He married Marguerite O'Connor Ellicott in 1902, but they divorced in 1905. *Colorado, County Marriage Records and State Index, 1862–2006* (online), and *Colorado, Divorce Index, 1851–1985* (online), Ancestry.com (viewed August 3, 2020). After moving to California, he joined the *Los Angeles Times* and became its film critic. By 1915, when he married the wife to whom AWA refers, his parents and most of his brothers had joined him in Los Angeles County, taking up residence in Huntington Park. Theresa Brunner, the woman he married, was the daughter of a merchant who built the Alhambra mansion called "Villa Brunner" after

making his fortune in Missouri as a "St. Louis capitalist." The story of Henry's marriage appeared under the headline: "Poet-Author Weds His Castle's Chatelaine." *Los Angeles Times,* March 15, 1915 (online), ProQuest Historical Newspapers (viewed May 28, 2020). The couple had two sons before Henry died November 2, 1927. Before his death, he became interested in motion pictures, worked for a film production company, and wrote several film scenarios. "H. C. Warnack, Writer, Dies: Poet and Author Formerly Was Editor of '*Times*' Dramatic Department," *Los Angeles Times,* Nov. 3, 1927 (online), ProQuest Historical Newspapers (viewed May 28, 2020). How AWA knew about his later life and death is not known. Parts of her memoir concerning him and his family are quoted in Campbell's thesis, 24.

10. Admiral George Dewey (1837–1917) visited Knoxville in May 1900 to dedicate a memorial to Admiral David Glasgow Farragut, under whom Dewey was serving during the Civil War battle of Mobile Bay (August 5, 1864) and at which Farragut reportedly gave his famous order: "Damn the torpedoes, full speed ahead!" Festivities on May 14, 1900, proclaimed "Dewey Day" in Knoxville, included a parade, speeches, a banquet, and the evening reception. The following day, May 15, Admiral Dewey unveiled a stone monument, commissioned by Bonny Kate Chapter DAR, marking the site of Admiral Farragut's birthplace near Lowe's Ferry (originally called Stoney Point) in west Knox County. Newspapers as far away as Washington, DC, and Detroit, Michigan, reported the story, headed "Dateline: Knoxville, Tennessee." The marker has since been moved to Farragut Memorial Plaza in the Town of Farragut (incorporated 1980) alongside a statue of the admiral. Rothrock, 417; "Dewey's Day in Knoxville," *Washington Post,* May 13, 1900, 3; "Welcome to Dewey," *Nashville American,* May 15, 1900, 6; "Hero of Mobile Bay: Memorial to Admiral Farragut Unveiled by Dewey," *Detroit Free Press,* May 16, 1900, 2; Farragut, TN - Official Website, s.v. "History," townoffarragut.org/251/History (viewed June 1, 2020).
11. Robert F. Armstrong's address was 517 Cumberland Avenue, W. *Knoxville City Directory,* 1900.
12. AWA does not mention that Adolph Simon Ochs (1858–1935), although born in Cincinnati, Ohio, spent most of his youth in Knoxville. He began delivering newspapers at a young age and then worked as a "printer's devil" (apprentice) under Captain William Rule at the Knoxville *Chronicle,* where he learned to set type and mastered other skills of the printing trade. After working briefly as a compositor at a Kentucky newspaper, he moved to Chattanooga where he bought the failing *Chattanooga Times* and turned it into a leading Southern newspaper. In 1896 he acquired the *New York Times* (near bankruptcy at the time) and, under his leadership, made it the nation's top newspaper. Rothrock, 463–464; Timothy P. Ezzell, "Ochs, Adolph Simon," in *Tennessee Encyclopedia of History & Culture,* ed. Carroll Van West (Nashville: Tennessee Historical Society / Rutledge Hill Press, 1998), 143–44; Jack Neely, "Night School," *From the Shadow Side, and Other Stories of Knoxville, Tennessee* (Oak Ridge, Tenn.: Tellico Books, 2003),

39–43; Neely, "Night School," *Knoxville: This Obscure Prismatic City* (Charleston, SC: History Press, 2009) [31]-37; *Encyclopaedia Britannica Online*, s.v. "Adolph Simon Ochs," https://www.britannica.com/biography/Adolph-Simon-Ochs (viewed April 30, 2020).

13. AWA earlier called this girl Jean Crawford.

14. Charles Albert Perkins (1867–1945) was Professor of Physics and Electrical Engineering at the University of Tennessee and the only faculty member who taught electrical engineering when that subject was added to the curriculum in the late 1800s. Dr. Perkins was a native of Massachusetts with a Ph. D. from Johns Hopkins. He taught at UT for more than fifty years; "Perkins Hall" engineering building, dedicated in 1950, is named for him. The Perkins lived on Clinch Avenue and were members of Second Presbyterian Church so it is no surprise that they were family friends. In addition, Mrs. Perkins (née Angie Warren) was active in Ossoli Circle, to which both AWA and her mother belonged. Rule, 383; "Min H. Kao Department of Electrical Engineering & Computer Science (Tickle College of Engineering, University of Tennessee, Knoxville): History" Web page, <eecs.utk.edu/about/history> (viewed May 21, 2020); Ben Winiger, "Ayres, Morgan, Perkins Halls Celebrate Major Anniversaries," UT Daily Beacon (online), March 11, 2019, http://www.utdailybeacon.com/campus_news/campus_events/ayres-morgan-perkins-halls-celebrate-major-anniversaries/ (viewed May 21, 2020); Rothrock, 466–67.

15. Laura and Hugh, born May 22, 1884. The Tylers also had a younger daughter, Paula, born August 27, 1893. Paul F. Brown, *Rufus: James Agee in Tennessee* (Knoxville: University of Tennessee Press, 2018), 16, 19.

16. Although the Tylers moved to Knoxville in 1891, they did not buy the house at the corner of West Clinch Avenue and Twelfth (formerly Fourth) Street until May 1898. Interestingly, the Tylers came to Knoxville from Michigan, just as the Wetzells had. Joel Tyler was in the lumber business with his father in Kalamazoo, Michigan, only about fifty miles from Grand Rapids, where Henry Wetzell and his brothers had their lumber business. Both men were attracted to East Tennessee by the vast timber resources available there at the time. Tyler bought timberland in Sevier County but later sold it, choosing instead to join William J. Savage in his Knoxville machine business, which became Savage & Tyler (later the Ty-Sa-Ma Machine Company, owned by Tyler, Savage's brother Arthur, and E. T. Manning). Paul F. Brown, *Rufus*, 16–19, 24, 54; Rule, 199; Deaderick, 599; J. C. (Jim) Tumblin, "Arthur Savage," *Fountain City: People Who Made a Difference* (Knoxville: Celtic Cat, 2016), 129.

17. James Agee (1909–1955)—poet, journalist, film critic, screenwriter, novelist—was the son of Laura Tyler and Hugh James "Jay" Agee. His prose poem, "Knoxville: Summer of 1915," was published in *Partisan Review* 5, no. 3 (Aug.-Sept. 1938): 22–25. However, it was American composer Samuel Barber who set Agee's text to music in a work for soprano and orchestra that premiered in Boston in 1948 and was performed in

Knoxville in 1949 by the Knoxville Symphony Orchestra. "Knoxville: Summer of 1915" was later used as the prologue in Agee's posthumously published novel *A Death in the Family* (1957), which won the Pulitzer Prize for Fiction in 1958. *All the Way Home,* a play adapted from the novel, also won a Pulitzer and was made into a movie which premiered in Knoxville in 1963. "A James Agee Chronology," in *James Agee Rediscovered,* ed. Michael A. Lofaro and Hugh Davis (Knoxville: University of Tennessee Press, 2005), xxxvii-xl; "City Orchestra to Play Tone Poem," *Knoxville Journal,* Nov. 20, 1949, cited in Brown, 239, 377n2.

18. Fort Loudon Lake was created when the Tennessee Valley Authority completed Fort Loudoun Dam in 1943. Joe Spence, "Loudon County," in *Tennessee Encyclopedia of History & Culture,* ed. West, 557.
19. E. E. McCroskey was President of the Board of Education from 1887–1899. Before that, he had been Secretary-Treasurer, 1881–1887. Rule, 406.
20. In addition to his work as an attorney on both the local and state levels, Joshua William Caldwell (1856–1909) was a lecturer in the department of law at the University of Tennessee and a member of the University's board of trustees. Not only was he a gifted orator and speaker, he was the author of two books, *Sketches of the Bench and Bar of Tennessee* (1898) and *Studies in the Constitutional History of Tennessee* (1895), and contributed to magazines. William Rule, editor of the *Standard History of Knoxville, Tennessee* (1900), credits Caldwell's work for much of the material in Chapter 18, "The Bench and Bar," although Rule states that the chapter was not written by Caldwell. The Irving Club, founded in 1886, was originally a men's club with membership limited to twenty-four. It is still active as a private literary group in Knoxville but, since 1993, has admitted women to its membership, which is still twenty-four, half from the University and half from the community. Caldwell was an early supporter of libraries in Knoxville and was one of the original trustees of Lawson McGhee Library. Rule, preface iii-iv, 384, 466; Rothrock, 241, 242, 244, 389; Deaderick, 441, 443.
21. An end-of-year newspaper article about Knoxville city schools mentions AWA's resignation from her teaching position. "One Perfect Attendance . . . ," *Knoxville Sentinel,* June 4, 1902, 6.
22. The 1902 *Knoxville City Directory* contains an entry for "The New School" at 620 West Cumberland Avenue (address of Lizzie Crozier French), and also includes the listing: "Mrs. Anna W. Waldron, tchr, 'The New School,' bds 620 Cumberland W." *Knoxville City Directory,* 1902. No other information about this school has been found.
23. Jenny Wetzell Williams was the daughter of Daniel M. Wetzell, brother of AWA's father.
24. Abingdon, in southwest Virginia.

Chapter Twenty-Four

Knoxville Thirty Years After

One fresh beautiful June morning, when the new century was still young, Bob Armstrong and I were married by the Rev. Ulysses Pierce, chaplain of the United States Senate, at the Church of All Souls in Washington, where Roger and I had been living for the past winter and spring.[1]

It was early morning, so that Bob and I could catch the train for New England to spend a couple of weeks in the lovely New England countryside in its lilac time.

The great empty church was cool and dim; our only witnesses to the simple ceremony Roger and two elderly women, Washington friends.

Knowing Bob and I had both been divorced, Dr. Pierce altered the usual words in the ceremony, "Those whom God hath joined together let no man put asunder," to "Those whom Love hath joined together let no man put asunder"; and Bob placed on my finger, not the conventional wedding-ring, but one set with a pearl encircled by diamonds, engraved inside it the word: *Fulfillment.*

Roger would stay with the women friends who were present while Bob and I were away, and when we returned it would be to a home in Washington, not far from Lafayette Square, and the happiest I had known since my early girlhood.[2]

But my most treasured memory of that June morning was when Bob and I, after the ceremony, as we stopped in the sacristy to sign our names and then were leaving by a side entrance to the church where a carriage was waiting, Roger, close beside me as we reached the pavement, whispered shyly in my ear, "Mother, I call it sacred ground where first they trod"—for now his beloved "Uncle Bob" had become "Father."[3]

In the something more than two years since that anguishing night when I left Atlanta for I knew not what, I had passed through deep waters—years that today, my sands running low, and when I am enjoying a long rich Indian Summer, I can not recall without asking myself: Did I ever really have such experiences, or is it only that "dark dream" of which Rimbaud wrote and which seemed to him his life—was it just a bad dream that now and then comes back to me?

I had found employment, it is true, and almost at once, in the Rialto Grain Company, with imposing offices, dealing with grain on paper, as a speculation, and which for a time had enjoyed considerable prestige in the business world, but which shortly after I was employed by it collapsed under a Grand Jury's investigation of its irregularities.[4]

From then on I lived mainly by my wits. I had made agreeable acquaintances in the city from the beginning; not only at the Rialto Grain Company but at one excellent boarding-house after another where I stayed. Soon these acquaintances were paying me attention. Soon I knew no little gaiety—if the picture be veracious—in fashionable cafés with their long wine-lists. I rode in hansom cabs. Went occasionally to concerts. Night after night danced the night away. I went to the best plays in the city's leading theatres; saw Duse, in her prime, in *Paola and Francesca*. I went to the races, where sometimes I won a small bet I had placed on this horse or that. I revelled in hot-house flowers and Houbigant's *Ideal*. But for the most part I knew only abject misery.

In these feverish years, even in my idlest hours—and I knew many idle ones—, books failed me. I read, I recall, only two books in all this time: Pierre Loti's *An Island* [i.e., Iceland] *Fisherman*, a tragic tale whose somber tone chimed with my own sad mood; and Eden Phillpotts' lovely *Children of the Mist*, which with its Dartmoor setting for a fleeting moment or so lifted me out of my misery and into that magic world of books on which I had drawn so heavily in my teaching years—now almost as if they had never been. During my life with Theodore I had not been able to read, and even less could I now.

I never knew a single moment of serenity, and in my desperation again and again all that saved me was looking at Roger's sweet innocent little face in the locket always hung on the hidden gold chain around my neck. Roger would save me, sooner or later, if anything could—Roger who (with my precarious existence) was seldom with me now, and then only for a few happy, if stabbing, days.

During this period, I became engaged again, and to a lovable Southerner, not a man who took possession of all my senses, but a charming companion and marvelous dancing partner, as a former leader of cotillions in his native Birmingham. Wasn't this perhaps a way out of my present existence, as I had once thought—in what different circumstances!—of Jim Ramsey? But here again, though not for the same reasons, after a few months I broke my engagement.

One night with a lively group in a smart restaurant, when I referred in some connection or other to Mark Twain's *The Prince and the Pauper*, the man to whom I was engaged laid his hand on mine and said in his good-natured indulgent way: "Honey, that's the first book you've ever mentioned that I've read!"

No, I couldn't marry him either. If his mind was not so feudal as Jim Ramsey's (of that I wasn't sure), yet except for our mutual love of gaiety, we had too little in common.

Finally, however, I found what promised to be a paying job, traveling for a well-established collecting agency which offered to doctors and dentists a special service in collecting for them their overdue bills.

This, at any rate, if not the most dignified employment, held out more than my first venture years before as a traveling agent, which had turned out so dismal a failure.

I started out with fresh hope. My first stop was Memphis, and though already ill, more seriously ill than I dared acknowledge to myself, I met straight off with success, landing one contract after another until one day I broke down completely, could no longer walk more than a few steps, those with assistance, and had barely strength enough for the further trip to Atlanta, where May would be near, and Mama, and the only place I knew to turn.

In Atlanta I lay for weeks and weeks in a private hospital for surgical cases.

After being near death and too weak even to lift my head, one morning the superintendent of nurses with a smiling face ushered into my room Bob Armstrong, who had never ceased to follow my movements, nor to keep in touch with Roger, now in a Christian Brothers boarding-school where I had placed him.

One look at my face on the pillow, and Bob fell on his knees beside my bed. Overcome with emotion, his head bowed, he put out his hand and covered my own thin and feeble one, resting on the counterpane.

"Annie, Annie!" burst from him convulsively. Then he took a chair close to me, and after a while, when he had control of himself, told me of his pending divorce, which I had not known of before. "Now," he said, "if you will have me, the rest of my life is dedicated to you!"

Looking back now—in what must, in the nature of things, be near the end of my own life—on those two dark years before Bob found me in the hospital in Atlanta, I am no longer inclined, as once, to look upon them as "lost years." I do not regret them. I am tempted to regard them the most valuable I have known. After them, I could never lament, as many a man and woman in their old age, "I have never lived!" I had had contact with all sorts and conditions of men and women; been exposed to ways of living I had previously hardly known existed. However high the cost—one I have never quite finished paying for—this experience nevertheless had broadened my understanding of my fellow human beings. It had deepened immeasurably my sympathy with them. Never again would I be surprised that people are so bad, but only that they are as good as they are.

Perhaps these years were part and parcel of the design of my own individual destiny. In any event, I can not deny that "I am part," as Tennyson says in his *Ulysses*, "of all I have met," and I may add, in this testament of age, that considering the complexity of human emotions and the power of forces which may deflect us—sweep us irresistibly into dubious courses, I am convinced myself that around us at all times, under whatever disguises, are heroes and heroines.

In the long years Bob and I lived together, partly propelled by circumstances, partly by what were probably our equally adventurous natures, we lived in many places, many houses. We lived in New York now and again, either in hotels or own apartment. We lived in one and another small town in Tennessee, towns which speedily seemed too small. For a time we owned and lived on a rice plantation on the borders of Louisiana, the most rash of all our adventures, as we lost in the end every cent we had invested in it.

We lived up and down, now in luxury, with a staff of servants; again, if not in poverty, our ménage much more modest; for in the course of time Bob lost most of his inherited and other fortune, through poor investments and his impetuous generosity, unable to see a friend in distress, and loaning thousands without proper security, if any at all; not to mention our mutual extravagance in the years when I thought there was no end to Bob's money.

Up or down, however, while there might at times be some anxiety, we seemed to get as much out of life in one condition as the other; indeed more, when we were down, for then we were closest to each other. Certainly never was there a moment for me in those long years—and I believe for Bob—that was not of intense interest, and our last years together the best of all.

Tired at last of big towns or small, on a fishing trip with Bob, more or less by accident we found a superb site in the mountains of upper East Tennessee. On the side of a wooded knob, virgin forest all around, facing the mountains (a spur of the Blue Ridge), only two miles away, not a human habitation, even a cabin, in sight, and below a river (that "river which goes with heaven"), not the broad Tennessee on which Bob had grown up, but one of its rushing roaring tributaries, visible for miles and miles from this height—here we built a home.

With ample room, we built it for summer occupancy only, but presently would not leave it at any season unless under absolute necessity; and at that, when in winter, at this elevation, it was sometimes half-buried in snow.

I do not believe that in all our years in this mountain domain (as we thought of it, for all [that] our acreage was not extensive) Bob ever mourned the splendors of Bleak House, which might have been ours had we not, when opportunity offered to acquire it, turned the chance down in favor of more liberty of movement and other expressions of our individual natures than we could find in any old Southern town the size of Knoxville, with its still predominantly provincial life, as it seemed to us at the time.

Here in the mountains, Bob knew some of that freedom, sense of boundless space, he had known when he was growing up on the great plantation then surrounding Bleak House, and to an infinitely greater degree in his wild years, as a mere stripling, with the Sioux Indians. Assuredly, never had I seen him so content as now.

* * *

But however idyllic our present existence, nevertheless a day came when the urge grew stronger and stronger in me to see once again the town where I had lived the morning of my life—the town inseparably linked with much that was dearest, as much that was saddest, in my girlhood and young womanhood.

Through the years Bob from time to time had been in Knoxville on business or for a brief visit with his sister at Westwood. But it was thirty years since I had been there unless for a necessary change of cars when I was going to Chicago, California, or somewhere else. Knoxville was becoming more and more unreal to me.

I only wanted to go there with Bob. Ten years my senior, Bob was old now. His hair had long been white, a mop of white curls, to his disgust, if he had been delayed in getting to a barber. Though still active, occupied with his customary concerns, his strong athletic figure still youthful, slim-waisted, without the hint of a paunch, yet his step had lost its spring, and I knew, though he was never ill, he had a lesion of the heart. One day when he had been as usual across the river for our mail, as he was climbing the zigzag path to our cottage and getting near, I noticed his sagging walk, his pausing to get his breath every few steps, and realized, for the first time, that Bob was a very old man, old even beyond his years.

He died within the year, sitting before our log fire in the study, reading the editorial page in the *New York Times*, suddenly his hand relaxed, the half-smoked cigarette in his fingers dropped to the rug underneath, and he was gone—the death, of all others, he would have most desired.

But now my whole thought, in the September before this, was that if Bob and I were ever to go together to Knoxville, we must not wait too long.

I planned it all out in my own mind. We would drive down to Knoxville and after a few days there drive to the neighboring Smokies, greatly changed since Bob's boyhood, when his grandfather owned fifty thousand acres in the Great Smokies; his tenants long distances apart, but one and all journeying to Knoxville to pay their annual rent in wild honey, venison and bear meat, the pelts of foxes and other wild animals. Now tourists by the thousands were invading it, with the inescapable disenchanting features tourists bring in their wake. Even so, it was a magnificent region and I had some slight curiosity to see it in its present state; although my real object in revisiting the scenes of Bob's and my youth was of course to see Knoxville again. It was like a gnawing hunger in me which would not be appeased until I had done so.

When I divulged my plan to Bob, he discouraged me. The very names of its streets had been changed. People we had known well—the whole family in some cases—were dead. Houses we had come and gone in, if near the heart of town, were tea-rooms now, funeral homes; the house on Main Street where Margaret and Charlton had lived long since razed and the new post office building standing on its former site. It was never safe, Bob sought to convince me, to go back to one's home town after so long a time. I was bound to be disappointed.

But I persisted. We stopped at the Andrew Johnson Hotel, built in recent years, facing Court House Square and the river not far below.[5]

Callers came, old acquaintances, most of whom I did not even recognize until they told me their names.

Old Major Webb I went to see because at ninety he would be too decrepit to be likely to come to see me. Once my father's chief legal counselor and intimate friend, the old Major did not even remember there had been such a man, although for a moment, when I was leaving, the fog in which his mind was enveloped lifted and a glimmer of light from the long past came through to him.

"Oh, Annie," he quavered, as his withered hand held mine, "how my Hugh did love you!"—Hugh, dead years and years ago, and his father only undead.[6]

The one person I saw who brought back even fleetingly the feel of the Knoxville I had known was lame, brilliant Miss Lucy Crozier, sister of Mrs. French, her mental faculties intact, and who still held forth in the intensely human, slightly mad and exciting fashion she always had. But save for Miss Lucy, only unseen ghosts flitted through the streets of Knoxville. Our visit could not end too soon.

On our last evening Bob and I stood looking down from the windows of our room on one of the upper floors in the hotel. It was getting dark, but we could still make out the river below.

"Bob, could it be possible," I said, after a long silence between us, "that you and I ever went to gay picnics—went boating on that river?"

Bob put his arm around me. "Knoxville," he said, "is not what you think it is," adding whimsically, "It never was!"

"But, Bob," I protested, my heart heavy, "Knoxville was my first great love, and I don't suppose I shall ever quite get over it!"

Andrew Johnson Hotel, with river below. Courtesy of Knoxville History Project.

NOTES

1. Annie W. Waldron and Robert F. Armstrong were married June 14, 1905, in Washington, D.C. "Marriage Licenses," *Washington Times*, June 13, 1905, 5; *District of Columbia, Compiled Marriage Index, 1830–1921,* Ancestry.com database on-line (viewed August 17, 2020).
2. Robert F. Armstrong's residence in Washington, D.C., was listed as The Sherman, an apartment house at 1101 15th St., (corner L) NW. *Washington, District of Columbia, City Directory,* 1906.
3. Roger assumed Bob Armstrong's middle and surnames, becoming Roger Franklin Armstrong. At some point while he was in school, he was nicknamed "Shad."
4. Although no definitive evidence documenting where AWA went has been found to date, the Rialto Grain and Securities Company was located in St. Louis, Missouri. In October 1903 its offices were raided, and the company president soon charged on five counts including fraud and "operating a bucket shop." "A St. Louis 'Securities Company' Raided," *New York Times* (online), Oct. 1, 1903 (viewed August 25, 2020); "Grain Operator Indicted: President of St. Louis Concern Held for Fraud," *New York Times* (online), Oct. 4, 1903 (viewed August 25, 2020).
5. The Andrew Johnson Hotel opened October 19, 1929, and is still standing at 912 South Gay Street across from the Courthouse near where the Gay Street Bridge crosses the Tennessee River. It was Knoxville's leading hotel for forty years and tallest building for nearly fifty years. In 1980 it was added to the National Register of Historic Places. Since the early 1990s, the Andrew Johnson building has housed the administrative offices of the Knox County Schools, but with the school system moving its headquarters to the TVA (Tennessee Valley Authority) East Tower, Knox County Commissioners voted in February 2020 to finalize sale of the building to a Nashville real estate development firm which plans to turn it into a boutique hotel with apartment units. "New Hotel Is Opened Today," *Knoxville News-Sentinel,* Oct. 19, 1929, 3; U.S. Dept. of the Interior. Heritage Conservation and Recreation Service. National Register of Historic Places Inventory – Nomination Form (online), npgallery.nps.gov/ (viewed Aug. 26, 2020); Tyler Whetstone, "Commission OKs Johnson Building Sale," *Knoxville News-Sentinel,* Feb. 26, 2020, A4.
6. Major Thomas Shepard Webb (1840–1930) practiced law in partnership with his brother-in-law, Hugh Lawson McClung, Jr. (1858–1936), from 1879 until 1908. It was to Hugh McClung's house that AWA fled when her first husband bloodied her face in the "little house near Bell Avenue" (Part 2, Chapter 6). Webb was in practice later on with Lewis M. G. Baker and Malcolm McDermott. It is not clear to whom Major Webb was referring when he said "my Hugh." Webb and his wife, the former Blanche McClung (1843–1894), had four children, including a son named Hugh McClung Webb (1871–1931), but he was still living at that time. If AWA and her husband *did*

make this trip in September 1930 (before RFA died in March 1931), it must have been early in the month because Major Webb died September 24, 1930, two days before he would have turned ninety on September 26. In the 1930 census, Major Webb was listed as 90 years old, head of the household, owner of the property (a farm), his son Hugh and daughter-in-law living with him. The family's home in the 1890s was Middlebrook, one of the oldest existing frame residences in east Tennessee (built by Gideon Morgan Hazen in 1845) and listed on the National Register of Historic Places. Rothrock, 447; Tumblin, *Fountain City*, 83ff; 1901 *Knoxville Cookbook*, 323; *U.S Census*, 1930, Eighth District of Knox County (Sheet 15A, enumerated April 11, 1930).

Epilogue

And so, Anne Wetzell Armstrong ends her remembrance of Knoxville at the Andrew Johnson Hotel, only about a block from where she began—at the Schubert Hotel which, at that time, was on the corner of Gay Street across Cumberland Avenue from the Lamar House (now the Bijou Theatre).

She has taken us on a tour of the town at the time she lived there—from downtown (Gay Street, the Custom House, Second Presbyterian Church, Market Square) to West End (now the historic Fort Sanders neighborhood). She has shown us North Knoxville, Old Gray Cemetery, and Fountain Head; told us of riding the streetcar out to Lake Ottosee. We have seen the stark contrast between Island Home and "a little house near Bell Avenue." She has taken us out Kingston Pike past Crescent Bend to Bleak House and Westwood (historic homes which Knoxville is fortunate to still have), built on land that once belonged to the family she married into. What a trip—and what a story this girl has told about coming to Knoxville at the beginning of her teen years and the experiences she had growing into adulthood!

In his interpretation of Knoxville's history, the opening section of *Heart of the Valley*, William J. MacArthur says: "Knoxville had grown, flourished, and matured in the sixty-five years after the Civil War; the city achieved its zenith and began to decline, for its greatest economic assets had lost their vitality. A prosperity built on railroads and wholesale merchandizing, on limited mineral resources and textile manufacturing began to fade. Still Knoxville had also developed a definite identity. . . . This image persisted, persists still, long after the economy of Knoxville changed and the social-cultural atmosphere began to change. . . . it still persists in the memories of the many who love the city as it was."[1]

And Anne Armstrong was obviously one who loved the city as it was!

Following their visit to Knoxville "thirty years after," she and her husband returned to their home in Sullivan County, where Robert F. "Bob" Armstrong died March 24, 1931. Mrs. Armstrong continued living at "Knobside," although she often traveled and spent extended periods of time elsewhere, until the early 1940s when the Tennessee Valley Authority (TVA) began construction of South Holston Dam, which created a lake that flooded her property and the surrounding area, forcing her to give up her home. After that, she lived in various places, including

DESCENDANTS OF ANNE WETZELL ARMSTRONG

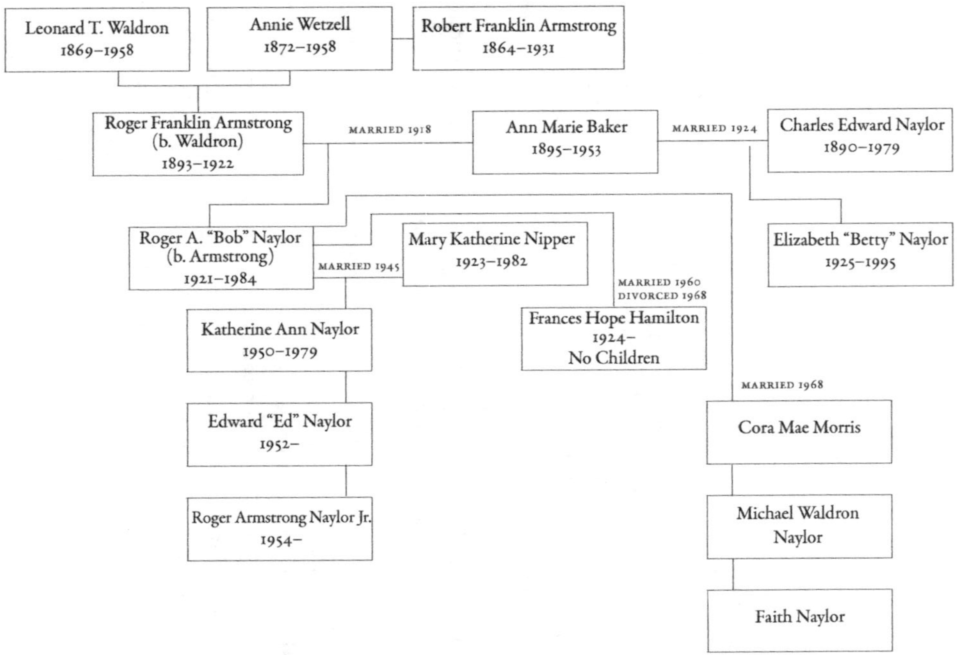

Bristol, Tennessee, and Asheville, North Carolina, ending up at the Barter Inn in Abingdon, Virginia, where she died March 17, 1958.

Her husband, Robert "Bob" Armstrong, had been buried on their land, but his grave was relocated by TVA in 1943 before South Holston Lake flooded the area. He and Anne Wetzell Armstrong are now buried together in Rooty Branch Church Cemetery near the Emmett Community in Sullivan County.

Anne Armstrong was survived by her sister, Mrs. Mary W. Peyton, Pasadena, California, and her grandson, Roger "Bob" Armstrong Naylor, of Houston, Texas. Her mother, Lorinda "Linnie" (Snyder) Wetzell, had died February 27, 1921, and was buried alongside her husband and son in Knoxville's Old Gray Cemetery. Mary "May" Wetzell Roach Peyton (who had divorced her first husband, remarried, and apparently divorced again) died October 30, 1969, in Los Angeles. Roger A. "Bob" Naylor died in November 1984.

NOTES

1. William J. MacArthur, "Knoxville's History: An Interpretation," in *Heart of the Valley: A History of Knoxville, Tennessee,* ed. Lucile Deaderick (Knoxville: East Tennessee Historical Society, 1976), 60.

Works Cited

ARCHIVES

Archives of Appalachia, East Tennessee State University
Calvin M. McClung Historical Collection, Knox County Public Library
Knox County Archives, East Tennessee History Center
Special Collections, University of Tennessee, Knoxville

NEWSPAPERS

Knoxville Daily Chronicle
Knoxville Daily Journal
Knoxville Journal
Knoxville News
Knoxville News-Sentinel

ONLINE SOURCES

Ancestry.com database.
FamilySearch database.
Find A Grave, database and images, https://www.findagrave.com.
Knox County Public Library, http://www.knoxlib.org.
Knox Heritage, http://www.knoxheritage.org.
Mount Holyoke Web site, https://www.mtholyoke.edu/.
National Register of Historic Places Digital Archive on NPGallery, npgallery.nps.gov/NRHP/.

SECONDARY SOURCES

Ahlstrom, Sydney E. *A Religious History of the American People.* New Haven: Yale University Press, 1972.

Allen, Ronald R., comp. *Knox-Stalgia: a preliminary encyclopedia of communities, schools, hotels, entertainment venues, historical buildings, organizations, sites and some historical events in Knoxville, Tennessee from the earliest times to 1950*. Knoxville, Tenn.: R. R. Allen, 1999.

———. *Knoxville Miscellany: People, Places and Events in Old Knoxville*. Knoxville, Tenn.: [R. R. Allen], 2008

———, comp. *The Street Has Changed*. Knoxville: R. Allen, 2003.

Anderson, Ronald, and Anne Koval. *James McNeill Whistler: Beyond the Myth*. New York: Carroll & Graf, 1994.

Annual Report of the Knoxville City Schools, Knoxville, Tennessee. Twenty-eighth (1898–99). Knoxville: Ogden Bros., 1900, [plus various other years].

Armstrong, Anne W. "As I Saw Thomas Wolfe," *Arizona Quarterly* 2 (Spring 1946): 5–15.

———. "The Branner House." *Yale Review* 27 (March 1938): 587–600.

———. "Half-Wit Mary's Lover: A Short Story." *Cavalier* 15, no. 1 (April 27, 1912): 90–96.

———. *The Seas of God*. New York: Hearst's International Library, 1915 [published anonymously]. London: Mills & Boon, 1916.

———. "The Southern Mountaineers," *Yale Review* 24 (March 1935): 539–54. Reprinted in *American Points of View, 1934–1935*. Edited by William H. Cordell and Kathryn Coe Cordell. Garden City, N.Y.: Doubleday, Doran & Co., 1936. Condensed in *Reader's Digest* (May 1935): 67–70.

———. *This Day and Time*. New York: Knopf, 1930. Reprinted, with a personal reminiscence by David McClellan. Johnson City: Research Advisory Council, East Tennessee State University, 1970.

[Armstrong, Anne W.] "A Woman in Wall Street / by One," *Atlantic Monthly*, vol. 136, no. 2 (August 1925): 145–158.

Armstrong, Zella. *Notable Southern Families*. Chattanooga: Lookout Press, 1918.

Baxter, Albert. *History of the City of Grand Rapids*. New York and Grand Rapids: Munsell & Company, Publishers, 1891. Online e-book, Internet Archive <archive.org>

Benét, William Rose. *The Reader's Encyclopedia*. 2nd ed. New York: Thomas Y. Crowell, 1965.

Broun, Heywood Hale. *Whose Little Boy Are You? A Memoir of the Broun Family*. New York: St. Martin's/Marek, 1983.

Brown, Paul F. *Rufus: James Agee in Tennessee*. Knoxville: University of Tennessee Press, 2018.

Bucke, Richard Maurice. *Walt Whitman*. Philadelphia: David McKay, 1883 (xerographic copy).

Campbell, Carl Edward. "The Knoxville Walt Whitman Fellowship." Master's thesis, University of Tennessee, 1956.

Chase, Philip M. "William Gibbs McAdoo: The Last Progressive (1863–1941)." PhD diss., University of Southern California, 2008.

Clayton, LaReine Warden. *Stories of Early Inns and Taverns of the East Tennessee Country*. Nashville, Tenn.: National Society of the Colonial Dames of America in the State of Tennessee, 1995.

Coggins, Allen R. *Tennessee Tragedies: Natural, Technological, and Societal Disasters in the Volunteer State*. Knoxville: University of Tennessee Press, 2011.

Cohn, David L. *Where I Was Born and Raised.* Boston: Houghton Mifflin, 1948.

Coleman, Lance. "Library History Lives Here," *Knoxville News Sentinel*, November 5, 2011.

Connelly, Cyril. *The Unquiet Grave: A Word Cycle by Palinurus.* 3rd ed. New York: Harper & Bros., 1945.

Creekmore, Betsey Beeler. *Knoxville!* 1st ed. Knoxville: East Tennessee Historical Society, 1991.

———. *Knox County, Tennessee: A History in Pictures*. Norfolk, Va.: Donning Company, 1988.

Deaderick, Lucile, ed. *Heart of the Valley: A History of Knoxville, Tennessee.* Knoxville: East Tennessee Historical Society, 1976.

Dykeman, Wilma. *The French Broad.* Rivers of America. New York: Rinehart & Co., 1955. Reprint, Newport, Tenn.: Wakestone Books, 1999.

Fanslow, Mary. "What Do They Do at the Springs?: An Overview of Five East Tennessee Resorts." *Journal of East Tennessee History* 80 (2008): 1–27.

Frost, William Goodell. "Our Contemporary Ancestors in the Southern Mountains." *Atlantic Monthly* 83 (March 1899): 311-319.

Fuson, Henry H. *History of Bell County, Kentucky.* 2 vols. New York: Hobson Book Press, 1947.

Giffen, Lowell L. *A History of Second Presbyterian Church*. Knoxville, Tenn.: *s.n.*, 1994.

Goldman, Robert. "Mark Twain as Playwright." In *Mark Twain: A Sumptuous Variety,* edited by Robert Giddings, 108–131. London: Vision / Totowa, NJ: Barnes & Noble, 1985.

Goodspeed's History of Tennessee: Containing Historical and Biographical Sketches of Thirty East Tennessee Counties. Reprinted from Goodspeed's *History of Tennessee* (1887). Nashville: Charles and Randy Elder, 1972.

Groce, W. Todd. *Mountain Rebels: East Tennessee Confederates and the Civil War, 1860–1870*. Knoxville: University of Tennessee Press, 1999.

Gunther, John. *A Fragment of Autobiography: The Fun of Writing the Inside Books*. 1st ed. New York: Harper & Row, 1962.

———. *Inside U.S.A.* New York: Harper & Bros., 1947.

House, Ellen Renshaw. *A Very Violent Rebel: The Civil War Diary of Ellen Renshaw House.* Edited by Daniel E. Sutherland. Voices of the Civil War series. Knoxville: University of Tennessee Press, 1996.

Herzberg, Max J., et al. *The Reader's Encyclopedia of American Literature.* New York: Thomas Y. Crowell, 1962.

Hess, Earl J. *The Knoxville Campaign: Burnside and Longstreet in East Tennessee.* Knoxville: Univ. of Tenn. Press, 2012.

Hill, Howard. *The Herbert Walters Story.* Morristown, Tenn.: Morristown Printing Co., 1963–1966.

Hoskins, Katherine B. *Anderson County*. Tennessee County History Series. Memphis: Memphis State University Press, 1979.

Humes, Thomas William. *The Loyal Mountaineers of Tennessee*. Knoxville: Ogden Brothers, 1888.

James, Henry. *Letters*. Vol. 1, *1843–1875*. Edited by Leon Edel. Cambridge, Mass.: Belknap Press of Harvard University Press, 1974.

James, William. *The Varieties of Religious Experience: A Study in Human Nature*. London: Longmans, Green, 1902.

Johnson, Jeff D., and Jim Stokely, eds. *An Encyclopedia of East Tennessee*. Oak Ridge, Tenn.: Children's Museum of Oak Ridge, 1981.

Kemble, Frances Anne. *Journal of a Residence on a Georgian Plantation in 1838–1839*. London: Longman, Green, Longman, Roberts, & Green, 1863.

Kingston Pike-Sequoyah Hills Association. *Reflections on Sequoyah Hills, as Told to Sandy Berwick, Chair...* Knoxville, TN: Kingston Pike-Sequoyah Hills Association, 1997.

Kleber, John E., Lowell Hayes Harrison, and Thomas Dionysius Clark, eds. *Kentucky Encyclopedia*. Lexington: University Press of Kentucky, 2015.

Knoxville City Directory. [various years], 1880/81–1903.

Knoxville Woman's Building Association, comp. and ed. *Knoxville Cook Book*. Knoxville, Tenn.: Bean, Warters, 1901. Reedited by Frank T. Rogers. Knoxville: V. B. Rogers, 1985.

LeMaster, J. R., and Donald D. Kummings, eds. *Walt Whitman: An Encyclopedia*. New York: Garland, 1998.

Lofaro, Michael A., and Hugh Davis, eds. *James Agee Rediscovered*. Knoxville: University of Tennessee Press, 2005.

Luttrell, Laura E. "One Hundred Years of a Female Academy: The Knoxville Female Academy, 1811–1846; the East Tennessee Female Institute, 1846–1911." *East Tennessee Historical Society's Publications*, no. 17 (1945): 71–83.

MacArthur, William Joseph, Jr. "Charles McClung McGhee, Southern Financier." PhD diss., University of Tennessee, 1975.

MacArthur, William J., Jr. "Knoxville's History: An Interpretation." In *Heart of the Valley: A History of Knoxville, Tennessee*, edited by Lucile Deaderick, 1-67. Knoxville: East Tennessee Historical Society, 1976.

Manning, Russ, and Sondra Jamieson. *Historic Knoxville and Knox County: City Center, Neighborhoods, and Parks*. Bicentennial ed. Norris, Tenn.: Laurel Place, 1990.

McDonald, Michael J., and William Bruce Wheeler. *Knoxville, Tennessee: Continuity and Change in an Appalachian City*. Knoxville: University of Tennessee Press, 1983.

McGinnis, Robert A., transcriber. *Graves of Old Gray Cemetery*. [Knoxville: R. A. McGinnis], 2007.

McKenzie, Robert Tracy. *Lincolnites and Rebels: A Divided Town in the American Civil War*. New York: Oxford University Press, 2006.

Miller, Jim, comp. *Knoxville Bicentennial Yesteryear II.* Knoxville Yesteryear Historical Society, [1976].

Mitchell, Ted. *Thomas Wolfe: A Writer's Life.* Rev. ed. Raleigh: North Carolina Division of Archives and History, 1999. Published in cooperation with the Appalachian Consortium.

Morrison, Andrew. *Knoxville, Tennessee.* Engelhardt series: American cities, vol. 25. A facsimile of the 1891 ed. by Charles A. Reeves, Jr. Knoxville: Charles A. Reeves, Jr., 2002.

The National Cyclopaedia of American Biography. Reprint. Ann Arbor: University Microfilms, 1967.

Neely, Jack. *Knoxville: This Obscure Prismatic City.* Charleston, SC: History Press, 2009.

———. *The Legend of the Gold Bricks, and Other Knoxville Stories,* edited by Paul James. Knoxville, Tenn.: Knoxville History Project, 2018.

———. *From the Shadow Side, and Other Stories of Knoxville, Tennessee.* Oak Ridge, Tenn.: Tellico Books, 2003.

———. *Market Square: A History of the Most Democratic Place on Earth.* 2nd ed. [Knoxville]: Market Square District Association, 2011.

———. *A Splendid Instinct: Robert Webb and the Founding of the Webb School of Knoxville.* Oak Ridge, Tenn.: Tellico Books, 2006.

O'Connor, Richard. *Heywood Broun: A Biography.* New York: Putnam's, 1975.

Osborn, Jamie. "Lawson McGhee Library Still Relevant after 125 Years," *Knoxville News Sentinel,* November 6, 2011.

Percy, William Alexander. *Lanterns on the Levee: Recollections of a Planter's Son.* 1st ed. New York: Knopf, 1941. Reprinted with an introduction by Walker Percy. Baton Rouge: Louisiana State University Press, 1973.

Peters, Lisa N. *James McNeill Whistler.* New York: Smithmark, 1996.

Pulliam, Walter T. *Harriman: The Town That Temperance Built.* [Harriman]: Walter T. Pulliam, 1978.

Rothrock, Mary U., ed. *The French Broad-Holston Country: A History of Knox County, Tennessee.* Knoxville, Tenn.: East Tennessee Historical Society, 1946.

Rule, William, ed. *Standard History of Knoxville, Tennessee.* Chicago: Lewis Publishing Co., 1900. Reproduction by Charles A. Reeves, Jr. Knoxville: Charles A. Reeves, Jr., Technical Illustration & Publishing, 2009.

Sand, George. *The Intimate Journal of George Sand.* Translation and notes by Marie Jenney Howe. New York: Haskell House, 1975.

Saxton, Sadie Boyd, and Elizabeth Skaggs Bowman. *Highlights of Ossoli Circle's History, 1885–1960. [Knoxville, 1960].*

Schirer, Thomas. *Mark Twain and the Theatre.* Erlanger Beiträge zur Sprach- und Kunstwissenschaft 71. Nürnberg: Verlag Hans Carl, 1984.

Schrock, Earl F., Jr. "An Examination of the Dialect in *This Day and Time.*" *Tennessee*

Folklore Society Bulletin 37 (June 1971): 31–39. (Reprinted in *Voices from the Hills: Selected Readings of Southern Appalachia*. Ed. Robert J. Higgs, Ambrose Manning. New York: Ungar, 1975.)

Seymour, Digby Gordon. *Divided Loyalties: Fort Sanders and the Civil War in East Tennessee.* 1st ed. Knoxville: University of Tennessee Press, 1963. 2nd ed., rev. Knoxville: East Tennessee Historical Society, 1982.

Still, Laura. *A Haunted History of Knoxville.* Asheville, N.C.: Stony River Media, 2014.

Sutherland, John. *Mrs. Humphry Ward: Eminent Victorian, Pre-eminent Edwardian.* Oxford: Clarendon Press, 1990.

Temple, Oliver P. *Notable Men of Tennessee from 1833 to 1875: Their Times and Their Contemporaries*, compiled and arranged by Mary B. Temple. New York: Cosmopolitan Press, 1912.

Thomason, Jerry, Tom Quirk. Introduction to "Col. Sellers: A Drama In Five Acts by Saml L. Clemens." *The Missouri Review*, 18, no. 3, (1995): 111–112. https://muse.jhu.edu/ (viewed February 14, 2019).

Tumblin, J. C. (Jim). *Fountain City: People Who Made a Difference.* Knoxville, Tenn.: Celtic Cat, 2016.

Turnbull, Andrew. *Thomas Wolfe.* New York: Charles Scribner's Sons, 1967.

Two Centuries of Knox County, Tennessee: A Celebration in Photographs. Knoxville: McClung Historical Collection, 1992.

U.S. Census [various years].

Wakefield, Larry. "Wetzell: Broom Handles and a Bank Robbery." In *Ghost Towns of Michigan*, 30–34. W. Bloomfield, Mich.: Northmont Publ., 1994.

Watkins, James H. "Percy, William Alexander," in *The New Encyclopedia of Southern Culture,* Charles Reagan Wilson, ed. Vol. 9, Literature, 385–87. Chapel Hill: University of North Carolina Press, 2008.

West, Carroll Van, ed. *The Tennessee Encyclopedia of History & Culture.* Nashville: Tennessee Historical Society / Rutledge Hill Press, 1998.

Wheeler, William Bruce. *Knoxville, Tennessee: A Mountain City in the New South.* 3rd ed. Knoxville: University of Tennessee Press, 2020.

Whitman, Walt. *Leaves of Grass,* edited by Emory Holloway. Inclusive ed. Garden City, N.Y.: Doubleday, 1926.

Yearbook of the Ossoli Circle, Knoxville, Tennessee . . . 5th season (1889–90), 6th season (1890–91), 7th season (1891–92), 8th season (1892–93), 9th season (1893–94), 10th season (1894–95), 11th season (1895–96), 12th season (1896–97).

Index

Page numbers in **boldface** refer to illustrations.